W9-ACB-651

THE SOCIAL HISTORY OF ART

VOLUME TWO

ARNOLD HAUSER

THE SOCIAL HISTORY OF ART

VOLUME TWO

ROUTLEDGE & KEGAN PAUL

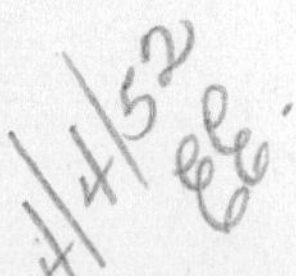

First published in 1951
by Routledge & Kegan Paul Limited
Broadway House, 68–74 Carter Lane
London E.C.4

Text Printed in Great Britain
by Butler & Tanner Limited
Frome and London
Plates Printed in Great Britain
by W. S. Cowell Limited
Ipswich and London

Translated in collaboration with the Author
by Stanley Godman, and now published for
the first time in any language

CONTENTS

VI. ROCOCO, CLASSICISM AND ROMANTICISM

1. THE DISSOLUTION OF COURTLY ART *page* 501
The end of the age of Louis XIV, page 503; *The Régence, page* 505; *The new wealth of the bourgeoisie, page* 509; *The Voltairian ideal of culture, page* 510; *Watteau, page* 513; *Pastoral poetry, page* 515; *The pastoral in painting, page* 520; *The heroic novel and the love novel, page* 523; *The psychological novel, page* 525; *The triumph of the love motif in literature, page* 526; *Marivaux, page* 527; *The concept of the rococo, page* 528; *Boucher, page* 532; *Greuze and Chardin, page* 533

2. THE NEW READING PUBLIC *page* 534
The English monarchy and the liberal strata of society, page 534; *Parliament, page* 536; *The new periodicals and the middle-class reading public, page* 540; *Literature in the service of politics, page* 543; *Defoe and Swift, page* 544; *The changes in the conditions of literary life, page* 545; *The revival and end of patronage, page* 546; *Subscription and publishing, page* 548; *Pre-romanticism, page* 550; *The Industrial Revolution, page* 552; *The new ethic of labour, page* 555; *The ideology of freedom, page* 555; *Individualism, page* 556; *Emotionalism, page* 557; *Moralism,* page 558; *The return to nature, page* 560; *Richardson, page* 562; *Rousseau, page* 568; *The stylistic consequence of public concerts, page* 576

CONTENTS

3. THE ORIGINS OF DOMESTIC DRAMA *page* 577

The drama in the service of the class struggle, page 578; *The social character of the dramatic hero, page* 580; *The significance of the milieu in the domestic drama, page* 582; *The problem of tragic guilt, page* 585; *Freedom and necessity, page* 588; *The tragic and the non-tragic attitude to life, page* 589

4. GERMANY AND THE ENLIGHTENMENT *page* 592

The political immaturity of the German bourgeoisie, page 594; *German particularism, page* 595; *The estrangement of the German intelligentsia from public life, page* 598; *The metropolis and the free literary life, page* 602; *The aestheticizing of the philosophical world-view, page* 608; *The new concept of genius, page* 610; *The 'vitalism' of the 'Storm and Stress', page* 613; *Rationalism, page* 614; *Herder, page* 615; *Goethe and the bourgeoisie, page* 617; *The idea of world literature, page* 621

5. REVOLUTION AND ART *page* 622

Naturalism, classicism and the bourgeoisie, page 623; *Baroque classicism, page* 627; *Rococo classicism, page* 630; *Archaeological classicism, page* 631; *Revolutionary classicism, page* 634; *David, page* 636; *The art programme of the Revolution, page* 638; *The renewal of the ceremonial and the historical picture, page* 640; *Art and political propaganda, page* 641; *The preparation of romanticism by the Revolution, page* 643; *Napoleon and art, page* 645; *The consolidation of the bourgeoisie as an art public, page* 648; *Art exhibitions and the Academy, page* 649; *The reform of art education, page* 651

6. GERMAN AND WESTERN ROMANTICISM *page* 653

The connection of romanticism with liberalism and reaction, page 653; *Historicism, page* 657;

The 'emanatistic' philosophy of history, page 659; *Historical materialism*, page 661; *The flight from the present*, page 663; *'Romantic irony'*, page 665; *Romanticism as a middle-class movement*, page 666; *The ambivalent relationship of the romantics to art*, page 668; *The idea of the 'second self'*, page 669; *Romanticism as a 'disease'*, page 670; *The dissolution of form*, page 671; *The 'occasionalism' of romanticism*, page 672; *The romanticism in Western Europe*, page 673; *The Restoration in France*, page 674; *The literature of the émigrés*, page 677; *The romantic coteries*, page 678; *The origins of the bohème*, page 681; *'Jeune France'*, page 683; *Victor Hugo and Béranger*, page 685; *The struggle for the theatre*, page 687; *The popular theatre of the revolutionary epoch*, page 688; *The melodrama*, page 690; *The vaudeville*, page 692; *Pixerécourt*, page 693; *English romanticism*, page 695; *The Byronic hero*, page 699; *Walter Scott and the new reading public*, page 703; *Romanticism and naturalism*, page 706; *Delacroix and Constable*, page 707; *The dissolution of classical form in music*, page 710

VII. NATURALISM AND IMPRESSIONISM

1. THE GENERATION OF 1830 page 714

The foundations of the nineteenth century, page 715; *The rule of capital*, page 721; *The permanent revolution*, page 723; *Journalism and literature*, page 725; *The serial novel*, page 726; *'L'art pour l'art'*, page 731; *Stendhal as spokesman of post-revolutionary youth*, page 740; *The idea of the class struggle*, page 742; *Classical-romantic and modern psychology*, page 751; *Balzac's sociology*, page 754; *The pathology of capitalism*, page 755; *The discovery of the ideological deter-*

mination of thought, page 758; The 'triumph of realism', page 761; The renewal of cyclical form, page 763; The secret of Balzac's art, page 766

2. THE SECOND EMPIRE *page* 768
Eclecticism, page 771; The naturalism of the mid-century, page 772; Courbet, page 774; Art as relaxation, page 778; The reinterpretation of 'l'art pour l'art', page 780; Flaubert's wrestling with the spirit of romanticism, page 782; Aesthetic nihilism, page 787; The struggle for the 'mot juste', page 788; 'Bovarysm', page 789; Flaubert's conception of time, page 791; Zola, page 792; The 'idealism' of the bourgeoisie, page 795; The new theatre public, page 797; The apotheosis of the family in the drama, page 798; The 'pièce bien faite', page 801; The operetta, page 804; 'Grand opera', page 809; Richard Wagner, page 810

3. THE SOCIAL NOVEL IN ENGLAND AND RUSSIA *page* 812
Idealists and utilitarians, page 813; The second romantic movement, page 815; The pre-Raphaelites, page 817; Ruskin, page 819; Morris, page 820; The cultural problem of technics, page 822; The antecedents of the social novel in England, page 824; The novel in monthly instalments and the new reading public, page 827; Dickens, page 828; The novel of the mid-Victorian period, page 835; The bourgeoisie and the intelligentsia, page 837; The Russian intelligentsia, page 841; Westernizers and Slavophils, page 844; The activism of the Russian novel, page 847; The psychology of self-estrangement, page 848; Dostoevsky, page 850; Tolstoy, page 861

4. IMPRESSIONISM *page* 869
The modern dynamic attitude to life, page 871; Impressionism and naturalism, page 873; The predominance of painting, page 877; The crisis of

naturalism, *page* 880; *Aesthetic hedonism*, *page* 883; *The 'vie factice'*, *page* 885; *The decadent movement*, *page* 888; *The artist and the bourgeois outlook on life*, *page* 890; *The escape from civilization*, *page* 891; *The transformation of the bohème*, *page* 892; *Symbolism*, *page* 895; *'Poésie pure'*, *page* 896; *Modernism in England*, *page* 901; *Dandyism*, *page* 904; *The aesthetic movement*, *page* 905; *Intellectualism*, *page* 906; *International impressionism*, *page* 907; *Chekhov*, *page* 909; *The problem of the naturalistic drama*, *page* 911; *Ibsen*, *page* 914; *Shaw*, *page* 917; *The psychology of exposure*, *page* 919; *Freud*, *page* 921; *Pragmatism*, *page* 924; *Bergson and Proust*, *page* 925

VIII. THE FILM AGE *page* 927

The crisis of capitalism, *page* 927; *'Mass democracy'*, *page* 929; *Anti-impressionism*, *page* 930; *'Terrorists' and 'rhetoricians'*, *page* 932; *Dadaism and surrealism*, *page* 933; *The crisis of the psychological novel*, *page* 938; *Space and time in the film*, *page* 940; *The experience of simultaneity*, *page* 944; *The problem of collectivism in art production*, *page* 947; *The cinema public*, *page* 949; *Russian montage*, *page* 953; *The film as an instrument of propaganda*, *page* 956; *Film and technics*, *page* 957; *The democratization of art*, *page* 958

INDEX OF SUBJECTS *page* 979

INDEX OF NAMES *page* 1002

CHAPTER VI

ROCOCO, CLASSICISM AND ROMANTICISM

1. THE DISSOLUTION OF COURTLY ART

THE fact that the development of courtly art, which had been almost uninterrupted since the close of the Renaissance, comes to a standstill in the eighteenth century and is superseded by the bourgeois subjectivism which, on the whole, still dominates our own conception of art today, is well known, but the fact that certain features of the new trend are already present in the rococo itself and that the break with courtly tradition really takes place in the first half of the eighteenth century is not so generally familiar. For, although we do not enter the bourgeois world before Greuze and Chardin appear, Boucher and Largillière already bring us very close to it. The tendency towards the monumental, the ceremonious and the solemn already disappears in the early rococo and makes room for a more delicate and intimate quality. In the new art preference is given to colour and shades of expression rather than to the great, firm, objective line and the note of sensuality and sentiment is to be heard in all its manifestations. Therefore, although in some respects the 'Dixhuitième' is nothing more than the continuation, indeed the consummation, of baroque splendour and pretension, the uncompromising way in which the seventeenth century insisted on the 'grand goût' as a matter of course is foreign to it. Even when they are intended for the highest classes of society, its creations lack the grand heroic mould. But, naturally, the art we are dealing with here is still a very aloof, very refined and essentially aristocratic art, an art which regards the criteria of the pleasant and the conventional as more decisive than those of spirituality and spontaneity, an art in which work is performed in accordance with a fixed, universally acknowledged and constantly repeated pattern, and of which nothing is more characteristic than the masterly, though all too often purely external technique of the execution. These conventional elements of the rococo, which derive from the baroque, are only gradually dissolved and replaced by the characteristics of bourgeois taste.

The attack on the baroque-rococo tradition ensues from two different directions, but is based in both cases on the same opposition to courtly taste. The emotionalism and naturalism represented by Rousseau and Richardson, Greuze and Hogarth, is one, the rationalism and classicism of Lessing and Winckelmann, Mengs and David, the other. Both oppose the ideal of simplicity and the earnestness of a puritan outlook on life to the courtly taste for ostentation. In England the transformation of courtly into bourgeois art takes place earlier and is carried out more thoroughly than in France itself where the baroque-rococo tradition continues underground and is still perceptible in the romantic movement. But, at the close of the century, the only important art in Europe is bourgeois. It is possible to differentiate between a progressive and a conservative trend within the middle class, but a living art expressing aristocratic ideals and serving court purposes no longer exists. In the whole history of art and culture, the transfer of leadership from one social class to another has seldom taken place with such absolute exclusiveness as here, where the aristocracy is completely displaced by the middle class and the change in taste, which puts expression in the place of decoration, could not possibly be any clearer.

To be sure, this is not the first time that the middle class appears on the scene as the upholder of taste. As early as the fifteenth and sixteenth centuries a leading position was held all over Europe by an art of a predominantly middle-class character. It was not until the later Renaissance and the age of mannerism and baroque that its place was taken by works in the courtly style. But in the eighteenth century, when the middle class again attains economic, social and political power, the ceremonial art of the courts, which had meanwhile come into its own, breaks up again and yields to the unrestricted sway of middle-class taste. It was only in Holland that there was already a middle-class art of high standing in the seventeenth century and one much more thoroughly and consistently middle-class than the Renaissance, which was interspersed with chivalric-romantic and mystical-religious elements. But this Dutch middle-class art remained an almost completely isolated phenomenon in the Europe of the time and, when the eighteenth century established modern middle-class art, it did not link up directly with this earlier manifestation. There could be no question of a continuous development, if only because Dutch painting itself lost much of its middle-class character in the course of the seventeenth century. Both in France and England, the art of the modern middle class had its real origins in social changes at home; these had inevitably to be the basis of the displacement of the courtly conception of art, and the stimulation received from contemporary philosophical and literary movements was bound to be stronger than that from the art of countries remote in time and space.

The development which reaches its political climax in the French Revolution, and its artistic objective in romanticism, begins in the Régence with the undermining of the royal power as the principle of absolute authority, with the disorganization of the court as the centre of art and culture and the dissolution of baroque classicism as the artistic style in which the power-strivings and power-consciousness of absolutism found their direct expression. The ground for this process is already prepared for during the reign of Louis XIV. The endless wars throw the finances of the country into confusion; the public exchequer becomes empty and the population impoverished, since it is impossible to create tax-payers by whippings and imprisonment and economic supremacy by wars and conquests. Even during the lifetime of the *roi soleil* critical remarks about the consequences of autocracy are heard. Fénelon is already quite candid in this respect, but Bayle, Malebranche and Fontenelle go so far that it has been rightly maintained that the 'crisis of the European spirit', the history of which fills the eighteenth century, was in full swing from 1680 onwards.[1] Simultaneously with this tendency, criticism of classicism also gains ground and prepares the way for the dissolution of courtly art. By about 1685 the creative period of baroque classicism has come to an end; Le Brun loses his influence, and the great writers of the age, Racine, Molière, Boileau and Bossuet, have spoken their last or their last decisive words.[2] The 'Quarrel between the Ancients and the Moderns' marks the beginning of the conflict between tradition and progress, classicism and modernism, rationalism and emotionalism, which was to be settled in the pre-romanticism of Diderot and Rousseau.

In the last years of Louis XIV's life the state and the court were governed by the devout Mme de Maintenon. The aristocracy no longer felt comfortable in the atmosphere of gloomy solemnity and narrow-minded piety at Versailles. When the King died a sigh of relief was uttered by everyone, above all by those who expected the regency of Philip of Orléans to bring liberation from despotism. The Regent had always considered his uncle's administrative system out of date,[3] and began his reign by reacting against the old methods all along the line. In the political and social spheres he strove for a renaissance of the nobility, in the economic sphere he favoured individual enterprises, such as that of Law, for example, he introduced a new style in the way of life of the upper classes and made a vogue of hedonism and libertinism. A condition of general disintegration began, which none of the old ties was able to resist. Some of them were reconstituted later on, but the old system was now shattered once and for all. The first act of state of Philip of Orléans was to annul the will of the departed king, which provided for the recognition of his illegitimate children. That was the beginning of the decline of the king's authority, which, in spite of the continuance of the absolute monarchy, was never to be restored to its former greatness. The exercise of supreme power became more and more arbitrary, but the confidence of those in power became more and more unsettled—a process best described in the often quoted words of Marshal Richelieu to Louis XVI: 'Under Louis XIV no one dared open his mouth, under Louis XV everyone whispered, now everyone speaks aloud and in a perfectly free and easy way.' To think of assessing the real power of the state on the basis of government orders and decrees would be, as Tocqueville remarks, a ridiculous error. Sanctions, such as the famous death penalty for the writing and spreading of books against religion and public order, remained on paper. The worst penalty the guilty had to pay was to leave the country, and they were often warned and protected by the very officials whose duty it was to prosecute them. In the age of Louis XIV the whole intellectual life was still under the protection of the king; there was no defence apart from him, much less any defence against him. New protectors, new patrons and new centres of culture now arise; art develops very largely, literature entirely, away from the court and the king.

Philip of Orléans transfers the residence from Versailles to Paris and, by so doing, virtually dissolves the court. The Regent loathes all restrictions, formalities and constraint; he feels really happy only in the company of his closest friends. The young King lives in the Tuileries, the Regent in the Palais Royal, the members of the nobility are dispersed in their castles and palaces and amuse themselves in the theatres, at balls and in the *salons* of the city. The Regent and the Palais Royal themselves represent the more unrestrained, more fluid taste of Paris, in contrast to the 'grand goût' of Versailles. The life of the 'city' is no longer subsidiary to that of the 'court', it displaces the court and takes over its cultural functions. The melancholy exclamation of the Countess Palatine Elizabeth Charlotte, the mother of the Regent, 'there is no longer a court in France!', is absolutely in accordance with the facts. And this situation is no passing episode; the court in the old sense has, in fact, now vanished for ever. Louis XV has similar tastes to the Regent, he, too, favours a small society of friends, and Louis XVI likes above all to live within the family circle. Both kings shun ceremony, etiquette bores and annoys them, and although it is still preserved to a certain extent, it, nevertheless, loses much of its solemnity and grandeur. At the court of Louis XVI the dominant tone is one of decided intimacy, and on six days of the week the social gatherings achieve the character of a private party.[4] The only place where anything like a court household develops during the Régence is the castle of the Duchess of Maine at Sceaux, which becomes the scene of brilliant, expensive and ingenious festivities and, at the same time, a new centre of art, a real Court of the Muses. But the entertainments arranged by the Duchess contain the germ of the ultimate dissolution of court life: they form the transition from the old-style court to the *salons* of the eighteenth century—the cultural heirs of the court. In this way, the court breaks up again into the private societies out of which it had developed into the centre of art and literature.

Philip's attempt to restore the old political rights and public functions of the aristocracy subdued by Louis XIV was one of the most important parts of his programme. From the members of the feudal nobility he formed the so-called 'Conseils', which were intended to take the place of the middle-class ministers. But the experiment had to be given up after only three years, because the nobles had lost the habit of conducting state affairs and no longer took any real interest in the government of the country. They stayed away from meetings and willy-nilly a return had to be made to the system of Louis XIV. Outwardly, therefore, the Régence marked the beginning of a new turn in the direction of aristocracy, as expressed in the growing rigidity of social barriers and the increasing isolation of the estates, but inwardly it represented the continuation of the triumphant progress of the middle class and the further decline of the nobility. A peculiar characteristic of the social development of the eighteenth century, already noted by Tocqueville, was the fact that, in spite of all the emphasis on the barriers dividing the various estates and classes, the process of cultural levelling could not be halted and that people, who were so anxious to keep themselves isolated from one another externally, were becoming more and more alike internally,[5] so that in the end there were merely two big groups: the common people and the community of those who stood above the common people. Those belonging to this latter group shared the same habits, the same taste and spoke the same language. The aristocracy and the upper bourgeoisie amalgamated into one single cultural élite, and in so doing the former upholders of culture were giving and taking at the same time. The members of the high nobility did not visit only occasionally and condescendingly the houses where the representatives of high finance and the bureaucracy were guests, on the contrary, they crowded into the *salons* of the rich middle-class gentlemen and cultured middle-class ladies. Mme Geoffrin brings together in her home the intellectual and social élite of her time, sons of princes, counts, watchmakers and small tradesmen, she corresponds with the Empress of Russia and with Grimm, she is friendly with the King of Poland and with Fontenelle, she declines the invitation of Frederick the Great and bestows the distinction of her personal attention on the plebeian d'Alembert. The adoption by the aristocracy of middle-class patterns of thought and moral conceptions and the intermingling of the highest classes with the bourgeois intelligentsia begins, moreover, precisely at the moment when the social hierarchy makes itself felt more sharply than ever before.[6] Perhaps there is, in fact, a causal relationship between the two phenomena.

Of all its feudal privileges, the nobility had retained in the seventeenth century only the property rights in its own land and its exemption from taxation; it had ceded its judicial and administrative functions to Crown officials. Ground-rent had lost a good deal of its value because of the steady diminution, before 1660, of the purchasing power of money. The nobility was forced in an increasing measure to sell its property; it became impoverished and decayed. This was certainly more the case in the medium and lower ranks of the landed nobility than amongst the high and court nobility, which was still very rich and regained its influence in the eighteenth century. The 'four thousand families' of the court nobility remained the only usufructuaries of the court offices, the high ecclesiastical dignities, the commissioned ranks in the army, the gouverneurs' posts and royal pensions. Almost a quarter of the total budget accrued to them. The old resentment of the Crown against the feudal nobility had cooled down; under Louis XV and Louis XVI, ministers were again chosen mostly from the hereditary nobility.[7] But the latter remained anti-dynastic in its outlook all the same, was insubordinate and a source of supreme danger to the monarchy in the hour of peril. It made a common stand with the middle class against the Crown, although the good relations between the two classes had greatly suffered since the beginning of centralization. Previously they had not only often felt themselves menaced by the same danger, they had frequently had common administrative problems to solve, and this had automatically brought them closer together. But the relationship deteriorated when the nobility realized that the middle class was its most dangerous rival. From then on the king had to intervene again and again and to reconcile the jealous nobility; for, although he apparently dominated both parties, he had to make constant concessions and show favour now to one now to the other.[8] A token of this policy of appeasement towards the nobility is also to be seen, for example, in the fact that under Louis XV it was already much more difficult for a commoner to attain a commission in the army than under Louis XIV. Since the Edict of 1781 the middle class had been totally excluded from the army. The situation with regard to high ecclesiastical posts was similar: in the seventeenth century there was still a number of Church leaders of plebeian origin, such as Bossuet and Fléchier, for example; in the eighteenth century that was hardly any longer the case. The rivalry between the aristocracy and the bourgeoisie became, on the one hand, more and more critical, but, on the other hand, it assumed the sublimated forms of intellectual emulation and created a complicated network of spiritual relationships in which attraction and repulsion, imitation and rejection, respect and resentment, were intermingled. The material equality and practical superiority of the middle class provoked the nobility to stress the unlikeness of their descent and the difference of their traditions. But with the increasing similarity of the external conditions of both classes, the hostility of the bourgeoisie towards the nobility also became more intense. So long as they were excluded from climbing the social scale, it never occurred to them to compare themselves with the upper classes; it was not until the possibility of rising was given them that they became really aware of the existing social injustice, and began to regard the privileges of the nobility as intolerable. In a word, the more the nobility lost of its real power, the more obstinately it clung to the privileges which it still enjoyed and the more ostentatiously it displayed them; on the other hand, the more material goods the middle class acquired, the more shameful it considered the social discrimination from which it was suffering and the more exasperatedly it fought for political equality.

As a result of the great state bankruptcies of the sixteenth century, the middle-class wealth of the Renaissance had been dispersed and was not able to recover during the golden age of absolutism and mercantilism when the monarchs and states themselves were doing the big business.[9] Not until the eighteenth century, when the world policy of mercantilism was given up and 'laissez-faire' introduced, did the middle class, with its individualistic economic principles, come into its own again and although the traders and industrialists were able to derive considerable advantages for themselves from the absence of the aristocracy from business life, big middle-class capital first arose during the Régence and the succeeding period. This régime was in fact the 'cradle of the third estate'. Under Louis XVI the bourgeoisie of the *ancien régime* reached the zenith of its intellectual and material development.[10] Trade, industry, the banks, the *ferme générale*, the liberal professions, literature and journalism, that is to say, all the key posts in society, with the exception of the leading positions in the army, the Church and at court, were in its possession. Commercial activities developed on an unprecedented scale, industries grew, the banks multiplied, enormous sums flowed through the hands of the employers and speculators. Material needs increased and spread; and not merely people like bankers and tax-farmers climbed higher up the social ladder and vied with the nobility in their style of life, but the middle sections of the bourgeoisie also profited from the boom and took an increasing part in cultural life. The country in which the revolution broke out was, therefore, by no means economically exhausted; it was rather merely an insolvent state with a rich middle class. The bourgeoisie gradually took possession of all the instruments of culture—it not only wrote the books, it also read them, it not only painted the pictures, it also bought them. In the preceding century it had still formed only a comparatively modest section of the art and reading public, but now it is the cultured class par excellence and becomes the real upholder of culture. Most of Voltaire's readers already belong to this class, and Rousseau's almost exclusively. Crozat, the greatest art collector of the century, comes from a commercial family, Bergeret, the patron of Fragonard, is of still more humble origin, Laplace is the son of a peasant, and no one knows whose son d'Alembert was. The same middle-class public that reads Voltaire's books also reads the Latin poets and the French classics of the seventeenth century and is just as decided about what it rejects as it is in the choice of its reading. It is not much interested in the Greek writers and these now gradually disappear from libraries; it despises the Middle Ages, Spain has become a more or less unknown territory, its relationship to Italy has not yet properly developed, and will never become so cordial as the relations between court society and the Italian Renaissance in the preceding two centuries. The *gentilhomme* has been considered the intellectual representative of the sixteenth century, the *honnête homme* that of the seventeenth, and the 'cultured' man, that is to say, the reader of Voltaire, that of the eighteenth.[11] It has been asserted that one cannot understand the French bourgeois without knowing Voltaire, whom he took for his eternal model;[12] but one cannot understand Voltaire, if one does not see how deeply rooted he is in the middle class not only by heredity but also in his whole outlook, despite his seignorial demeanour, his royal friends and his enormous fortune. His sober classicism, his renunciation of the solution of the great metaphysical problems, indeed his mistrust of anyone who even discusses them, his acute, aggressive and yet thoroughly urbane mind, his anticlerical religiosity, with its dislike of any kind of mysticism, his anti-romanticism, his distaste for everything obscure, unclarified and inexplicable, his self-confidence, his conviction that everything can be grasped, everything solved, everything decided by the powers of the reason, his wise scepticism, his sensible acceptance of the nearest and the accessible, his understanding of the 'demands of the day', his 'mais il faut cultiver notre jardin', all that is middle-class, profoundly middle-class, even if it does not exhaust the characteristics of the bourgeoisie, and even if the subjectivism and sentimentalism, which Rousseau is to proclaim is the other, perhaps just as important side of the bourgeois mind. The great antagonism within the middle class was a given fact from the very beginning; Rousseau's later supporters had not yet become a regular reading public, when Voltaire was acquiring his readers, but they were already an exactly definable section of society and they merely had to discover their spokesman in Rousseau.

The French middle class of the eighteenth century is by no means any more uniform than was the Italian middle class of the fifteenth and sixteenth centuries. To be sure, there is nothing corresponding to the struggle for the control of the guilds, but there is just as intense a conflict between the various economic interests as there was then. It is only that the habit has grown of speaking of the struggle for liberation and the revolution of the 'third estate' as a homogeneous movement, but, in reality, the unity of the middle class is restricted to its common front against the aristocracy and against the peasantry and the urban proletariat; within these frontiers it is divided into a positively and negatively privileged section. There is never any mention in the eighteenth century of the privileges of the middle class, people pretend never to have heard of them, but the privileged resist every reform that would extend their opportunities to the lower classes.[13] All the middle class wants is a political democracy, and it leaves its fellow-combatants in the lurch as soon as the revolution begins to take economic equality seriously. The society of the time is, therefore, full of contradictions and tensions; it produces a royal house which is forced to represent the interests of the nobility and those of the bourgeoisie by turns, and ends by having both against it; an aristocracy which is inimical to both the Crown and the middle class, and adopts ideas which lead to its own downfall; and, finally, a middle class which brings its revolution to a triumphant conclusion with the help of the lower classes, but makes a stand against its own allies and on the side of its former enemies. So long as these elements dominate the intellectual life of the nation in equal proportions, that is, until the middle of the century, art and literature are in a state of transition and are full of contradictory, often scarcely reconcilable tendencies; they waver between tradition and freedom, formalism and spontaneity, ornamentalism and expression. And even in the second half of the century, when liberalism and emotionalism get the upper hand, the ways only divide more sharply, but the different tendencies remain side by side. To be sure, they undergo a change of function, and classicism in particular, which was a courtly-aristocratic style, becomes the vehicle of the ideas of the progressive middle class.

The Régence is a period of extraordinarily lively intellectual activity, which not only criticizes the previous epoch but is highly creative and raises questions which are to occupy the whole century. The dissolution in art of the 'grand', ceremonial style goes hand in hand with the slackening of general discipline, the growing lack of religion, the more unrestrained and personal conduct of life. It begins with the criticism of the academic doctrine, which attempted to represent the classical ideal in art as a timelessly valid principle established, as it were, by God himself, quite in the same terms as the official political theory of the time interpreted the absolute monarchy. Nothing better describes the liberalism and relativism of the new age than the statement made by Antoine Coypel, which no previous director of the Academy would have approved, that painting, like all human things, is subject to the change of fashion.[14] The new outlook expressed in these words makes itself felt everywhere in art production; art becomes more human, more accessible, more unassuming—it is no longer intended for demigods and supermen, but for ordinary mortals, for weak, sensual, pleasure-seeking individuals. It no longer expresses grandeur and power but the beauty and grace of life, and no longer wants to impress and overwhelm but to charm and please. In the final period of the reign of Louis XIV, circles are formed at the court itself, in which the artists find new patrons, who are often more generous and have more feeling for art than the monarch, who is already struggling against material difficulties and is dominated by Mme de Maintenon. The Duke of Orléans, the nephew of the King, and the Duke of Bourgogne, the son of the Dauphin, are the leading personalities in these circles. The later Regent already turns against the artistic trend favoured by Louis XIV and demands more lightness and fluidity from his artists, a more sensual and more delicate formal language than is in use at the court. Often the same artists work for the King and the Duke and change their style according to the particular patron, as, for example, Coypel, who decorates the palace chapel in Versailles in the correct court style, paints the ladies in the Palais Royal in coquettish négligé and sketches classicistic medals for the 'Académie des Inscriptions'.[15] The 'grande manière' and the grand, ceremonial genres decay during the Régence. The religious devotional picture, which even in the days of Louis XIV had already become a mere pretext to portray the King's relations, and the great narrative painting, which was, above all, an instrument of monarchist propaganda, are neglected. The place of the heroic landscape is taken by the idyllic scenery of the pastorals, and the portrait which hitherto had been intended for the public, becomes a trivial, popular genre serving mostly private purposes; everybody who can afford it has his portrait painted now. Two hundred portraits are exhibited in the Salon of 1704, as compared with fifty in the Salon of 1699.[16] Largillière already prefers to paint the bourgeoisie and no longer the court nobility as did his predecessors; he lives in Paris, not in Versailles, and thereby again gives expression to the victory of the 'city' over the 'court'.[17]

The 'galant social' scenes of Watteau take the place of the religious and historical ceremonial pictures in the favour of the progressive art public, and this transition from Le Brun to the master of the 'fêtes galantes' expresses in the most acute fashion the change of taste which occurs at the turn of the century. The formation of the new public made up of the progressively-minded aristocracy and the art-minded upper middle class, the doubt that is now cast on hitherto acknowledged authorities in the world of art, the bursting of the bounds of the old, narrowly restricted subject-matter, all this contributes to make possible the emergence of the greatest French painter before the nineteenth century. The genius whom the age of Louis XIV, with its state commissions, scholarships and pensions, its Academy, its school of Rome and its royal manufactory, was not able to produce, is begotten by the bankrupt, headless, frivolous Régence with its lack of piety and discipline. Watteau, who was born in Flanders and continues the Rubens tradition, is, incidentally, also the first thoroughly 'French' master of painting since the Gothic period. In the last two centuries before his arrival, art had been under foreign influence in France: the Renaissance, mannerism and the baroque were imported from Italy and the Netherlands. In France, where the whole court life was guided, to begin with, by foreign models, court ceremonial and monarchist propaganda were also expressed in foreign, especially Italian art forms. These forms then became so intimately bound up with the idea of royalty and the court that they acquired an institutional tenacity and remained valid as long as the court was the centre of artistic life.

Watteau painted the life of a society into which he could look only from outside, he portrayed an ideal that obviously had only external points of contact with his own aims in life, and he gave form to a Utopia of freedom which was probably no more than merely analogous to his own subjective idea of freedom, but he created these visions from the elements of his own direct experience, from sketches of the trees in the Luxembourg, of theatre scenes which he could and certainly did see every day, and of types of character of his own, albeit enchantingly disguised environment. The profundity of his art is due to the ambivalence of his relationship to the world, to the expression of both the promise and the inadequacy of life, to the always present feeling of an inexpressible loss and an unattainable goal, to the knowledge of a lost homeland and the Utopian remoteness of real happiness. In spite of the delight in the senses and the beauty, the joyful surrender to reality and the pleasure in the good things of the earth, which form the immediate theme of his art, what he paints is full of melancholy. In all his pictures he describes a society menaced by the unrealizable nature of its desires. But what is expressed here is still by no means the Rousseauish feeling, by no means the yearning for the state of nature, but, on the contrary, a longing for the perfect culture, for the tranquil and secure joy of living. In the 'fête galante', the conviviality of lovers and courts of love, Watteau discovers the appropriate form for the expression of his own attitude to life, which is a compound of optimism and pessimism, joy and boredom. The predominant element of the 'fête galante', which is always a 'fête champêtre' and portrays the amusements of young people leading the carefree life of Theocritan shepherds and shepherdesses with music, dancing and singing, is bucolic. It describes the peace of the countryside, the haven of security from the great world and the self-forgetting happiness of lovers.

It is, however, no longer the ideal of an idyllic, contemplative and frugal life that the artist has in his mind's eye, but the Arcadian ideal of the identity of nature and civilization, beauty and spirituality, sensuousness and intelligence. This ideal is, of course, by no means new; it is merely a variation on the formula of the poets of the Roman Empire, who combined the legend of the Golden Age with the pastoral idea. The only novelty, as compared with the Roman version, is that the bucolic world is now disguised in the fashions of polite society, the shepherds and shepherdesses wear the stylish costume of the age, and all that remains of the pastoral situation are the conversations of the lovers, the natural framework and the remoteness from the life of the court and the city. But is even all that new? Was not the pastoral from the very beginning a fiction, a playful dissimulation, a mere coquetting with the idyllic state of innocence and simplicity? Is it conceivable that ever since there has existed a pastoral poetry, that is, since the existence of a highly developed urban and court life, anyone has ever really wanted to lead the simple, modest life of shepherds and peasants? No, the shepherd's life in poetry has always been an ideal in which the negative features, the tearing of oneself away from the great world and the disregarding of its customs, have been the decisive elements. It was a kind of sport to imagine oneself in a situation which held the promise of liberation from the fetters of civilization whilst retaining its advantages. The attractions of the painted and perfumed ladies were intensified by attempting to represent them, painted and perfumed as they were, in the guise of fresh, healthy and innocent peasant maidens, and by enhancing the charms of art with those of nature. The fiction contained from the outset the preconditions which allowed it to become the symbol of freedom in every complicated and sophisticated culture.

It is not without good reason that the literary tradition of pastoral poetry can look back on an almost uninterrupted history of over two thousand years since its beginnings in Hellenism. With the exception of the early Middle Ages, when urban and court culture was extinguished, there have been variants of this poetry in every century. Apart from the thematic material of the novel of chivalry, there is probably no other subject-matter that has occupied the literature of Western Europe for so long and maintained itself against the assaults of rationalism with such tenacity. This long and uninterrupted reign shows that 'sentimental' poetry, in Schiller's sense of the word, plays an incomparably greater part in the history of literature than 'naïve' poetry. Even the idylls of Theocritus himself owe their existence not, as might be imagined, to genuine roots in nature and a direct relationship to the life of the common people, but to a reflective feeling for nature and a romantic conception of the common folk, that is, to sentiments which have their origin in a yearning for the remote, the strange and the exotic. The peasant and the shepherd are not enthusiastic about their surroundings or about their daily work. And interest in the life of the simple folk is, as we know, to be sought neither in spatial nor social proximity to the peasantry; it does not arise in the folk itself but in the higher classes, and not in the country but in the big towns and at the courts, in the midst of bustling life and an over-civilized, surfeited society. Even when Theocritus was writing his idylls, the pastoral theme and situation were certainly no longer a novelty; it will already have occurred in the poetry of the primitive pastoral peoples, but doubtless without the note of sentimentality and complacency, and probably also without attempting to describe the outward conditions of the shepherd's life realistically. Pastoral scenes, although without the lyrical touch of the *Idylls*, were to be found before Theocritus, at any rate, in the mime. They are a matter of course in the satyr plays, and rural scenes are not unknown even to tragedy.[18] But pastoral scenes and pictures of country life are not enough to produce bucolic poetry; the preconditions for this are, above all, the latent conflict of town and country and the feeling of discomfort with civilization.

But Theocritus still took a delight in simple descriptions of pastoral life, whereas his first independent successor, Virgil, no longer takes any pleasure in realistic description, and the pastoral poem acquires with him that allegorical form which marks the most important turning point in the history of the genre.[19] If the poetic conception of the pastoral life represented merely an escape from the bustle of the world even in earlier times, and the desire to live a shepherd's life was never to be taken quite literally, the unreality of the motifs is now intensified still further in so far as not only the yearning for the pastoral life but also the pastoral situation itself becomes a fiction which enables the poet and his friends to appear disguised as shepherds and to be, thereby, poetically removed from ordinary life, although the initiated are still able to recognize them straight away. The attraction of this new formula, already heralded by Theocritus, was so great that Virgil's *Eclogues* not only had the greatest success of all the poet's works, but there is probably no literary masterpiece the influence of which has been so lasting and so deep. Dante and Petrarch, Boccaccio and Sannazzaro, Tasso and Guarini, Marot and Ronsard, Montemayor and d'Urfé, Spenser and Sidney, and even Milton and Shelley are directly or indirectly dependent on them in their pastoral poetry. It appears that Theocritus only felt alarmed by the court with its constant struggle for success and the big city with the agitated pace of its life; Virgil already had more grounds for escaping from his contemporary world. The century-long civil war was hardly over, his own youth was contemporaneous with the bloodiest of the fighting, and the Augustan peace was more a mere hope than a reality, when he was writing his *Eclogues*.[20] His escape into the world of idyll was in perfect accordance with the reactionary movement initiated by Augustus, which, in representing the patriotic past as the Golden Age, tried to divert attention from the political events of the present.[21] Virgil's new conception of the pastoral poem was actually nothing more than the fusion of his own wish-fulfilment dream of peace with the propaganda for a policy of appeasement.

The medieval pastoral links up directly with the Virgilian allegory. It is true that there are only scanty remains of pastoral poetry from the centuries between the downfall of the ancient world and the rise of medieval court and city culture, and what has come down to us of the genre is the product of mere learning and the deposit of mere reminiscences of classical poets, above all of Virgil. Even Dante's eclogues are learned imitations and there are still traces of the old pastoral allegory in Boccaccio, the author of the first modern idyll. Simultaneously with the rise of the pastoral novel, which gives a new turn to the development, bucolic motifs also occur in the Italian Renaissance short story, but they lack the romantic traits with which they are connected in the idyll, the pastoral novel and the pastoral drama.[22] This phenomenon is readily understandable, however, if one considers that the short story is middle-class literature par excellence and as such has a naturalistic tendency, whereas pastoral poetry represents a courtly-aristocratic genre and inclines to romanticism. This romantic tendency is predominant throughout the pastorals of Lorenzo di Medici, Jacopo Sannazzaro, Castiglione, Ariosto, Tasso, Guarini and Marino, and proves that literary fashion at the courts of the Italian Renaissance, whether in Florence, Naples, Urbino, Ferrara or Bologna, conforms to one and the same model. Pastoral poetry is everywhere the mirror of court life and serves the reader as a sample of courtly manners. No one any longer takes the shepherd's life literally; the conventionality of the shepherd's costume is obvious and as the original purpose of the genre, the repudiation of over-civilized life, falls into the background, courtly forms are rejected only on account of their constraint, but not on account of their artificiality and sophistication. It is understandable that this pastoral poetry with its refinement and allegory, its intermingling of the far and near, of the immediate and the unusual, is one of the most popular genres of mannerism and that it is cultivated with particular affection in Spain, the classical land of courtly etiquette and mannerism. To begin with, the Italian models, which spread all over Europe along with courtly modes of life, are followed even here; but the individuality of the country soon breaks through and is expressed in the combination of the elements of the novel of chivalry and the pastoral. This Spanish hybrid of romantic and bucolic elements then becomes the bridge between the Italian and the French pastoral novel by which the further development of the genre is dominated.

The beginnings of French pastoral poetry go back to the Middle Ages and first appear in the thirteenth century in a complicated, heterogeneous form, dependent on the courtly-chivalric lyric. As in the idylls and eclogues of classical antiquity, the bucolic situation in the French *pastourelles* is also a wish-fulfilment dream of redemption from the all too rigid and conventional forms of eroticism.[23] When the knight declares his love to the shepherdess, he feels exempt from the commands of courtly love, fidelity, chastity and discretion. His desire is thoroughly unproblematical and, in spite of all its impulsiveness, it makes an impression of innocence compared with the forced purity of high courtly love. But the scene where the knight tries to win the favour of the shepherdess is absolutely conventional and no longer bears a trace of the natural note sounded by Theocritus. Apart from the two principal figures, and maybe the jealous shepherd, the only stage properties are a few sheep; there is nothing left of the atmosphere of the meadows and woods, of the mood of harvest and vintage, of the smell of milk and honey.[24] Certain elements of classical bucolics will probably have percolated into the *pastourelles* with the drifting sand of reminiscences from classical poets, but it is impossible to establish a direct influence of classical pastoral poetry on French literature before the diffusion of the Italian Renaissance and Burgundian court culture. And this influence does not go deep until the universal vogue of the Italian and Spanish pastoral novels and the victory of mannerism.[25] Tasso's 'Aminta', Guarini's 'Pastor fido' and Montemayor's 'Diana' are the models imitated by the French, especially by Honoré d'Urfé, who, following the example of the Italians and the Spaniards, wanted his 'Astrée' to be, first of all, a manual of international social etiquette and a mirror of cultivated manners. The work is rightly regarded as the school in which the coarse feudal lords and soldiers of the age of Henri IV were trained to become members of a cultured French society. It owes its existence to the same movement that produced the first *salons* and from which the precious culture of the seventeenth century arose.[26] The 'Astrée' is certainly the climax of the development which began with the pastorals of the Renaissance. No one any longer dreams of thinking of simple folk as he watches the fine ladies and gentlemen who, disguised as shepherds and shepherdesses, carry on spirited conversations and discuss ticklish questions of love. The fiction has lost all relation to reality and has become a pure social game. The shepherd's life is nothing but a masquerade, which enables the reader to withdraw for a moment from triviality and the everyday self.

Of course, Watteau's 'fêtes galantes' bear little resemblance to this poetry. In the pastoral novel the rural love scenes, with their erotic fulfilments and love ritual, are the perfect happiness, whereas in Watteau's pictures the whole erotic situation is an intermediary station on the progress to the real goal—only the preparation for the journey to that 'Cythère' which always lies in a nebulously mysterious remoteness. But pastoral poetry in France is on the decline when Watteau is painting his pictures; the master receives no direct stimuli from it. Before the eighteenth century, scenes from pastoral life do not occur at all as the real theme of the representation in painting itself. It is true that bucolic motifs are no rarity as accessories in biblical and mythological pictures, but they have an origin of their own, absolutely different from the pastoral idea. The elegiac mood of the 'Giorgionesque' version is certainly strongly reminiscent of Watteau,[27] but it lacks both the erotic undertone and the tormenting feeling of tension between nature and civilization. Even in Poussin the relationship with Watteau is only apparent. Poussin portrays Arcadia very impressively but with no direct reference to the shepherd's life; the subject remains classical and mythological and makes an essentially heroic impression, in keeping with the spirit of Roman classicism. In seventeenth-century French art pastoral subjects appear independently only on tapestries which have always displayed a fondness for portraying scenes of country life. Such motifs are, of course, not in harmony with the official character of the great art of the baroque period. They are still admissible in pictorial representations of a decorative nature, as in a novel or an opera or a ballet, but they would seem just as out of place in a big ceremonial picture as in a tragedy. 'Dans un roman frivole aisément tout s'excuse . . . Mais la scène demande une exacte raison.'[28] Nevertheless, as soon as painting takes hold of it, the pastoral acquires a subtlety and a depth which it never possessed in poetry, where it was always merely a genre of second-rate importance. As a literary genre, it represented an extremely artificial form from the very beginning, and remained the exclusive possession of generations whose relationship to reality was thoroughly reflective. The bucolic situation itself was always merely a pretext, never the real purpose of the representation, which had, in consequence, always a more or less allegorical, never a symbolical character. In other words, the pastoral had an all too clear purpose and allowed of only one valid interpretation. It was immediately exhausted, it kept no secrets back, and resulted, even in a poet like Theocritus, in a rather undifferentiated though extraordinarily attractive picture of reality. It could never overcome the limitations of allegory and it remained sportive, lacking in tension and pregnancy. Watteau is the first to succeed in giving it a symbolical depth, and he does so, above all, by excluding from it all those features which cannot also be conceived as a simple, direct reproduction of reality.

The eighteenth century was bound, by its very nature, to lead to a renaissance of the pastoral. For literature the formula had become too narrow, but in painting it still had enough life in it for a new beginning to be made. The upper classes were living in extremely artificial social conditions in which everyday relationships were very largely metamorphosed and sublimated; but they no longer believed in the deeper purpose of these forms, and merely regarded them as the rules of the game. Gallantry was one of the rules of the game of love, just as the pastoral had always been a sportive form of erotic art. Both desired to keep love at a distance, to divest it of its directness and passionateness. Nothing was, therefore, more natural than that the pastoral should reach the zenith of its development in the century of gallantry. But just as the costume worn by Watteau's figures became a fashion only after the master's death, so the genre of the 'fête galante' only found a wider public in the later rococo. Lancret, Pater and Boucher enjoyed the fruits of the innovation which they themselves merely trivialized. All his life, Watteau himself remained the painter of a comparatively small circle: the collectors Julienne and Crozat, the archaeologist and art patron Count Caylus, the art dealer Gersaint, were the only faithful supporters of his art. He was mentioned but seldom in contemporary art criticism and then usually reprovingly.[29] Even Diderot failed to recognize his importance and rated him lower than Teniers. The Academy did not make things difficult for him, it is true, even though, faced with an art such as his, it held fast to the traditional hierarchy of the genres and continued to regard the 'petits genres' with contempt. But it was in no way any more dogmatic than the educated public in general, which still conformed, in theory at least, to the classical doctrine. In all practical questions the attitude of the Academy was extremely liberal. The number of its members was unrestricted and admission was by no means dependent on acceptance of its doctrine. It was not perhaps so indulgent of its own accord, but, at any rate, it recognized that it was only by adopting such a liberal attitude that it could keep itself alive in this period of ferment and renewal.[30] Watteau, Fragonard and Chardin became members of the Academy without any difficulty, just like all the other famous artists of the century, to whatever school they belonged. To be sure, the Academy still represented the 'grand goût' as much as ever, but in practice it was only a small group of its members that kept to this principle. Those artists who could not count on public commissions, and had their buyers outside court circles, did not worry much about official recognition and cultivated the 'petits genres' which, although theoretically they did not enjoy much esteem, were all the more sought after in practice. To these belonged the 'fêtes galantes', which were intended from the very outset for a more liberal circle than the court, although it was only for a short time longer that those interested in this kind of picture represented the artistically most progressive section of the public.

But painting still kept to erotic subjects for a long time after literature, above all the novel, as the more mobile and, for economic reasons, more popular type of art, had already turned its attention to subjects of more general importance. The libertinism of the century did find its representatives in literature in Choderlos de Laclos, Crébillon *fils* and Restif de la Bretonne, but it played no decisive part in the work of the other novelists of the age. In spite of the audacity of their subjects, Marivaux and Prévost never attempt to produce grossly erotic effects. Whilst, therefore, in painting the connection with the upper classes continues unimpaired for the time being, the novel approaches the world-view of the middle classes. The transition from the novel of chivalry to the pastoral novel marked the first step in this direction, in which the foregoing of certain medieval-romanesque elements was already expressed. The pastoral novel discusses, though in a thoroughly fictitious framework, problems of real life, and describes, though in a fantastic disguise, real contemporary people; from the historical point of view, these are important features, pointing to future developments. The pastoral novel also approaches modern realism in so far as the action, above all in d'Urfé, is historically localized.[31] But the most important fact in relation to the further history of literature is that d'Urfé writes the first genuine love novel. It goes without saying that love already occurs in the novel earlier than this, but before d'Urfé there is no work of any considerable size with love as the main subject. Only from now onwards does the love theme become and remain for over three centuries the driving force in the novel as well as in the drama.[32] Since the baroque, epic and dramatic literature has always been essentially love poetry; only in the most recent period are there any signs of a change. Love gets the better of heroism even in the 'Amadis', but Céladon is the first love-hero in our sense, the first unheroic, the first defenceless slave of his passions, the precursor of the Chevalier Des Grieux and the ancestor of Werther.

The French pastoral novel of the seventeenth century is the literature of a tired age; the society which has been exhausted in the civil wars rests from its exertions as it reads the beautiful and affected conversations of the amorous shepherds. But as soon as it has recovered and the wars of conquest of Louis XIV awaken it to new ambitions, the reaction against the precious novel begins, and this goes hand in hand with the attacks on preciosity which are being made by Boileau and Molière. The pastoral novel of d'Urfé is succeeded by the heroic and love novel of La Calprenède and Mlle de Scudéry, a genre which picks up the broken thread of the Amadis novels. The novel again deals with important events, describes foreign lands and strange peoples, represents significant and impressive schemes and characters. Its heroism is, however, no longer the romantic recklessness of the novels of chivalry but rather the stern sense of duty of the tragedies of Corneille. Like the court drama, La Calprenède's heroic novel set out to be a school of will-power and magnanimity; and the same tragi-heroic ethic was also expressed in Mme de la Fayette's *Princesse de Clève*. Here, too, the question was one of the conflict between honour and passion, and here, too, duty was triumphant over love. In this age of heroic stimuli, we are everywhere confronted by the same clear analysis of volitional motifs, the same rationalistic dissection of the passions, the same stern dialectic of moral ideas. Perhaps there is to be found a more intimate trait, a more personal nuance, a more fleeting aspect of the development of the feelings in Mme de la Fayette occasionally, but even in her work everything seems to be moved into the sharp light of consciousness and analytical reason. The lovers never for a moment find themselves the defenceless victims of their passion; they are not incurably, not irretrievably lost, as are René and Werther, and even Des Grieux and Saint-Preux.

But in addition to all these bucolic-idyllic and heroic-amorous forms, there are certain phenomena even in the seventeenth century which herald the later middle-class novel. There is, above all, the picaresque novel, which differs from the fashionable types mainly in the everyday reality of its motifs and its preference for the lowlands of life. *Gil Blas* and the *Diable Boiteux* still belong to this genre and certain traits even in Stendhal's and Balzac's novels are reminiscent of the motley mosaic of the picaresque view of life. Precious novels are still read for a long time in the seventeenth century, they are actually read far into the eighteenth century, but they are no longer written after 1660.[33] The witty, artificial, aristocratically affected style yields to a more natural, more middle-class tone. Furetière already gives to his unheroic unromantic novel in the picaresque manner the specific title *Le Roman bourgeois*. This description is, however, justified only by the motifs dealt with, for this work is still a mere juxtaposition of episodes, sketches and caricatures, a form, in other words, which has nothing in common with the concentrated 'dramatic' novel of modern times, where the action revolves around the fate of a principal character completely absorbing the reader's interest.

The novel, which, despite its popularity, represents an inferior and in some respects still backward form in the seventeenth century, becomes the leading literary genre in the eighteenth, to which belong not only the most important literary works, but in which the most important and really progressive literary development takes place. The eighteenth century is the age of the novel, if only because it is an age of psychology. Lesage, Voltaire, Prévost, Laclos, Diderot, Rousseau, are brimful of psychological observations, and Marivaux is obsessed with a mania for psychology; he explains, analyses and comments on the spiritual attitudes of his figures incessantly. He takes every manifestation of life as an occasion for psychological considerations, and he never misses an opportunity of exposing the motives of his characters. The psychology of Marivaux and his contemporaries, above all of Prévost, is much richer, finer and more differentiated than was the psychology of the seventeenth century; the characters lose much of their earlier stereotyped quality, they now become more complicated, more contradictory and make the character drawing of classical literature seem, for all its acuteness, somewhat schematic. Even Lesage still provides us almost exclusively with types, eccentrics and caricatures, and it is not until Marivaux and Prévost that we have real portraits with indistinct, fleeting contours and the graded, toned-down colours of real life before us. If there is any border-line at all separating the modern from the older novel, then it runs here. From now on the novel is spiritual history, psychological analysis, self-unravelling, previously it was the representation of external happenings and spiritual processes as mirrored in concrete actions. It is true that Marivaux and Prévost still move within the limitations of the analytical and rationalistic psychology of the seventeenth century and really stand closer to Racine and La Rochefoucauld than to the great novelists of the nineteenth century. Like the moralists and dramatists of the classical period, they still split up the characters into their components and develop them from a few abstract principles, instead of the total context of life in which they stand. It is not until the nineteenth century that the decisive step towards this indirect, impressionistic psychology is taken and, thereby, a new conception of psychological probability created, which makes the whole of previous literature seem out of date. What strikes us as modern in the writers of the eighteenth century is the de-heroizing and humanizing of their heroes. They reduce their size and bring them closer to us; therein lies the essential progress of psychological naturalism since the description of love in the work of Racine. Prévost already shows the reverse side of the great passions, above all the humiliating and shaming situation for a man of being in love. Love is once again a disaster, a disease, a disgrace as it was described by the Roman poets. It gradually develops into the 'amour-passion' of Stendhal and takes on the pathological features which are to characterize love in the literature of the nineteenth century. Marivaux does not yet know the power of this love which attacks its victims like a ravenous animal and never leaves go of them again; but with Prévost it has already taken possession of the mind. The age of knightly love is over; the fight against mésalliance begins. The degradation of love here serves merely as a social defence-mechanism. The stability of medieval feudal society and even that of the courtly society of the seventeenth century was not threatened by the dangers of love; they needed no such defence against the excesses of prodigal sons. But now, when the frontiers between the social castes are crossed more and more frequently and not only the nobility but also the bourgeoisie has to defend a privileged position in society, the excommunication of the wild, incalculable love-passion, which threatens the prevailing social order, begins, and a literature arises which finally leads to the *Dame aux camélias* and to our Garbo films. Prévost is doubtless still the unconscious instrument of the conservatism which a Dumas *fils* already serves consciously and with conviction.

Rousseau's exhibitionism is already heralded in Prévost's *Manon Lescaut*. The hero of the novel no longer spares himself in the least with the description of his inglorious love and even shows a masochistic delight in making confession of the weakness of his character. The fondness for such 'mixtures of smallness and greatness, of the contemptible and the estimable', as Lessing was to call them, with special reference to Werther, is already shown in Marivaux. The author of the *Vie de Marianne* is already conversant with the little weaknesses of even great souls, and not only draws his M. de Climal as a nature in whom attractive and repulsive features are mixed, but also describes his heroine as a character who cannot be summed up on the spur of the moment. She is an honest and sincere girl, but she is never so careless as to do or say anything that might injure her. She knows her trump-cards and plays them cleverly. Marivaux is the typical representative of an age of transition and reconstruction. As a novelist, he gives his full support to the progressive, middle-class trend, but as a writer of comedy, he clothes his psychological observations in the old forms of intrigue. The new departure, however, is that love, which had previously always played only a secondary rôle in comedy, moves into the centre of the action,[34] and, with the conquest of this last important stronghold, it completes its triumphal progress in modern literature, a development which is attributable to the fact that now even characters in comedy become more complicated and love itself acquires such a differentiated structure that the comic features which it receives are not able to damage its serious and sublimated quality. But the new characteristic in Marivaux the writer of comedy is, above all, his attempt to describe his figures as socially conditioned beings acting on impulses derived directly from their social position.[35] For, just as Molière's characters are in love, but their being in love is never the theme around which his plays revolve, so, too, the social conditioning of their nature is certainly evident, but never the origin of the dramatic conflict. In Marivaux's *Jeu de l'amour et du hasard*, on the other hand, the whole action hinges on a play with social appearances, namely on the question whether the principal characters are in fact the servants they disguise themselves to be or the masters whose identity they conceal.

Marivaux has often been compared with Watteau, and the similarity of their witty and piquant styles certainly suggests the comparison. But they also confront us with the same problem of art sociology, for they both express themselves, in full harmony with the conventions of good society, in extremely cultivated forms, and yet neither of them is so successful as one would expect in the circumstances. Throughout his life, Watteau was really appreciated by only a few, and it is well known that Marivaux repeatedly failed with his plays. His contemporaries found his language complicated, affected and obscure and stamped his glittering, sparkling, nimble dialogue as 'marivaudage', which was not intended as an appreciation, although Sainte-Beuve asserts, with some justification, that it is no small matter when the name of a writer becomes a household word. And even if, in the case of Watteau, one were to allow the explanation, which is no explanation, to stand, that he was too great for his age, and that great art 'goes against human instincts', that kind of explanation is in no way applicable to Marivaux, who was not a great writer. They were both the representatives of an age of transition, and were never understood during their lifetime; this had nothing to do with their artistic quality, but was bound up with their historical rôle as precursors and pioneers. Artists of this kind never find an adequate public. Their contemporaries do not understand them, the next generation enjoys their artistic ideas usually in the diluted form of the epigones, and posterity, which is sometimes in a more favourable position to appreciate their works, can hardly any longer bridge the historical gap which separates them from the present. Both Watteau and Marivaux were not discovered until the nineteenth century, by connoisseurs whose taste was schooled by impressionism and at a time when their art had been long since out of date thematically.

The rococo is not a royal art, as was the baroque, but the art of an aristocracy and an upper middle class. Private patrons displace the king and the state in the field of building activity; 'hôtels' and 'petites maisons' are erected instead of castles and palaces; the intimacy and elegance of boudoirs and cabinets are preferred to cold marble and heavy bronze; grave and solemn colours, brown and purple, dark blue and gold, are replaced by light pastel colours, grey and silver, mignonette green and pink. In contrast to the art of the Régence, the rococo gains in preciousness and brilliance, playful and capricious charm, but also in tenderness and spirituality; on the one hand, it develops into the society art par excellence, but, on the other, it approaches the middle-class taste for diminutive forms. It is a highly-skilled decorative art, piquant, delicate, nervous, by which the massive, statuesque, realistically spacious baroque is replaced; but it is sufficient to think of artists like La Tour or Fragonard, to remember that the facility and the verve of this art is, at the same time, a triumph of naturalistic observation and representation. Compared with the wild, excited visions of the baroque, with their tumultuous overflowing of the boundaries of ordinary life, everything produced by the rococo seems feeble, petty and trifling, but no master of the baroque can wield a brush with greater ease and assurance than Tiepolo, Piazzetta or Guardi. The rococo really represents the last phase of the development which starts with the Renaissance, in that it leads to victory the dynamic, resolving and liberating principle, with which this development began and which had to assert itself again and again against the principle of the static, the conventional and the typical. It is not until the rococo that the artistic aims of the Renaissance finally succeed in establishing themselves; now the objective representation of things attains that exactness and effortlessness which it was the aim of modern naturalism to achieve. The middle-class art, which begins after and partly even in the midst of the rococo, is already something fundamentally new, something absolutely different from the Renaissance and subsequent periods in the history of art. It marks the beginning of our present cultural epoch, which is conditioned by the democratic idea and by subjectivism and which is, no doubt, directly related to the élite cultures of the Renaissance, the baroque and the rococo from an evolutionary point of view, but is opposed to them in principle. The antinomies of the Renaissance and of the artistic styles dependent on it, the polarity of formal rigorism and naturalistic formlessness, of tectonics and pictorial dissolution, of statics and dynamics, are now replaced by the antagonism between rationalism and sentimentalism, materialism, and spiritualism, classicism and romanticism. The earlier antitheses very largely lose their meaning, since both forms of the artistic achievement of the Renaissance period have become indispensable; the naturalistic accuracy of the representation is taken for granted as much as the compositional harmony of the elements in a picture. The real question now is whether precedence is to be given to the intellect or the feeling, to the world of objects or the subject, to rationalistic insight or intuition. The rococo itself prepares the way for the new alternative, by undermining the classicism of late baroque and by creating with its pictorial style, its sensitiveness to picturesque detail and impressionistic technique an instrument which is much better suited to express the emotional contents of middle-class art than the formal idiom of the Renaissance and the baroque. The very expressiveness of this instrument leads to the dissolution of the rococo, which is bent, however, by its own way of thinking on offering the strongest resistance to irrationalism and sentimentalism. Without this dialectic between more or less automatically developing means and original intentions it is impossible to understand the significance of the rococo; not until one comes to see it as the result of a polarity which corresponds to the antagonism of the society of the same period, and which makes it the connecting link between the courtly baroque and middle-class pre-romanticism, can one do justice to its complex nature.

The epicureanism of the rococo stands, with its sensualism and aestheticism, between the ceremonial style of the baroque and the emotionalism of the pre-romantic movement. Under Louis XIV the court nobility still extolled an ideal of heroic and rational perfection, even though in reality it mostly lived for its own pleasure. Under Louis XV the same nobility professes a hedonism which is also in harmony with the outlook and the way of life of the rich bourgeoisie. The dictum of Talleyrand: 'No one who did not live before 1789 knows the sweetness of life', gives one an idea of the kind of life which these classes lead. The 'sweetness of life' is, of course, taken as meaning the sweetness of women; they are, as in every epicurean culture, the most popular pastime. Love has lost both its 'healthy' impulsiveness and its dramatic passionateness; it has become sophisticated, amusing, docile, a habit where it used to be a passion. There is a universal and constant desire to see pictures of the nude; it now becomes the favourite subject of the plastic arts. Wherever one looks, whether at the frescoes in state apartments, the gobelins of the *salons*, the paintings in boudoirs, the engravings in books, the porcelain groups and bronze figures on mantelpieces, everywhere one sees naked women, swelling thighs and hips, uncovered breasts, arms and legs folded in embraces, women with men and women with women, in countless variations and endless repetitions. Nudity in art has become so habitual that the ingénues of Greuze produce an erotic effect merely by putting their clothes on again. But the ideal of female beauty itself has also changed, it has become more piquant, more sophisticated. In the age of the baroque, mature and well-developed women were preferred, now slender young girls, often still almost children, are painted. The rococo is, in fact, an erotic art intended for rich and blasé epicureans—a means of intensifying the capacity for enjoyment, where nature has set limits to it. It is only to be expected that with the art of the middle classes, the classicism and romanticism of David, Géricault and Delacroix, the more mature, more 'normal' type of woman comes back into fashion again.

The rococo develops a striking form of 'l'art pour l'art'; its sensual cult of beauty, its affected and highly-skilled, graceful and melodious formal language, surpasses every kind of Alexandrinism. Its 'l'art pour l'art' is in some respects even more genuine and more spontaneous than that of the nineteenth century, since it is no mere programme and no mere demand but the natural attitude of a frivolous, tired and passive society, which turns to art for pleasure and rest. The rococo actually represents the final phase in a culture of taste, in which the principle of beauty still holds unrestricted sway, the last style in which 'beautiful' and 'artistic' are synonymous. In the work of Watteau, Rameau and Marivaux, and even in that of Fragonard, Chardin and Mozart, everything is 'beautiful' and melodious; in Beethoven, Stendhal and Delacroix this is by no means any longer the case—art becomes active, combative, and the striving for expression violates the formal structure. But the rococo is also the last universal style of Western Europe; a style which is not only universally recognized and moves within a generally speaking uniform system over the whole of Europe, but is also universal in the sense that it is the common property of all gifted artists, and can be accepted by them without reserve. After the rococo there is no such canon of form, no such universally valid trend of art. From the nineteenth century onwards the intentions of each single artist become so personal that he has to struggle for his own means of expression and can no longer accept ready-made solutions; he regards every pre-established form as a fetter rather than a help. Impressionism again acquires fairly universal recognition, but the relation of the individual artist to that movement is no longer wholly unproblematical, and there is no such thing as an impressionistic formula in the rococo sense. In the second half of the eighteenth century a revolutionary change took place; the emergence of the modern middle class, with its individualism and its passion for originality, put an end to the idea of style as something consciously and deliberately held in common by a cultural community, and gave the idea of intellectual property its current significance.

Boucher is the most important name in connection with the rise of the rococo formula and the masterly technique which gives the art of a Fragonard and Guardi that quality of unfailing certainty in the execution. He is the individually insignificant representative of an extraordinarily significant artistic convention, and he represents this convention in such a perfect way that he attains an influence unlike that of any artist since Le Brun. He is the unrivalled master of the erotic genre, of the genre of painting most sought after by the *fermiers généraux*, the *nouveaux riches* and the more liberal court circles, and the creator of that amorous mythology which, next to Watteau's 'fêtes galantes', provides the most important subject-matter of rococo painting. He transfers the erotic motifs from painting to the graphic arts and the whole of industrial art, and makes a national style out of the 'peinture des seins et des culs'. Naturally, it is not the whole of the art-minded public in France that sees Boucher as its leading painter; there is a cultured middle section of the bourgeoisie, which has already been having its say in literature for a long time past, and which now goes its own ways in art. Greuze and Chardin paint their didactic and realistic pictures for this public. To be sure, their supporters do not all belong to the middle classes but also to those who provide the public of Boucher and Fragonard. Fragonard, for his part, often conforms to the taste which the 'bourgeois' painters strive to satisfy, and motifs are to be found even in Boucher which are not so far removed from the world of these painters. His 'Breakfast' in the Louvre, for example, can be described as a scene from middle-class, albeit upper middle-class life; it is, at least, already genre painting and no longer the representation of a ceremony.

The break with the rococo takes place in the second half of the century; the cleft between the art of the upper classes and that of the middle classes is obvious. The painting of Greuze marks the beginning not only of a new attitude to life and a new morality, but also of a new taste—possibly a 'bad taste'—in art. His sentimental family scenes, with the cursing or blessing father, the prodigal or the good and grateful sons, are of little artistic value. They lack originality in the composition, they are unremarkably drawn, their colours are unattractive and, furthermore, the technique has an unpleasant smoothness. The impression they make is cold and empty, despite their exaggerated solemnity, and mendacious, despite the emotions they display. The interests they attempt to satisfy are almost entirely non-artistic, and they present their unpainterly, in most cases purely narrative, subject-matter quite crudely, with no attempt to transfer it into genuine pictorial forms. Diderot praises them for portraying events which contain the germs of whole novels;[36] but one might perhaps assert with more justification that they contain nothing that a story could not contain. They are 'literary' painting in the bad sense of the word, banal, moralizing, anecdotic painting, and as such the prototype of the most inartistic products of the nineteenth century. But the works of Greuze are not in bad taste merely on account of their 'middle-class' character, although the change in the groups which are the upholders of taste is, naturally, bound up with an undermining of the old well-tried albeit schematized standards. The pictures of Chardin are, at any rate, among the best artistic products of the eighteenth century, in spite of their bourgeois plainness. And they are a much more genuine and honest middle-class art than that of Greuze, who, with his stereotyping of simple, chaste folk, his apotheosis of the middle-class family, his idealization of the artless maiden, expresses more the ideas and conceptions of the upper than those of the middle and lower classes. In spite of that, the historical importance of Greuze is no less than that of Chardin; in the struggle against the aristocratic and upper middle-class rococo, his weapons proved even more effective. Diderot may have over-estimated him as an artist, but his recognition of the political propagandistic value of his painting was well grounded. He was, at any rate, aware that the 'l'art pour l'art' of the rococo was under fire here, and if he asserted that it was the task of art 'to honour virtue and expose vice', if he wanted to make art, the great match-maker, a school of virtue, if he condemned Boucher and Vanloo on account of their artificiality, their empty, easy, thoughtless dexterity and their libertinage, then he always had in mind the 'punishment of the tyrants', or, more concretely, the introduction of the middle class into the world of art, in order to lead it to a place in the sun. His crusade against the art of the rococo was merely a stage in the history of the revolution which was already under way.

2. THE NEW READING PUBLIC

Intellectual leadership in the eighteenth century passes from France to economically, socially and politically more progressive England. The great romantic movement starts here about the middle of the century, but the enlightenment also receives its decisive impulse from this country. The French writers of the period see in English institutions the quintessence of progress and build up a legend around English liberalism—a legend which only partly corresponds to reality. The displacement of France as the upholder of culture by England proceeds hand in hand with the decadence of the French royal house as the leading European power and, hence, the eighteenth century sees the ascent of England both in politics and in the arts and sciences. The weakening of the king's authority, which in France results in national decline, becomes a source of power in England, where enterprising classes with an understanding of the trend of economic development and a capacity for adapting themselves to it stand ready to take over the reins of government. Parliament, which is now the expression of the liberal political aspirations of these classes and their strongest weapon against absolutism, supported the Tudors in their fight against the feudal aristocracy, the foreign foe and the Roman Church, since the commercial and industrial middle classes, represented in Parliament, as well as the liberal nobility, with interests in the commercial activities of the bourgeoisie, recognized that this fight was promoting their own designs. Until towards the end of the sixteenth century, there was a close community of interests between the monarchy and these classes. English capitalism was still in a primitive, adventurous stage of its development and the merchants gladly supported the confidential advisers of the Crown in joint piratical enterprises. The parting of the ways took place only when capitalism began to follow more rationalistic methods and the Crown no longer needed the assistance of the middle class against the crippled aristocracy. The Stuarts, encouraged by the example of continental absolutism and believing that they had an ally in the French king, carelessly threw away both the loyalty of the middle classes and the support of Parliament. They rehabilitated the old feudal nobility as a court nobility and laid the foundations of a new period of ascendancy for this class, to whom they were bound by stronger feelings and more permanent common interests than to their predecessors' comrades in arms in the ranks of the middle class and the liberal gentry. Until 1640 the feudal nobility enjoyed considerable privileges and the state not only provided for the continuance of the latifundia, but tried to assure the great landowners of a share in the profit of capitalistic enterprises by monopolies and other forms of protectionism. This very practice, however, was fraught with disastrous consequences for the whole system. The economically productive classes were by no means prepared to share their profits with the favourites of the Crown and protested against interventionism in the name of freedom and justice, slogans which they continued constantly to use when they themselves had become the beneficiaries of economic privilege.

There is, as Tocqueville remarks, almost no political question which is not connected in some way with the imposition or the granting of taxes. At any rate, problems of taxation dominated public life in England from the end of the Middle Ages and became in the seventeenth century the immediate cause of the revolutionary movements. The same middle class that granted taxes to the Tudors without any fuss, and was ready to bear them in even greater measure in the years of the Civil War, refused them to Charles I because of his reactionary, anti-middle-class policy. When James II, a generation later, called on the council of the City of London to protect him against William of Orange, the citizens of London refused him their help and preferred to supply the intruder with the means necessary for success. This was the beginning of that alliance between the monarchy and the commercial classes which guaranteed the victory of capitalism and the continuance of the royal house in England.[37] The remains of feudalism, of which a clean sweep was only made a hundred years later in France, were already destroyed in England in the period of revolution between 1640 and 1660; but in both countries the Revolution was a class struggle, in which the classes tied to capital defended their economic interests against absolutism, pure landed property and, above all, against the Church.[38]

The great conflict, which dominates the political life of the seventeenth and eighteenth centuries, was waged in England between the Crown and the court nobility, on the one side, and the classes interested in capitalism, on the other, but in reality at least three different, economically antagonistic groups stood against each other: the big landowners, the bourgeoisie in alliance with the capitalistically-minded nobility and the already very complex group of small tradesmen, town labourers and peasants. But in the eighteenth century this latter category was not mentioned much either in Parliament or literature.

The Parliament that met after 1688 was by no means a 'representation of the people' in our sense of the term; its task was to establish capitalism on the ruins of the old feudal order and to stabilize the predominance of the economically productive elements over the parasitic classes in sympathy with absolutism and the ecclesiastical hierarchy. The Revolution did not result in a new distribution of economic property, but it created rights to freedom which finally benefited the whole nation and the whole civilized world. For, even if these rights could at first be exercised only imperfectly, they signified, nevertheless, the end of absolute royal power and the beginning of a development which bore within it the seeds of democracy. Parliament wanted, above all, to exert a conserving influence, that is, to create conditions under which the elections would remain dependent on commercially based landed property and the commercial capital associated with it. The antagonism between the Whigs and Tories was a conflict of secondary importance within the common cause of the classes represented in Parliament. Whichever of the two parties was at the helm, political life was led by the aristocracy, which had far-reaching influence on the elections and made the middle class its satellite. When power passed from the Tories to the Whigs, it merely meant that the administration encouraged commercialism and dissent rather than pure landed property and the Anglican Church; parliamentary government was, however, as much the rule of an oligarchy as ever. The Whigs no more wanted a Parliament without a monarch and without aristocratic privileges, than did the Tories a monarchy without a Parliament. Neither party thought of Parliament as a democratic corporation; they regarded it merely as the guarantee of their own privileges against the Crown. Furthermore, Parliament retained this class character throughout the eighteenth century. The country was ruled alternately by a few dozen Whig and Tory families who, with their first-born in the House of Lords and their younger sons in the Commons, monopolized the whole of political life. Two-thirds of the Members of Parliament were simply nominated and the rest chosen by not more than 160,000 electors, and some of their votes were acquired corruptly. The census, which made the franchise dependent in the first place on ground rent, secured a predominant place in Parliament for the land-owning classes from the very outset. But in spite of the limited franchise, the buying of votes and corruptibility of Members of Parliament, England was already in the eighteenth century a modern nation in gradual process of liberation from the relics of medievalism. At any rate, its citizens enjoyed a personal freedom still unknown in the rest of Europe; and the social privileges themselves, which in England were based on the mere ownership of land and not, as in France, on mystical birthrights,[39] made it easier to reconcile the lower classes to the intrinsically more elastic class distinctions.

The English social order of the eighteenth century has often been compared with conditions in Rome in the last period of the Republic; the fact, however, that the organization of Roman society, with its senator class, its *equites* and its plebeians, is repeated, to a certain extent, in the categories of the parliamentary aristocracy, the moneyed classes and the 'poor' in England, can hardly be said to be remarkable in itself—this tripartition is in fact characteristic of all more advanced societies where the process of equalization has not yet begun. What gives special significance to the parallel between England and Rome is the emergence of the aristocracy as the class by which parliament is dominated, and the thoroughly fluid boundaries between the patricians and the capitalists. But the relationship between these classes and the plebs is rather different in the two countries. It is true that the Roman authors of the period mention the poor just as seldom as do the English writers of the eighteenth century,[40] but whilst the proletariat constantly occupies public attention in Rome, it plays almost no part at all in English politics. Another peculiarity distinguishing English from Roman society —and not only from Roman—is that the nobility, which normally becomes impoverished under similar conditions, increases its wealth and remains the well-to-do class in England.[41] The ruling class in this country shows its political wisdom not only by allowing the bourgeoisie to earn and by itself earning alongside of it, but by renouncing of its own accord the fiscal privileges to which the French aristocracy clings most firmly of all.[42] In France only the poor pay taxes, in England only the rich,[43] which does not mean that the situation of the poor is essentially any better, but the budget remains balanced and the most disgraceful privilege of the nobility disappears. In England power is held by a commercial aristocracy which probably does not feel and think more humanely than the aristocracy in general, but which, thanks to its business experience, has more sense of reality and understands in good time that its interests are identical with those of the state. The universal levelling tendency of the age, which influences everything except the difference between rich and poor, assumes more radical forms in England than elsewhere, and creates for the first time modern social relationships based essentially on property. The lack of distance between the different levels of the social hierarchy is guaranteed not only by a series of intermediary grades, but also by the indefinable nature of the individual categories themselves. The English 'nobility' is a hereditary nobility, but the title of a peer always passes only to the eldest son; there is hardly any difference between the younger sons and the ordinary gentry. But the boundaries dividing the lower nobility from the immediately inferior classes are also fluid. Originally the gentry was identical with the 'squirearchy'; gradually, however, it absorbed not only the local notabilities but also all the elements of society which were differentiated from the manufacturing classes, the small tradesmen and the 'poor' by reason of property and culture. Hence the concept of the gentleman lost all legal significance and became indefinite even with reference to a certain fixed standard of life. Membership of the ruling class was more and more dependent on a common cultural level and ideological agreement. That explains, above all, why the transition from the aristocratic rococo to bourgeois romanticism in England was not bound up with the kind of violence to cultural values that occurred in France or Germany.

The cultural levelling process in England is expressed most strikingly in the rise of the new and regular reading public, by which is to be understood a comparatively wide circle reading and buying books regularly and thereby assuring a number of writers a livelihood free from personal obligations. The existence of this public is due, first of all, to the increasing prominence of the well-to-do middle class, which breaks the cultural prerogatives of the aristocracy and shows a lively and ever-growing interest in literature. The new upholders of culture can produce no individual personalities ambitious and rich enough to come forward as patrons on the grand scale, but they are numerous enough to guarantee a sale of books sufficient to provide writers with a living. The objection to the explanation of the existence of this public as being due to the presence of an economically, socially and politically influential middle class, and the argument that the middle class had already become important in the seventeenth century and that its cultural function in the eighteenth cannot, therefore, be derived simply from the improvement of its social position,[44] are easily refuted. In the seventeenth century artistic culture was limited to the court aristocracy above all because of the puritanical outlook of the middle class. Circles outside the court themselves gave up the function they had fulfilled in Elizabethan culture; they had first to regain their place in cultural life, that is, to traverse a road which could follow on from their fresh economic and social rise only after a certain interval. The prosperity of the middle class had to spread and become firmly established before it could again become the basis of intellectual leadership. Finally, the aristocracy itself had to adopt certain aspects of the bourgeois outlook on life, in order to form a homogeneous cultural stratum with the middle class and in order adequately to strengthen the reading public, and this could not happen until after it had begun to participate in the business life of the bourgeoisie.

The former court aristocracy had not constituted a real reading public; it is true that it somehow looked after its writers, but it did not regard them as the producers of indispensable goods, only as servants whose service could also be dispensed with in certain circumstances. It supported them more for reasons of prestige than because of the real value of their accomplishments. At the end of the seventeenth century the reading of books was not yet a very widespread recreation; as far as secular belles-lettres were concerned, which consisted very largely of old-fashioned stories of love and marvels, only people of the upper classes with no other occupation could be considered potential readers; and learned books were read only by scholars. The literary education of women, who were to play such an important part in the literary life of the following century, was still defective. We know, for example, that Milton's elder daughter could not write at all and that Dryden's wife, who, incidentally, came from an aristocratic family, had a desperate struggle to master the grammar and spelling of her mother tongue.[45] The only kind of book that had a wider public in the seventeenth and the beginning of the eighteenth century was the edifying religious tract; secular fiction formed only an unimportant fraction of the total book-production.[46] The turning away of the reading public from devotional books to secular belles-lettres, which until about 1720 still dealt mainly with moral subjects and only later began to treat more trivial themes, can, contrary to Schoeffler's assumption,[47] be attributed only indirectly to Walpole's politicizing of the Church and to the free-thinking activities of the Anglican clergy. The liberal policy and secular outlook of the High Church were merely symptoms of the enlightenment, which, in its turn, was nothing more than the ideological expression of the dissolution of feudalism and the arrival of the middle classes. But the evidence proving that the Protestant clergy played a highly important part in the dissemination of secular literature and the education of the new reading public[48] is, nevertheless, one of the most significant results of the modern sociology of literature. Without the publicity they received from the pulpit, the novels of Defoe and Richardson would scarcely have achieved the popularity accorded to them.

Towards the middle of the century the number of readers grows to a marked degree; more and more books appear which, judging by the prosperity of the book trade, must have found their buyers. Around the turn of the century reading is already one of the necessities of life for the upper classes, and the possession of books is, as has been noted, just as much taken for granted in the circles described by Jane Austen as it would have caused surprise in the world of Fielding.[49] Of the cultural media on which the new reading public thrives, the periodicals which spread from the beginning of the century onwards—the great invention of the age—are the most important. From them the middle class receives both its literary and its social culture, both of which are still based fundamentally on aristocratic standards. The aristocracy has also changed a good deal since the days of its absolute power, and has learnt its lesson from the victory of the urban middle-class over the courtly mind. A tension between the forms of thinking and feeling of the aristocratic and the middle classes still continues for a long time, however. The coolly intellectual, sceptically superior mentality of the aristocracy does not vanish from one day to the next; on the contrary, it still makes its influence felt in the affected style and stoic moral philosophy of the periodicals. In literature proper classicistic taste prevails longer than in the press; here intellect and wit, clever ideas and highly-skilled technique, clarity of thought and purity of language, as represented by the supporters of Pope and the 'Wits', are regarded as the literary qualities par excellence right up to the middle of the century. Nothing is more typical of the transitional character of this semi-court, semi-bourgeois culture, than the thin intellectual stratum of writers and amateurs who try to distinguish themselves from ordinary mortals by their classical education, their fastidious taste and their playful and complacent wit. How these intellectuals then gradually disappear, how certain qualities of their mental equipment become the accepted precondition of literary culture, whilst others come to seem all the more ridiculous, how, above all, coquettish wit is displaced by common sense and formal elegance by emotional directness, all that belongs to the later development and to the complete emancipation of the middle-class spirit in literature. In the end the tension between the two directions ceases entirely and middle-class literature is no longer opposed by anything that could be called courtly. That does not mean, however, that all tension comes to an end and that literature is dominated by a single, undivided taste. On the contrary, a new antagonism develops, a tension between the literature of the cultured élite and that of the general reading public, and lapses of good taste are to be observed, in which the weaknesses of the light fiction of a later age are already discernible.

Steele's *Tatler*, which begins to appear in 1709, Addison's *Spectator*, by which it is replaced two years later, and the 'moral weeklies' which follow them, first create the preconditions of a literature which bridges the gap between the scholar and the more or less educated general reader, between the aristocratic *bel esprit* and the matter-of-fact bourgeois, a literature which is, therefore, neither courtly nor really popular, and which stands, with its stern rationalism, its moral harshness and its ideal of respectability, halfway between the knightly-aristocratic and the bourgeois-puritanical outlook on life. Through these periodicals, which, with their short pseudo-scientific dissertations and ethical enquiries, form the best introduction to the reading of real books, the public becomes accustomed for the first time to the regular enjoyment of serious literature; through them reading becomes a habit and a necessity for comparatively wide sections of society. But the periodicals themselves are already the product of a development connected with the alteration in the social position of the writer. After the glorious Revolution it is no longer at court that authors find their patrons; the court has ceased to exist in the old sense and will never again take up its earlier cultural function.[50] The rôle of court circles as patrons of literature is taken over by the political parties and the government, which is now dependent on public opinion. Under William III and Anne, power is divided between the Tories and the Whigs and the two parties have, therefore, to wage an incessant war for political influence, in which they cannot forgo the weapon of literary propaganda. The writers themselves are forced to undertake this task, whether they like it or not, since, as the old form of patronage is on the point of disappearing altogether and the free book market cannot yet depend on a sufficient public, they have no reliable source of income apart from political propaganda. Just as Steele and Addison become journalists representing directly or indirectly the interests of the Whigs, so Defoe and Swift are also active as political pamphleteers and pursue political aims even in their novels. The idea of 'l'art pour l'art' would have had something irresponsible and immoral about it for them, if they had been able to conceive such an idea at all. *Robinson Crusoe* is a novel with a socially instructive purpose, and *Gulliver* is a topical social satire; both are political propaganda in the strictest sense of the term and nothing but propaganda. This is probably not the first time that we are confronted by a militant literature with direct social purposes, but the 'paper canon-balls' of Swift and his contemporaries would have been unthinkable before the introduction of the freedom of the press and the public discussion of political questions of the day. Now for the first time writers emerge as a regular social phenomenon, making ad hoc weapons of their pens and hiring them out to the highest bidder.

The fact that they no longer face a single compact phalanx of power, but two different parties, makes them independent, for they can now choose their employers more or less in accordance with their own inclinations.[51] But if the politicians regard them simply as their confederates, then in most cases that is based on a pure illusion, the maintenance of which flatters and profits both sides. Now, as for the two greatest publicists of the age, Defoe usually defends his own real convictions, and, at any rate, the hatred in Swift's passionate utterances is genuine. The former, a Whig, is a profound optimist, whereas the latter, as goes without saying for a Tory under Walpole, is a bitter pessimist; the one proclaims a puritanical middle-class philosophy of life based on faith in the world and faith in God, the other exhibits a sarcastically superior, misanthropic and world-despising attitude to life. They are the most conspicuous literary representatives of the two political camps into which England is divided. Defoe is the son of a London butcher and dissenter; the suppressed but stubborn puritanism of his fathers still comes through in his writings. He himself suffered at the hands of High-Church-inspired Tory rule. The victory of the Whigs finally vindicates the expectations of his social compeers and co-religionists and it is the optimistic outlook of this middle class that is expressed through him for the first time in secular literature. Robinson, who, thrown back on his own resources, triumphs over the stubbornness of nature and creates prosperity, security, order, law and custom out of nothing, is the classical representative of the middle class. The story of his adventures is one long hymn in praise of the industry, endurance, inventiveness and common sense which overcomes all difficulties, in a word, the practical middle-class virtues; it is the confession of faith of a class with keen social aspirations and conscious of its strength, and it is, at the same time, the manifesto of a young, enterprising nation fighting its way to world-dominion. Swift sees only the reverse of all this; not only because he looks at it from another social standpoint from the outset, but also because he has already lost Defoe's simple confidence. He is one of the first to experience the disillusionment of the period of enlightenment and he moulds his experience into the super-Candide of the age. He is one of the minds that hatred turns into genius, and he sees things that others cannot see, because he hates better than others and because, as he writes to Pope, he wants to torment and not delight the world. Hence he becomes the author of the most cruel book of a century which, for all its humanity and sentiment, is by no means lacking in cruel books. It is hardly possible to imagine anything more opposed to the philanthropic 'Robinson' than this second great 'youth novel' of English literature, the cruelty of which is perhaps surpassed only by the third classical example of the genre, *Don Quixote*. Nevertheless, there are certain features common to *Gulliver* and *Robinson Crusoe*. First of all, they both have their literary origin in those phantastic travel novels and Utopian stories of marvels, which were so popular in the Renaissance and the best-known representatives of which are Cyrano de Bergerac, Campanella and Thomas More. But they also hinge on the same philosophical problems, namely the origin and validity of human culture. These problems could become so important, as they did become for Defoe and Swift, only in an age in which the social foundations of civilization had begun to totter, and it was only under the direct impact of the passing of leadership in cultural affairs from one class to another, that it was possible to formulate so pointedly the idea of the dependence of civilizations on social conditions.

With the development of political propaganda in literature, the economic and social position of writers undergoes a fundamental change. Now that they are compensated for their services with high office and abundant reward, their moral value also rises in the estimation of the public. Addison marries a Countess of Warwick, Swift stands in friendly relationship with such personalities as Bolingbroke and Harley in the 'Kitcat Club', a Count of Sunderland and a Duke of Newcastle associate with Vanbrugh and Congreve on equal terms. But one must not forget that these writers are appreciated and rewarded solely on account of their political services and not because of their literary or moral qualities.[52] And since the politicians now have the means of reward, above all, high office, at their disposal, the parties and the government take over the position in literature once occupied by court coteries and the king. Only the price they pay is higher and the honours they award to their authors greater than the rewards formerly bestowed on a writer. Locke is a Commissioner of the Court of Appeal and the Board of Trade, Steele holds a similar office at the Stamp Office, Addison becomes a Secretary of State and retires with a pension of £1,600, Granville is a member of the House of Commons, becomes Minister of War and Treasurer of the Royal Household, Prior obtains the post of an ambassador and Defoe is entrusted with various political missions.[53] At no other time and in no other country have writers been honoured with so many high offices and dignities as in England at the beginning of the eighteenth century.

This exceptionally favourable situation for authors reaches its climax in the last years of the reign of Queen Anne, and comes to an end completely when Walpole enters office in 1721. The assumption of office by the Whigs creates conditions in which writers become unprofitable to the government and which bring political patronage to a sudden end. The power of the government party seems so consolidated that it is able to forgo all propaganda; the influence of the Tories, on the other hand, is so small that they are not in a position to pay authors for their services. Walpole, who has no personal relation to literature, also does not find any surplus money and vacant offices for authors. The more lucrative appointments have to be given to Members of Parliament whose support is needed, or to constituencies it is desired to reward for services rendered. It has been realized, after all, that there are always dissatisfied writers, however many have been satisfied, and that Halifax, the most generous of all patrons, had the greatest number of literary enemies.[54] Public interest in writers cools down. Pope, Addison, Steele, Swift, Prior, withdraw from the capital and from public life and continue to write, if at all, in rural solitude. The economic situation of the younger writers becomes worse from day to day. Thomson is so poor that he is forced to sell one canto of his 'Seasons', in order to buy himself a pair of shoes, and Johnson fights against the most bitter poverty at the beginning of his career. The man of letters is no longer a gentleman; and his public esteem and self-respect decline along with the security of his existence. He acquires bad manners, falls into untidy habits, becomes unreliable and, finally, breeds types like Savage, who would have been impossible in the age of courtly culture, and who are really already the precursors of the modern bohemian.

Fortunately, private patronage does not stop so abruptly as political subvention. The old aristocratic tradition had never entirely broken down, and now that writers can and must turn again to private customers, it experiences a kind of renaissance. The new system of patronage is not so widespread as the old, but, in general, it is guided by more adequate considerations, so that sooner or later every gifted writer finds a patron if he tries.[55] At any rate, there were few authors who would have been in a position to forgo private support in this transitional period between the age of political propaganda and free-lance activity in the literary world. Complaints about the system of patronage are constantly heard, but there is hardly any mention of a writer ever having had the courage to part from his patron. Being dependent on a patron was after all less uncomfortable than being dependent on a publisher, although it was a more personal relationship and, therefore, often seemed to be more humiliating. Even Johnson, who struggled throughout his life against the system of canvassing for patrons and did not think much of the institution, admitted that it was, nevertheless, possible to be the protégé of a lord and yet preserve one's independence. Fielding's relationship to his protector proves that it actually was feasible. Writers who had not enjoyed any private support usually had to hire themselves out as day-labourers and take on the work of translation, making excerpts, preparing revised editions, proof-reading, writing contributions to periodicals and popular works of reference. Even Johnson, the later arbiter of English literature, begins his career as a hack. Pope cannot, it is true, be included in any of these categories, and seems to remain free of external ties, but, in fact, he is in the service of the aristocracy that subscribes to his books and that rightly regards him as its own. With the revival of private patronage, the esteem in which the professional author is held declines once again, as even the attitude of men with such a high literary culture as Horace Walpole and Lord Chesterfield proves. The latter's famous words: 'We, my lords, may thank Heaven that we have something better than our brains to depend upon', are a perfect expression of the dominant view. But some authors also share this view and pretend that for them writing is simply a noble passion. Congreve, who desired Voltaire to regard him, above all, as a 'gentleman' and not as a writer, belongs to this category.

After the middle of the century, patronage comes to an absolute end, and round about the year 1780 no writer any longer counts on private support. The number of independent poets and men of letters living on their writing increases from day to day, just as does the number of people who read and buy books and whose relation to the author is purely impersonal. Johnson and

Goldsmith now write only for such readers. The patron's place is taken by the publisher; public subscription, which has very aptly been called collective patronage, is the bridge between the two.[56] Patronage is the purely aristocratic form of the relationship between author and public; the system of public subscription loosens the bond, but still maintains certain features of the personal character of the relationship; the publication of books for a general public, completely unknown to the author, is the first form of the relationship to correspond to the structure of a middle-class society based on the anonymous circulation of goods. The publisher's rôle, as the mediator between author and public, begins with the emancipation of middle-class taste from the dictates of the aristocracy and is itself a symptom of this emancipation. It forms the historical starting point of literary life in the modern sense, as typified not only by the regular appearance of books, newspapers and periodicals, but, above all, by the emergence of the literary expert, the critic, who represents the general standard of values and public opinion in the world of literature. The forerunners of the eighteenth-century men of letters, especially the humanists of the Renaissance, were not in a position to fulfil that kind of function, because they had no periodical press at their disposal and, therefore, no appropriate means of influencing public opinion.

Until the middle of the eighteenth century writers did not live on the direct profit accruing from their works but on pensions, beneficies and sinecures, which often bore no relationship to the intrinsic value or general attraction of their writings. Now, for the first time, the literary product becomes a commodity, the value of which conforms to its saleableness on the free market. One can welcome or deplore this change; but the development of authorship into an independent and regular profession would have been unthinkable in the age of capitalism without the transformation of personal service into an impersonal commodity. It was only in this way that authorship was able to attain a firm material footing and its present public esteem; for the buyer of a book that appears in an edition of a thousand copies is obviously not doing the author a favour, whereas rewarding him for a manuscript always seems like making a present. In an age of courtly and aristocratic society a man's reputation depended on the standing of his protector, but now, in the epoch of liberalism and capitalism, the freer he is from personal ties and the more successful he is in his impersonal dealings with other people, based on mutual service, the greater is the esteem he enjoys. The literary hack does not disappear entirely, it is true, but there is such a great demand for literary entertainment and instruction, especially for historical, biographical and statistical encyclopaedias, that the average author can count on an assured income.[57] In organizations like Smollet's 'literary factory', where work is in progress, at one and the same time, on a translation of *Don Quixote*, a *History of England*, a *Compendium of Voyages* and a translation of the works of Voltaire, there is employment for anyone who can write.[58] A lot is heard about the exploitation of writers in this period, and the publishers were certainly in no sense charitable institutions; but Johnson says to their credit that they were punctilious and generous partners and we know that recognized and marketable authors received considerable sums for their works even judged by present-day standards. Hume, for example, earned £3,400 from his *History of Great Britain* (1754–61) and Smollett £2,000 from his historical work (1757–65). Conditions have undergone a big change since the days of Defoe, who, to begin with, could not find any publisher at all for his *Robinson Crusoe* and, in the end, received £10 for the manuscript. With the achievement of material independence, the moral esteem of writers now rises to unprecedented heights. In the age of the Renaissance famous writers and scholars were certainly extolled, but the average man of letters was put in the same category as the clerk and the private secretary. Now for the first time the writer as such enjoys the regard due to the representative of a higher sphere of life. 'Nous protégeons les grands, protecteurs d'autrefois' says a philosopher in a comedy by Dorat.[59] Now for the first time the ideal of the creative personality arises, of the artistic genius with his originality and subjectivism, as already characterized by Edward Young in his *Conjectures on Original Composition* (1759).

The element of genius in artistic creation is in most cases merely a weapon in the competitive struggle, and the subjective mode of expression often only a form of self-advertisement. The subjectivism of the pre-romantic poets is partly, at any rate, a consequence of the growing number of writers, of their direct dependence on the book market and their competition against one another, just as the romantic movement in general, with its middle-class emphasis on the sentiments, is nothing more than the product of intellectual rivalry and an instrument in the fight against the classicistic world-view of the aristocracy with its tendency to the normative and the universally valid. Hitherto the middle class had striven to adopt the artistic idiom of the upper classes, now, however, that it has become so well-to-do and influential that it can afford a literature of its own, it tries to make its own individuality felt, in opposition to these upper classes, and to speak its own language, which, if only out of mere antagonism to the intellectualism of the aristocracy, develops into a language of sentimentality. The revolt of the emotions against the coldness of the intellect is as much a part of the ideology of the ambitious and progressive classes in their fight against the spirit of conservatism and convention, as is the rebellion of the 'genius' against the constraint of rules and forms. The rise of the modern middle class is connected, like that of the *ministeriales* in the Middle Ages, with a romantic movement; in both cases the redistribution of social power leads to the dissolution of formal ties and produces a sudden heightening of sensibility.

The turning away from the intellectual culture of classicism to the emotional culture of romanticism has often been described as a change of taste expressing the weariness and disgust felt by the cultured circles of society with the sophisticated and decadent art of the period. Against this view it has rightly been pointed out that the mere desire for novelty plays a relatively small part in the alternation of styles, and that the older and the more developed a tradition of taste is, the less liking for change it shows of its own accord. Hence a new style can make its way only with difficulty, if it does not address itself to a new public.[60] At any rate, the aristocracy of the eighteenth century would have had small reason for surrendering its old aesthetic discernment, if the middle class had not taken over the intellectual leadership in Western Europe. It was also by no means prepared to entrust itself to this new leadership and to share the emotionalism of the lower classes. But, as we know, the dominant tendency of an age often presses the very classes into its service that it threatens with destruction. And the eighteenth century offers the classical example of precisely this phenomenon. The aristocracy played an outstanding part in the preparatory stages of the Revolution and shrunk back from it only when it became clear what its victory would entail. The upper classes played a similar part in the development of anti-classical culture. In the assimilation and propagation of the ideas of the enlightenment they vied with the middle class and often even surpassed it; it was only Rousseau's frankly plebeian and irreverent way of thinking that brought them to their senses and drove them into opposition. Voltaire's dislike for Rousseau is already an expression of the resistance of this social élite. But in most of the leading personalities the elements of rationalism and emotionalism are intermingled from the very outset; their intellectual sensibility makes them, to some extent, indifferent to their own class interests. The development of art, which was already rather heterogeneous in the seventeenth century, becomes now, in the age of pre-romanticism, even more complicated and presents an even more obscure picture than in the succeeding period. The nineteenth century is, in fact, already absolutely dominated by the middle class, in which there are certainly acute differences of wealth, but no very acute differences in cultural standards; the only deep rift here is between the classes that share the privileges of culture and those that are wholly excluded from them. In the eighteenth century, on the other hand, both the aristocracy and the bourgeoisie are divided into two camps; in both there is a progressive and a conservative group, with many points of contact but with its own personal identity intact.

In its origins, romanticism is an English movement, just as the modern middle class, which here speaks for itself for the first time in literature independently of the aristocracy, is a result of English conditions. Thomson's nature poetry, Young's 'Night Thoughts' and Macpherson's Ossianic laments as well as the sentimental novel of manners of Richardson, Fielding and Sterne are all only the literary form of the individualism which also finds expression in *laissez-faire* and the Industrial Revolution. They are phenomena of the age of commercial wars, which brings the thirty years' peaceful hegemony of the Whigs to an end and leads to the loss of French leadership in Europe. At the end of the struggle the British Empire is not only the leading world power and not only plays the same part in world commerce as Venice in the Middle Ages, Spain in the sixteenth century and France and Holland in the seventeenth, but remains strong internally, in contrast to its predecessors,[61] and is able to continue the fight for economic supremacy with the technical acquisitions of the Industrial Revolution. England's military triumphs, the geographical discoveries, the new markets and ocean-routes, the relatively great capital sums on the look-out for investments, all that is part of the background which is the precondition of this revolution. The mass of new inventions cannot be explained by the mere progress of the exact sciences and the sudden emergence of technical abilities. The inventions are made because they can be put to good use, because there is a mass demand for industrial goods which it is impossible to satisfy with the old production methods and because the material means for effecting the necessary technical alterations are available. In the previous history of the sciences, considerations for industry had played a relatively small part; it is not until the last third of the eighteenth century that research comes to be dominated by the technological outlook. Nevertheless, the Industrial Revolution does not signify an absolutely new beginning. It is, in fact, the continuation of a development which had already started at the end of the Middle Ages. Neither the divorce between capital and labour nor the businesslike organization of goods production is new; machines had been known for centuries, and ever since there had existed a capitalistically based economy, the rationalization of production had been constantly progressing. But the mechanization and rationalization of production now enters a decisive phase of its development in which the past is entirely liquidated. The gulf between capital and labour becomes unbridgeable; the power of capital, on the one hand, and the suppression and misery of the working class, on the other, reach a stage in which the whole atmosphere of life is changed. However old the beginnings of this development are, at the end of the eighteenth century it leads to a new world.

The Middle Ages, with all its relics, its corporative spirit, its particularistic forms of life, its irrational, traditional methods of production, disappears once and for all, to make room for an organization of labour based solely on expediency and calculation and a spirit of ruthless competitive individualism. With the thoroughly rationalized factory, run on these principles, the 'modern age' in the real sense of the word—the machine age—begins. There arises a new type of working system conditioned by mechanical methods, the strict division of labour and an output adapted to meet the needs of mass consumption. As a consequence of the depersonalization of labour, its emancipation from the personal capacities of the worker, a far-reaching matter-of-factness in the relationship between employee and employer arises. Harder conditions and more constrained forms of life arise with the concentration of the working class in the industrial cities and their dependence on the fluctuating labour market. As a result of being tied to one definite factory, the capitalist develops a new and stricter morality of work; for the labourer, however, who feels no kind of personal link between himself and the factory, the ethical value of work disappears. Finally, a new social structure comes into being: a new capitalist stratum (the modern employers), a new urban middle class, threatened with extinction (the heirs of the small and medium tradesmen and manufacturers), and a new working class (the modern industrial proletariat). Society loses the former differentiation of professional types and, especially in the lower grades, the levelling process is terrifying. Craftsmen, day labourers, propertyless and uprooted peasants, skilled and unskilled workmen, men, women and children, all become mere drudges in a great, mechanically functioning factory run on the lines of a barracks. Life loses its stability and continuity, all its forms and institutions are dislocated and always shifting. The mobilization of society is conditioned, above all, by the migration to the towns. Whilst the enclosures and the commercialization of agriculture lead to unemployment, the new industries create new opportunities for labour; the result is the depopulation of the village and the overpopulation of the industrial city, which, with its dreary routine and its overcrowding, represents a completely unfamiliar and bewildering background to life for the uprooted masses. The cities are like great labour camps and prisons, they are uncomfortable, unclean, unhealthy and ugly beyond all conception.[62] The living conditions of the urban working class sink to such a low level that the existence of the medieval serf seems quite idyllic in comparison.

The amount of capital necessary to run an industrial undertaking capable of standing up to competition leads to the fundamental divorce between labour and the means of production, and brings about the typically modern struggle between capital and labour. Since the means of production are only within the reach of the capitalist, all the worker can do is to offer his labour for sale and make his existence entirely dependent on the chances of the prevailing market, in other words, to run the risk of a situation in which he is threatened by the constant fluctuation of wages and by periodical unemployment. It is not, however, only the destitute labouring class that succumbs in the competitive struggle against the factory, but also the small independent master craftsmen—they, too, lose their independence and the feeling of security. The new method of production also deprives the propertied classes of their peace of mind and their confidence. The most important form of wealth was formerly landed property, which became transformed only slowly and hesitantly into commercial and banking capital; but even mobile capital participated in industry only to a very small extent.[63] It is only from about 1760 onwards that the industrial undertaking becomes a popular form of capital investment. But the running of a factory, with its machines, its consumption of raw material and its army of workmen, presupposes more and more considerable means and leads to a more intense accumulation of capital than was required by the previous forms of goods production. With the new concentration of wealth and its investment in means of production the era of high capitalism truly begins.[64] But the highly speculative phase of capitalist development also begins. In the older agrarian economy capital risks and speculation were unknown, and to indulge in risky transactions even in industrial and financial business had hitherto been rather exceptional; but the new industries gradually become too much for the capitalists, and factory owners often play with bigger stakes than they can afford to lose. An existence endangered in this way produces, for all its actual prosperity, an outlook on life from which the optimism of an earlier age vanishes beyond recall.

The new type of capitalist—the industrial leader—develops new talents with his new function in economic life and, above all, a new discipline and evaluation of labour. He allows commercial interests to recede to a certain extent and concentrates on the internal organization of his factory. The principle of expediency, methodical planning and calculability, which had become very important in the economy of the leading countries since the fifteenth century, now becomes all-powerful. The employer disciplines himself just as ruthlessly as he does his workmen and employees, and becomes just as much the slave of his concern as his staff.[65] The raising of labour to the level of an ethical force, its glorification and adoration, is fundamentally nothing but the ideological transfiguration of the striving for success and profit and an attempt to stimulate even those elements who share least in the fruits of their labour into enthusiastic co-operation. The idea of freedom is part of the same ideology. In view of the risky nature of his business, the industrial employer must enjoy absolute independence and freedom of movement, he must not be hampered in his activity by any outside interference, must not be injured in favour of his rivals by any measures of state. The essence of the Industrial Revolution consists in the triumph of this principle over the medieval and mercantilist regulations.[66] Modern economy first begins with the introduction of the principle of *laissez-faire*, and the idea of individual freedom first succeeds in establishing itself as the ideology of this economic liberalism. These connections do not, of course, prevent both the idea of labour and the idea of freedom from developing into independent ethical forces and from often being interpreted in a really idealistic sense. But to realize how small a part was played by idealism in the rise of economic liberalism, it is only necessary to recall that the demand for freedom of trade was directed, above all, against the skilled master, in order to take away from him the only advantage he had over the mere contractor. Adam Smith himself was still far from claiming such idealistic motives for the justification of free competition; on the contrary, he saw in human selfishness and the pursuit of personal interests the best guarantee for the smooth functioning of the economic organism and the realization of the general weal. The whole optimism of the enlightenment was bound up with this belief in the self-regulating power of economic life and the automatic adjustment of conflicting interests; as soon as this began to disappear, it became more and more difficult to identify economic freedom with the interests of the general weal and to regard free competition as a universal blessing.

The author's aloofness towards his characters, his strictly intellectual approach to the world, the reserve in his relationship to the reader, in a word, his classicistic-aristocratic restraint, comes to an end, as economic liberalism begins to establish itself. The principle of free competition and the right of personal initiative are paralleled by the author's desire to express his subjective feelings, to make the influence of his own personality felt and to make the reader the direct witness of an intimate conflict of mind and conscience. This individualism, however, is not simply the translation of economic liberalism into the literary sphere, but also a protest against the mechanization, levelling-down and depersonalization of life connected with an economy left to run itself. Individualism transfers the system of *laissez-faire* to the moral life, but, at the same time, protests against a social order in which human beings are severed from their personal inclinations and become the bearers of anonymous functions, the buyers of standardized goods and mere tools in a world growing more and more uniform every day. The two basic forms of social causality, imitation and opposition, now combine to produce the romantic mood. The individualism of this romanticism is, on the one hand, a protest of the progressive classes against absolutism and state interventionism, but, on the other, it is also a protest against this protest, that is to say, against the concomitant phenomena and consequences of the Industrial Revolution, in which the emancipation of the bourgeoisie was completed. The polemical character of romanticism is expressed, above all, in the fact that it does not merely move in individualistic forms, but makes its individualism the basis of a definite programme. To start with, it is able to formulate its ideal of personality and its world-view only in terms of contradiction and negation. There have always been strong, self-willed individuals, and Western man had already become conscious of his individuality in the Renaissance, but it is only since the middle of the eighteenth century that individualism as a challenge and a protest against the depersonalization inherent in the process of civilization has existed. It goes without saying that conflicts between the individual and the world, between the personality and society, between the citizen and the state, had also occurred in earlier periods of literature, but the antagonism had never been felt to flow from the individual character of the person in conflict with the collective unit. In the drama, for example, the conflict did not result from the motif of a fundamental estrangement of the individual from society or the conscious revolt of the individual against social ties, but from a concrete, personal antithesis between the different characters in the play. It is entirely arbitrary to explain the tragedy in the older drama as resulting from the idea of individuation; such an interpretation turns out on closer analysis to be an untenable, if ever so pleasant, construction of romantic aesthetics. Before the romantic period, individualism as an attitude had never become problematical, it could, therefore, not become the theme of a dramatic conflict either.

Like individualism, emotionalism, too, serves the middle class as a means of expressing its intellectual independence of the aristocracy. Sentiments are asserted and emphasized, not because they are suddenly experienced more strongly and more deeply, but are exaggerated by auto-suggestion, because they represent an attitude opposed to the aristocratic outlook on life. The so long despised bourgeois looks at himself admiringly in the mirror of his own spiritual life, and the more seriously he takes his feelings, moods and impulses, the more important he appears to himself. In the middle and lower strata of the bourgeoisie, where this emotionalism has the deepest roots, the cult of the sentiments is, however, not merely a premium put on success but, at the same time, a compensation for lack of success in practical life. As soon, however, as the culture of the feelings has found its objective expression in art, it makes itself more or less independent of its origin and goes its own ways. The sentimentalism which was originally the expression of bourgeois class-consciousness, and due to the repudiation of aristocratic aloofness, leads to a cult of sensibility and spontaneity, the connection of which with the anti-aristocratic frame of mind of the middle class is increasingly lost to sight. At first people were sentimental and exuberant, because the aristocracy was reserved and self-controlled, but soon inwardness and expressiveness become artistic criteria, the validity of which is recognized even by the aristocracy. There is a deliberate hunt for spiritual shocks and gradually a real emotional virtuosity is achieved, the whole soul is dissolved in pity and, in the end, the only aim pursued in art is the excitement of the passions and the rousing of the sympathies. Sentiment becomes the most reliable medium between artist and public and the most expressive means of interpreting reality; to hold back from the expression of feeling now means to forgo artistic influence altogether, and to be without feeling means to be dull.

The moral rigorism of the middle class is, like its individualism and emotionalism, another weapon directed against the aristocratic outlook. It is not so much the continuation of the old middle-class virtues of simplicity, honesty and piety, as more a protest against the frivolity and extravagance of a social stratum whose levity has to be made good by others. The middle class plays off its prudery, especially in Germany, first of all against the immorality of the princes, which it only dares to attack in this indirect way. But it is quite unnecessary to mention their moral corruption directly; it is sufficient to praise the pure morals of the middle class, and everyone knows what is meant.[67] Now a regular occurrence in the eighteenth century repeats itself: the aristocracy accepts the viewpoint and standards of value of the middle class; virtue becomes a fashion in the upper classes, just as sentimentality had become a vogue. With the exception of a few specialists of obscenity, not even the French novelists have any longer a desire to be described as frivolous; what the public looks for now is the praise of virtue and the condemnation of vice. Perhaps Rousseau himself might not have given so much space in his works to moralizing sermons, if he had not known that Richardson owed his success very largely to such digressions.[68]

But if the tendency to individualism, emotionalism and moralism still lay to some extent in the very nature of the middle-class mind, the literature of pre-romanticism called forth qualities in it which were foreign to its earlier disposition, thus, above all, the proneness to melancholy which was in contradiction to the former middle-class optimism, to elegiac moods and even to a decided pessimism. This phenomenon cannot be explained by a spontaneous change of mind, but only by social displacements and restratifications. The upholders of the romantic movement are, first of all, not quite the same elements of the middle class as in the first half of the century had formed the bourgeois contingent of the reading public. The new strata, which make themselves heard now, have no intellectual contacts with the aristocracy and less reason for optimism than the economically privileged bourgeoisie. But even the old reading public, the bourgeoisie which had intermingled with the aristocracy, has altered in its spiritual outlook. Its elation with victory, its confidence, its self-assurance, which were almost boundless at the time of its first successes, dwindle and evaporate. It now begins to take its achievements for granted, to become conscious of what has been denied it, and it already feels perhaps that it is menaced by the classes that are climbing up from below. The misery of the exploited has a disturbing and depressing effect in any case. A deep melancholy possesses men's souls; the shady sides and the inadequacies of life are seen everywhere; death, night, loneliness and the yearning for a distant, unknown world, removed from the present, become the main theme of poetry and literature, and a surrender is made to the intoxication of suffering, just as a surrender had been made to the voluptuousness of sentimentalism.

In the first half of the century middle-class literature still had a thoroughly practical and realistic character; it was borne by a healthy common sense and filled with a love for immediate reality. After the middle of the century it suddenly comes to consist of nothing but escapism, above all the attempt to escape from strict rationality and watchful consciousness into turbid emotionalism, from culture and civilization into the irresponsibility of the state of nature and from the clear present into the infinitely ambiguous past. Spengler once remarked how strange and unprecedented was the cult of the ruin in the eighteenth century;[69] but the longing of the educated man for the primitive state of nature was no less strange and the suicidal self-dissolution of reason in the chaos of sentiment no less unprecedented—all tendencies, however, which make themselves felt in English literature even before the appearance of Rousseau. In contrast to the yearning for the historical past, which was a product of romanticism itself, the yearning for nature as an escape from conventionality had a long history behind it. It had appeared repeatedly, as we know, in the form of bucolic poetry at the height of the urban and courtly cultures, and as an artistic trend independent of naturalism, often indeed in opposition to it. Even in the eighteenth century the love for nature bears more a moral than an aesthetic character, and has practically nothing to do with the later naturalistic interest in reality. For the poets of pre-romanticism there is a direct relationship between the simple, honest man, living in modest middle-class circumstances, who now appears for the first time as an ideal in literature—for example in Goldsmith—and the 'innocence of nature'; they regard the countryside as the most suitable and most harmonious background for the activities of such a man. But they do not see nature more exactly nor do they enter into more intimate details in their descriptions than would be in keeping with a normally progressing development of the means of aristic expression. Their relationship to nature merely has different moral presuppositions than that of their predecessors. Nature for them is still the expression of the divine idea, and they continue to interpret it according to the principle of 'Deus sive natura'; it is not until the nineteenth century that a more direct, more unprejudiced approach to nature was achieved. But the generation of the pre-romantics experiences nature, in contrast to earlier times, in any case, as the revelation of moral powers, ruling in accordance with human moral concepts. The changing seasons of the day and year, the quiet moonlit night and the raging tempest, the mysterious mountain landscape and the unfathomable sea, all this they see as a great drama, a play in which the manifestations of human destiny are transferred to the wider setting of nature. Nature now takes up much more space in literature than formerly, and in this respect, too, romanticism paves the way for a new development, in opposition to classicism, which is limited to the purely human world; it still does not signify, however, a break with the anthropocentrism of older literature, but, at most, the transition from the humanism of the enlightenment to the naturalism of the present time. The heterogeneous make-up of the pre-romantic conception of nature is also expressed in the English garden, the great symbol of the age, that combines within itself perfectly natural and thoroughly artificial characteristics. It is a protest against all straight lines, against everything rigid and geometrical, and it is a profession of faith in the organic, the irregular and the picturesque; but with its artificial hills, ponds, islands, bridges, grottoes and ruins, it also represents just as unnatural a pattern as the French park, the only difference being that it is guided by different rules of taste. How far removed this generation still was from a clear rejection of classicism is best shown by the fact that the same artists who design romantically picturesque gardens follow the manneristic trend of Palladio when they have to build palaces. The Gothicizing style, which now emerges, is used, to start with, only in buildings of lesser importance, such as villas and country-house-like castles.[70] The upper classes make a fundamental distinction in art between public and private purposes, and realize that the anti-classicistic and romantic form is only suitable for the latter. A Horace Walpole, who has his castle, Strawberry Hill, built in the Gothic style and, at the same time, introduces the fashion of medieval subjects in the novel with his *Castle of Otranto*, is anything but a romantic spirit; as far as grand, representative art is concerned, he continues to acknowledge traditional classical ideals. But even if his experimenting with medieval themes is only the expression of a fondness for innovation, the romantic trend of these experiments is no less significant as a symptom of the age.[71]

In the case of intellectual movements, such as the romantic, it is almost impossible to establish a definite beginning; they often have their source in tendencies which suddenly emerge and, for lack of adequate response, are dropped again, in a word, in tendencies which remain individual experiments with no particular sociological relevance. There are already 'romantic' phenomena in the style of the seventeenth century, and in the first half of the eighteenth century we meet them on every hand. But it is hardly possible to speak of a romantic movement in the real sense before the appearance of Richardson; he is the first to combine the most essential characteristics of the style. And he finds such a felicitous formula for the new trend of taste that the whole of romantic literature, with its subjectivism and sentimentalism, seems to depend on him. At any rate, such a mediocre artist has never exerted such a deep and lasting influence; or, to put it in other words, the historical importance of an artist has never been determined by reasons lying so entirely outside his own artistic genius. The decisive reason for Richardson's influence was that he was the first to make the new middle-class man, with his private life, living within the framework of the home, absorbed by his family affairs, unconcerned with fictitious adventures and marvels, the centre of a literary work. The stories he tells are those of ordinary middle-class people, not heroes and rogues, and what he is concerned with are the simple, intimate affairs of the heart, not lofty and heroic deeds. He forgoes the amassing of colourful and fantastic episodes and concentrates on the spiritual life of his heroes. The epic material of his novels is based on a slender plot, which is nothing more than a pretext for analysing the emotions and examining the conscience. His characters are thoroughly romantic, but free of all romanesque and picaresque traits.[72] He is also the first to stop creating exactly definable types; he portrays the mere flow and fluctuation of feelings and passions—the characters as such do not interest him particularly.

With the contraction of the world of the novel to the modest and often idyllic private life of the middle class, with the limitation of the motifs to the great and simple fundamentals of family life and the fondness for unpretentious, unobtrusive destinies and characters, in a word, with the reduction of the novel to the domestic scene, it also becomes more ethical in its purpose. This process is connected not merely with the shift in the composition of the reading public and the entry of the middle classes into the literary world, but also with the general 'repuritanization' of English society, which takes place about the middle of the century and adds substantially to the public for the new literature.[73] The main purpose of the family novel and the novel of manners is didactic, and Richardson's novels are fundamentally moral tracts in the form of pathetic love stories. The author takes on the rôle of a spiritual adviser, discusses the great problems of life, forces the reader to examine himself, clears up his doubts and helps him with fatherly counsel. He has been rightly called a 'Protestant father confessor', and it was not for nothing that his books were recommended from the pulpit. Their influence can only be understood if one takes into account their double function as light reading and as devotional literature, and remembers that, as the family reading of the middle class, they not only satisfied a new need but eliminated an old one and displaced the reading of the Bible and Bunyan.[74] Today, in an age in which the subjective approach in literature has long since established itself, it is difficult to explain what it was in these novels that fascinated the contemporary public so greatly and affected it so deeply; but one must not forget that there was as yet nothing in the literature of the time to compare with the directness and intensity of the psychological descriptions in these novels. Their expressionism acted as a revelation and the frankness of the self-exposure of their characters seemed to be unsurpassable, however affected and forced the tone of these confessions seems to us today. But at that time it was a new tone, a tone sounding from the depth of a Christian soul that had lost its bearings in the struggle of life and was seeking a new foothold. The middle class immediately grasped the importance of the new psychology and understood that its own deepest qualities were finding expression in the emotional intensity and inwardness of these novels. It knew that a specifically middle-class culture could only be constructed on this foundation and it therefore judged Richardson's novels not according to traditional criteria of taste, but according to the principles of the bourgeois ideology. It developed new standards of aesthetic value from them, such as subjective truth, sensibility and intimacy, and laid the foundations of the aesthetic theory of modern lyricism. But the upper classes were also perfectly conscious of the significance of this confessional literature, and rejected its plebeian exhibitionism with disgust. Horace Walpole calls Richardson's novels dreary tales of woe, which describe life as if through the eyes of a bookseller or a Methodist preacher. Voltaire is silent about Richardson and even a d'Alembert is very reserved about him. Good society does not adopt the subjective view of art held by the romantics until its social origins have already become effaced and its social function has partly changed.

Richardson's success-morality is just as foreign to the upper classes as his subjectivism. The recommendations and admonitions which he bestows, to show the aspiring middle class how to make its way in society, form a moral philosophy which means nothing to the aristocracy and the upper bourgeoisie. It is the morality of the hard-working apprentice who marries his master's daughter, as Hogarth portrayed him, or of the virtuous maiden who is finally married by her master, as Richardson himself describes her, establishing one of the most popular themes of modern literature. *Pamela* is the prototype of all such modern wish-fulfilment stories. The development of the motif leads from Richardson to the films of our day, in which the irresistible private secretary withstands all the wiles of seduction and induces her presumptuous boss to marry her in the proper manner. Richardson's moralizing novels contain the germ of the most immoral art that has ever existed, namely the incitement to indulge in those wish-fantasies in which decency is only a means to an end, and the inducement to occupy oneself with mere illusions instead of striving for the solution of the real problems of life.[75] They also, for that reason, denote one of the most important dividing lines in the history of modern literature; previously the works of an author were either really moral or immoral, but since his time the books which want to appear moral in most cases merely moralize. In the struggle against the upper classes the bourgeois loses his innocence, and, as he has to emphasize his virtue all too often, he becomes a hypocrite.

The autobiographical form of the modern novel, whether a

story told in the first person or in letter or diary form, merely serves to intensify its expressionism and is only a means of stressing the shift of attention from outside to inside. From now onwards the diminution of the distance between the subject and the object becomes the principal aim of all literary effort. With the striving for this psychological directness, all the relations between the author, the hero and the reader are changed: not only the author's relation to his public and the characters of his work, but also the reader's attitude to these characters. The author treats the reader as an intimate friend and addresses himself to him in a direct, so to say, vocative style. His tone is constrained, nervous, embarrassed, as if he were always speaking about himself. He identifies himself with his hero and blurs the dividing line between fiction and reality. He creates a middle-kingdom for himself and his characters, which is sometimes remote from the reader's world, sometimes fused with it. Balzac's attitude to the characters of his novels, of whom he was in the habit of speaking as if they were personal acquaintances, has its origin here. Richardson falls in love with his heroines and sheds bitter tears over their fate; but his readers also speak and write about Pamela, Clarissa and Lovelace as if they were real, living persons.[76] There arises a hitherto unheard of intimacy between the public and the heroes of novels; the reader not only invests them with a greater spaciousness of life than the life enclosed within the limits of the particular work, he not only imagines them in situations which have nothing to do with the work itself, he also brings them constantly into relationship with his own life, his own problems and ambitions, his own hopes and disappointments. His interest in them becomes entirely personal, and in the end he can only understand them at all in relation to his own personality. It is true that even in earlier times the heroes of the great novels of knighthood and adventure were taken as models; they were ideals—idealizations of real men and ideal patterns for men of flesh and blood. But it would never have occurred to the ordinary reader to measure himself by their standards and to relate their privileges to himself. The heroes moved *ab ovo* in a different sphere; they were mythical figures and their stature in matters of good and evil was of superhuman quality. The remoteness of the symbol, of the allegory, of the legend, separated them from the reader's own world and prevented an all too direct relationship with them. Now, on the contrary, the reader has the feeling that the hero of the novel is merely consummating his—the reader's—unfulfilled life and realizing his neglected opportunities. For, at some time or other, everyone has been on the point of experiencing a novel in real life and of becoming something like the hero of a novel. From such illusions the reader derives his right to put himself on the same level as the hero and to claim for himself his exceptional position, his extra-territorial rights in life. Richardson invites the reader to put himself in the position of the hero, to romanticize his existence, and encourages him to absent himself from the fulfilment of the duties of the unromantic daily round. In this way, the author and the reader become the principal actors in the novel; they flirt with each other all the time and maintain an illegal relationship in which all the rules of the game are broken. The author speaks to the public over the footlights and the readers often find him more interesting than his characters. They enjoy his personal comments, reflections, 'stage directions' and do not take it amiss, for example, when Sterne becomes so preoccupied with his marginal comments that he never reaches the story itself.

Both for the author and the public the work is, above all, the expression of a spiritual situation, the value of which lies in the immediacy and personal quality of the experiences described. The reader is moved only by what is represented as a stirring, exciting, introverted event involving the destiny of a well-defined, interesting individual. To make an impression, the work must be a homogeneous, self-contained drama, made up entirely of a series of smaller 'dramas', each of which moves towards its own particular climax. In other words, an effective work develops in a rising crescendo, from point to point, from climax to climax. Hence the loaded, forced, often violent quality of expression that characterizes the productions of modern art and literature. Everything is bent on immediate effect, on surprise and stupefaction. Novelty is desired for novelty's sake; the piquant and the extraordinary is sought after, because it stimulates the nerves. It is this need which gives rise to the first thrillers and the first 'historical' novels with their mysterious atmosphere, filled with the false grandeur of history. All this signifies a lowering of the prevailing standard of taste and heralds the beginning of a decline in quality. In many respects the artistic culture of the nineteenth century is superior to that of the eighteenth, but it shows a weakness which was unknown to the age of the rococo: it lacks the safe and balanced, if not always the most flexible criteria of courtly art. It goes without saying that even before the romantic movement weak and unimportant artistic products existed, but everything that was not purely dilettante had a certain level and there arose neither literary works which had anything in common with the cheap psychology and trashy sentimentality of later light fiction, nor works in the plastic arts which had anything in common with the insipidity of the neo-Gothic, for example. These phenomena do not appear until leadership in cultural affairs passes from the upper classes to the middle class, although they do not always arise in the lower classes themselves. But in judging a turning point like the one under consideration here, the criterion of taste proves perhaps to be too narrow and sterile to be worth abiding by. 'Good taste' is not merely an historically and sociologically relative concept, but it has also only limited significance as a category of aesthetic valuation. The tears which are shed in the eighteenth century over novels, plays, musical compositions, are not only the sign of a change in taste and of the shift of aesthetic value from the exquisite and the reserved to the drastic and the importunate, they mark, at the same time, the beginning of a new phase in the development of that European sensibility of which the Gothic was the first triumph and of which the nineteenth century was to be the climax. This turning point signifies a much more radical break with the past than the enlightenment itself, which, in fact, represents merely the continuation and completion of a development that had been in progress since the end of the Middle Ages. The criterion of mere taste breaks down in face of a phenomenon like the beginning of this new emotional culture, which leads to a wholly new concept of poetry. 'La poésie veut quelque chose d'énorme et sauvage', as Diderot says,[77] and although this wildness and audacity is not realized immediately, nevertheless, it stands before the poet as an artistic ideal, as the imperative demand that poetry should move, overwhelm and infatuate the human heart. The 'bad taste' of the pre-romantics is the origin of a development to which we owe, to some extent, the most valuable qualities of nineteenth-century art. Balzac's impetuosity, Stendhal's complexity, Baudelaire's sensibility, are just as inconceivable without it as Wagner's sensualism, Dostoevsky's spirituality or Proust's neurasthenia.

The romantic tendencies which appear in Richardson were first given European significance and a universally applicable form by Rousseau. The irrationalism, which was able to make its way in England only slowly, was developed by a Swiss, whom Mme de Staël described with good reason as the representative of the Nordic, that is, of the German spirit in French literature. The Western European nations were permeated so deeply by the ideas of the enlightenment, by its rationalism and materialism, that the emotional and spiritualistic trend met with strong opposition, to begin with, and found a bitter enemy even in a man like Fielding, who, after all, represented the same middle class as Richardson. Rousseau approached the problems of the time with much less prejudice than the intellectual leaders of the enlightened West. He not only belonged to the comparatively traditionless petty bourgeoisie, he was also a déclassé who did not feel tied even to the conventions of this class. Such conventions were, moreover, on the whole more elastic in Switzerland, which had remained unaffected by court life and uninfluenced by the aristocracy, than in France or England. The emotionalism which in Richardson and the other representatives of English pre-romanticism was not always directly aimed at the rationalism of the enlightenment, and in which the antithesis to this movement was often only latent, assumed the character of open rebellion in Rousseau. His *Back to Nature!* had only one motive in the last analysis: to strengthen resistance to a development which had led to social inequality. He turned against reason, because he saw in the process of intellectualization also that of social segregation. Rousseau's primitivism was only a variant of the Arcadian ideal and a form of those dreams of redemption which one meets in all exhausted cultures,[78] but in Rousseau that feeling of 'discomfort with culture', which so many generations before him had felt, became conscious for the first time and he was also the first to develop a philosophy of history from this cultural weariness. The real originality of Rousseau consisted in his thesis, so monstrous in its implications for the humanism of the enlightenment, that the cultured man is degenerate and the whole history of civilization a betrayal of the original destination of mankind, that, therefore, the basic doctrine of the enlightenment, the belief in progress, turned out on closer examination to be a superstition. Such a revaluation of standards could only take place along with a radical change in the whole social philosophy of the time, and can only be explained by the fact that the strata represented by Rousseau no longer considered it possible to fight the artificiality and mendacity of court culture with the instruments of the enlightenment; they sought for weapons which did not derive from the intellectual arsenal of their enemies. In the criticism which Rousseau directed against the culture of the rococo and the enlightenment, in his exposure of their mechanical and often soulless formalism, to which he opposed the idea of the spontaneous and the organic, he was not merely expressing his awareness of the cultural crisis in which Europe had been involved ever since the destruction of the Christian unity of the Middle Ages, but also the modern concept of culture in general, with its inherent antagonism of spirit and form, spontaneity and tradition, nature and history. The discovery of this tension is Rousseau's epoch-making achievement. But the danger of his teaching was that, with his one-sided championing of life against history, his escape to the state of nature which was nothing more than a leap into the unknown, he prepared the way for those nebulous 'philosophies of life' which, out of despair at the apparent powerlessness of rational thinking, argue that reason should commit suicide.

Rousseau's ideas were in the air; he only expressed what many of his contemporaries knew, namely that they were faced with a choice and had to decide either for Voltairianism, with its reasonableness and respectability, or for the surrender of historical traditions and a completely new beginning. There is no personal relationship in the whole history of European culture with more profound symbolic significance than that between Voltaire and Rousseau. These two contemporaries, if not precisely members of the same generation, who were bound to one another by innumerable material and personal ties, who had mutual friends and supporters, both of whom were contributors to such an ideologically sharply defined literary undertaking as the *Encyclopédie* and were regarded as the most influential precursors of the Revolution, stood on the two opposite sides of the great watershed which divided modern, individualistic and anarchic Europe from a world in which the ties of the old formalistic culture were not yet wholly dissolved. Rousseau's naturalism implies the denial of everything that Voltaire considered the quintessence of civilization, above all, of the limitations of a subjectivism which, in his opinion, was only permitted as long as it was reconcilable with the rules of decency and self-respect. Before Rousseau, except in certain forms of lyric poetry, a writer had spoken only indirectly about himself, but after him writers spoke of hardly anything else, and in the most free and easy manner. It is since that time that that idea of a literature of experience and confession first arose which was uppermost in Goethe's mind when he declared that all his works were only the 'fragments of a great confession'. The mania for self-observation and self-admiration in literature and the view that a work is the more true and the more convincing, the more directly the author reveals himself in it, are part of the intellectual inheritance of Rousseau. In the next hundred to hundred and fifty years everything of importance in European literature is stamped with this subjectivism. Not only Werther, René, Obermann, Adolphe, Jacopo Ortis, are among the successors of Saint-Preux, but also the heroes in later novels—from Balzac's Lucien de Rubempré, Stendhal's Julien Sorel, Flaubert's Frédéric Moreau and Emma Bovary to Tolstoy's Pierre, Proust's Marcel and Thomas Mann's Hans Castorp—are derived from it. They all suffer from the discrepancy between dream and reality and are the victim of the conflict between their illusions and practical, commonplace, middle-class life. The motif first finds full expression in *Werther* —and one must recall the impact of this new experience, to understand the unparalleled impression the work made on the contemporary public—but the antithesis is already latent in the *Nouvelle Héloïse*. Here, too, the hero no longer faces individual opponents but a necessity, which he does not yet, however, regard as absolutely soulless and bereft of all intelligible purpose, like the hero of the later novel of disillusionment, but which he also by no means raises to a higher level than himself, as does the tragic hero the fate that destroys him. But without Rousseau's pessimistic approach to history and without his doctrine of the depravity of the present, the nineteenth-century novel of disillusionment is just as inconceivable as the conception of tragedy held by Schiller, Kleist and Hebbel.

The depth and extent of Rousseau's influence are without precedent. He is one of those minds which, like Marx and Freud in more recent times, change the thinking of millions within a single generation, and of many who do not even know them by name. By the end of the eighteenth century, at any rate, there were very few thinking men who had remained unaffected by Rousseau's ideas. Such an influence is possible only when a writer is in the deepest sense the representative and spokesman of his generation. With Rousseau the wider classes of society, the petty bourgeoisie and the undifferentiated mass of the poor, the oppressed and the outlawed, found expression for the first time in literature. It is true that the 'philosophes' of the enlightenment often sided with the common people, but they merely came forward as its intercessors and protectors. Rousseau is the first to speak as one of the common people himself, and to speak for himself when he is speaking for the people; the first to induce others to rebellion, because he is a rebel himself. His predecessors were reformers, world-improvers, philanthropists—he is the first real revolutionary. They hated 'despotism', agitated against the Church and positive religion, were enthusiastic about England and freedom, but continued to live the life of the upper class and felt that they belonged to it, in spite of their democratic sympathies; Rousseau, on the other hand, not only stands on the side of the poorest and lowliest, not only fights for absolute equality, but remains all his life the same petty bourgeois as he was born and the déclassé into which the conditions of his life had made him. In his youth he comes to know the real misery which none of the gentleman 'philosophers' knew from personal experience, and even later on he continues to lead the life of a man from the lower ranks of the middle class, for a time even that of a peasant. Before him, however lowly their origins may have been, writers were considered as belonging to the higher ranks of society; however deep their sympathy with the common people, they tried rather to keep their descent from the common people a secret than to make a show of it. Rousseau, on the other hand, stresses on every possible occasion that he has nothing at all in common with the upper classes. Whether this is simply 'plebian pride' and whether it is a mere feeling of resentment are questions which may be left undecided, the decisive point is that the differences between Rousseau and his opponents are not merely questions of opinion but vital class antagonisms. Voltaire said of Rousseau that he wanted to make civilized mankind creep on all fours again; and that must have been the opinion of the whole of the educated and conservative upper class. For them Rousseau was not only a fool and a charlatan but also a dangerous adventurer and criminal. But Voltaire was protesting not merely, as the bourgeois and the rich gentleman that he was, against Rousseau's plebeian emotionalism, vulgar enthusiasm and lack of historical understanding, he was also resisting, as a sober, critical, realistically-minded citizen and scholar, the abyss of irrationalism which Rousseau had torn open and which threatened to swallow up the whole structure of the enlightenment. How great this danger in fact was, and how justified Voltaire's fears were, is shown by the fate of the enlightenment in Germany. In France, Voltaire under-estimated perhaps the fruits of his own influence; here the achievements of rationalism and materialism could no longer be undermined.

In spite of his unmixed democratic feelings, to classify Rousseau sociologically is not easy. Social relationships are now so complicated that a writer's subjective attitude is not always an adequate criterion when it is a question of considering his rôle in the social process. Voltaire's rationalism turned out to be in some respects more progressive and more fruitful than Rousseau's irrationalism. The latter takes up a more radical point of view than the encyclopaedists, it is true, and represents wider circles of society politically not only than Voltaire but also than Diderot, yet in his religious and moral views he is less progressive than they.[79] Just as his sentimentalism is profoundly middle-class and plebeian, but his irrationalism reactionary, so his moral philosophy also contains an inner contradiction: on the one hand, it is saturated with strongly plebeian characteristics, but on the other, it contains the germ of a new aristocratism. The concept of the 'beautiful soul' presupposes the complete dissolution of kalokagathia and implies the perfect spiritualization of all human values, but it also implies an application of aesthetic criteria to morality and is bound up with the view that moral values are the gift of nature. It means the recognition of a nobility of soul to which everyone has a right by nature, but in which the place of irrational birthrights is taken by an equally irrational quality of moral genius. The way of Rousseau's 'spiritual beauty' leads, on the one hand, to characters like Dostoevsky's Myshkin, who is a saint in the guise of an epilectic and an idiot, on the other, to the ideal of individual moral perfection which knows no social responsibility and does not aspire to be socially useful. Goethe, the Olympian, who thinks of nothing but his own spiritual perfection, is a disciple of Rousseau just as much as the young freethinker who wrote *Werther*.

The change of style which takes place in literature with English pre-romanticism and the work of Rousseau, the replacement of objective and normative by more subjective and less restrained forms, is probably expressed most clearly of all in music, which now, for the first time, becomes an historically representative and leading art. In no other form did the change-over occur so suddenly and so violently as here, and to such a degree that even the contemporary public spoke of a 'great catastrophe' having taken place in music.[80] The acute conflict between Johann Sebastian Bach and his immediate successors, above all the irreverent way in which the younger generation made fun of his out-of-date fugal form, reflects not only the change from the lofty and conventional style of the late baroque to the intimate and simple style of the pre-romantics, but also the transition from a still fundamentally medieval method of juxtaposition, which the rest of the arts had already overcome in the Renaissance, to an emotionally homogeneous, concentrated, dramatically developed form. Not only Bach himself but the whole music of his time seems, measured by the standard of the other arts, conservative. Bach's immediate successors could rightly describe the master's style as 'scholastic', for however deeply felt this style is and however often its very emotional depth thrills the listener, the rigid, rigorous form, the learned, pedantic counterpoint and the whole impersonally conventional mode of expression of Bach's compositions could not but appear antiquated to the representatives of the new subjective trend, if they took their own concept of simplicity, directness and intimacy as the criterion. The essential point for them, as for the representatives of the romantic movement in literature, was the expression of the flow of the emotions as a unified process with a gradual intensification and a climax, if possible with a conflict and a solution, in contrast to a constant feeling spreading itself out equally over the whole movement.[81] Their feelings were neither deeper nor more intensive than those of their predecessors, they merely took them more seriously and wanted to make them seem more important, and for that reason they dramatized them. This tendency towards dramatization was the real distinction between the new self-contained forms of the Lied and the sonata and the old sequential forms of the fugue, the passacaglia, the chaconne and the other forms based on imitation and variation.[82] The impression made by the older music was controlled and measured, if only as a result of the uniform treatment of the emotional content, whereas that made by the more modern music, with its constant rising and falling, tension and solution, exposition and development, was intrinsically disturbing and exciting. The 'dramatic' mode of expression, aiming at piquant climaxes, is to be explained, first of all, by the fact that the composer found himself faced with a public whose attention had to be roused and captivated by more effective means than those to which the older public had responded. Simply because he was afraid of losing contact with his audience, he developed the musical composition into a series of constantly renewed impulses, and worked it up from one expressive intensity to another.

Until the eighteenth century all music was written more or less for a specific occasion; it was commissioned by a prince, by the

Church or by a town council, and had the task of entertaining a court society, of adding depth to public worship or enhancing the splendour of public festivities. Composers were court musicians, church musicians or town musicians; their artistic activity was limited to the fulfilment of the duties connected with their office,—it probably occurred to them but rarely to compose on their own responsibility, without a commission. Apart from church services, festivities and dance entertainments, the middle class had seldom any opportunity of hearing music; it was only by way of an exception that they were able to attend the performances of the orchestras in the employ of the nobility and the courts. About the middle of the century people began to feel that this was a weakness and town concert societies were founded.[83] The originally private 'Collegia musica' paved the way for public concerts and with them there developed a musical life which the middle class could call its own. The concert societies hired large halls and the musicians played for payment to ever-increasing audiences.[84] This led to the creation of a free market for musical products, corresponding to the literary market with its newspapers, periodicals and publishers. But whereas literature, like painting, had already made itself more or less independent of the practical utilization of its products, music remained functional until the eighteenth century. Anything in the nature of useless music had not existed at all before this time and pure concert music, the only purpose of which was to express feelings, only existed from the eighteenth century onwards. The audiences which attended the public concerts were different in several essential respects from those before whom musical performances at court were given: they had, first of all, less practice in the criticism of music written for its own sake and not for a religious purpose; it was a public which paid for its music from concert to concert and, therefore, one that had to be satisfied and won over again and again; it gathered simply to enjoy the music as music, that is to say, unrelated to any other purpose, such as had hitherto been the case in church, at the dance, at civic festivities or even in the social framework of court concerts. These peculiar characteristics of the new concert public brought about that fight for success in which the main weapon was the concentration, the forcing and piling up of effects and which conditioned that loaded style struggling constantly to intensify the expressiveness of the composition, which typifies the music of the nineteenth century.

The middle class becomes the chief consumer of music and music the favourite art of the middle class, the form in which it can express its emotional life more directly and with less hindrance than in any other. And as music now comes to be written not for a set purpose, but to express feelings, the composer not only begins to feel a dislike for all music written for specific occasions and in fulfilment of commissions, but to despise composition as an official activity altogether. Philip Emmanuel Bach already considers the pieces he writes merely for himself his best. This announces a conflict of conscience and a crisis where in earlier times no antithesis of any kind had been suspected to exist. The best-known and the most blatant example of the conflicts to which the new subjectivism leads is the estrangement of Mozart from his employer, the Archbishop of Salzburg. Nothing is more typical of the opposition which now arises between the musician in official employment and the creative artist than the differentiation of the virtuoso from the composer and the ordinary orchestral player from the leader of the orchestra. The development proceeds extraordinarily quickly and it is surprising that the lack of absolute mastery of even a single instrument, which is so characteristic of the modern composer, is already evident in the case of Haydn.[85]

But the rise of the middle-class concert public changes not merely the nature of artistic effects and the social position of the artist, but also gives a new direction to musical composition and a new significance to the individual work within the total output of a composer. The fundamental difference between composing for a nobleman or a personal patron in general and working for the anonymous concert public is that the commissioned work is usually intended for a single performance, whereas the concert piece is written for as many repeats as possible. That explains not only the greater degree of care with which such a work is often composed but also the more exacting way in which the composer presents it. Now that it is possible to create works which would not be consigned to oblivion so quickly as commissioned works, he sets out to create 'immortal' works. Haydn already composes much more cautiously and slowly than his predecessors. But even he writes over a hundred symphonies; Mozart writes only half as many and Beethoven only nine. The final change-over from objective composing done to commission to composition as a personal confession takes place somewhere between Mozart and Beethoven, or still more precisely, at the beginning of Beethoven's maturity, that is, immediately before the 'Eroica'—at a time, therefore, when the organization of public concerts is already fully developed and the music trade, which first gains ground with the need for repeat performances, forms the composer's chief source of income. In the case of Beethoven, from this time onward every new work of any size is the expression not only of a new idea but also of a new phase in the artist's development. Such a development can, of course, also be discerned in the case of Mozart, but with him the precondition of a new symphony is by no means always to be sought in a new stage of his artistic evolution; he writes a new symphony when he has use for one or when something new occurs to him, but this novelty need not be in any way stylistically different from his earlier symphonic ideas. Art and craft, which are not wholly divorced in him, are completely separate in Beethoven, and the idea of the unique, unrepeatable, utterly individual work of art is realized even more purely in music than in painting, although the latter had made itself independent of craftwork centuries ago. In literature, as well, the emancipation of the artistic purpose from the practical task had already been perfectly accomplished in Beethoven's day and become so much a matter of course that Goethe was able to assert with something of the pride of the practical craftsman that all his poetry was occasional in its origins. Beethoven, who was still the direct pupil of Haydn, the servant of princes, would not have been so proud of the fact.

3. THE ORIGINS OF DOMESTIC DRAMA

The middle-class novel of manners and family life represented a complete innovation compared with the various forms of heroic, pastoral and picaresque novel, which had dominated the whole field of light fiction until the middle of the eighteenth century, but it was by no means so deliberately and methodically opposed to the older literature as the middle-class drama, which arose in conscious antithesis to classical tragedy and became the mouthpiece of the revolutionary bourgeoisie. The mere existence of an elevated drama, the protagonists of which were all members of the middle class, was in itself an expression of the claim of this class to be taken just as seriously as the nobility from which the heroes of tragedy had sprung. The middle-class drama implied from the very outset the relativizing and belittling of the heroic and aristocratic virtues and was in itself an advertisement for bourgeois morality and the middle-class claim to equality of rights. Its whole history was determined by its origins in bourgeois class-consciousness. To be sure, it was by no means the first and only form of the drama to have its source in a social conflict, but it was the first example of a drama which made this conflict its very theme and which placed itself openly in the service of a class struggle. The theatre had always propagated the ideology of the classes by which it had been financed, but class differences had never before formed more than the latent, never the manifest and explicit content of its productions. Such speeches as, shall we say, the following had never been heard before: 'Ye Athenian aristocrats, the injunctions of your kinship morality are inconsistent with the principles of our democratic state: your heroes are not only fratricides and matricides, they are also guilty of high treason.' Or: 'Ye English barons, your reckless manners threaten the peace of our industrious cities; your crown-pretenders and rebels are no more than imposing criminals.' Or: 'You Paris shopkeepers, money-lenders and lawyers, know that if we, the French nobility, go under, a whole world will go under which is too good to compromise with you.' But now such things were stated quite frankly: 'We, the respectable middle class, will not and cannot live in a world dominated by you parasites, and even if we ourselves must perish, our children will win the day and live.'

Because of its polemical and programmatical character, the new drama was burdened from the very outset with problems unknown to the older forms of the drama. For, although these also were 'tendentious', they did not result in plays with a thesis to propound. It is one of the peculiarities of dramatic form that its dialectical nature makes it a ready vehicle for polemics, but the dramatist himself is prevented from taking sides in public by its 'objectivity'. The admissibility of propaganda has been disputed in this form of art more than in any other. The problem first arose, however, after the enlightenment had turned the stage into a lay-pulpit and a platform and had in practice completely renounced the Kantian 'disinterestedness' of art. Only an age which believed as firmly as this one in the educable and improvable nature of man could commit itself to purely tendentious art; every other age would have doubted the effectiveness of such clumsy moral teaching. The real difference, however, between the bourgeois and the pre-bourgeois drama did not consist exactly in the fact that the political and social purpose which was formerly latent was now given direct expression, but in the fact that the dramatic conflict no longer took place between single individuals but between the hero and institutions, that the hero was now fighting against anonymous forces and had to formulate his point of view as an abstract idea, as a denunciation of the prevailing social order. The long speeches and indictments now usually begin with a plural 'Ye' instead of the singular 'You'. 'What are your laws, of which you make your boast,' declaims Lillo, 'but the fool's wisdom, and the coward's valour, the instrument and screen of all your villainies? By them you punish in others what you act yourselves, or would have acted, had you been in their circumstances. The judge who condemns the poor man for being a thief, had been a thief himself, had he been poor.'[86] Speeches like that had never been heard before in any serious play. But Mercier goes even further: 'I am poor, because there are too many rich'—says one of his characters. That is already almost the voice of Gerhart Hauptmann. But, in spite of this new tone, the middle-class drama of the eighteenth century no more implies the criteria of a people's theatre than does the proletarian drama of the nineteenth; both are the result of a development in which all connection with the common people has long been lost, and both are based on theatrical conventions which have their source in classicism.

In France the popular theatre, which had masterpieces like *Maître Pathelin* to its credit, was completely forced out of literature by the court theatre; the biblical-historical play and the farce were supplanted by high tragedy and the stylized, intellectualized comedy. We do not precisely know what had survived of the old medieval tradition on the popular stage in the provinces in the age of classical drama, but in the literary theatre of the capital and the court hardly any more of it had been preserved than was contained in the plays of Molière. The drama developed into the literary genre in which the ideals of court society in the service of absolute monarchy found the most direct and imposing expression. It became the representative genre, if only for the reason that it was suitable for presentation with an impressive social framework and theatrical performances offered a special opportunity for displaying the grandeur and splendour of the monarchy. Its motifs became the symbol of a feudalistic-heroic life, based on the idea of authority, service and loyalty, and its heroes the idealization of a social class which, thanks to its exemption from the trivial cares of everyday life, was able to see in this service and loyalty the highest ethical ideals. All those who were not in a position to devote themselves to the worship of these ideals were regarded as a species of humanity beyond the pale of dramatic dignity. The tendency to absolutism, and the attempt to make court culture more exclusive and more like the French model, led in England, too, to the displacement of the popular theatre that, at the turn of the sixteenth century, had been still completely fused with the literature of the upper classes. Since the reign of Charles I, dramatists had limited themselves more and more to producing for the theatre of the court and the higher ranks of society, so that the popular tradition of the Elizabethan age had soon been lost. When the Puritans proceeded to close down the theatres, the English drama was already on the decline.[87]

The peripeteia had always been regarded as one of the essentials of tragedy and until the eighteenth century every dramatic critic had felt that the sudden turn of destiny makes the deeper impression, the higher the position from which the hero falls. In an age like that of absolutism this feeling must have been particularly strong, and in the poetic theory of the baroque, tragedy is simply defined as the genre whose heroes are princes, generals and suchlike notabilities. However pedantic this definition may appear to us today, it does lay hold of a basic characteristic of tragedy and even points perhaps to the ultimate source of the tragic experience. It was, therefore, really a decisive turning point when the eighteenth century made ordinary middle-class citizens the protagonists of serious and significant dramatic action and showed them as the victims of tragic fates and the representatives of high moral ideas. In earlier times this kind of thing would never have occurred to anyone, even though the assertion that middle-class persons had always been portrayed on the older stage merely as comic figures is by no means in accordance with the facts. Mercier is slandering Molière when he reproaches him for having tried to 'ridicule and humiliate' the middle class.[88] Molière generally characterizes the bourgeois as honest, frank, intelligent and even witty. He usually combines such descriptions, moreover, with a sarcastic thrust at the upper classes.[89] In the older drama, however, a person from the middle class had never been made to bear a lofty and soul-stirring destiny and to accomplish a noble and exemplary deed. The representatives of the bourgeois drama now emancipate themselves so completely from this limitation and from the prejudice of considering the promotion of the bourgeois to the protagonist of a tragedy as the trivialization of the genre, that they can no longer understand a dramaturgical sense in raising the hero above the social level of the average man. They judge the whole problem from the humanitarian angle, and think that the high rank of the hero only lessens the spectator's interest in his fate, since it is possible to take a genuinely sympathetic interest only in persons of the same social standing as oneself.[90] This democratic point of view is already hinted at in the dedication of Lillo's *Merchant of London*, and the middle-class dramatists abide by it on the whole. They have to compensate for the loss of the high social position held by the hero in classical tragedy by deepening and enriching his character, and this leads to the psychological overloading of the drama and creates a further series of problems unknown to earlier playwrights.

Since the human ideals followed by the pioneers of the new middle-class literature were incompatible with the traditional conception of tragedy and the tragic hero, they emphasized the fact that the age of classical tragedy was past and described its masters, Corneille and Racine, as mere word-spinners.[91] Diderot demanded the abolition of the tirades, which he considered both insincere and unnatural, and in his fight against the affected style of the *tragédie classique*, Lessing also attacked its mendacious class character. It was now discovered for the first time that artistic truth is valuable as a weapon in the social struggle, that the faithful reproduction of facts leads automatically to the dissolution of social prejudices and the abolition of injustice, and that those who fight for justice need not fear the truth in any of its forms, that there is, in a word, a certain correspondence between the idea of artistic truth and that of social justice. There now arose that alliance, so familiar in the nineteenth century, between radicalism and naturalism, that solidarity which the progressive elements felt existed between themselves and the naturalists even when the latter, as in the case of Balzac, thought differently from them in political matters.

Diderot already formulated the most important principles of naturalistic dramatic theory. He requires not merely the natural, psychologically accurate motivation of spiritual processes but also exactness in the description of the milieu and fidelity to nature in the scenery; he also desires, as he imagines, still in accordance with the spirit of naturalism, that the action should lead not to big scenic climaxes but to a series of optically impressive tableaux, and here he seems to have in mind 'tableaux vivants' in the style of Greuze. He obviously feels the sensual attractiveness of the visual more strongly than the intellectual effects of dramatic dialectics. Even in the linguistic and acoustic field he favours purely sensual effects. He would prefer to restrict the action to pantomime, gestures and dumb-show and the speaking to interjections and exclamations. But, above all, he wants to replace the stiff, stilted Alexandrine by the unrhetorical, unemotional language of every day. He attempts everywhere to tone down the loudness of classical tragedy and to curb its sensational stage effects, guided as he is by the bourgeois fondness for the intimate, the direct and the homely. The middle-class view of art, which sees in the representation of the immanent, self-sufficient present the real aim, strives to give the stage the character of a self-contained microcosm. This approach also explains the idea of the fictitious 'fourth wall', which is first hinted at by Diderot. The presence of spectators on the stage had been felt to be a disturbing influence in earlier times, it is true, but Diderot goes so far as to desire that plays should be performed as if no audience were present at all. This marks the beginning of the reign of total illusion in the theatre—the displacement of the play-element and the concealment of the fictitious nature of the representation.

Classical tragedy sees man isolated and describes him as an independent, autonomous intellectual entity, in merely external contact with the material world and never influenced by it in his innermost self. The bourgeois drama, on the other hand, thinks of him as a part and function of his environment and depicts him as a being who, instead of controlling concrete reality, as in classical tragedy, is himself controlled and absorbed by it. The milieu ceases to be simply the background and external framework and now takes an active part in the shaping of human destiny. The frontiers between the inner and the outer world, between spirit and matter, become fluid and gradually disappear, so that in the end all actions, decisions and feelings contain an element of the extraneous, the external and the material, something that does not originate in the subject and which makes man seem the product of a mindless and soulless reality. Only a society that had lost its faith in both the necessity and the divine ordinance of social distinctions and in their connection with personal virtue and merit, that experiences the daily growing power of money and sees men becoming merely what external conditions make them, but which, nevertheless, affirms the dynamism of human society, since it either owes its own ascendancy to it or promises itself that it will lead to its ascendancy, only that kind of society could reduce the drama to the categories of real space and time and develop the characters out of their material environment. How strongly this materialism and naturalism was conditioned by social factors is shown most strikingly by Diderot's doctrine of the characters in the drama—namely, the theory that the social standing of the characters possesses a higher degree of reality and relevance than their personal, spiritual habitus and that the question whether a man is a judge, an official or a merchant by profession is more important than the sum total of his individual qualities. The origin of the whole doctrine is to be found in the assumption that the spectator is able to escape from the influence of a play much less easily, when he sees his own class portrayed on the stage, which he must acknowledge to be his class if he is logical, than when he merely sees his own personal character portrayed, which he is free to disown if he wants to.[92] The psychology of the naturalistic drama, in which the characters are interpreted as social phenomena, has its origin in this urge which the spectator feels to identify himself with his social compeers. Now, however much objective truth there may be in such an interpretation of the characters in a play, it leads, when raised to the status of an exclusive principle, to a falsification of the facts. The assumption that men and women are merely social beings results in just as arbitrary a picture of experience as the view according to which every person is a unique and incomparable individual. Both conceptions lead to a stylization and romanticizing of reality. On the other hand, however, there is no doubt that the conception of man held in any particular epoch is socially conditioned and that the choice as to whether man is portrayed in the main as an autonomous personality or as the representative of a class depends in every age on the social approach and political aims of those who happen to be the upholders of culture. When a public wishes to see social origins and class characteristics emphasized in the human portraiture, that is always a sign that that society has become class-conscious, no matter whether the public in question is aristocratic or middle-class. In this context the question whether the aristocrat is only an aristocrat and the bourgeois only a bourgeois is absolutely unimportant.

The sociological and materialistic conception of man, which makes him appear to be the mere function of his environment, implies a new form of drama, completely different from classical tragedy. It means not only the degradation of the hero, it makes the very possibility of the drama in the old sense of the term questionable, since it deprives man of all autonomy and, therefore, to some extent of responsibility for his actions. For, if his soul is nothing but the battle-ground for contending anonymous forces, for what can he himself still be called to account? The moral evaluation of actions must apparently lose all significance or at least become highly problematical, and the ethics of the drama become dissolved into mere psychology and casuistry. For, in a drama in which the law of nature and nothing but the law of nature predominates, there can be no question of anything beyond an analysis of the motives and a tracking down of the psychological road at the end of which the hero attains his deed. The whole problem of tragic guilt is in question. The founders of the bourgeois drama renounced tragedy, in order to introduce into the drama the man whose guilt is the opposite of tragic, being conditioned by everyday reality; their successors deny the very existence of guilt, in order to save tragedy from destruction. The romantics eliminate the problem of guilt even from their interpretation of earlier tragedy and, instead of accusing the hero of wrong, make him a kind of superman whose greatness is revealed in the acceptance of his fate. The hero of romantic tragedy is still victorious in defeat and overcomes his inimical destiny by making it the pregnant and inevitable solution of the problem with which his life confronts him. Thus Kleist's Prince of Homburg overcomes his fear of death, and thereby abolishes the apparent meaninglessness and inadequacy of his fate, as soon as the decisive power over his life is put into his own hands. He condemns himself to death, since he recognizes therein the only way to resolve the situation in which he finds himself. The acceptance of the inevitability of fate, the readiness, indeed the joyfulness, with which he sacrifices himself, is his victory in defeat, the victory of freedom over necessity. The fact that in the end he does not have to die, after all, is in accordance with the sublimation and spiritualization which tragedy undergoes. The acknowledgement of guilt, or of what remains over of guilt, that is, the successful struggle to escape from the throes of delusion into the clear light of reason, is already equivalent to expiation and the restoration of the balance. The romantic movement reduces tragic guilt to the wilfulness of the hero, to his mere personal will and individual existence, in revolt against the primal unity of all being. According to Hebbel's interpretation of this idea, it is absolutely indifferent whether the hero falls as a result of a good or evil action. The romantic conception of tragedy, culminating in the apotheosis of the hero, is infinitely remote from the melodramas of Lillo and Diderot, but it would have been inconceivable without the revision to which the first bourgeois dramatists submitted the problem of guilt.

Hebbel was fully aware of the danger by which the form of the drama was threatened by the middle-class ideology, but, in contrast to the neo-classicists, he in no way failed to recognize the new dramatic possibilities inherent in middle-class life. The formal disadvantages of the psychological transformation of the drama were obvious. The tragic deed was an uncanny, inexplicable, irrational phenomenon in Greek drama, in Shakespeare and still, to some extent, in French classical drama; its shattering effect was due, above all, to its incommensurability. The new psychological motivation gave it a human measure and, as the representatives of the domestic drama intended, it was made easier for the audience to sympathize with the characters on the stage. The opponents of the domestic drama forget, however, when they deplore the loss of the terrors, the incalculability and inevitability of tragedy, that the irrational effect of tragedy went not as a consequence of the invention of psychological motivation and that the irrational content of tragedy had already lost its influence, when the need for that kind of motivation was first felt. The greatest danger with which the drama, as a form, was threatened by psychological and rational motivation was the loss of its simplicity, of its overwhelmingly direct, brutally realistic character, without which 'good theatre' in the old sense was impossible. The dramatic treatment became more and more intimate, more and more intellectualized and withdrawn from mass effects. Not merely the action and stage procedure but also the characters themselves lost their former sharpness of definition; they became richer but less clear, more true to life but less easy to grasp, less immediate to the audience and more difficult to be reduced to a directly evident formula. But it was precisely in this element of difficulty that the main attraction of the new drama resided, though it thereby became increasingly remote from the popular theatre.

The ill-defined characters were involved in obscure conflicts, situations in which neither the opposing figures nor the problems with which they were concerned were fully brought to light. This indefiniteness was conditioned, above all, by the comprehensive and conciliatory bourgeois morality which attempted to discover explanatory and extenuating circumstances and stood for the view that 'to understand everything is to forgive everything'. In the older drama a uniform standard of moral values had prevailed, accepted even by the villains and scoundrels;[93] but now that an ethical relativism had emerged from the social revolution, the dramatist often wavered between two ideologies and left the real problem unsolved, just as Goethe, for example, left the conflict between Tasso and Antonio undecided. The fact that motives and pretexts were now open to discussion weakened the element of inevitability in the dramatic conflict, but this was compensated for by the liveliness of the dramatic dialectic, so that it is by no means possible to maintain that the ethical relativism of the domestic drama merely had a destructive influence on dramatic form. The new bourgeois morality was all in all dramatically no less fertile than the feudal-aristocratic morality of the old tragedy. The latter knew of no other duties than those owed to the feudal lord and to honour, and it offered the impressive spectacle of conflicts in which powerful and violent personalities raged against themselves and each other. The domestic drama, on the other hand, discovers the duties which are owed to society,[94] and describes the fight for freedom and justice waged by men who are materially more narrowly tied, but are, nevertheless, spiritually free and brave—a fight which is perhaps less theatrical but in itself no less dramatic than the bloody conflicts of heroic tragedy. The outcome of the struggle is not, however, inevitable to the same degree as hitherto, when the simple morality of feudal loyalty and knightly heroism allowed of no escape, no compromise, no 'having it both ways'. Nothing describes the new moral outlook better than Lessing's words in *Nathan der Weise*: 'Kein Mensch muss muessen'—words which do not, of course, imply that man has no duties at all, but that he is inwardly free, that is to say, free to choose his means, and that he is accountable for his actions to none but himself. In the older drama inward, in the new drama outward ties are stressed; but oppressive as the latter are in themselves, they allow absolutely free play to the dramatically relevant action. 'The old tragedy rests on an unavoidable moral duty'—Goethe says in his essay *Shakespeare and No End*: '. . . All duty is despotic . . . the will, on the other hand, is free . . . It is the god of the age . . . Moral duty makes tragedy great and strong, the will makes it weak and slight.' Goethe here takes a conservative standpoint and evaluates the drama according to the pattern of the old, quasi-religious immolation, instead of according to the principles of the conflict of will and conscience into which the drama has developed. He reproaches the modern drama for granting too much freedom to the hero; later critics usually fall into the opposite error and think that the determinism of the naturalistic drama makes any question of freedom, and therefore of dramatic conflict, impossible. They do not understand that it is dramaturgically completely irrelevant where the will originates, by what motives it is guided, what is 'intellectual' and what 'material' in it, provided that a dramatic conflict takes place one way or another.[95]

These critics put quite a different interpretation on the principle which they oppose to the hero's will from that of Goethe; it is a matter of two entirely different kinds of necessity. Goethe is thinking of the antinomies of the older drama, the conflict of duty and passion, loyalty and love, moderation and presumption, and deplores that the power of the objective principles of order has diminished in the modern drama, in comparison with that of the subjectivity. Later, necessity is usually taken as meaning the laws of empirical reality, especially those of the physical and social environment, the inescapability of which was discovered by the eighteenth century. In reality, therefore, three different things are in question here: a wish, a duty and a compulsion. In the modern drama individual inclinations are confronted by two different objective orders of reality: an ethical-normative and a physical-factual order. Philosophical idealism described the conformity to law of experience as accidental, in contrast to the universal validity of ethical norms, and in accordance with this idealism, modern classicistic theory regards the predominance of the material conditions of life in the drama as depraving. But it is no more than a prejudice of romantic idealism to assert that the hero's dependence on his material environment thwarts all dramatic conflict, all tragic effects and makes the very possibility of true drama problematical. It is true, however, that, as a consequence of the conciliatory morality and non-tragic outlook of the middle class, the modern world offers tragedy less material than former ages. The modern bourgeois public likes to see plays with a 'happy ending' more than great, harrowing tragedies, and feels, as Hebbel remarks in his preface to *Maria Magdalene*, no real difference between tragedy and sadness. It simply does not understand that the sad is not tragic and the tragic not sad.

The eighteenth century loved the theatre and was an extraordinarily fertile period in the history of the drama, but it was not a tragic age, not an epoch which saw the problems of human existence in the form of uncompromising alternatives. The great ages of tragedy are those in which subversive social displacements take place, and a ruling class suddenly loses its power and influence. Tragic conflicts usually revolve around the values which form the moral basis of the power of this class and the ruinous end of the hero symbolizes and transfigures the ruinous end which threatens the class as a whole. Both Greek tragedy and the English, Spanish and French drama of the sixteenth and seventeenth centuries were produced in such periods of crisis and symbolize the tragic fate of their aristocracies. The drama heroizes and idealizes their downfall in accordance with the outlook of a public that still consists for the most part of members of the declining class itself. Even in the case of the Shakespearian drama, the public of which is not dominated by this class, and where the poet does not stand on the side of the social stratum threatened with destruction, tragedy draws its inspiration, its conception of heroism and its idea of necessity from the sight afforded by the fate of the former ruling class. In contrast to these ages, the periods in which the fashion is set by a social class which believes in its ultimate triumph are not favourable for tragic drama. Their optimism, their faith in the capacity of reason and right to achieve victory, prevents the tragic outcome of dramatic entanglements, or seeks to make a tragic accident out of tragic necessity and a tragic error out of tragic guilt. The difference between the tragedies of Shakespeare and Corneille, on the one hand, and those of Lessing and Schiller, on the other, is that in the one case the destruction of the hero represents a higher and in the other case a mere historical necessity. There is no conceivable order of society in which a Hamlet or Antony would not inevitably come to ruin, whereas the heroes of Lessing and Schiller, Sara Sampson and Emilia Galotti, Ferdinand and Luise, Carlos and Posa, could be happy and contented in any other society and any other time except their own, that is to say, except that of their creator. But an epoch which sees human unhappiness as historically conditioned, and does not consider it an inevitable and inescapable fate, can certainly produce tragedies, even important ones; it will, however, in no way utter its final and deepest word in this form. It may, therefore, be right that 'every age produces its own necessity and thus its own tragedy',[96] yet the representative genre of the age of the enlightenment was not tragedy but the novel. In the ages of tragedy the representatives of the old institutions combat the world-view and aspirations of a new generation; in times in which the non-tragic drama prevails, a younger generation combats the old institutions. Naturally, the single individual can be wrecked by old institutions just as much as he can be destroyed by the representatives of a new world. A class, however, that believes in its ultimate victory, will regard its sacrifices as the price of victory, whereas the other class, that feels the approach of its own inevitable ruin, sees in the tragic destiny of its heroes a sign of the coming end of the world and a twilight of the gods. The destructive blows of blind fate offer no satisfaction to the optimistic middle class which believes in the victory of its cause; only the dying classes of tragic ages find comfort in the thought that in this world all great and noble things are doomed to destruction and wish to place this destruction in a transfiguring light. Perhaps the romantic philosophy of tragedy, with its apotheosis of the self-sacrificing hero, is already a sign of the decadence of the bourgeoisie. The middle class will, at any rate, not produce a tragic drama in which fate is resignedly accepted until it feels threatened with the loss of its very life; then, for the first time, it will see, as happens in Ibsen's play, fate knocking at the door in the menacing shape of triumphant youth.

The most important difference between the tragic experience of the nineteenth century and that of earlier ages was that, in contrast to the old aristocracies, the modern middle class felt itself threatened not merely from outside. It was a class made up of such multifarious and contrary elements that it seemed menaced by the danger of dissolution from the very outset. It embraced not only elements siding with reactionary groups and others who felt a sense of solidarity with the lower ranks of society, but, above all, the socially rootless intelligentsia that flirted now with the upper now with the lower classes, and, accordingly, stood partly for the ideas of the anti-revolutionary and anti-rationalist romantics, partly agitated for a state of permanent revolution. In both cases it aroused in the mind of the middle class doubts about its right to exist at all and about the lasting quality of its own social order. It bred a 'super-bourgeois' attitude to life—a consciousness that the middle class had betrayed its original ideals and that it now had to conquer itself and struggle to attain a universally valid humanism. On the whole, these 'super-bourgeois' tendencies had an anti-bourgeois origin. The development through which Goethe, Schiller and many other writers passed, especially in Germany, from their revolutionary beginnings to their later, conservative and often anti-revolutionary attitude, was in accordance with the reactionary movement in the middle class itself and with its betrayal of the enlightenment. The writers were merely the spokesmen of their public. But it often happened that they sublimated the reactionary convictions of their readers and, with their less robust conscience and their greater readiness to sham, simulated higher, super-bourgeois ideals, when they had really sunk back to a pre- and anti-bourgeois level. This psychology of repression and sublimation created such a complicated structure that it is often difficult to differentiate the various tendencies. It has been possible to establish that in Schiller's *Kabale und Liebe*, for example, three different generations and, therefore, three ideologies intersect each other: the pre-bourgeois of the court circles, the bourgeois of Luise's family and the 'super-bourgeois' of Ferdinand.[97] But the super-bourgeois world here differs from the bourgeois merely by reason of its greater breadth and lack of bias. The relation between the three attitudes is really much more complicated in a work like *Don Carlos*, in which the super-bourgeois philosophy of Posa enables him to understand Philip and even to sympathize to a certain degree with the 'unhappy' king. In a word, it becomes increasingly difficult to ascertain whether the dramatist's 'super-bourgeois' ideology corresponds to a progressive or a reactionary disposition, and whether it is a question of the middle class achieving victory over itself or simply one of desertion. However that may be, the attacks on the middle class become a basic characteristic of the bourgeois drama, and the rebel against the bourgeois morality and way of life, the scoffer at bourgeois conventions and philistine narrow-mindedness, becomes one of its stock figures. It would shed an extraordinarily revealing light on the gradual alienation of modern literature from the middle classes, to examine the metamorphoses this figure underwent from the 'Storm and Stress' right up to Ibsen and Shaw. For he does not represent simply the stereotyped insurgent against the prevailing social order, who is one of the basic types of the drama of all times, nor is he merely a variant of rebellion against the particular ruler of the moment, which is one of the fundamental dramatic situations, but he represents a concrete and consistent attack on the bourgeoisie, on the basis of its spiritual existence and on its claim to stand for a universally valid moral norm. To sum up, what we are here confronted with is a literary form which from being one of the most effective weapons of the middle class developed into the most dangerous instrument of its self-estrangement and demoralization.

4. GERMANY AND THE ENLIGHTENMENT

All over Europe the romantic movement of the eighteenth century was a very conflicting phenomenon sociologically. On the one hand, it represented the continuation and the climax of that emancipation of the middle class which began with the enlightenment; it was the expression of plebeian emotionalism and, therefore, the opposite of the fastidious and unobtrusive intellectualism of the higher levels of society. On the other hand, however, it represented the reaction of these same higher levels against the undermining influences of the rationalism and the reformative tendencies of the enlightenment. It developed, to begin with, in the broad middle sections of the bourgeoisie which had been only superficially influenced by the enlightenment, and amongst that section which regarded the enlightenment as still all too closely allied with the old classical culture; gradually, however, it became the property of those classes which were using the emotional tendencies of the age for the attainment of their own anti-rational, socially and politically reactionary ends. But whilst the middle class in France and England remained fully conscious of its own position in society and never entirely abandoned the achievements of the enlightenment, the German middle class came under the sway of romantic irrationalism before it had passed through the school of rationalism. That is not to say that rationalism as a doctrine was without its protagonists in Germany; as a matter of fact, it was probably championed more vigorously in the German universities than anywhere else, but, characteristically, it remained a doctrine and the speciality of professional scholars and academic poets. Rationalism in Germany had never completely penetrated public life, the social and political thinking of the broad masses or the attitude to life of the middle classes. Germany could certainly boast the possession of several quite outstanding representatives of the enlightenment, such as Lessing, to name the greatest of them all and perhaps the most genuine and the most attractive personality in the whole movement, but the honest, clear-sighted and steadfast supporters of the ideas of the enlightenment were here always exceptions even among the intellectuals. The majority of the middle class and the intelligentsia were incapable of grasping the significance of the enlightenment in relation to their own class interests; it was easy to present a distorted picture of the nature of the movement to them and to caricature the limitations and inadequacies of rationalism. We must not, of course, think of the process as a kind of conspiracy, in which writers were acting as the hirelings and accomplices of the politicians in office. Probably not even the real controllers of public opinion admitted to themselves that an ideological falsification of the facts was taking place; at any rate, the intellectual leaders of the middle classes were far from any awareness that they were perpetrating a fraud, nor in fact were they even remotely aware of anything fraudulent or treasonable in the whole proceeding.

Now, how did this faulty awareness, this political naïvety of the intelligentsia, which led in the end to the final German tragedy, come about? Why was the enlightenment never properly assimilated by the German middle classes, and why did the progressively-minded class-conscious intelligentsia fail so completely as a compact social unit? We may call the enlightenment the political elementary school of the modern middle class, without which the part it has played in the cultural history of the last two centuries would be inconceivable. It was Germany's calamity that she missed attending this school at the time and was unable to make up for lost time later on. When the enlightenment became the leading intellectual movement in Europe, the German intelligentsia was not yet sufficiently mature to take part in it, and later on it was no longer so easy to overlook the limitations and prejudices of the movement. The backwardness of the German intelligentsia is, naturally, no explanation, it must first be explained itself. In the course of the sixteenth century the German middle classes had lost their economic and political influence, which had been rising steadily since the end of the Middle Ages, and, consequently, they forfeited their importance in the cultural sphere as well. International trade shifted from the Mediterranean to the Atlantic Ocean, the Hanseatic League and the North German cities were displaced by the Dutch and English trading centres, and the South German cities, particularly Augsburg, Ratisbon and Ulm, then the main centres of German culture, declined at the same time as the Italian trading centres had their lines of communication in the Mediterranean cut off by the Turks. This decline of the German cities meant the decline of the German middle classes; the princes no longer had anything to hope or to fear from them. It is true that the power of the princes was also considerably strengthened in the West from the end of the sixteenth century and a new process of aristocratization took place, but the Western monarchies derived part of their support in the struggle against the feudal nobility from the bourgeoisie, and as for the nobility itself, it either left trade and industry entirely to the middle classes, as happened in France, or allied itself with them, in order to make the most of the economic boom, as was the case in England. The German princes, on the other hand, who after the suppression of the peasant revolts were the undisputed masters of the country, saw a possible threat to their sovereignty not in the nobility, to which they themselves belonged and whose policies they defended before the Emperor, but in the peasantry and the middle classes. Unlike the French and English kings, the German territorial princes were great landowners with predominantly feudal interests and no particular concern for the prosperity of the bourgeoisie and the peasantry. The Thirty Years War had brought the final collapse of German commerce and destroyed the German cities economically as well as politically.[98] The Peace of Westphalia set the seal on German particularism and confirmed the sovereignty of the territorial princes; by so doing, it sanctioned conditions in contrast to which the West, where the king represented to some extent the unity of the nation and in certain circumstances defended its interests even against the nobility, can be described as progressive. Even after their reconciliation, there still remained a certain tension between the king and the stubborn nobility, from which the middle classes profited in any case. In Germany, on the other hand, the princes and the nobility always stood together, when it was a question of depriving other classes of their rights. In the West the middle classes had established themselves in the administration and could in future never be completely forced out of it again; but in Germany, where the loyalty of the army and the bureaucracy was the basis of a new feudalism, government posts were reserved, except for subordinate offices, for the nobility and the junkers. The common people were oppressed by the officials of the Crown, high and low, as much and even more than by the manorial stewards in former days. The German peasants had never known anything but serfdom, but now the middle classes, as well, lost everything they had gained in the course of the fourteenth and fifteenth centuries. First of all, they were impoverished and deprived of their privileges, then they lost their self-confidence and self-respect. Finally, out of their misery, they developed those ideals of submissiveness and unquestioning loyalty which made it possible for any cringing philistine to think of himself as the servant of a 'higher Idea'.

Just as the development of mercantilism into free trade took place only very slowly in Germany and was hardly complete before 1850,[99] centralized political control over the territorial princes came to full fruition only in the second half of the nineteenth century. In fact, as a French historian has remarked, the interregnum lasted until 1870.[100] In the sixteenth century, the Empire recovered for a time and, supported by the absolutist tendency of the age, Charles V succeeded in consolidating the imperial power, but even he did not succeed in breaking the authority of the princes. His activities were too widely dispersed to devote himself properly to the improvement of conditions in Germany. Furthermore, with his European interests, he had to sacrifice the cause of the German Reformation out of consideration for the pope and so he missed the unique opportunity of creating a unified Germany out of a genuinely popular movement.[101] He ceded the advantages accruing to the patrons of the Reformation to the German princes, to whom Luther readily surrendered the instruments of spiritual power. He made them the heads of the established Churches and gave them authority to control the spiritual life of their subjects and to take upon themselves the cure of souls. The princes seized the ecclesiastical properties, made the official ecclesiastical appointments, took over the control of religious education, and it is, therefore, not surprising that the established Churches developed into the most reliable supports of the power of the princes. They preached the duty of obedience to the government, confirmed the 'divine right' of their illustrious overlords, and bred the stuffy, strait-laced conservative mentality which is so typical of seventeenth-century Lutheranism in Germany. The despotic particularism, which was now completely unopposed, thus estranged the progressive strata of society from the Church.

The bourgeois spirit of the fifteenth and sixteenth centuries disappeared from German art and culture, in so far as any art and culture survived the Peace of Westphalia at all. For the Germans not only followed the courtly-aristocratic style of the French, but adopted it quite openly by importing artists and works of art from France or by slavishly imitating French models. All the two hundred petty principalities made it their great ambition to emulate the French king and the court of Versailles. Thus arose, in the first half of the eighteenth century, the most magnificent castles and palaces of the German princes: Nymphenburg, Schleissheim, Ludwigsburg, Pommersfelden, the Zwinger in Dresden, the Orangery in Fulda, the Residence in Würzburg, Bruchsal, Rheinberg, Sanssouci—all built to the same overriding pattern and furnished with a luxury out of all proportion to the means and resources of the mostly very small and very poor principalities. Thanks to this extravagance, there developed, however, something approaching a German species of the Italian and French rococo. Literature, on the other hand, gained little support and inspiration from them, except from a few outstanding patrons of the arts, and that was only towards the end of the century. 'Germany is swarming with princes, of whom three-quarters are mentally sub-normal and a disgrace to mankind,' writes a contemporary, 'small as their kingdoms are, they imagine, nevertheless, that humanity was made for them.'[102] There was, of course, a variety of different types among the German princes, more or less cultured, despotic and less despotic, art-loving and merely splendour-loving persons, but probably not a single one among all of them doubted for one moment that the only purpose in life for the average mortal was to be ruled and exploited by them.

What resources were left after the princes had indulged in all this insane luxury and extravagant building, and had covered the expense of the upkeep of the court and of their mistresses, were spent on the army and the bureaucracy. The army could, of course, only perform police duties and cost comparatively little; the burden of maintaining an expensive bureaucracy lay all the heavier on the nation. All this petty particularism occasioned in itself a multiplication of official machinery, and this was still more intensified by the bureaucratization of the state, by the transfer of the functions of autonomous corporations to government offices, by the fondness for issuing decrees and orders and by the general tendency to regiment the whole of public and private life. It is true that the same political, economic and social system predominated in France and that the citizen was hampered by the same kind of interventionism in his business undertakings, injured by the same kind of governmental mismanagement and had to endure the same deprivation of his rights and the same lack of consideration as in Germany. In the small-scale conditions which prevailed in the German principalities, however, all these restrictions were far more oppressive and humiliating than in France. Living in direct proximity to the court, suffering from the pressure of a petty governmental machine and of a pretentious and extravagant prince, watched and supervised by less influential but no less inhuman officials, the German citizen lived an even more harassed and even more threatened life. It is true that the civil service, on its lower levels, absorbed a considerable part of the middle class, but these petty officials were corrupted from the very beginning, because government employment was the only opening compatible with their status in society. For a member of the middle class not engaged in trade or in craft, there was nothing else possible but to become a civil servant, a legal official in government service, a clergyman of the established Church or a teacher in a publicly controlled school.

The powerlessness of the middle class, their exclusion from the government of the country and from practically every kind of political activity, induced a passive mentality which affected the whole cultural life of the time. The intelligentsia, which consisted of subordinate officials, schoolmasters and unpractical poets, accustomed itself to drawing a line of demarcation between its private life and the world of politics, and to renouncing any kind of practical influence on public affairs. It made up for all this by an excess of idealism, by the emphatic disinterestedness of its ideas, and by leaving the direction of state affairs to the holders of power. This renunciation was the expression of not only a complete indifference towards apparently unalterable social conditions but also of a definite contempt for professional politics. In this way, the middle-class intelligentsia lost all contact with social reality and became more and more isolated, eccentric and crack-brained. Its thinking became purely contemplative and speculative, unreal and irrational, its mode of expression self-willed, high-flown, incommunicable, incapable of taking others into consideration and always resisting any correction from outside. These people retired to what they called the level of the 'universally human', a level above all classes, ranks and groups, made a virtue of their lack of practical-mindedness and called it 'idealism', 'inwardness', triumph over the limitations of time and space. Out of their involuntary passivity, they developed an ideal of the idyllic private life, and out of their lack of external freedom, the idea of inward freedom and of the sovereignty of the spirit over common empirical reality. The result of this development in Germany was the complete divorce of literature from politics, and the disappearance of that representative of public opinion, so well known in the West, the writer who is a politician, a scholar and a publicist, a good philosopher and a good journalist, all at the same time.

The social development which had divided the German middle class since the end of the Middle Ages into different clearly graduated strata came to a halt in the sixteenth century. The retrograde process of a new integration set in, and led to the formation of the somewhat undifferentiated middle class that we meet in the seventeenth century. The broader strata had given up their cultural pretensions and the upper middle class had diminished to such an extent that it no longer had much significance as a cultural factor in society. It was hardly any longer possible to speak of a special select middle-class way of life, or of a special middle-class outlook as expressed in art and literature. What developed was rather a uniformly low and unpretentious level of culture reminiscent of the primitive conditions of the early Middle Ages. The revolutionary events of the sixteenth century, in particular the shifting of the centres of world economy and the strengthening of the power of the princes, destroyed the fruits of the bourgeois late Gothic and Renaissance. There was nothing left of the culture based on the middle-class standard of life; nothing left of the standards of a specifically middle-class education and of a specifically middle-class conception of art; nothing of the intellectual atmosphere of an age in which the main stream of cultural development and the most progressive artistic and philosophical tendencies were expressed in the idiom of the middle class, and in which the leading personalities, like Dürer and Altdorfer, Hans Sachs and Jacob Böhme, were, above all, representatives of the middle-class outlook.

The middle classes which acquired wealth and esteem, as a result of the development of a money economy and as a result of the rising prosperity of the cities and the decline of the feudal aristocracy, obtained control, by a hard struggle and by using their financial power, of the larger urban municipalities, took over the administration and occupied important positions in the state government, in the princes' privy councils and in the legal senates as well. The later decline of the German cities, the consequent loss of prestige sustained by the middle classes and the steadily advancing economic ruin of the aristocracy led, however, as early as the end of the sixteenth century, to the exclusion of the middle-class element from official positions in the state and at the courts and to their replacement by members of the nobility.[103] The Thirty Years War, which also worsened the position of the feudal classes, renewed and accelerated the drift of the nobility into official posts and closed the higher reaches of the bureaucracy to the middle classes. In France the official aristocracy, which had mostly worked its way up from the middle class, developed side by side with the landed and court aristocracy; in Germany, however, the land-owning nobility itself became an official caste and the middle class was pushed back in an even more ruthless fashion than anywhere else into the ranks of the subordinate civil service. The victory of the princes meant the end of the estates as a political factor, that is to say, it meant the liquidation of the rights of both the nobility and the middle class; from that time on, there was only *one* political force, that of the princes. What happened, however, was what usually happens in such cases: the princes indemnified the nobility and sent the middle classes away empty-handed. German society was now dominated by two groups: the high state and court officials, forming a kind of new vassalage around the princes, and the lower bureaucracy, consisting of the princes' most obedient servants. Some made up for servility towards superiors by unlimited brutality towards inferiors, whilst others made a cult of discipline, regarding their superiors as spiritual directors of their own conduct and making a religion of their performance of official duty.

In the long run, however, it was impossible to hold up the progress of trade and industry for ever, despite the obstacles placed in the way of economic development by particularism with its petty interests and neglected finances. The middle classes enriched themselves once again and began to divide up into income-groups. First of all, there arose a bourgeoisie, distinct from the lower middle class, which could afford to pay for the patronage of court officials and follow the French fashions of the court. Through the influence of this upper middle class, which became, together with the court nobility, the only cultured élite left, French taste and a contempt for all native traditions spread amongst the whole intelligentsia. French literature dominated the universities and found its most fervid advocate in Gottsched, the best-known academic poet of the age; the bourgeois art of the German Renaissance, and the few traces still surviving as a living tradition, seemed coarse, undeveloped and in bad taste as compared with French ideals in art. Nevertheless, it would be quite wrong to describe Gottsched as the literary spokesman of the aristocracy; he was rather the protagonist of the bourgeoisie, which still had no artistic ideals of its own, however, and neither a distinct national character nor a clearly defined class-consciousness. It must not be forgotten, of course, that the aristocratic culture which served as a model for the middle classes and even the culture of the court aristocracy itself was merely a pseudo-culture based on stereotyped and often completely lifeless patterns.[104] The secular light reading, the only cultural need of these classes of society, was still confined around 1700 to those genres which were also popular in the French court aristocracy, above all the heroic, the pastoral and the love novel and heroic tragedy. Their authors were, however, unlike their French and English counterparts, in most cases academically educated persons, that is to say, university teachers, lawyers and court officials generally belonging to the upper middle class. Some of them were aristocrats, like Baron von Canitz, Friedrich von Spee and Friedrich von Logau, but hardly any were representatives of the lower classes.[105] Apart from the men of high social degree, who wrote poetry for their own amusement and to pass the time, all these writers were directly or indirectly dependent on the courts. They were either in the immediate service of the princes or they worked at one of the universities and were thus hangers-on.

The first German professional poet, in the European connotation of the term, was Klopstock, although even he was unable to make himself completely independent of private patronage. The fact is that before the arrival of Lessing and the development of the metropolis as fertile literary soil, there were no independent writers in Germany at all. The upper middle class long remained loyal to French taste and the courtly forms of poetry. We know that even in a commercial city like Leipzig, and as late as the period when Goethe was a student there, rococo taste still prevailed in undisputed supremacy. Nevertheless, it was such commercial cities, as above all Hamburg and Zürich, which were the first to free themselves from the tyranny of the courts in matters of taste, and which had provided a home for middle-class literature. After the middle of the century there still existed residences where poetry was cultivated—Weimar is the classical example—but there was no more court poetry. Not only because of his origins and sympathies but also because of the very nature of his literary activity, which was chiefly critical and journalistic, Lessing was the representative of the middle classes and of urban life. When he settled in Berlin, that city was already beginning to assume the appearance of a great metropolis. It had a hundred thousand inhabitants and, partly as an after-effect of the Seven Years War, it enjoyed a certain freedom of criticism and discussion, which was suppressed, however, by Frederick II as soon as it bordered on provinces beyond the confines of religion.[106] Lessing himself referred to this characteristic limitation of the questions allowed for discussion, in a letter to Nicolai: 'Your Berlin freedom', he writes, 'reduces itself . . . to the freedom to bring to market as many absurdities against religion as you like . . . But let someone come on the scene who wants to raise his voice on behalf of the rights of subjects and against exploitation and despotism . . . and you will soon discover which is the most servile land in Europe to this very day.' Nevertheless, Lessing knew very well what made him go to Berlin; in this great city the air was different, when all is said and done, from the air in the stuffy residences and in the walled-up universities, which were the only choice open to a writer who wanted somewhere to work.[107] It is true that Lessing led the life of a literary hack, put libraries in order, carried out secretarial duties, prepared translations, but, on the whole, he was independent. One does not begin to realize what his independence cost him, until one reads the answer he once gave to someone who asked him why he wrote such small letters; his reply was that his income from fees would not cover the expense of the paper and ink he would require, if he wrote his letters bigger. When he was over forty, nothing remained even for him, however, but to take upon himself the yoke against which he had resisted for a lifetime. He entered the service of a prince and spent the last tortured years of his life in Wolfenbüttel as librarian to the Duke of Brunswick. German literature was, nevertheless, on the upward grade by now. The number of writers increased (in 1773 there were about 3,000 authors in Germany, but in 1787 already twice as many) and in the final decades of the eighteenth century many of them could live on the proceeds of their literary work.[108] Right into the romantic period, however, most of them still found it necessary to take up a professional career. Gellert, Herder and Lavater were clergymen, Hamann, Winckelmann, Lenz, Hoelderlin and Fichte were private tutors, Gottsched, Kant, Schiller, Goerres, Schelling and the Grimm brothers were university professors, whilst Novalis, A. W. Schlegel, Schleiermacher, Eichendorff and E. T. A. Hoffmann were state officials.

With the 'Storm and Stress' movement, German literature becomes entirely middle-class, even though the young rebels are anything but lenient towards the bourgeoisie. But their protest against the encroachments of despotism and their enthusiasm for freedom is just as genuine and sincere as their anti-rationalist attitude. And even if they are merely a loosely connected group of fantasts, ignorant of the world and crazy social misfits, they are deeply rooted in the middle class and cannot deny their origins. The whole period of German culture which extends from the 'Storm and Stress' to the romantic movement is borne by this class; the intellectual leaders of the age think and feel in accordance with middle-class attitudes and the public to which they turn consists mainly of middle-class elements. It does not by any means embrace the whole of the middle class, it is true, and is often restricted, in fact, to a not very numerous élite, but it, nevertheless, represents a progressive tendency and accomplishes the final dissolution of courtly culture. The bourgeoisie develops into a cultured class, distinct not only from the nobility but also from the academic class, and provides a bridge between the intellectual leaders and the broad masses of the nation. Germany now becomes the 'land of the middle class', in which the aristocracy shows itself to be increasingly unproductive, whereas the bourgeoisie makes its way intellectually, in spite of its political weakness, and undermines the non-bourgeois forms of culture with its rationalism. The rationalism of the eighteenth century is one of those movements the progress of which can be retarded but not brought to a standstill by reactionary counter-currents. No social group is able to keep itself wholly aloof from it, and the German intelligentsia all the less, as its irrational tendencies are derived from a misunderstanding of its real interests. The situation in Germany is, therefore, briefly as follows: the attitude to life of the upholders of culture becomes middle-class, their ways of thinking and modes of experience become rationalized and revolutionized, a new type of intellectual arises, who is inwardly without ties, that is, free of traditions and conventions, without being able or often even wanting to exert a corresponding influence on political and social reality. He fights against the rationalism of which he is the involuntary supporter, and becomes, to some extent, the pioneer of the conservatism which he imagines he is struggling against. Thus conservative and reactionary are everywhere mixed up with progressive and liberal tendencies.[109]

Lessing knew that the 'overcoming' of rationalism by the 'Storm and Stress' was an aberration of the middle class; that also explains the reserve he showed towards Goethe's early works, especially *Goetz* and *Werther*.[110] The criticism of the rationalistic popular philosophy was certainly justified, but, in the given situation, it needed more intelligence to disregard the inadequacies of rationalism than to be obsessed by them. In its fight against the Church, which was inseparably allied with absolutism, the enlightenment had become insensitive to everything connected with religion and the powers of the irrational in history. The representatives of the 'Storm and Stress' movement now played off these powers against the 'disenchanted', sober reality of their time, to which they felt themselves to be in no way bound. But in so doing, they merely conformed to the wishes of the ruling classes, who were endeavouring to divert attention from the reality of which they had made themselves masters. They encouraged any idea representing the purpose of the world as inexplicable and incalculable, and promoted the spiritualizing of the problems, hoping thereby to deflect the revolutionary tendency of developments in the intellectual sphere and to induce the middle class to content itself with an ideological instead of a practical solution.[111] Under the influence of this opiate, the German intelligentsia lost its feeling for positive and rational knowledge and replaced it by intuition and metaphysical vision. Irrationalism was certainly a universal European phenomenon, but it was expressed everywhere essentially as a form of emotionalism, and first received its special quality of idealism and spiritualism in Germany; it was only here that it developed into a philosophy of contempt for empirical reality, based on the timeless and the infinite, on the eternal and the absolute. As a form of emotionalism, the romantic movement still had a direct link with the revolutionary tendencies at work in the middle class, as a form of idealism and super-naturalism, on the other hand, it became increasingly remote from progressive middle-class thought. It is true that the starting point of German idealism was Kant's anti-metaphysical theory of knowledge, with its roots in the enlightenment, but it developed the subjectivism of this doctrine into an absolute renunciation of objective reality and reached a position of decided opposition to the realism of the enlightenment. German philosophy in the person of Kant had already become estranged from the cultured lay public of the period, above all because of its jargon, which it was simply impossible for the uninitiated to understand and which identified profundity with difficulty. German scientific style successively assumed that often vague, coquettish character, iridescent with half-expressed intimations, which differentiates it so sharply from the style of Western European scientific language. At the same time, the Germans also lost the feeling for the simple, sober and certain truths which are so highly honoured in the West, and their fondness for speculative constructions and complications developed into a real passion.

The intellectual habit, described as 'German thinking', 'German science', 'German style', must not, however, be regarded as the expression of an unchanging national character, but merely as a mode of thinking and writing which arose in a definite period of German history, that is to say, in the second half of the eighteenth century, and was created by a definite social stratum, the middle-class intelligentsia which was excluded from the government of the country and was practically without influence. This stratum played just as important a part in the development of the German cultured class as did the litterateurs of the enlightenment in that of the French reading public. What Tocqueville asserts of the origins of the typical French mentality, namely that it owes its tendency to rational, evident and general ideas to the enormous influence of the literature of the enlightenment,[112] can also be applied mutatis mutandis to the origins of the German frame of mind with its eccentricity and its passion for surprises and complications. Both are the creation of an epoch in which the literary class in process of self-emancipation exerted a more lasting influence than ever before on the intellectual development of the nations. In the whole of the West, in France and England as well as in Germany, the eighteenth century was the age which saw the beginnings of modern scientific thinking and of the criteria of education to some extent still regarded as valid today. They arose with the modern middle class and to it owe their tenacity. Thus, for example, in his *Zauberberg*, Thomas Mann still judges the enlightenment from the same point of view as did the 'Storm and Stress'. He, too, speaks of the 'shallow optimism' of the pedagogical century, and, in the character of Settembrini, he typifies the West European rationalist as an idle speechifier and complacent humanitarian.

The unreality expressed in the abstract thinking and esoteric language of the German poets and philosophers is also apparent in their exaggerated individualism and mania for originality. Their desire to be absolutely different from everyone else is, like their jargon, merely a symptom of their a-social nature. Mme de Staël's words, 'trop d'idées neuves, pas assez d'idées communes', are a most succinct diagnosis of the German mind. What the Germans lacked was not Sunday cake but daily bread. They lacked that healthy, alert, universally acknowledged public opinion, which in the Western European countries set a limit on individual aspirations from the very beginning and created a common trend of thought. Mme de Staël already recognized that the individual freedom, or as Goethe called it, the 'literary sansculottism', of the German poets was nothing more than a compensation for their exclusion from active political life. But their esoteric language and their 'profundity', their cult of the difficult and the complicated, were derived from the same source. It was all the expression of an attempt to make up for the political and social influence, denied to the German intelligentsia, by cultivating intellectual exclusiveness and making the higher forms of intellectual life just as much the reserve of an élite as political rights.

The German intellectuals were incapable of grasping that rationalism and empiricism were the natural allies of the progressive middle class and the best preparation for a social order in which oppression would sooner or later have to come to an end. They could have done the forces of conservatism no greater service than to bring the 'sober language of the reason' into discredit. These intellectuals were confused in their aims, on the one hand, because the German princes took a patronizing interest in the enlightenment for the sake of appearance and adapted the rationalism of the old absolute régime to the new cultivation of the reason, and on the other hand, because of the religious traditions of the petty bourgeois homes from which they came and which were often intellectually conditioned by the father's pastoral calling. Most of the representatives of the intelligentsia inherited these traditions, which now see an important revival under the influence of Pietism. In its campaign against the enlightenment, the intelligentsia confined itself, above all, to those fields in which anti-rationalism had the broadest scope, and borrowed its intellectual weapons mainly from the religious and aesthetic sphere. The religious experience was in itself irrational and the experience of art became irrational to the extent that the aesthetic criteria of court culture were left behind. Following the example of Neoplatonism, the two spheres were first of all allowed to merge into each other, but later the primacy in the new world-view was given to the aesthetic categories. The features of a work of art, which are impenetrable by the reason and not to be defined in logical terms, had already been observed and emphasized by the Renaissance: they did not have to wait until now to be discovered; but the eighteenth century first drew attention to the fundamental irrationality and irregularity of artistic creation. This anti-authoritarian age, with its deliberate and planned opposition to courtly academicism, was the first to deny that the reflexive and rationalized intellectual functions, the artistic intelligence and the critical faculty, had any part in the origins of a work of art. The establishment of anti-rationalism met, at any rate, with less opposition in this sphere than in the theoretical field. The tendencies opposed to the enlightenment, therefore, withdrew, to begin with, to the aesthetic line, and conquered the intellectual world from this vantage ground. The harmonious structure of the work of art was transferred from the aesthetic sphere to the whole cosmos, and an artistic plan was ascribed to the creator of the universe, as had already been done by Plotinus. That 'the beautiful is a manifestation of secret powers of nature' was asserted even by the otherwise in no way mystically inclined Goethe, and the whole natural philosophy of the romantic movement revolved around this idea. Aesthetics became the basic discipline and the organ of metaphysics. Even in Kant's theory of knowledge, experience was the creation of the knowing subject, just as the work of art had always been considered the product of the artist tied to but master of reality. Kant thought he was in a position to say practically nothing about the constitution of the object in itself but a great deal about the spontaneity of the subject, and he transformed knowledge, which had been understood by the whole of classical antiquity and the Middle

Ages as an image of reality, into a function of the reason. The opposition of objectivity to the freedom of the subject diminished in the course of time, and reality, as the object of knowledge, finally became the unrestricted domain of the creative subject. How could such a change in the conception of the world take place? Philosophical systems are committed to paper in libraries and studies, it is true, but they do not originate in them; and if this, nevertheless, does occur once in a while, as it actually did in the case of German idealism, then there are solid, practical reasons for that too. The studies of the German philosophers were impenetrably walled up and the experience out of which these philosophers developed their systems was precisely their isolation, their loneliness, their lack of influence on practical affairs. Their aestheticism was partly the expression of their aloofness from the world in which the 'mind' had proved itself to be powerless, partly the roundabout way towards the realization of a human ideal that could not be realized by the direct way of political and social education.

Voltaire and Rousseau became household words in Germany almost simultaneously, but the influence of Rousseau was incomparably deeper and wider than that of Voltaire. Even in France, Rousseau did not find so many and such enthusiastic supporters as he did in Germany. The whole 'Storm and Stress' movement, Lessing, Kant, Herder, Goethe and Schiller were dependent on him and acknowledged their indebtedness to him. Kant saw in Rousseau the 'Newton of the moral world', and Herder called him a 'saint and prophet'. The authority which Shaftesbury attained in Germany stood in a similar relationship to the fame he enjoyed in his own country. English specialists of the eighteenth century ascribe no particular importance to him and find it impossible to understand how this 'second-rate' writer was able to acquire such celebrity in Germany.[113] But with a closer knowledge of conditions there, it is not so difficult to explain why an anti-rationalist like Shaftesbury, with his belief in spiritual values and his opposition to Locke, his Platonic enthusiasm and his Neoplatonic idea of beauty as the innermost essence of the divine, made such a deep impression on the Germans. Shaftesbury was a typical Whig aristocrat and his intellectual peculiarity was best expressed in the kalokagathia of his pedagogic ideal and his aestheticizing moral philosophy. His 'self-breeding' was nothing more than the translation of aristocratic selection from the physical to the intellectual and moral sphere. The sociological origin of his ideal of personality was just as unmistakably reflected in the idea that the conflict between egoistic and altruistic instincts, by which the lower classes of humanity are morally depraved, is settled in the higher 'educated' classes, as in the identification of the true and the good with the beautiful. The idea that life is a work of art at which one works, guided by an infallible instinct ('moral sense'), just as the artist is guided by his genius, was an aristocratic conception which was taken up with such enthusiasm by the German intelligentsia, merely because it was so completely open to misunderstanding and its aristocratic quality could be interpreted as an awareness of intellectual nobility.

To the enlightenment the world appeared as something thoroughly intelligible, explicable and open to explanation, whereas the 'Storm and Stress' regarded it as something fundamentally incomprehensible, mysterious and, from the standpoint of the human reason, without meaning. Such views are not simply the product of excogitation and are not conditioned by logical rules. The one is the result of a consciousness of being able to control or, at any rate, to conquer reality, the other is the expression of the feeling of being lost and forsaken in this reality. Whole classes of society and generations do not voluntarily relinquish the world; and if they are forced into doing so, they often invent the most beautiful philosophies, fairy tales and myths, in order to raise the compulsion to which they have succumbed into the sphere of freedom, spirituality and pure inwardness. In this way, there arose the theories of the self-realization of the Idea in history, of the categorical imperative of the moral person, the self-imposed law of the creative artist and other similar doctrines. But perhaps nothing reflects so acutely and comprehensively the motives from which the 'Storm and Stress' develops its world-view as the concept of the artistic genius, which it places at the summit of human values. The concept contains, first of all, the criteria of the irrational and the subjective, which pre-romanticism emphasizes in opposition to the generalizing and dogmatic enlightenment, the conversion of external compulsion into inward freedom, which is rebellious and despotic at one and the same time, and, finally, the principle of originality, which, in this natal hour of the free man of letters and of an hourly increasing competitiveness, becomes the most important weapon in the intelligentsia's struggle for existence. Artistic creation, which was a clearly definable intellectual activity, based on explicable and learnable rules of taste, for both courtly classicism and the enlightenment, now appears as a mysterious process derived from such unfathomable sources as divine inspiration, blind intuition and incalculable moods. For classicism and enlightenment the genius was a higher intelligence bound by reason, theory, history, tradition and convention; for pre-romanticism and the 'Storm and Stress' he becomes the personification of an ideal characterized, above all, by the lack of all these ties. The genius is rescued from the wretchedness of everyday life into a dream-world of boundless freedom of choice. Here he lives not merely free from the fetters of reason, but in possession of mystic powers which enable him to dispense with ordinary sense experience. 'The genius has presentiments, that is to say, his feelings outrun his powers of observation. The genius does not observe. He *sees*, he feels'—says Lavater. To be sure, the irrational and unconscious aspects of the concept of genius are to be found, to begin with, in the pre-romanticism of Western Europe, first of all, in Edward Young's *Conjectures on Original Composition* (1759), but here the genius still appears alongside the mere talent, as a 'magician' alongside a good 'master builder', whereas in the art philosophy of the 'Storm and Stress' he becomes the rebellious, godlike Titan. We are no longer confronted with a necromancer, whose tricks are impossible to follow, though by no means unnatural, but with the guardian of a mysterious wisdom, the 'speaker of unspeakable things' and the law-giver of a world of his own, with laws of its own.[114] What distinguishes this concept of genius from that of Young is, above all, the extreme subjectivism which it owes to the special German situation. The personal aspects of artistic creativity were already well known both to Hellenism and the Renaissance, but neither of these epochs attained a concept of art comparable in its subjectivity to that of the eighteenth century.[115] It is, however, even in the eighteenth century only in Germany that artistic subjectivism developed into that mania for originality, which cannot be explained merely as a protest against the dogmatism of the enlightenment and as the self-advertisement of literary men competing against each other. To understand it, one must also consider the boundless veneration in which the 'energetic man', the 'fine fellow' was held. This overstrained subjectivism, which has been called, not without justification, an 'excess of bourgeois frenzy',[116] could, naturally, only arise in a relatively free bourgeois world, independent of the class morality and solidarity of the aristocracy and dominated by the spirit of free competition, but without the psychological antagonism of the suppressed, intimidated German intelligentsia, which was always searching for compensations and wavered irresolutely between submissiveness and presumption, pessimism and exuberance, it would hardly have assumed the pathological form peculiar to the 'Storm and Stress'. Without this inner contradiction and this tendency to overcompensate for the limitations of practical life, however, not only subjectivism but also the dissolution of formal structures in art which took place in German pre-romanticism, its escape into extravagance and shapelessness, its doctrine of the fundamental falsehood and inadequacy of any form, would be unthinkable. The world that had become foreign and inimical did not propose to offer itself as material for the pre-romantics to mould into a finished shape, and so they made the atomized structure of their world-view and the fragmentary nature of their motifs symbols of life itself. Goethe's dictum on the mendacity of all forms is derived from the outlook of this generation and is absolutely in harmony with the words of Hamann, who said that all systems are 'in themselves an obstruction of the truth'.[117]

The 'Storm and Stress' was even more complicated in its sociological structure than the West European forms of pre-romanticism, and not merely because the German middle class and the German intelligentsia had never identified themselves closely enough with the enlightenment to keep their eyes sharply fixed on the aims of the movement and not to deviate from it, but also because their struggle against the rationalism of the abolutist régime was at the same time a struggle against the progressive tendencies of the age. They never became aware of the fact that the rationalism of the princes represented a less serious danger for the future than the anti-rationalism of their own compeers. From being the enemies of despotism they, therefore, became the instruments of reaction and merely promoted the interests of the privileged classes with their attacks on bureaucratic centralization. To be sure, their struggle was not directed against the social levelling tendencies of the system, with which aristocratic and upper middle-class interests were in conflict, but against its generalizing influence and violation of all intellectual distinction and variety. They championed the rights of life, of individual being, natural growth and organic development, against the rigid formalism of the rationalized administration, and meant not only the denial of the bureaucratic state with its mechanical generalization and regimentation, but also the repudiation of the planning and regulating reformism of the enlightenment. And although the idea of the spontaneous, irrational life was still of an indefinite and fluctuating nature and certainly hostile to the enlightenment, but not yet markedly conservative in its purpose, nevertheless, it already contained the essence of the whole philosophy of conservatism. It did not need much now to ascribe a mystical superrationality to this principle of 'life', in contrast to which the rationalism of enlightened thought seemed unnatural, inflexible and doctrinaire, and to represent the rise of political and social institutions from historical 'life' as a 'natural', that is to say, superhuman and superrational growth, in order to protect these institutions against all arbitrary attacks and to secure the continuance of the prevailing system.

At first sight it is surprising that conservatism, which we are in the habit of associating with the idea of continuity and persistency, here stresses the value of life and growth, whereas liberalism, which we usually connect with the idea of movement and dynamics, bases its claims on reason. The attempt has been made to attribute this apparent paradox to the fact that the revolutionary thinking of the middle class developed in a clear, unambiguous alliance with rationalism and that the counter-current took up the opposite ideological standpoint for the sake of 'mere opposition'.[118] But the difficulty of the problem is that the relation to rationalism of the various political tendencies of the eighteenth century is by no means clear-cut, and that even the conservatism of the age contains a certain streak of rationalism. The peculiar situation of the 'Storm and Stress' between the enlightenment and the romantic movement is conditioned by the fact that it is impossible simply to identify rationalism and anti-rationalism with progress and reaction, and that modern rationalism is not an unequivocal and specific phenomenon, but, to some extent, a general characteristic of modern history. Since the Renaissance it has made its influence felt in all periods of development and all classes of society and has sometimes shown a tendency to intellectual flexibility and mobility, at others a striving for the permanent and the universally valid. The rationalism of the Italian Renaissance was of a different kind from that of French classicism, and that of the enlightenment was again completely different from that of the court aristocracy and the absolute monarchy. There was a progressive middle-class rationalism, but there was also a rationalism peculiar to the conservative class. The middle class of the Renaissance had to fight against paralysing habits and traditions; its rationalism was, therefore, dynamic and anti-traditional in character, tending towards maximum efficiency. The aristocracy of the same period was of a knightly-romantic, unreasoning and unpractical nature, but, chiefly under the pressure of economic developments, from the end of the sixteenth century onwards, it adapted itself increasingly to the rationalism of the middle class, though not without modifying certain manifestations of this mode of thought and experience. Thus, first of all, it dropped the anti-traditionalism of the middle-class rationalist ideology, making up for that by eliminating all the elements of the fanciful and the romanesque from its own medieval conception of the world, and, in the course of the seventeenth century, it developed a philosophy of order and discipline, that was fundamentally as 'undynamic' as it was 'reasonable'. To begin with, the middle class of the enlightenment period was under the influence of this rationalistically thinking aristocracy and took over from it the ideal of a strictly regulated, normative standard of life, even though, in other respects, it held fast to the older form of rationalism derived from the Renaissance and consistently developed the doctrine of economic efficiency and competition. But the middle class of the second half of the eighteenth century turned away from rationalism in some respects and, for the time being, left its interpretation to the nobility and the upper middle class. The middle sections of the bourgeoisie became Rousseauistic, sentimental and romantic, whereas the upper classes despised all this sentimental rubbish and remained loyal to their own intellectualism. The progressive middle class, nevertheless, preserved the anti-traditionalist and dynamic character of its outlook on life, just as the conservative classes held fast to the traditionalism of their social philosophy, in spite of the rationalism of their moral principles and their attitude to art. On closer examination, however, the specifically dynamic character, which is habitually ascribed to the liberal and progressive outlook, turns out to be just as metaphorical as the static quality ascribed to rationalism. Liberalism and conservatism are both dynamic and rationalistic at the same time, and in this phase of development, in which the Middle Ages are liquidated once and for all, it is quite impossible for them to be anything else. The only anti-rationalists left now are the idealists, who have become confused by the complex social situation, and—according to what they pass themselves off for—the propagandists of conservatism. The latter champion the rights of 'life' against reason, not because rationalism had in fact lost its authority and influence, but because concrete thinking, based on reality, of which both parties will soon claim to have a monopoly, has won a new and enhanced value.

Herder is perhaps the most characteristic figure in eighteenth-century German literature. He combines within himself the most important currents of the age and expresses most clearly that ideological conflict, that mixture of progressive and reactionary tendencies, by which the society of this time is dominated. He despises the 'matter-of-fact intellectual culture' of the enlightenment, but, on the other hand, he speaks of his age as 'a truly great century' and imagines that it is possible to reconcile his anti-rationalist convictions with an enthusiasm for the French Revolution, just as the majority of the German intelligentsia and most German writers, including Kant, Wieland, Schiller, Friedrich Schlegel and Fichte, are unconditional supporters of the Revolution, to begin with, and only renounce it after the Convention. Herder's development follows the course taken by the German intelligentsia from the rebelliousness of the 'Storm and Stress' to the more clear-sighted, though more resigned, bourgeois attitude of the classical period. His example sheds the clearest possible light on the significance of Weimar for German literature. Goethe's influence on him displaces that of Hamann and Jacobi and brings him nearer to rationalism. He writes an enthusiastic obituary notice of Lessing, the fearless fighter for the truth, and not only overcomes his earlier orthodoxy, but even gives his religion an aesthetic twist and applies his theory of the nature of folk song to the original documents of religion, so that, in the end, the Bible becomes for him merely a prototype of folk poetry. On the other hand, he finds it impossible entirely to renounce his past; the ecclesiastical ties of his youth are transformed into a moralizing philistinism, and how deeply rooted he remains in the world of conservative thought is proved by his philosophy of history, which comes very close to the ideas of Burke. What he has in common with him is, above all, his desire not to domineer, change and violate, but to understand, interpret and surrender himself to the varied forms of historical life.[119] In spite of his loving piety, Herder's morphological conception of history, which takes vegetal rotation as its starting point and sees a development from seed into bud and blossom and from flowering to withering and dying, wherever it looks, is the expression of an intrinsically pessimistic outlook on the world, that already contains the germ of Spengler's theory of the decline of civilizations.[120]

The classicism of Herder, Goethe and Schiller has been described as the belated German Renaissance and the equivalent of French classicism. But its main difference from all similar movements outside Germany is that it represents a synthesis of classicistic and romanticizing tendencies and, especially from the French point of view, appears to be absolutely romantic.[121]. But the German classicists, almost all of whom were members of the 'Storm and Stress' movement in their youth and would be inconceivable without Rousseau's gospel of nature, also represent a renunciation of Rousseau's hostility to culture and to his nihilism. They live in a frenzy of culture and education, like hardly any generation of writers since the humanists, and regard the civilized society, not the gifted individual, as the real upholder of culture.[122] Above all, Goethe's educational ideal finds its true realization only in the culture of a society as a whole, and the measure in which the individual achievement fits into the bourgeois pattern of life becomes for him the very criterion of its value. Now that is the conception of culture held by a literary class which has already attained success and esteem, which is resting on its laurels and no longer feels any kind of resentment towards society. But this success in no way implies that the German classicists ever became popular; their works did not even penetrate so deeply into the national life as did the classical creations of French and English literature. And Goethe was the least popular writer of them all. In his lifetime his fame extended only to a quite exiguous cultured stratum, and even later on his writings were hardly read at all outside the ranks of the intelligentsia. He repeatedly complains about his loneliness, in spite of the fact that he was really, as Schiller says, 'the most communicative of all men' and longed for sympathy, understanding and influence on others. The mass of letters that have survived and the conversations that have been recorded show what intellectual communication, exchange and the mutual development of ideas meant to him. Goethe was, however, perfectly aware of his lack of influence, and attributed not only the character of German literature in general but also that of his own writings to the lack of social intercourse in German intellectual life. The period of his real popularity was his youth, when he published *Goetz* and *Werther*. After his move to Weimar and the beginning of his official activities, he disappeared to some extent from literary life.[123] In Weimar his public was made up of half a dozen persons —the Duke, the two Duchesses, Frau von Stein, Knebel and Wieland—to whom he read aloud his new and not particularly numerous or extensive works, that is to say, single chapters and fragments from his works. One must not imagine that even this public was especially understanding.[124] The incident with the dog-trainer, who, in spite of Goethe's energetic protests, was allowed to perform in the court theatre, best describes the situation. One can imagine the state of affairs at the other courts, if things were as bad as this in Weimar! No particular attention was paid to German literature as such in Weimar; here, too, as in court circles and the nobility in general, reading was mostly confined to the latest French books.[125] In the wider public, in so far as it took any notice of serious literature at all, Schiller became the centre of interest during the time that Goethe spent in Italy; *Don Carlos*, for example, was received much more warmly than *Tasso*. But the greatest literary success was achieved not by Goethe or Schiller, but by Gessner and Kotzebue. It was not until the appearance of the romantics and their enthusiasm, above all, for *Wilhelm Meister* that Goethe attained his unique position in German literature.[126] The romantics' championing of Goethe is the most striking symptom of the deep and, in spite of all personal and ideological disagreements, inviolable community of interest which binds together into a single unity not only the classical and romantic movements, but the whole period of German culture from the 'Storm and Stress' onwards. Art is the great experience which they share in common, and not only as the object of supreme intellectual delight, not only as the one remaining practicable road to personal perfection, but also as the instrument by which humanity is to regain its lost innocence and achieve the simultaneous possession of nature and culture. For Schiller, aesthetic education is the only salvation from the evil recognized by Rousseau, and Goethe actually goes still further, when he maintains that art is the individual's attempt 'to preserve himself against the destructive power of the whole'. The experience of art here acquires the function which up till then only religion had been able to fulfil; it becomes the bulwark against chaos.

A sentence like this is sufficient to give one an idea of Goethe's absolutely a-religious, though perhaps not irreligious outlook on life. For, in spite of his 'Faustian' idealism, his aristocratic aestheticism and his fanatically conservative worship of order, he was one of the most uncompromising representatives of the enlightenment in Germany, and even if he cannot exactly be called a matter-of-fact rationalist, he must be considered, nevertheless, the sworn enemy of all obscurantism and the impassioned opponent of all nebulosity and mysticism, of all reactionary and retarding forces. In spite of his connection with the 'Storm and Stress', he felt a deep dislike for all romanticism, for all reckless suppression of reason, and an equally deep sympathy for the solid realism, discipline, moral appreciation of work and tolerance of the middle class. The impetuosity of the Werther period, its blazing protest against the prevailing social order and conventional morality, calmed down in the course of time, but Goethe remained an enemy of all oppression and a fighter against all injustice that threatened the middle class as a living intellectual community. It was only later in his life that he recognized the real value of this community and only in *Wilhelm Meister* that he gave an appreciation of it. It is not at all necessary to deny or to conceal Goethe's intellectually aristocratic inclinations and ambitions at court, his Olympian egocentricity and his political indifference, or even the embarrassing phrase 'rather injustice than disorder'. In spite of everything, Goethe remained a man of freedom and progress, and not only as a writer and poet whom the very realism of his art, his 'ins Reale verliebte Beschraenktheit', made into such. There are, in fact, different ways in which the fight against reaction and for progress can be carried on. One man hates the pope and parsons, another the princes and their vassals, a third the exploiters and oppressors of the people, but there are also those who experience the meaning of reaction most intensely in the deliberate obscuration of human minds and the prevention of truth, for whom all forms of social injustice are felt most acutely to be the 'sin against the spirit', and who, when they stand up for freedom of conscience, of thought and speech, fight for the indivisible freedom which is the same in all forms of life. Goethe had not much sympathy for tyrannicides, but he was very sensitive to threats to freedom of thought, and was never a party to its restriction. When, in 1794, the German intelligentsia, and especially Goethe himself, were called upon by the conservatives to place themselves at the disposal of the new league of princes, and thereby rid the country of the threatening 'anarchy', Goethe answered that he considered it impossible to bring together princes and writers in this way.[127]

Everything that contributed to the education of the young Goethe, his descent, his childhood impressions, the imperial city of Frankfurt, the commercial and university town of Leipzig, Gothic Strasburg, the Rhineland milieu, Darmstadt, Duesseldorf, the home of Fraeulein Klettenberg and the Schoenemanns, was thoroughly middle-class in the best sense, partly upper middle-class, and often bordering on the sphere of the aristocracy, but never without an inner connection with the spirit of the middle class.[128] Goethe's middle-class character was, however, not a militant attitude of mind, was never directed against the nobility as such, not even in his youth, not even in *Werther*.[129] He regarded it as more important to preserve the bourgeois way of life from obscurantism and unreality than from the influence of the higher ranks of society. The most interesting and original point about Goethe's conception of the bourgeois attitude to life was that it reflected the modern artist's awareness of his own middle-class frame of mind and that it stressed the ethical standards of ordinary work even in relation to artistic production. Goethe repeatedly emphasizes the workmanlike nature of poetic creation and demands from the artist, above all, professional reliability. Since the Renaissance, art and literature had been practised mostly by middle-class persons. The workmanlike relationship of the producer to his art was taken so much for granted that it would have been senseless to lay special stress on it. What had to be done was rather to stimulate artists and writers to raise themselves above the level of mere technical skill. It was not until the eighteenth century when, on the one hand, the middle class became more intensely conscious of its class characteristics, and, on the other hand, the unbridled subjectivism of the 'original geniuses', their repudiation of all rules and disciplines, began to act as an excrescence of bourgeois emancipation and a kind of wild competition, that it seemed advisable to remind them of the bourgeois and artisan-like origins of their profession. It was certainly no longer necessary to draw special attention to the high rank of a writer, but it was expedient to preserve the literary class from the spread of dilettantism and charlatanism. Behaving like a 'genius' was a competitive method used by writers when they were fighting for emancipation; protests against the application of such methods were first heard when they were no longer needed. To be allowed to be 'genius-like' was a symptom of the attainment of independence; no longer to want and have to be 'genius-like' was the mark of a situation in which artistic freedom had become a matter of course. The self-consciousness of the respectable burgher and recognized artist is already so strong in Goethe that he strives to avoid all extravagance both in his art and in his behaviour and feels a particular aversion for the lack of solidity and thoroughness, for the tendency to the chaotic and the pathological, which are, to some extent, constant traits in the artist's character.[130] He thereby anticipates a feature of the nineteenth century and of the successful modern artist, who reacts against the nonsense of bohemianism with exaggerated prudence, and adopts a normal bourgeois, indeed an almost petty bourgeois, way of life for fear of seeming unreliable.

In accordance with the dislike of successful classes for all wilfulness and exaggerated individualism, the art ideal of German classicism shows a predominant trend towards the typical and the universally valid, the regular and the normative, the permanent and the timeless. In contrast to the 'Storm and Stress', it feels form to be the expression of the essence and the very idea of the work of art, in no sense any longer identical with a purely external harmony of relationships, with euphony and beauty of line. By form it understands 'inward form', the microcosmic equivalent of the totality of existence. Goethe finally succeeds in overcoming even this variety of aestheticism, and finds the road to a more realistic philosophy based on the idea of the bourgeois society. The content of *Wilhelm Meister* is precisely this way leading from art to society, from the artistic-individualistic attitude to life to the experience of intellectual community, from the aesthetic-contemplative relation to the world to an active, socially useful life.[131] In his later period, Goethe turns away from the purely personal approach to literature and comes nearer to a super-individual, super-national conception of art, concentrated on tasks of general importance to civilization. The name and partly the concept of 'world literature' comes from him; but the thing had existed before anyone was conscious of it. The literature of the enlightenment, the works of Voltaire and Diderot, Locke and Helvétius, Rousseau and Richardson, were already 'world literature' in the strictest sense of the word. Since the first half of the eighteenth century a 'European conversation' had been in progress, in which all civilized nations had been participating, though most of them only in a passive capacity. The literature of the period was that of Europe as a whole, the expression of a European community of ideas, such as had not been known since the end of the Middle Ages. But it was almost as acutely different from medieval literature as it was from the international literary movements of more recent times. The literature of the Middle Ages owed its universality to the Latin, that of the baroque and the rococo to the French language; the former was limited to the learned clerical class, the latter to aristocratic court cricles. Both were undifferentiated products originating in a more or less uniform intellectual outlook, not the consort of several voices, as Goethe desired, and as the enlightenment produced from the literatures of the great nations of Europe. The theory and practice of world literature was the creation of a civilization dominated by the aims and methods of world trade. The words of Goethe himself, when he compares the exchange of intellectual goods between the nations with international trade, touch on this connection and point to the origin of the concept. When Goethe goes on to speak of the 'velociferic' character of intellectual and material production and the accelerated tempo with which intellectual and material goods are exchanged, one sees how directly the whole orbit of ideas is connected with the experience of the Industrial Revolution.[132] The only curious thing is that the Germans, who of the great nations had contributed least of all to this world literature, were the first to understand its significance and to develop the idea.

5. REVOLUTION AND ART

The eighteenth century is full of contradictions. It is not only that its philosophical attitude wavers between rationalism and anti-rationalism, but its artistic aims are also dominated by two opposite tendencies and at some times approach a strictly classicistic, at others a more unrestrained pictorial conception. And like the rationalism of the period, its classicism is also difficult to define and open to various sociological interpretations, since it is sustained alternately by courtly-aristocratic and middle-class strata of society and ends by developing into the representative artistic style of the revolutionary bourgeoisie. The fact that David's painting becomes the official art of the Revolution only seems strange or even inexplicable, if one conceives the concept of classicism too narrowly and restricts it to the artistic aims of the upper, conservatively-minded classes. Classicistic art certainly tends towards conservatism and is well suited to represent authoritarian ideologies, but the aristocratic outlook often finds more direct expression in the sensualistic and exuberant baroque than in abstemious and matter-of-fact classicism. The rationalistically-minded, moderate and disciplined middle class, on the other hand, often favours the simple, clear, uncomplicated forms of classicistic art and is no more attracted by the indiscriminate and shapeless imitation of nature than by the whimsical imaginative art of the aristocracy. Its naturalism moves in most cases within relatively narrow limits and is usually restricted to the rationalistic portrayal of reality, that is to say, of a reality without internal contradictions. Naturalness and formal discipline are almost one and the same thing here. It is only in the classicism of the aristocracy that the bourgeois principle of order becomes transformed into a strict conformity to rigid norms, its striving for simplicity and economy into coercion and subordination, and its healthy logic into a cool intellectualism. In Greek classicism or in that of Giotto, fidelity to nature is never felt to be incompatible with formal concentration; it is only in the art of the court aristocracy that form holds sway at the expense of naturalness, and only here that it is regarded as a limitation and a barrier. But, intrinsically, classicism no more represents an expansive, naturalistic tendency than a typical bourgeois outlook,[133] although it often begins as a bourgeois movement and derives its formal principles from conformity to nature. It extends, however, beyond both the frontiers of the bourgeois view of art and the presuppositions of naturalism. The art of Racine and

Claude Lorrain is classicistic without being either bourgeois or naturalistic.

The history of modern art is marked by the consistent and almost uninterrupted progress of naturalism; the tendencies towards rigorous formalism emerge comparatively seldom and never for more than a short period at a time, although they are always present as an undercurrent. The consistent association of naturalism and classical form in the work of Giotto is already dissolved in the Trecento, and in the essentially bourgeois art of the following two centuries naturalism is developed at the expense of form. The High Renaissance turns its attention again to the principles of form, without regarding the composition, however, as Giotto did, merely as an instrument of clarification and simplification but, in accordance with its aristocratic temper, as a means of enhancing and idealizing reality. And yet the art of the High Renaissance is, as we know, by no means anti-naturalistic; it is only poorer in naturalistic details and less concentrated on the differentiation of the empirical material than the art of the preceding period, but it is in no way less true and exact. Mannerism, on the other hand, which corresponds to the further progress of the process of aristocratization, connects its classicism with a series of anti-naturalistic conventions, and thereby influences the taste of the upper classes so deeply that its arty concept of beauty is accepted more or less as the standard by which all later courtly art is judged. In the second half of the sixteenth century mannerism is the leading style just as much in France as in Italy and Spain. In France its progress is suddenly interrupted, however, by the religious and civil wars under Henry IV, and this disturbance, which is prolonged by the anti-aristocratic government policy of the succeeding period, makes it possible for the middle class to exert a decisive, albeit passing influence on the further development of art. The Renaissance tradition of court culture breaks down and with the retrogression of court life, first of all, theatrical performances at court become more and more infrequent and finally come to an end altogether. The popular theatre, on the other hand, continues its modest existence even during this time of crisis. In addition to the mysteries and moralities, humanist plays are now performed on the popular stage, though they have to adapt themselves to the scenic mobility of the medieval theatre and assume its characteristic shapelessness. The middle class that enjoys the favour of the Crown under Louis XIII, and Richelieu and even in the first period of the reign of Louis XIV and gives employment to the literary men of the period, finally succeeds in reforming this theatre, which was still suffering from a medieval lack of rules and restrictions. It develops a literary style of its own fundamentally different from the mannerism of the aristocracy, and establishes in the genre with which it has the longest and deepest connections—the drama—a new classicism based on naturalness and reasonableness. The *tragédie classique* is, therefore, not the creation of the learned humanists with their courtly taste and of the aristocratic Pléiade, as has so often been asserted, but grows out of the living and commonplace bourgeois theatre. Its formal limitations, especially its unities of time and place, do not result from the study of classical tragedy, or at least not directly, but develop, first of all, as the artistic means by which an attempt is made to heighten the stage effect and the probability of the action. Increasing bewilderment is felt that the scenery of actions taking place in different houses, cities and countries should be separated by a mere board and that the short interval between two acts should be supposed to represent months and years. On the basis of such rationalistic considerations, a dramatic action begins to be regarded as all the more probable the shorter the time and the more uniform the space is in which it takes place. The duration of the events and the distances between the various scenes is, therefore, reduced, in order to attain a more perfect illusion, and a gradual approach is made to the most obvious form of illusionism: the identification of the actual time of the performance with the imaginary time of the action. The unities accordingly conform to a perfectly naturalistic requirement, and are also represented by the dramaturgists of the period as the criteria of dramatic probability. But it is, to say the least, strange that an artistic device which led to the most far-reaching stylization and most ruthless violation of reality originally meant the victory of the naturalistic outlook and of rationalistic thought over the unbridled and indiscriminate curiosity of a theatre public whose feelings were still essentially medieval.

And as in the drama, so also in the other arts, classicism is synonymous with the triumph of naturalism and rationalism: on the one hand, over the fantasy and lack of discipline, on the other hand, over the affectedness and conventionalism of art as practised hitherto. To the poetry of du Bartas, d'Aubigné and Théophile de Viau the middle class opposes the drama of men like Hardy, Mairet and Corneille and follows up the mannerism of Jean Cousin and Jacques Bellange with the naturalism and classicism of Louis Le Nain and Poussin. The fact that naturalistic classicism never becomes so predominant in the plastic arts as in the drama is to be attributed, above all, to the much less close historical relationship of the French bourgeoisie with painting than with the theatre and to the fact that it still has not the resources at its disposal necessary in order to exert such an overwhelming influence. It is true that mannerism gradually falls out of fashion in painting and sculpture too, but, in this case, it is superseded by a style that inclines more to the baroque than to classicism. In the drama, however, bourgeois classicism is entirely successful with its enforcement of the unities. The *Cid* by the Rouen solicitor Corneille, which appears in 1636, can be regarded as its final triumph. To begin with, it meets with the opposition of court circles, but the realistic and rationalistic thinking that dominates the economic and political life of the age proves to be irresistibly victorious. The aristocracy, which is subject to the influence of Spanish taste, is forced to overcome its penchant for the adventurous, the extravagant and the fantastic and to resign itself to the aesthetic criteria of the matter-of-fact and unpretentious bourgeoisie. This does not take place, however, without this philosophy of art being modified by the aristocracy, to fit in with its own ideals and aims. It preserves the harmony, the regularity and the naturalness of bourgeois classicism, since the new court etiquette regards all shrillness, noisiness and wilfulness as in bad taste, in any case, but it reinterprets the artistic economy of this aesthetic trend, in order to bring it into line with a philosophy in which concentration and precision are understood not as principles of puritanical discipline but as fastidious rules of taste and in which they are opposed to 'coarse', unruly and incalculable nature as the norms of a higher, purer reality. Classicism, which was originally intended only to preserve and stress the organic unity and stern 'logic' of nature, in this way becomes a brake on the instincts, a defence against the flood of the emotions and a veil over the ordinary and the all-too-natural.

This reinterpretation was already partly achieved in the tragedies of Corneille, which are among the ripest manifestations of the new artistic rationalism, but which arose obviously not without regard for the requirements of the court theatre. In the succeeding period the sober, matter-of-fact, puritanical tendencies recede increasingly in court art, on the one hand, because alongside and often against its severity, the desire for a heightened display makes itself felt, on the other hand, because a general change is taking place in the whole conception of art in this century, and this leads to the freer, more emotional, more sensualistic aspirations of the baroque gaining the upper hand. In this way, there arises in French art and literature a curious proximity and interaction of classicistic and baroque tendencies, and a resulting style that is a contradiction in itself—baroque classicism. The high baroque of Racine and Le Brun contains—in the one case absolutely resolved, in the other absolutely unresolved—the conflict between the new courtly ceremonial style and the formal severity that has its roots in bourgeois classicism. It is classicistic and anti-classicistic at the same time it acts; equally through the material and the form, through fullness and restriction, expansion and concentration. Around 1680 a countertendency sets in against this courtly and academic style: in opposition as much to its grandiose attitudes and pretentious themes as to its alleged fidelity to classical models. The conception of art that now holds good, as a result, is less restrained, more individualistic, more intimate and it turns its liberalism, above all, against the classicism, not the baroque tendencies of court art. The success of the modernists in the 'Quarrel between the Ancients and the Moderns' is merely a symptom of this development. The Régence decides the victory of the anti-classical trend and brings about an absolute re-orientation of the prevailing fashions of taste. The social origins of the new art, however, are not wholly evident. The change is carried through partly by the liberal-minded aristocracy, partly by the upper middle class. But as the art of the Régence gradually develops into the rococo, it more and more assumes the characteristics of a courtly-aristocratic style, although it bears within it from the very outset the elements of the dissolution of court culture. At any rate, it loses the concentrated, precise and solid character of classicism, shows an increasingly strong dislike for everything regular, geometrical and tectonic, and tends more and more to favour the improvization, the aperçu and the epigram. 'Si quelqu'un est assez barbare—assez classique!'—as even the by no means courtly-minded Beaumarchais says. Since the Middle Ages, art had never been so far removed from classical purity, never had it been more sophisticated and more artificial. And then, around 1750, in the midst of the rococo, a new reaction sets in. The progressive elements of society stand, in opposition to the prevailing trend, for an artistic ideal which once again bears a rationally classicistic character. No classicism had ever been more strict, more sober, more methodical than this; in none had the reduction of forms, the straight line and the tectonically significant been carried through more consistently, in none had the typical and the normative been emphasized more strongly. None had possessed the unmistakable clarity of this classicism, because none had had its strictly programmatical character, its aggressive determination to break up the rococo. Even now it is not immediately clear by which strata of society the new movement is initiated. Its first representatives, men like Caylus and Cochin, Gabriel and Soufflot, are rooted in courtly-aristocratic culture, but it soon becomes perceptible that the most progressive elements of society are the motive power behind them. The sociological derivation of the new classicism is so difficult, because the tradition of the old baroque classicism had never entirely broken down, and is just as active in the elegance of Vanloo or Reynolds as in the correctness of Voltaire or Pope. Certain classicistic formulae remain current both in painting and literature during the whole period of courtly style covering the seventeenth and eighteenth centuries, and, as regards poetic diction, the following passage from Pope, for example, illustrates the classicism of this period just as perfectly as any text from the century of Louis XIV:

> See, through this air, this ocean, and this earth,
> All matter quick, and bursting into birth,
> Above, how high, progressive life may go!
> Around, how wide! how deep extend below!
> Vast chain of being! which from God began,
> Natures ethereal, human, angel, man,
> Beast, bird, fish, insect, what no eye can see,
> No glass can reach; from infinite to thee,
> From thee to nothing.[134]

The aloof rationalism and smooth crystalline form of these lines are different, however, even at first sight, from the vibrant tone of the following lines by Chénier which are just as perfectly classicistic but are filled with a new passion:

> Allons, étouffe tes clameurs;
> Souffre, o cœur gros de haine, affamé de justice.
> Toi, Vertu, pleure, si je meurs.

Pope's lines are still a reminiscence of the intellectual culture of the court aristocracy, whereas Chénier's are already the expression of the new bourgeois emotionalism and come from the lips of a poet who stands in the shadow of the guillotine and becomes the victim of that revolutionary middle class whose classicistic taste finds in him its first important, though involuntary, mouthpiece.

The new classicism does not arrive so unheralded as has often been assumed.[135] Ever since the end of the Middle Ages conceptions of art had developed between the two poles of a strictly tectonic trend and formal freedom, that is, between an outlook related to classicism and one opposed to it. No change in modern art represents a completely new beginning; they all link up with one or other of these two tendencies, each of which takes over the lead from the other, but neither of which is ever entirely supplanted. Those scholars who represent neo-classicism as a complete innovation usually regard it as peculiar that the development does not proceed from the simple to the complicated, in other words, from the linear to the pictorial, or from the pictorial to the more pictorial, but that the process of differentiation 'breaks off' and the development 'jumps back' to a certain extent. Woelfflin is of the opinion that in this retrogression 'the initiative is more clearly grounded in outward circumstances' than in the uninterrupted process of increasing complication. In reality, there is no fundamental difference, however, between the two types of development, the influence of 'outward circumstances' is only more obvious in the case of an intermittent than in that of a straightforward development. In fact, outward circumstances always play the same decisive rôle. At every point and in every moment of the development it is an open question what direction artistic creation will take. The maintenance of the course already set represents a dialectical process which is just as much the result of 'outward circumstances' as a change in the prevailing trend. The attempt to hold up or interrupt the progress of naturalism does not presuppose any factors fundamentally different from those underlying the desire to maintain or accelerate its progress. The art of the age of the Revolution differs from earlier classicism, above all, by the fact that it leads to a more exclusive predominance of the strictly formal conception of art than had ever occurred since the beginning of the Renaissance, and that it represents the final conclusion of the three hundred year long development extending from the naturalism of Pisanello to the impressionism of Guardi.[136] It would, nevertheless, be unjustifiable to assert a complete lack of tension and stylistic conflict in the art of David; the dialectic of the various trends of style pulsates in it just as feverishly as in the poetry of Chénier and all the important artistic creations of the revolutionary period.

The classicism which extends from the middle of the eighteenth century to the July revolution is not a homogeneous movement but a development that, although it proceeds without interruption, takes place in several clearly distinguishable phases. The first of these phases, which lasts roughly from 1750 to 1780 and is usually called 'rococo classicism' on account of the mixed character of its style, represents what is historically probably the most important of the tendencies united in the 'Louis-Seize', but is only an undercurrent in the real artistic life of the period. The heterogeneousness of the competing stylistic tendencies is expressed most forcibly of all in the architecture of the age, in which rococo interiors are combined with classicistic façades, a mixture of styles which never disturbs the contemporary public. In no phenomenon is the indecision of the period, its inability to choose between the given alternatives, expressed so clearly as in this eclecticism. The baroque was already marked by a wavering between rationalism and sensualism, formalism and spontaneity, classical and modern, but it still attempted to resolve the conflict in a single, albeit not wholly uniform style. Here, on the other hand, we are confronted with an art in which there is not even an attempt to reduce the different stylistic elements to a common denominator. For just as in architecture stylistically different façades and interiors are combined, so in painting and poetry works of utterly different formal character stand side by side—the works of Boucher, Fragonard and Voltaire beside those of Vien, Greuze and Rousseau. The age produces, at most, hybrid forms, but no adjustment of the opposing formal principles. This eclecticism corresponds to the general structure of a society in which the different classes intermingle and often co-operate, but still remain absolute strangers to each other. The prevailing power relationships are expressed in the world of art above all in the fact that the courtly rococo is, in practice, still the predominant style and enjoys the favour of the overwhelming majority of the art public, whereas classicism merely represents the art of an artistic opposition and constitutes the programme of a comparatively sparse group of amateurs hardly big enough to make any difference in the art market.

This new movement, which has also been called 'archaeological classicism', is more directly dependent on the antiquarian approach to Greek and Roman art than the older cognate tendencies. But even here, the theoretical interest in classical antiquity is not the primary factor; it rather presupposes a change of taste, which in its turn presupposes a shift of values in the whole outlook on life. Classical art acquires a topical interest for the eighteenth century, because once again the attraction of a more stern, more serious and more objective artistic style is felt after the reign of a pictorial technique that had become all too flexible and fluid, and all too playful with charming colours and tones. When the new classicistic trend emerged around the middle of the century, the classicism of the 'grand siècle' had been dead for fifty years; art had surrendered itself to the voluptuousness that dominates the whole century. The anti-sensualism of the classicistic ideal, which now comes into its own again, is not a question of taste and aesthetic evaluation, or not primarily, but a matter of morals, the expression of a striving for simplicity and sincerity. The change of taste which consigns to oblivion the charms of the sensual, richness and gradations of colour, the streaming profusion and sweeping flight of impressions, and questions the value of everything that all connoisseurs had for half a century considered the quintessence of art, this unheard of simplification and levelling down of aesthetic criteria, signifies the triumph of a new puritanical idealism directed against the hedonism of the age. The yearning for the pure, clear-cut, uncomplicated line, for regularity and discipline, harmony and rest, for Winckelmann's 'noble simplicity and calm greatness', is above all a protest against the insincerity and sophistication, the empty virtuosity and brilliance, of the rococo, qualities that now begin to be regarded as depraved and degenerate, diseased and unnatural.

Beside the artists who, like Vien and Falconet, Mengs and Battoni, Benjamin West and William Hamilton, support the new trend with enthusiasm all over Europe, there are innumerable artists and amateurs, critics and collectors, who only flirt with the revolt against the rococo and join in the fashionable imitation of classical antiquity in a purely superficial way. For the most part they are merely the supporters of a movement the real origin and ultimate aim of which remains hidden from them. Theoretically, Antoine Coypel, the Director of the Academy, takes his stand alongside classicism, and Count Caylus, the cultured art patron and archaeologist, even places himself at the head of the movement. The Surintendant de Marigny, the brother of Madame de Pompadour, sets out on a journey to Italy in 1748 with Soufflot and Cochin for purposes of study and thereby initiates the new series of pilgrimages to the South. Systematic archaeological research begins with Winckelmann, through Mengs the new classicistic trend becomes predominant in Rome, and in Piranesi's work the experience of archaeology becomes the very subject of artistic treatment. The main difference between the new classicism and the older classicistic movements is that it regards the classical and the modern as two hostile, mutually irreconcilable tendencies.[137] Whilst in France, however, a compromise between the conflicting trends is reached, and classicism represents, above all in the work of David, at the same time an advance of naturalism, the new movement produces, in the other countries of Europe, mostly an anaemic, academic art, which regards the imitation of classical antiquity as an aim in itself.

It is usual to look on the excavations of Pompeii (1748) as the decisive stimulus to the new archaeological classicism; but this enterprise must itself have been stimulated by a new interest and a new point of view, to have made such an impression, since the first excavations, which took place in Herculaneum in 1737, had had no results worth mentioning. The change in the intellectual climate does not occur in fact until around the middle of the century. From this time onward the international scientific pursuit of archaeology first begins alongside the international movement of classicism, which is no longer dominated by the French, even though the school of David will have its affiliations all over Europe. The 'scavi' become the slogan of the day; the whole intelligentsia of Western Europe shows an interest in them. The collecting of 'antiques' becomes a real passion; considerable sums are spent on classical works of art, and everywhere collections of works of sculpture and of gems and vases are started. A journey to Italy is now not only a mark of good breeding, but is looked upon as an essential part of the training of a young man of the world. There is no artist, no writer, no person of intellectual interests who does not promise himself the supreme enhancement of his capabilities from the direct experience of the monuments of classical art in Italy. Goethe's Italian journey, his collection of antiques, the Hera-room in his house in Weimar, with the colossal bust of the goddess threatening to explode the walls of the bourgeois interior, serve as a symbol of this cultural epoch. But the new cult of antiquity is, precisely like the almost simultaneous enthusiasm for the Middle Ages, an essentially romantic movement; for even classical antiquity now seems to have become an inaccessible springtime of human culture, that has, as Rousseau would have it, disappeared for ever. Winckelmann, Lessing, Herder, Goethe and the whole of German romanticism are absolutely unanimous in holding this conception of antiquity. They all see in it a source of recovery and renewal—an example of genuine and full, though never again to be realized, humanity. It is no accident that the pre-romantic movement coincides with the beginnings of archaeology and that Rousseau and Winckelmann are contemporaries; the basic intellectual characteristic is expressed in one and the same nostalgic philosophy of culture—concentrated in the one case on classical antiquity, in the other on the Middle Ages. The new classicism is just as much directed against the frivolity and sophistication of the rococo as is the pre-romantic movement; both are inspired by the same bourgeois outlook on life. The Renaissance conception of classical antiquity was conditioned by the ideology of the humanists and reflected the antischolastic and anticlerical ideas of the intellectual stratum; the art of the seventeenth century interpreted the world of the Greeks and Romans according to the feudal standards of morality professed by the absolute monarchy; the classicism of the revolutionary period is dependent on the stoic ideals of the progressive and republican middle class and remains faithful to them in all its manifestations.

The third quarter of the century was still pervaded by the conflict of styles. Classicism found itself involved in a fight and was the weaker of the two competing tendencies. Until about 1780, it limited itself for the most part to a theoretical dispute with court art; only after this date, especially after the appearance on the scene of David, can the rococo be considered vanquished. The success of David's 'Oath of the Horatii', in 1785, signifies the end of a thirty years' conflict and the victory of the new monumental style. With the art of the revolutionary era, which extends roughly from 1780 to 1800, a new phase of classicism begins. On the eve of the Revolution, generally speaking, the following tendencies were represented in French painting: (1) the tradition of the sensualistic-coloristic rococo in the art of Fragonard; (2) the sentimentalism represented in the work of

Greuze; (3) the bourgeois naturalism of Chardin; and (4) the classicism of Vien. The Revolution chose this classicism as the style most in harmony with its outlook, although one would have thought the artistic trends represented by Greuze and Chardin would have been more in accordance with its taste. But the decisive factor in its choice was not the question of taste and form, not the principle of intimacy and inwardness derived from the bourgeois philosophy of art of the late Middle Ages and the early Renaissance, but the consideration as to which of the existing trends was best able to portray the ethos of the Revolution with its patriotic-heroic ideals, its Roman civic virtues and republican ideas of freedom. Love of freedom and fatherland, heroism and the spirit of self-sacrifice, Spartan hardness and stoic self-control, are now set in the place of the moral concepts developed by the bourgeoisie in the course of its climb to economic power, which were finally so weakened and undermined that it was possible for the bourgeoisie to be one of the most important supporters of rococo culture. The pioneers and precursors of the Revolution, therefore, had to turn just as sharply against the ideals of the *fermiers généraux* as against the 'douceurs de vivre' of the aristocracy. But they were also unable to rely on the easy-going, patriarchal, unheroic bourgeois attitude of earlier centuries and could expect their aims to be promoted only by an absolutely militant art. But of all the trends they had to choose from, the classicism of Vien and his school was most qualified to meet their requirements.

The art of Vien himself was, however, still full of triviality and prettiness, and just as closely connected with the rococo as the bourgeois sentimentality of Greuze. Classicism was in this case nothing more than a tribute to the fashion in which the artist joined with pedantical zeal. In his coquettishly erotic paintings only the motifs were classical and the manner pseudo-classical, the spirit and the disposition were pure rococo. No wonder that the young David began his Italian journey with the determination not to be taken in by the seductions of classical antiquity.[138] Nothing shows more strikingly how deep was the gulf between rococo classicism and the revolutionary classicism of the following generation than this resolution of David's. If, in spite of it, David became the pioneer and greatest representative of classicistic art, then the reason for this was the change of meaning which classicism had undergone and as a result of which it lost its aestheticizing character. David did not, however, immediately succeed in imposing his new interpretation of classicism. To begin with, there was nothing to suggest that he would ever occupy the unrivalled position which he held after the 'Horatii' and did not lose until after the Restoration. At the same time as David, a whole group of young French artists sojourned in Rome, and they went through a similar development to David himself. The Salon of 1781 was dominated by these young 'Romans' who were moving towards a stricter classicism, and of whom Ménageot was considered the real leader. David's pictures were still too severe, too serious for contemporary taste. Criticism only gradually realized that these very pictures meant the triumph of the ideas which were being proclaimed in the attempts to destroy the rococo.[139] But the times soon became ripe for David and the amends that were made to him left nothing to be desired. The 'Oath of the Horatii' was one of the greatest successes in the history of art. The triumphant progress of the work already began in Italy where David exhibited it in his own studio. Pilgrimages were made to the picture, flowers placed before it, and Vien, Battoni, Angelika Kaufmann and Wilhelm Tischbein, that is to say, the most esteemed artists in Rome, joined in the universal praise of the young artist. In Paris, where the public became acquainted with the work in the Salon of 1785, the triumph continued. The 'Horatii' was described as the 'most beautiful picture of the century' and David's achievement was regarded as really revolutionary. The work appeared to the contemporary world as the most novel and daring feat imaginable—as the perfect realization of the classicistic ideal. The scene portrayed was here reduced to a few figures, almost without 'supers', without accessories. The protagonists of the drama were, as a sign of their unanimity and determination, if necessary, to die together for their common ideal, brought into one single, unbroken, rigid line; this formal radicalism enabled the painter to achieve an effect unparalleled by anything in the artistic experience of his generation. He developed his classicism into a purely linear art, completely renouncing mere pictorial effects and all the concessions that would have made the picture a pure feast for the eyes. The artistic means which he employed were strictly rational, methodical, puritanical, and subordinated the whole organization of the work to the principle of economy. The precision and the objectivity, the restriction of the work to the barest essentials and the intellectual energy expressed in this concentration were more in harmony with the stoicism of the revolutionary bourgeoisie than any other artistic trend. Here was the unity of greatness and simplicity, dignity and sobriety. The 'Horatii' have rightly been called the 'classicistic picture par excellence'.[140] The work represents the stylistic ideal of its age just as perfectly as, for example, Leonardo's 'Last Supper' represents the Renaissance conception of art. If it is admissible to interpret pure artistic form sociologically, then here is a case in point. This clarity, this uncompromising rigour, this sharpness of expression, has its origin in the republican civic virtues; form is here really only the vehicle, the means to an end. The fact that the upper classes join in this classicism is, in view of what we know of the infectious power of successful movements, nothing like so astonishing as the fact that even the government gave their support to it. 'The Oath of the Horatii' was, as is known, painted for the Ministry of Fine Arts. The general attitude to the subversive tendencies in art was just as unsuspecting or undecided as in politics.

When 'Brutus', the picture with which David attains the height of his fame, is exhibited in 1789, formal considerations no longer play any conscious part in the reception of the work. Roman costume and Roman patriotism have become the ruling fashion and a universally acknowledged symbol of which use is made all the more readily as any other analogy, any other historical parallel, would be a reminder of the knightly-heroic ideal. The presuppositions from which modern patriotism arose are not, however, connected with the Romans. This patriotism is the product of an age in which France no longer has to defend her freedom against a greedy neighbour or a foreign feudal sovereign but against a hostile surrounding world of which the whole social structure is different from hers, and which is up in arms against the Revolution. Revolutionary France quite ingenuously enlists the services of art to assist her in this struggle; the nineteenth century is the first to conceive the idea of 'l'art pour l'art' which forbids such a practice. The principle of 'pure', absolutely 'useless' art first results from the opposition of the romantic movement to the revolutionary period as a whole, and the demand that the artists should be passive derives from the ruling class's fear of losing its influence on art. In the attainment of its practical aims, the eighteenth century continues to exploit art as unscrupulously as all previous centuries had done; but until the outbreak of the Revolution artists themselves had hardly become conscious of this practice and they thought much less of turning it into a programme. It is only with the Revolution that art becomes a confession of political faith, and it is now emphasized for the first time that it has to be no 'mere ornament on the social structure', but 'a part of its foundations'.[141] It is now declared that art must not be an idle pastime, a mere tickling of the nerves, a privilege of the rich and the leisured, but that it must teach and improve, spur on to action and set an example. It must be pure, true, inspired and inspiring, contribute to the happiness of the general public and become the possession of the whole nation. The programme was ingenuous, like all abstract reforms of art, and its sterility proved that a revolution must first change society before it can change art, although art itself is an instrument of this change and stands in a complicated relationship of reciprocal action and reaction to the social process. The real aim of the Revolution was, incidentally, not the participation in the enjoyment of art of the classes excluded from the privileges of culture, but the alteration of society, the deepening of the feeling of community and the arousing of an awareness of the achievements of the Revolution.[142] From now on the cultivation of art constituted an instrument of government and enjoyed the attention given only to important affairs of state. As long as the Republic was in danger and fighting for its very existence, the whole nation was called upon to serve it with all its combined strength. In an address given to the Convention by David, we find these words: 'Each one of us is responsible to the nation for the talents he has received from nature.'[143] And Hassenfratz, a juror of the Salon of 1793, formulates the corresponding aesthetic theory in the following terms: 'The whole talent of an artist dwells in his heart; what he achieves with his hands is without significance.'[144]

David plays an unprecedented part in the art politics of his time. He is a member of the Convention and as such already exerts a considerable influence; but, at the same time, he is the confidant and mouthpiece of the Revolutionary government in all matters of art. Since the days of Le Brun no artist had had such a wide sphere of activity; but David's personal prestige is incomparably greater than was the respect in which Louis XIV's factotum was held. He is not merely the artistic dictator of the Revolution, not merely the authority to whom all artistic propaganda, the organization of all great festivities and ceremonies, the Academy with all its functions, the whole system of museums and exhibitions, are subject, he is the creator of a revolution of his own, of that 'révolution Davidienne' which was, to some extent, the starting point of modern art. He is the founder of a school, the authority, extent and stability of which are almost without parallel in the history of art. Nearly all the talented young artists of the time belong to it and, in spite of the adversities which the master had to suffer, in spite of flight and banishment and the dwindling of his own creative powers, it remains, right up to the July revolution, not only the most important school but *the* 'school' of French painting. In fact, it becomes the school of European classicism as a whole, and its founder, who has been called the Napoleon of painting, thereby exercises an influence which may, in his own sphere, be compared to that of the world conqueror. The master's authority outlasts the 9 Thermidor, the 18 Brumaire and Napoleon's accession to the throne, and not simply because David is the greatest contemporary French painter, but because his classicism represents the conception of art most in harmony with the political aims of the Consulate and the Empire. The uniform development of artistic work and policy is interrupted only during the Directoire, which, in contrast to both the Revolution and the Empire, is frivolous, hedonistic and aesthetically epicurean in character.[145] Under the Consulate, when the French are constantly being reminded of the heroic virtues of the Romans, and under the Empire, in whose political propaganda the comparison with the Roman Imperium plays a similar rôle to the analogy with the Roman Republic during the Revolution, classicism remains the representative style of French art. But, despite the consistency of its development, David's painting bears the marks of the transformation which the society and government of the country are undergoing. Even during the Directoire his style shows, above all in the 'Sabine Women', a softer and more pleasing character, a turning away from the uncompromising artistic severity of the revolutionary period. And under the Empire, although he again surrenders the flattering elegance and artistry of his Directoire style, he diverges from the aims of his early period in a different direction. The master's Empire style contains, translated into artistic terms, the whole internal conflict implicit in Napoleon's rule. For, just as this régime never altogether denies its origins in the Revolution and destroys the hope of a revival of the hereditary privileges once and for all, but relentlessly continues the liquidation of the Revolution which had begun with the 9 Thermidor, and not only guarantees the powerful position of the capitalistic bourgeoisie and the landed peasantry, but sets up a political dictatorship which restricts the freedoms of these very classes to the code of civil law, so the Empire art of David is likewise an unbalanced synthesis of contradictory tendencies in which the ceremonial and the conventional gradually gain the upper hand over naturalism and spontaneity.

The tasks imposed on David as Napoleon's 'premier peintre' further his art by bringing him into direct touch with historical reality again and by offering him an opportunity of grappling with the formal problems of great official historical pictures, but at the same time they stiffen his classicism and bring out in him the marks of that academicism which was to become so fateful for himself and his school. Delacroix called David 'le père de toute l'école moderne' and that he was in a double respect: not only as the creator of the new bourgeois naturalism which, especially in the portrait, gave expression to the seriousness and dignity of a stern, simple, absolutely untheatrical outlook on life, but also and above all as the man who restored the narrative painting and the pictorial representation of great historical occasions. Thanks to such tasks, David regains, after the superficial elegance and trifling treatment of formal problems, characteristic of his Directoire period, much of his earlier objectivity and simplicity. The problems which he now has to solve no longer hover in the air, like the theme of the 'Sabine Women', but result from direct, topical reality. In commissions like those that lead to the painting of the 'Sacre' (1805–8) or to the 'Distribution of the Eagles' (1810), he finds more artistic stimulation than he himself would have perhaps expected. What these pictures lack in verve and dramatic quality, compared with the 'Oath in the Tennis Court', they make up for by the more simple, more realistic treatment of the subject. With them David turns farther away from the eighteenth century and the rococo tradition and creates, in contrast to the prevailing individualism of his early works, a more objective style, which it was possible to misappropriate academically, but which it was, at any rate, possible to continue. Even now, however, he does not entirely overcome the inner conflict which had been threatening the intellectual unity of his art since the Directoire. Besides the official ceremonies, for which he finds a thoroughly satisfactory solution, he paints scenes from the ancient world, such as the 'Sappho' (1809) or the 'Leonidas' (1812), which are just as affected and mannered as were the 'Sabine Women'. The classical world has ceased to be a source of inspiration for David and becomes a mere convention, as it does with all his contemporaries. When he is confronted with practical tasks, he continues to produce masterpieces, but when he tries to soar above reality, he fails.

The conflict in David's art between the abstract, anaemic idealism of his mythological and antique-historical compositions and the full-blooded naturalism of his portraits, becomes still more intense during his exile in Brussels. Whenever he enters into direct contact with real life, that is to say, when he has to paint portraits, he is still the great old master, but in so far as he gives way to his classical illusions, which lack all relationship to the present and have become an artistic game, the impression he makes is not only old-fashioned but often also in bad taste. The case of David is of special importance for the sociology of art, for he probably provides the most convincing refutation of the thesis according to which practical political aims and genuine artistic quality are incompatible. The more intimately connected he was with political interests and the more completely he placed his art at the service of propagandistic aims, the greater was the artistic worth of his creations. During the Revolution, when all his thoughts revolved around politics and he painted his 'Oath in the Tennis Court' and his 'Marat', he was at the height of his powers artistically. And under the Empire, when he was at least able to identify himself with Napoleon's patriotic aims and was doubtless aware what the Revolution owed to the dictator, in spite of everything, his art remained creative and alive, whenever it was concerned with practical tasks. Later, however, in Brussels, when he had lost all connection with political reality and was nothing but a painter, he sank to the lowest point in his artistic development. Now, although these correlations do not prove that an artist must be politically interested and progressively-minded to paint good pictures, yet they do, none the less, prove that such interests and such aims by no means prevent the creation of good pictures.

It has often been asserted that the Revolution was artistically sterile and that its creations moved within the limits of a style which was nothing more than the continuation and culmination of the old rococo classicism. It has been emphasized that the art of the revolutionary epoch can be described as revolutionary only in relation to its subjects and ideas but not in relation to its forms and stylistic principles.[146] It is a fact that the Revolution had found classicism more or less ready-made when it came on the scene, but it gave it a new content and a new meaning. The classicism of the Revolution seemed unoriginal and uncreative only from the levelling perspective of posterity; the contemporary world was quite aware of the stylistic difference between the classicism of David and that of his predecessors. How daring and revolutionary David's innovations appeared to them is best proved by the words of the Academy Director Pierre, who described the composition of the 'Horatii' as an 'attack on good taste' because of their deviation from the usual pyramidal pattern.[147] The real stylistic creation of the Revolution is, however, not this classicism but romanticism, that is to say, not the art that it actually practised but the art for which it prepared the way. The Revolution itself was unable to realize the new style, because it possessed new political aims, new social institutions, new standards of law, but so far no new society speaking its own language. Only the bare presupposition for the rise of such a society existed at that time. Art lagged behind political developments and still moved partly, as Marx already noted, in the old antiquated forms.[148] Artists and writers are, in fact, by no means always prophets and art falls behind the times just as often as it hastens on in advance of them.

Even the romanticism for which the Revolution prepared the way is based on an earlier kindred movement; but pre-romanticism and romanticism proper have not even as much in common with each other as have the two forms of modern classicism. They represent in no sense a uniform romantic movement, which merely happened to be interrupted in its development.[149] Pre-romanticism suffers a decisive and final defeat at the hands of the Revolution. It is true that anti-rationalism revives again, but the sentimentality of the eighteenth century does not outlast the Revolution. Post-revolutionary romanticism reflects a new outlook on life and the world and, above all, it creates a new interpretation of the idea of artistic freedom. This freedom is no longer a privilege of the genius, but the birthright of every artist and every gifted individual. Pre-romanticism allowed only the genius to deviate from the rules, romanticism proper denies the validity of objective rules of any kind. All individual expression is unique, irreplaceable and bears its own laws and standards within itself; this insight is the great achievement of the Revolution for art. The romantic movement now becomes a war of liberation not only against academies, churches, courts, patrons, amateurs, critics and masters, but against the very principle of tradition, authority and rule. The struggle is unthinkable without the intellectual atmosphere created by the Revolution; it owes both its initiation and its influence to the Revolution. The whole of modern art is to a certain degree the result of this romantic fight for freedom. However much talk there is about supra-temporal aesthetic norms, of eternally human artistic values, of the need of objective standards and binding conventions, the emancipation of the individual, the exclusion of all extraneous authority, a reckless disregard for all barriers and prohibitions, is and remains the vital principle of modern art. However enthusiastically the artist of our time acknowledges the authority of schools, groups, movements, and professes faith in his companions in arms, as soon as he begins to paint, to compose or to write, he is and feels alone. Modern art is the expression of the lonely human being, of the individual who feels himself to be different, either tragically or blessedly different, from his fellows. The Revolution and the romantic movement mark the end of a cultural epoch in which the artist appealed to a 'society', to a more or less homogeneous group, to a public whose authority he acknowledged in principle absolutely. Art ceases to be a social activity guided by objective and conventional criteria, and becomes an activity of self-expression creating its own standards; it becomes, in a word, the medium through which the single individual speaks to single individuals. Until the romantic period it was more or less irrelevant whether and in what measure the public consisted of real connoisseurs; artists and writers made it their endeavour at all costs to meet the wishes of this public, in contrast to the romantic and post-romantic period, in which they no longer submit to the taste and demands of any collective group and are always on the point of appealing against the verdict of one forum of opinion to another. Their work brings them into a constant state of tension and opposition towards the public; certainly, groups of connoisseurs and amateurs are constantly being formed, but this formation of groups is in a state of endless flux and destroys all continuity in the relationship between art and public.

That David's classicism and romantic painting have a common source, namely the Revolution, is also expressed in the fact that romanticism does not begin as an attack on classicism and does not undermine the David school from outside, but first comes on the scene in the work of the nearest and most gifted pupils of the master himself, Gros, Girodet and Guérin. The rigid separation of the two trends does not begin until the period from 1820 to 1830, when romanticism becomes the style of the artistically progressive, whilst classicism becomes that of the elements who still swear by the absolute authority of David. The hybrid of classicism and romanticism invented by Gros was most in accordance with Napoleon's personal taste and with the nature of the problems which he set his artists to solve. Napoleon sought relaxation from his practical rationalism in romantic works of art and inclined to sentimentalism, when he was not judging art as an instrument of propaganda and display. That explains his fondness for Ossian and Rousseau in literature and for the picturesque in painting.[150] When Napoleon made David his court painter, he was merely following public opinion; his own sympathies belonged to Gros, Gérard, Vernet, Prudhon and the 'anecdotal painters' of his time.[151] They were, by the way, all compelled to paint his battles and victories, festivities and ceremonies—the supersensitive Prudhon just as much as the robust David. The real painter of the Empire, Napoleon's painter par excellence, however, was Gros, who owed his fame, of which both the supporters and the opponents of the David school approved, partly to his ability to represent a scene strikingly, often with a waxwork-like directness, partly to his new moral conception of the battle picture. He was, in fact, the first to portray war from a humanitarian point of view and to show the unspectacular sides of battle. The miseries of war were so great that they could no longer be glossed over; the most sensible thing was to make no attempt at all to do so.

The Empire found the artistic expression of its outlook on life in an eclecticism which combined and permuted already existing stylistic trends. The contradictory characteristics of this art were in accordance with the political and social antinomies of the Napoleonic government. The great problem that the Empire tried to solve was the reconciliation of the democratic achievements of the Revolution with the political forms of the absolute monarchy. To return to the *ancien régime* was just as unthinkable for Napoleon as to remain tied to the 'anarchy' of the Revolution. A form of government had to be found which would combine them both and create a compromise between the old and the new state, the old and the new nobility, and between the process of social levelling and the new wealth. The idea of freedom was as foreign to the *ancien régime* as the idea of equality. The Revolution undertook to realize both of them but, finally, dropped the principle of equality. Napoleon wanted to rescue this principle, but only succeeded in establishing it juridically; economically and socially the old, pre-revolutionary inequality continued to prevail. What political equality there was consisted in the fact that all were equally without rights. Of the achievements of the Revolution nothing remained but the civic freedom of the person, equality before the law, the abolition of feudal privileges, freedom of belief and the 'carrière ouverte aux talents'. That was no mean attainment, but the logic of Napoleon's authoritarian government and court ambitions led to the rehabilitation of the nobility and the Church and created, in spite of the attempt to hold fast to the basic principles of the Revolution, an anti-revolutionary atmosphere.[152] The romantic movement received an enormous impetus from the conclusion of the Concordat and the religious renaissance connected with it. Romanticism had already gone hand in hand with the idea of a Catholic revival and monarchist tendencies in the work of Chateaubriand. The 'Génie du Christianisme', which appeared a year after the Concordat had been concluded and which was the first representative work of French romanticism, had a more stupendous success than any literary production of the eighteenth century. The whole of Paris read it and the 'premier consul' had parts of it read aloud to him on several evenings. The appearance of the book marks the initiation of the clerical party and the end of the reign of the 'philosophes'.[153] With Girodet the romantic-clerical reaction spreads to art and speeds up the dissolution of classicism. During the years of the Revolution no pictures with a religious content were seen at all in exhibitions.[154] David's school began by taking a thoroughly negative attitude to the genre; but with the spread of romanticism the number of religious paintings increased and religious motifs finally invaded academic classicism itself.

The religious renaissance begins at the same time as the political reaction under the Consulate. It, too, is part of the liquidation of the Revolution and is taken up with enthusiasm by the ruling class. The general rejoicing soon becomes silent, however, under the burden of the oppressive sacrifices which the Napoleonic adventure imposes on the nation, and the high spirits of the bourgeoisie are also substantially restrained by the creation of the new military nobility and the attempts at conciliation with the old aristocracy. The golden days of the army contractors, corn merchants and speculators are only just beginning, however, and in the fight for supremacy in society the bourgeoisie remains victorious after all, even though it is no longer quite the old revolutionary bourgeoisie. The aims which it pursued through the Revolution were, incidentally, never so altruistic as they are usually made out to be. The well-to-do middle class had already been the creditor of the state long before the Revolution and, in view of the persistent mismanagement of the court, it had more and more to fear the collapse of the state finances. If it was fighting for a new order, then its main purpose was to make certain of its rents. This circumstance explains the apparent paradox that the Revolution was realized by one of the richest and not least privileged of all classes.[155] It was in no sense a revolution of the proletariat and the propertyless petty bourgeoisie but of the rentiers and the commercial contractors, that is to say, of a class that was certainly harassed in its economic expansion by the privileges of the feudal nobility but in no way vitally menaced by them.[156] The Revolution was fought for, however, with the help of the working class and the lower strata of the middle class and would scarcely have been successful without their help. Yet as soon as the bourgeoisie had achieved its aims, it left its former comrades in arms in the lurch and wanted to enjoy the fruits of the common victory alone. In the end, all the classes deprived of civic rights and all the oppressed did benefit, nevertheless, from the victory of the Revolution, which after so many unsuccessful rebellions and revolts was the first to lead to a radical and lasting reconstruction of society. The immediate after-effect of the events was, however, by no means encouraging. Hardly had the Revolution ended, than a boundless disillusion seized men's souls and not a trace remained of the optimistic philosophy of the enlightenment. The liberalism of the eighteenth century had been based on the idea of the identity of freedom and equality. The belief in this equation was the source of liberal optimism, and the loss of faith in the compatibility of the two ideas the origin of the pessimism of the post-revolutionary period.

The most striking sign of the victory of the liberal idea is that the influence of the coercion, limitation and regimentation of the mind is not felt to be a paralysing one until after the Revolution. Hitherto the greatest achievements of art had often been connected with the most rigid despotism; from now on all attempts to set up an authoritarian culture meet with invincible resistance. The Revolution had demonstrated that no human institution is unalterable; any idea imposed on the artist had lost its claim to represent a higher norm, and all compulsion only awakened his doubts and suspicion. The principles of order and discipline lost their stimulating influence and the liberal idea became from now on—yes, indeed, only from now on—a source of artistic inspiration. In spite of the prizes, gifts and distinctions which he bestowed on them, Napoleon was unable to spur on his artists and writers to achieve anything of importance. The really productive authors of his time, people like Mme de Staël and Benjamin Constant, were dissidents and outsiders.[157]

The most important achievement of the Empire in the sphere of art consisted in the stabilization of the relations between producer and consumer which had been created by the enlightenment and the Revolution. The middle-class public that had arisen in the eighteenth century became consolidated and from now on it also played a leading part as a party interested in the plastic arts. The public of the seventeenth-century French literature consisted of a few thousand people; it was a group of amateurs and connoisseurs estimated by Voltaire to number some two to three thousand.[158] That did not mean, of course, that this public was made up exclusively of people capable of independent artistic judgement and an assured sense of quality, but merely that it was in possession of certain aesthetic criteria which enabled its members to distinguish the valuable from the valueless within definite, usually rather restricted, limits. The public for the plastic arts was, naturally, even more circumscribed than the literary public and was made up purely of collectors and connoisseurs. It was not until the period in which the quarrel between the Poussinistes and the Rubénistes took place, that an art public arose no longer consisting entirely of such specialists,[159] and not until the eighteenth century that it embraced people interested in pictures with no thought of buying them. This trend of development becomes more and more marked after the Salon of 1699, and in 1725 the Mercure de France already reports that an enormous public of every class and every age is to be seen in the Salon admiring, praising, criticizing and finding fault.[160] According to contemporary reports, the crowds are unprecedented, and even if most of them only want to be there because visiting Salons has become a fashion, nevertheless, the number of serious art lovers is also growing. That is indicated, first of all, by the mass of new art publications, art journals and reproductions.[161]

Paris, which had long been the centre of social and literary life, now becomes the art capital of Europe and takes over in its totality the rôle played by Italy since the Renaissance in the artistic life of Western Europe. It is true that Rome continues to be the centre of the study of classical art, but Paris is the place where people go to study modern art.[162] Parisian art life, which now keeps the whole educated world busy, gains its strongest impulse, however, from the art exhibitions which are by no means limited to the Salon. Exhibitions had been held in Italy and the Netherlands in earlier times, but it was only in seventeenth- and eighteenth-century France that they became an indispensable factor in artistic activity.[163] It was only after 1673 that art exhibitions were arranged regularly, that is to say, from the time when diminished state support forced French artists to look round for buyers. Only members of the Academy were allowed to exhibit in the Salon, non-academicians had to show their works to the public in the much less distinguished 'Academy' of the Guild of St. Luke or in the 'Exposition de la Jeunesse'. These secessionist exhibitions did not become superfluous until the Revolution opened the Salon to all artists in the year 1791 and artistic life, which had acquired its restless and stimulating character from them and from the many private, studio and pupils' exhibitions, became more organized and healthy, though less lively and interesting.

The Revolution meant the end of the dictatorship of the Academy and the monopolization of the art market by the court, the aristocracy and high finance. The old ties which had stood in the way of the democratization of art were loosened; they vanished with rococo society and rococo culture. It is, however, by no means accurate to claim, as has been done so often, that all the strata of the public which had had the keys of culture in its hands and had represented 'good taste' disappeared overnight. As a result of the far-reaching participation of the middle class in artistic life long before the Revolution, there was a certain continuity of development, in spite of the profound revulsion. It is true that an unprecedented democratization of artistic life took place, that is to say, not merely an enlargement but also a levelling down of the public—even this tendency had begun, however, before the Revolution. In his *Thoughts on Beauty and on Taste* (1765), Mengs had already asserted that the beautiful is what appeals to the majority. The real change that came to light after the Revolution consisted in the fact that the old public represented a class in which art fulfilled a direct function in daily life and was one of those forms by means of which this class expressed, on the one hand, its aloofness from the lower classes of society and, on the other, its fellowship with the court and the monarch, whereas the new public developed into one of amateurs with aesthetic interests, for whom art became an object of free choice and changing tastes.

After the Legislative Assembly had abolished the privileges of the Academy as early as 1791 and bestowed on all artists the right to exhibit in the Salon, two years later the Academy itself was completely suppressed. The decree corresponded in the sphere of art to the abolition of feudal privileges and the realization of democracy. But this development had, like the corresponding social development, also begun before the Revolution. The Academy had always been regarded as the quintessence of conservatism by all liberals; in reality, it had been, especially since the end of the seventeenth century, by no means so narrow-minded and inaccessible as it was represented to be. The question of admission to membership was treated very liberally in the eighteenth century. That is a well-known fact. Only the limitation of the right to exhibit in the Salon to members of the Academy was strictly observed. But it was precisely against this practice that

WATTEAU: EMBARKATION FOR CYTHERA. *Paris, Louvre. Between 1716 and 1718.—Watteau's art signifies the triumph of the stylistic freedom which, with the Régence, supersedes the formalism and academicism of the "grand siècle".*

1. BOUCHER: NUD
A SOFA. *Munich,*
Pinakothek. 17
Works of this kin
most in demand
the rich bourgeois
the aristocracy in
cess of emancip
itself from the co

2. BOUCHER: THE B
FAST. *Paris, Lo*
1738.—Boucher,
leading master o
rococo, already
a certain emphas
the bourgeois ele
in art. His 'Brea
in the Louvre exp
an intimacy remin
of Chardin.

ARDIN: LA POURVOYEUSE. , *Louvre. 1739.—Chardin 'he great, unduly neglected eois painter of the 18th 'y whom not even Diderot 'ately appreciated.*

EUZE: THE PUNISHED SON. *Louvre. About 1761.— ot saw in pictures of this kind enuine artistic expression of urgeois attitude to life.*

1. DAVID: THE OATH OF THE HORATII. *Paris, Louvre. 1784.—The main work of the classicism of the revolutionary period.*

2. CONSTABLE: STUDY FOR 'THE HAY WAIN'. *London, Victoria and Albert Museum. About 1821.—With Constable the decisive turning-point in the development towards the modern naturalistic landscape takes place.*

1. DELACROIX: LIBERTY LEADING THE PEOPLE. *Paris, Louvre. 1831.—The great representative painting of the generation of 1830.*

2. DELACROIX: THE DEATH OF SARDANAPAL. *Paris, Louvre. 1827.—The spirit of 'grand opera', of the demonism and molochism of the romantics is not lacking even in the art of Delacroix.*

1. COURBET: THE
BREAKERS. *Dresden, G
degalerie. 1849.—A
portant work of the n
ism of the mid-centur*

2. DAUMIER: WASHERV
*Paris, Louvre. About
—Like Courbet and
Daumier also pain
praises of manual lat*

HEODORE ROUSSEAU: THE OAK TREES. *Paris, Louvre.—One of the most successful tions of the new naturalistic landscape painting.*

ROYON: OXEN GOING TO WORK. EARLY MORNING. *Paris, Louvre.—The 'Cuyp' of bizon.*

1. PAUL BAUDRY: ALLEGORY. *Musée de Luxembourg.—The i beauty cherished by the Second*

2. D. G. ROSSETTI: THE DAY- *London, Victoria and Albert M —The ideal of beauty cherished Pre-Raphaelites.*

progressive artists under David's leadership fought most bitterly of all. The Academy was dissolved abruptly, but it was much more difficult to find a substitute for it. As early as 1793, David founded the 'Commune des Arts', a free and democratic artists' association without special groups, classes and privileged members. But owing to the subversive activities of the royalists in its midst, it had to be replaced in the very next year by the 'Société populaire et républicaine des Arts', the first truly revolutionary association whose duty it was to take over the functions of the suppressed Academy. It was, however, in no sense an Academy but a club of which anyone could become a member without regard to position and calling. In the same year the 'Club révolutionnaire des Arts' arose to which, amongst others, David, Prudhon, Gérard and Isabey belonged and which, thanks to its famous members, enjoyed great prestige. All these associations were directly dependent on the 'Committee for Public Instruction' and were under the aegis of the Convention, the Welfare Committee and the Paris Commune.[164] The Academy was suppressed, to begin with, merely as owner of the monopoly of exhibition, it continued to exercise its monopoly of instruction for some time and thereby preserved much of its influence.[165] Soon, however, its place was taken by the 'Technical School for Painting and Sculpture' and art instruction began to be given in private schools and evening classes as well. In addition, drawing instruction was also introduced into the curriculum of the high schools (*écoles centrales*). Nothing, however, had probably contributed so much to the democratization of art education as the formation and extension of the museums. Until the Revolution those artists who were not in a position to undertake a journey to Italy had had little chance of seeing much of the works of the famous masters. They had mostly been kept in the private galleries of the king and the great collectors, and were not accessible to the general public. The Revolution changed all that. In 1792 the Convention decided to create a museum in the Louvre. Here, in the immediate neighbourhood of the studios, young artists could henceforward daily study and copy the great works of art and here, in the galleries of the Louvre, they found the best completion of the teaching of their own masters.

After the 9 Thermidor the principle of authority was also gradually restored in the sphere of art and the Academy of Fine Arts was finally replaced by the IVth section of the Institute. Nothing is more characteristic of the undemocratic spirit in which the reform was carried through than the fact that the old Academy had 150, whereas the new one had only 22 members. Nevertheless, David, Houdon and Gérard belonged to it and it soon regained its old authority. The whole body of artists revised its relation to the Revolution, of course, but it was never an entirely uniform relationship. Some artists were honest and sincere revolutionaries from the outset, and not only those, like David, who had his wife's money to fall back on and did not have to worry about the momentary state of business on the art market, but also such men as Fragonard, who was financially ruined by the turn of events, and remained loyal to the Revolution all the same. It goes without saying that convinced anti-revolutionists were also to be found among artists, such as Mme Vigée-Lebrun, for instance, who left the country with her high-born clientèle. Most of them were, however, on the right as well as on the left, merely fellow-travellers who sided with the émigrés or the revolutionaries according to the way they judged their chances. Artists as a whole saw themselves profoundly menaced by the Revolution, to begin with; the emigration robbed them of their wealthiest and most competent buyers.[166] The number of émigrés grew from day to day and the old art public that stayed behind was neither in a position nor in a mood to buy works of art. Most artists were exposed to dire privation at the outset, and thus it was no wonder that they were not always able to feel enthusiastic about the Revolution. If they, nevertheless, took up their stand on its side in such great numbers, then it was because they had felt humiliated and exploited during the old régime, under which they had usually been regarded as domestic servants. The Revolution meant the end of this situation and it also brought them, after all, material compensation. For, apart from the government's growing interest in art, the number of private persons interested also grew, and suddenly a new public existed with a lively interest in the work of famous artists.[167] During the Revolution attendances at the Salon in no way diminished, in fact, they increased. At auctions works of art soon reached just as high prices as before the Revolution, and under the Empire prices even rose considerably.[168] The number of artists increased and critics complained that there were already too many artists. Artistic life had recovered quickly—too quickly—from the shocks of the Revolution. The art machine was back to normal, before a new art had come into existence. The old institutions were revived, but those who revived them had no aesthetic criteria of their own and not even the courage to have them. That explains the artistic decadence of the post-revolutionary period, and the reason why it was another twenty years before romanticism could be realized in France.

6. GERMAN AND WESTERN ROMANTICISM

Nineteenth-century liberalism identified romanticism with the Restoration and reaction. There may have been a certain justification for this emphasis, especially in Germany, but in general it led to a false conception of the historical process. It was not corrected until scholars began to distinguish between German and Western romanticism and to derive the one from reactionary and the other from progressive tendencies. The resulting picture certainly came much nearer to the truth but still contained a considerable simplification of the facts, for, from a political point of view, neither the one nor the other form of romanticism was clear and consistent. In the end a distinction was made, in accordance with the real situation, between an early and a later phase both in German and in French and English romanticism, a romanticism of the first and another of the second generation. It was ascertained that the development followed different directions in Germany and Western Europe and that German romanticism proceeded from its originally revolutionary attitude to a reactionary standpoint, whereas Western romanticism proceeded from a monarchist-conservative point of view to liberalism. This account of the situation was intrinsically correct, but it did not prove to be particularly fruitful for the task of defining romanticism. The characteristic feature of the romantic movement was not that it stood for a revolutionary or an anti-revolutionary, a progressive or a reactionary ideology, but that it reached both positions by a fanciful, irrational and undialectical route. Its revolutionary enthusiasm was based just as much on ignorance of the ways of the world as its conservatism, its enthusiasm for the 'Revolution, Fichte and Goethe's Wilhelm Meister' was just as ingenuous, just as remote from an appreciation of the real motives behind the historical issues, as its frenzied devotion to the Church and the Crown, to chivalry and feudalism. Perhaps events themselves would have taken a different turn, if the intelligentsia had not, even in France, left it to others to think and act realistically. Everywhere there was a romanticism of the Revolution, just as there was a romanticism of the Counter-Revolution and the Restoration. The Dantons and the Robespierres were just as unrealistic dogmatists as the Chateaubriands and the de Maistres, the Goerres and Adam Muellers. Friedrich Schlegel was a romantic in his youth with his enthusiasm for Fichte, Wilhelm Meister and the Revolution, as he was in his old age with his enthusiasm for Metternich and the Holy Alliance. But Metternich himself was no romantic, despite his conservatism and traditionalism; he left it to the literary men to consolidate the mythos of historicism, legitimism and clericalism. A realist is a man who knows when he is fighting for his own interests and when he is making concessions to those of others; and a dialectician is one who is aware that the historical situation at any given moment consists of a complex of different irreducible motives and tasks. Despite all his appreciation of the past, the romantic judges his own time unhistorically, undialectically; he does not grasp that it stands midway between the past and the future and represents an indissoluble conflict of static and dynamic elements.

Goethe's definition, according to which romanticism embodies the principle of disease—a verdict that is hardly to be accepted in the way it was meant—gains a new significance and a new confirmation in the light of modern psychology. For, if romanticism, in fact, sees only one side of a total situation fraught with tension and conflict, if it always considers only one factor in the dialectic of history and stresses this at the expense of the other, if, finally, such a one-sidedness, such an exaggerated, overcompensating reaction, betrays a lack of spiritual balance, then romanticism can rightly be called 'diseased'. Why should one exaggerate and distort things, if one does not feel disturbed and frightened by them? 'Things and actions are what they are, and the consequences of them will be what they will be; why then should we wish to be deceived?' says Bishop Butler, and thereby gives the best description of the serene and 'healthy' eighteenth-century sense of reality with its aversion to all illusion.[169] From this realistic point of view, romanticism always seems a lie, a self-deception, which, as Nietzsche says in reference to Wagner, 'does not want to conceive antitheses as antitheses', and shouts the loudest about what it doubts the most profoundly. The escape to the past is only one form of romantic unreality and illusionism—there is also an escape into the future, into Utopia. What the romantic clings to is, in the final analysis, of no consequence, the essential thing is his fear of the present and of the end of the world.

Romanticism was not only of epoch-making importance, it was also aware of its importance.[170] It represented one of the most decisive turning points in the history of the European mind, and it was perfectly conscious of its historical rôle. Since the Gothic, the development of sensibility had received no stronger impulse and the artist's right to follow the call of his feelings and individual disposition had probably never been emphasized with such absoluteness. The rationalism that had been steadily progressing since the Renaissance, and was given a position of dominating importance in the whole civilized world by the enlightenment, suffered the most painful setback in its history. Never since the dissolution of the supernaturalism and traditionalism of the Middle Ages had reason, alertness and sobriety of mind, the will to and the capacity for self-control, been spoken of with such contempt. 'Those who restrain desire do so because theirs is weak enough to be restrained'—as is said even by Blake, who was in no sense in agreement with the uncontrolled emotionalism of a Wordsworth. Rationalism, as a principle of science and practical affairs, soon recovered from the romantic onslaught, but European art has remained 'romantic'. Romanticism was not merely a universal European movement, seizing one nation after another and creating a universal literary language which was finally just as intelligible in Russia and Poland as in England and France, it also proved to be one of those trends which, like the naturalism of the Gothic or the classicism of the Renaissance, have remained a lasting factor in the development of art. There is, in fact, no product of modern art, no emotional impulse, no impression or mood of the modern man, which does not owe its delicacy and variety to the sensitiveness which developed out of romanticism. The whole exuberance, anarchy and violence of modern art, its drunken, stammering lyricism, its unrestrained, unsparing exhibitionism, is derived from it. And this subjective, egocentric attitude has become so much a matter of course for us, so absolutely inevitable, that we find it impossible to reproduce even an abstract train of thought without talking about our feelings.[171] The intellectual passion, the fervour of reason, the artistic productivity of rationalism have been so completely forgotten that we are only able to understand classical art itself as the expression of a romantic feeling. 'Seuls les romantiques savent lire les ouvrages classiques, parce qu'ils les lisent comme ils ont été écrits, romantiquement,' says Marcel Proust.[172]

The whole nineteenth century was artistically dependent on romanticism, but romanticism itself was still a product of the eighteenth century and never lost the consciousness of its transitional and historically problematical character. Western Europe had gone through several other—similar and more serious—crises, but it had never had so much the feeling of having reached a turning point in its development. This was by no means the first time that a generation had taken a critical attitude to its own historical background and rejected the traditional patterns of culture, because it was unable to express its own outlook on life in them. Previous generations had had the feeling of growing old and the desire for renewal, but to none had it occurred to make a problem of the meaning and *raison d'être* of its own culture and to ask whether it was entitled to its own frame of mind and whether it represented a necessary link in the total chain of human culture. The romantic feeling of rebirth was by no means new; the Renaissance had already experienced it and even the Middle Ages had toyed with ideas of renewal and visions of resurrection of which ancient Rome had been the theme. But no generation had had such a strong awareness of being the heir and descendant of previous ages, none had had so decidedly the desire simply to repeat and to awaken to new life a past age and a lost culture. The romantics are constantly searching for reminiscences and analogies in history and they derive their greatest inspiration from ideals which they believe have already been realized in the past. Their relationship to the Middle Ages does not completely correspond, however, to the classicistic sense of antiquity, since classicism simply takes the Greeks and Romans as an example, whereas romanticism always has the feeling of 'déjà vécu' in connection with the past. It remembers past time as if it were a previous existence. But this feeling by no means proves that romanticism had more in common with the Middle Ages than classicism had with classical antiquity—it proves rather the contrary. 'When a Benedictine studied the Middle Ages', we read in a recent and very clever analysis of romanticism, 'he did not ask himself how it could be of service to him and whether people lived happier and more pious lives in the Middle Ages. As he himself stood within a continuity of faith and ecclesiastical organization, he could take up a more critical attitude to religion than a romantic living in a century of revolution, in which all faith had been shaken and laid open to question.'[173] It is unmistakable that the romantic experience of history gives expression to a psychotic fear of the present and an attempt to escape into the past. But no psychosis has ever been more fruitful. Romanticism owes it its historical sensitivity and clairvoyance, its feeling for relationships, however remote and however difficult to interpret. Without this hypersensitiveness, it would hardly have succeeded in restoring the great historical continuities of culture, in marking the boundary between modern culture and classical antiquity, in recognizing in Christianity the great dividing line in the history of the West and discovering the common 'romantic' nature of all the individualistic, reflective, problematical cultures derived from Christianity.

Without the historical consciousness of romanticism, without the constant questioning of the meaning of the present, by which the thinking of the romantics was dominated, the whole historicism of the nineteenth century and one of the deepest revolutions in the history of the human mind would have been inconceivable. In spite of Heraclitus and the Sophists, the nominalism of scholastic philosophy and the naturalism of the Renaissance, the dynamic approach of capitalism and the progress of historical science in the eighteenth century, the world-view of the West had been essentially static, Parmenidean and unhistorical until the advent of romanticism. The most important factors in human culture, the principles of the natural and supernatural world order, the laws of morality and logic, the ideals of truth and right, the destiny of man and the purpose of social institutions, had been regarded as fundamentally unequivocal and immutable in their significance, as timeless entelechies or as innate ideas. In relation to the constancy of these principles, all change, all development and differentiation had appeared irrelevant and ephemeral; everything that occurred in the medium of historical time seemed to touch merely the surface of things. Only from the time of the Revolution and the romantic movement did the nature of man and society begin to appear as essentially evolutionistic and dynamic. The idea that we and our culture are involved in eternal flux and endless struggle, the notion that our intellectual life is a process with a merely transitory character, is a discovery of romanticism and represents its most important contribution to the philosophy of the present age.

It is a well-known fact that the 'historical sense' was not only alive and astir in the pre-romantic movement, but was a motive force in the intellectual development of the time. We know that the enlightenment produced not merely historians like Montesquieu, Hume, Gibbon, Vico, Winckelmann and Herder and emphasized the historical as opposed to the revealed source of cultural values, but that it already had an inkling of the relativity of these values. In any case, it was a familiar notion in the aesthetics of the time that there are several equivalent types of beauty, that the conceptions of beauty are just as varied as the physical conditions of life and that 'a Chinese god has just as stout a belly as a mandarin'.[174] But, in spite of these insights, the philosophy of history of the enlightenment was based on the idea that history reveals the unfolding of an immutable Reason and that the development of history moves towards a fixed goal discernible from the very beginning. The unhistorical character of the eighteenth century was not, therefore, expressed in a lack of interest in history or a failure to recognize the historical character of human culture, but in the fact that it misunderstood the nature of historical development and thought of it as a straightforward continuum.[175] Friedrich Schlegel and Novalis are the first to recognize that historical relationships are not of a logical nature and that 'philosophy is fundamentally anti-historical'. Above all, the insight that there is such a thing as historical destiny, and that 'we are precisely who we are, because we look back on a particular kind of past history', is an achievement of romanticism. Thoughts of this kind and the historicism they reflect were absolutely alien to the enlightenment. The idea that the nature of the human mind, of political institutions, of law, language, religion and art are understandable only on the basis of their history, and that historical life represents the sphere in which these structures become incarnate in the purest and most substantial form, would have been simply unthinkable before the romantic movement. Where this historicism led to, however, is seen most strikingly perhaps in the paradoxically exaggerated formulation which Ortega y Gasset has given to it: 'Man has no nature, what he has is history.'[176] That sounds by no means encouraging at first sight; but here, too, we are confronted, as in the whole romantic movement, with an ambivalent approach midway between optimism and pessimism, activism and fatalism, and which can be claimed by both.

With the hermeneutic art of romanticism, its eye for historical affinities and its sensitiveness to the problematical and disputable in history, we have also inherited its historical mysticism, its personification and mythologization of historical forces, in brief, the idea that historical phenomena are nothing but the functions, manifestations and incarnations of independent principles. This mode of thinking has been called, very illuminatingly and expressively, an 'emanatistic logic',[177] and attention has thereby been drawn not merely to the abstract conception of history but, at the same time, to the often unconscious metaphysic that such a method involves. According to this logic, history appears as a sphere dominated by anonymous powers, as a substratum of higher ideas, which are only incompletely expressed in the individual historical phenomena. And this Platonic metaphysic finds expression not only in the already out-of-date romantic theories of the folk-spirit, the folk epic of national literatures and Christian art, but even in the still current concept of the 'artistic intention' (Kunstwollen). For even Riegl is, to some extent, under the influence of the romantics and their pneumatic conception of history. He imagines the artistic approach of an epoch as if it were an active person obtaining recognition for his purposes often against the strongest resistance, and sometimes succeeding without the knowledge, even against the will, of his supporters. He regards the great historical styles as independent individuals, unexchangeable and incomparable, living or dying, going under and being replaced by another style. The concept of the history of art as the contiguity and succession of such stylistic phenomena, the value of which resides in their individuality and which have to be judged by their own standards, is in some respects the purest example of the romantic view with its personification of historical forces. In reality, the most significant and comprehensive creations of the human spirit are hardly ever the result of a deliberately willed, straightforward development directed towards a final goal from the very outset. Neither the Homeric epic and the Attic tragedy, nor the Gothic style of architecture and the art of Shakespeare, represent the realization of a uniform and clear-cut artistic purpose, but are the chance result of special needs, conditioned by time and place, and of a whole series of pre-existing, often extraneous and inadequate means. They are, in other words, the product of gradual technical innovations, leading away from the original aim as often as they approach it, of motifs derived from the passing moment, sudden whims and individual experiences, which sometimes have no connection at all with the underlying artistic problem. The theory of the 'artistic intention' hypostasizes as a leading idea what is, in fact, the final result of a thoroughly incoherent and heterogeneous development. But even the doctrine of the 'history of art without names' is, precisely because it excludes real personalities as influential factors from the development of art, only a form of this hypostasis, in which historical forces are personified. The history of art thereby acquires the character of a process following its own inner principle, and no more tolerating the success of independent artistic personalities than, shall we say, an animal body the emancipation of its single organs. If one intends—finally—to imply by historical materialism that nothing but the quality of the actual means of production is expressed in cultural structures, and that economic reality reigns in history just as absolutely as, according to the idealistic interpretation of the romantics, Riegl, and Woelfflin, the 'artistic intention' or the 'immanent formal law', then one is still romanticizing and simplifying what is in reality a much more complex process, and making of historical materialism a mere variant of the emanatistic logic of history. The real meaning of historical materialism, and at the same time, the most important advance of the philosophy of history since the romantic movement, consists rather in the insight that historical developments have their origin not in formal principles, ideas and entities, not in substances which unfold and produce in the course of history mere 'modifications' of their fundamentally unhistorical nature, but in the fact that historical development represents a dialectical process, in which every factor is in a state of motion and subject to constant change of meaning, in which there is nothing static, nothing timelessly valid, but also nothing one-sidedly active, and in which all factors, material and intellectual, economic and ideological, are bound up together in a state of indissoluble interdependence, that is to say, that we are not in the least able to go back to any point in time, where a historically definable situation is not already the result of this interaction. Even the most primitive economy is already an organized economy, which does not, however, alter the fact that, in our analysis of it, we must start with the material preconditions, which, in contrast to the forms of intellectual organization, are independent and comprehensible in themselves.

Historicism, which was connected with a complete reorientation of culture, was the expression of deep existential changes, and corresponded to an upheaval which shook the very foundations of society. The political revolution had abolished the old barriers between the classes and the economic revolution had intensified the mobility of life to a previously inconceivable degree. Romanticism was the ideology of the new society and the expression of the world-view of a generation which no longer believed in absolute values, could no longer believe in any values without thinking of their relativity, their historical limitations. It saw everything tied to historical suppositions, because it had experienced, as part of its own personal destiny, the downfall of the old and the rise of the new culture. The romantic awareness of the historicity of all social life was so deep that even the conservative classes were able to produce only historical arguments to justify their privileges, and based their claims on seniority and the fact of being firmly rooted in the historical culture of the nation. But the historical world-view was by no means the creation of conservatism, as has repeatedly been asserted; the conservative classes merely appropriated it to themselves and developed it in a special direction and one opposite to its original purpose. The progressive middle class saw in the historical origin of social institutions evidence against their absolute validity, whereas the conservative classes, who, in their endeavour to justify their privileges, had nothing to appeal to but their 'historical rights', their age and their priority, gave historicism a new meaning—they disguised the antithesis between historicity and supra-temporal validity, and created in its stead an antagonism between the product of historical growth and steady evolution, on the one hand, and the individual, rational, reform is tact of volition, on the other. The antithesis here was not between time and timelessness, history and absolute being, positive law and natural law, but between 'organic development' and individual arbitrariness.

History becomes the refuge of all the elements of society at variance with their own age, whose intellectual and material existence is threatened; and the refuge, above all, of the intelligentsia, which now feels disillusioned in its hopes and tricked out of its rights, not only in Germany but also in the countries of Western Europe. The lack of influence on political developments, which had hitherto been the fate of the German intellectuals, now becomes a European-wide fate shared by intellectuals in general. The enlightenment and the Revolution had encouraged the individual to cherish exorbitant hopes; they had seemed to promise the unrestricted reign of reason and the absolute authority of writers and thinkers. In the eighteenth century, writers were the intellectual leaders of the West; they were the dynamic element behind the reform movement, they embodied the ideal of personality by which the progressive classes were guided. The upshot of the Revolution changed all that. They were now made responsible by turns for the Revolution having done too much and too little, and were in no way able to maintain their prestige in this period of stagnation and mental eclipse. Even when they were in agreement with the prevailing forces of reaction and were serving them faithfully, they felt none of the satisfaction enjoyed by the 'philosophes' of the eighteenth century. Most of them saw themselves condemned to absolute ineffectiveness and had the feeling of being quite superfluous. They took refuge in a past which they made the place where all their dreams and wishes came true and from which they excluded all the tensions between idea and reality, the self and the world, the individual and society. 'Romanticism is rooted in the torment of the world, and so one will find a people the more romantic and elegiac, the more unhappy its condition is' says a liberal critic of German romanticism.[178] The Germans were probably the most unhappy people in Europe; soon after the Revolution, however, no Western people—or at least the intelligentsia of no people—felt comfortable and secure in its own land. The feeling of homelessness and loneliness became the fundamental experience of the new generation; their whole outlook on the world was influenced by it. It assumed innumerable forms and found expression in a whole series of attempts to escape, of which turning to the past was merely the most pronounced. The escape to Utopia and the fairy tale, to the unconscious and the fantastic, the uncanny and the mysterious, to childhood and nature, to dreams and madness, were all disguised and more or less sublimated forms of the same feeling, of the same yearning for irresponsibility and a life free from suffering and frustration—all attempts to escape into that chaos and anarchy against which the classicism of the seventeenth and eighteenth centuries had fought at times with alarm and anger, at others with grace and wit, but always with the same determination. The classicist felt himself to be master of reality; he agreed to be ruled by others, because he ruled himself and believed that life can be ruled. The romantic, on the other hand, acknowledged no external ties, was incapable of committing himself, and felt himself to be defencelessly exposed to an overwhelmingly powerful reality; hence his contempt for and simultaneous deification of reality. He either violated it or surrendered himself to it blindly and unresistingly, but he never felt equal to it.

Whenever the romantics describe their outlook on art and the world, the word or the idea of homelessness creeps into their sentences. Novalis defines philosophy as 'home-sickness', as the 'urge to be at home in all places', and the fairy tale as a dream of 'that homeland which is everywhere and nowhere'. He praises in Schiller all 'that is not of this earth' and Schiller himself calls the romantics 'exiles pining for a homeland'. That is why they speak so much of wandering, wandering aimlessly and endlessly, of the 'blue flower' which is unattainable and is to remain unattainable, of the solitude that one seeks and shuns, of the infinity which is nothing and everything. 'Mon coeur désire tout, il veut tout, il contient tout. Que mettre à la place de cet infini qu'exige ma pensée . . . ?'—we read in Senancour's *Obermann*. But it is clear that this 'tout' contains nothing and this 'infini' is to be found nowhere. A longing for home and a longing for what is far off—these are the feelings by which the romantics are torn hither and thither; they miss the near-at-hand, suffer from their isolation from men, but, at the same time, they avoid other men and seek zealously for the remote, the exotic and the unknown. They suffer from their estrangement from the world, but they also accept and desire it. Thus Novalis defines romantic poetry as 'the art of appearing strange in an attractive way, the art of making a subject remote and yet familiar and pleasant', and he asserts that everything becomes romantic and poetic, 'if one removes it in a distance', that everything can be romanticized, if one 'gives a mysterious appearance to the ordinary, the dignity of the unknown to the familiar and an infinite significance to the finite'. 'The dignity of the unknown'—what sensible man would have uttered such nonsense a generation or even only a few years before! People had spoken of the dignity of reason, of knowledge, of common sense, of wise and sober matter-of-factness, but who would have dreamt of talking about the 'dignity of the unknown'! They wanted to master the unknown and make it harmless; to praise it and make it superior to man would have been intellectual suicide and self-destruction. Novalis here gives not merely a definition of the romantic, but also a recipe for 'romanticizing'; for the romantic is not content to be romantic, he makes romanticism an ideal and a policy for the whole of life. He not only wants to portray life romantically, he wants to adapt life to art and to indulge in the illusion of an aesthetic-Utopian existence. But this 'romanticization' means, above all, simplifying and unifying life, freeing it from the tormenting dialectic of all historical being, excluding from it all the indissoluble contradictions and mitigating the opposition which it offers to all romantic wish-fulfilment dreams and fantasies. Every work of art is a vision and a legend of reality, all art replaces actual life with a Utopia, but in romanticism the Utopian character of art is expressed more purely and more fully than elsewhere.

The concept of 'romantic irony' is based essentially on the insight that art is nothing but autosuggestion and illusion, and that we are always aware of the fictitiousness of its representations. The definition of art as 'deliberate self-deception'[179] has its source in romanticism and in ideas like Coleridge's 'willing suspension of disbelief'.[180] The consciousness and deliberateness of this attitude are, however, still a characteristic of the classicistic rationalism which romanticism only gives up in the course of time and replaces with *unconscious* self-deception, with the anaesthesia and intoxicating of the senses, with the forgoing of irony and critical aloofness. The effect of the film has been compared to that of alcohol and opium, and the crowds staggering out from the cinemas into the dark night have been described as drunken narcotics, neither able nor willing to account for the state in which they find themselves. But this effect is not peculiar to the film; it has its origin in romantic art in general. Classicism, naturally, also desired to be stimulating and arouse feelings and illusions in the reader or the beholder—what art has not desired to do so!—but its representations were always in the nature of an instructive example, an analogy or a symbol full of implications.

The audience reacted not with tears, raptures and fainting fits but with reflections, fresh insights and a deeper understanding of man and his destiny.

The post-revolutionary period was an age of general disappointment. For those who were only superficially connected with the ideas of the Revolution this disillusion began with the Convention, for the real revolutionaries with the 9 Thermidor. The first group gradually came to hate everything that reminded it of the Revolution, for the latter every new stage in the development only confirmed the treachery of their former confederates. But it was also a painful awakening for those for whom the dream of the Revolution had been a nightmare from the very beginning. To all of them the present age seemed to have become stale and empty. The intellectuals isolated themselves more and more from the rest of society, and the intellectually productive elements already lived a life of their own. The concept of the philistine and the 'bourgeois', in contrast to the 'citoyen', arose, and the curious and almost unprecedented situation came about that artists and writers were filled with hatred and contempt for the very class to which they owed their intellectual and material existence. For romanticism was essentially a middle-class movement, indeed, it was the middle-class literary school par excellence, the school which had broken for good with the conventions of classicism, courtly-aristocratic rhetoric and pretence, with elevated style and refined language. Despite its revolutionary trend, the art of the enlightenment was still based on the aristocratic tastes of classicism. Not only Voltaire and Pope, but also Prévost and Marivaux, Swift and Sterne, were nearer to the seventeenth than to the nineteenth century. Romantic art is the first to consist in the 'human document', the screaming confession, the open wound laid bare. When the literature of the enlightenment praises the bourgeois, it is always done merely in order to attack the upper classes; the romantic movement is the first to take it for granted that the bourgeois is the measure of man. The fact that so many of the representatives of romanticism were of noble descent no more alters the bourgeois character of the movement than does the anti-philistinism of its cultural policy. Novalis, von Kleist, von Arnim, von Eichendorff and von Chamisso, Vicomte de Chateaubriand, de Lamartine, de Vigny, de Musset, de Bonald, de Maistre and de Lamennais, Lord Byron and Shelley, Leopardi and Manzoni, Pushkin and Lermontov, were members of aristocratic families and manifested aristocratic views to some extent, but from the time of the romantic movement, literature was intended exclusively for the free market, that is to say, for a middle-class public. It was occasionally possible to persuade this public to accept political opinions contrary to its real interests, but it was no longer possible to present the world to it in the impersonal style and abstract intellectual patterns of the eighteenth century. The world-view that was really suited to it was expressed most clearly of all in the idea of the autonomy of the mind and the immanence of the individual spheres of culture, which had predominated in German philosophy since Kant and which would have been unthinkable without the emancipation of the middle class.[181] Until the romantic movement the concept of culture had been dependent on the idea of the subordinate rôle of the human mind; no matter whether the world-view of the moment happened to be of an ecclesiastical-ascetic, a secular-heroic, or an aristocratic-absolutist nature, the mind had always been considered a means to an end and had never seemed to pursue immanent aims of its own. It was only after the dissolution of the earlier ties, after the disappearance of the feeling of the absolute nullity of the mind in relation to the divine order and its relative nullity in relation to the ecclesiastical and secular hierarchy, that is, after the individual had been referred back to himself, that the idea of intellectual autonomy became conceivable. It was in harmony with the philosophy of economic and political liberalism, and remained current until socialism created the idea of a new obligation and historical materialism again abolished the autonomy of the mind. This autonomy was, therefore, like the individualism of romanticism, the result and not the cause of the conflict which shook the foundations of eighteenth-century society. Neither of these ideas was absolutely new, but this was the first time that the individual had been incited to revolt against society and against everything that stood between him and his happiness.[182]

Romanticism pushed its individualism to extremes as a compensation for the materialism of the world and as a protection against the hostility of the bourgeoisie and the philistines to the things of the mind. As the pre-romantics had already tried to do, the romantics proper wanted to create with their aestheticism a sphere withdrawn from the rest of the world in which they could reign unhindered. Classicism based the concept of beauty on that of truth, that is, on a universally human standard controlling the whole of life. But Musset turned Boileau's words inside out and proclaimed: 'Rien n'est vrai que le beau.' The romantics judged life according to the criteria of art, because they wanted thereby to raise themselves as a new aristocracy above the rest of men; but the ambivalent attitude on which their whole world-view was based also found expression in their relationship to art. The Goethean problem of the nature of the artist continued to torment them; art was looked upon, on the one hand, as an instrument of higher knowledge, of religious ecstasy, of divine revelation, but, on the other, its value in the practice of daily life was questioned. 'Art is a seducing, forbidden fruit'—as Wackenroder had already said—'whoever has once tasted its innermost, sweetest juice, is irretrievably lost for the active, living world. He creeps more and more closely into his own little corner of pleasure . . .' And: 'That is the poison of art that the artist becomes an actor who regards the whole of life as a part, his stage as the model world and the kernel, and real life as the husk, as a miserable patched-up imitation.'[183] Schelling's 'system of identity' was just as much an attempt to overcome this contradiction as Keats's message: 'Beauty is truth, truth beauty.' Nevertheless, aestheticism remains the basic characteristic of the romantic outlook, and Heine's summing up of classicism and romanticism as the 'art period' (Kunstperiode) of German literature is absolutely correct.

Nothing presented itself to the romantics free from conflicting features; the problematical nature of their historical situation and the inner strife of their feelings is reflected in all their utterances. The moral life of humanity has taken place in conflicts from time immemorial; the more differentiated man's social life has been, the more violent have been the clashes between the ego and the world, between instinct and reason, past and present. But in romanticism these conflicts become the basic form of consciousness. Life and mind, nature and culture, history and eternity, solitude and society, revolution and tradition, no longer appear as logical correlatives or as moral alternatives, between which one has to choose, but as possibilities which one strives to realize simultaneously. They are not yet, however, set in dialectical opposition to one another, there is no search for a synthesis which would express their interdependence, they are merely experimented and played with. Neither idealism and spiritualism nor irrationalism and individualism reign unopposed; on the contrary, they alternate with an equally strong tendency to naturalism and collectivism. The spontaneity and consistency of philosophical attitudes has ceased; all that exist now are reflexive, critical, problematical attitudes, the antitheses of which are always present and capable of realization. The human mind has now lost even that last remnant of spontaneity which the eighteenth century was still able to call its own. The inner discord and ambivalence of spiritual relationships goes so far that it has been rightly asserted that the romantics, or at least the early German romantics, endeavoured to keep the 'romantic' itself at a distance from themselves.[184] Friedrich Schlegel and Novalis, at any rate, tried to overcome all the sensitivity inside them and, for all their subjectivity and sensibility, to found their world-view on something solid and universally valid. That was, in fact, precisely the great, basic difference between pre-romanticism and romanticism, that the sentimentalism of the eighteenth century was replaced by a heightened sensibility, an enhanced 'impressionability of the heart and the soul', and, although plenty of tears continued to be shed, emotional reactions began to lose their moral value and sank down to lower and lower cultural strata.

The inner strife of the romantic soul is reflected nowhere so directly and expressively as in the figure of the 'second self' which is always present to the romantic mind and recurs in innumerable forms and variations in romantic literature. The source of this *idée fixe* is unmistakable: it is the irresistible urge to introspection, the maniacal tendency to self-observation and the compulsion to consider oneself over and over again as one unknown, as an uncannily remote stranger. The idea of the 'second self' is, of course, again merely an attempt to escape and expresses the inability of the romantics to resign themselves to their own historical and social situation. The romantic rushes headlong into his 'double', just as he rushes headlong into everything dark and ambiguous, chaotic and ecstatic, demonic and dionysian, and seeks therein merely a refuge from the reality which he is unable to master by rational means. On this flight from reality, he discovers the unconscious, that which is hidden away in safety from the rational mind, the source of his wish-fulfilment dreams and of the irrational solutions of his problems. He discovers that 'two souls dwell in his breast', that something inside him feels and thinks that is not identical with himself, that he carries his demon and his judge about with him—in brief, he discovers the basic facts of psychoanalysis. For him, the irrational has the inestimable advantage of not being subject to conscious control, which is why he praises the unconscious, obscure instincts, dreamlike and ecstatic states of soul, and looks in them for the satisfaction which is not vouchsafed him by the cool, cold, critical intellect. 'La sensibilité n'est guère la qualité d'un grand génie . . . Ce n'est pas son coeur, c'est sa tête qui fait tout', as even a writer as late as Diderot said;[185] now, on the other hand, everything is expected to come from the *salto mortale* of the reason. Hence the belief in direct experiences and moods, the surrender to the moment and the fleeting impression, hence that adoration of the 'chance occurrence' of which Novalis speaks. The more bewildering the chaos, the more radiant the star, it is hoped, that will emerge from it. Hence the cult of the mysterious and nocturnal, of the bizarre and the grotesque, the horrible and the ghostlike, the diabolical and the macabre, the pathological and the perverse. If one describes romanticism as 'hospital-poetry', as Goethe did, that is certainly to do it a great injustice, but a revealing injustice, even if one does not think just of Novalis and the aphorisms in which he says that life is a disease of the mind, and that it is disease that distinguishes man from the plants and animals. For the romantic disease is again only an escape from the rational mastery of the problems of life, and being ill only a pretext for withdrawing from the duties of daily routine. If one maintains that the romantics were 'diseased', one has not said very much; but the statement that the philosophy of disease constituted an essential element of their world-view implies a good deal more. For them disease represented the negation of the ordinary, the normal, the reasonable and contained the dualism of life and death, nature and non-nature, continuance and dissolution, which dominated their whole conception of life. It meant the depreciation of everything sharply defined and abiding, and was in accordance with their hatred for all limitations, all solid and definite form.

We know that Goethe had already spoken of the untruth and inadequacy of forms, and if we recall his saying, we shall understand why the French have always reckoned him among the romantics. But Goethe felt the restricted forms of art to be untrue only when measured against the concrete richness of life; the romantics, on the other hand, considered everything clear-cut and definite as intrinsically of less value than the open, unfulfilled possibility, on which they bestowed the characteristics of infinite growth, of the eternal movement, change and fertility of life. They regarded all solid forms, all unequivocal thoughts, all determinate utterance as dead and false; hence they inclined, despite their aestheticism, to disparage the work of art as a controlled and self-sufficient form. Their extravagances and arbitrariness, their mingling and combining of the arts, the improvised and fragmentary nature of their style, were merely symptoms of this dynamic approach to life, to which they owed all their genius, all their intensified sensibility and historical clairvoyance. Since the Revolution, the individual had lost all external supports; he was dependent on himself, had to seek for help within himself, and became an object of infinite importance and infinite interest to himself. He replaced experience of the world more and more with self-experience and finally came to feel that spiritual activity, the current of thoughts and feelings, the way leading from one spiritual state to another, is more real than external reality. He regarded the world merely as the raw material and substratum of his own experiences and used it as a pretext for talking about himself. 'All the accidents of our life', Novalis thought, 'are materials out of which we can make what we like, everything is a link in an unending chain.' This implies a disparagement of both the beginning and the end of the stream of experience, of both the content and the form of the finished work of art. The world becomes a mere occasion for spiritual movement, and art the accidental vessel in which the contents of experience achieve definition for a moment. There arises the mode of thought which has been called the 'occasionalism' of romanticism[186]—the approach which dissolves reality into a series of unsubstantial, inherently undefinable occasions, into mere stimuli to intellectual creation, into situations which apparently exist simply in order that the subject may make sure of his own existence, of his own substantiality. The more indefinite, iridescent, atmospherical and 'musical' the stimuli are, the more vigorously does the experiencing subject vibrate in response; the more intangible, inconstant, unsubstantial the world appears, the stronger, freer and more autonomous will be the feeling of the individual fighting for authority. Only in a historical situation in which the individual was already free and dependent on himself, but still felt that he was menaced and endangered, could such an attitude arise. The whole ostentatious subjectivism, the irresistible urge to spiritual enlargement, the never satisfied, self-surpassing lyricism of the new art, can only be explained by this split of the ego. Romanticism cannot be understood unless one's explanation of it is based on this dissension and on the over-compensations typical of the emancipated and disillusioned individual of the post-revolutionary period.

The political conversion of romanticism in Germany from liberalism to the monarchist-conservative point of view, the opposite trend of development in France and in England, too, in a probably more complicated way, wavering between Revolution and Restoration, but on the whole in harmony with the French development, was possible only because romanticism had an equivocal relationship to the Revolution and was at all times ready to change over to the opposite of its previous attitude. German classicism had sympathized with the ideas of the French Revolution, and this affection became still deeper in German romanticism, which, as Haym and Dilthey have already noted, was never wholly unpolitical.[187] It was only during the Napoleonic Wars that the ruling classes succeeded in winning over the romantics to the side of reaction. Until Napoleon's invasion of Germany the conservative powers felt absolutely safe and were 'enlightened' and tolerant in their own way; but now that with the victorious French army the institutions of the French Revolution threatened to spread, they set to work to suppress every kind of liberalism, and fought against Napoleon, above all, as the exponent of the Revolution. The really progressively and independently minded people, like Goethe, did not allow themselves to be taken in by the anti-Napoleonic propaganda; but they formed only a vanishing minority of the middle class and the intelligentsia. The revolutionary spirit was always of a different character in Germany from what it was in France. The German poets' enthusiasm for the Revolution was abstract and fact-distorting in its approach and no more did justice to the meaning of events than the thoughtless tolerance of the ruling classes. The poets thought of the Revolution as a great philosophical discussion, the holders of power regarded it as a mere play that, in their opinion, could never become a reality in Germany. This lack of understanding explains the complete change that comes over the whole nation after the Wars of Liberation. The change of front of Fichte, the republican and rationalist, who suddenly sees the period of the Revolution as the age of 'absolute sinfulness', is supremely typical. The initial romanticization of the Revolution only brings about an all the more violent repudiation and results in the identification of romanticism with the Restoration. At the time when the romantic movement reached its really creative and revolutionary phase in the West, there was no longer a single romantic in Germany who had not transferred his allegiance to the conservative and monarchist camp.[188]

French romanticism, which in its beginnings was an 'émigré literature',[189] remained the mouthpiece of the Restoration until after 1820. It is only in the second half of the 20's that it develops into a liberal movement formulating its artistic aims after the analogy of the political Revolution. In England romanticism is, as in Germany, pro-revolutionary, to begin with, and becomes conservative only during the war against Napoleon; after the war years, however, it takes a fresh turn, and again approaches its earlier revolutionary ideals. Romanticism, therefore, finally turns against the Restoration and reaction both in France and England—and, indeed, much more decidedly than the course of political events themselves. For, although the liberal idea apparently gains the upper hand in the constitutions and institutions of the West, modern Europe, with its pro-capitalist economic policy, its militaristic-imperialistic monarchies, its centralistic-bureaucratic administrative systems, its rehabilitated Churches and state religions, is just as much the creation of the Restoration as it is of the enlightenment and it is equally justifiable to see in the nineteenth century a period of opposition to the spirit of the Revolution as the triumph of the ideas of freedom and progress.[190] If the Napoleonic empire had already meant the dissolution of the individualistic ideals of the Revolution, the victory of the allies over Napoleon, the Holy Alliance and the Restoration of the Bourbons led to the final break with the eighteenth century and with the idea of basing state and society on the individual. But the spirit of individualism could no longer be displaced from the modes of thought and experience of the new generation; that explains the contradiction between the anti-liberal politics and the liberal artistic tendencies of the age.

For the Restoration, Napoleon's military adventure was nothing more than the counterpart to the political crime of 1789 and the first Empire merely the continuation of lawlessness and anarchy. The monarchists regarded the whole revolutionary-Napoleonic epoch as a unity, as the consistent undermining of the old order, of the old hierarchy, of the old rights of property. And the Empire was, in spite of its reactionary tendencies, all the more dangerous, as it appeared to consolidate the achievements of the Revolution and to create a new state of equilibrium. In contrast to this whole revolutionary epoch, the Restoration meant the beginning of a new era. It rescued what there was to rescue, and tried to create an adjustment between what it was no longer possible to restore of the old institutions and what it was no longer possible to alter in the new. But in this respect, the Restoration was only the continuation of the Napoleonic period; it represented the same antagonism between the principles of the Revolution and the ideas of the *ancien régime*—though with the difference that Napoleon wanted to preserve as much as possible of the achievements of the Revolution, whereas the Restoration wanted to undo them as much as possible. One must not underestimate this difference, although the Restoration began by introducing a certain relaxation in the use of force which both the Revolution, always in danger of losing its life, and the Empire, threatened from left and right, were compelled to apply. There was, of course, no question of a renaissance of middle-class freedom, in contrast to Napoleon's military dictatorship; the semblance of one arose only because now, instead of individual persons, whole classes and groups were persecuted and prejudiced, but within the framework of this class rule statutory freedom was considered to some extent. The Restoration was able to allow itself the luxury of being more tolerant than its predecessors. Reaction had triumphed in the whole of Europe and liberal ideas were losing their danger; the peoples of Europe were tired of revolutionary and warlike undertakings and yearned for peace and quiet. A freer exchange of ideas than hitherto became possible and it was no longer necessary to make the following of certain trends subject to sanctions, even though the political background of the various artistic approaches was perceived with great exactness.

In France the romantics profess themselves legitimists and clericalists, to begin with, whereas the classical tradition in literature is represented mainly by the liberals. Not all the classicists are liberal, but all the liberals are classicists.[191] There is probably no other example in the history of art which makes it so clear that a conservative political disposition is directly compatible with a progressive artistic outlook, indeed, that conservatism and progressiveness are, properly speaking, incommensurable in the two spheres. No understanding is possible between the classicistically-minded liberals and the romantic 'ultras', but amongst the legitimists there is a whole group of believers in the classicistic view of art, although, in contrast to the liberals, they have in mind not the classicism of the eighteenth century but that of the age of Louis XIV. In their fight against romanticism, however, the liberal and conservative classicists are in complete agreement; that is why the Academy rejects Lamartine, despite his conservatism. Incidentally, the Academy no longer represents the taste prevailing among the literary public; a large section of the reading public supports the romantics and, indeed, with a hitherto unknown fervour. The success of Chateaubriand's *Génie du Christianisme* was already unprecedented for a work of its kind, but never before or since has a small collection of lyrical poems been received with such enthusiasm as Lamartine's *Méditations*. After the long stagnation of literature, there now begins a lively, extremely productive era, rich in unusual talents and successful works. To be sure, the reading public is not big, but it is a grateful public with a passionate interest in and enthusiasm for literature.[192] A relatively large number of books is bought, the press follows literary events with the greatest attention, the *salons* open up again and celebrate the intellectual heroes of the day. As a result of the relatively high degree of freedom, a disintegration of literary effort takes place and the homogeneous culture of the 'grand siècle' gradually recedes into a mythical past. It is true that there had already been a quarrel between the 'ancients' and the 'moderns' in the seventeenth century, a conflict between the academic trend of Le Brun and the pictorial conception of art of his opponents, and in the eighteenth century there was the far more violent antagonism between the courtly rococo and bourgeois pre-romanticism, but during the whole of the *ancien régime* a fundamentally homogeneous taste had prevailed in art —an orthodoxy the enemies of which had always been regarded as dissidents and outsiders. There had never been, in a word, any real rivalry between artistic tendencies. Now, on the other hand, there are two equally strong groups, or at least, two groups enjoying equal prestige. Neither of the competing trends has an authoritarian character and dominates the intellectual élite exclusively or overwhelmingly; and even after the victory of romanticism there is no standard 'romantic taste' in the sense that there had been a normative classicistic taste. Certainly, no one escapes from its influence, but by no means everyone acknowledges it, and a fight begins against this taste in the camp of its own representatives almost simultaneously with its victory. The conflict between competing aesthetic tendencies is now just as characteristic a feature of artistic life as the intolerance of the public towards the new movements. In everything that it cannot understand the bourgeoisie scents the presence of scorn and contempt and finally rejects innovations on principle. The dividing line between aesthetic orthodoxy and unorthodoxy is gradually obliterated and the distinction ultimately loses all its significance. Soon there are merely literary 'parties' and something approaching a democracy of literary life comes into being. The sociological innovation of romanticism is the politicization of art and not merely in the sense that artists and writers join political parties, but also that they carry on party politics within artistic life itself. 'Vous verrez qu'il faudra finir par avoir une opinion' are the melancholy words of an eclectic of the period[193] and Balzac characterizes the situation in the *Illusions perdues* in the following terms: 'Les royalistes sont romantiques, les libéraux classiques . . . Si vous êtes éclectiques vous n'aurez personne pour vous.' The unavoidable necessity of taking sides in the great controversy was seen quite accurately by Balzac, only the situation was somewhat more complicated than he described it here.

The most important representative of the 'émigré literature' is Chateaubriand. With Rousseau and Byron, he is one of the most influential forces in the moulding of the new romantic type and, as such, he plays an incomparably more important rôle than would be justified by the intrinsic value of his works. Like his predecessor and his successor, he is merely the exponent, not the sustainer and creator, of an intellectual movement, and enriches it only with a new form of expression, not with a new content of experience. Rousseau's Saint-Preux and Goethe's Werther were the first embodiments of the disillusion which seized men's minds in the romantic era, Chateaubriand's René is the expression of the despair into which this disillusion now develops. The sentimentalism and melancholy of pre-romanticism was in accordance with the emotional condition of the bourgeoisie before the Revolution, the pessimism and weariness of life of the émigré literature is in accordance with the mood of the aristocracy after the Revolution. This mood becomes a universal European phenomenon after the fall of Napoleon and gives expression to the feelings of all the upper classes. Rousseau still knew why he was unhappy; the complaints from which he suffered were modern culture and the inability of conventional social forms to meet his spiritual needs. He imagined a quite concrete, though unrealizable, situation in which he would be cured of his complaints. René's melancholy, on the other hand, is indefinable. For him the whole of life has become meaningless; he feels an infinite, exalted desire for love and fellowship, an everlasting yearning to embrace everything, to be embraced by everything; but he knows that this yearning is incapable of fulfilment and that his soul would still remain unsatisfied, if all his wishes could be fulfilled. Nothing is worth being desired, all striving and fighting is useless; the only sensible action is suicide. And the absolute separation of the internal and external world, of the poetry and prose of life, the solitude, the contempt for the world and the misanthropy, the unreal, abstract, desperately egoistic existence, which the romantic natures of the new century lead, is already suicide.

Chateaubriand, Mme de Staël, Senancour, Constant, Nodier, all stand alongside Rousseau and feel a marked dislike for Voltaire. But most of them feel themselves in opposition only to the rationalism of the eighteenth century, not to that of the seventeenth. Only because of this distinction does Chateaubriand succeed in combining his progressive view of art with his political conservatism, his royalism and clericalism, his enthusiasm for throne and altar. And only because romanticism feels its connection with the more distant more strongly than with the more recent past, is it possible to explain why Lamartine, Vigny and Hugo remained loyal to legitimism for so long. The first signs of a change in their political views do not become apparent until about 1824. It is then that the first of the romantic coteries ('cénacles') comes into being, the famous circle around Charles Nodier in the 'Arsenal', and it is not until then that the movement amalgamates into something in the nature of a school. The social framework within which eighteenth-century French literature had developed was the *salons*, that is, the regular meetings of writers, artists and critics with members of the upper classes in the homes of the aristocracy and the upper middle class. These were closed circles, in which the manners of cultured society set the fashion and which, however many concessions were made to the way of life of the intellectual 'stars', preserved their 'social' character. But the influence of the *salons* on literature was, for all the stimulation which they gave to the writers of the time, not directly creative. They constituted a forum to which most people submitted without question, a school of good taste and a tribunal which was called upon to decide the fate of literary fashions, but in no way a suitable milieu for the creative co-operation of a group. The 'cénacles' of the romantics are, in contrast, friendly artistic gatherings, in which the 'social' element recedes very much into the background, above all because in every case they are formed round a particular artist and are much less strictly closed than even the most liberal *salons*. Here not only is every writer, artist and critic, who is prepared to join the movement, welcome, but sympathetic members of the public are also admitted. It is true that this open-mindedness and intermingling impairs the scholastic character of the movement, but it in no way prevents the development of a homogeneous conception of art and of a common art policy. In contrast to earlier groupings, the circle in which literary life now develops is no centreless party, as in eighteenth-century France, nor a club or a coffee-house, as in England, but a group assembled round a personality, whom the group regards as its master, and whose authority it acknowledges unconditionally, though not always within the terms of a definite master-disciple relationship. This is the first time in the history of modern literature that the form of a school exerts a decisive influence on the course of events. This form is known neither to the seventeenth nor to the eighteenth century, although it would have been more in accordance with the normative character of classical literature. Romanticism, on the other hand, develops, in spite of or perhaps precisely because of the problematical validity of its artistic principles, a school with a strictly formulatable and teachable doctrine. In the age of classicism, the whole of French literature formed one great school, one uniform taste prevailed in the whole of France; the dissidents and rebels represented much too atomized a group to join forces within the framework of a common programme. But now that French literature has become the battleground of two great and almost equal parties, now that the example of political life induces writers to formulate party programmes and rouses in them the desire for a leader, now that, finally, the artistic aims of the new trend are still so unclarified and contradictory that they have to be summarized and codified, now the time for the founding of literary schools has arrived.

In France the romantic movement was more in the nature of a literary school than in Germany, where the classical ideal in art had never been realized so purely, where the romantics still very largely continued to follow the cultural ideals of classicism and where even the outlook of classicism was to some extent romantic in character. At any rate, the party structure of literary life was much less marked than in France and, consequently, the grouping of writers according to literary 'schools' was also less pronounced. In England, where the distinction between classicism and romanticism had become pointless since the second half of the eighteenth century, because there was, so to say, nothing but romantic literature, no literary school of any kind was formed and no personality with the authority of an acknowledged master appeared on the scene.[194] Even the French 'cénacles', however, are often no more than literary cliques kept together only by a common jargon and seem from outside to be a conspiracy and from inside a jealous troop of actors. They are, indeed, often merely warlike sects or heated debating societies, for whom doctrine is more important than practice and being different from one another more interesting than mutual adaptation. Nevertheless, both in France and Germany the romantic movement is marked by a deep conception of community and a strong tendency towards collectivism. The romantics spend their lives in a fellowship of mutual philosophizing, writing, criticizing and discussion; they find the deepest meaning in life in the relationships of love and friendship; they found periodicals, publish year-books and anthologies, deliver lectures and hold courses, make propaganda for themselves and for one another; try, in a word, to work together in a community, even though this symbiotic urge is only the reverse side of their individualism and the compensation for their loneliness and rootlessness.

The amalgamation of the French romantics into a homogeneous group takes place at the same time as public opinion takes a turn to liberalism. About 1824 the *Globe* begins to strike a new note and that is also the date of the first regular meetings in the 'Arsenal'. The leading romantics, above all Lamartine and Hugo, are, it is true, still loyal supporters of the Church and the Throne, but romanticism ceases from being exclusively clerical and monarchistic. The real change does not occur, however, until 1827, when Victor Hugo writes the famous Preface to his *Cromwell* and propounds the thesis that romanticism is the liberalism of literature. In this year, too, the pictures of the leading romantic painters are seen in the Salon for the first time in greater numbers; besides twelve paintings by Delacroix, representative works of Devéria and Boulanger are exhibited. The public is confronted with a broad, compact movement, which seems to be embracing the whole intellectual life of the country and to be securing complete and final victory for romanticism. The composition of the new 'cénacle' around Victor Hugo is in accordance with this quality of universality and he is regarded from now on as the master of the romantic school. The writers Deschamps, Vigny, Sainte-Beuve, Dumas, Musset, Balzac, the painters Delacroix, Devéria, Boulanger, the graphic artists Johannot, Gigoux, Nanteuil and the sculptor David d'Angers are among the regular guests in the rue Notre-Dame-des-Champs. To this circle Hugo reads aloud his dramas *Marion Delorme* and *Hernani* in 1829. It is true that the group is dissolved in the very same year, but the school continues. The movement becomes even more concentrated and clarified, more and more radical and clear-cut. From the second 'cénacle' in Nodier's home, which comes into being in 1829, the still semi-classical elements already disappear entirely, whereas the plastic artists become regular members of the circle. The absolute unity of the movement, as well as its anti-bourgeois tendency, which gradually hardens into a dogma, are expressed most incisively in the last romantic 'cénacle' which gathers in the studios inhabited by Théophile Gautier, Gérard de Nerval and their friends in the rue de Doyenné. This artists' colony with its anti-philisitinism and its theory of 'l'art pour l'art' is the hot-house of modern bohemianism.

The bohemian character with which romanticism is usually associated was by no means characteristic of the movement from the outset. From Chateaubriand to Lamartine, French romanticism was represented almost exclusively by aristocrats, and if, after 1824, it no longer stood up unanimously for the monarchy and the Church, nevertheless, it remained to some extent aristocratic and clerical. Only very gradually does the leadership of the movement pass into the hands of the plebeians Victor Hugo, Théophile Gautier and Alexandre Dumas, and only shortly before the July revolution do the majority of the romantics change their conservative attitude. The emergence into prominence of the plebeian elements is, however, more a symptom than the cause of the political change. Formerly the middle-class writers adapted themselves to the conservatism of the aristocrats, whereas now even the aristocratic Chateaubriand and Lamartine go over to the opposition. The ever-advancing restriction of personal freedom under Charles X, the clericalization of public life, the introduction of the death penalty for blasphemy, the dissolution of the Garde Nationale and the Chamber, government by decree, only accelerate the radicalization of intellectual life. They only make more obvious what had already been unmistakable since 1815, namely that the Restoration meant the definitive end of the Revolution. Men's minds have now at last recovered from their post-revolutionary apathy and it was this change of mood which forced Charles X to take more and more reactionary measures, if he wanted to keep to the direction imperative for a government based on anti-revolutionary elements. The romantics, who gradually became conscious of where the Restoration was really leading to, recognized at the same time that the wealthy bourgeoisie was the strongest support of the régime—a much stronger support than the old, partly dispossessed, disabled aristocracy. Their whole hatred, their whole contempt, was now heaped on the middle class. The avaricious, narrow-minded, hypocritical bourgeois became their public enemy No. 1 and, in contrast to him, the poor, honest, open-hearted artist struggling against all the humiliating ties and conventional lies of society appears as the human ideal par excellence. The tendency to remoteness from practical life with firm social roots and political commitments, which had been characteristic of romanticism from the very beginning and had become apparent in Germany even in the eighteenth century, now becomes predominant everywhere; even in the Western nations an unbridgeable gulf opens up between the genius and ordinary men, between the artist and the public, between art and social reality. The bad manners and impertinences of the bohemians, their often childish ambition to embarrass and provoke the unsuspecting bourgeois, their frantic attempt to differentiate themselves from normal, average men and women, the eccentricity of their clothes, their head-dress, their beards, Gautier's red waistcoat and the equally conspicuous, though not always so dazzling masquerade of his friends, their free and easy and paradoxical language, their exaggerated, aggressively formulated ideas, their invectives and indecencies, all that is merely the expression of the desire to isolate themselves from middle-class society, or rather of the desire to represent the already accomplished isolation as intentional and acceptable.

With the *Jeune-France*, as the rebels now call themselves, everything revolves around their hatred for philistinism, around their contempt for the strictly regulated and soulless life of the bourgeoisie, around their fight against everything traditional and conventional, everything capable of being taught and learnt, everything mature and serene. The system of intellectual values is enriched by a new category: the idea of youth as more creative than and intrinsically superior to age. This is a new idea, alien, above all, to classicism, but to a certain extent to all previous cultures. There had naturally been a competition between the generations and victorious youth had been the power sustaining artistic developments in earlier ages. But youth had not triumphed simply because it was 'young'; the general attitude to youth had been one rather of guarded prudence than of excessive confidence. It is not until the romantic movement that the idea prevails of regarding the 'young' as the natural representatives of progress, and not until the victory of romanticism over classicism that any mention is made of the fundamental injustice in the older generation's attitude to youth.[195] The emphasis on the unity of the arts is, incidentally, like this solidarity of youth, merely a symptom of the isolation of romanticism from the world of the inartistic philistine. Whilst the connection of belles-lettres with philosophy was stressed in the eighteenth century, literature is now described, quite consistently, as an 'art'.[196] So long as the plastic artists had aspired to be reckoned as belonging to the upper middle class, they had underlined the similarity of their profession to that of the men of letters, but now writers themselves want to be different from the bourgeoisie and stress, therefore, their affinity to the craftsmanlike arts.

The complacency and vanity of the romantics goes so far that, in contrast to their former aestheticism, which turned the poet into a god, they now turn God into a poet. 'Dieu n'est peut-être que le premier poète du monde,' says Gautier. Even the theory of 'l'art pour l'art', which is, however, an extremely complex phenomenon, and gives expression, on the one hand, to a liberal, on the other, to a quietistic-conservative attitude, has its origin in the protest against bourgeois values. When Gautier stresses the pure formalism and play character of art, when he desires to free it from all ideas and all ideals, his supreme wish is to emancipate it from the dominion of the bourgeois order of life. When Taine once praised Musset at the expense of Hugo, Gautier is said to have remarked to him: 'Taine, you seem to have fallen into bourgeois idiocy. Fancy demanding feeling from poetry! That's not the main thing at all. Radiant words, words of light, full of rhythm and music, that's poetry.'[197] In the 'l'art pour l'art' of Gautier, Stendhal and Mérimée, in their emancipation from the ideas of the time, in their programme of pursuing art as a sovereign game and enjoying it as a secret paradise forbidden to ordinary mortals, opposition to the bourgeois world even plays a more important part than in the later 'l'art pour l'art', whose renunciation of all political and social activity is thoroughly welcomed by the parvenu bourgeoisie. Gautier and his comrades in arms refused the bourgeoisie their help in the moral subjugation of society; Flaubert, Leconte de Lisle and Baudelaire, on the other hand, promote the interests of the bourgeoisie by shutting themselves up in their ivory towers and not bothering any further about the course of the world.

The romantics' struggle to obtain control of the theatre, especially their fight for Victor Hugo's *Hernani*, was a war waged by the rue de Doyenné, the bohemians and youth. It did not in any sense end with a striking victory for the romantics; the opposition had not disappeared overnight and it was a long time yet before it gave up its control of the most distinguished theatres in Paris. The movement's fate no longer depended, however, on the reception of a play; as a stylistic trend, romanticism had long since conquered the world. The period about 1830 brings about a change only in so far as romanticism now becomes entirely politicized and allies itself with liberalism. After the July revolution, the intellectual leaders of the time abandon their passivity and many of them exchange a literary for a political career. But even the writers who, like Lamartine and Hugo, remain faithful to their literary profession, take a more active and direct part in political events than hitherto. Victor Hugo is no rebel, no bohemian, and is not directly concerned in the romantic campaign against the bourgeois. In his political development he treads rather the path of the French bourgeoisie. To begin with, he is a loyal adherent of the Bourbons, then he takes part in the July revolution and is the devoted servant of the July monarchy, finally, he supports the aspirations of Louis Napoleon and becomes a radical republican only after the majority of the French bourgeoisie has already become liberal and anti-monarchistic. His relation to Napoleon is also merely in keeping with the changes in public opinion. In 1825 he is still an embittered opponent of Napoleon and curses his memory; it is only around 1827 that he alters his attitude and begins to speak of the glory that is bound up for France with the name of Napoleon. Finally, he becomes the noisiest spokesman of the Bonapartism that represents such a queer mixture of naïve hero-worship, sentimental nationalism and sincere, though not always consistently thought-out, liberalism. How extremely complex the motives of this movement are is best shown by the fact that such different spirits as Heine and Béranger are amongst its supporters and that it is based, on the one hand, on the genuine Voltairians and the heirs of the enlightenment, on the other hand, on the petty bourgeoisie that certainly has a tinge of Voltairianism about it, is anti-clerical and anti-monarchist but, at the same time, sentimental and inclined to build up legends. The fact that a single publisher, the famous Touquet, sells thirty-one thousand copies, that is, a million and six hundred thousand volumes, of Voltaire's works between 1817 and 1824,[198] is the most striking token of the renaissance of the enlightenment and a proof that the middle class constitutes an important contingent of the buyers. It is characteristic of this class that it acquires Voltaire's collected works and sings the free-thinking, though intellectually and artistically not very exacting songs of Béranger. These songs are heard everywhere, their refrains sound in every ear and, as has been said, they contribute more to the undermining of the prestige of the Bourbons than all the other intellectual products of the age. It goes without saying that the middle class had had its songs in earlier ages: its table- and dancing-songs, its patriotic and political songs, its topical verses and street-ballads, which were in no respect more remarkable than the songs of Béranger. But they led their life outside 'literature' and exercised no more than a superficial influence on the poets of the cultured classes. The Revolution not only introduced a much richer production in this popular genre, but also promoted the infiltration of the taste which it expressed into the literature of more fastidious circles. Victor Hugo's development as a poet is the best example of the process by which literature assimilated this influence and shows with the greatest possible clarity the advantages and disadvantages which it involved. The patriotic poetry of later romanticism is just as inconceivable without Béranger's songs as is the romantic drama without the popular theatre. Victor Hugo even as a poet trod the bourgeois path; his lyrical style oscillated between the popular taste of the period of the Revolution and the lofty, ostentatious, pseudo-baroque approach of the Second Empire. Victor Hugo was in no sense a revolutionary, in spite of the conflicts which raged about him. Even the definition of romanticism as the liberalism of literature, as he formulated it, was no longer new; the idea occurs, before him, in Stendhal. The conformity between Hugo's conception of art and the taste of the ruling middle class became more and more complete. They coincide, finally, in the cult of grandiosity, from which they were, in reality, both entirely remote, and in the fondness for a pompous, noisy, rapturous and highly emotional style of which there are still echoes in Rostand, for example.

The most important achievement of the romantic revolution

was the renewal of the poetic vocabulary. The French literary language had become poor and colourless in the course of the seventeenth and eighteenth century, owing to the strict convention regarding permissible expressions and stylistic forms recognized as 'correct'. Everything that sounded commonplace, professional, archaic or provincial was taboo. The simple, natural expressions used in everyday language had to be replaced with noble, choice, 'poetic' terms or artistic paraphrases. It was not considered correct to say 'warrior' or 'horse', but 'héros' and 'coursier', it was not permitted to say 'water' and 'storm', one had to say 'the damp element' and 'the raging of the elements'. The conflict about *Hernani* broke out, as is well known, over the passage: 'Est-il minuit?'—'Minuit bientôt.' That sounded too commonplace, too direct, too listless. Stendhal thought that the answer should have run:

> ' . . . l'heure
> Atteindra bientôt sa dernière demeure'.

The advocates of the classical style knew quite well, however, what the fundamental issue was. Victor Hugo's language was really nothing new; it was, in fact, the language of the boulevard theatres. But the classicists were merely concerned with the 'purity' of the literary theatre; they did not bother themselves about the boulevards and the entertainment of the masses. So long as an elevated theatre and cultivated writing existed, it was possible confidently to disregard what was happening on the boulevards, but once it was permitted to speak from the stage of the Théâtre-Français as one chose, then there was no longer any recognizable difference between the various cultural and social strata. Since Corneille, tragedy had been the representative literary genre; one made one's début as a poet with a tragedy and reached the pinnacle of fame as a tragic poet. Tragedy and the literary theatre were the domain of the intellectual élite; as long as it remained inviolate, people were still able to feel themselves the heirs of the 'grand siècle'. What was at stake now, however, was the invasion of the literary theatre by a drama based on the popular theatre, which was indifferent to the psychological and moral problems of classical tragedy and was more concerned to seek, in their stead, for exciting actions, picturesque scenery, piquant characters and highly coloured descriptions of sentiments. The fate of the theatre was a topic of daily conversation; the antagonists in both camps knew very well that they were fighting for the conquest of a key position. Owing to his theatrical temperament, his mania for the theatre, his loud and demonstrative nature and his feeling for the popular, the trivial, the brutally effective, Victor Hugo was the born exponent, though not entirely the motive power in the struggle for this position.

Romanticism found a very complex situation in the theatre when it arrived on the scene. The popular stage, as the heir of the old mime, the medieval farce and the *commedia dell'arte*, had been displaced by the literary theatre in the seventeenth and eighteenth century. During the Revolution, however, popular productions received a new impulse and again took possession of some of the Paris theatres with forms which still owed a good deal to the influence of the literary drama. It is true that in the Comédie-Française and the Odéon the tragedies and comedies of Corneille, Racine and Molière, and the works of writers who had either adapted themselves to the classical tradition and the court taste or had kept to the literary principles of the domestic drama, continued to be performed. In the theatres of the boulevards—in the Gymnase, the Vaudeville, the Ambigu-Comique, the Gaieté, the Variétés and the Nouveautés—on the other hand, plays were performed which were in accordance with the taste and cultural level of the broader masses. Contemporary records report in detail on the change that came over the theatre public during and immediately after the Revolution and stress the lack of artistic pretensions and culture in the ranks of society that now filled the Paris theatres. The new public is made up for the most part of soldiers, workers, shop-assistants and youngsters of whom, as one of our sources remarks, hardly a third are able to write.[199] And this auditorium dominates not merely the plebeian theatres of the boulevards but, at the same time, threatens the existence of the distinguished literary theatres, by absorbing the better public, so that the actors of the Comédie-Française and the Odéon play before empty houses.[200]

At the time of the first Empire, the Restoration and the July monarchy the following genres are represented in the repertoire of the Paris theatres: (1) The '*comédie en 5 actes et en vers*', which represents the literary genre par excellence and is intended, as such, for the Comédie-Française and the Odéon (as, for example, Ducis's *Othello*). (2) The '*comédie de mœurs en prose*', that is to say, the play of manners, which, as the heir of the domestic drama, occupies a more modest position, but still enjoys sufficient prestige to be performed in the leading theatres (example: Scribe's *Mariage d'argent*). (3) The '*drame en prose*', that is to say, the sentimental drama that likewise originates in the domestic drama, but stands on a lower level of taste than the 'comédie de mœurs' (example: Bouilly's *L'Abbé et l'épée*). (4) The '*comédie historique*', which no longer treats historical events and personalities as examples to be followed, but as curiosities, and desires rather a review of spectacular scenes than a homogeneous dramatic process (examples are manifold: they embrace, from Mérimée's *Cromwell* to Vitet's *Barricades*, all the experiments to which Dumas's *Henri III* owes its origin). (5) The '*vaudeville*', that is, the musical comedy, or more exactly the comedy with songs interpolated, which is to be reckoned among the direct predecessors of the operetta (to this category belong most of the plays of Scribe and his collaborators). (6) '*mélodrame*', a mixed form which shares its musical accessories with the vaudeville, but its serious and often tragic plot with the other lowly genres, especially with the sentimental drama and the historical show-piece.

The enormous productivity in the popular genres, particularly in the two last-named, and the gradual displacement of the literarily more pretentious drama is to be explained, along with the fact that the Revolution opened the theatres to the broad masses of the people and that the success of the plays performed was determined by these classes, above all by the influence of the censorship on the development of the repertoire. The censorship of Napoleon and the Restoration prevented questions of the day and the manners of the ruling class being discussed and described in the serious literary drama. The farce, the musical comedy and the melodrama, on the other hand, enjoyed more freedom, because they were not taken so seriously and were not considered worth bothering about. In the boulevard theatres no obstacles were put in the way of the ruthless description of manners and conditions which was forbidden in the Comédie-Française; this was the source of the attraction of these theatres both for the playwrights and the public.[201] The most important and interesting dramatic forms of the age are, from the historical point of view, the vaudeville and the melodrama; they represent the real turning point in the history of the modern stage and form the transition between the dramatic genres of classicism and romanticism. Through them the theatre regains its character, catering for entertainment, its bustle, its direct appeal to the senses and its obviousness. Of the two, the melodrama has the more complex structure and the more ramified pedigree. One of its many predecessors is the monologue delivered with musical accompaniment, the original form of the hybrid genre that one still comes across in the programmes of amateur performances and the first well-known example of which was Rousseau's *Pygmalion* (1775). This is the starting point of the revival of the dramatic recitation with musical accompaniment—an intrinsically very old form. Another, technically much more fertile, source of the 'mélodrame' is the domestic drama of de la Chaussée, Diderot, Mercier and Sedaine, that had become very popular with the lower classes since the Revolution, owing to its maudlin and moralizing nature. But the most important prototype of the melodrama is the pantomime. The '*pantomimes historiques et romanesques*', as they are called, first appear in the last third of the eighteenth century. They begin by treating mythological and fairy-tale subjects, such as *Hercules and Omphale*, *The Sleeping Beauty* and *The Iron Mask*, but later on contemporary themes as well, such as the *Bataille du Général Hoche*. These pantomimes usually consist of agitated and stormy scenes put together revue fashion without organic coherence or dramatic development, and aim at creating situations in which the mysterious and miraculous element, ghosts and spirits, dungeons and graves play a leading part. In the course of time short explanatory notes and dialogues are inserted into the single scenes and in this way they develop during the Revolution into the curious '*pantomimes dialoguées* and, finally, into the '*mélodrame à grand spectacle*', that gradually loses both its showpiece-like character and its musical elements, and becomes the play of intrigues which is of fundamental importance in the history of the theatre in the nineteenth century. The most important influence exerted on the melodrama in this transformation is that of the thrillers of Mrs. Radcliffe and her French imitators. This is the source not only of its *Grand Guignol*-like effects but also of its criminalistic touch.

All these influences, however, only result in the modification and amplification of the kernel of the melodramatic form, the kernel itself is the conflict of the classical drama. The melodrama is nothing but the tragedy popularized, or, if one likes, corrupted. Pixerécourt, the chief representative of the genre, is perfectly aware of the affinity of his art with the popular theatre, he is merely mistaken in assuming that there is an historical continuity and essential likeness between the melodrama and the mime.[202] He recognizes the real continuity between the medieval mysteries, the pastoral play, Molière's art and the mime, but he overlooks the fundamental difference between the genuinely popular nature of the mime and the derived character of the literary theatre that has sunk to the level of the broad strata of the urban public. The melodrama is anything but a spontaneous and naïve art; it follows rather the sophisticated formal principles of the tragedy, acquired in the course of a long and consistent development, even though it reflects them in a coarsened style lacking the psychological subtleties and poetic beauties of the classical form. On the purely formal plane, the melodrama is the most conventional, schematic and artificial genre imaginable—a canon into which new, spontaneously invented, naturalistically straightforward elements can hardly find an entry. It has a strictly tripartite structure, with a strong antagonism as the initial situation, a violent collision and a dénouement representing the triumph of virtue and the punishment of vice, in a word, an easily understood and economically developed plot; with the priority of plot over characters; with sharp figures: the hero, persecuted innocence, the villain and the comic;[203] with the blind and cruel fatefulness of events; with a strongly emphasized moral, which, owing to its insipid, conciliatory tendency based on reward and punishment, is not in accordance with the moral character of tragedy, but shares with it a high, albeit exaggerated, solemnity. The melodrama betrays its dependence on tragedy above all in its observation of the three unities, or at least in its tendency to take them into consideration. Pixerécourt allows a change of scene to take place between two acts, but the jump is never a painful one and he does not introduce a change of scene within one and the same act until *Charles-le-Téméraire* (1814). On the other hand, he apologizes for it in a note the text of which is extremely revealing of his classicistic disposition: 'This is the first time that I have allowed myself this infringement of the rules,' he avers. On the whole, Pixerécourt preserves even the unity of time; in his plays everything usually takes place within twenty-four hours. It is not until 1818 that he introduces a new method in his *Fille de l'exilé ou huit mois en deux heures*, but, here again, he apologizes for it.[204] In contrast to these characteristics of the melodrama, the mime consisting of a naturalistic commonplace scene, or a loose sequence of such scenes, has no stereotyped plot reducible to a fixed pattern, no typical or extraordinary characters, no rigid moral, no idealized style differing from colloquial language. All that the melodrama has in common with the mime is the drive of its scenes and the crudeness of its effects, the lack of discrimination in its choice of means and the popular character of the motifs; otherwise it keeps to the stylistic ideal of classical tragedy. Obviously, the strict conventionality of a form is in itself by no means the sign of a higher purpose.

The modern species of the mime is not the melodrama but the vaudeville, which with its episodic plot divided into separate scenes, its interpolated songs, its popular types taken from daily life, its fresh, piquant, apparently spontaneous style, is much nearer to the old popular theatre than the melodrama, in spite of the literary influences which it by no means lacks. The period between 1815 and 1848 displays an unprecedented fertility in this genre, to which, apart from the numerous comedies by Scribe, an endless number of small, light, amusing plays and playlets belong. One can only get an idea of the literary practitioners' alarm at the extent and success of these productions by remembering the reaction which accompanied the triumphant progress of the film. During the Revolution and the Restoration, comedy became exhausted, just as tragedy had already proved itself sterile in an earlier age. The vaudeville came forward as a corrupt, externalized form of comedy, just as the melodrama represented a corrupt, externalized form of tragedy. The vaudeville and the melodrama did not mean the end of the drama, however, but rather its revival, for the romantic drama—the form of Hugo's *Hernani* or Dumas's *Antony*—was nothing but the 'mélodrame parvenu' and the modern drama of manners of Augier, Sardou and Dumas *fils* only a species of the vaudeville.[205]

Between 1798 and 1814, Pixerécourt wrote about a hundred and twenty plays, of which some were performed many thousands of times. The melodrama dominated theatre life for three decades and its popularity did not abate until after 1830, when the level of public taste began to rise and the crudities of the plays, their lack of logic, the insufficiency of their motivation and unnatural language, were felt to be more and more upsetting. The romantics had a weakness for the melodrama, however, not only on account of their hostility to the conservative strata of the cultured public, but also because, owing to their less prejudiced outlook, they showed more understanding for the unliterary, purely theatrical qualities of this genre. Charles Nodier at once declared himself an enthusiastic supporter of the melodrama and called it 'la seule tragédie populaire qui convienne à notre époque';[206] and Paul Lacroix described Pixerécourt as the dramatist who was the first to finish the process begun by Beaumarchais, Diderot, Sedaine and Mercier.[207] The unprecedented success, the opposition of official circles, as well as the romantics' own fondness for melodramatic effects, for shrill colours, crudely sensational situations, violent accents, all this contributed to the preservation in the romantic drama of so many of the most characteristic features of the plebeian theatre. But romanticism only received back from the melodrama what had belonged to it from the very beginning, what had been contained in the bud in pre-romanticism and the 'Storm and Stress' and had been taken over by the theatre partly from English tales of horror, partly from German penny-dreadfuls, novels of brigandage and chivalry. The common elements between the romantic theatre and the melodrama are, above all, the sharp conflicts and violent clashes, the involved, adventurous, bloody and brutal plot; the predominance of miracle and chance, the sudden, usually unmotivated twists and turns, the unforeseen encounters and recognitions, the constant alternation of tension and relaxation; the violent, irresistibly brutal tricks, the assaults on the audience by the horrible, the uncanny and the demonic; the ready-made mechanical development of the plot, the disguises and deceptions, the conspiracies and traps; finally, the *coups de théâtre* and stage requisites, without which a romantic drama is quite inconceivable: the arrests and seductions, the kidnappings and rescues, the attempts to escape and the assassinations, the corpses and coffins, the cellars and tombs, the castle-towers and dungeons, the daggers, swords and poison phials, the rings, amulets and family heirlooms, the intercepted letters, lost wills and stolen secret contracts. Romanticism was certainly not very fastidious, but one has only to think of Balzac, the greatest and, from the point of view of taste, most problematical writer of the century, to realize how narrow and, in the long run, unimportant the aesthetic criteria of classicism had become.

The development of the theatre in the direction of popular taste was not, however, expressed so much in the mere existence of the melodrama but in the good conscience with which Pixerécourt offered his wares for sale. He considered the romantics' plays bad, false, immoral and dangerous, and was profoundly convinced that his pretentious rivals had neither so much heart nor so much feeling of moral responsibility as he.[208] On this point Faguet comments quite rightly that one must believe in trash, to produce good, successful trash. D'Ennery, for example, was a better writer and a more intelligent person than Pixerécourt, but he wrote his melodramas without conviction, purely and simply to make money with them, and thus he did not even succeed in writing good melodramas.[209] Pixerécourt, on the other hand, believed in his mission and protested that he had not had anything to do with the rise of the wicked romantic drama. But the romantics owed him, first of all, their feeling for the requirements of the stage and their contact with the broader masses of the public. They owed him the part they played in the development of the 'pièce bien faite', and the whole nineteenth century owed him the rebirth of the living popular theatre, that certainly lacked discrimination and was often trivial in comparison with the seventeenth and eighteenth centuries, but prevented the development of the drama into mere literature. It was part of the fate of this century that every time the poetic element came into its own in the drama, its entertainment value, its theatrical effectiveness and the immediacy of its appeal threatened to wither. Even in the romantic movement the two elements came into conflict and their antagonism prevented either the stage success or the poetic perfection of the drama. Alexandre Dumas inclined to the good sturdy play, Victor Hugo to the linguistically overwhelming dramatic poem, and their successors were constantly faced with the same choice; it was not until Ibsen that the two antithetical tendencies were harmoniously resolved, and then only for a time.

England had its political revolution in the seventeenth century, its industrial and artistic revolution a century later; whilst the great war between classicism and romanticism was raging in France, hardly anything of the classical tradition survived in England. English romanticism developed more continuously, more consistently and met with less public resistance than French romanticism; its political evolution was also more homogeneous than the corresponding movement in France. To begin with, it was absolutely liberal and thoroughly well disposed towards the Revolution; it was only the war against Napoleon which led to an understanding between the romantics and the conservative elements and only after his fall that liberalism became predominant in romantic literature once again. The earlier uniformity, however, never returned. There was no desire to forget so soon the 'lessons' learnt from the Revolution and the rule of Napoleon, and many former liberals, among others the members of the Lake School, remained anti-revolutionary. Walter Scott was and remained a Tory; Godwin, Shelley, Leigh Hunt and Byron, on the other hand, represented the radicalism that was predominant in the younger generation. English romanticism had its origins essentially in the reaction of the liberal elements to the Industrial Revolution, whereas French romanticism arose from the reaction of the conservative classes to the political revolution. The connection between romanticism and pre-romanticism was much closer in England than in France where the continuity between the two movements was completely disrupted by the classicism of the revolutionary period. In England the same relation existed between romanticism and the successful completion of the Industrial Revolution as between pre-romanticism and the preparatory stages of the industrialization of society. Goldsmith's *Deserted Village*, Blake's 'Satanic Mills' and Shelley's 'Age of Despair' are all the expression of an essentially identical mood. The romantics' enthusiasm for nature is just as unthinkable without the isolation of the town from the countryside as is their pessimism without the bleakness and misery of the industrial cities. They realize perfectly what is going on and are acutely aware of the significance of the transformation of human labour into a mere commodity. Southey and Coleridge see in periodical unemployment the necessary consequence of uncontrolled capitalist production and Coleridge already stresses the fact that, in accordance with the new conception of work, the employer buys and the employee sells something that neither of them has the right to buy or sell, namely 'the labourer's health, life and well-being'.[210]

After the end of the struggle against Napoleon, England finds herself, if in no sense exhausted, at least weakened and intellectually bewildered—in a condition especially calculated to make the middle class aware of the problematical bases of its existence. The younger romantics, the generation of Shelley, Keats and Byron, are the leading influences in this process. Their uncompromising humanism is their protest against the policy of exploitation and oppression; their unconventional way of life, their aggressive atheism and their lack of moral bias are the different modes of their struggle against the class that controls the means of exploitation and suppression. Even in its conservative representatives, Wordsworth and Scott, the English romantic movement is to some extent a democratic movement, aiming at the popularization of literature. Wordsworth's aim above all to bring poetic diction nearer to everyday language is a characteristic symptom of this popularizing tendency, even though the 'natural' poetic diction which he uses is, in reality, no more spontaneous than the older literary language which he renounces because of its artificiality. If it is less learned, its subjective psychological presuppositions are all the more complicated. And as for the enterprise of describing himself and his own intellectual development in a poem the length of the Homeric epics, it certainly represents a revolutionary experiment compared with the objectivity of the older literature and is just as typical of the new subjectivism as, for instance, Goethe's *Dichtung und Wahrheit*, but the 'popularity' and 'naturalness' of such an undertaking is more than doubtful. In his essay on Wordsworth, Matthew Arnold remarks, in speaking of certain of the poet's inadequacies, that it goes without saying that even Shakespeare has his weak passages, but if one should call him to account for them in the Elysian Fields, he would certainly reply that he was perfectly aware of them. 'After all'—he would add smilingly—'what is the harm in letting oneself go occasionally!' In contrast, the modern poet's concentration on his own ego is bound up with a humourless over-estimation of every personal utterance, with the appreciation of the tiniest detail according to its expressive value and the loss of that unconcerned facility with which the older poet simply let his lines flow on.

For the eighteenth century, poetry was the expression of ideas; the meaning and purpose of poetic images was the explanation and illustration of an ideal content. In romantic poetry, on the other hand, the poetic image is not the result but the source of ideas.[211] The metaphor becomes productive and we feel as though language were making itself autonomous and were composing of its own accord. The romantics abandon themselves to language without resistance and give expression in this way, too, to their anti-rationalistic conception of art. The origin of Coleridge's *Kubla Khan* may have been an extreme case; but it was, at any rate, symptomatic. The romantics believed in a transcendental, world-pervading spirit as the source of poetic inspiration and identified it with the spontaneous creative power of language. To allow oneself to be controlled by it was considered by them to be the sign of the highest artistic genius. Plato had already spoken of the 'enthusiasm', of the divine inspiration of poets, and the belief in inspiration had always appeared on the scene whenever poets and artists had wanted to give themselves the appearance of a priestly caste. But this was the first time that inspiration had ever been regarded as a self-kindling flame, as a light that has its source in the soul of the poet himself. The divine origin of inspiration was, therefore, now a purely formal, not a substantial attribute; it brought nothing into the soul that was not already there. Thus both principles, the divine and the individual, were preserved—and the poet became his own god.

Shelley's ecstatic pantheism is the classical example of this self-deification. It lacks all trace of self-forgetting devotion and any sign of readiness to obliterate the self before a higher being. The absorption of the self in the universe is now the expression of a desire to dominate, not a willingness to be dominated. The world ruled over by poetry and the poet is considered the higher, purer, more divine world, and the divine itself seems to have no other criteria than those derived from poetry. It is true that Shelley's world-view, wholly in accordance with that of Friedrich Schlegel and German romanticism, is based on a mythology; but not even the poet himself believes in this mythology. Metaphor now becomes myth and not the other way round, as with the Greeks. This mythologizing is again merely an instrument of flight from ordinary, common, soulless reality—a bridge to the poet's own spiritual depths and sensibility. It is only a means whereby the poet can come to himself. The myths of classical antiquity arose from a sympathy and a genuine relationship with reality; the mythology of the romantics arises from its ruins and to some extent as a substitute for reality. Shelley's cosmic vision revolves around the idea of a great, world-embracing conflict between the good and the evil principle and represents the monumentalization of the political antagonism which constitutes the poet's deepest and most decisive experience. His atheism is, as has been said, more a revolt against God than a denial of God; he is fighting an oppressor and a tyrant.[212] Shelley is the born rebel, who sees in everything legitimate, constitutional and conventional the work of a despotic will and for whom oppression, exploitation and violence, stupidity, ugliness and mendacity, kings, the ruling classes and the Churches, form a single compact power with the God of the Bible. The abstract, indefinite character of this conception best shows how similar English and

German poets had become. The anti-revolutionary hysteria has poisoned the intellectual atmosphere in which the English writers of the eighteenth century had freely developed their abilities; the intellectual manifestations of the period take on an unreal, world-shunning and world-denying character which was absolutely alien to earlier English literature. The most gifted poets of Shelley's generation are not appreciated by the public;[213] they feel homeless and they take refuge abroad. This generation is doomed in England as well as in Germany or Russia; Shelley and Keats are worried to death by their age just as mercilessly as Hoelderlin and Kleist or Pushkin and Lermontov. Ideologically, too, the result is the same everywhere: idealism in Germany, 'l'art pour l'art' in France, aestheticism in England. Everywhere the struggle ends with a turning away from reality and the abandonment of any effort to change the structure of society. In Keats this aestheticism is already accompanied by a profound melancholy, by a mourning for the beauty that is not life, that is, indeed, the negation of life, the negation of a life and reality which are everlastingly separated from the poet, the lover of beauty, and which remain beyond his grasp, like everything ingenuous, natural and purely instinctive. This is a foreshadowing of Flaubert's renunciation, the resignation of the last great romantic, who knew only too well that the price of poetry is life.

Of all the famous romantics, Byron exerts the deepest and most far-reaching influence on his contemporaries. But he is by no means the most original of them, he is merely the most successful in the formulation of the new ideal of personality. Neither the 'mal du siècle' nor the proud and lonely hero marked by destiny, in other words, neither of the two basic elements of his poetry, is his own original intellectual property. The Byronic *Weltschmerz* has its source in Chateaubriand and the French émigré literature, the Byronic hero in Saint-Preux and Werther. The incompatibility of the moral claims of the individual with the conventions of society had already been part of the new concept of man defined by Rousseau and Goethe, and the portrayal of the hero as an eternally homeless wanderer, doomed by his own unsociable nature, is already to be found in Senancour and Constant. But in these authors the estrangement of the hero was still combined with a certain feeling of guilt and manifested itself in a complicated, inconsistent relationship to society; it is only in Byron that it becomes transformed into open, unscrupulous mutiny, into a self-righteous, self-pitying, doleful indictment of man. Byron externalizes and trivializes the spiritual problem of romanticism; he makes a social fashion of the spiritual disintegration of his time. Through him romantic restlessness and aimlessness becomes a plague, the 'disease of the century'; the feeling of isolation develops into a resentful cult of solitude, the loss of faith in the old ideals into anarchic individualism, cultural weariness and ennui becomes a flirtation with life and death. Byron bestows a seductive charm on the curse of his generation and turns his heroes into exhibitionists who openly display their wounds, into masochists who publicly load themselves with guilt and shame, flagellants who torment themselves with self-accusations and pangs of conscience and confess both their evil and their good deeds with the same intellectual pride of ownership.

The Byronic hero, this late successor of the knight-errant, who is just as popular and almost as hardy as the hero of the novels of chivalry, dominates the whole literature of the nineteenth century and still haunts the crime and gangster films of our own time. Certain features of the type are extremely old, that is to say, at least as old as the picaresque novel. For the outlaw, who declares war on society and is a fearless enemy of the great and the mighty but a friend and benefactor of the weak and the poor, is already a familiar figure in this genre; he seems an unpleasantly rough customer from outside, but turns out to be true-hearted and generous in the end, a man whom only society has made into what he is. On the journey from Lazarillo di Tormes to Humphrey Bogart, the Byronic hero merely marks an intermediary station. Long before Byron, the rogue had become the restless wanderer setting out for the starry heights, the eternal stranger among men seeking but not finding his lost happiness on earth, the embittered misanthrope bearing his destiny with the pride of a fallen angel. All these features were already present in Rousseau and Chateaubriand—the only really new characteristics in the picture painted by Byron are the emonic and narcissistic. The romantic hero whom Byron intro-uces into literature is a mysterious man; in his past there is a ecret, an awful sin, a disastrous error or an irreparable omission. Ie is an exile—every one feels it, but no one knows what is idden behind the veil of time, and he does not lift the veil. He oes around in the secret of his past as in a royal robe: lonely, lent and unapproachable. Perdition and destruction go forth om him. He is unsparing towards himself and merciless towards thers. He knows no pardon and asks no forgiveness, either from iod or man. He regrets nothing and, in spite of his disastrous fe, would not wish to have anything different, do anything ifferent from what he has been and from what has happened. Ie is rough and wild but of high descent; his features are hard nd impenetrable but noble and beautiful; a peculiar charm manates from him which no woman can resist and to which all nen react with friendship or enmity. He is the man pursued by lestiny who becomes other men's destiny, the prototype not only f all the irresistible and fateful love heroes of modern litera-ure but, to some extent, of all the female demons from Mérimée's Carmen to the vamps of Hollywood.

If Byron did not discover the 'demonic hero' who, possessed nd deluded, hurls himself and all who come in contact with him o destruction, he turned him into the 'interesting' man par excellence. He bestowed on him the piquant and enticing char-acteristics which have stuck to him ever since, transformed him nto the immoralist and the cynic whose influence is so irre-istible, not despite but precisely because of his cynicism. The dea of the 'fallen angel' possessed an incomparable power of ttraction for the disillusioned world of romanticism struggling for a new faith. There was a general feeling of guilt, of having fallen away from God, but at the same time, a desire to be something like a Lucifer, if one was already damned anyway. Even the seraphic poets Lamartine and Vigny went over to the satanists in the end and became followers of Shelley and Byron, Gautier and Musset, Leopardi and Heine.[214] This satanism originated in the ambivalence of the romantic attitude to life and undoubtedly proceeded from the feeling of religious dissatisfac-tion, but, particularly in Byron, it turned into scorn for all the sacred things venerated by the middle class. The only difference between the aversion of the French bohème to the bourgeoisie and Byron's attitude was that the plebeian anti-conventionalism of Gautier and his friends was an attack from below, whereas Byron's immoralism was directed from above. Every more or less important utterance of Byron's betrays the snobbishness which was combined with his liberal ideas, every record reveals the aristocrat who is no longer firmly rooted in his social position, but still preserves the pose of his class. Above all, the hysterical passion with which, in his later works, he rages against the aristocracy that is excommunicating him shows how deeply he feels tied to this class and how much of its authority and attractiveness it still holds for him, in spite of everything.[215] 'Death is no argument,' Hebbel says somewhere. Byron, at any rate, proved nothing by his heroic death. Despite the poet's revolutionary convictions, it was no appropriate death. Byron committed suicide, 'while the balance of his mind was disturbed', and died 'with vine-leaves in the hair', as Hedda Gabler wanted to die.

The fact that Byron always held to the classicistic view of art and that Pope was his favourite poet is in accordance with his aristocratic inclinations. He did not care for Wordsworth because of his soberly solemn, prosaically unctuous tone and he despised Keats on account of his 'vulgarity'. The supercilious, mocking spirit and playful form of his works, above all the easy-going conversational tone of *Don Juan*, was only an aspect of his classical ideal of art. The connection between the fluency of his style and Wordsworth's 'natural' poetic diction is, nevertheless, unmistakable; both are symptoms of the reaction against the high-flown rhetorical poetry of the seventeenth and eighteenth centuries. The common aim was a greater flexibility of language, and it was precisely as the master of such a fluid, brilliantly skilful, apparently improvised style that Byron made the greatest impression on his contemporaries. Neither the graceful ease of Pushkin nor the elegance of Musset would be conceivable without this new note. *Don Juan* became not only the model of the witty and insolent topical satire but, at the same time, the origin of the whole of modern feuilletonism.[216] Byron's first readers may have belonged to the aristocracy and the upper middle class, but he found his real public in the ranks of that dissatisfied, resentful, romantically inclined middle class whose unsuccessful members regarded themselves as so many unrecognized Napoleons. The Byronic hero was so conceived that every disillusioned youth, every love-sick girl could identify him- or herself with him. The fact that Byron encouraged the reader to indulge in such intimacy with the hero, in doing which he was, of course, merely continuing a tendency already evident in Rousseau and Richardson, was the deepest reason for his success. With the closer personal relationship between the reader and the hero, the reader's interest in the author himself also increased. This tendency too already existed in the age of Rousseau and Richardson, but until the romantic movement the poet's private life had remained, on the whole, unknown to the public. It was only after the self-advertisement contrived by Byron that the poet became the 'favourite' of the public and it was only from then onwards that his readers, and especially his female readers, entered into the peculiar relationship with him which resembled the connection between the psycho-analyst and his patients, on the one hand, and the filmstar and his fans, on the other.

Byron was the first English poet to play a leading rôle in European literature, Walter Scott the second. Through them what Goethe understood by 'world literature' became a full reality. Their school embraced the whole literary world, enjoyed the highest authority, introduced new forms, new values, set intellectual traffic flowing backwards and forwards between the countries of Europe, carrying along with it new talents and often raising them above their masters. One only needs to think of Pushkin and Balzac to realize the extent and the importance of this school. The vogue of Byron was perhaps more feverish and more obtrusive, but the influence of Walter Scott, who has been described as the 'most successful writer in the world',[217] was more solid and more profound. It was his work that inspired the revival of the naturalistic novel, the modern literary genre par excellence, and thereby led to the transformation of the whole modern reading public. The number of readers had been rising steadily in England since the beginning of the eighteenth century. One can distinguish three stages in this process of growth: the phase that begins around 1710 with the new periodicals and culminates in the novels of the middle of the century; the period of the pseudo-historical thriller from 1770 to roughly 1800; and the period of the modern romantic-naturalistic novel that begins with Walter Scott. Each of these periods produced a considerable increase in the reading public. In the first, only a comparatively small section of the middle class was enlisted for secular belles-lettres, people who up till then had never read books at all or at best the products of devotional literature; in the second, this public was enlarged by wide sections of the increasingly wealthy bourgeoisie, mostly women; in the third, elements belonging partly to the higher, partly to the lower strata of the middle class, looking for entertainment as well as instruction in the novel, were added. Walter Scott succeeded in achieving the popularity of the thriller by the more fastidious methods of the great novelists of the eighteenth century. He popularized the portrayal of the feudal past that had hitherto been exclusively the reading of the upper classes,[218] and, at the same time, raised the pseudo-historical shocker to a really literary level.

Smollett was the last great novelist of the eighteenth century. The wonderful development which corresponded in the English novel to the political and social achievements of the middle class comes to a standstill about 1770. The sudden growth of the reading public leads to a sharp decline in the general standard. The demand is much greater than there are good writers to meet it, and as the production of novels is an extremely paying concern, they are turned out in wild and indiscriminate profusion. The needs of the lending libraries dictate the pace and determine the quality of the output. Apart from the thriller, the subjects most in demand are the scandals of the day, famous 'cases', fictitious and semi-fictitious biographies, travel descriptions and secret memoirs, in a word, the usual types of sensational literature. The result is that cultured circles begin to speak of the novel with a disdain that was hitherto unknown.[119] The prestige of the novel is first restored by Scott, above all by the way he handles the genre to accord with the historicism and scientific outlook of the intellectual élite. He not only tries to give an inherently true picture of a historical situation, but also provides his novels with introductions, notes and appendices, to prove the scientific trustworthiness of his descriptions. Though Walter Scott cannot be regarded as the real creator of the historical novel, he is, without any doubt, the founder of the novel dealing with social history, a genre of which no one before him had had an inkling. The French novelists of the eighteenth century, Marivaux, Prévost, Laclos and Chateaubriand, enormously advanced the psychological novel, but still placed their characters in a sociological vacuum or into a social milieu that had no essential share in their development. Even the English novel of the eighteenth century can be described as a 'social novel' only in so far as it lays more emphasis on human relationships; but it pays no particular attention to class differences or to the social causality of character formation. Walter Scott's characters, on the other hand, always bear the marks of their social origin.[220] And as, on the whole, Scott describes the social background of his stories accurately, he becomes, in spite of his conservative outlook in politics, the pioneer of liberalism and progress.[221] However critical he was of the Revolution politically, his sociological method would be unthinkable without this change in affairs. For it was the Revolution that first developed a feeling for class differences and made it imperative for the honest artist to describe reality in accordance with them. At any rate, as a writer, Scott, the conservative, is more deeply connected with the Revolution than Byron, the radical. On the other hand, one must not over-estimate this 'triumph of realism', as Engels called the trick of art which often makes conservative minds useful instruments of progress. The appreciation of and enthusiasm for the 'folk' is usually no more than a non-committal gesture with Scott and his description of the lower classes is, generally speaking, conventional and schematic. But Scott's conservatism is, at least, less aggressive than the anti-revolutionism of Wordsworth and Coleridge, which is the expression of a disillusionment and of an all too sudden change of mind. It is true that Scott is as enthusiastically devoted to medieval chivalry as the reactionary romantics in general and that he regrets its decline, but at the same time he also criticizes, as do Pushkin and Heine, for example, the whole effusiveness of the romantics. He recognizes, with the same clear-sightedness with which Pushkin establishes the spuriousness of Onegin's character, 'the brilliant but useless character of a knight of romance' in Richard Coeur de Lion,[222] and by no means conceals his apprehensions in this connection.

Delacroix, the first great and, at the same time, greatest representative of romantic painting, is also one of the enemies and conquerors of romanticism. He already represents the nineteenth century, whilst romanticism is still an essentially eighteenth-century movement, not only because it is the continuation of pre-romanticism, but also because, although full of contradictions, it is by no means so disintegrated as the nineteenth century. The eighteenth century is dogmatic—there is a dogmatic streak even in its romanticism—the nineteenth century is sceptical and agnostic. The men of the eighteenth century strive to extract a clearly definable doctrine and world-view from everything, even from their emotionalism and irrationalism; they are systematists, philosophers, reformers, they make up their minds either for or against a cause, often they alternate between support and opposition, but they know where they stand, they follow principles and are guided by a plan for the improvement of life and the world. The intellectual representatives of the nineteenth century, on the other hand, have lost their faith in systems and programmes and see the meaning and purpose of art in a passive surrender to life, in seizing hold of the rhythm of life itself, in preserving the atmosphere and mood of it; their faith consists in an irrational, instinctive affirmation of life, their morality in a resigned acceptance of reality. They want neither to regiment nor to overcome reality; they want to experience it and to reproduce their experience as directly, as faithfully and perfectly as possible. They have the indomitable feeling that the life of the immediate present, the contemporary and the surrounding world, time and place, experience and impressions are slipping away from them daily and hourly and being lost for ever. For them, art becomes a pursuit of the 'temps perdu', of life which is for ever evaporating and beyond our grasp. The periods of absolute naturalism are not the centuries in which men imagine they are in firm and secure possession of reality, but those in which they are afraid of losing it; hence the nineteenth is the classical century of naturalism.

Delacroix and Constable stand on the threshold of the new era. They are partly still romantic expressionists struggling to express ideas, but partly they are already impressionists striving to hold fast the fleeting object and no longer believing in any perfect equivalent of reality. Of the two, Delacroix is the more romantic artist; if one compares him with Constable, what connects classicism and romanticism in a historical unity, and distinguishes them from naturalism, becomes quite clearly apparent. As opposed to naturalism, the two older stylistic tendencies have in common, above all, the fact that they confer more than life-size dimensions on life and man, give them a tragi-heroic format and a passionately emotional expression, which is still present in Delacroix, but completely absent from Constable and nineteenth-century naturalism. In Delacroix this conception of art is also expressed in the fact that man still stands in the centre of his world, whilst in Constable he becomes a thing amongst other things, and is absorbed by his material environment. Hence Constable is, if not the greatest, at any rate, the most progressive artist of his time. With the displacement of man from the centre of art and the occupation of his place by the material world, painting not only acquires a new content, but is reduced more and more to the solution of technical and purely formal problems. The subject-matter of pictures gradually loses all aesthetic value, all artistic interest, and art becomes formalistic to a hitherto unknown extent. What is painted becomes quite unimportant; the only question is how it is painted. Not even the most flippant mannerism had ever shown such indifference to the motif. Never before had a head of cabbage and the head of a Madonna been considered of equal value as artistic subjects. It is only now, when the pictorial quality forms the real content of painting, that the old academic distinctions between the different subjects and genres come to an end. Even in Delacroix, in spite of his deep romantic affection for poetry, literary motifs constitute merely the occasion for, not the content of his pictures. He rejects the literary as the aim of painting and strives to express, instead of literary ideas, something of his own, something irrational and similar to music.[223]

The transfer of the pictorial interest from man to nature has its source, apart from the shaken self-confidence of the new generation, its bewilderment and homelessness, above all in the victory of the dehumanized philosophy of natural science. Constable overcomes classical-romantic humanism more easily than Delacroix and becomes the first modern landscape painter, whilst Delacroix remains essentially a 'narrative painter'. But by their scientific approach to the problems of painting, and the pre-eminence which they give to optics over vision, they both embody the spirit of the new century in equal measure. The development of the 'painterly' style, which began in France with Watteau and was interrupted by the classicism of the eighteenth century, is taken up again and continued by Delacroix. Rubens revolutionizes French painting for the second time; for the second time an irrational, anti-classicistic sensualism emanates from him. Delacroix's dictum, that a picture should be above all a feast for the eyes,[224] was also the message of Watteau and remains the gospel of painting until the conclusion of impressionism. The vibrant dynamics of the composition, the movement of line and form, the baroque convulsion of the bodies and the dissolution of the local colours into their components, all this is merely the instrument of a sensualism which now makes it possible to combine romanticism with naturalism and to oppose both of them to classicism.

Delacroix was still to some extent subject to the romantic 'mal du siècle'. He suffered from serious fits of depression, knew the feeling of aimlessness and emptiness, fought against an indefinable and incurable ennui. He was the victim of melancholia, discontent and the feeling of eternal imperfection. The mood in which Géricault found himself in London and of which he wrote home: 'Whatever I do, I wish that I had done something different,' tormented Delacroix throughout his life.[225] He was still so deeply rooted in the romantic outlook on life that not even its most brutal temptations were foreign to him. It is sufficient to think of a work like the 'Sardanapal' (1829), to realize the place which the theatrical demonism and molochism of the romantics occupied in his thought. But he was always fighting against romanticism as an attitude to life, acknowledged its representatives only with strong reservations, and accepted it as an artistic trend above all on account of the greater range of its subject-matter. Just as Delacroix undertook a voyage to the East, instead of the traditional journey to Rome, he also used, in place of the classics of antiquity, the poets of earlier and later romanticism, Dante and Shakespeare, Byron and Goethe, as his sources. This thematic interest was the only common element between him and artists like Ary Scheffer and Louis Boulanger, Decamps and Delaroche. He hated moonshine romanticism and the incorrigible dreamers, like Chateaubriand, Lamartine and Schubert, to repeat his own rather wilful assortment of names.[226] He himself had not the slightest desire to be called a romantic, and protested against being regarded as the master of the romantic school. Incidentally, he felt no inclination at all to train artists and never opened a generally available studio; at most, he took on a few assistants, but no pupils.[227] There was no longer anything in French painting corresponding to the David school; the master's place remained unoccupied. Artistic aims had become much too personal, the criteria of artistic quality much too differentiated, for schools in the old sense to arise.[228]

Delacroix's dislike of bohemianism is in line with his aversion to romanticism. Rubens is not only his artistic but also his human model and he is in fact, as has been said, the first and perhaps the only painter since Rubens and the great artistic personalities of the Renaissance to combine the highest intellectual culture with the mode of life of a grand seigneur.[229] His strictly upper-bourgeois and gentlemanly inclinations make all exhibitionism and ostentation odious to him. He only preserves one feature from the intellectual inheritance of bohemianism: contempt for the public. At twenty-six, he is already a famous painter, but a generation later he still writes: 'Il y a trente ans que je suis livré aux bêtes.' He had his friends, his admirers, his patrons, his state commissions, but he was never understood, never loved by the public. There was no trace of warmth in the recognition that was accorded him. Delacroix is a solitary and an isolated individual, and in a much stricter sense than the romantics in general. There is only one contemporary whom he esteems and loves unreservedly: Chopin. Neither Hugo and Musset, nor Stendhal and Mérimée are particularly near to him; he does not take George Sand very seriously, the negligent Gautier repels him and Balzac makes him nervous.[230] The extraordinary significance that music holds for Delacroix, and which contributes most to his admiration for Chopin, is a symptom of the new hierarchy of the arts and the prominent position which music occupies in it. It is the romantic art par excellence and Chopin the most romantic of all the romantics. In his relation to Chopin, Delacroix's intimate connection with romanticism is brought most clearly to light. His judgement of the other masters of music reveals, however, the inconsistency of his relationship to romanticism. He always speaks of Mozart with the greatest admiration, but Beethoven often appears to him too despotic, too romantic. Delacroix has a classicistic taste in music;[231] Chopin's stereotyped sentimentalism does not disturb him, but Beethoven's 'despotism', which should, one would think, appeal much more to him as an artist, he finds bewildering.

Romanticism in music signifies the antithesis not merely to classicism but also to pre-romanticism, in so far as they represent the principle of formal unity and consistently developed musical ideas. The concentrated structure of musical form, based on dramatic climaxes, gradually breaks up in romanticism and gives way again to the cumulative composition of the older music. Sonata form falls to pieces and is replaced more and more often by other, less severe and less schematically moulded forms—by small-scale lyrical and descriptive genres, such as the Fantasy and the Rhapsody, the Arabesque and the Étude, the Intermezzo and the Impromptu, the Improvisation and the Variation. Even extensive works are often made up of such miniature forms, which no longer constitute, from the structural point of view, the acts of a drama, but the scenes of a revue. A classical sonata or symphony was the world in parvo: a microcosm. A succession of musical pictures, such as Schumann's *Carnaval* or Liszt's *Années de Pèlerinage*, is like a painter's sketch-book; it may contain magnificent lyrical-impressionistic details, but it abandons the attempt to create a total impression and an organic unity from the very beginning. Even the fondness for the symphonic poem, which displaces the symphony in Berlioz, Liszt, Rimsky-Korsakov, Smetana and others, shows, above all, that the composers are unable or hesitate to represent the world as an organic whole. This change of form is accompanied by the literary inclinations of the composers and their bias towards programme music. The intermingling of forms also makes itself felt in music and is expressed most conspicuously in the fact that the romantic composers are often very gifted and important writers. In the painting and poetry of the period the disintegration of form does not proceed anything like so quickly, nor is it so far-reaching as in music. The explanation of the difference is partly that the cyclical 'medieval' structure had long since been overcome in the other arts, whereas it remained predominant in music until the middle of the eighteenth century, and only began to yield to formal unity after the death of Bach. In music it was therefore much easier to revert to it than, for example, in painting where it was completely out of date. The romantics' historical interest in old music and the revival of Bach's prestige had, however, only a subordinate part in the dissolution of strict sonata form, the real reason is to be sought in a change of taste which was in essentials sociologically conditioned.

Romanticism is the culmination of the development which began in the second half of the eighteenth century: music becomes the exclusive property of the middle class. Not only the orchestras move from the banqueting-halls of the castles and palaces into the concert-halls filled by the middle class, but chamber music also finds a home, not in aristocratic salons but in bourgeois drawing-rooms. The broader masses, who take a growing interest in musical entertainments, demand, however, a lighter, more ingratiating, less complicated music. This demand in itself promotes the creation of shorter, more entertaining, more varied forms, but leads, at the same time, to a division of musical output into serious and light music. Hitherto compositions serving purposes of entertainment had not been different qualitatively from the rest; there had been, of course, a great difference in quality between individual works, but this difference in no way corresponded to the difference in their respective purposes. As we know, the generation immediately following that of Bach and Handel had already made a distinction between composing for one's own amusement and producing for the public; but now distinctions are made between the different categories of the public itself. In the oeuvre of Schubert and Schumann a corresponding division is already feasible;[232] in Chopin and Liszt regard for the musically less pretentious section of the public influences every single work; and in Berlioz and Wagner this regard often leads to definite flirtation. When Schubert declares that he knows no 'cheerful' music, it sounds as if he were trying to defend himself against the charge of frivolity from the very outset; for since the advent of romanticism all cheerfulness seems to have a superficial, frivolous character. The combination of carefree light-heartedness with the most profound seriousness, of playful exuberance with the highest, purest ethos transfiguring the whole of life, which was still present in Mozart, breaks up; from now on everything serious and sublime takes on a gloomy and careworn look. It is sufficient to compare the serene, clear and calm humanity of Mozart, its freedom from all mysticism and turbid emotionalism, with the violence of romantic music, to realize what had been lost with the eighteenth century.

With the concessions to the public there is combined, at the same time, a marked recklessness and arbitrariness of expression. Compositions become markedly difficult: they are no longer intended to be performed by middle-class amateurs. Even Beethoven's later piano and chamber music works were only able to be executed by professional artists, and appreciated by a musically highly educated public. With the romantics, first of all, the technical difficulties of performance increased. Weber, Schumann, Chopin, Liszt, compose for the virtuosos of the concert-halls. The brilliant execution which they presuppose in the performer has a double function: it restricts the practice of music to the expert, and it deludes the layman. In the case of the virtuoso-composers, the prototype of whom is Paganini, the dazzling style is intended above all to flabbergast the listener, but with the real masters the technical difficulty is merely the expression of an inner difficulty and complication. Both tendencies, the enlargement of the distance between the amateur and the virtuoso as well as the deepening of the gulf between lighter and more difficult music, lead to the dissolution of the classical genres. The virtuoso mode of writing inevitably atomizes the big, massive forms; the bravura piece is relatively short, sparkling, pointed. But the intrinsically difficult, individually differentiated style, based on the sublimation of thoughts and feelings, also promotes the dissolution of universally valid, stereotyped and long-winded forms.

The inherent propensity with which music comes to meet this dissolution of forms, the irrationality of its content and the independence of its means of expression, explain the pre-eminence which it now enjoys among the arts. For classicism poetry was the leading art; early romanticism was partly based on painting; later romanticism is, however, entirely dependent on music. For Gautier painting was the perfect art, for Delacroix music is already the source of the deepest artistic experience.[233] This development reaches its climax in Schopenhauer's philosophy and Wagner's message. Romanticism celebrates its greatest triumphs in music. The fame of Weber, Meyerbeer, Chopin, Liszt and Wagner fills the whole of Europe, and surpasses the success of the most popular poets. Music remained romantic until the end of the nineteenth century, more completely, more unreservedly romantic than the other arts. And the fact that this century experienced the nature of art above all in music shows most conspicuously how deeply involved it was in romanticism. Thomas Mann's confession that it was the music of Wagner that first revealed to him the meaning of art is supremely symptomatic. The romantic intoxication of the senses and the *salto mortale* of reason signified the quintessence of art even at the turn of the century. The nineteenth century's struggle against the spirit of romanticism remained undecided; the decision was first achieved in the century to come.

CHAPTER VII

NATURALISM AND IMPRESSIONISM

1. THE GENERATION OF 1830

If the purpose of historical research is the understanding of the present—and what else could it be?—then this enquiry is approaching its goal. What we are now to be concerned with is modern capitalism, modern bourgeois society, modern naturalistic art and literature, in short, our own world. Everywhere we are faced with new situations, new ways of life and feel as if we were cut off from the past. But the incision is probably nowhere so deep as in literature, where the frontier between the older works which are merely of historical interest to us and those that arise from now onwards and are still more or less topical today represents the most remarkable breach in the whole history of art. It is only the works produced on our side of the divide that constitute the living, modern literature directly concerned with our own contemporary problems. We are separated from all the older works by an unbridgeable gulf—to understand them, a special approach and a special effort on our part are necessary and their interpretation is always involved in the danger of misunderstanding and falsification. We read the works of the older literature differently from those of our own age; we enjoy them purely aesthetically, that is, indirectly, disinterestedly, perfectly aware of their fictitiousness and of our self-deception. This presupposes points of view and abilities which the average reader in no way has at his command; but even the historically and aesthetically interested reader feels there is an irreconcilable difference between works which have no immediate relationship to his own age, his own feelings and aims in life and such as have grown out of these very feelings and seek an answer to the question: How can one, how should one, live in this present age?

The nineteenth century, or what we usually understand by that term, begins around 1830. It is only during the July monarchy that the foundations and outlines of this century are developed, that is to say, the social order in which we ourselves are rooted, the economic system, the antagonisms and contradictions of which still continue, and the literature in whose forms we on the whole still express ourselves today. The novels of Stendhal and Balzac are the first books concerned with our own life, our own vital problems, with moral difficulties and conflicts unknown to earlier generations. Julien Sorel and Mathilde de la Mole, Lucien de Rubempré and Rastignac are the first modern characters in Western literature—our first intellectual contemporaries. In them we meet for the first time the sensibility which throbs in our own nerves, in the delineation of their characters we find the first outlines of the psychological differentiation which for us is part of the nature of contemporary man. From Stendhal to Proust, from the generation of 1830 to that of 1910, we are witnesses of a homogeneous, organic intellectual development. Three generations struggle with the same problems; for seventy to eighty years the course of history remains unchanged.

All the characteristic features of the century are already recognizable around 1830. The bourgeoisie is in full possession and awareness of its power. The aristocracy has vanished from the scene of historical events and leads a purely private existence. The victory of the middle class is undoubted and undisputed. It is true that the victors form a thoroughly conservative and illiberal capitalist class adopting the administrative forms and methods of the old aristocracy often without alteration, but a class that is absolutely unaristocratic and untraditionalistic in its way of life and thought. Romanticism was, no doubt, already an essentially bourgeois movement, which would have been inconceivable without the emancipation of the middle classes, but the romantics often behaved rather aristocratically and flirted with the idea of appealing to the nobility as their public. After 1830 these whims come to an end entirely and it becomes obvious that there is in fact no massive public apart from the middle class.

But as soon as the emancipation of the middle class is accomplished, the struggle of the working class for its rights already begins. And that is the second of the decisively important movements which proceed from the July revolution and monarchy. Hitherto the class struggles of the proletariat had been fused with those of the middle class, and it had been mainly the political aspirations of the middle classes for which the working class had fought. The developments after 1830 first open its eyes and supply it with the proof that, in fighting for its rights, it can rely on no other class. Simultaneously with the awakening class-consciousness of the proletariat, socialist theory acquires its first more or less concrete form and there also arises the programme of an artistic activist movement which for radicalism and consistency surpasses all previous movements of a similar nature. 'L'art pour l'art' goes through its first crisis and has from now on to fight not only against the idealism of the classicists but also against the utilitarianism of both 'social' and 'bourgeois' art.

The economic rationalism which goes hand in hand with advancing industrialization and the total victory of capitalism, the progress of the historical and exact sciences and the general philosophical scientism connected with it, the repeated experience of an unsuccessful revolution and the political realism which results—all this paves the way for the great fight against romanticism which pervades the history of the next hundred years. The preparation and institution of this fight is a further contribution of the 1830 generation to the foundations of the nineteenth century. Stendhal's wavering between 'logique' and 'espagnolisme', Balzac's ambivalent relationship to the middle class, the dialectic of rationalism and irrationalism in both of them, shows the fight already in full swing; Flaubert's generation deepens the conflict, but finds it already under way. The artistic outlook of the July monarchy is partly bourgeois, partly socialistic, but unromantic on the whole. The public is, as Balzac remarks in the preface to *Peau de Chagrin* (1831), 'fed up with Spain, the Orient and the history of France à la Walter Scott', and, as Lamartine laments, the age of poetry, that is, of 'romantic' poetry, is past.[1] The naturalistic novel, the most original creation of this period and the most important art form of the nineteenth century, gives expression, despite the romanticism of its founders, despite Stendhal's Rousseauism and Balzac's melodramatics, to the unromantic spirit of the new generation. Both economic rationalism and political thinking in terms of the class struggle refer the novel to the study of social reality and socio-psychological mechanisms. The subject and the point of view are both in full accord with the aspirations of the middle class and the result, the naturalistic novel, serves this rising class as a kind of textbook in its endeavour to secure complete control of society. The writers of the period turn it into an instrument for sounding man and dealing with the world and thereby conform to the taste and needs of a public that they hate and despise. They strive to satisfy their middle-class readers, no matter whether they are Saint-Simonites and Fourierites or not, and believe in social art or 'l'art pour l'art'—for there is no proletarian reading public, and even if there were, its existence would only embarrass them.

Until the eighteenth century, authors had been nothing but the mouthpiece of their public;[2] they looked after their readers' minds, just as servants and officials managed their material goods. They accepted and confirmed the generally recognized moral principles and criteria of taste; they did not invent them and they did not alter them. They produced their works for a clearly defined and clearly limited public and made no attempt whatsoever to gain new readers. Thus there was no tension of any kind between the real and an ideal public.[3] The writer knew neither the tormenting problem of having to choose between different subjective possibilities, nor the moral problem of having to choose between different strata of society. It is not until the eighteenth century that the public divides into two different camps and art into two rival tendencies. From now on every artist stands between two opposing orders, between the world of the conservative aristocracy and that of the progressive bourgeoisie, between a group that holds fast to the old, traditional, allegedly absolute values and one based on the view that even, and above all, these values are historically conditioned and that there are other, more up-to-date values, more in accordance with the general good. The middle class renounces its aristocratic models and the aristocracy itself begins to doubt the validity of its own standards; partly it goes over to the bourgeois camp, in order to promote a literature which is hostile and pernicious to its own interests. For writers an absolutely new situation develops; those who continue in the service of the conservative classes, the Churches, the court and the court nobility, betray their own social compeers; those, on the other hand, who represent the world-view of the rising bourgeoisie fulfill a function never before discharged by representative writers, apart from isolated individuals—they fight for an oppressed class, or at least for a class that is not yet in possession of power.[4] They no longer find the ideology of this public ready and waiting for them, they have themselves to contribute to its conceptual system, its philosophical categories and standards of value. They are, therefore, no longer merely the mouthpiece of their readers, they are at the same time their advocates and teachers, and even regain something of that long-lost priestly dignity which neither the poets of antiquity nor of the Renaissance had enjoyed, least of all the clerics of the Middle Ages, whose readers were themselves merely clerics and who came into no contact at all with the lay public. During the Restoration and the July monarchy the littérateurs lose the unique position they had occupied in the eighteenth century; they are no longer either the protectors or the teachers of their readers, they are, on the contrary, their unwilling, constantly revolting, but none the less very useful, servants. Once again they proclaim a more or less ready-made, prescribed ideology, namely, the liberalism of the victorious middle class, derived from the enlightenment, but falsifying it in many ways. They are compelled to base themselves on this philosophy, if they want to find readers and sell their books. The peculiar thing is, however, that they do it without identifying themselves with their public. Even the authors of the enlightenment counted only a part of the literary public among their supporters; they, too, were surrounded by a hostile and dangerous world, but at least they were in the same camp as their own readers. Even the romantics still felt themselves related to one or other stratum of society, in spite of their homelessness, and were always able to say which group, which class they were supporting. But to what section of the public does Stendhal feel himself related? At best to the 'happy few'—the outsiders, the outlaws, the defeated. And Balzac? Does he identify himself with the nobility, with the bourgeoisie, or the proletariat?—with the class for which he has certain sympathies, but which he abandons without turning an eyelash, or with the class whose inexhaustible energy he recognizes, but for which he feels a loathing, or with the masses by whom he is as frightened as he is by fire? The writers who are not merely the 'maîtres de plaisir' of the bourgeoisie have no real public—Balzac, the successful, no more than Stendhal, the failure.

Nothing reflects the tense, discordant relationship between the literarily productive and the receptive sections of the 1830 generation more sharply than the new type of novel hero appearing in Stendhal and Balzac. The disillusionment and *Weltschmerz* of the heroes of Rousseau, Chateaubriand and Byron, their remoteness from the world and their loneliness, are transformed into a forgoing of the realization of their ideals, into a contempt for society and often into a desperate cynicism concerning current norms and conventions. The romantic novel of disillusionment becomes the novel of hopelessness and resignation. All the tragic and heroic characteristics, the self-assertiveness, the belief in the perfectibility of one's own nature, yield to a readiness to compromise, to the readiness to live aimlessly and die obscurely. The romantic novel of disillusionment still contained something of the idea of the tragedy which allows the hero fighting against trivial reality to be victorious even in defeat; in the nineteenth-century novel, on the other hand, he appears inwardly defeated even, and often precisely, when he has reached his actual goal. Nothing was further from the minds of the young Goethe, Chateaubriand or Benjamin Constant than to let their heroes doubt the *raison d'être* of their own personalities and aims in life; the modern novel first creates the bad conscience of the hero in conflict with the bourgeois social order, and demands that he accept the customs and conventions of society at least as the rules of the game. Werther is still the exceptional personality to whom the poet grants the right to revolt against the unappreciative and prosaic world from the very outset; Wilhelm Meister, on the other hand, ends his years of apprenticeship with the realization that one has to adapt oneself to the world as one finds it. External reality is more bereft of meaning and more soulless, because it has become more mechanical and self-sufficient; society, which had hitherto been the individual's natural milieu and only field of activity, has lost all significance, all value from the point of view of his higher aims, but the requirement that he should comply with society, live in and for it, has become more imperative.

The politicization of society, which began with the French Revolution, reaches its climax under the July monarchy. The quarrel between liberalism and reaction, the struggle for the reconciliation of the achievements of the Revolution with the interests of the privileged classes, continues and embraces every sphere of public life. Finance capital triumphs over landed property, and both the feudal aristocracy and the Church cease to play a leading rôle in political life; the progressive elements are opposed by the bankers and industrialists. The old political and social antagonism has not become any less, but the positions have shifted. The deepest antitheses are now between industrial capitalism, on the one side, and the wage-earning workers with the petty bourgeoisie, on the other. The aims of the class struggle are clarified and the methods of warfare intensified; everything seems to point to the imminence of a new revolution. In spite of constant setbacks, liberalism gains ground and the way for Western European democracy is gradually prepared. The electoral law is altered and the number of electors is increased from some 100,000 to two and a half times its previous size. The rudiments of the parliamentary system and the foundations of the coalition of the working class come into being. In parliament, in spite of the electoral reforms, the possessing classes continue to be represented exclusively, and the liberalism that comes to power represents merely a liberalism within the bounds of the upper middle class. The July monarchy is, in brief, a period of eclecticism, of compromise, of the middle way—if not precisely the period of the 'right' middle way, as Louis-Philippe calls it and as it is now called by everyone, sometimes approvingly, sometimes ironically. It is outwardly a period of moderation and tolerance, but inwardly one marked by the most severe struggle for existence, an epoch of moderate political progress and economic conservatism after the English pattern. The Guizots and the Thiers extol the idea of the constitutional monarchy, desire that the king should merely reign, not rule, but they are the instrument of a parliamentary oligarchy, of a small government party which keeps the broader strata of the middle class spellbound with the magic formula of 'Enrichissez-vous!'. The July monarchy is a period of glorious prosperity, a flowering time for all industrial and commercial undertakings. Money dominates the whole of public and private life; everything bows before it, everything serves it, everything is prostituted—exactly, or almost, as Balzac described it. It is true that the rule of capital does not in any sense begin now, but hitherto the possession of money had been only one of the means by which a man had been able to gain a position for himself in France, and neither the most refined nor the most effective method either. Now, on the other hand, all rights, all power, all ability, are suddenly expressed in terms of money. In order to be understood, everything has to be reduced to this common denominator. From this point of view, the whole previous history of capitalism seems no more than a mere prelude. Not only politics and the higher strata of society, not only parliament and the bureaucracy, are plutocratic in character, France is dominated not merely by the Rothschilds and the other 'juste-millionaires', as Heine called them, but the king himself is a wily and unscrupulous speculator. For eighteen years the government represents, as Tocqueville says, a kind of 'trading company'; the king, the parliament and the administration share the tasty morsels amongst themselves, exchange information and tips, make each other a present of transactions and concessions, speculate in shares and rents, bills of exchange and mortgages. The capitalist monopolizes the leadership of society and gains a position for himself that he had never had before. Hitherto, in order to play this part, the man of property had to have some kind of ideological halo; the rich man had to come forward as a patron of the Church, the Crown or the arts and sciences, but now he enjoys the highest honours simply because he is rich. 'From now on the bankers will rule!'—Laffitte prophesies after Louis-

Philippe has been elected king. And: 'No society can continue without an aristocracy'—a deputy says in parliament in 1836.—'Do you want to know who the aristocrats of the July monarchy are? The captains of industry; they are the basis of the new dynasty.'[5] But the bourgeoisie is still fighting for its position, for the social prestige that the nobility concedes to it reluctantly and hesitantly. It is still a 'rising class' and still has the dashing offensive spirit and unbroken self-consciousness of the disfranchised. But it is so certain of victory that its self-consciousness already begins to turn into self-satisfaction and self-righteousness. Its good conscience is based partly on self-deception and develops into a state of mind in which the exposures of socialism will later break its self-confidence. It becomes more and more intolerant and illiberal, and takes for the foundations of its philosophy its worst inadequacies, its narrow-mindedness, its shallow rationalism and its idealistically disguised striving for profit. It suspects all real idealism and laughs at all unworldliness; it struggles against all intransigence and radicalism, persecutes and suppresses all opposition to the spirit of the 'juste-milieu' and the prudent concealment of antagonisms. It trains its satellites to be hypocrites, and shelters all the more desperately behind the fictions of its ideology the more dangerous the attacks of socialism become.

The basic tendencies of modern capitalism, which had been becoming increasingly apparent ever since the Renaissance, now emerge in all their blatant and uncompromising clarity, unmitigated by any tradition. The most conspicuous of these tendencies is the attempt to withdraw the whole mechanism of an economic undertaking from all direct human influence, that is, from all consideration for personal circumstances. The undertaking becomes an autonomous organism, pursuing its own interests and aims, conforming to the laws of its own internal logic, a tyrant turning everyone who comes into contact with it into its slave.[6] The absolute devotion to business, the self-sacrifice of the entrepreneur in the interest of the competitive system, the prosperity and extension of the firm, his abstract, ruthless, self-centred striving for success, acquires an alarming monomaniacal character.[7] The system becomes independent of those who sustain it, and transformed into a mechanism whose progress no human power is able to restrain. This automobility of the apparatus is the uncanny thing about modern capitalism; it gives it that demonism which Balzac described so terrifyingly. To the extent that the means and presuppositions of economic success are withdrawn from the individual's sphere of influence, the feeling of insecurity, the feeling of being at the mercy of a despotic monster, becomes ever stronger. And as economic interests become intertwined and interwoven, the struggle becomes more and more wild, more and more desperate, the monster more and more multiform, and ultimate ruin more and more inescapable. In the end, people find themselves surrounded on every side by rivals and enemies, everyone fights against everyone else, everyone stands in the front line of an unremitting, universal, really 'total' war.[8] All property, all position, all influence, have to be newly acquired, conquered and enforced from day to day; everything seems provisional, unreliable and unstable.[9] Hence the general scepticism and pessimism, hence the feeling of choking anxiety which fills the world of Balzac and remains the predominant characteristic of the literature of the capitalist era.

Louis-Philippe and his financial aristocracy are faced by a powerful and extensive opposition which embraces, in addition to the aristocratic and clerical legitimists, all the elements who feel that the hopes they placed in the July revolution have been disappointed, that is, it embraces, on the one hand, the patriotic and Bonapartist but fundamentally liberal-minded petty bourgeoisie, on the other hand, the left wing consisting of the bourgeois republicans and the socialists, with the progressive intelligentsia in one camp or the other. The so-called 'liberal' government party is therefore surrounded by a whole circle of opposition and revolutionary groups, whilst Louis-Philippe, the 'citizen king', is opposed by the overwhelming majority of his people.[10] The radical tendencies are expressed and discharge themselves in the formation of democratic associations, parties and sects, in strikes, hunger revolts and attempted murders, in brief, in what has been rightly described as a state of permanent revolution. These disturbances are by no means simply the continuation of the earlier revolutions and revolts. Even the Lyons rising of 1831 is different from the older revolutionary movements by reason of its non-political character;[11] it is the prelude and beginning of that mass movement whose symbol, the red flag, first appears in the year 1832. The change begins with a discovery typical of socialistic thinking. 'The bourgeois economic doctrine of the identity of the interests of capital and labour, of universal harmony and universal national prosperity as the results of free competition, is', as Engels remarks, 'confounded more and more conclusively by the facts.'[12] Socialism as a theory develops from the recognition of the class character of this economy. Of course, we already come across socialistic ideas and tendencies in the great French Revolution, especially in the Convention and the Babeuf conspiracy, but there can be no question of a proletarian mass movement and a corresponding class-consciousness until after the victory of the Industrial Revolution and the introduction of the large-scale, completely mechanized factory. The human contacts in these factories are the origin of working-class solidarity and of the whole modern labour movement.[13] The modern proletariat, as the integration of the hitherto dispersed small labour-units, is first created by the nineteenth century and industrialism; nothing similar had been known to former ages.[14] The socialistic theory, founded by isolated philanthropists and Utopians, which arose from the economic sufferings of the people, from the desire to relieve this suffering and find a way to distribute wealth more equitably, only becomes an effective weapon with the consolidation of the urban factory and the social struggles which take place from 1830 onwards; now it first begins to tread the path described by Engels as its development 'from Utopia to science'. The social criticism of Saint-Simon and Fourier had already sprung from the experience of industrialism and the recognition of its devastating effects, but the realism of these thinkers was still combined with a good deal of romanticism and the right questions with fantastic attempts to achieve a solution. The religious tendencies appearing after the Restoration, indeed, to some extent as soon as the Concordat, and which become deeper after 1830, determined the character of their whole reforming and missionary activity. From Saint-Simon to Auguste Comte a romantic goal hovers before the mind of the socialists and social philosophers: they would all like to put a new order, a new organization of society in the place of the medieval Church as an organic, synthetic form, and set up the 'new Christianity' with the aid of the poets and artists.

Along with the advancing politicization of life, between 1830 and 1848, the political tendency in literature is also intensified. During this period there are hardly any works without some political interest; even the quietism of 'l'art pour l'art' has, of course, a political tinge. The new trend is expressed most strikingly in the fact that politics and literature are now combined by the same men, and that it is usually the members of the same social stratum who practise politics or literature as a profession. Literary abilities are regarded as the obvious precondition of a political career and political influence is often the reward for literary services. The literary politicians and the political littérateurs of the July monarchy—men like Guizot, Thiers, Michelet, Thierry, Villemain, Cousin, Jouffroy, Nisard—are the last descendants of the 'philosophes' of the eighteenth century; the writers of the next generation have no political ambitions and its politicians no longer have any intellectual influence. Until the February revolution, however, political life absorbs all the intellectual forces of the time. The gifted young people who are barred from a political career owing to lack of means devote themselves to journalism; that is now the usual beginning and the typical form of a literary career. As a journalist, one not only builds oneself a bridge to the world of politics and the world of real literature, one often secures a considerable influence, income and reputation through journalism itself. Bertin, the chief editor of the *Journal des Débats*, is, with his complacency and self-confidence, the very embodiment of the July monarchy. He is the incarnation of the bourgeois littérateur and the literary bourgeois. But literary activity not only becomes a business for men like Bertin, but, as Sainte-Beuve remarks, it develops into an 'industry' for all concerned in its production.[15] It becomes simply a means of acquiring advertisements and subscribers. The connection of literature with the daily press has, according to one contemporary, just as revolutionary an effect as the use of steam for industrial purposes; the whole output of literature changes its character.[16] Even if this analogy is exaggerated and the industrialization of literature is only a symptom of a universal intellectual development, that is, only expresses a general trend to which the artistic production of the period inclines in any case, nevertheless, it must be described as an historical event, when Émile de Girardin, an unimportant writer but an imaginative business man, adopts the idea of the previously completely unknown Dutacq and founds the newspaper *La Presse* in 1836. The epoch-making innovation is that he fixes the subscription at forty francs per annum, that is, at half the usual rate, and plans to cover the loss with the income from announcements and advertisements. In the same year, Dutacq founds the *Siècle* with the same programme, and the rest of the Paris newspapers follow his example. The number of subscribers grows and amounts to 200,000 in 1846, compared with 70,000 ten years before. The new undertakings force the editors to compete with each other in improving the contents of their papers. They have to offer their readers as tasty and varied fare as possible, in order to increase the attraction of their papers, above all with an eye on the income from advertisements. From now on everyone is to find in his paper articles in accordance with his taste and interests; it is to become everyman's private library and encyclopaedia.

Apart from specialist contributions, the newspapers carry articles of general interest, particularly travel descriptions, scandal stories and law reports. But serial novels are their greatest attraction. Everyone reads them, the aristocracy and the bourgeoisie, polite society and the intelligentsia, young and old, men and women, masters and servants. The *Presse* opens the series of its 'feuilletons' with the publication of works of Balzac, who supplies it with a new novel every year from 1837 to 1847, and of Eugène Sue, who lets it have most of his works. The *Siècle* plays off Alexandre Dumas against the authors of the *Presse*, the Dumas whose *Three Musketeers* is enormously successful and brings considerable profit to the paper. The *Journal des Débats* owes its popularity above all to the *Mystères de Paris* by Eugène Sue, who is, after the publication of this novel, one of the best-paid authors and one of those most in demand. The *Constitutionnel* offers him 100,000 francs for his *Juif Errant*, and henceforth this amount is regarded as his standard fee. But Alexandre

Dumas still has the biggest income, earning roughly 200,000 francs yearly and receiving an annual sum of 63,000 francs for 220,000 lines from the *Presse* and the *Constitutionnel.* To satisfy the enormous demand, popular authors now join forces with the literary hacks who give them invaluable help in turning out standardized products. Whole factories of literature are set up and novels are produced almost mechanically. In a court action it is proved that Dumas publishes more under his own name than he could write even if he were to work day and night without a break. In fact, he employs seventy-three collaborators, and amongst them one August Maquet, whom he allows to work quite independently. Literary work now becomes a 'commodity' in the fullest sense of the word; it has its price tariff, is produced according to a pattern and delivered on a day fixed in advance. It is a commercial article for which one pays the price it is worth—the price it returns. It does not occur to any editor to pay Mr. Dumas or Mr. Sue any more than he must and can. The authors of the newspaper serials are therefore no more 'overpaid' than the filmstars of today; their prices conform to the demand and have nothing to do with the artistic value of what they produce.

The *Presse* and the *Siècle* are the first daily papers to print serials, but the idea of publishing a novel in serial form is not their property. It comes from Véron, who already puts it into practice in his *Revue de Paris* founded in 1829.[17] Buloz takes the idea over from him in the *Revue des Deux Mondes* and in this form publishes, amongst other things, novels by Balzac. The 'feuilleton' in itself is, however, older than these periodicals; we come across it as early as 1800. The newspapers, which are very scanty during the Consulate and the first Empire, owing to the censorship and the other restrictions on the press, publish a literary supplement, in order to offer something to their readers. To begin with, this represents a kind of chronicle of the social and artistic worlds, but develops into a real literary supplement during the Restoration. From 1830 stories and travel descriptions are its main contents and after 1840 it only carries novels. The Second Empire, which imposes a tax of one centime on every copy of a paper with a 'feuilleton', soon brings the serial novel to an end. It is true that the genre is revived later on, but it has no further influence on the development of literature, compared with the deep tracks which it leaves behind in the literature of the 'forties.

The serial novel is intended for just as mixed and recently constituted a public as the melodrama or the vaudeville; it conforms to the same formal principles and aesthetic criteria as the contemporary popular stage. The fondness for exaggeration and raciness, for the crude and the eccentric, is just as decisive an influence on its style of presentation; the most popular subjects revolve around seductions and adulteries, acts of violence and cruelty. Here, too, as in the melodrama, the characters and the plot are stereotyped and constructed in accordance with a set pattern.[18] The interruption of the story at the end of each instalment, the problem of creating a climax every time and making the reader curious for the next instalment, induces the author to acquire a kind of stage technique and to take over from the dramatist the discontinuous method of presentation in separate scenes. Alexandre Dumas, the master of dramatic tension, is also a brilliant exponent of the technique of the serial; for the more dramatic the development of a serial novel, the stronger the effect it has on its public. But the continuation of the plot from day to day, the publication of the separate parts usually without an exact plan and without the possibility of altering what has already appeared and bringing it into harmony with the later instalments, produces, on the other hand, an 'undramatic', episodic and improvising narrative style, a never-ending stream of events and an unorganic, often contradictory portrayal of the characters. The whole art of 'preparation', the technique of seemingly natural, unforced, unintentional motivation, is lost. The turns in the plot and the changes of purpose in the characters often seem to be far-fetched, and the secondary characters, who turn up in the course of the story, often appear much too suddenly, as the author has failed to 'introduce' them in time. Even Balzac is often guilty of introducing characters without preparing the reader for them in advance, although it is precisely this improvising technique that he finds fault with in the *Chartreuse de Parme*. With Stendhal, however, the careless, loose construction is the result of an intrinsically episodic, picaresque and essentially undramatic narrative method,[19] whereas with Balzac, whose ideal is a novel with a dramatic form, it is an inadequacy ensuing from his journalistic mode of writing, from his hand-to-mouth existence. Whether the industrialization of literature is a consequence of journalism, however, and the light novel owes its rigid, stereotyped character entirely to the newspaper serial, must be left an open question; for, as the Empire and Restoration style proves, the conventionalization of this form had already been in progress for a long time past.[20]

The serial novel signifies an unprecedented democratization of literature and an almost complete reduction of the reading public to one level. Never has an art been so unanimously recognized by such different social and cultural strata and received with such similar feelings. Even a Sainte-Beuve praises the author of the *Mystères de Paris* for qualities that he regrets to find missing in Balzac. The spread of socialism and the growth of the reading public go hand in hand, but Eugène Sue's democratic approach and his belief in the social purpose of art only partly explain the success of his novels. It is, on the contrary, peculiar to hear the favourite of a very largely bourgeois public waxing enthusiastic about the 'noble labourer' and storming furiously about the 'cruelties of capitalism'. The humanitarian aim that he pursues, the revelation of the wounds of the diseased social body that he sets himself in his works, explains at most the sympathy with which he is treated by the progressive press, the *Globe*, the *Démocratie pacifique*, the *Revue indépendante*, the *Phallange* and their followers. The majority of his readers probably merely take his socialistic tendencies into the bargain. But there is no doubt that even this section of the public takes for granted the literary treatment of the social problems of the day. The idea emphasized by Mme de Staël, that literature is the expression of society, finds universal recognition and becomes an axiom of French literary criticism. From 1830 onwards it is quite normal to judge a literary work from the point of view of its relation to topical political and social problems, and, with the exception of the comparatively small group behind the 'l'art pour l'art' movement, no one is annoyed at seeing art subordinated to political ideals. There was probably never a time when so little purely formal, non-utilitarian art criticism was practised as now.[21]

Until 1848 the most important and the major part of the works of art belong to the activistic, after 1848 to the quietistic school. Stendhal's disillusionment is still aggressive, extroverted, anarchistic, whereas Flaubert's acquiescence is passive, egocentric and nihilistic. Even within the romantic movement, the 'l'art pour l'art' of Théophile Gautier and Gérard de Nerval is no longer the leading tendency. The old unworldly, mystical and mystifying kind of romanticism is dead. Romanticism is continued, but transformed and reinterpreted. The anti-clerical and anti-legitimist tendency which makes itself felt at the end of the Restoration develops into a more revolutionary philosophy. Most of the romantics fall away from 'pure art' and go over to the Saint-Simonites and Fourierites.[22] The leading personalities—Hugo, Lamartine, George Sand—profess an artistic activism and place themselves at the disposal of the 'popular' art demanded by the socialists. The people has triumphed, and the call is now to give expression to the revolutionary change in art as well. Not only George Sand and Eugène Sue become socialists, not only Lamartine and Hugo become enthusiastic about the people, even writers like Scribe, Dumas, Musset, Mérimée and Balzac flirt with socialistic ideas.[23] This flirtation soon comes to an end, however; for, just as the July monarchy turns away from the democratic ideals of the revolution and becomes the régime of the conservative bourgeoisie, the romantics also fall away from socialism and return to their former conception of art, though in a modified form. In the end not a single important writer remains loyal to the socialist ideal and, for the moment, the cause of 'popular art' seems to be lost. Romantic art quietens down, becomes more disciplined and more middle-class. Under the leadership of Lamartine, Hugo, Vigny and Musset, there arises, on the one hand, a conservatively academic, on the other, an elegant salon romanticism. The wild and violent rebelliousness of earlier days is subdued and the bourgeoisie takes an enthusiastic interest in this new romanticism, now partly subject to academic restraints and almost 'classical' in its outlook, partly fused with the dandysm of Byron's disciples.[24] Sainte-Beuve, Villemain, Buloz, are the highest authorities, the *Journal des Débats* and the *Revue des Deux Mondes* the official organs of the new, romantically tinged, but academically-minded bourgeois literary world.[25]

To some sections of the public, however, romanticism still seems too wild and despotic. A new, matter-of-fact, strictly bourgeois classicism is put in its place, the art of the so-called 'école de bon sens' and the aesthetic 'juste-milieu'. Ponsard's success, the revival of the 'tragédie classique' and the Rachel vogue are the most striking expression of this new school of taste. After the 'morbid' exaggerations and overheated atmosphere there is a desire to breathe fresh air again. There is a desire for balanced, measured, exemplary characters, for normal, universally understandable feelings and passions, for a philosophy of balance, order and the middle way, in short, for a literature that forgoes the piquancy, bizarre ideas and eccentric style of romanticism. 1843 is the year in which *Lucrèce* is a success and the *Burgraves* a fiasco; and this implies not only the victory of Ponsard over Hugo, but also that of Scribe, Dumas and Ingres and their ilk over Stendhal, Balzac and Delacroix. The middle class does not expect to get violent shocks but entertainment from art; it does not see a 'vates' in the poet but a 'maître de plaisir'. Ingres is followed by the endless succession of orthodox but drearily academic painters, Ponsard by the reliable but unimportant caterers for the state and municipal theatres. Amusement and peace and quiet are what is wanted and there is a corresponding change in the attitude to 'pure', non-political art.

'L'art pour l'art' sprang from romanticism and represents one of the weapons in its struggle for freedom; it is the result and to some extent the sum-total of romantic aesthetic theory. What was originally merely a revolt against the classical rules has become a revolt against all external ties, an emancipation from all non-artistic, moral and intellectual values. For Gautier artistic freedom already means independence from the criteria of the middle class, a lack of interest in its utilitarian ideals and the refusal to co-operate in the realization of these ideals. For the romantics 'l'art pour l'art' becomes the ivory tower in which they shut themselves off from all practical affairs. They buy the peace and superiority of a purely contemplative attitude at the price of an understanding with the prevailing order. Until 1830 the middle class hoped that art would promote its ideals, it therefore accepted art as a vehicle of political propaganda. 'Man is not created only to sing, believe and love . . . Life is no exile, but a call to action . . .'—writes the *Globe* in 1825.[26] After 1830, however, the bourgeoisie becomes suspicious of the artist, and prefers neutrality to the former alliance. The *Revue des Deux Mondes* is now of the opinion that it is not necessary, that it is in fact undesirable for the artist to have his own political and social ideas; and that is the standpoint represented by the most authoritative critics, amongst others Gustave Planche, Nisard and Cousin.[27] The middle class makes 'l'art pour l'art' its own; it stresses the ideal nature of art and the high, superpolitical status of the artist. It locks him up in a golden cage. Cousin goes back to the idea of autonomy in Kant's philosophy and revives the theory of the 'disinterestedness' of art, and here the tendency to specialization which becomes ascendant with capitalism proves very useful. 'L'art pour l'art' is, in fact, partly the expression of the division of labour which advances hand in hand with industrialization, partly the bulwark of art against the danger of being swallowed up by industrialized and mechanized life. It signifies, on the one hand, the rationalization, disenchantment and contraction of art, but simultaneously the attempt to preserve its individual quality and spontaneity, in spite of the universal mechanization of life.

'L'art pour l'art' indubitably represents the most involved problem in the whole field of aesthetics. Nothing expresses so acutely the dualistic, spiritually divided nature of the artistic outlook. Is art its own end or only the means to an end? This question will be answered differently, not only according to the particular historical and social situation in which one happens to find oneself, but also according to which element in the complex structure of art one concentrates on. The work of art has been compared to a window through which life can be seen without the necessity of accounting for the structure, transparency and colour of the window-pane itself.[28] According to this analogy, the work of art appears to be a mere vehicle of observation and knowledge, that is, a pane of glass or an eye-glass of no consequence in itself and merely serving as a means to an end. But just as one can concentrate one's attention on the structure of the window-pane, without paying any attention to the picture displayed on the other side of the window, so the work of art can be thought of as an independent formal structure existing for its own sake, as a coherent and significant entity, complete and perfect in itself, and in which all transgressing interpretations, all 'looking through the window', prejudices the appreciation of its spiritual coherence. The purpose of the work of art constantly wavers between these two points of view, between an immanent being, detached from all reality beyond the work itself, and a function determined by life, society and practical necessity. From the standpoint of the direct aesthetic experience, autonomy and self-sufficiency appear to be the essence of the work of art, for only by cutting itself off from reality and putting itself completely in the place of reality, only by forming a total, self-contained cosmos, is it able to produce a perfect illusion. But this illusion is in no way the whole content of art and often has no share in the effect it produces. The greatest works of art forgo the deceptive illusionism of a self-contained aesthetic world and point beyond themselves. They stand in an immediate relationship to the great problems of their age and are always searching for an answer to the questions: How can a purpose be gained from human life? and: How can we participate in this purpose?

The most inexplicable paradox of the work of art is that it seems to exist for itself and yet not for itself; that it addresses itself to a concrete, historically and sociologically conditioned public, but seems, at the same time, to want to have no knowledge at all of a public. The 'fourth wall' of the stage seems at times the most natural premise, at others the most arbitrary fiction of aesthetics. The destruction of the illusion by a thesis, a moral purpose, a practical intention, which prevents, on the one hand, the pure and perfect enjoyment of art, first leads, on the other hand, to the real participation of the beholder or the reader in the work, taking hold of his whole being. This alternative has, however, nothing to do with the actual intention of the artist. Even the politically and morally most tendentious work can be regarded as pure art, that is, as a mere formal structure, provided it is a work of art at all; on the other hand, every artistic product, even one with which its creator has connected no practical intention of any kind, can be considered the expression and instrument of social causality. Dante's activism no more excludes a purely aesthetic interpretation of the *Divine Comedy*, than Flaubert's formalism a sociological explanation of *Madame Bovary* and the *Éducation sentimentale.*

The main artistic trends around 1830—'social' art, the 'école de bon sens' and 'l'art pour l'art'—are correlated to one another in complicated and usually contradictory ways. The Saint-Simonites and the Fourierites are conditioned by these contradictions both in their relationship to romanticism and to bourgeois classicism. They reject romanticism because of its fondness for the Church and monarchy, its unreal, romanesque outlook, its selfish individualism, but chiefly on account of its quietistic principle of 'l'art pour l'art'. On the other hand, they sympathize with romanticism on account of its liberalism, its principle of artistic freedom and spontaneity, its revolt against the classical rules and authorities. But they also feel strongly drawn by the naturalistic efforts of romanticism; they recognize in this naturalism an affinity with their own positive, affirmative, open-minded disposition. The affinity between socialism and naturalism explains above all their sympathetic attitude to Balzac, whose works they judge very kindly especially at the beginning of his career.[29] An equally contradictory attitude to bourgeois classicism is connected with these conflicting feelings about romanticism. The acknowledgement of the liberalism in the romantic conception of art implies the simultaneous condemnation of the return to classical models in bourgeois art, whereas the dislike for the caprices and extravagances of romantic poetry, above all of the romantic theatre, expresses itself in a partial approval of Ponsard's classicism.[30] Corresponding to this indecision of the socialists, we find, on the one hand, the favours of the bourgeoisie divided between academic romanticism and Ponsard's drama, and, on the other hand, the wavering of the romantics themselves between activism and 'l'art pour l'art'. These three tendencies are crossed by yet a fourth and historically the most important of them all: the naturalism of Stendhal and Balzac. The relationship of this naturalism to romanticism is also ambivalent. The ambivalence here corresponds above all to the rift which usually exists between two successive generations or two consecutive intellectual trends. Naturalism is both the continuation and the dissolution of romanticism; Stendhal and Balzac are its most legitimate heirs and its most violent opponents.

Naturalism is not a homogeneous, clear-cut conception of art, always based on the same idea of nature, but changes with the times, always aiming at a particular and immediate goal, always concerned with a concrete task and confining its interpretation of life to particular phenomena. One professes a belief in naturalism, not because one considers a naturalistic representation more artistic *a priori* than a stylizing, but because one discovers a trait, a tendency in reality on which one would like to put more emphasis, which one would like either to promote or fight against. Such a discovery is not itself the result of naturalistic observation, on the contrary, the interest in naturalism is the result of such a discovery. The 1830 generation begins its literary career with the recognition that the structure of society has completely changed; partly it accepts, partly it opposes this change, but, in any case, it reacts to it in an extremely activistic fashion and its naturalistic approach is derived from this activism. Naturalism is not aimed at reality as a whole, not at 'nature' or 'life' in general, but at social life in particular, that is, at that province of reality which has become specially important for this generation. Stendhal and Balzac make it their task to portray the new and changed society; the aim of giving expression to its novelties and peculiarities leads them to naturalism and determines their conception of artistic truth. The social consciousness of the generation of 1830, its sensitiveness to phenomena in which social interests are at stake, its quick eye for social changes and revaluations, make its writers the creators of the social novel and modern naturalism.

The history of the novel begins with the medieval epic of chivalry. It is true that this has little to do with the modern novel in general, but its cumulative structure, its continuative narrative method stringing together one adventure and one episode after another, are the source of a tradition which is maintained not only in the picaresque novel, the heroic and pastoral novels of the Renaissance and the baroque, but even in the adventure novel of the nineteenth century and, to some extent, in the representation of the stream of life and experience in the novels of Proust and Joyce. Apart from the general tendency, characteristic of the whole Middle Ages, towards the cumulative form, and apart from the Christian conception of life as a non-tragic phenomenon which does not come to a head in isolated dramatic conflicts, but is more in the nature of a journey with many stages, this structure is connected, above all, with the recitation of medieval poetry and the medieval public's naïve hunger for new material. Printing, that is, the direct reading of books, and the more concentrated Renaissance conception of art bring it about that the expansive narrative style of the Middle Ages begins to yield to a more compact, less episodic method of presentation. In spite of its still essentially picaresque structure, *Don Quixote* constitutes a criticism of the extravagant novel of chivalry even from a purely formal point of view. But the decisive change towards a unification and simplification of the novel is first brought about by French classicism. It is true that the *Princesse de Clèves* is an isolated example, for the heroic and pastoral novels of the seventeenth century still belong to the category of the medieval adventure stories with their avalanche-like cumulation of episodes; but in Mme de Lafayette's masterpiece the idea of the love novel, with a uniform plot and a dramatic climax, and of the psychological analysis of a single conflict had been realized and had become a possibility capable of realization at any time. The adventure novel now represents a second-rate literary genre; it stands outside the frontiers of representative art and enjoys the advantages of insignificance and irresponsibility. The *Grand Cyrus* and *Astrée* form the main reading of the court aristocracy, but people read them, so to say, in their private capacity and indulge in them as it were in a vice, or, at any rate, a weakness of which there is no reason to be proud. In his funeral oration on Henriette d'Angleterre, Bossuet mentions it as praiseworthy in the deceased that she cared little for fashionable novels and their silly heroes; that is enough to show how this genre was judged in public. Where their private amusements were concerned, the aristocracy did not allow themselves, however, to be guided by the classicistic rules of art, but indulged in the enjoyment of adventures and extravaganzas as unrestrainedly as ever.

The novel of the eighteenth century still belongs very largely to the diffuse, picaresque genre. Not only *Gil Blas* and the *Diable boiteux* but also Voltaire's novels, in spite of their limited size, are constructed episodically, and *Gulliver* and *Robinson* are a complete embodiment of the cumulative principle. Even *Manon Lescaut*, the *Vie de Marianne* and the *Liaisons dangereuses* still represent transitional forms between the old adventure stories and the love novel, which gradually becomes the leading genre and begins to dominate the literature of pre-romanticism. With *Clarissa Harlowe*, the *Nouvelle Héloïse* and *Werther*, the dramatic principle triumphs in the novel and a development begins which is to reach its climax in works like Flaubert's *Madame Bovary* and Tolstoy's *Anna Karenina*. Attention is now concentrated on the psychological movement of the story; the external events are only taken into consideration in so far as they produce spiritual reactions. The psychologization of the novel is the most striking evidence of the spiritualization and subjectivization through which the culture of the age is passing. The novel of character-formation (*Bildungsroman*), which represents the next stage in the development and the stylistically most important literary form of the century, gives even stronger expression to the spiritualizing tendency. The story of the hero's development now becomes the story of the formation of a world. Only an age in which individual culture had become the most important source of culture altogether could have produced this form of the novel, and it had to arise in a country like Germany where the roots of a common culture were shallowest. At any rate, Goethe's *Wilhelm Meister* is the first *Bildungsroman* in the strict sense of the word, even if the origins of the genre are to be found in earlier works, mainly of a picaresque character, such as Fielding's *Tom Jones* and Sterne's *Tristram Shandy*.

The novel becomes the leading literary genre of the eighteenth century, because it gives the most comprehensive and profound expression to the cultural problem of the age—the antithesis between individualism and society. In no other form do the antagonisms of bourgeois society make themselves felt so intensely, in none are the struggles and defeats of the individual described so thrillingly. It was not without reason that Friedrich Schlegel called the novel the romantic genre par excellence. Romanticism sees in it the most satisfactory representation of the conflict between the individual and the world, dreams and real life, poetry and prose, and the deepest expression of the acquiescence which it regards as the only solution of this conflict. In *Wilhelm Meister*, Goethe finds a solution diametrically opposed to the romantic; and his work is not only the culmination of the history of the novel in the eighteenth century, not only the prototype from which the most representative creations of the genre, the *Rouge et Noir*, the *Illusions perdues*, the *Éducation sentimentale* and the *Gruene Heinrich*, can be derived directly or indirectly, but also the first important criticism of romanticism as a way of life. Goethe here points, and this is the real message of the work, to the absolute sterility of the romantic turning away from reality; he emphasizes that one can only do the world justice if one is spiritually bound up with it, and that one can only reform it from inside. He by no means conceals and glosses over the discrepancy between the inner spirit and the outer world, between the spiritual self and conventional reality, but he recognizes and proves that the romantic contempt for the world is an evasion of the real problem.[31] The Goethean demand that man should live with the world and in accordance with the rules of the world was trivialized by later bourgeois literature and turned into a summons to co-operate unconditionally with the world. The peaceable, but by no means absolute adaptation of the individual to the given situation was transformed into a cringing spirit of indiscriminate tolerance and a utilitarian secularism. Goethe had a share in this development only in so far as he did not perceive the impossibility of a peaceful reconciliation of the antitheses and only in so far as his somewhat frivolous optimism offered itself automatically as the ideology of the bourgeois policy of appeasement. Stendhal and Balzac saw the prevailing tensions much more acutely and judged the situation with a greater sense of reality than Goethe. The social novel, in which they recorded their insights, was a step which not only led beyond the romantic novel of disillusionment but also beyond Goethe's *Bildungsroman.* In their attitude both the romantic contempt for the world and Goethe's criticism of romanticism were quashed. Their pessimism resulted from an analysis of society which was quite clear of illusions about the possibility of solving the social problem.

The realism with which Stendhal and Balzac described the situation, their understanding of the dialectic which was moving society, was unparalleled in the literature of their time, but the idea of the social novel was in the air. Sub-titles like 'Scenes from polite society' or 'Scenes from private life' are met with long before Balzac.[32] 'Many young people describe things just as they happen daily in the provinces . . . Not much art but a good deal of truth results,' writes Stendhal with reference to the society novel of his day.[33] There had long been omens and experiments everywhere, but with Stendhal and Balzac the social novel becomes *the* modern novel and it now appears quite impossible to portray a character in isolation from society and to allow him to develop outside a definite social milieu. The facts of social life make their way into the human consciousness and can no longer be displaced from it. The greatest literary creations of the nineteenth century, the works of Stendhal, Balzac, Flaubert, Dickens, Tolstoy and Dostoevsky, are social novels, whatever other category they may belong to. The social definition of the characters becomes the criterion of their reality and credibility and the social problems of their life first make them suitable subjects for the new naturalistic novel. It is this sociological conception of man that the writers of the 1830 generation discovered for the novel and which was what most interested a thinker like Marx in the works of Balzac.

Stendhal and Balzac are both stern, often malicious critics of the society of their time; but the one criticizes it from the liberal, the other from the conservative standpoint. In spite of his reactionary views, Balzac is the more progressive artist; he sees the structure of middle-class society more acutely and describes the tendencies at work in it more objectively than the politically more radical but in his whole thinking and feeling more contradictory Stendhal. There is probably no other example in the whole history of art which makes it so clear that the service an artist renders to progress depends not so much on his personal convictions and sympathies as on the power with which he portrays the problems and contradictions of social reality. Stendhal judges his age according to the already out-of-date concepts of the eighteenth century, and fails to recognize the historical significance of capitalism. It is true that Balzac considers even these concepts much too progressive, but he cannot help describing society in his novels in such a way as to make a return to pre-revolutionary conditions and ideas appear absolutely unthinkable. Stendhal regards the culture of the enlightenment, the intellectual world of Diderot, Helvétius and Holbach, as exemplary and immortal; he considers its decline a passing phenomenon and dates its future revival from the day when he expects his own rehabilitation as an artist to take place. Balzac, on the other hand, sees that the old culture has already broken up, recognizes that the aristocracy itself has furthered the process and regards this in itself as a sign of the irresistible progress of capitalism. Stendhal's outlook is essentially political and, in his descriptions of society, he concentrates his attention on the 'mechanism of the state'.[34] Balzac, on the other hand, bases his social structure on economics, and, to some extent, anticipates the doctrines of historical materialism. He is perfectly aware that the actual forms of science, art and morality, as well as of politics, are functions of material reality and that bourgeois culture, with its individualism and rationalism, has its roots in the economic structure of capitalism. The fact that feudal conditions are more in accordance with his ideal than bourgeois-capitalist conditions does not in any way affect the fruitfulness of this insight. In spite of his enthusiasm for the old monarchy, the Catholic Church and aristocratic society, the realism and materialism of this world-view acts as one of the intellectual ferments by which the last remains of feudalism are dissolved.

Stendhal's novels are political chronicles: *Rouge et Noir* is the story of French society during the Restoration, the *Chartreuse de Parme* a picture of Europe under the rule of the Holy Alliance, *Lucien Leuwen* the socio-historical analysis of the July monarchy. Novels with a historical and political background had also existed in earlier times, of course, but it would never have occurred to anyone before Stendhal to make the political system of his own age the real subject of a novel. No one before him had been so conscious of the historical moment, no one felt so strongly as he did that history is made up purely and simply of such moments and constitutes a continuous chronicle of the generations. Stendhal experiences his own age as a time of unfulfilled promise and expectations, of unexploited energies and disappointed talents. He experiences it as an awful tragi-comedy, in which the parvenu middle class plays just as pitiable a rôle as the conspiring aristocracy, as a cruel political drama, in which all the players are only intriguers, no matter whether they are called ultras or liberals. He asks himself whether in a world like this, in which everyone lies and plays the hypocrite, any means is not good enough, provided it leads to success? The main thing is not to be the deceived, that is, to lie and simulate better than the others. All Stendhal's great novels revolve around the problem of hypocrisy, around the secret of how to deal with men and how to rule the world; they are all in the nature of text-books or political realism and courses of instruction in political amoralism. In his critique of Stendhal, Balzac already remarks that the *Chartreuse de Parme* is a new *Principe*, which Machiavelli himself, if he had lived as an émigré in the Italy of the nineteenth century, would not have been able to write any differently. Julien Sorel's Machiavellian motto, 'Qui veut les fins veut les moyens', here acquires its classical formulation, as used repeatedly by Balzac himself, namely that one must accept the rules of the world's game, if one wants to count in the world and to take part in the play.

For Stendhal the new society differs from the old above all by reason of its forms of government, the shift of power and the change in the political significance of the classes; for him the capitalistic system is the result of the political reconstruction. He describes French society at a stage of development where the middle class has already achieved economic supremacy, but still has to fight for its position in society. Stendhal portrays this struggle from a subjective, personal point of view, in the way that it presents itself to the rising intelligentsia. Julien Sorel's homelessness is the leitmotif of his whole work, the theme that he merely varies and modulates in his other novels, above all in the *Chartreuse de Parme* and in *Lucien Leuwen*. The social problem consists for him in the fate of those ambitious young people, rising from the lower classes and uprooted by their education, who find themselves without money and without connections at the end of the revolutionary period, and who, deluded, on the one hand, by the opportunities of the Revolution, on the other, by Napoleon's good fortune, want to play a rôle in society in accordance with their talents and ambitions. But they now discover that all power, all influence, all important posts are held by the old nobility and the new financial aristocracy and that superior gifts and greater intelligence are being displaced everywhere by mediocrity. The principle of the Revolution, that everyone is the architect of his own fortune, an idea that was absolutely foreign to the *ancien régime* but all the more familiar to the revolutionary youth of the time, loses its validity. Twenty years earlier the fate of Julien Sorel would have shaped itself quite differently; at twenty-five he would have become a colonel, at thirty-five a general—that is what we are told again and again. He was born too late or too early, and stands between the times, just as he stands between the classes. Where does he belong, whose side is he really on? It is the old familiar question, the problem of romanticism, coming up again and it remains as unsolved as ever. The romantic source of Stendhal's political ideas is probably revealed most clearly in the fact that he bases his hero's claim to success and position merely on the prerogative of talent, intelligence and energy. In his criticism of the Restoration and in his apologia for the Revolution, he bases his argument on the conviction that it is only in the people that real vitality and energy are still to be found. He regards the circumstances of the notorious murder committed by the seminarist Berthet, which he uses as a motif in *Rouge et Noir*, as evidence that the great men will henceforth proceed from those vigorous lower classes which are still capable of real passion, and to which not only Berthet, but also, as he now stresses, Napoleon, belonged.

In this way, the conscious class struggle is now ushered into literature proper. The conflict between the various strata of society had already been described by great writers in earlier ages, of course; to be true to life, no portrayal of social realities could omit to consider it. But the real meaning of the struggle was not realized either by the literary characters or even by their creators. The slave, the serf and the peasant even appeared comparatively frequently in the older literature—usually as comic figures—and the plebeian was described not only as the representative of a sluggish element of society, but also, as for example in Marivaux's *Paysan parvenu*, as an upstart; a representative of the lower classes, that is, of the classes below the middle section of the bourgeoisie, never came forward, however, as the pioneer of a disfranchized class. Julien Sorel is the first hero in a novel to be constantly aware of his plebeian birth, and to regard every success as a victory over the ruling class and every defeat as a humiliation. He cannot even forgive Mme de Rênal, the one woman he really loves, for being rich and belonging to the class against which he imagines he must for ever be on his guard. In his relation to Mathilde de la Mole the class conflict can no longer be distinguished at all from the conflict between the sexes. And the speech which he addresses to his judges is nothing but a proclamation of the class war, a challenge to his enemies with his neck already under the axe: 'Gentlemen,' he says, 'I have not the honour to belong to your social class. You see in me a peasant in revolt against the baseness of his fate . . . I see men who would like in my person to punish and dishearten for ever that class of young people who, born in a lowly and poverty-stricken class, had the chance to educate themselves and the courage to associate with those circles which the arrogance of the rich calls society . . .' And yet, the author is not only and perhaps not even primarily concerned with the class struggle; his sympathy is bestowed not simply on the poor and the disfranchised, but on society's brilliantly gifted, sensitive stepchildren, on the victims of the heartless, unimaginative ruling class. Hence Julien Sorel, the peasant's son, Fabrice del Dongo, the descendant of an age-old aristocratic family, and Lucien Leuwen, the heir of a fortune of millions, appear as allies, as fellow-combatants and fellow-sufferers sharing a feeling of strangeness and homelessness in this common and prosaic world. The Restoration created conditions in which conformity is the only way to success and in which no one can any longer breathe and move about freely, whatever his descent.

The common destiny of Stendhal's heroes does not, however, alter the fact that the class struggle is the sociological source of the new type of hero and that Fabrice and Lucien are nothing but ideological transcriptions of Julien, variations of the 'indignant plebeian', species of the 'unfortunate who wages war against the whole of society'. The figure of Fabrice del Dongo would be no more conceivable than that of Julien Sorel without the existence of a middle class threatened by reaction and of that intelligentsia condemned to passivity, to which Stendhal himself belongs. Henri Beyle, the functionary of the Imperial army, is placed on half-pay in 1815; for years he applies for a new position, but cannot even get a job as librarian. He lives in voluntary exile far away from France and the possibilities of a career, as one whose life has been shipwrecked. He hates reaction, but always, whenever he speaks of freedom, thinks only of himself, always of the right to 'pursue his happiness'. The happiness of the individual, happiness in a purely epicurean sense, is for him the aim of all political endeavour. His liberalism is the result of his personal destiny, of his education, of the antagonism to society bred by childhood experiences, of his lack of success in life, not of a genuinely democratic feeling. He is an 'enfant de gauche'[35]—partly as the victim of his Oedipus complex, but also as the pupil of his grandfather who, as a faithful disciple of the eighteenth-century 'philosophes', transmits the spirit of the enlightenment to him. His failures keep this spirit alive in him, turn him into a rebel; but emotionally he is an individualist and an aristocrat, a stranger to all herd instincts. His romantic hero-worship, his glorification of the strong, gifted, extraordinary personality, his conception of the 'happy few', his morbid aversion to everything plebeian, his aestheticism and dandyism are all expressions of a supersensitive, complacently aristocratic taste. He is afraid of the republic, refuses to have anything to do with the masses, loves comfort and luxury, and sees the ideal political state of affairs in a constitutional monarchy which assures the intellectual of a carefree existence. He loves the cultured salons, a life of leisure and enjoyment, well-bred, frivolous and intelligent people. He fears that the republic and democracy will impoverish and shed a pall of gloom over life, lead to the victory of the coarse, uncultivated masses over refined, cultured society with its sophisticated pleasure in the beauties of life. 'I love the people and hate the oppressors,' he said, 'but it would be torture for me always to have to live with the people.'

Despite the sympathy that Stendhal feels for Julien Sorel, he follows him with a strictly critical eye, and, for all his admiration for the genius and purity of the young rebel, does not allow us to overlook his reservations concerning his plebeian nature. He understands his bitterness, he shares his contempt for society, he approves his unscrupulous hypocrisy and his refusal to co-operate with the people surrounding him, but what he in no way understands and approves of is the 'folle méfiance', the morbid degrading suspicions of the plebeian tormented by inferiority complexes and feelings of resentment, his impotent, blind vindictiveness, his ugly, disfiguring jealousy. The description of Julien's feelings after the letter with Mathilde's declaration of love shows most unmistakably the distance separating Stendhal from his hero. It actually constitutes the key to the whole novel and reminds us that the story of Julien Sorel is no mere personal confession on the part of the author. Confronted with this monomaniacal suspicion, the writer is overcome rather by a feeling of strangeness, awe and horror. 'Julien's look was cruel, his countenance hideous,' he says quite unsympathetically, without the slightest attempt to excuse him. Can it never have occurred to Stendhal that society's greatest sin against Julien was precisely that it made him so suspicious, and so unhappy, so inhuman in his suspiciousness?

Stendhal's political views are just as full of contradictions as the circumstances of his life. By descent he belongs to the upper middle class, but, as a result of his education, he becomes its antagonist. He holds quite an important official position under Napoleon, takes part in the Emperor's last campaigns, is perhaps deeply impressed but by no means enthusiastic—he still has his reservations about the violent despot and the ruthless conqueror.[36] For him, too, the Restoration at first means peace and the end of the long, restless, uncertain period of the Revolution; to begin with, he feels in no way strange and uncomfortable in the new France. But as he gradually becomes aware of the hopelessness of his existence on half-pay and the Restoration reveals its true face, his hatred and loathing of the new régime grows and, at the same time, his enthusiasm for Napoleon. His weakness for the good, comfortable life makes him an opponent of social levelling, but his poverty and lack of success keep alive his mistrust and hostility towards the prevailing order and prevent him from coming to terms with reaction. These two tendencies are constantly present in Stendhal's mind and, according to the particular circumstances of his life, now one, now the other comes into the foreground. During the period of the Restoration, which is unsuccessful for him, his dissatisfaction and political radicalism grow; but as soon as his personal circumstances improve, he calms down and the rebel becomes the champion of order and a moderate conservative.[37] *Rouge et Noir* is still the confession of an uprooted rebel, whereas the *Chartreuse de Parme* is already the work of a man who has found inward peace and quiet strength in renunciation.[38] A tragedy has turned into a tragi-comedy, the genius of hatred into a philanthropic, almost conciliatory wisdom and frank, superior sense of humour, surveying everything with relentless objectivity, but recognizing at the same time the relativity of all things and the weakness of everything human. There is no doubt that this results in a note of frivolity creeping into his writing, something of the tolerance of 'to understand all is to forgive all'; but how remote Stendhal is from the conformity of the later bourgeoisie that forgives everything within and nothing outside its conventions. What a difference of values! What enthusiasm in Stendhal for youth, courage, intellect, the need for happiness, for the talent to enjoy and to create happiness, and what weariness, what boredom, what fear of happiness in the successful and established bourgeoisie! 'I should be happier than the others, because I possess everything that they have not . . .' says Count Mosca. 'But let us be honest, this idea must disfigure my smile . . . must give me an expression of selfishness and self-satisfaction . . . How charming, on the other hand, is his smile! [He means Fabrice.] He has the expression of the easy happiness of early youth and creates it in others.' And yet Mosca is by no means a scoundrel. He is only weak and he has sold himself. But Stendhal makes a great effort to understand him. Indeed, he already asked himself in *Rouge et Noir*: 'Who knows what one goes through on the way to a great deed?'—'Danton stole, Mirabeau sold himself. Napoleon stole millions in Italy, without which he would hardly have made any progress . . . Only Lafayette never stole. Must one steal, must one sell oneself?' Stendhal is here obviously not merely worried about Napoleon's millions: he discovers the inexorable dialectic of actions conditioned by material reality, the materialism of all existence and all practical life. A shattering discovery for a born, though inhibited, romantic.

In no representative of the nineteenth century are the seductions of romanticism and resistance to it distributed so equally as in Stendhal. This is the origin of the lack of harmony in his political philosophy. Stendhal is a strict rationalist and positivist; he finds all metaphysics, all mere speculation and idealism of the German kind, strange and loathsome. For him the embodiment of morality, the essence of intellectual integrity, consists in the effort 'to see clearly in that which is', that is to say, it consists in resistance to the temptations of superstition and self-deception. 'Her fiery imagination sometimes veiled things from her eyes,' he says of one of his favourite characters, the Duchess Sanseverina, 'but the arbitrary illusions prompted by cowardice were foreign to her.' In his eyes, the highest ideal in life is that cherished by Voltaire and Lucretius: to live free from fear. His atheism consists in the fight against the despot of the Bible and mythology, and is only one form of the passionate realist's constant struggle against lies and deception. His loathing for all rhetoric and emotionalism, for big words and phrases, for the colourful, luxuriant, emphatic style of Chateaubriand and de Maistre, his fondness for the clear, objective, dry style of the 'civil code', for 'good definitions', for short, precise, colourless sentences, all this is the expression of his stern, uncompromising and, as Bourget says, 'heroic' materialism—of the desire to see clearly and to make others see clearly in that which is. All exaggeration and ostentation is suspect and alien to him, and even though he is often enthusiastic, he is never bombastic. It has been noted, for example, that he never says 'freedom' but always merely 'the two chambers and the freedom of the press';[39] this, too, is a sign of his dislike for everything that is unreal and sounds over-excited and it is also part of his fight against romanticism and his own romantic feelings.

For, emotionally, Stendhal is a romantic; 'it is true that he thinks like Helvétius, but he feels like Rousseau'.[40] His heroes are disillusioned idealists, passionate dare-devils and unspoilt children, unsullied by the filth of life. They are, like their famous ancestor Saint-Preux, lovers of solitude and secluded heights, where they can dream in peace and devote themselves to their memories. Their dreams, their recollections, their most secret thoughts, are filled with tenderness. That is the great power counter-balancing reason in Stendhal, the source of the purest poetry and the deepest magic in his work. But his romanticism is by no means always pure poetry and pure, unmixed art. It is, on the contrary, full of romanesque, fantastic, morbid and macabre traits. His cult of genius does not in any way consist merely in an enthusiasm for greatness and the superhuman, but at the same time in a joy in the extravagant and the strange; his glorification of the 'dangerous life' does not signify merely a reverence for fearlessness and heroism, but also a toying with wickedness and crime. *Rouge et Noir* is, if you like, a thriller with a spicy and creepy ending, the *Chartreuse de Parme* an adventure novel full of surprises, miraculous rescues, cruelties and melodramatic situations. 'Beylism' is not merely a religion of power and beauty, but also a cult of pleasure and a gospel of force—a variant of romantic satanism. The whole of Stendhal's analysis of present-day culture is romantic; it is inspired by Rousseau's enthusiasm for the state of nature, but it constitutes, at the same time, an exaggerated and a negative Rousseauism, lamenting, as it does, not only the loss of spontaneity in modern civilization but also the drying up of the courage needed to commit great and picturesque crimes. Stendhal's Bonapartism is the best illustration of the complex and to some extent still very romantic character of his mind. Apart from the aestheticising glorification of the genius, this cult of Napoleon consists, on the one hand, in an appreciation of the upstart and the will to rise in society, on the other, in a sense of solidarity with the defeated, with the victim of reaction and the powers of darkness. For Stendhal, Napoleon is partly the little lieutenant who becomes the ruler of the world, the youngest son of the fairy tale, who solves the riddle and obtains the king's daughter, partly the eternal martyr and spiritual hero who is too good for this corrupt world and perishes as its victim. The immoralism and satanism of the romantic attitude are also intermingled in this cult of Napoleon and transform it from an apotheosis of greatness in good and evil, from an admiration of greatness, in spite of the evil that it is often forced to cause, into a cult of greatness precisely because of its readiness to commit evil and even crime. Stendhal's Napoleon is, like his Sorel, one of the ancestors of Raskolnikov; they are the embodiment of what Dostoevsky understood by Western individualism and made the cause of his hero's ruin.

Stendhal's resignation, too, has many romantic characteristics and is more directly connected with the romantic novel of disillusionment than Balzac's cold, clear-headed pessimism. But Stendhal's novels end just as badly as Balzac's; the difference lies in the manner, not in the degree, of the resignation. His heroes are also defeated: they, too, perish miserably or, what is still worse, are forced to capitulate and compromise; they die young or withdraw in disillusionment from the world. But in the end they are all tired of life, exhausted, worried to death, burnt out, they all give up the struggle and come to terms with society. Julien's death is a kind of suicide, and the end of the *Chartreuse de Parme* is just as melancholy a defeat. The note of renunciation is already sounded in *Armance*, where the motif of impotence is the unmistakable symbol of the estrangement from which all Stendhal's heroes suffer. The motif has its after-effect in the conviction of the young Fabrice that he is incapable of real love and in Julien's doubts as to his talent for love. In any case, he is a stranger to the bliss and self-extinguishing power of the erotic, the complete absorption in the moment and perfect self-forgetfulness of devotion to the beloved. For Stendhal's heroes the present has no blessedness; happiness always lies behind them and they think of it only when it is already past. There is no more moving evidence of Stendhal's tragic conception of life than the grief that lies in Julien's realization that the days of Vergy and Verrières, which were lived through unconsciously and unappreciated, which have vanished inevitably and for ever, were the most beautiful, the best and the most precious thing that life had to offer. Only the passing of things makes us aware of their value; only in the shadow of death does Julien learn to value life and the love of Mme de Rênal, and only in prison does Fabrice discover genuine happiness and real, spiritual freedom. Who knows, Rilke once asked in front of a lion's cage, where freedom is—in front of or behind the railings?—a genuinely Stendhalien and extremely romantic question.

In spite of his dislike for the colourful and emphatic style, Stendhal is an heir of romanticism even from a formal point of view, and in a much stricter sense than more or less every modern artist. The classical ideal of unity, concentration and subordination of the parts under the control of a leading idea and of the steady development of the theme, free from subjective arbitrariness and always taking the reader into consideration, is completely displaced in his work by a conception of art which is dominated entirely by self-expression and which strives to reproduce the material of experience as directly, as genuinely and as authentically as possible. Stendhal's novels seem like a collection of entries in a diary and sketches, attempting above all to hold fast the motions of the mind, the mechanism of the feelings and the intellectual labour of the author. Expression, confession, subjective communication, is the real aim, and the stream of experience, the rhythm of the stream of experience itself, the real subject of the novel; what the stream carries and drags along with it seems almost immaterial.

Practically all modern, post-romantic art is the fruit of improvisation; it is all contingent on the idea that feelings, moods and inspirations are more fruitful and more directly related to life than artistic intelligence, critical deliberation and the preconceived plan. Consciously or unconsciously, the whole modern conception of art is based on the belief that the most valuable elements of the work of art are the product of windfalls and flights of fancy, in a word, gifts of a mysterious inspiration, and that the artist does best to allow himself to be carried along by his own power of invention. That is why the invention of details plays such a pre-eminent part in modern art, and why the impression that it arouses is dominated by the wealth of unexpected turns and unanticipated secondary motifs. Compared with those of his predecessors, Beethoven's works already seem the product of improvisation, although the creations of the older masters, and above all those of Mozart, arose more unconcernedly, more easily and more in accordance with direct inspiration than the carefully prepared compositions of Beethoven, which are often based on numerous preliminary sketches. Mozart always seems to be guided by an objective, inevitable and unalterable plan, whereas in Beethoven's work every theme, every motif and every note sounds as if the composer were saying 'because I feel it like this', 'because I hear it like this' and 'because I wish to have it so'. The works of the older masters are well-articulated and well-constructed compositions, with plain, neat, well-rounded melodies, whereas the creations of Beethoven and later composers are recitatives, outcries from the depths of a troubled heart.

In his *Port-Royal*, Sainte-Beuve remarks that in the age of classicism that writer was regarded as the greatest, who created the most finished, the clearest and the most pleasant work, whereas we, the moderns, look in a writer above all for stimulation, that is, for opportunities to join in the writer's dreams and creative activity.[41] Our most popular writers are those who only hint at many things and always leave something unsaid that we have to guess, explain and complete for ourselves. For us the uncompleted, inexhaustible, indefinable work is the most attractive, the most profound and the most expressive. Stendhal's whole psychological art is aimed at stimulating the reader to co-operate, to take an active part in the author's observations and analyses. There are two different methods of psychological analysis. French classicism is based on a uniform conception of character, and develops the various spiritual attributes from an inherently invariable substance. The convincing force of the resulting portrait is due to the logical consistency of the features, but the picture itself represents more the 'mythos' than the portrait of the person. The characters of classical literature do not gain in interest and probability from the reader's self-observation; they are impressive on account of the greatness and acuteness of their lines, they are intended to be looked at and admired, not to be verified and interpreted. Stendhal's psychological method, which is equally described as analytical, although it is diametrically opposed to the classical method, is not based on the unity of the personality, but on his or her various manifestations, and does not stress the outlines, but the shades and valeurs of the picture. The portrait is here made up of a mass of details which, in association, usually make such a contradictory and unfinished impression on the reader that he is constantly directed to add the traits of his self-observation and to interpret the complex and chaotic picture in his own way. For the age of classicism the uniformity and clarity of a character was the criterion of its authenticity, whereas now the impression made by a character is all the more live and convincing, the more complicated and rhapsodic it is, the more scope it leaves for the reader to add details from his own experience.

The Stendhalien technique of 'petits faits vrais' does not imply that spiritual life is made up of a mass of small, ephemeral, intrinsically irrelevant phenomena, but that human character is incalculable and indefinable, and that it contains innumerable features apt to modify the abstract idea of its nature and to break up its unity. To stimulate the reader to join in the process of observation and composition, and to admit the inexhaustibility of the subject, signifies one and the same thing, namely, doubt in the ability of art to master the whole of reality. The complexity of modern psychology is merely a sign of our impotence to understand the modern man in the way that classicism understood the man of the seventeenth and eighteenth centuries. But to exclaim in the face of this inadequacy, as Zola did, 'life is simpler',[42] would amount to sheer blindness to the complex nature of modern life. For Stendhal, the psychological complication results from the growing self-consciousness of contemporary man, from his passionate self-observation, from the vigilance with which he follows all the motions of his heart and mind. When it is said, in *Rouge et Noir*, that 'man has two souls within himself', the author does not yet mean, however, the discord and self-estrangement of Dostoevsky, but simply the dualism which consists in the fact that the intellectual of our day is both a man of action and an observer, an actor and also his own audience. Stendhal knows the source of his greatest happiness and his worst misery: the reflexivity of his spiritual life. When he loves, enjoys beauty, feels free and unconstrained, he realizes not only the bliss of these feelings but, at the same time, the happiness of being aware of this happiness.[43] But now that he ought to be completely absorbed by his happiness and feel redeemed from all his limitations and inadequacies, he is still full of problems and doubts: Is that the whole story?—he asks himself. Is that what they call love? Is it possible to love, to feel, to be delighted and yet to observe oneself so coolly and so calmly? Stendhal's answer is by no means the usual one, which assumes the existence of an insurmountable gulf between feeling and reason, passion and reflexion, love and ambition, but is based on the assumption that modern man simply feels differently, is enraptured and enthusiastic differently from a contemporary of Racine or Rousseau. For them, spontaneity and reflexivity of the emotions were incompatible, for Stendhal and his heroes they are quite inseparable; none of their passions is so strong as the desire to be constantly calling themselves to account for what is going on inside them. Compared with the older literature, this self-consciousness implies just as profound a change as Stendhal's realism, and the overcoming of classical-romantic psychology is just as strictly one of the preconditions of his art as the abolition of the alternative between the romantic escape from the world and the anti-romantic belief in the world.

Balzac's characters are more coherent, less contradictory and problematical than Stendhal's; they signify to some extent a return to the psychology of classical and romantic literature. They are monomaniacs ruled by a single passion, who seem, with every step they take and with every word they speak, to follow an absolute command. But it is curious that their credibility is not in any way prejudiced by this compulsion and that they are more real than Stendhal's characters, despite the fact that the latter correspond, with their antinomies, much more exactly to our psychological ideas. We are here, as everywhere in Balzac, faced by the mystery of an art the overwhelming influence of which is, in view of the absolutely unequal value of its constituent elements, one of the most inexplicable phenomena in the history of literature. Incidentally, Balzac's characters are by no means always so simple as they are usually described; their maniacal one-sidedness is often connected with an extraordinary wealth of individual traits. They are certainly less complex and 'interesting' than Stendhal's heroes, but they make a more lively, more unmistakable and unforgettable impression.

Balzac has been called the literary portraitist par excellence, and the incomparable effect of his art has been attributed to the power of his character descriptions. In fact, one thinks, in speaking of Balzac, above all of the human jungle of his novels, of the abundance and variety of the characters he sets in motion; but he is not interested primarily in the psychological aspect. If one attempts to explain the sources of his world, one is forced constantly to revert to his sociology and to speak of the material presuppositions of his intellectual cosmos. For him, in contrast to Stendhal, Dostoevsky or Proust, there is something more essential and irreducible than spiritual reality. For him a character in itself is unimportant; he only becomes interesting and significant as the agent of a social group, as the bearer of a conflict between antithetical, class-conditioned interests. Balzac himself always speaks of his characters as of natural phenomena, and when he wants to describe his artistic intentions, he never speaks of his psychology, but always of his sociology, of his natural history of society and of the function of the individual in the life of the social body. He became, anyhow, the master of the social novel, if not as the 'doctor of the social sciences', as he described himself, yet as the founder of the new conception of man, according to which 'the individual exists only in relation to society'. In the *Recherche de l'absolu*, he says that just as one can reconstruct a whole world from a geological find, so every monument of culture, every dwelling house, every mosaic, is the expression of a whole society; everything is an expression of and bears witness to the great universal social process. He is overcome by a transport of ecstasy, as he considers this social causality, this inescapable conformity to law, which is his only clue to the meaning of the present age and the only solution of the problems around which his whole work revolves. For the *Comédie humaine* owes its inner unity not to the intertwinements of its plot, not to the recurrence of its characters, but to the predominance of this social causality and to the fact that it is actually one single great novel, namely the history of modern French society.

Balzac frees the narrative from the limitations of the autobiography and mere psychology to which it had been subject since the second half of the eighteenth century. He breaks through the framework of individual destinies to which both the novels of Rousseau and Chateaubriand and those of Goethe and Stendhal were confined, and liberates himself from the confessional style of the eighteenth century, even though he is, naturally, unable all at once to strip away everything lyrical and autobiographical. Balzac discovers his style very slowly in any case; to begin with, he merely continues the fashionable literature of the Revolution, Restoration and romanticism, and even his most mature work still suffers from reminiscences of the trashy novels of his predecessors. He can no more deny the descent of his art from the mystical novel of terror and the melodramatic 'roman-feuilleton' than from the romantic love and historical novel, and his style presupposes the works of Pigault-Lebrun and Ducray-Duminil just as much as those of Byron and Walter Scott.[44] Not only Ferragus and Vautrin but also Montriveau and Rastignac are among the rebels and outlaws of romanticism and not only the lives of adventurers and criminals but also bourgeois life is, as has been said, treated by him as material for a thriller.[45] Modern middle-class society, with its politicians, bureaucrats, bankers, speculators, men about town, cocottes and journalists, seems to him like a nightmare, like the relentless procession of a *danse macabre*. He regards capitalism as a social disease and toys for some time with the idea of treating it from a medical point of view in a 'Pathologie de la vie sociale'.[46] He diagnoses it as a hypertrophy of the striving for profit and power and attributes the evil to the egoism and irreligiosity of the age. He sees it all as the consequence of the Revolution and traces back the dissolution of the old hierarchies, especially that of the monarchy, the Church and the family, to individualism, free competition and inordinate, unrestrained ambition. Balzac describes with astonishing acuteness the symptoms of the boom period in which he finds himself with his generation, he sees through the fateful internal contradictions of the capitalistic system, but he presupposes too many arbitrary circumstances in its origins, and even he himself does not really believe in the cure which he prescribes. Gold, the Louis d'or and the five-franc piece, shares, bills of exchange, lottery tickets and playing cards are the idols and fetishes of the new society; the 'golden calf' has become a more frightening reality than it was in the Old Testament and the millions sound more seductively in the ears than the call of the apocalyptic woman. Balzac considers his tragedies of bourgeois life, although they merely revolve around money, more cruel than the drama of the Atridae, and the words of the dying Grandet to his daughter, 'You will give me an account of this down there', are indeed more dreadful than the gloomiest notes sounded in Greek tragedy. Numbers, sums, balances, are here the formulae of exorcism and the oracles of a new mythology, of a new world of magic. Millions spring from nothing and vanish, melt away again like the gifts of evil spirits in fairy tales. Balzac easily falls into the fairy-tale style, when the subject under discussion is money. He likes to play the part of the genii who give presents to beggars and is always ready to escape with his heroes into the world of day-dreams. But he never hides from himself the ultimate effect of gold, the devastation it causes and the poisoning of human relationships to which it leads; on this point his sense of reality never forsakes him.

The pursuit of money and profit destroys family life, estranges wife from husband, daughter from father, brother from brother, turns marriage into a mutual benefit society, love into a business and chains the victims one to another with the bonds of slavery. Can one imagine anything more sinister than the way old father Grandet is bound to his daughter as the inheritress of his fortune! Or the Grandet characteristics in Eugénie which emerge as soon as she becomes mistress of the house. Is there anything more uncanny than this power of nature, this mastery of matter over human souls! Money alienates men and women from themselves, destroys ideals, perverts talents, prostitutes artists, poets and scholars, turns geniuses into criminals and born leaders into adventurers and gamblers. The social class which bears the heaviest responsibility for the relentlessness of money economy and which makes the biggest profit out of it, is, of course, the bourgeoisie, but all classes are involved in the wild, bestial struggle for existence which it unleashes, the aristocracy, its bloodiest victim, no less than the other classes. Nevertheless, Balzac finds no other way out of the anarchy of the present than by reviving this aristocracy, educating it to the rationalism and realism of the middle class and opening its ranks to the talents striving up from below. He is an enthusiastic supporter of the feudal classes, he admires the intellectual and moral ideals which they embody and regrets their decline, but he describes their degeneration with an all the more merciless objectivity, above all their deference to the money-bags of the bourgeoisie. Balzac's snobbery is certainly very embarrassing, but his political capers are perfectly harmless, for, however zealous the interest he takes in the cause of the aristocracy, he is, nevertheless, no aristocrat and, as has been pointed out, the difference is fundamental.[47] His aristocratism is a speculative idea; it does not come from the heart or the instincts.

Balzac is not only a thoroughly bourgeois writer, all of whose spontaneous feelings are rooted in the outlook of his class, he is at the same time the most successful apologist of the bourgeoisie and he in no way conceals his admiration for the achievements of this class. He is only full of a hysterical fear and scents disorder and revolution everywhere. He attacks everything that threatens the stability of the status quo and defends everything that appears to protect it. He sees the strongest bulwark against anarchy and chaos in the monarchy and the Catholic Church; he regards feudalism as merely the system which follows from the dominion of these powers. He is not in any way concerned with the forms which the monarchy, the Church and the nobility have assumed since the Revolution, but only with the ideals which they represent, and he attacks democracy and liberalism only because he knows that the whole structure of the hierarchies of society must collapse, once they begin to be criticized. He is of the opinion that 'a power that is a subject for discussion is non-existent'.

Equality is a chimera; it has never been realized anywhere in the world. And just as every community, above all the family, is based on authority, so the whole of society must be founded on the principle of sovereign rule. Democrats and socialists are unrealistic dreamers, not merely because they believe in freedom and equality, but also because they idealize the common people and the proletariat inordinately. Men are, however, fundamentally all the same; they are all out for their own advantages and pursue only their own interests. Society is entirely dominated by the logic of the class struggle; the conflict between rich and poor, strong and weak, the privileged and the underdog, knows no limits. 'Self-preservation is the aim of all power' (*Le Médecin de campagne*), and the destruction of its oppressors that of every suppressed class—these are unalterable facts. But Balzac is not only familiar with the concepts of the class struggle, he is already in possession of the method of exposure of historical materialism. 'They send a criminal to the galley,' says Vautrin in the *Illusions perdues*, 'whereas a man who ruins whole families by fraudulent bankruptcy gets a few months. . . . The judges who sentence a thief are guarding the barriers dividing rich and poor . . . they know, of course, that the bankrupt causes at most a shift in the distribution of wealth.'

But the fundamental difference between Balzac and Marx lies in the fact that the writer of the *Comédie humaine* judges the struggle of the proletariat in just the same way as that of the other classes, that is to say, as a struggle for benefits and privileges, whereas Marx sees in the proletariat's fight for power and in its victory the beginning of a new epoch in the world's history, the realization of an ideal and final situation.[48] Balzac discovers before Marx, and in a form which Marx himself can accept as authoritative, the ideological nature of all thinking. 'Virtue begins with prosperity,' he says in the *Rabouilleuse*, and in the *Illusions perdues*, Vautrin speaks of the 'luxury of honourable conduct', which one can only afford when one has reached a suitable position and acquired the money that goes with it. In his *Essai sur la situation du parti royaliste* (1832), Balzac already refers to the way ideologies are formed: 'Revolutions take place', he maintains, 'first of all in material things and interests, then they extend to ideas and finally become transformed into principles.' He already discovers the material ties which condition our ideas and the dialectic of being and consciousness in *Louis Lambert*, the hero of which becomes, as he remarks, more and more aware, after the spiritualism of his youth, of the material texture of all thinking. It was, obviously, no coincidence that Balzac and Hegel recognized the dialectical structure of history almost simultaneously. Capitalistic economy and the modern bourgeoisie were full of contradictions and gave clearer expression to the antithetical definition of historical developments than earlier cultures. But the material foundations of bourgeois society were not only intrinsically more transparent than those of feudalism, the new upper class also attached, for the time being, less importance to putting an ideological disguise on the material precondition of its power. In any case, its ideology was still far too recent to be able to hide its origin.

The outstanding feature in Balzac's world-view is his realism, his sober and honest examination of the facts. His historical materialism and his theory of ideologies are merely the applications of his sense of reality. And Balzac maintains his realistic, critical standpoint even when considering those phenomena to which he has an emotional attachment. Thus, in spite of his conservative outlook, he emphasizes the irresistibility of the development which has led to modern, bourgeois-capitalist society, and never lapses into the provincialism which conditions the idealists' approach to technical culture. His attitude to modern industry, as the new world-uniting power, is thoroughly positive.[49] He admires the modern metropolis with its standards, its dynamism and its élan. Paris enchants him; he loves it, despite its viciousness, indeed perhaps precisely because of the monstrosity of its vices. For when he speaks of the 'grand chancre fumeux, étalé sur les bords de la Seine', he betrays in every word the fascination that lies hidden behind his strong language. The mythos of Paris, as the new Babylon, the city of light and secret paradises, the home of Baudelaire and Verlaine, Constantin Guys and Toulouse-Lautrec, the mythos of dangerous, seductive, irresistible Paris, has its origins in the *Illusions perdues*, the *Histoire des Treize* and *Père Goriot*. Balzac is the first writer to speak about a modern metropolis with enthusiasm and to find pleasure in an industrial plant. It had never occurred to anyone before him to describe such a plant in the midst of a charming valley as a 'délicieuse fabrique'.[50] This admiration for the new, creative, albeit mercilessly impetuous life of the industrial age is the compensation for his pessimism and the awakening of his hope and confidence in the future. He knows that it is quite impossible to return to the patriarchal and idyllic life of the small town and village; but he also knows that this life was by no means so romantic and poetic as it is usually made out to be, and that its 'naturalness' meant nothing but ignorance, disease and poverty (*Le Médecin de campagne, Le Curé de village*). In spite of his own romanesque inclinations, Balzac is a complete stranger to the 'social mysticism' of the romantics,[51] and as for the 'moral purity' and 'unspoilt nature' of the peasants in particular, he indulges in no illusions on that score. He judges the good and the bad qualities of the common people with the same objectivity as the virtues and vices of the aristocracy, and his relation to the masses is just as undogmatic and full of contradictions as his mingling of hatred and affection for the bourgeoisie.

Balzac is a revolutionary writer without wanting to be and without knowing that he is. His real sympathies make him an ally of the rebels and nihilists. Most of his contemporaries recognize his political unrealiability; they know that he is essentially an anarchist who always feels in absolute agreement with the enemies of society, with those who have come off the rails and the uprooted. Louis Veuillot remarks that he defends the throne and altar in such a way as to make the enemies of these institutions grateful to him.[52] Alfred Nettement writes in the *Gazette de France* (February, 1836) that Balzac wanted to take revenge on society for all the wrongs he had suffered in his youth, and that his glorification of antisocial natures is simply one expression of this revenge. In his memoirs (October, 1833), Charles Weiss emphasizes that, although Balzac passed himself off for a legitimist, he always spoke as a liberal. Victor Hugo asserts that whether he wanted to or not he was a revolutionary writer, and that his works revealed the heart of a genuine democrat. Finally, Zola establishes the antithesis between the manifest and the latent elements in his outlook on life and notes, anticipating the Marxist interpretation, that a writer's talent may well be in conflict with his convictions. Engels is the first, however, to discover and define the real significance of this antagonism. He is the first to treat in a scientifically exploitable way the contradiction between the political views and the artistic creations of the writer and he thereby formulates one of the most important heuristic principles in the whole sociology of art. It has since become quite clear that artistic progressiveness and political conservatism are perfectly compatible and that every honest artist who describes reality faithfully and sincerely has an enlightening and emancipating influence on his age. Such an artist helps involuntarily to break up those conventions and clichés, taboos and dogmas on which the ideology of the reactionary, anti-liberal elements is based. In his famous letter to Miss Harkness of April, 1888, Engels writes as follows:

'The realism I allude to may creep out even in spite of the author's views. . . . Balzac, whom I consider a far greater master of realism than all the Zolas, past, present, or future, gives us in his *Comédie humaine* a most wonderfully realistic history of French "society", describing, chronicle fashion, almost year by year from 1816 to 1848, the ever-increasing pressure of the rising bourgeoisie upon the society of nobles that established itself after 1815 and that set up again, as far as it could, the standard of the *vieille politesse française*. He describes how the last remnants of this, to him, model society gradually succumbed before the intrusion of the vulgar moneyed upstart or was corrupted by him. . . . Well, Balzac was politically a legitimist; his great work is a constant elegy on the irreparable decay of good society; his sympathies are with the class that is doomed to extinction. But for all that, his satire is never keener, his irony never more bitter, than when he sets in motion the very men and women with whom he sympathizes most deeply—the nobles. . . . That Balzac was thus compelled to go against his own class sympathies and political prejudices, that he *saw* the necessity of the downfall of his favourite nobles and described them as people deserving no better fate; that he *saw* the real men of the future where, for the time being, they alone were to be found—that I consider one of the greatest triumphs of realism, and one of the greatest features in old Balzac.'[53]

Balzac is a naturalist who concentrates on the enrichment and differentiation of his experience. But if one understands by naturalism the absolute levelling of all the data of reality, the same criterion of truth in all the parts of an artist's work, then one will hesitate to call him simply a naturalist. One will rather be forced to face the fact that he is carried away by his romantic imagination and his inclination to melodrama again and again, and that he not only often goes out of his way to find the most eccentric characters and the most improbable situations, but also builds up the settings of his stories so that they are impossible to imagine in the concrete and only contribute by the colours and tones of the description to the atmosphere intended. To pronounce Balzac a naturalist pure and simple can only lead to disappointments. It is meaningless and useless to compare him as a psychologist or as a painter of milieu with the masters of the later naturalistic novel, with Flaubert or Maupassant, for example. If one cannot enjoy his works as descriptions of reality and, at the same time, as the most audacious and wildest visions, and if one expects to get from them anything but the indiscriminate mixture of these elements, one will never get to like them at all. Balzac's art is dominated by the passionate desire to be completely surrendered to life, but it owes almost nothing to direct observation; its most fundamental qualities are invented, the product of conscious thought and fictitious feeling.

Every work of art, even the most naturalistic, is an idealization of reality—a legend, a kind of Utopia. Even with the most unconventional style we accept certain characteristics, as for example the bright colours and blobs of impressionistic painting or the incoherent and inconsistent characters of the modern novel, as true and accurate *a priori*. But Balzac's portrayal of reality is much more arbitrary than that of most naturalists. He awakens the impression of truth to life mainly by the despotism with which he subjects the reader to his own mood and the microcosmic totality of his fictitious world, from which the possibility of competition with the world of empirical reality is excluded from the very outset. His characters and settings do not seem so genuine, because their individual features correspond to real experience, but because they are drawn so sharply and circumstantially as if they had in fact been observed and copied from reality. We feel as though we were being confronted by a closely packed reality, because the individual elements of this microcosm all cohere in an indivisible unity, because the figures are inconceivable without their environment, the characters without their physical constitution and the bodies without the objects by which they are surrounded.

Classical and classicist works of art are cut off from the outside world and stand beside each other in strict isolation within their own aesthetic sphere. Naturalism in all its forms, that is to say, all art that is obviously dependent on a real model, breaks through the immanence of this sphere, and all cyclic forms which embrace a variety of artistic representations abolish the autocracy of the individual work of art. Most of the creations of medieval art arose in this cumulative fashion comprising several independent unities. With their lengthy, never-ending stories and their partly recurring characters, the epics of chivalry and the novels of adventure belong to this category no less than the cycles of medieval painting and the innumerable episodes of the mysteries. When Balzac discovered his system and came on the idea of the *Comédie humaine* as a framework embracing the individual novels, he returned to some extent to this medieval method of composition and adopted a form for which the self-sufficiency and crystalline definiteness of the classical works of art had lost their meaning and value. But how did Balzac alight on this 'medieval' form? How could it again become a matter of urgent topical interest in the nineteenth century?—The artistic method of the Middle Ages was completely displaced by the classicism of the Renaissance, by the idea of the unity and formal concentration of the work of art. As long as this classicism was alive, the cyclical method of composition could never regain its old position, but it remained alive only so long as men were confident of their ability to master material reality. The predominance of classicistic art gradually comes to an end as the feeling of dependence on the material conditions of life grows. In this respect, too, the romantics are Balzac's direct predecessors.

Zola, Wagner and Proust mark the further stages in this development and give more and more currency to the cyclic, encyclopedic, world-embracing style, in contrast to the principle of unity and selection. The modern artist wants to participate in a life that is inexhaustible and cannot be reduced to a single work. He can express greatness only by size, and power only by boundlessness. Proust was obviously conscious of his relationship to the cyclical form of Wagner and Balzac. 'The musician (that is, Wagner)', he writes, 'inevitably felt the same intoxication as Balzac, when he looked at his creations with the eyes of a stranger and at the same time with those of a father. . . . He then observed that they would be much more beautiful if united by recurring figures into a cycle, and he added a final stroke of the brush, the most sublime of them all, to his work . . . an additional but by no means artificial . . . an unrecognized but all the more real, all the more vital unity. . . .'[54]

Of the two thousand characters of the *Comédie humaine* four hundred and sixty recur in several novels. Henry de Marsay, for example, appears in twenty-five different works, and in the *Splendeurs et misères des courtisanes* alone one hundred and fifty-five figures appear, who also play a more or less prominent rôle in other parts of the cycle.[55] All these characters are broader and more substantial than the individual works, and we always feel that Balzac is not telling us everything he knows about them and could tell. When Ibsen was once asked why he gave the heroine of his *Doll's House* such a foreign-sounding name, he answered that she was named after her grandmother who was Italian. Her real name was Eleonora, but she had been pampered as a child and called Nora. To the objection that all this played no part in the play itself, he replied in amazement: 'But facts are still facts.' Thomas Mann is perfectly right, Ibsen belongs to one and the same category as the two other great theatrical talents of the nineteenth century, Zola and Wagner.[56] With him, too, the individual work lost the microcosmic finality of classicistic form.

There is an extraordinary number of anecdotes about Balzac's relationship to his characters, similar to the one about Ibsen. The best known is the incident with Jules Sandeau who, while telling him about his sister's illness, was interrupted by Balzac saying: 'That's all very well, but let's get back to reality: to whom are we going to marry Eugénie Grandet?' Or there is the question with which he surprises one of his friends: 'Do you know whom Félix de Vaudeville will marry? A de Grandville. That's quite a good match, isn't it?' But the most beautiful and the most characteristic is Hofmannsthal's anecdote, in which Balzac is made to say in an imaginary dialogue: 'My Vautrin considers it (the *Venice Preserved* by Otway) the most beautiful of all plays. I set great store by the judgement of such a man.' [57] His characters' existence outside the novels is such an unmistakable reality for Balzac, and one which he takes so much for granted, that he would have been able to say of any play or book what Vautrin or de Marsay or Rastignac would think of it. The transcending of the immediate sphere of the work itself goes so far with Balzac that he often refers to individual characters in the *Comédie humaine* even when they do not appear at all in the work in question and quotes the titles of certain parts of the total work simply as references.

It is well known how fond Paul Bourget was of browsing in the 'Répertoire' of the *Comédie humaine*, this 'Who's Who' of Balzac's characters.[58] His hobby is regarded today almost as the passport of a real 'Balzacien'; it is, at any rate, the sign of an appreciation of the fact that the conception and effect of the *Comédie humaine* are only partly aesthetic and that it is inseparable from real life. Balzac represents a passing moment in the development leading from the pure artistic quality of classicistic and romantic writing to the aestheticism of Flaubert and Baudelaire—the brief hour of an art completely absorbed by the topical problems of the day. There is no nineteenth-century writer further removed from 'l'art pour l'art' and who was less concerned with artistic purism than he. Balzac's works can never be enjoyed in peace and with a good conscience, if the fact is not faced from the very outset that they are an ill-balanced, partly crude mixture with nothing in common with the classicistic principles of 'no more and no less' and the transference of the data of experience on to a single level. The idea of the work of art as a perfect whole is always a fiction—even the most accomplished works are full of chaotic and disparate elements, but Balzac's novels are simply the classical example of a successful evasion of all the rules of aesthetics. If one takes the classical works of literature as a standard, one will be bound to find in them the most flagrant transgressions of even the most liberal rules of art. Still completely under their spell, with the self-destructive ravings of their characters, the terrible words of their rebels and desperados still burning in one's soul, one will be compelled to admit that in these works practically everything open to rational analysis has been 'bungled'; that Balzac can neither construct not develop a plot tidily; that his characters are often just as vaguely and heterogeneously put together as his milieus and settings; that his naturalism is not only incomplete, but also clumsy and summary. And, above all, one will be forced to confess that hair-raising examples of bad taste are concomitant with all these inadequacies; that the writer lacks all power of self-criticism and is prepared to go to any lengths to surprise and overwhelm the reader; that he no longer has anything of the aesthetic culture of the eighteenth century, its reserve, its elegant, playful casualness; that his taste is on the same level as the serial-reading public, and the worst serials at that; that nothing can be too overladen, exaggerated and exuberant for him; that he is incapable of expressing without emphasis and without superlatives anything that is near to his heart; that he always has his mouth full; that he brags and swindles; that he is a loathsome charlatan the moment he tries to give the impression of being a scholar and a philosopher; and that he is certainly greatest as a thinker, when he is least conscious of being one, when he thinks and reasons spontaneously, in accordance with his personal interests and historical situation.

The most embarrassing evidence of his bad taste are the lapses of his style: his confused torrent of words, his thickly laid-on solemnity, his affected and pompous metaphors, his raving enthusiasm and pseudo-sublime emotions. Not even his dialogues are irreproachable; here, too, there are dead passages and notes that sound 'wrong', just as one can sing wrong notes. The train of thought with which Taine attempts to explain and justify Balzac's stylistic peculiarities is well known. He remarks that there are different styles in literature, all entitled to the same rights, and he emphasizes that the author of the *Comédie humaine* no longer addresses himself to the public of the seventeenth- and eighteenth-century *salons*, to a public that reacted to the slightest hints and did not need loud colours and shrill sounds to have its attention attracted, but that, on the contrary, he writes for people who are impressed only by novelties, sensations and exaggerations, that is to say, for the readers of the serialized novels.[59] This is, no doubt, a splendid example of sociological literary criticism; for, although many of the writers of Balzac's generation had avoided his stylistic mistakes, few of them were so intimately engrossed in their own time as he. But should we not, instead of justifying Balzac's weaknesses, rather attempt to understand the abrupt proximity of the great and the inferior in his work? And for a sociological explanation should we not attribute the peculiarities of his style above all to the fact that he himself was a plebeian and the intellectual expression of the new, comparatively uncultivated but extraordinarily active and efficient middle class?

It has repeatedly been remarked that, in his works, Balzac draws more the picture of the succeeding than of his own generation and that his 'nouveaux riches' and parvenus, his speculators and adventurers, his artists and cocottes, are more typical of the Second Empire than the July monarchy. In his case it certainly seems as if life had imitated art. Balzac is one of the literary prophets in whom vision was stronger than observation. 'Prophet' and 'visionary' are, of course, mere words used in an attempt to cloak the dilemma presented by an art the magical influence of which seems only to increase with every fresh inadequacy. But what else can one say about a work like the *Chef-d'œuvre inconnu*, which combines the deepest insight into the meaning of life and the present age with an incredible naïvety?—Frenhofer, we read there, is the greatest pupil of Mabuse, the only one to whom the master has transmitted his art of infusing life into painted figures. He has been labouring for ten years on a work, the picture of a woman, in a struggle to achieve the highest object of all art, the secret of Pygmalion. He feels that every day is bringing him nearer to his goal, but there always remains something invincible, something insoluble and unattainable. He believes that reality is keeping it back from him, that he has not yet found the right model. Then, one day Poussin, in his enthusiasm for art, brings him his mistress, who is supposed to have the most perfect body ever painted. Frenhofer is carried away by the girl's beauty, but his eyes pass from her young body back to the uncompleted and uncompletable picture. Reality no longer holds him fast, he has killed the life within himself. But the picture, his life-work, that, more jealous than Poussin of his mistress, he had never wanted to reveal to any stranger's eyes, contains nothing but an unintelligible muddle of curling lines and blobs, which he has painted one over the other and piled up one upon the other in the course of the years, and among which only the forms of a perfectly shaped leg are still discernible. Balzac foresaw the fate of the art of the last century and described it incomparably. He recognized the results of its estrangement from life and society, and understood the aestheticism, the nihilism, the danger of self-destruction which threatened it, and which was to become a dreadful reality under the Second Empire, more perfectly than even the most learned and sharp-sighted of his contemporaries.

2. THE SECOND EMPIRE

The romantics were perfectly aware of the loss of prestige which writers had suffered since the Revolution and sought a refuge from the unfriendly public in individualism. Their feeling of homelessness expressed itself in an embittered mood of contention; but they did not consider their fight against society by any means hopeless. The writers of the generation of 1830 were the first to lose the pugnacious attitude of their predecessors and begin to resign themselves to their isolation; their only protest consisted in emphasizing the difference between themselves and the public they served. The writers of the next generation then became so arrogant that they forewent even this demonstration of independence and shrouded themselves in an ostentatious impersonality and insensitiveness. Their reserve was, however, quite different from the objectivity of the seventeenth and eighteenth centuries. The writers of the classicistic age wanted to amuse or instruct their readers or converse with them about certain problems of life. But since the advent of romanticism, literature had developed from an entertainment and a discussion between the author and his public into a self-revelation and self-glorification of the author. When, therefore, Flaubert and the Parnassiens try to hide their personal feelings, their reserve does not in any way imply a return to the spirit of pre-romantic literature; it represents rather the most overbearing and arrogant form of individualism—an individualism which does not even consider it worth while to unbosom itself to others.

1848 and its consequences completely estranged the real artists from the public. As in 1789 and 1830, the revolution again followed a period of supreme intellectual activity and productivity and ended, like the earlier revolutions, with the ultimate defeat of democracy and intellectual freedom. The victory of reaction was accompanied by an unprecedented intellectual decline and a complete brutalization of taste. The conspiracy of the bourgeoisie against the revolution, the denunciation of the class struggle as high treason, as having split the ostensibly peaceful nation into two camps,[60] the suppression of the freedom of the press, the creation of the new bureaucracy as the strongest support of the régime, the establishment of the police state as the most competent judge in all questions of morals and taste, brought about a cleavage in French culture, such as no previous age had known. This was also the beginning of that conflict between meekness and the spirit of revolt in the intelligentsia which has still not been settled today and that opposition to the state which made a part of the intelligentsia into an element of demoralization.

Socialism fell victim to the newly restored order without resistance of any kind. In the first ten years after the *coup d'état* there is no labour movement in France worth mentioning. The proletariat is exhausted, intimidated, confused, its unions have been dissolved, its leaders locked up, expelled or reduced to silence.[61] The elections of 1863, which lead to a considerable increase in the opposition, are the first sign of a change. The working class again combines in associations, strikes multiply and Napoleon III sees himself forced to make more and more new concessions. But socialism would not have reached its goal for a long time, if it had not found an involuntary aid in the liberal upper middle class which saw in Napoleon's caesarism a threat to its own power. This conflict at the heart of the régime explains the political development after 1860, the decay of the authoritarian government and the decadence of the Empire.[62] Napoleon III's rule was based on finance capital and big industry; the army was very useful in the struggle against the proletariat, but all the more useless against the bourgeoisie as its very life depended on the favour of this class. The Second Empire is unthinkable without the wave of economic prosperity with which it coincided. Its strength and its justification were in the wealth of its citizens, in the new technical inventions, the development of the railways and waterways, the consolidation and speeding up of goods traffic, the spread and growing flexibility of the credit system. During the July monarchy it was still politics that most attracted the younger talents, now commerce absorbs the best men. France becomes capitalistic not merely in the latent conditions, but also in the outward forms of its culture. It is true that capitalism and industrialism develop on long familiar lines, but it is only now that they exert their full influence, and from 1850 onwards daily life, the homes of the people, means of transport, the techniques of illumination, food and clothing undergo more radical changes than in all the centuries since the beginning of modern urban civilization. Above all, the demand for luxury and the mania for amusement become incomparably greater and more widespread than ever before.

The bourgeois becomes self-confident, fastidious, arrogant, and imagines he can hide the humbleness of his origins and the hybrid constitution of the new fashionable society, in which the *demi-monde*, actresses and foreigners play an unprecedented rôle, by mere externals. The dissolution of the *ancien régime* enters its final stage and, with the disappearance of the last representatives of the good old society, French culture goes through a more severe crisis than when it received its first violent shock. In art, above all in architecture and interior decoration, bad taste had never set the fashion so much as now. For the newly rich, who are wealthy enough to want to shine, but not old enough to shine without ostentation, nothing is too expensive or pompous. They have no discrimination in the choice of means, in the use of genuine and false materials, and none in the styles which they adopt and mix up. Renaissance and baroque are just as much merely means to an end as marble and onyx, satin and silk, mirror and crystal. They imitate Roman palaces and the castles on the Loire, Pompeian atriums, baroque salons, the furniture of the Louis-Quinze cabinet-makers and the tapestries of the Louis-Seize manufactories. Paris acquires a new splendour, a new metropolitan air. But its grandeur is often only an outward appearance, the pretentious materials are often only a substitute, the marble only stucco, the stone only mortar; the magnificent façades are merely splashed on, the rich decoration is unorganic and amorphous. An unreliable element comes into architecture, corresponding to the parvenu set-up of the prevailing society. Paris again becomes the capital of Europe, not, however, as formerly, the centre of art and culture, but the metropolis of the world of entertainment, the city of opera, operetta, balls, boulevards, restaurants, department stores, world exhibitions, and cheap, ready-made pleasures.

The Second Empire is the classical period of eclecticism—a period without a style of its own in architecture and the industrial arts, and with no stylistic unity in its painting. New theatres, hotels, tenement-houses, barracks, department stores, market-halls, come into being, whole rows and rings of streets arise, Paris is almost rebuilt by Haussmann, but apart from the principle of spaciousness and the beginnings of iron construction, all this takes place without a single original architectural idea. Even in earlier ages different competing styles had, of course, existed side by side and the discrepancy between the historically important style, which was not in accordance with the taste of the leading classes of society, and an inferior, historically insignificant but popular style was a well-known phenomenon. The artistically important tendencies had, however, never met with so little approval as now, and in no other period do we feel so strongly that the art and literary history, which speaks only of the aesthetically valuable and historically significant phenomena, gives an inadequate picture of the real art life of the age; that, in other words, the history of the progressive trends which point to the future and the history of the tendencies which predominate on account of their momentary success and influence refer to two absolutely different sets of facts. An Octave Feuillet or a Paul Baudry, who are given ten lines in our textbooks, occupied incomparably more space in the consciousness of the contemporary public than Flaubert or Courbet, to whom we devote as many pages. The art life of the Second Empire is dominated by easy and agreeable productions, destined for the comfortable and lazy-minded bourgeoisie. The bourgeoisie which calls into being the pretentious architecture of the period, based on the greatest models but usually empty and unorganic, and which fills its homes with the most expensive but often completely superfluous, pseudo-historical articles, favours a style of painting that is nothing more than a pleasant decoration for the walls, a literature that is nothing more than a leisurely entertainment, a music that is easy and ingratiating, and a drama that celebrates its triumphs with the tricks of the 'pièce bien faite'. A bad, uncertain, easily satisfied taste now sets the fashion, whilst real art becomes the possession of a stratum of connoisseurs, who are not in a position to offer the artists any adequate compensation for their achievements.

The naturalism of the period, which contains the whole later development in the bud and can claim the most important artistic creations of the century, remains the art of an opposition, that is to say, the style of a small minority both among the artists themselves and in the public. It is the object of a concentrated attack on the part of the Academy, the University and the critics, in fact, of all official and influential parties. And the hostility becomes more intense as the aims and principles of the movement become more specific and the so-called 'realism' develops into 'naturalism'. In view of the fact that their boundaries are quite fluid, to separate the two phases of the development in this way proves, however, to be absolutely useless from a practical point of view, if not directly misleading. At any rate, it is more expedient to call the whole artistic movement under discussion here naturalism and to reserve the concept of 'realism' for the philosophy opposed to romanticism and its idealism. Naturalism as an artistic style and realism as a philosophical attitude are perfectly clear-cut, but the distinction between naturalism and realism in art only complicates the situation and presents us with a pseudo-problem. Furthermore, the antithesis to romanticism is given too much stress in the concept of 'realism', and both the fact that what we are dealing with here is the direct continuation of the romantic approach, and the fact that naturalism represents more a constant wrestling with the spirit of romanticism than a victory over it, are neglected. Naturalism is a romanticism with new conventions, with new, but still more or less arbitrary, presuppositions of verisimilitude. The most important difference between naturalism and romanticism consists in the scientism of the new trend, in the application of the principles of the exact sciences to the artistic portrayal of facts. The predominance of naturalistic art in the second half of the nineteenth century is altogether only a symptom of the victory of the scientific outlook and of technological thought over the spirit of idealism and traditionalism.

Naturalism derives almost all its criteria of probability from the empiricism of the natural sciences. It bases its concept of psychological truth on the principle of causality, the proper development of the plot on the elimination of chance and miracles, its description of milieu on the idea that every natural phenomenon has its place in an endless chain of conditions and motives, its utilization of characteristic details on the method of scientific observation in which no circumstance, however trifling, is neglected, its avoidance of pure and finished form on the inevitable inconclusiveness of scientific research. But the main source of the naturalistic outlook is the political experience of the generation of 1848: the failure of the revolution, the suppression of the June insurrection and the seizure of power by Louis Napoleon. The disappointment of the democrats and the general disillusionment caused by these events finds its perfect expression in the philosophy of the objective, realistic, strictly empirical natural sciences. After the failure of all ideals, of all Utopias, the tendency is now to keep to the facts, to nothing but the facts. The political origins of naturalism explain in particular its anti-romantic and ethical features: the refusal to escape from reality and the demand for absolute honesty in the description of facts; the striving for impersonality and impassibility as the guarantees of objectivity and social solidarity; activism as the attitude intent not only on knowing and describing but on altering reality; the modernism which keeps to the present as the sole subject of consequence; and, finally, its popular trend both in the choice of subject and in the choice of public. Champfleury's saying, 'le public du livre à vingt sous, c'est le vrai public',[63] shows the direction in which the Revolution of 1848 had influenced literature, and how different the new concept of popularity is from that of the old serial writers. The latter wrote for the broad masses, because they wanted to write for everyone, whereas the naturalists, that is, Champfleury and his circle, want to write above all for the masses. Nevertheless, there are two different trends within naturalistic literature: the naturalism of the writers who come from the bohemian circle, Champfleury, Duranty and Murger, and the naturalism of the 'rentiers', the Flauberts and the Goncourts.[64] The two camps confront each other as absolute adversaries; the bohemians hate all traditionalism, whilst Flaubert and his friends suspect any writer who strives for popular favour.

Naturalism begins as a movement of the artistic proletariat; its first master is Courbet, a man of the people, and an artist lacking all feeling for bourgeois respectability. After the old bohème had broken up and its members had become the favourites of the romanticizing bourgeoisie or the occupants of good bourgeois positions themselves, a new circle forms around Courbet, a second bohemian cénacle. The painter of the 'Stone-breakers' and the 'Burial at Ornans' owes his position as leader chiefly to human, not to artistic qualities, above all to his descent, to the fact that he describes the life of the common people and appeals to the people or, at any rate, to the broader strata of the public, that he leads the uncertain and unrestrained life of the artistic proletariat, despises the bourgeois and bourgeois ideals, and is a convinced democrat, a revolutionary and the victim of persecution and contempt. Naturalistic theory arises directly in defence of his art against traditionalistic criticism. On the occasion of the exhibition of the 'Burial at Ornans' (1850), Champfleury declares: 'From now on the critics must decide for or against *realism.*' The great word had now been spoken.[65] Intrinsically, neither the concept nor the practice of this art is new, even if everyday life had perhaps never been portrayed with such directness and brutality; but its political bias, the social message which it contains, the representation of the people with a complete lack of condescension and any supercilious interest in folkways and customs—all this is new. But however new this social outlook is, and however much talk there is in Courbet's circle about the humanitarian aims and political tasks of art, bohemianism is and remains an heir of aestheticizing romanticism. It often ascribes a significance to art which it did not have even in the most exalted theories of the romantics and makes a prophet out of a confusedly chattering painter and a historical event out of the exhibition of an unsaleable picture.

The passion which fills Courbet and his supporters is, however, fundamentally political; their self-assurance comes from the conviction that they are the pioneers of truth and the forerunners of the future. Champfleury asserts that naturalism is nothing more than the artistic trend corresponding to democracy, and the Goncourts simply identify bohemianism with socialism in literature. In the eyes of Proudhon and Courbet, naturalism and political rebellion are different expressions of the same attitude, and they see no essential difference between social and artistic truth. In a letter of 1851, Courbet declares: 'I am not only a socialist, but also a democrat and a republican, in a word, a partisan of revolution and, above all, a realist, that is, the sincere friend of the real truth.'[66] And Zola merely continues Courbet's idea, when he says: 'La République sera naturaliste ou elle ne sera pas.'[67] By rejecting naturalism, the ruling classes, therefore, only give expression to their instinct of self-preservation: their perfectly correct feeling that every art that describes life without bias and without restraint is in itself a revolutionary act. In reference to this danger, conservatism has clearer ideas at its disposal than the opposition itself.[68] Gustave Planche declar quite frankly in the *Revue des Deux Mondes* that the resistanc to naturalism is a confession of faith in the prevailing order an that by rejecting naturalism, one is also rejecting the materialisn and democracy of the age.[69]

The conservative critics of the 'fifties already quote all th well-known arguments against naturalism and try to cloak th political and social prejudices which condition their anti-natural istic attitude with aesthetic objections. Naturalism, they say lacks all idealism and morality, luxuriates in ugliness and vul garity, in the diseased and the obscene, and represents an in discriminate, slavish imitation of reality. But what disturbs th conservative critics is, naturally, not the degree but the subjec of the imitation. They know only too well that with the destruc tion of the classical-romantic kalokagathia and the abolition c the old ideal of beauty, which had survived almost unchange until 1850, in spite of the revolutions and restratifications o society, Courbet is fighting for a new type of man and a nev order. They feel that the ugliness of his peasants and workers the corpulence and vulgarity of his middle-class women, are a pro test against prevailing society and that his 'contempt for idealism and his 'wallowing in filth' are all part of naturalism's revolu tionary armoury. Millet paints the apotheosis of physical worl and makes the peasant the hero of a new epic. Daumier describe the state-supporting bourgeois in his obtuseness and hardness o heart, scoffs at his politics, his justice, his amusements and un covers the whole phantom-like comedy hidden behind bourgeoi respectability. It is unmistakably clear that the choice of motifs i here conditioned more by political than by artistic considerations

Even landscape painting becomes a demonstration against th culture of the prevailing society. The modern landscape aros from the very beginning as a contrast to the life of the industria town, it is true, but romantic landscape painting still represente an autonomous world, the picture of an unreal, ideal existence that did not need to be brought in any direct relationship to th life of the present and the life of everyday. This world was sc different from the scenes of real, contemporary life that it wa certainly understood as its antithesis, but hardly as a protes against it. The 'paysage intime' of modern painting, on the other hand, describes a milieu that, in its quietness and intimacy, is utterly different from the town, but is yet so close to it on account of its simple, unromantic, everyday character that we are inevitably prompted to compare them. The romantic mountain-tops and sea-levels and even Constable's woods and skies had something fabulous and mythical about them, whereas the forest clearings and forest fringes of the painters of Barbizon seem so natural and familiar, so easy to reach and so completely possessable, that the modern townsman must necessarily feel them as a warning and a reproach. In this choice of trivial, 'unpoetic' motifs the same democratic spirit is expressed as in the choice of the human types of Courbet, Millet and Daumier—with the sole difference that the landscape painters seem to say: nature is beautiful at all times and in all places, no 'ideal' motifs are necessary to do justice to its beauty, whereas the figure painters want to prove that man is ugly and pitiable no matter whether he is oppressing others or being oppressed himself. But, in spite of its sincerity and simplicity, the naturalistic landscape soon becomes just as conventional as the romantic had been. The romantics painted the poetry of the sacred grove, the naturalists paint the prose of rural life—the clearing with the grazing cattle, the river with the ferry, the field with the hayrick. Progress here consists, as so often in the history of art, more in the renewal than in the diminution of the stock motifs. The most radical changes follow from the principle of open-air painting, which is, incidentally, by no means put into practice all at once and hardly ever consistently, and is usually limited to creating the mere semblance that the picture has arisen in the open air. Apart from its obvious scientific elements, this technical idea also has a political and moral content and seems to be trying to say: Out into the open, out into the light of truth!

The social character of the new art is also expressed in the tendency towards a closer amalgamation of the painters, in their efforts to found artists' colonies and to adapt themselves to one another in their way of life. The 'School of Fontainebleau', which is no school at all and no coterie, but an incoherent group whose members go their own ways and are bound to one another merely by the earnestness of their artistic aims, already represents the collective spirit of the new age. And the later artist fraternities and settlements, the joint reformative efforts and *avant-garde* formations of the nineteenth century, all express the same tendency towards coalition and co-operation. The epochal consciousness, the awareness of the significance and the requirements of the hour, that came into the world with romanticism, now completely dominates the minds of artists. Courbet's dictum about 'faire de l'art vivant' and Daumier's alleged motto 'Il faut être de son temps' express one and the same idea, namely, the desire to break through the isolation of the romantic and redeem the artist from his individualism. The introduction of lithography as an artistic medium is likewise a symptom of this social aspiration. But it is not only in harmony with that democratization of the enjoyment of art which was attained in literature by the serial novel, it implies the victory of popular taste and journalism on an incomparably higher level. Daumier's 'journalistic' painting marks a culminating point in the art of his time, whereas Balzac's serial novel writing represents a lowering of his own level without a rise in the general standard.

But did the naturalists really represent the contemporary world, or at least an important part of the contemporary art public? They certainly did not represent the majority of the people who ordered, bought or publicly criticized pictures, who directed the art academies and had to decide which works were to be exhibited. The views of these people were fairly liberal on the whole, but their tolerance stopped short of naturalism. They liked and promoted the academic idealism of Ingres and his school, the romantic anecdotal painting of Decamps and Meissonier, the elegant portrait art of Winterhalter and Dubufe, the pseudo-baroque narrative painting of Couture and Boulanger, the mythological and allegorical decorations of Bouguereau and Baudry,[70] that is to say, large-scale, resplendent and empty form in all its varieties. But they had no room for the creations of naturalistic painting either in their homes crammed with furniture and draperies, nor in their official halls built in one or the other of the favourite historical styles. Modern art became homeless and began to lose all practical function. The same distance that separated the naturalistic painting and the elegant 'wall decoration' of the time also divided serious and light literature, serious and light music, from each other. The literature or music which did not serve to entertain was just as devoid of function as the progressive painting of the time. Previously even the most valuable and most serious productions of literature, such as the novels of Prévost, Rousseau and Balzac, had formed the reading of relatively large strata of society, some of which were quite indifferent to literature as such. The dual rôle of literature as an art and an entertainment at the same time, and the satisfaction of the requirements of different levels of culture by means of the same works, now comes to an end. The artistically most valuable literary products are hardly any longer suitable for light reading and have no attraction at all for the general reading public, unless they draw public attention to themselves for some reason and become successful by creating a scandal, like Flaubert's *Madame Bovary*, for example. Only a quite small stratum of intellectuals appreciates such works adequately and therefore even this literature may be classed as 'studio art', like the whole school of progressive painting: it is intended for specialists, for artists and connoisseurs. The estrangement of the whole body of progressive artists from the contemporary world and their refusal to have anything to do with the public goes so far that they not only accept lack of success as something perfectly natural, but regard success itself as a sign of artistic inferiority and consider being misunderstood by their contemporaries a precondition of immortality.

Romanticism still contained a popular element appealing to the broader masses of society, whereas naturalism, at least in its most important productions, has nothing to attract the general public. The death of Balzac marks the end of the romantic age; Victor Hugo is still at the height of his artistic development, but as a literary movement romanticism has ceased to play any part in cultural life. The leading writers' renunciation of the romantic ideal also means a complete break with the most influential circles in the general public and the world of criticism. The 'partie de résistance', which in literature corresponds to the party of order in politics, takes up a more positive attitude to the romantic school than naturalism, despite the latter's direct historical connection with romanticism. It is true that conservative critics fight the spirit of rebellion in every form, romantic as well as naturalistic, and put reasonableness above every kind of spontaneity, but they demand that literature should express 'genuine feelings' and they regard the 'depth of the heart' as the criterion of the real artist. This new aesthetic of the emotions is, however, only a new, though not always entirely clear form of the old kalokagathia; it is based on the alleged identity of the emotionally spontaneous and the morally valuable elements of the spiritual life, and postulates a mystical harmony between the good and the beautiful. The moral effect of art is its most important axiom and the educational rôle of the artist its supreme ideal. The bourgeois attitude to the principle of 'l'art pour l'art' has changed once more. After its original rejection and later recognition of 'pure', morally neutral art, its approach is now relentlessly hostile. The rebelliousness of the artist has been broken, there is no longer any cause to fear his intervention in questions of practical life; 'l'art pour l'art' can be thrown overboard and the competence of the artist as an intellectual leader recognized again. Naturalism is the only surviving source of possible danger; but since its representatives declare themselves in favour, if not of 'l'art pour l'art' as such, at least of the unprejudiced and unsentimental treatment of moral questions, in other words, of an a-moral approach in art, the rejection of 'l'art pour l'art' is also directed against them. The government fits art and artists into its educational and correctional system. The editors-in-chief and the critics of the great periodicals and newspapers, men like Buloz, Bertin, Gustave Planche, Charles Rémusat, Arnauld de Pontmartin, Émile Montégut, are its highest authorities; Jules Sandeau, Octave Feuillet, Émile Augier and Dumas *fils* its most respected authors; the University and the Academy its teaching and research institutes for intellectual hygiene; the public prosecutor and the prefect of the Paris police the guardians of its moral principles. The representatives of naturalism have to fight against the hostility of the critics until about 1860, and against that of the University all their lives. The Academy remains barred to them and they are never able to count on help from the state. Flaubert and the Goncourt brothers are impeached for offences against morality, and a considerable fine is imposed on Baudelaire.

The lawsuit against Flaubert and the sensational success of *Madame Bovary* (1857) decide the struggle for naturalism in favour of the new trend. The public shows itself interested and soon the critics also lay down their arms; only the most obstinate and short-sighted reactionaries remain in opposition. The progressive trend is this time forced on the critics by the reading public, although the reasons for the public's interest are by no means purely artistic. Sainte-Beuve, who has a very subtle feeling for changes in intellectual fashions, finds the way back to the liberalism of his youth. He joins the circle which includes Taine, Renan, Berthelot and Flaubert, criticizes the government and proclaims the victory of naturalism. The fact that his political and artistic conversion takes place at the same time is extremely symptomatic of the intellectual situation; it proves that, in spite of its internal division into the two camps of the bohemians and the 'rentiers', naturalism is rooted in liberalism. One cannot even maintain that Flaubert, whose political views are thoroughly conservative, represents a reactionary, anti-social and anti-liberal point of view. The opposition to the political system of the Second Empire and the opportunism of the bourgeoisie, as expressed above all in the *Éducation sentimentale*, is at any rate more characteristic of his way of thinking than the abusive references to democracy in his often all too impulsive and contradictory letters. Anti-government social criticism is common to all naturalistic literature, and Flaubert, Maupassant, Zola, Baudelaire and the Goncourts are, in spite of all the differences in their political outlook, in complete agreement as regards their nonconformity.[71] The 'triumph of realism' is repeated and its representatives all contribute to destroy the foundations of the prevailing society. In his letters, Flaubert complains repeatedly about the suppression of freedom and the hatred for the traditions of the great Revolution.[72] He is undeniably an opponent of the universal franchise and the rule of the uneducated masses,[73] but he is by no means an ally of the ruling bourgeoisie. His political views are often vague and childish, but they always express an honest endeavour to be rational and realistic, and manifest an attitude from which all Utopias, including those of the prophets of universal happiness and progress, are far removed. He rejects socialism not so much because of its materialistic as because of its irrational elements.[74] In order to be immune from all dogmatisms, all blind faiths and all ties, he refuses to accept any kind of political activism and fights against every temptation which might cause him to venture beyond the circle of purely private relationships and interests.[75] He becomes a nihilist for fear of self-deception. But he feels that he is the legitimate heir of the Revolution and the enlightenment and attributes the intellectual decline to the fateful victory of Rousseau over Voltaire.[76]

Flaubert clings to rationalism as the last relic of the unromantic eighteenth century, and one only needs to think of the anxiety neuroses of our own time, to understand the meaning of his warning about the irrational, self-destructive tendencies of Rousseauist romanticism. 'What is the offence for which men are supposed to be responsible' —he asks a neurotic woman correspondent tortured with religious hallucinations and self-reproach.[77] That sounds like a cry of distress and seems like the writer's last attempt to keep his equilibrium in the midst of a world in jeopardy on every side. Flaubert's wrestling with the spirit of romanticism, the constant changes in his attitude towards it, in the course of which he always has the feeling of being a traitor, are nothing but a manoeuvre to preserve this balance. His whole life and work consists in a wavering between two poles, between his romantic inclinations and his self-discipline, between his yearning for death and his desire to remain alive and sound. His very provincialism keeps him nearer to romanticism, already somewhat old-fashioned, than his contemporaries in Paris,[78] and right up to and beyond his twentieth year he lives in the fictitious world and overheated spiritual atmosphere of a youth without roots and behind the times. In later years he often refers to the terrible frame of mind, under the constant threat of madness and suicide, in which he found himself with his friends at that time,[79] and from which he was able to save himself only by an extraordinary exertion of the will, and a merciless self-discipline. Until the crisis which he goes through when he is twenty-two, he is a man tortured by visions, fits of depression, wild outbursts of emotion, a sick man whose irritability and sensibility contain the seeds of inevitable catastrophe. His life in and for art, the regularity and uncompromising character of his work, the inhumanity of his 'l'art pour l'art' and the impersonality of his style, in a word, the whole of his artistic theory and practice, is nothing but a desperate effort to save himself from certain destruction. In him aestheticism plays the same rôle psychologically as it had played in romanticism sociologically; it is a kind of escape from a reality that has become unbearable.

Flaubert writes himself free from romanticism; he overcomes it by giving it literary shape, and by developing from its lover and victim into its analyst and critic. He confronts the world of romantic dreams with the reality of everyday life and becomes a naturalist, in order to expose the mendacity and unwholesomeness of these extravagant delusions. But he never tires of affirming his hatred of humdrum everyday life, his loathing of the naturalism of *Madame Bovary* and the *Éducation sentimentale* and his contempt for the 'childishness' of the whole theory. Nevertheless, he remains the first real naturalistic writer, the first whose works give a picture of reality in harmony with the doctrines of naturalism. With a sure eye, Sainte-Beuve recognizes the results of the climacteric in the history of French literature represented by *Madame Bovary*. 'Flaubert wields the pen', he writes in his review, 'as others wield the scalpel,' and he describes the new style as the victory of the anatomist and physiologist in art.[80] Zola derives his whole theory of naturalism from the works of Flaubert and regards the author of *Madame Bovary* and the *Éducation sentimentale* as the creator of the modern novel.[81] Flaubert signifies above all, compared with the exaggerations and violent effects of Balzac, the complete renunciation of the melodramatic, adventurous and, in fact, of even the merely thrilling plot; the fondness for describing the monotony, flatness and lack of variety of everyday life; the avoidance of all extremes in the moulding of his characters, the refusal to lay any emphasis on the good or bad in them; the forgoing of all theses, propaganda, moral lessons, in brief, of all direct intervention in the proceedings and all direct interpretation of the facts.

But Flaubert's impersonality and impartiality by no means follow from the presuppositions of his naturalism, and do not correspond merely to the aesthetic requirement that the objects in a work of art should owe the impression they make to their own life, not to the author's recommendation; his 'impassibilité' in no way constitutes merely a reaction against Balzac's importunity and a return to the idea of the work of art as a self-contained microcosm, as a system in which 'the author, like God in the universe, should be always present but never visible';[82] it is also not merely the result of the knowledge, since repeated and confirmed so often by the Goncourts, by Maupassant, Gide, Valéry and others, that the worst poems are made from the most beautiful feelings and that personal sympathy, genuine emotion, twitching nerves and tear-filled eyes only impair the sharpness of the artist's vision—no, Flaubert's impassibility is not only a technical principle, it contains a new idea, a new morality of the artist. His 'nous sommes faits pour le dire, et non pour l'avoir' is the most extreme and most uncompromising formulation of that renunciation of life which was the starting point of romanticism as an aesthetic doctrine and a philosophy, but it is, in accordance with the ambivalence of Flaubert's feelings, at the same time the sharpest possible rejection of romanticism. For, when Flaubert exclaims that literature is not the 'dregs of the heart', he is trying to preserve both the purity of the heart and the purity of literature.

From the knowledge that the chaotic, eccentric, romantic disposition of his youth was on the point of destroying him both as an artist and as a human being, Flaubert derived a new way of life and a new aesthetic. 'There are children', he wrote in 1852, 'on whom music makes an adverse impression; they have great abilities, remember tunes after only hearing them once, get excited when they hear a piano being played, get palpitations, lose flesh, become pale, fall ill and their poor nerves are convulsed with agony, like the nerves of dogs when they hear music. One will search in vain for the Mozarts of the future amongst such children. Their talents have become deranged, the idea has worked its way into the flesh where it is sterile and where it also destroys the flesh itself . . .'[83] Flaubert did not realize how romantic his separation of the 'idea' from the 'flesh' and his renunciation of life in favour of art was and never recognized that the real, unromantic solution of his problem can only grow out of life itself. Nevertheless, his own attempt at a solution is one of the great symbolical attitudes of Western man; it represents the last relevant form of the romantic outlook on life, the form in which it obliterates itself and in which the bourgeois intelligentsia becomes aware of its inability to master life and to make art an instrument of life. The self-disparagement of the middle class is actually part of the very nature of the bourgeois attitude to life, as Brunetière has pointed out,[84] but this self-criticism and self-denial only becomes a decisive factor in cultural life from Flaubert's time onwards. The bourgeoisie of the July monarchy still believed in itself and in the mission of its art.

Flaubert's criticism of the romantics, his loathing for the display and prostitution of their most personal experiences and most intimate feelings, is reminiscent of Voltaire's aversion to Rousseau's exhibitionism and crude naturalism. But Voltaire was still completely uncontaminated by romanticism and, in fighting against Rousseau, he did not have to fight against himself at the same time; his middle-classness was unproblematical and not exposed to any danger. Flaubert, on the other hand, is full of contradictions and his antithetical relationship to romanticism corresponds to an equally conflicting relationship to the middle class. His hatred of the bourgeois is, as has often been said, the source of his inspiration and the origin of his naturalism. In his persecution mania, he allows the bourgeois principle to expand into a metaphysical substance, into a kind of 'thing-in-itself', something unfathomable and inexhaustible. 'For me the bourgeois is something without definition', he writes to a friend—a saying in which, along with the idea of the indefinite, that of the infinite can also be heard. The discovery that the bourgeoisie itself had become romantic and in fact, to a certain extent, the romantic element in society par excellence, that romantic verse is declaimed by no one with so much feeling and emotion as by this class, and that the Emma Bovarys are the last representatives of the romantic ideal, contributed much to turning Flaubert away from his romanticism. But Flaubert himself is a bourgeois in the very depths of his nature and he knows it. 'I refuse to be classed a man of letters,' he declares, '. . . I am simply a bourgeois, living a quiet life in the country and occupying himself with literature.'[85] During the period when he stands accused on account of his book and is preparing his defence, he writes to his brother: 'It must be known at the Home Office that we in Rouen are what is called a *family* and that we have deep roots in the country.' But Flaubert's bourgeois character finds expression above all in his methodical and strictly disciplined habits of work, his distaste for the disorderly ways of the so-called genius-like creation. He quotes Goethe's words about the 'demands of the day' and makes it his duty to practise writing as a systematic, bourgeois profession, independent of likes and dislikes, moods and inspiration. His monomaniacal struggle to achieve formal perfection and his matter-of-fact philosophy of art originate in this bourgeois and workmanlike conception of artistic activity. 'L'art pour l'art' results, as we know, only partly from the romantic outlook and its estrangement from society and practical life; in some respects it is the direct expression of a genuinely bourgeois and workmanlike attitude, concentrated wholly on the efficient performance of the work in hand.[86] Flaubert's dislike for romanticism is closely connected with his aversion to the 'artist' as a type, with his loathing of the irresponsible dreamer and idealist. In the artist and the romantic he attacks the embodiment of a way of life by which he knows that his whole moral existence is threatened. He hates the bourgeois, but he hates the tramp even more. He knows that there is a destructive element in all artistic activity, an antisocial, disintegrating force. He knows that the artistic way of life tends to anarchy and chaos and that artistic work is apt to neglect discipline and order, perseverance and steadiness, if only because of the irrational factors involved in it. That which Goethe had already felt,[87] and Thomas Mann makes the central problem of his criticism of the artistic way of life, the artist's tendency to the pathological and the criminal, his shameless exhibitionism and his undignified trade of playing the fool, in a word, the whole histrion's and vagabond's existence that he leads, must have disturbed and depressed Flaubert deeply. The asceticism which he imposes on himself, his workmanlike assiduity, the monastic seclusion in which he shelters behind his work, are intended, in the final analysis, to bear witness only to his seriousness, his bourgeois respectability and reliability, and to prove that he has absolutely nothing in common with Gautier's 'red waistcoat'. The artistic proletariat has become a social fact which it is impossible to neglect any longer; the bourgeoisie considers it a revolutionary danger and the bourgeois writers feel as unanimous with their own class about this danger as they do later, when faced with the Commune, which rouses into action all their suppressed bourgeois instincts.

A doctrine like Flaubert's aestheticism is, however, no clear-cut, unequivocal, final solution, but a dialectical force, altering its direction and questioning its own validity. Flaubert looks in art for reassurance and protection from the romantic impetuosity of his youth; but in fulfilling this function, it assumes fantastic proportions and a demonic power, it not only becomes a substitute for everything else that can satisfy and content the soul, but the basic principle of life itself. Only in art does there seem to be any stability, any fixed point in the stream of evanescence, corruption and dissolution. The self-surrender of life to art here acquires a quasi-religious, mystical character; it is no longer a mere service and a mere sacrifice, but an ecstatic, spellbound gazing at the only real Being, a total, self-denying absorption in the Idea. 'L'art, la seule chose vraie et bonne de la vie', Flaubert writes at the beginning of his career,[88] 'l'homme n'est rien, l'oeuvre tout', at the end.[89] The doctrine of 'l'art pour l'art' as the glorification of technical mastery, in contrast to romantic dilettantism, was originally the expression of a desire to adapt oneself to a firm social order, but the aestheticism to which Flaubert comes in the end, represents an antisocial and life-negating nihilism, an escape from everything connected with the practical, materially conditioned existence of ordinary human beings. It is the expression of mere contempt and absolute denial of the world. 'Life is so horrible', Flaubert groans, 'that one can only bear it by avoiding it. And that can be done by living in the world of art.'[90] The 'nous sommes faits pour le dire, et non pour l'avoir' is a cruel message, the acceptance of an unblessed and inhuman fate. 'You will only be able to describe wine, love, women and fame, if you are neither a drinker, neither a lover neither a husband, nor a soldier', writes Flaubert and adds that the artist 'is a monstrosity, something standing outside nature'. The romantic was too intimately connected with life, that is to say, with a yearning for life; he was mere feeling, mere nature. Flaubert's artist no longer has any direct relationship to life; he is nothing but a puppet, an abstraction, something thoroughly inhuman and unnatural.

Art lost its spontaneity in its conflict with romanticism and became the prize in the artist's fight against himself, against his romantic origins, against his inclinations and instincts. Hitherto artistic activity had been regarded, if not as a process of letting oneself go, at any rate, as that of letting oneself be guided by one's own talent; now every work seems to be a 'tour de force', an achievement that has to be wrung from oneself, obtained by fighting against oneself. Faguet remarks that Flaubert writes his letters in an absolutely different style from his novels, and that good style and correct language by no means come to him naturally and as a matter of course.[91] Nothing sheds a more piercing light on the distance between the natural man and the artist in Flaubert than this statement. There are few writers of whose working methods we know so much, but there has certainly never been a writer who wrote his works with such torture, with such convulsions and so much against his own instincts. His constant wrestling with language, his struggle for the 'mot juste', is, however, only a symptom—the sign of the unbridgeable gulf between the 'possession' of life and the 'expression' of it. The 'mot juste', the uniquely correct word, no more exists than does the uniquely correct form; they are both the invention of aesthetes for whom art as a vital function has ceased to have any meaning. 'I prefer to die like a dog rather than hasten by a single moment any sentence of mine before it is mature'—no writer with a spontaneous human relationship to his work would have spoken like that. Matthew Arnold's Shakespeare smiled at such scrupulousness in the Elysian Fields. Complaints about the daily, heart-, brain- and nerve-deadening struggle, about the life of the fettered galley-slave that he leads, are the leitmotif of Flaubert's letters. 'For three days I have been tossing about on all my urniture trying to get ideas', he writes to Louise Colet in 1853.[92] I can no longer distinguish the days of the week one from nother . . . I am leading a mad, absurd life. . . . This is pure, bsolute nothingness', he writes to Ernest Feydeau in 1858.[93] You don't know what it means to sit all day long with your head n both hands, trying to squeeze a word out of your brain', he vrites to George Sand in 1866.[94] Working regularly for seven ours, he writes one page a day, then twenty pages in a month, hen again two pages in a week. It is pitiable. 'La rage des hrases t'a désséché le cœur', his mother tells him, and probably o one ever spoke a more cruel and truer word about him. The vorst of all is that, in spite of his aestheticism, Flaubert also lespairs of art. Perhaps in the end it is nothing but a kind of laying at skittles, perhaps everything is mere humbug, he emarks on one occasion.[95] His whole uncertainty, the forced, ortured features of his work, his absolute lack of the light-nindedness of the old authors, come from the fact that he always eels his works are endangered and that he never really believes n them. 'What I am doing now', he declares while he is at work n *Madame Bovary*, 'can easily develop into something like Paul le Kock. . . . In a book like this the displacement of a single line an divert one from the goal.'[96] And while he is working at the *Éducation sentimentale*, he writes: 'What drives me to despair is he feeling that I am doing something useless and contrary to art. . . .'[97] It becomes a standing formula in his letters that he is ccupying himself with things for which he is not suited, and hat he never succeeds in writing what he would really like to write and in the way he would like to write it.[98]

Flaubert's statement, '*Madame Bovary*, c'est moi', is true in a double sense. He must often have had the feeling that not merely the romanticism of his youth, but also his criticism of romanticism, the judicial mantle which he presumed to don in literary matters, was a life-fantasy. *Madame Bovary* owes its artistic veracity and opportuneness to the intensity with which he experienced the problem of this life-fantasy, the crises of self-deception and the falsification of his own personality. When the meaning of romanticism became problematical, the whole questionableness of modern man was revealed—his escape from the present, his constant desire to be somewhere different from where he has to be, his unceasing yearning for foreign lands because he is afraid of the proximity and responsibility for the present. The analysis of romanticism led to the diagnosis of the disease of the whole century, to the recognition of the neurosis the victims of which are incapable of giving an account of themselves, and would always prefer to be inside other peoples' skins who do not, in other words, see themselves as they really are but as they would like to be. In this self-deception and falsification of life, this 'Bovarysm', as his philosophy has been called,[99] Flaubert seizes hold of the essence of the modern subjectivism that distorts everything with which it comes in contact. The feeling that we possess only a deformed version of reality and that we are imprisoned in the subjective forms of our thinking is first given full artistic expression in *Madame Bovary*. A straight and almost uninterrupted road leads from here to Proust's illusionism.[100] The transformation of reality by the human consciousness, already pointed out by Kant, acquired in the course of the nineteenth century the character of an alternately more or less conscious and unconscious illusion, and called forth attempts to explain and unmask it, such as historical materialism and psycho-analysis. With his interpretation of romanticism, Flaubert is one of the great revealers and unmaskers of the century, and, therefore, one of the founders of the modern, reflexive outlook on life.

Flaubert's two main novels, the story of the romantic and futile provincial woman and of the well-to-do, tolerably gifted young bourgeois who squanders his intellectual powers and talents, are closely connected. Frédéric Moreau has been called the intellectual child of Emma Bovary; but both are the children of that 'tired civilization'[101] in which the life of the successful middle class moves and has its being. Both embody the same emotional confusion and represent the same type of 'ratés' so characteristic of this generation of heirs. Zola called the *Éducation sentimentale* the modern novel par excellence, and, as the story of a generation, it does in fact form the climax of the development which begins with the *Rouge et Noir* and is continued in the *Comédie humaine*. It is an 'historical' novel, that is, a novel in which the hero is time, in a double sense. In the first place, time appears in it as the element which conditions and gives life to the characters, and then as the principle by which they are worn out, destroyed and devoured. Creative, productive time was discovered by romanticism; corrupting time, which undermines life and hollows man out, was discovered in the fight against romanticism. The realization that it is, as Flaubert says, 'not the great disasters but the small ones of which one has to be afraid',[102] in other words, that we are not destroyed by our greatest and most shattering disappointments, but perish slowly with our faded hopes and ambitions, is the saddest fact of our existence. This gradual, imperceptible, irresistible pining away, this silent undermining of life, which does not even produce the startling bang of the great, imposing catastrophe, is the experience around which the *Éducation sentimentale* and practically the whole modern novel revolves—an experience that, owing to its non-tragic and undramatic character, can only be portrayed in the epic mode. The unrivalled position of the novel in the literature of the nineteenth century is, no doubt, to be explained above all by the fact that the feeling that life is being irresistibly hackneyed and mechanized, and the conception of time as a destructive force, had completely taken hold of men's minds. The novel develops its formal principle from the idea of the corrosive effects of time, just as tragedy derives the basis of its form from the idea of the timeless fate which destroys man with one fell blow. And as fate possesses a superhuman greatness and a metaphysical power in tragedy, so time attains an inordinate, almost mythical dimension in the novel. In the *Éducation sentimentale*—and this is the very reason for the novel's historical importance—Flaubert discovers the constant presence of passing and past time in our life. He is the first to realize that, with their relation to time, things also change their meaning and value—they can become significant and important for us only because they form a part of our past—and that their value in this function is absolutely independent of their effective content and objective bearings. This revaluation of the past, and the consolation that lies in the fact that time, which buries us and the ruins of our life, 'leaves buds and traces of the lost meaning everywhere',[103] is, however, still an expression of the romantic feeling that the present, that every present, is barren and without significance, and that even the past was lacking all value and importance so long as it was the present. That is, in fact, the meaning of the final pages of the *Éducation sentimentale*, which contain the key to the whole novel and to Flaubert's whole conception of time. That is the reason why the author singles out an episode from his hero's past life at random, and calls it the best he probably ever had from life. The absolute nothingness of this experience, its complete triviality and emptiness, means that there is always one link missing in the chain of our existence, and that every detail of our life is replete with the melancholy of objective purposelessness and a purely subjective significance.

Flaubert marks one of the lowest points in the curve which describes the emotional outlook of the nineteenth century. In spite of its sombre notes, Zola's work already expresses a new hope, a turning towards optimism. And, although he is just as bitter, Maupassant is, nevertheless, more light-hearted and more cynical than Flaubert; ideologically, his stories form the transition to the light fiction of the bourgeoisie. As far as its optimistic and pessimistic elements are concerned, this ideology is just as complicated and contradictory as that of the lower classes; to form a correct judgement here one must differentiate strictly between the emotional attitude of the individual strata of society to the present and the future. The rising classes are confident about the future, however pessimistically they regard the present, whereas the ruling classes, for all their power and glory, are often filled with the choking feeling of their own imminent destruction. In the minds of the ascending classes a pessimistic attitude to the present is connected with optimism about the future, for they have every confidence in themselves and their advancement in society; in the minds of the classes doomed to destruction the conception of present and future is just as conflicting, but the signs are reversed. For this reason Zola, who identifies himself with the oppressed and the exploited and whose attitude to the present is thoroughly pessimistic, is by no means hopeless about the future. This antagonism is also in accordance with his scientific outlook. He is, as he himself declares, a determinist, but not a fatalist, in other words, he is perfectly conscious of the fact that men are dependent on the material conditions of their life in their whole behaviour, but he does not believe that these conditions are unalterable. He accepts Taine's milieu theory unreservedly and presses it even further, but he considers it the real task and the absolutely attainable goal of the social sciences to transform and improve the external conditions of human life —to plan society, as we should say today.[104]

The whole of Zola's scientific thinking is stamped with this utilitarian character and is filled with the reforming and civilizing spirit of the enlightenment. His psychology itself is dependent on practical aims; it stands in the service of a spiritual hygiene and is based on the theory that as soon as their mechanism is understood, even the passions can be influenced. The scientism peculiar to naturalism reaches its summit in Zola and begins to veer into its opposite. Hitherto the representatives of naturalism had regarded science as the handy-man of art; Zola sees art as the servant of science. Flaubert also believes that art has reached a scientific stage in its development and endeavours not merely to describe reality in accordance with the most meticulous observation, but stresses the scientific and especially the medical character of his observation. But he never claims other than artistic merits for himself, whereas Zola desires to be regarded as a research worker and to support his reputation as an artist by his realiability as a scientist. This is an expression of the same apotheosis of science, the same scientific fetish-worship which is characteristic of socialism in general and is peculiar to the social strata which expect the improvement of their position in society to come from science. For Zola, as for the scientific and socialistic ideology in general, man is a being whose qualities are conditioned by the laws of heredity and environment, and, in his enthusiasm for the natural sciences, he goes so far as to define naturalism in the novel as simply the application of the experimental method to literature. But in this context experiment is only a big word with no meaning at all, or at least no more exact meaning than mere observation.[105] Zola's literary theories are not entirely free of charlatanism, but his novels have, nevertheless, a certain theoretical value, for, even if they do not contain any new scientific insights, they are, as has rightly been said, the creations of a considerable sociologist. And they are, and this is extremely remarkable from the point of view of artistic development, the result of a systematic scientific method previously quite unknown in art. The artist's experience of the world is without plan and system; he gathers his empirical material as it were in passing by the features and data of life, which he carries around with him, which he allows to grow and mature, in order one day to draw unknown, undreamt-of treasures from this store. The scholar chooses to take the opposite way. He starts with a problem, that is, with a fact of which he knows nothing or does not know the very thing he would really like to know. The gathering and sifting of the material begins with the setting of the problem, that is, a closer acquaintance with the section of life to be treated begins with the setting of the problem. It is not the experience which leads him to the problem, but the problem which leads him to the experience. That is also Zola's method and procedure. He begins a new novel as the German professor of the anecdote begins a new course of lectures, in order to obtain more exact information about a subject with which he is unfamiliar. What Paul Alexis has related about the origins of *Nana*, about Zola's voyages of discovery into the world of prostitution and the theatre, is, at any rate, reminiscent of this anecdote.

The whole idea on which Zola bases his cycle of novels seems like the plan for a scientific undertaking. The individual works constitute, in accordance with the programme, the parts of a great, encyclopedic system, a kind of Summa of modern society. 'I want to explain how a family, that is, a small group of human beings, behaves in a society', he writes in the preface to the *Fortune des Rougon*. And by society he means the decadent and corrupt France of the Second Empire. No artistic programme could sound more exact, more objective, more scientific. But Zola does not escape the fate of his century; in spite of his scientific attitude he is a romantic, and indeed much more whole-heartedly so than the other less radical naturalists of his day. His one-sided, undialectical rationalization and schematization of reality is already boldly and ruthlessly romantic. And the symbols to which he reduces motley, many-sided, contradictory life—the city, the machine, alcohol, prostitution, the department store, the market-hall, the stock exchange, the theatre, etc.—are all the more the visions of a romantic systematizer, who sees allegories instead of concrete individual phenomena everywhere. To this fondness of Zola's for the allegorical is added the fascination which everything big and excessive exerts on him. He is a fanatical devotee of the masses, of numbers, of raw, compact, inexhaustible factual reality. He is enchanted by material abundance, the luxuriance and the great 'tutti' of life. It is not for nothing that he is a contemporary of the 'grand opera' and Baron Haussmann.

It is, in fact, not naturalism but the idealistic light reading of the bourgeoisie which is sober and unromantic in this age of the upper middle class and high capitalism. In spite and, indeed, often precisely because of its radical materialism, naturalistic literature offers a wildly fantastic picture of reality. Bourgeois rationalism and pragmatism, on the other hand, strive towards a balanced, harmonious, peaceful picture of the world. By 'ideal' subjects the middle class means such as have a calming and soothing influence. The task which it sets literature is to reconcile the unhappy and the discontented to life, to conceal reality from them, and to dangle before them the possibility of attaining an existence in which they actually have and can have no part. The goal that it pursues is the deluding, not the enlightenment of the reader. To the naturalistic novel of Flaubert, Zola and the Goncourts, which always excites and agitates the reader, the social élite opposes the novel of the *Revue des Deux Mondes*, above all the novels of Octave Feuillet. Works which describe the life of polite society and represent its aims as the supreme ideal of civilized humanity; works in which there are still real heroes, strong, brave and selfless knights, ideal characters who are either members of the higher ranks of society or are embodied in youths whom this society is prepared to adopt. Hitherto, in spite of revolutions and the social upheavals, the life of the aristocracy had always been described with a certain naturalness and ease; in spite of its being behind the times, it still preserved a certain spontaneity and common sense. But now the existence led by the great world of genteel society in novels loses all relationship to real life and suddenly appears in the pale, indistinct, elegantly softened drawing-room lighting of our Hollywood films. Feuillet sees no difference between elegance and culture, between good manners and good character; to his mind good education is synonymous with a noble disposition, and a loyal attitude to the higher classes a proof that one is 'something better' oneself. The hero of his *Roman d'un jeune homme pauvre* (1858) is the embodiment of this good breeding and noblesse; he is generous and handsome, sportsmanlike and intelligent, virtuous and sensitive, and only proves by his poverty that the distribution of the material goods of life sets no limits to the realization of aristocratic ideals. Just as the plays of Augier and Dumas propound a thesis, so this is a novel with a thesis. The dictates of Christian morality, of political conservatism and social conformism are proclaimed and extolled; the danger of vast, chaotic passions, wild despair and passive resistance is fought against.

The hypocrisy of the bourgeoisie is accompanied by an unprecedented lowering of the general cultural level. The Second Empire, which produces the art of Flaubert and Baudelaire, is at the same time the period in which the bad taste and inartistic trash of modern times are born. There had, of course, been bad painters and untalented writers, rough-hewn and quickly finished works, diluted and bungled artistic ideas, in earlier times; but the inferior had been unmistakably inferior, vulgar and tasteless, unpretentious and insignificant—the elegant rubbish, inartistic trifle turned out with dexterity and a show of skill had never existed before, or at most as a by-product. Now, however, these trifles become the norm, and the substitution of quality by the mere appearance of quality the general rule. The aim is to make the enjoyment of art as effortless and agreeable as possible, to take from it all difficulty and complication, everything problematical and tormenting, in short, to reduce the artistic to the pleasant and the ingratiating. Art as a form of 'relaxation' in which the public knowingly and deliberately sinks below its own level is the invention of this period; it dominates all forms of production, but above all that which is most resolutely and unscrupulously a public art: the theatre.

In the novel and in painting, naturalism prevails alongside the tendencies which are in accord with bourgeois taste, whereas nothing opposed to the interests and ideas of the bourgeoisie appears in the theatre at all. In warding off the tendencies which may threaten it, the government by no means relies only on the majority of the 'pro-government' forces in the auditorium, but combats such tendencies with all possible regulations and prohibitions. The theatre, as the art of the broad masses, is handled more strictly than the other genres, just as today the film is subjected to restrictions which are not applied to the theatre. From the middle of the century the efforts of the playwrights are concentrated, in accordance with the intentions of the government, on the creation of a propaganda instrument for the ideology of the bourgeoisie, for their economic, social and moral principles. The ruling classes' hunger for amusement, their weakness for public entertainments, their pleasure in seeing and being seen, make the theatre the representative art of the period. No previous society had ever taken such delight in the theatre, for none had a première ever meant so much, as for the public of Augier, Dumas *fils* and Offenbach.[106] The passion of the middle class for the theatre is highly satisfactory to those who shape public opinion; they are encouraged to hold fast to this enthusiasm and they are confirmed in their standards of aesthetic value. The judgement passed on the public by Sarcey, the most influential dramatic critic of the day, is undoubtedly connected with this tendency. For it is not merely in keeping with the general progress of the social sciences and the concentration of interest on collective intellectual phenomena, when he asserts that the public is the essence of the theatre and that one could more easily imagine a play being performed without anything than without the audience.[107] For Sarcey the principle that the public is always right is the criterion of all criticism and he keeps to this touchstone, although he knows perfectly well that the old cultivated public has already disintegrated and that of the old habitués, amongst whom a real consensus of taste prevailed, only a small group of regular theatre-goers exists—the public of the first-nights.[108] Sarcey regards the social changes which have produced the theatre public of the modern metropolis as a comparatively new process taking place within the framework of the middle class itself. The rapid increase in this public as a result of the development of the railways, which enables people from the provinces and abroad to stream to Paris and replaces the comparatively homogeneous circle of the old habitués with the mixed society of ad-hoc visitors—a phenomenon which other contemporary critics beside Sarcey draw attention to and represent as the most important reason for the change of style in the drama[109]—marks, however, only the last, by no means the most important, stage in a process that had already begun with the French Revolution.

The decisive turning point in the history of the modern French drama is represented by Scribe, who is not only the first to give dramatic expression to the money-based bourgeois ideology of the Restoration, but also creates, with his play of intrigues, the instrument best calculated to serve the bourgeoisie as a weapon in its struggle to enforce its ideology. Dumas and Augier represent merely a more highly developed form of his 'bon sens' and signify for the middle class of 1850 what he had meant for the bourgeoisie of the Restoration and the July monarchy. They both proclaim the same shallow rationalism and utilitarianism, the same superficial optimism and materialism, the only difference being that Scribe was more honest than they are, and spoke without false modesty and affectation about money, careers and marriages de convenance, where they speak about ideals, duties and eternal love. The middle class, which in the days of Scribe was a rising class still fighting for its position, has now attained a recognized status and is already threatened from below, imagines that it must dress up its materialistic aims in a cloak of idealism and thereby shows a timidity which classes still fighting for position never feel.

Nothing was so well calculated to serve as a basis for the idealization of the middle class as the institution of marriage and the family. It was possible to represent it in all good faith as one of those social forms in which the purest, most selfless and most noble feelings are respected, but no doubt, it was the only institution which, since the dissolution of the old feudal ties, still guaranteed permanence and stability to property. However that may have been, the idea of the family, as the bulwark of bourgeois society against dangerous intruders from without and destructive elements from within, became the intellectual foundation of the drama. It was all the more suited for this function as it could be brought into direct relationship with the love motif. This did not happen, however, until the idea of love had been reinterpreted and freed of its romantic features. It could no longer be allowed to be the great wild passion or be accepted and extolled as such. Romanticism had always understood and forgiven unbridled, rebellious, triumphant love—it was justified by its intensity; for the bourgeois drama, on the other hand, the meaning and value of love consists in its permanence, in its standing the test of daily married life. This transformation of the idea of love can be followed step by step from Hugo's *Marion de Lorme* to Dumas's *Dame aux Camélias* and *Demi-Monde*. Already in the *Dame aux Camélias* the hero's love for the fallen girl is incompatible with the moral principles of a bourgeois family, but the author still stands, at any rate with his feelings, if not with his mind, on the side of the victim; in the *Demi-Monde* his attitude to the woman with the doubtful reputation is already entirely negative—she must be removed from the social body as a centre of infection. For she constitutes an even greater danger for the bourgeois family than a poor but respectable girl, who can after all become a good mother, a faithful companion and a trustworthy guardian of the family property. If one has already seduced such a girl, then one should also marry her, not only to make amends for the error committed, but also in order to settle things and—as Zola sums up the moral of Augier's *Fourchambaults*—in order not to finish up a bankrupt. If one has, however, brought an illegitimate child into the world, and there is nothing praiseworthy about that either, then one should, as Dumas pleads in the *Fils naturel* and in *Monsieur Alphonse*, legitimize it, above all, in order not to add to the uprooted elements which are a constant danger to bourgeois society. The only point of view from which adultery is judged is whether it endangers the family as an institution. In certain circumstances a man can be forgiven for it, a woman never. A woman who is morally of any account at all is, incidentally, quite incapable of adultery (*Francillon*). In short, everything is permitted that can be reconciled with the idea of the family, everything taboo that conflicts with it. These are the norms and ideals with which the plays of Augier and Dumas are concerned; they were written to justify them and their success proves that the writers had read the public's inmost thoughts.

The inferior quality of the plays—for they are inferior—is not due to the fact that they serve a special purpose and propound a thesis—even the comedies of Aristophanes and the tragedies of Corneille did that—but to the fact that the purpose is attached to them from outside and does not become flesh and blood in any of the characters. Nothing is more typical of the unorganic combination of thesis and exposition in these plays than the stock figure of the 'raisonneur'. The mere fact that a character has no other function than to be the author's mouthpiece shows that the moral doctrine never gets beyond the stage of the purely abstract and that the ideology in the background does not form a unity with the body of the play. The authors concern themselves with or rather accept the views of the ruling classes on the good and bad habits of the time and have, independently of these ideas, a certain gift for entertainment, a certain ability to arouse interest and create tension by means of the stage. They now combine these data and use their theatrical talents to sell the views and theories which they have to proclaim. But they do it in an all too direct and brutal way and unwittingly contribute much to justify the principle of 'art for art's sake'. For propaganda in art is most disturbing when it does not completely permeate the work and when the idea to be proclaimed does not entirely coincide with the artist's vision.

In contrast to romanticism, the Second Empire is an age of rationalism, reflection and analysis.[110] Everywhere technical problems are in the foreground, in all genres the critical intellect is predominant. In the novel this spirit of criticism is represented by Flaubert, Zola and the Goncourt brothers, in lyric poetry by Baudelaire and the Parnassiens, in the drama by the masters of the 'pièce bien faite'. The formal problems, which counterbalance the emotional romantic trend in most of the genres, are preponderant on the stage. And it is not merely the external conditions of the representation, its narrow temporal and spatial limits, the mass character of the public and the directness of the reaction to the impression it receives, which induce the dramatist to attend to the problems of order and artistic economy, the didactic and propagandist intention itself makes for a formally clarified and closely packed, technically efficient and purposeful treatment of the material from the very outset. Authors and critics become more and more conscious of the fact that the theatre is intrinsically not concerned with literature, that the stage conforms to its own laws and its own logic, and that the poetic element of a drama often runs directly counter to its effectiveness on the stage. What Sarcey understands by theatrical perspective ('optique de théâtre') and theatrical instinct ('génie de théâtre') or simply what he means when he says 'c'est du théâtre', is suitability for the stage quite apart from literary considerations, a drastic use of purely theatrical methods, an all-out effort to win the public at any price, in short, an attitude which identifies the 'stage' with the 'platform'. Voltaire already knew that it is more important in the theatre 'de frapper fort que de frapper juste', but the practitioners and theoreticians of the 'well-made play' are the first to establish the rules of this hard-hitting and well-aimed type of drama. Their most important discovery consists in the recognition that stage effectiveness, indeed the mere possibility of the performance of a play at all, depends on a series of conventions and tricks of the trade, 'tricheries', as Sarcey says, and that the tacit agreement between the productive and receptive elements is even more decisive in the drama than in the other genres. The most important convention of the theatre is the public's readiness to be taken by surprise by the turns of the plot: its conscious self-deception, its unresisting acceptance of the rules of the game. Without this readiness we should not only be unable to see a play operating with purely theatrical means a second time, we could not even enjoy it once. For in such a play everything must seem surprising, although everything is foreseeable. Its 'scènes à faire' are the inevitable discussions of which, as Sarcey points out, the public knows exactly that they must and will come,[111] and its 'dénouement' is the solution which the audience expects and which it hankers after.[112] Consequently, the theatre becomes a party game played according to the strictest conventions and with the greatest possible skill, but with something naïve and primitive about it, all the same. The difficulties result not from the differentiation of the material with which the playwright is concerned, but from the complication of the rules of the game. It is their task to compensate the more fastidious members of the audience for the poverty and dullness of the contents of the play. The precision with which the machine functions is intended to divert attention from the fact that it is running empty. The public, and even the better-educated public, wants light, unexacting entertainment; it does not want obscurities, insoluble problems and unfathomable depths. Hence the strong emphasis now laid on strictness of construction and logical consistency. The development of the plot must be like a mathematical operation; the internal must be replaced by an external inevitability, just as the inner truth of the thesis is replaced by the jugglery of the argumentation.

The 'dénouement' is the final solution of the problem. If the result is wrong, the whole operation is wrong, says Dumas. Therefore one must, as he thinks, begin working on the end, the solution, the last word of the play. Nothing sheds a more piercing light than this crab's walk on the difference between the calculating intelligence with which a 'pièce bien faite' is constructed, and the impulses by which the true poet allows himself to be carried away. To take a step forwards, the playwright has to take two steps back at the same time; he has to compare every idea, every new motif, every new move with the already firmly established motifs and moves and to make them agree. Writing plays means a constant forestalling and referring back, a continual arranging and rearranging, a groping forwards and building upwards with one capacity-test after another and with the gradual consolidation and safeguarding of the several strata of the play. A rationalism of this kind is more or less characteristic of every palatable artistic product and especially of every performable dramatic work—the works of Shakespeare, which are based on the genius of the stage, as much as the plays of Augier and Dumas—but the effectiveness of a 'well-made play' rests solely on the succession of its tricks and trump cards, whereas that of a Shakespearian drama depends on an infinity of components beyond the sphere of purely mathematical relationships. Emerson preferred to read

Shakespeare's plays in the reverse order of the scenes and deliberately renounced all interest in their effectiveness as stage plays, in order to concentrate entirely on their poetic contents. Read in this way, a real 'pièce bien faite' would not only be unpalatable, it would also be unintelligible, for the details of that kind of play have no inner value of their own, but merely in relation to the whole of which they are part. In developing them, the playwright's eye is fixed on the final constellation, as in a game of chess; and how mechanically this constellation can be developed is best demonstrated by the method with the aid of which Sardou adopted Scribe's technique. According to his own assertion, he always read only the first act of the master's plays and then tried to derive the 'right' sequel from the premises thus acquired. In the course of time, this 'purely logical exercise', as he calls it, brought him nearer and nearer to the solution chosen by Scribe in the second and third acts of his plays, and at the same time he came to the view, also held by Dumas, that the whole plot follows with a certain inevitability from the situation from which one starts out. Dumas was of the opinion that there is no art at all in inventing a dramatic situation and thinking out a conflict; the art consists rather in the due preparation of the scene in which the plot culminates and in the smooth unravelling of the knot. The plot, which seems at first sight to be the most spontaneous, most unproblematical and most immediate datum of the drama, thus proves to be its most artificial and most laboriously acquired ingredient. It is by no means mere raw material or a pure product of the imagination, but consists of a series of moves which leave no scope at all for the playwright's spontaneous inventions and sovereign discretion.

One can, if one cares to, regard the scaffolding of a well-constructed work as the ladder leading upwards into the region of wonderful heights or merely as the schedule of a routine that has nothing to do with genuine art and humanity. One can extol, with Walter Pater, the artistic intelligence that 'foresees the end in the beginning and never loses sight of it, and in every part is conscious of all the rest, till the last sentence does but, with undiminished vigour, unfold and justify the first', but one can also, like Bernard Shaw, fear the worst for the dramatist from the tyranny of the logic, of which he writes that 'it is almost impossible for its slaves to write tolerable last acts to their plays, so conventionally do their conclusions follow their premises'. But, in order to believe that Shaw really despises and scorns the tricks and dodges of this artistic intelligence, one would have to forget that he is the author of plays like *The Devil's Disciple* and *Candida*, which on closer examination turn out to be regular 'pièces bien faites'. Not only Shaw, however, but Ibsen and Strindberg as well, and with them the whole theatrically effective drama of the present age, are based more or less on the French 'pièce bien faite'. The art of producing entanglements and tension, of tying the knot and delaying its unravelling, of preparing the turns in the plot and, nevertheless, surprising the audience with them, the rules of the proper distribution and timing of the 'coups de théâtre', the casuistry of the big discussions and the curtain-lines, the sudden sensation of the falling curtain and the last-minute solution—all these things they learnt from Scribe, Dumas, Augier, Labiche and Sardou. That does not mean at all that modern stage technique is entirely the creation of these playwrights. On the contrary, the line of development can be traced back through the melodrama and the vaudeville of the post-revolutionary period, the domestic drama and the comedy of the eighteenth century, the 'commedia dell'arte' and Molière, to the Roman comedy and the medieval farce. Nevertheless, the contribution to this tradition of the masters of the 'pièce bien faite' is extraordinary.

The most original and in many respects the most expressive artistic product of the Second Empire is the operetta.[113] It too is, of course, in no sense an absolute innovation—this would be unthinkable in such an advanced stage in the history of the theatre—it represents rather the continuation of two older genres, the *opera buffa* and the vaudeville, and it transmits to this ponderous and humourless age something of the light-hearted, cheerful, unromantic spirit of the eighteenth century. It is the only playful, light and airy form of the period. Alongside the conformist trends in keeping with sober bourgeois taste and the naturalistic art of the opposition, it constitutes a world of its own—a middle kingdom. It is much more attractive than the contemporary drama or the popular novel, sociologically more representative than naturalism and, as such, the only genre in which popular works with both a wide appeal and a certain artistic value are produced.

The most conspicuous and, from the naturalistic point of view, the most peculiar characteristic of the operetta is its absolute improbability, the unreal, entirely imaginative nature of its whirling scenes. It has the same significance for the nineteenth century as the pastoral play had had for earlier centuries; the set formulae of its contents, the conventionality of its entanglements and dénouements, are pure play forms unrelated to reality. Both the marionette-like nature of the characters and the apparently improvised form of the presentation only heighten the impression of fictitiousness. Sarcey already notes the similarity between the operetta and the 'commedia dell'arte',[114] and points out the impression of dreamlike unreality that Offenbach's works make on him; by which he only intends to say, however, that they have a quite peculiar fantastic quality. An admirer of Offenbach in our own time, the Viennese writer Karl Kraus, was the first to give a more definite meaning to this quality by pointing out that in the Offenbach operetta life is just as improbable and nonsensical, just as grotesque and uncanny as reality itself.[115] Such an interpretation would, naturally, have been absolutely foreign to Sarcey and it would have been altogether inconceivable before the expressionism and surrealism of modern art had emphasized the dream- and phantom-like character of life. Only the eye with its vision sharpened by these artistic trends was able to see that the operetta was not only an image of the frivolous and cynical society of the Second Empire but, at the same time, a form of self-mockery, that it not only expressed the reality, but also the unreality of this world, that it arose, in a word, out of the operetta-like nature of life itself[116]—so far as one may speak of the 'operetta-like nature' of such a serious, sober and critical age as this. The peasants at the plough, the workers in the factories, the merchants in their offices, the painters in Barbizon, Flaubert in Croisset, they were what they were, but the ruling class, the court in the Tuileries and the world of carousing bankers, dissolute aristocrats, parvenu journalists and pampered beauties, had something improbable, something phantom-like and unreal, something ephemeral about it—it was a land of operetta, a stage whose wings threatened to collapse at any moment.

The operetta was the product of a world of 'laissez faire, laissez passer', that is, a world of economic, social and moral liberalism, a world in which everyone was able to do what he liked, so long as he abstained from questioning the system itself. This limitation meant, on the one hand, very wide, on the other, very narrow frontiers. The same government that summoned Flaubert and Baudelaire to a court of law tolerated the most insolent social satire, the most disrespectful ridiculing of the authoritarian régime, the court, the army and the bureaucracy, in the works of Offenbach. But it tolerated his frolics only because they were not or did not seem to be dangerous, because he confined himself to a public whose loyalty was beyond doubt and needed no other safety-valve, in order to be quite happy, than this apparently harmless banter. The joke seems mischievous only to us; the contemporary public missed the sinister undertone which we can hear in the frantic rhythm of Offenbach's galops and cancans. The entertainment was, however, not quite so harmless. The operetta demoralized people, not because it scoffed at everything 'venerable', not because its deriding of antiquity, of classical tragedy, of romantic opera was only criticism of society in disguise, but because it shattered the belief in authority without denying it in principle. The immorality of the operetta consisted in the thoughtless tolerance with which it conducted its criticism of the corrupt system of government and the depraved society of the time, in the appearance of harmlessness which it gave to the frivolity of the little prostitutes, the extravagant gallants and the lovable old 'viveurs'. Its lukewarm, hesitant criticism merely encouraged corruption. One could, however, expect nothing else but an ambiguous attitude from artists who were successful, who loved success more than anything and whose success was bound up with the continuance of this indolent and pleasure-seeking society. Offenbach was a German Jew, a homeless, vagrant musician, an artist whose existence was doubly threatened; he inevitably felt a stranger, a déraciné, an apathetic spectator in a double and manifold sense in the French capital, in the midst of this corrupt and yet so alluring world. He inevitably felt the problematical position of the artist in modern society, the contradiction between his ambitions and his resentment, his beggar's pride and his courting of the public, even more intensely than most of his professional colleagues. He was no rebel, not even a genuine democrat, on the contrary, he welcomed the rule of the 'strong hand', and enjoyed with the greatest peace of mind the advantages which he derived from the political system of the Second Empire; but he regarded all the bustling activity around him with the astonished, cold and piercing eye of an outsider, and involuntarily hastened the fall of the society to which he owed his success in life.

The rise of the operetta marks the penetration of journalism into the world of music. After the novel, the drama and the graphic arts, it is now the turn of the musical stage to comment on the events of the day. But the journalism of the operetta is not restricted to the topical references in the songs and jokes of the comics; the whole genre is rather like a gossip column devoted to the scandals of genteel society. Heine has rightly been called the predecessor of Offenbach. The origins, the temperament and the social position of both are more or less the same; they are both born journalists, critical and practical natures, who do not wish to live outside but in and with society, if not by any means always in agreement with its aims and methods. Heine had intrinsically the same chances of success in the cosmopolitan Paris of the July monarchy and the Second Empire as Meyerbeer and Offenbach, only he did not have at his disposal the international means of communication used by his more fortunate countrymen. His fame remained confined to a comparatively narrow circle, whilst Meyerbeer and Offenbach conquered the French capital and the whole civilized world. They not only created two of the most characteristic genres of French art, but represented the Parisian taste of the time more faithfully and more comprehensively than their French colleagues. Offenbach can be regarded as the very epitome of his age; his work contains its most characteristic and original features. His contemporaries already felt him to be so representative that they identified him with the spirit of Paris and described his art as the continuation of the classical French tradition. His music united Western Europe in a mood of exuberance.[117] *The Grand Duchess of Gerolstein* proved to be the greatest and most lasting attraction of the World Exhibition of 1867; the sovereigns and princes who visited Paris were just as enthusiastic about the play, with the irresistible Hortense Schneider in the title rôle, as the libertines of the French capital and the petty bourgeois from the provinces. Three hours after his arrival in Paris the Russian Czar was already sitting in a box in the 'Variétés', and, although he was apparently better able to control his impatience, Bismarck was just as enchanted as the crowned heads themselves. Rossini called Offenbach the 'Mozart of the Champs Elysées' and Wagner confirmed this judgement—though only after the death of his envied rival.

The heyday of the operetta was the period between the two world exhibitions of 1855 and 1867. After the political unrest at the end of the 'sixties it lacked an appropriately light-hearted public or even one deluding itself with light-heartedness and security. With the Second Empire the best days of the operetta came to an end; the pleasure which later generations took in it was not derived from the genre as the living, spontaneous and direct expression of the present, but from the 'good old times' which were associated with this genre more directly than with any other. Thanks to this association of ideas, the operetta survived the upheavals of the 'fin de siècle' and, in such an intellectually unstable city as Vienna, it remained the most popular vehicle of idealization of the past right up to the Second World War. The experiences of the last ten years were necessary to bring about a revision of the idea of the 'good old times' connected in one part of Europe with Napoleon III and Offenbach, in the other with the Emperor Franz Joseph and Johann Strauss. The class struggle, which was suppressed everywhere between 1848 and 1870, blazed up again at the end of this period and threatened the rule of the bourgeoisie as the beneficiaries of reaction. The operetta now seemed to be the picture of a happy life free from care and danger—of an idyll which had, however, never existed in reality.

The Goncourts were right when they prophesied that the circus, the variety show and the revue would displace the theatre. The film, which, owing to its pictorial quality and display, can be reckoned among these visual forms, entirely confirms their prediction. The operetta came nearest to the revue, but it by no means represented the oldest form in which spectacle had triumphed over the drama. The real turning point occurred with the emergence of 'grand opera' during the July monarchy, even though spectacle had always formed an integral component of the theatre and had repeatedly gained the upper hand over its dramatic and acoustic elements. This was above all the case in the baroque theatre, in which the festive character of the performance, the decorations, costumes, dances and processions, often overran everything else. The bourgeois culture of the July monarchy and the Second Empire, which was a parvenu culture, also looked for the monumental and the imposing in the theatre and exaggerated the appearance of greatness, the more so as it lacked true spiritual greatness itself. There are, in fact, two different impulses which drive society to ceremonial, grandiose and pretentious forms; on the one hand, it may be impelled to seek for grandeur because that is in line with its natural way of life, or the rage for the colossal may be due to a need to compensate for a more or less painfully felt weakness. The baroque of the seventeenth century corresponded to the grand proportions in which the court and the aristocracy of the period naturally breathed and moved, the pseudo-baroque of the nineteenth century corresponded to the ambitions with which the risen bourgeoisie was trying to fill out these proportions. Opera became the favourite genre of the bourgeoisie because no other art offered such great possibilities for ostentation, for display and scenery, for the accumulation and working up of effects. The type of opera realized by Meyerbeer combined all the allurements of the stage, and created a heterogeneous mixture of music, song and dance that demanded to be seen as well as to be heard and in which all the elements were intended to beguile and overwhelm the audience. The Meyerbeer opera was a great variety show, the unity of which consisted more in the rhythm of the moving spectacle on the stage than in the absolute predominance of the musical form.[118] It was intended for a public whose connection with music was purely external.

The idea of the 'universal work of art' (*Gesamtkunstwerk*) made its mark here long before Wagner, and expressed a need before anyone had thought of formulating it in a set programme. Wagner sought to justify the complex nature of opera by means of the analogy of Greek tragedy, which was actually nothing more than an oratorio, but the desire for such a justification arose from the baroque heterogeneity of the genre, which ever since Meyerbeer had been threatening to become more and more 'styleless and formless'. 'Grand opera' owed its authority, which is still perceptible in *The Mastersingers* and *Aïda* and which probably represented a more rigid convention than that of earlier Italian opera,[119] to the fact that the culture of the French bourgeoisie served the whole continent as a model and everywhere met genuine needs rooted in social conditions. Nothing satisfied these needs more perfectly and more readily than the concerted ensemble of this opera, the organization of the means at its disposal—the gigantic orchestra, the enormous stage and the huge choir—into a whole, which was intended only to impress, overwhelm and subjugate the audience. That was above all the aim of the great finales, which often invented new and strong effects, but had nothing in common with the deep humanity of Mozart's and the sprightly grace of Rossini's final scenes. What we usually call 'operatic'—monumental scenery, empty emphases, blustering heroics, artificial emotions and language—is, however, in no sense Meyerbeer's creation and is in no way limited to the opera of the age. Even an artist of such fastidious taste as Flaubert is not wholly free of theatricality. It is part of the romantic legacy inherited by this generation, and Victor Hugo had no less a share in its development than Meyerbeer.

Of all the important representatives of the age, Richard Wagner stands nearest to Meyerbeer's operatic style, not only because he wants to link his work on to a living art, but also because no one is more keen on success than he. He accepts the predominant convention without opposition and, as has been said, only gradually fights his way through to originality, in contrast to the typical development, which starts with an individual experience, a personal discovery and ends with a more or less stereotyped manner.[120] Much more remarkable, however, than Wagner's setting out from 'grand opera' is his continual attachment to a form which combines the expression of the most inward, most intimate and most sublimated feelings with the ostentation of the Second Empire. For it is not only *Rienzi* and *Tannhaeuser* that are still thorough-going spectacular operas in which the scenic apparatus predominates, but *The Mastersingers* and *Parsifal* are also to some extent musical show-pieces, intended to engage all the senses and surpass all expectations. The fondness for the magnificent and the massive is just as strong in Wagner as in Meyerbeer or Zola, and he is, no less than Victor Hugo and Dumas, a born man of the theatre, a 'histrion' and 'mimomaniac', as Nietzsche called him.[121] But his theatricality is by no means simply the result of his writing operas; on the contrary, his operas are themselves the expression of his undiscriminating theatrical taste and his loud ostentatious nature. Like Meyerbeer, Napoleon III, la Païva or Zola, he loves the obtrusive, the precious, the voluptuous, and it is easy to realize what his operas and the *salons* of the period, filled with silk, velvet, gold brocade, upholstered furniture, carpets and door curtains, have in common, even without knowing that he wanted to have stage-scenes painted by Makart.[122] The mania for grandeur and exuberance has more complicated origins in Wagner, however; its strands lead back not merely to Makart but also to Delacroix. The connections between the 'Death of Sardanapal' and the *Twilight of the Gods* are just as close as between the lavish splendour of Parisian 'grand opera' and the celebrations of the Bayreuth festivals. But even that does not complete the story; Wagner's sensualism is not only more elemental than mere ostentation, but also more genuine and spontaneous than the whole 'blood, death and lust' mysticism of his time. It was not without reason that for many of the most sensitive minds of the century his work signified the very essence of art—the paradigm which first revealed the meaning and underlying principle of music to them. It was certainly the last and perhaps the greatest revelation of romanticism, the only form of it that is still alive today. No other allows us to apprehend so intimately with what intoxication of the senses it impressed itself on the contemporary public, and how much it was felt to be a revolt against all dead conventions and the discovery of a young, blissful and forbidden world. It is comprehensible, although at first surprising, that Baudelaire, who was himself not musical at all, but the only one of Wagner's contemporaries whose accents create in us the same feeling of happiness as the Tristan music, was the first to recognize the significance of Wagner's art.

Apart from his overstrained nerves, his passion for narcosis and narcotizing effects, Wagner shares with Baudelaire the same quasi-religious feelings, the same romantic yearning for redemption. And apart from a weakness for glowing colours and exuberant forms, he is related to Flaubert by a kind of dilettantism and a thoroughly reflexive relationship to his own work. He has just as little natural, spontaneous talent, he forces his works just as violently and desperately from himself and has just as little genuine faith in art as Flaubert. Nietzsche points out that none of the great masters was still such a bad musician as Wagner at twenty-eight, and, with the exception of Flaubert, certainly no great artist doubted his own ability for so long. Both felt that art was the torment of their life, that it stood between them and the enjoyment of life, and both regarded the gulf between reality and art, between 'avoir' and 'dire', as unbridgeable. They were members of the same late romantic generation that fought a fight as unremitting as it was hopeless against their egotism and aestheticism.

3. THE SOCIAL NOVEL IN ENGLAND AND RUSSIA

The Industrial Revolution began in England, had the most fruitful results and called forth the loudest and most passionate protests there. The charges levelled against it did not, however, by any means prevent the ruling classes from opposing the social revolution with all the greater energy and success. The failure of the revolutionary endeavours then brought it about that, whilst in France a section of the intelligentsia and the literary élite began to adopt an anti-democratic attitude after the experiences of the Revolution, by and large the opinions of the English intellectuals remained, if not always revolutionary, at any rate radical. But the most striking difference between the frame of mind of the intellectual élite in the two countries was that the French were and remained unflinching rationalists, whatever their attitude to the Revolution and democracy, whereas the English became desperate irrationalists, in spite of their radical outlook and opposition to industrialism, indeed often precisely because of their opposition to the ruling class, and took refuge in the nebulous idealism of German romanticism. Strange to say, here in England the capitalists and the utilitarians were more closely in touch with the ideas of the enlightenment than their opponents, who denied the principle of free competition and the division of labour. At any rate, from the point of view of the history of ideas, the machine-breaking idealists were the reactionaries and the materialists and capitalists the representatives of rationalism and progress.

Economic freedom had the same historical roots as political liberalism; both were among the achievements of the enlightenment and were logically inseparable. The moment one adopted the standpoint of personal freedom and individualism, one had to allow the validity of free competition as an integral component of human rights. The emancipation of the middle class was a necessary step in the liquidation of feudalism and presupposed in its turn the liberation of economic life from medieval ties and restrictions. The middle class's participation in equality of rights can only be explained as the result of a development in which pre-capitalist forms of economy had become outmoded. Only after economic life had reached the stage of absolute autonomy and the middle class had pierced the rigid frontiers of the feudal class system, was it possible to think of emancipating society from the anarchy of free competition. It was also pointless to attack individual aspects of capitalism without questioning the system itself. So long as capitalist economy remained undisputed there could be no question of anything more than purely philanthropic mitigation of its abuses. And to keep to the principle of rationalism and liberalism was the only way of making an ultimate remedy of the abuses possible; all that was necessary was to understand the concept of freedom as surpassing its bourgeois limitations. The abandonment of reason and the liberal idea led inevitably, however good and honest the original intention, to an uncontrollable intuitionism and a loss of intellectual maturity. One is always conscious of this danger in Carlyle, but it threatens the idealism of most Victorian thinkers, and the proverbial compromise of the age, the middle course which it pursued between tradition and progress, is nowhere expressed so forcibly as in the romantic hankering for the past of its intellectual leaders. None of the representative Victorians is entirely free from the readiness to compromise and the resulting ambiguity impairs the political influence of even such a genuine radical as Dickens. In France, the intelligentsia felt itself compelled to choose between the Revolution and the bourgeois attitude, and even though the choice was often accompanied by divided feelings, it was, nevertheless, clear-cut and final. In England, on the other hand, the section of the intellectual élite that opposed industrialism based itself on just as conservative an ideology as the capitalistic bourgeoisie itself, an ideology that was in fact often even more reactionary.

The utilitarians, who represented the economic principles of industrialism, were the pupils of Adam Smith and proclaimed the doctrine that an economy left to run itself was most in accordance not merely with the spirit of liberalism but also with the interest of the general public. What aroused the strongest opposition to them on the part of the idealists was, however, not so much the indefensibility of this thesis, as the fatalism with which they represented the egoistic instincts as the ultimate principle of human action and the mathematical inevitability with which they imagined they could derive the laws of economic and social life from the fact of human egoism. The protest of the idealists against the reduction of man to 'homo economicus' was the eternal protestation of the romantic 'philosophy of life'—of the belief in the logical inexhaustibility of life and the impossibility of subduing it to man's design—against rationalism and thought abstracted from immediate reality. The reaction against utilitarianism was a second romanticism, in which the fight against social injustice and the opposition to the actual theories of the 'dismal science' played a much smaller part than the urge to escape from the present, whose problems the anti-utilitarians had no ability and no desire to solve, into the irrationalism of Burke, Coleridge and German romanticism. The cry for state intervention was, especially in the case of Carlyle, just as much the sign of anti-liberal, authoritarian tendencies as an expression of humanitarian and altruistic feeling, and his lament about the atomic disintegration of society was both the expression of a desire for real community and of a yearning for the beloved and dreaded leader.

With the end of the heyday of English romanticism, a current of anti-romantic rationalism sets in about 1815 and reaches its climax with the electoral reform of 1832, the new Parliament and the triumph of the middle class. The successful bourgeoisie becomes more and more conservative and starts a reaction to democratic aspirations, which is again essentially romantic in character. Alongside rationalistic England a sentimental England makes itself felt and the hard-boiled, clear- and sober-minded capitalists flirt with ideas of philanthropic reform. The theoretical reaction against economic liberalism therefore proves to be an internal affair, a kind of self-deliverance, of the bourgeoisie. It is supported by the same stratum as in practice represents the principle of economic freedom and it merely serves to counterbalance the materialism and egoism in the Victorian compromise.

The years between 1832 and 1848 are a period of the most acute social crises, full of unrestrained bloody conflicts between capital and labour. After the Reform Bill, the English working class received the same treatment from the bourgeoisie as their brethren received in France after 1830. The aristocracy and the common people thus become, to a certain extent, fellow-sufferers and fellow-victims in a struggle against the common enemy, the capitalistic middle class. To be sure, this ephemeral relationship can never lead to a real community of interests and comradeship in arms, but it is sufficient to hide the real state of affairs from such an emotionally inclined thinker as Carlyle and to turn his fight against capitalism into a romantic and reactionary enthusiasm for history. In contrast to France, where hatred for the bourgeoisie is expressed in a strict and sober naturalism, the above-mentioned second romantic movement arises in England, where there had been no revolution since the seventeenth century and where the political experiences and disappointments of the French were lacking. In France, romanticism as a movement had been overcome by the middle of the century and the tussle with it takes on a more or less private character. In England, the situation develops differently: here the antagonism between the rationalistic and irrationalistic trends is by no means limited to an internal struggle, as it is in Flaubert for example, but divides the country into two camps, which are in reality much more heterogeneous in character than Disraeli's 'two nations'. Here too, as in the whole of Western Europe, the main line of development is positivistic, that is to say, in harmony with the principles of rationalism and naturalism. Not merely the political and economic rulers, not merely the technicians and scientists, but also the common man and the practical man, with his roots in ordinary professional life, think rationalistically and untraditionalistically. But the literature of the period is replete with a romantic nostalgia, a yearning for the Middle Ages and a Utopia in which the laws of capitalistic economy, of commercialism, of mercilessly impersonal competition and all the unpleasant realities of modern society have no place. Disraeli's feudalism is political romanticism, the 'Oxford Movement' religious romanticism, Carlyle's attacks on contemporary culture social romanticism and Ruskin's philosophy of art aesthetic romanticism; all these theories repudiate liberalism and rationalism and take refuge from the complicated problems of the present in a higher, superpersonal and supernatural order, in an enduring state beyond the anarchy of liberal and individualistic society. The loudest and most seductive voice is that of Carlyle, the first and most original of the pied pipers who prepared the way for Mussolini and Hitler. For, however important and fruitful the influence that he exerted in certain respects and however much the last century owed him in its fight for the spiritual immediacy of cultural forms, he was, nevertheless, a muddle-headed fellow, who succeeded for generations in obscuring and hiding facts with the clouds of smoke and vapour which belched forth from his enthusiasm for infinity and eternity, his superman morality and mystical hero-worship.

Ruskin is Carlyle's direct heir; he takes over his arguments against industrialism and liberalism, repeats his jeremiads about the soullessness and godlessness of modern culture and shares his enthusiasm for the Middle Ages and the communal culture of the Christian West. But he transforms the abstract hero-worship of his master into a concrete philosophy of beauty, his vague social romanticism into an aesthetic idealism with definite tasks and exactly definable aims. Nothing proves the timeliness and realism of Ruskin's doctrines better than the fact that he was able to become the spokesman of such an important and historically representative movement as Pre-Raphaelitism. His ideas and ideals, above all his rejection of the art of the Renaissance, of grandiose, dashing, self-satisfied and autocratic forms, and the return to pre-classical, 'Gothic' art, to the timid and inspired way of the 'primitives', were in the air; they were the symptoms of a general cultural crisis affecting the whole of society. Ruskin's doctrine and the art of the Pre-Raphaelites spring from the same spiritual condition and find expression in the same protest against the conventional outlook on art and the world of Victorian England. In the academicism of their age the Pre-Raphaelites recognize and combat what Ruskin interprets as the degeneration of art since the Renaissance. Their attack is aimed at the classicism, the aesthetic canon of the school of Raphael, that is to say, at the empty formalism and smooth routine of an art with which the bourgeoisie wants to provide the proof of its respectability, puritanical morality, high ideals and feeling for poetry. The Victorian middle class is obsessed with the idea of 'high art',[123] and the bad taste which dominates its architecture, its painting, its arts and crafts is partly the result of its self-deception—of the ambitions and pretensions which muffle the spontaneous expression of its nature.

Victorian painting swarms with historical, poetic, anecdotal motifs; it is 'literary' painting par excellence, a hybrid art, in which it is more to be regretted, however, that it contains so little pictorial value than that it contains so much literature. It is, above all, the fear of any kind of sensuality and spontaneity that here stands in the way of that genuine, luxuriant style of painting which is so typical of the French conception of art. Expelled nature creeps in again, however, by the backstairs.—In the Chantrey Collection, that unique monument of Victorian bad taste, there is a picture of a young nun who, in renouncing the world, has also stripped off all her worldly clothes. She kneels stark naked before the altar of a chapel dim with nocturnal light and turns the alluring forms of her delicate body towards the monks standing behind her. It is difficult to imagine anything more embarrassing than this picture, for it belongs to the worst, because most insincere, kind of pornography.

Pre-Raphaelite painting is just as literary, just as 'poetic' as the whole of Victorian art, but it combines with its intrinsically non-pictorial subjects, that is, subjects which can never be completely mastered in terms of painting, certain pictorial values, which are often not only very attractive but also new. With its Victorian spiritualism, its historical, religious and poetic themes, its moral allegories and fairy-tale symbolism, it unites a realism which finds expression in a delight in minute details, in the playful reproduction of every blade of grass and every pleat in a skirt. This meticulousness is in accordance not only with the naturalistic tendency of European art in general, but at the same time with that bourgeois ethic of good workmanship which sees a criterion of aesthetic value in flawless technique and careful execution. In keeping with this Victorian ideal, the Pre-Raphaelites exaggerate the signs of technical ability, imitative skill and the finishing touch. Their pictures are turned out just as neatly as those of the academic painters and we feel any antithesis between the Pre-Raphaelites and the rest of the Victorian painters much less acutely than, for example, the difference between the naturalists and the academicians in France. The Pre-Raphaelites are idealists, moralists and shamefaced erotics, like most Victorians. They have the same contradictory conception of art, betray the same embarrassment, the same inhibitions in giving artistic expression to their experiences, and their puritanical abashment in face of the medium in which they express themselves goes so far that we always have the feeling of a timid, though supremely gifted dilettantism when considering their works. This distance between the creator and his work deepens still more the impression of decorative art which adheres to all Pre-Raphaelite painting. This is why this painting seems so affected, so dainty and pretty and always has about it something of the unreal and ornamental quality of mere tapestries. The precious, intellectual and, in spite of its lyrical nature, cold note of modern symbolism, the austere gracefulness and somewhat affected angularity of neo-romanticism, the studied shyness and restraint, the secrecy and secretiveness of the art at the turn of the century, partly have their source in this artificial style.

Pre-Raphaelitism was an aesthetic movement, an extreme cult of beauty, an assessment of life based on art; but it must no more be identified with 'l'art pour l'art' than Ruskin's philosophy itself. The thesis that the highest value of art consists in the expression of a 'good and great soul'[124] accorded with the conviction of all the Pre-Raphaelites. It is true that they were playful formalists, but they lived in the faith that their playing with forms had a higher purpose and an elevating educational effect. There is just as great a contradiction between their aestheticism and their moralism as between their romantic archaism and their naturalistic treatment of details.[125] It is the same Victorian contradiction which also produces a cleft in Ruskin's writings; his epicurean enthusiasm for art is by no means always compatible with the social gospel which he proclaims. According to this gospel, perfect beauty is possible only in a community in which justice and solidarity reign supreme. Great art is the expression of a morally healthy society; in an age of materialism and mechanization the feeling for beauty and the ability to create art of a high quality must wither. Carlyle had already brought the stereotyped charge against modern capitalistic society that it blunts and kills the souls of men with its 'cash nexus' and mechanical methods of production; Ruskin merely repeats his predecessor's fierce words. The lamentations over the decay of art are not new either. Ever since the legend of the Golden Age the art of the present had always been felt to be inferior to the creations of the past, and it was believed that signs of the same decay could be detected in it as were evident in the morals of the time. But artistic decay had never been regarded as the symptom of a disease involving the whole body of society and there has never been such a clear awareness of the organic relationship between art and life as since Ruskin.[126] He was indubitably the first to interpret the decline of art and taste as the sign of a general cultural crisis, and to express the basic, and even today not sufficiently appreciated, principle that the conditions under which men live must first be changed, if their sense of beauty and their comprehension of art are to be awakened. On the strength of this insight Ruskin exchanged the study of the history of art for that of economics and moved away from Carlyle's idealism in so far as he did greater justice to the materialism of this science. Ruskin was also the first person in England to emphasize the fact that art is a public concern and its cultivation one of the most important tasks of the state, in other words, that it represents a social necessity and that no nation can neglect it without endangering its intellectual existence. He was, finally, the first to proclaim the gospel that art is not the privilege of artists, connoisseurs and the educated classes, but is part of every man's inheritance and estate. But for all that, he was by no means a socialist, indeed, he was not even a democrat.[127] Plato's philosophers' state, in which beauty and wisdom reigned supreme, came nearest to his ideal and his 'socialism' was limited to a belief in the educability of human beings and in their right to enjoy the blessings of culture. According to him, real wealth consists not in the possession of material goods, but in the ability to enjoy the beauty of life and art. This aesthetic quietism and the renunciation of all violence mark the limits of his reformism.[128]

William Morris, the third in the series of representative social critics of the Victorian age, thinks much more consistently and advances much further in the practical sphere than Ruskin. In some respect he is, in fact, the greatest,[129] that is to say, the bravest, the most intransigent of the Victorians, although even he is not completely free of their contradictions and compromises. But he drew the ultimate conclusion from Ruskin's doctrine of the involvement of the fate of art in that of society, and became convinced that 'to make socialists' is a more urgent task than to make good art. He pursued to the very end Ruskin's idea that the inferiority of modern art, the decline of artistic culture and the bad taste of the public are only the symptoms of a more deeply rooted and more far-reaching evil, and realized that there is no point in trying to improve art and taste and leaving society unchanged. He knew that directly to influence artistic development is useless and that all one can do is to create social conditions which will facilitate a better appreciation of art. He was quite aware of the class struggle within which the social process and, consequently, the development of art takes place and he regarded it as the most important task to imbue the proletariat with consciousness of this fact.[130] For all their clarity on fundamental issues, his theories and demands still contain, as we have said, numerous contradictions. In spite of his sound conception of social reality and the function of art in the life of society, he is a romantic lover of the Middle Ages and the medieval ideal of beauty. He preaches the need for an art created by and intended for the people, but he is and remains a hedonistic dilettante producing things which only the rich can afford and only the well-educated can enjoy. He points out that art arises from work, from practical craftsmanship, but he fails to recognize the significance of the most important and most practical modern means of production—the machine. The source of the contradictions which exist between his teachings and his artistic activity is to be sought in the petty bourgeois traditionalism behind the judgement passed on the technical age by his teachers, Carlyle and Ruskin, and from whose provincialism he is never able entirely to free himself.

Ruskin attributed the decay of art to the fact that the modern factory, with its mechanical mode of production and division of labour, prevents a genuine relationship between the worker and his work, that is to say, that it crushes out the spiritual element and estranges the producer from the product of his hands. With him the fight against industrialism lost the barb directed against the proletarianization of the masses and became transformed into a romantic enthusiasm for something irretrievable, for handicraft, the home industry, the guild, in short, for the medieval forms of production. But the service rendered by Ruskin was that he drew attention to the ugliness of the Victorian arts and crafts and recalled his contemporaries to the charms of solid, careful craftsmanship as opposed to the spurious materials, senseless forms and crude, cheap execution of Victorian products. His influence was extraordinary, almost beyond description. Production within the framework of a comparatively small workshop, maintaining the personal relationship of the workers with one another and the absolute predominance of handicraft, with individual tasks concentrated on the single, self-contained work, became the ideal in the production of modern art and applied art. The purposefulness and solidity of modern architecture and industrial art are very largely the result of Ruskin's endeavours and doctrines, although his direct influence brought about a rather exaggerated cult of manual labour which failed to recognize the tasks and possibilities of machine industry and led to the awakening of an unrealizable hope. It was mere romanticism to believe that technical achievements, which had arisen from real economic needs and which secured tangible economic advantages, could simply be pushed aside; and it was extremely childish to try and arrest the progress of technical and economic developments with polemical pamphlets and protests. Ruskin and his disciples were right inasmuch as man did in fact lose control over the machine, that technics became autonomous and produced, especially in the field of industrial art, the most insipid and respulsive objects; but they forgot that there was no other way to control the machine than to accept it and to conquer it spiritually.

The logical mistake they made consisted in an all too narrow definition of technics, in failing to recognize the technical nature of every kind of material production, of every manipulation of things, of every contact with objective reality. Art always makes use of a material, technical, tool-like device, of an appliance, a 'machine', and does so so openly that this indirectness and materialism of the means of expression can even be described as one of its most essential characteristics. Art is perhaps altogether the most sensual, the most sensuous 'expression' of the human spirit, and already bound as such to something concrete outside itself, to a technique, to an instrument, no matter whether this instrument is a weaver's loom or a weaving machine, a paint brush or a camera, a violin or—to mention something really frightful—a cinema organ. Even the human voice—and even the vocal apparatus of a Caruso—is a material instrument, not a spiritual reality. It is only in mystical ecstasy, in the happiness of love, in compassion—perhaps only in compassion—that the soul flows directly, without mediation and without instrumentality, to other souls—but it never flows thus in the experience of a work of art.

The whole history of industrial art can be represented as the continuous renewal and improvement of the technical means of expression, and when this is developing normally and smoothly it can be defined as the complete exploitation and control of these means, as the harmonious adjustment of ability and purpose, of the vehicles and the contents of expression. The obstruction which has occurred in this development since the Industrial Revolution, the lead that technical achievements have gained over intellectual, is to be attributed not so much to the fact that more complicated and more diverse machines began to be used, as to the phenomenon that technical development, spurred on by prosperity, became so rapid that the human mind had no time to keep pace with it. In other words, those elements which might have transferred the tradition of craftsmanship to mechanical production, the independent masters and their apprentices, were eliminated from economic life before they had had any chance of adapting themselves and the traditions of their craft to the new methods of production. What produced the disturbance of the balance in the relationship between technical and intellectual developments was, therefore, a crisis of organization, and by no means a basic change in the nature of technics—all of a sudden there were too few experts in the industries rooted in the old traditions of craftsmanship.

Morris shared Ruskin's prejudices on the subject of mechanical production as well as his enthusiasm for handicraft, but he assessed the function of the machine much more progressively and rationally than his master. He upbraided the society of his time with having misused technical inventions, but he already knew that in certain circumstances they might prove a blessing to humanity.[131] His socialistic optimism only enhanced this hope in technical progress. He defines art as 'man's expression of his joy in labour';[132] for him, art is not only a source of happiness but, above all, the result of a feeling of happiness. Its real value lies in the creative process; in his work the artist enjoys his own productivity and it is the joy of work which is artistically productive. This autogenesis of art is rather mysterious and contains a strong dose of Rousseauism, but it is in no way more mystical and more romantic than the idea that mechanical techniques mean the end of art.

The social phenomena which occupy the art critics and the social critics of the Victorian age also form the subject of the English novel of the time. This too revolves around what Carlyle called the 'condition-of-England' problem, and it describes the social conditions which arose with the Industrial Revolution. But it turns to a more mixed public than the art criticism of the period, is more heterogeneous and speaks a more colourful, less fastidious language. It tries to interest the strata of society into which the works of Carlyle and Ruskin never penetrated and to win for itself readers for whom social reforms are no mere problems of conscience but questions of vital consequence. But, as such readers are still in a minority, the novel remains based in the main on the interests of the upper and middle strata of the bourgeoisie, and provides an outlet for the moral conflicts in which the victors in the class struggle are involved. The stimulus may proceed, as with Disraeli, from patriarchal-feudalistic wish-fulfilment dreams, or, as with Kingsley and Mrs. Gaskell, from a Christian-socialist ideal, or, as with Dickens, from concern about the pauperization of the petty bourgeoisie, but the final result is always a fundamental acceptance of the prevailing order. They all begin with the most violent attacks on capitalistic society, but come in the end to accept its presuppositions in either an optimistic or a quietistic frame of mind, as if they had merely wanted to expose and fight against the abuses, in order to prevent deeper revolutionary upheavals. In the case of Kingsley the conciliatory tendency finds expression in an openly confessed change of mind, with Dickens it is merely concealed by the author's radical and increasingly leftish attitude. Some writers sympathize with the upper classes, others with the 'insulted and injured', but there are no revolutionaries among them. At best, they waver between genuine democratic impulses and the reflection that, in spite of everything, class differences are justified and have a beneficent influence. The differences between them are, at any rate, of subordinate importance in comparison with the common features of their philanthropic conservatism.[133]

The modern social novel arises in England, as in France, in the period around 1830, and enjoys its heyday in the turbulent years between 1840 and 1850, when the country stands on the brink of revolution. Here, too, it becomes the most important literary form of the generation which has come to question the aims and standards of bourgeois society and which wants to explain the sudden rise and threatening ruin of it. But in the English novel the problems discussed are more concrete, of more general significance, less intellectualistic and sophisticated than in the French; the authors' standpoint is more humane, more altruistic, but, at the same time, more conciliatory and opportunistic. Disraeli, Kingsley, Mrs. Gaskell and Dickens are Carlyle's first disciples and are among the writers who accept his ideas most readily.[134] They are irrationalists, idealists, interventionists, they scoff at utilitarianism and national economy, condemn liberalism and industrialism, and place their novels at the service of the fight against the principle of 'laissez-faire' and the economic anarchy which they derive from this principle. Before 1830 the novel as a vehicle of this kind of social propaganda was absolutely unknown, although in England the modern novel had been 'social' from the very beginning, that is, from Defoe and Fielding onwards. It was much more directly and deeply connected with the essays of Addison and Steele than with the pastoral and love novel of Sidney and Lyly, and its first masters owed their insight into the contemporary situation and their moral feeling for the social problems of the day to the stimuli which they had received from journalism. It is true that this feeling becomes blunted at the end of the first great period of the English novel, but it was by no means lost. The novel of terror and mystery, which took the place of Fielding's and Richardson's works in the public favour, had no direct connection with the facts of society or with reality in general, and in Jane Austen's novels social reality was the soil in which the characters were rooted, but in no sense a problem which the novelist made any attempt to solve or interpret. The novel does not become 'social' again until Walter Scott, though in quite a different sense from what it had been in Defoe, Fielding, Richardson or Smollett. In Scott the sociological background is stressed much more consciously than in his predecessors; he always shows his characters as the representatives of a social class, but the picture of society that he draws is much more programmatic and abstract than in the novel of the eighteenth century. He founds a new tradition and is only very loosely connected with the Defoe–Fielding–Smollett line of development. But Dickens, the nearest heir of Walter Scott and, above all, his successor as the best story-teller and the most popular author of his age, resumes a direct connection with this line, for even if he is a pupil of Scott—and who of the novelists of the first half of the century is not?—nevertheless, the genre that he creates is much more similar to the picaresque form of the old writers than to Scott's dramatic mode of writing. Dickens is also closely connected with the eighteenth century by reason of the moralistic-didactic tendency of his art; apart from the picaresque tradition of Fielding and Sterne, he revives the philanthropic trend of Defoe and Goldsmith, which had been equally neglected by Scott.[135] He owes his popularity to the resuscitation of both these literary traditions and he meets the taste of the new reading public halfway both by the picaresque colourfulness and the sentimental-moralistic tone of his works.

Between 1816 and 1850 an average of a hundred novels appear in England every year,[136] and the books published in 1853, most of which are narrative literature, are three times as many as the works that had appeared twenty-five years previously.[137] The increase in the reading public in the eighteenth century was connected with the development of the lending libraries; but they merely led to a more lively activity among publishers and did not contribute in any way to the reduction of book prices. With their growing needs, they helped rather to stabilize the prices on a comparatively high level. The price of a novel in the usual three-volume edition amounted to one and a half guineas, a sum which only extremely few people were in a position to pay for a novel. Hence the readership of light fiction was restricted in the main to the subscribers to lending libraries. It was not until novels began to be published in monthly instalments that a fundamental change in the composition and size of the reading public took place. Payment by instalments, even though this reduced the price only by a third, allowed many people, who had hardly ever been able to buy books before, to purchase the works of their favourite authors. The publication of novels in monthly numbers represented a book-selling innovation, which was in fundamental accordance with the introduction of the serial novel and had similar results both sociologically and artistically. The return to the picaresque form of the novel was one of these results.

Dickens, whose successes also mean the triumph of the new method of publication, enjoys all the advantages and suffers from all the disadvantages connected with the democratization of literary consumption. The constant contact with broad masses of the public helps him to find a style which is popular in the best sense of the word; he is one of the none too numerous artists who are not only great and popular, not merely great, although they are popular, but great, because they are popular. To the loyalty of his public and the feeling of security with which the affection of his readers inspires him, he owes his grand epic style, the evenness of his language and that spontaneous, unproblematical, almost entirely artless mode of creation, which is quite unparalleled in the nineteenth century. On the other hand, his popularity only partly explains his greatness as a writer, for Alexandre Dumas and Eugène Sue are just as popular as he, without being great in any sense. And his greatness explains his popularity even less, for Balzac is incomparably greater, just as vulgar and yet much less successful, although he produces his works under quite similar outward conditions. The disadvantages of popularity for Dickens are much easier to explain. Fidelity to his readers, intellectual solidarity with the great masses of simple followers, and the desire to maintain the affection of this relationship produce in him a belief in the absolute artistic value of the methods which go down well with the emotionally inclined masses and, consequently, also a belief in the infallible instinct and soundness of the great public's unisonously beating heart.[138] He would never have admitted that the artistic quality of a work often stands in an inverse relationship to the number of people who feel moved by it. There are certain means by which we can all be moved to tears, even though we are afterwards ashamed of not having resisted the 'universally human' appeal of these means. But we shed no tears over the fate of the heroes of Homer, Sophocles, Shakespeare, Corneille, Racine, Voltaire, Fielding, Jane Austen and Stendhal, whereas in reading Dickens we feel the same thoughtless, complacent emotions with which we react to the films of today.

Dickens is one of the most successful writers of all time and perhaps the most popular great writer of the modern age. He is, at any rate, the only real writer since romanticism whose work did not spring from opposition to his age, nor from a strained relationship to his environment, but coincided absolutely with the demands of his public. He enjoys a popularity for which there is no parallel since Shakespeare and which approaches nearest to the idea we have of the popularity of the old mimes and minstrels. Dickens owes the totality and integrity of his world-view to the fact that he does not need to make any concessions, when he speaks to his public, that he has just as narrow a mental horizon, just as undiscriminating taste and just as artless, though incomparably richer, an imagination as his readers. Chesterton remarks that, in contrast to Dickens, the popular writers of our day always feel they must climb down to their public.[139] Between them and their readers there exists just as painful, though quite differently constituted and much less deeply founded a breach as between the great writers and the average public of the period. There is no question of any such breach in Dickens. He is not only the creator of the most comprehensive gallery of figures ever to have penetrated the general consciousness and imaginative world of the English reading public, his inner relationship to these figures is the same as that of his public. His readers' favourites are also his favourites and he talks of little Nell or little Dombey with the same feelings and in the same tone as the most harmless little grocer or the simplest old maid.

The series of triumphs began for Dickens with his first full-length work, the *Pickwick Papers*, forty thousand copies of the separate instalments of which were sold from the fifteenth number onwards. This success determined the style of bookselling in which the English fiction of the succeeding quarter of a century was to develop. The power of attraction of the author, who had become famous all of a sudden, never slackened throughout his whole career. The world was always hungry for more and he worked almost as feverishly and breathlessly as Balzac to meet the enormous demand. These two colossi belong together; they are exponents of the same literary boom, they supply the same book-hungry public, which, after the upheavals of an age filled with revolutionary agitation and disillusionments, seeks in the fictitious world of the novel for a substitute for reality, a signpost in the chaos of life and a compensation for lost illusions. But Dickens penetrates into wider circles than Balzac. With the aid of the cheap monthly instalments he wins a completely new class for literature, a class of people who had never read novels before, and beside whom the readers of the older novel literature seem like so many beaux esprits. A charwoman tells how where she lived the people met on the first Monday of every month at the house of a snuff shop proprietor and received tea on payment of a small sum; after tea the master read aloud the latest instalment of *Dombey* and all the occupants of the house were admitted to the reading without charge.[140] Dickens was a purveyor of light fiction for the masses, the continuer of the old 'shilling-shocker' and the inventor of the modern 'thriller',[141] in short, the author of books which, apart from their literary quality, corresponded in all respects to our 'best-sellers'. But it would be wrong to assume that he wrote his novels merely for the uneducated or the half-educated masses; a section of the upper middle class and even a section of the intelligentsia were part of his enthusiastic public. His novels were the up-to-date, topical literature of the time, just as the film is the 'contemporary art' of our age, and has even for people who are perfectly aware of its artistic inadequacies the inestimable value of being a living form, pregnant with the future.

From the very start, Dickens was the representative of the new type of artistically and ideologically progressive literature; he aroused interest even when he did not please, and even when people found his social gospel anything but agreeable, they found his novels entertaining. It was, in any case, possible to separate his artistic from his political philosophy. He raged with flaming words against the sins of society, the heartlessness and the insolence of the rich, the harshness and lack of sympathy of the law, the cruel treatment of children, the inhuman conditions in the prisons, factories and schools, in short, against the lack of consideration for the individual which is the property of all institutional organizations. His accusations rumbled in all ears and filled all hearts with the uneasy feeling of an injustice of which the whole of society was guilty. But the cry of distress and the satisfaction that always follows after a good cry did not lead to anything more tangible. The author's social message was politically fruitless, and even artistically his philanthropy bore very mixed fruits. It deepened his sympathetic insight into the psychology of his characters, but it produced, at the same time, a sentimentalism which was liable to cloud his vision. His uncritical benevolence, his 'Cheeryblism', his confidence in the ability of private charity and the kind-heartedness of the propertied class to repair social defects, sprang, in the final analysis, from his vague social consciousness, from his undecided position between the classes as a petty bourgeois. He was never able to overcome the shock of having been slung out of the middle class in his youth and having reached the brink of the proletariat; he always felt that he had fallen in the social scale, or rather was in danger of falling.[142] He was a radical philanthropist, a liberal-minded friend of the people, a passionate opponent of conservatism, but he was by no means a socialist and a revolutionary—at most a petty bourgeois in revolt, a victim of humiliation who never forgot what had been inflicted on him in his youth.[143] And he remained the life-long petty bourgeois who imagined he was under the necessity of protecting himself not only against a danger from above but also against one from below. He felt and thought like a petty bourgeois, and his ideals were those of the petty bourgeoisie. He regarded work, perseverance, thrift, the ascent to security, lack of worry and respectability as forming the true substance of life. He thought that happiness consisted in a state of modest prosperity, in the idyll of an existence protected from the hostile outside world, in the family circle, in the sheltered comfort of a well-heated room, of a cosy parlour or of the stage-coach taking its passengers to a safe destination.

Dickens is incapable of overcoming the inner contradictions of his social ideology. On the one hand, he hurls the bitterest charges at society, on the other, however, he under-estimates the extent of the social evils, because he refuses to admit it.[144] Actually, he still holds fast to the principle: 'everything for the people—nothing with the people', for he is unable to get away from the prejudice that the people is incompetent to rule.[145] He is afraid of the 'rabble' and identifies the 'people', in the ideal sense of the term, with the middle class. Flaubert, Maupassant and the Goncourts are, despite their conservatism, unbending rebels, whereas, in spite of his political progressiveness and his opposition to existing conditions, Dickens is a peace-loving citizen, who accepts the presuppositions of the prevailing capitalistic system without question. He knows only the burdens and grievances of the petty bourgeoisie, and fights only against evils which can be remedied without shaking the foundations of bourgeois society. Of the situation of the proletariat and life in the great industrial cities, he knows almost nothing and he has a very queer conception of the labour movement. He is only troubled about the fate of the crafts, the small independent masters and tradesmen, the assistants and apprentices. The demands of the working class, that great and constantly growing power of the future, only frighten him. He is not particularly interested in the technical achievements of his age, and the romanticism with which he adheres to antiquated ways of life is much more spontaneous and genuine than Carlyle's and Ruskin's enthusiasm for the Middle Ages with its monasteries and guilds. Compared with Balzac's metropolitan, technicistic outlook, with his delight in inventions and innovations, all this seems to indicate a paltry, sluggish provincialism. In the works of his later period, especially in *Hard Times*, a certain widening of his outlook can no doubt be observed: the problem of the industrial city enters into his range of ideas, and he discusses with growing interest the fate of the industrial proletariat as a class. But how inadequate is his conception of the inner structure of capitalism, how prejudiced and childish his judgement on the aims of the labour movement, how philistine his view that socialistic agitation is nothing but demagogy and the strike parole nothing but blackmail![146] The author's sympathy is with good Stephen Blackpool, who does not take part in the strike and feels an unconquerable, although strongly concealed, sense of solidarity with his master, based on an atavistic, cringing loyalty. The 'dog's morality' plays a great part in Dickens. The further removed an attitude is from the mature, critical, intellectual approach of a serious-minded man, the more understanding and sympathy he has for it. The uneducated, simple folk are always closer to his heart than the educated, and children more so than grown-ups.

Dickens absolutely misunderstands the significance of the conflict between capital and labour; he simply does not grasp that two irreconcilable forces confront each other here, and that the settlement of the quarrel does not depend on the good will of the individual. The gospel truth that man does not live by bread alone does not seem very convincing in a novel describing the struggle of the proletariat for daily bread. But Dickens cannot give up his childish belief in the possibility of reconciling the classes. He indulges in the illusion that patriarchal-philanthropic feelings, on the one, and a patient, self-sacrificing attitude, on the other side, guarantee social peace. He preaches the renunciation of violence, because he regards insurrection and revolution as greater evils than suppression and exploitation. If he never uttered such a harsh phrase as Goethe's 'rather injustice than disorder', it was only because he was not so brave and had not come to anything like such a clear understanding with himself as Goethe. He transformed the healthy, unsentimental egoism of the older bourgeoisie into an adulterated, sugary 'philosophy of Christmas', best summarized as follows by Taine: 'Be good and love one another; the feeling of the heart is the one real joy. . . . Leave science to the scholars, pride to the noble, luxury to the rich. . . .'[147] Dickens did not know how hard the kernel of this gospel of love really was, and what the peace it promised would have cost the weaker classes of society. But he felt it, and the inner contradictions of his philosophy are unmistakably reflected in the serious neurotic disturbances which tormented him. The world of this apostle of peace is by no means a peaceful and harmless world. His sentimentality is often only the mask hiding a terrifying cruelty, his humour smiles in the midst of tears, his good temper fights against a choking fear of life, a grimace is hidden behind the features of his most good-natured characters, his bourgeois decorum is always on the verge of criminality, the scenery of his beloved old-fashioned world is an uncanny lumber-room, his enormous vitality, his joy of life stand in the shadow of death and his fidelity to nature is a feverish hallucination. This apparently so decent, correct, respectable Victorian turns out to be a desperate surrealist tormented by fear-ridden dreams.

Dickens is not merely a representative of truth to life and fidelity to nature in art, not only a consummate master of the 'petits faits vrais', but the artist to whom English literature owes the most important naturalistic achievements. The whole modern English novel derives its art of milieu description, its character drawing and its mastery of dialogue from him. But, in reality, all the characters of this naturalist are caricatures, all the features of real life are exaggerated, pushed to extremes, overstrained, everything becomes a fantastic shadow-play and puppet-show, everything is transformed into the stylized, simplified and stereotyped relationships and situations of the melodrama. His most lovable figures are notorious fools, his most harmless petty bourgeois impossible cranks, monomaniacs and sprites; his carefully drawn milieus seem like romantic opera scenes and his whole naturalism often produces merely the sharpness and the dazzling light of apparitions in a dream. Balzac's worst absurdities are more logical than some of his visions. The Victorian repressions and compromises create an absolutely unbalanced, uncontrolled 'neurotic' style in him. But neuroses are by no means always complicated and there was in fact nothing complicated and sublimated about Dickens. He was not only one of the most uneducated English writers, not only just as ill-informed and unlettered as, for example, Richardson or Jane Austen, but, in contrast above all to the last-named, primitive and in some respects obtuse, a big child with no feeling for the deeper problems of life.

There was nothing intellectual about him and he never thought much of intellectuals. Whenever he had occasion to describe an artist or a thinker, he made fun of them. He maintained the puritan's hostile attitude to art and added to it the unintellectual and anti-artistic convictions of the matter-of-fact bourgeoisie; he regarded art as unnecessary and immoral. His hostility to the things of the mind was worse than bourgeois, it was petty bourgeois and narrow-minded. He refused to have any intercourse with artists, poets and suchlike wind-bags, as if he wanted thereby to bear witness yet again to the sense of solidarity with his public.[148]

In the Victorian age the reading public was already divided into two precisely definable circles and, in spite of his adherents in the upper classes, Dickens was regarded as the author of the uneducated, undiscriminating public. This cleavage had already existed in the eighteenth century, of course, and Richardson can be considered to represent the more elevated middle-class taste, especially in contrast to Defoe and Fielding; but the readers of Richardson, Defoe and Fielding were still on the whole the same people. From 1830 onwards, however, the gulf between the two cultural strata became much more perceptible, and it was fairly easy to mark off Dickens's public from that of Thackeray and Trollope, even though many readers were still on the borderline. It is quite clear that there had already been people in the eighteenth century who found it easier to identify themselves with Richardson's heroes and heroines than with those of Fielding, but there are now readers who can simply not endure Dickens and others who can hardly understand Thackeray or George Eliot. The phenomenon, so characteristic of the present-day situation, that alongside the educated, critical reading public there exists a circle of equally regular readers, who seek for nothing more in literature than easy, ephemeral entertainment, was unknown before the Victorian age. The public interested only in literary entertainment was still made up very largely of casual readers, whereas the regular reading public was restricted to the cultured class. But in Dickens's day, as in our own, there are two groups of people interested in belles-lettres. The only difference between that age and our own is that the popular light literature of that time still embraced the works of a writer like Dickens and that there were still many people who were able to enjoy both kinds of literature,[149] whereas today good literature is fundamentally unpopular and popular literature is unbearable to people of taste.

The World Exhibition of 1851 marks a turning point in the history of England; the mid-Victorian age is, in contrast to the early Victorian period, an age of prosperity and pacification. England becomes the 'workshop of the world', prices rise, the living conditions of the working class are improved, socialism is rendered harmless, the political ascendency of the bourgeoisie is consolidated. It is true that the social problems are not solved, but their sharp edge is removed. The catastrophe of 1848 produces a fatigue and passivity in the progressive strata of society and the novel thereby loses its intolerant and aggressive character. Thackeray, Trollope, and George Eliot no longer write 'social novels' as understood by Kingsley, Mrs. Gaskell and Dickens. Certainly, they draft great pictures of society, but they seldom discuss the social problems of the day, and renounce the propagation of a social-political thesis. With George Eliot, whose outlook on the world is particularly characteristic of the intellectual atmosphere of this period,[150] society is no longer in the foreground of the exposition, although it is, as in the novels of Jane Austen, the vital element in which the characters move and determine each other's fate. George Eliot always describes the mutual dependence of human beings, the magnetic field that they create around themselves, the influence of which they increase with every action and every word;[151] she shows that no one can lead an isolated, autonomous life within modern society,[152] and in this sense her works are social novels. The accent has shifted however: society appears as a positive, all-embracing reality, but as a fact that has to be endured.

The turning towards introversion in the history of the English novel is accomplished in the works of George Eliot. The most important events in her novels are of an intellectual and moral nature, and the soul, the inner citadel, the moral consciousness of man is the scene of the great conflicts of destiny. In this sense her works are psychological novels.[153] Instead of external happenings and adventures, instead of social questions and conflicts, moral problems and crises are central in her plots. Her heroes are thoughtful people for whom intellectual and moral experiences are as immediate as physical facts. Her works are to some extent psychological-philosophical essays which more or less conform to the ideal of the novel that the German romantics had in mind. In spite of that, her art signifies a break with romanticism and, in addition, the first successful attempt to replace the spiritual values created by the romantics with different, fundamentally unromantic values. With George Eliot, the novel acquires a new intellectual-emotional content—that intellectual content, the emotional value of which had been lost since the days of classicism; it hinges not on sentimental experiences of an irrational nature, but on an attitude which George Eliot herself calls 'intellectual passion'.[154] The real subject of her novels is the analysis and interpretation of life, the knowledge and appreciation of intellectual values. Understanding is a word that constantly recurs in her works;[155] to be alert, to be responsible, to deal uncompromisingly with oneself, is the demands he is always repeating. 'The highest calling and election is to do without opium, and live through all our pain with conscious, clear-eyed endurance,' she writes in a letter of 1860.[156]

The destiny of thoughtful people, with its problems and contradictions, its tragedies and defeats, could only attain the immediacy and force that it has in *Middlemarch*, in the work of a writer who was so deeply involved in the intellectual life of her time as George Eliot. The best and most progressive thinkers of the England of that period, including J. S. Mill, Spencer and Huxley, are among George Eliot's friends; she translates Feuerbach and D. F. Strauss and stands at the centre of the rationalistic and positivistic movement of her age. The serious, critical purpose, free from all frivolity and credulity, which informs her moral outlook, is typical of her whole thinking. She is the first to be able adequately to describe an intellectual in the English novel. Apart from her, none of the contemporary novelists can speak of an artist or a scholar without ridiculing him or making himself ridiculous. Even Balzac really regards them as strange, exotic creatures, who fill him with naïve amazement and force a more or less good-natured smile out of him. Compared with George Eliot, he seems a half-educated autodidact, even though, as in the *Chef-d'oeuvre inconnu*, he opens up perspectives the depth and breadth of which lie far beyond George Eliot's artistic powers. Balzac's strength is description, George Eliot's the analysis of experience. She knows from her own experience the torment of wrestling with intellectual problems, she knows or has some idea of the tragedies connected with spiritual defeats, otherwise she would never have been able to create a character like Dr. Casaubon.[157] Thanks to her intellectuality, she attains a new ideal and a new conception of the 'abortive life', and she adds a new type to that series of 'manqués' to which, almost without exception, the heroes of the modern novel belong.

George Eliot's intellectualism is, however, not the real and final reason for the psychologizing of the social novel, but itself only a symptom of the recession of social in favour of psychological problems. The psychological novel is the literary genre of the intelligentsia as the cultural stratum in process of emancipating itself from the bourgeoisie, just as the social novel was the literary form of the cultural stratum which was still fundamentally one with the bourgeoisie. It is not until the beginning of the mid-Victorian period that the intelligentsia comes forward in England as a group without ties, 'socially unattached',[158] 'beyond all class distinctions',[159] 'mediating' between the various classes.[160] Until this time there had never been an intelligentsia here with any feeling of being an independent social group in revolt against the bourgeoisie. The cultured stratum maintains its connection with the bourgeoisie so long as this class allows it to have its own way. The estrangement which set in with romanticism between the progressive literary élite and the conservative middle class was smoothed over again with the conversion of the romantics to the idea of conservatism. The writers of the early Victorian period fought for reforms within bourgeois society, but never thought of destroying this society. The bourgeoisie had also never regarded them in any way as traitors or even as foreigners; on the contrary, it followed their activities in the field of social and cultural criticism with sympathy and goodwill. The cultural stratum fulfilled a function in bourgeois society of the importance of which the ruling classes were on the whole quite aware. It formed the safety-valve that prevented an explosion and, by giving expression to conflicts of conscience which were in danger of being repressed, it provided an outlet for tensions within the bourgeoisie itself.

It was only after its victory over the Revolution and the defeat of Chartism that the bourgeoisie felt so safely entrenched that it no longer had any qualms and twinges of conscience and imagined that it was no longer in any need of criticism. But the cultural élite, and especially its literarily productive section, thereby lost the feeling of having a mission to fulfil in society. It saw itself cut off from the social class of which it had hitherto been the mouthpiece and it felt completely isolated between the uneducated classes and the bourgeoisie. It was this feeling that first gave rise to the replacement of the earlier cultural stratum with its roots in the middle class by the social group that we call the 'intelligentsia'. But this development really formed only the final stage in a process of emancipation in the course of which the representatives of culture had gradually detached themselves from the representatives of power. Humanism and the enlightenment are the first stations in this development; they complete the emancipation of culture, on the one hand, from the dogma of the Church, on the other, from the aesthetic dictatorship of the aristocracy. The French Revolution marks the end of the cultural monopoly that had been exercised until then by the two higher estates and it paves the way for the cultural monopoly of the bourgeoisie, which appears to be absolutely assured with the advent of the July monarchy. The conclusion of the revolutionary era around the middle of the century marks the final step towards the emancipation of the cultural stratum from the ruling classes and the first step towards the creation of the 'intelligentsia' in the narrower meaning of the word.

The intelligentsia arose out of the bourgeoisie and its predecessor was that vanguard of the middle class which paved the way for the French Revolution. Its cultural ideal is enlightened and liberal, its human ideal is based on the concept of the free, progressive personality unrestrained by convention and tradition. When the bourgeoisie spurns the intelligentsia and the intelligentsia deserts the class from which it had arisen and to which it is bound by innumerable ties of common interest, what takes place is really an unnatural and absurd proceeding. The emancipation of the intelligentsia can be regarded as a phase of the universal process of specialization, that is to say, as part of that process of abstraction which, since the Industrial Revolution, has been abolishing the 'organic' relationship between the various strata of society, between the different professions and provinces of culture, but it can also be interpreted as a direct reaction against this very specialization, as an attempt to realize the ideal of the total, all-round human being in whom the values of culture are combined in an integrated whole. The intelligentsia's apparent independence of the middle class, and consequently, of all social ties, is in accordance with the illusion, cherished by both the bourgeoisie and the intelligentsia, that the things of the mind live in a realm beyond the distinctions of class. The intellectuals try to believe in the absoluteness of truth and beauty, because that makes them seem the representatives of a 'higher' reality and because it compensates for their lack of influence in society; the bourgeoisie again allows this claim of the intelligentsia to a position between and above the classes to stand, because it fancies it can see therein a proof of the existence of universally human values and the possibility of class differences being forgotten. But like 'art for art's sake', science for science's sake or truth for truth's sake is merely a product of the estrangement of the intellectuals from practical affairs. The idealism which it contains costs the bourgeoisie the overcoming of its hatred for the things of the mind; the intelligentsia, on the other hand, thereby gives expression to its jealousy of the mighty middle class. The resentment of the cultured strata towards their masters is nothing new; the humanists had already suffered from it and had produced all the neurotic symptoms of an inferiority complex. But how could a class that imagined it was in possession of the truth help feeling jealousy, envy and hatred for the class that was in possession of all economic and political power? In the Middle Ages, the clergy had all the sanctions of 'truth' at their disposal, but partly the instruments of economic and political power as well. Thanks to this coincidence, the pathological phenomena which resulted from the later division of these spheres of authority were still unknown.

In contrast to the medieval clergy, the modern intelligentsia is recruited from various financial and professional classes and represents the interests and views of various and often antagonistic strata of society. This heterogeneity strengthens its feeling of standing above class differences and of representing the living conscience of society. As a result of its mixed descent, it feels the boundaries dividing the various ideologies and cultures more strongly than the earlier cultured strata and it gives a sharper edge to the social criticism, which it already felt called upon to make as the ally of the middle class. From the very beginning its task consisted in making clear the presuppositions of cultural values; it formulated the ideas which were at the root of the bourgeois outlook, it worked out the ideological content of the bourgeois attitude to life, in a world of practical business it fulfilled the function of contemplative thinking, of introversion and sublimation—it was, in short, the mouthpiece of the bourgeois ideology. But now that the bonds between the intelligentsia and the middle class have slackened, the self-imposed censorship of the ruling class turns into destructive criticism, and the principle of dynamics and renewal into that of anarchy. The cultural stratum still at one with the bourgeoisie was the pioneer of reforms; the intelligentsia which had deserted the bourgeoisie becomes an element of revolt and decomposition. Until about 1848 the intelligentsia is still the intellectual vanguard of the bourgeoisie, after 1848 it becomes, consciously or unconsciously, the champion of the working class. As a result of the insecurity of its own existence, it feels that it is to a certain extent in the same boat as the proletariat, and this feeling of solidarity increases its readiness to conspire, when occasion offers, against the bourgeoisie and to take part in preparing the anti-capitalistic revolution.

With the bohème the points of contact between the intelligentsia and the proletariat go far beyond this general feeling of sympathy. The bohemians are in fact themselves only a part of the proletariat. In certain respects they represent the consummation, but at the same time also a caricature of the intelligentsia. They complete the emancipation of the intelligentsia from the middle class, but at the same time they transform the fight against bourgeois conventions into an obsession, often into a kind of persecution mania. They realize, on the one hand, the ideal of absolute concentration on spiritual aims, but, on the other hand, they neglect the remaining values of life and deprive the mind, victorious over life, of the very purpose of its victory. Their independence of the bourgeois world turns out to be only a semblance of freedom, for they feel their estrangement from society as a heavy burden of guilt, unconfessed though it may be; their arrogance proves an overcompensation for an excess of weakness; their exaggerated self-assertion as a doubt in their own creative powers. In France this development takes place earlier than in England where, around the middle of the century, with Ruskin, J. S. Mill, Huxley, George Eliot and their adherents, the first representatives of an 'unattached', 'independently thinking' intelligentsia appear, but where, for the time being, there is no question either of a turning to proletarian revolution, or of the formation of a bohème. The connection with the middle class here continues to be so close that the intelligentsia prefers to take refuge in an 'aristocratic moralism',[161] than to make common cause with the broad masses. Even George Eliot regards as an essentially psychological and moral problem what is in reality a sociological problem, and looks in psychology for the answer to questions which can only be answered sociologically. She thereby leaves the path which is now trodden by the Russian novel and on which it achieves its consummation.

The modern Russian novel is in essentials the creation of the Russian intelligentsia, that is to say, of that intellectual élite which renounces official Russia and interprets literature as meaning above all social criticism and the novel as the 'social' novel. In Russia the novel as mere entertainment or pure analysis of character, with no claim to social significance and usefulness, is unknown until the beginning of the 'eighties. The nation is in such a violent ferment and political and social consciousness is so strongly developed in the reading public that it is quite impossible for a principle like 'art for art's sake' to arise here at all. In Russia the concept of the intelligentsia is always related to that of activism, and its connection with the democratic opposition is much more intimate than in the West. The conservative nationalists can in no sense be reckoned as belonging to this intransigent intelligentsia with its sectarian exclusiveness,[162] and even the greatest masters of the Russian novel, Dostoevsky and Tolstoy, only belong to it to a limited extent; in their critical attitude to society they are, however, very largely influenced by the way of thinking of the intelligentsia, and with their art they contribute to its destructive work, although they refuse personally to have anything to do with it.[163]

The whole of modern Russian literature arises from the spirit of opposition. It owes its first golden age to the literary activities of the progressive, cosmopolitan gentry who strive to obtain recognition for the ideas of the enlightenment and of democracy as against the despotism of the czars. In the age of Pushkin the liberal nobility, with its tendency to Western ideas, is the only cultured stratum of society in Russia. It is true that with the rise of commercial and industrial capitalism the class of intellectual workers, which had previously been made up mainly of officials and doctors, received a considerable influx of technicians, lawyers and journalists,[164] but literary production remained in the hands of the aristocratic officers who, finding no satisfaction in their profession, promised themselves more from the free bourgeois world than from the tottering feudalism of their time.[165] The reaction, which sets in with renewed strength after the defeat of the Decembrist Revolt, succeeds in scattering the rebels, but it does not succeed in preventing the formation of a new political and literary vanguard—that of the intelligentsia. With the rise of this cultured class the predominance of the nobility in Russian literature, which was all-powerful until the end of the 'eighties, comes to an end. The death of Pushkin marks the close of an age: intellectual leadership passes into the hands of the intelligentsia and remains there right up to the Bolshevist revolution.[166]

The new cultural élite is a mixed group, consisting of noble and plebeian elements, recruited from déclassés from above and below. Its members are, on the one hand, so-called 'conscious-stricken noblemen' whose outlook is still fairly close to that of the Decembrists and, on the other, the sons of small shopkeepers, subordinate civil servants, urban clergymen and emancipated serfs who are usually described as 'people of mixed descent' and most of whom lead the uncertain life of 'free artists', students, private tutors and journalists. Until the middle of the century these plebeians are in a minority compared with the gentry, but they gradually increase in numbers and they end by absorbing all the other elements of the intelligentsia. The most important part in the new pattern is played by clergymen's sons who, owing to the natural antagonism between father and son, give most pointed expression to the anti-religious and anti-traditionalist convictions of the intelligentsia. They fulfil the same function as the pastors' sons in eighteenth-century Europe, where during the enlightenment the situation was similar to that prevailing in pre-revolutionary Russia. It is therefore no accident that two of the most important pioneers of Russian rationalism, Chernyshevsky and Dobrolyubov, are the sons of priests and emerge from the middle-class population of the great commercial cities.

Moscow University, with its student associations and cultural societies, is the centre of the new 'classless' intelligentsia. The contrast between the old, pleasure-seeking and blasé residence with its high officials and generals, and the modern university city with its youth capable of enthusiasm and eager for knowledge, denotes the origin of the cultural change that now takes place.[167] The poor student, dependent on himself, is the prototype of the new intelligentsia, just as the noble officer in the Guards was the representative of the old intellectual élite. The cultured society of Moscow continues to preserve its semi-aristocratic stamp for a time, however, and philosophical discussions still take place very largely in the *salons* until about the end of the 'forties,[168] but the latter no longer have an exclusive character and gradually lose their former importance. In the 'sixties, the democratization of literature and the formation of the new intelligentsia is complete. After the emancipation of the peasants it is considerably extended by the masses that crowd in from the ranks of the impoverished lower nobility, but the new elements do not alter the inner structure of the group. The ruined landowners are to some extent forced to do intellectual work and to adapt themselves to the way of life of the bourgeois intelligentsia, in order to support themselves. It is to be noted, however, that they not only add to the number of the progressive, cosmopolitan Westernizers, but to an equal, if not to a higher degree that of the Slavophils as well, thereby creating a certain balance between the two groups.

The intellectual reaction which the rationalism of the Westernized intelligentsia calls forth corresponds to the romantic historicism and traditionalism with which Western Europe had reacted to the Revolution half a century earlier. The Slavophils are the indirect and mostly unconscious intellectual heirs of Burke, de Bonald, de Maistre, Herder, Hamann, Moeser and Adam Mueller, just as the Westernizers are the disciples of Voltaire, the Encyclopaedists, German idealism and later, on the one hand, of the socialists Saint-Simon, Fourier and Comte, and on the other, of the materialists Feuerbach, Buechner, Vogt and Moleschott. They stress, in opposition to the cosmopolitan and atheistic free thought of the Westernizers, the value of national and religious traditions, and proclaim their mystical belief in the Russian peasant and their fidelity to the orthodox Church. As opposed to rationalism and positivism, they declare themselves believers in the irrational idea of 'organic' historical growth, and they represent the old Russia, with its 'genuine Christianity' and its freedom from Western individualism, as the ideal and the salvation of Europe, just as the Westernizers, for their part, see the ideal and salvation for Russia in Europe. Slavophilism itself is very old, indeed even older than the resistance to Peter the Great's reforms, but it begins its official existence only with the struggle against Belinsky. At any rate, the movement owes its fervour and its definite programme to the opposition to the 'men of the 'forties'. The leaders of this theoretically clarified and programmatically conscious Slavophilism are, to begin with, mainly aristocratic landowners, still living under the old feudal conditions, who clothe their political and social conservatism in the ideology of 'holy Russia' and the 'messianic task of the Slav peoples'. Their cult of national traditions is mostly no more than a means of fighting the progressive ideas of the Westernizers, and their Rousseauist and romantic enthusiasm for the Russian peasant only the ideological form of their endeavour to hold fast to patriarchal-feudal conditions.

The Slavophil movement is not, however, wholly identical with conservatism and reaction. There are many real friends of the people among the Slavophils, just as there are many enemies of democracy among the Westernizers. Herzen himself is well known to have had certain reservations against the democratic institutions of the West. The first Slavophils, however, are opponents of czarist autocracy and attack the government of Nicholas I. It is true that the later Slavophils adopt a more positive attitude to czardom, the idea of which forms an integral component of their political theory and philosophy of history, but they continue to count democrats among their supporters. The Slavophil movement as a whole has to be divided into two stages, just as there are two different generations of Westernizers. For, just as the reformism and rationalism of the 'forties develops into the socialism and materialism of the 'sixties and 'seventies, so the Slavophilism of the feudal landowners changes into the pan-slavism and populism of Danilevsky, Grigoriev and Dostoevsky. The modern democratic trend is sharply opposed to the former aristocratic tendency.[169] After the liberation of the peasants many of the older writers turn away from the Westernized intellectuals and join the nationalists; so that it is hardly any longer possible to assert that 'conservative literature is notably weaker than progressive literature, both quantitatively and qualitatively'.[170]

The Slavophils and the Westernizers now differ more in their fighting methods than in their aims. The whole of intellectual Russia adopts the 'Slav idea'; all the intellectuals are patriots and prophets of the 'Russian mission'. They 'kneel in mystic adoration before the Russian sheepskin',[171] they study the Russian soul and develop an enthusiasm for 'ethnographical poetry'. Peter the Great's dictum, 'We need Europe for a few decades, then we shall be able to turn our backs on it', still accords with the opinion of most of the reformers. The very word 'narod', which means both 'people' and 'nation', makes it possible for the difference between democrats and nationalists to become blurred.[172] The Slavophil inclinations of the radicals are to be explained above all by the fact that the Russians, still in the very earliest stages of capitalism, are much more homogeneous as a nation, that is to say, much less divided by class differences, than the peoples of the West. The whole intellectual élite in Russia is Rousseauist in its outlook and is more or less hostile to art and sophisticated culture; it feels that the cultural traditions of the West, classical antiquity, the Roman Church, medieval scholasticism, the Renaissance and the Reformation, and partly even modern individualism, scienticism and aestheticism are an obstacle to the realization of its own aims.[173] The aesthetic utilitarianism of Belinsky, Chernyshevsky and Pisarev is just as anti-traditionalistic as Tolstoy's hostility to art. The rôles are not even exactly divided between Westernizers and Slavophils in the great controversy between subjectivism and objectivism, individualism and collectivism, freedom and authority, although the Westernizers naturally incline more to the liberal and the Slavophils more to the authoritarian ideal. But Belinsky and Herzen wrestle just as desperately and often just as helplessly with the problem of individual liberty as Dostoevsky or Tolstoy. The entire philosophical speculation of the Russians hinges on this problem and the danger of moral relativism, the spectre of anarchy, the chaos of crime, occupy and frighten all the Russian thinkers. The Russians see the great and crucial European question of the estrangement of the individual from society, the loneliness and isolation of modern man, as the problem of freedom. Nowhere has this problem been lived through more deeply, more intensively and more disturbingly than in Russia, and no one felt the responsibility involved in the attempt to solve it with greater anguish than Tolstoy and Dostoevsky. The hero of the *Memoirs from Underground*, Raskolnikov, Kirilov, Ivan Karamazov—they all wrestle with this problem, they all fight against the danger of being swallowed up in the abyss of unrestricted freedom, individual discretion and egoism. Dostoevsky's rejection of individualism, his criticism of rationalistic and materialistic Europe, his apotheosis of human solidarity and love, have no other purpose than to impede a development which must lead inevitably to Flaubert's nihilism. The Western novel ends with the description of the individual estranged from society and collapsing under the burden of his loneliness; the Russian novel depicts, from beginning to end, the fight against the demons which induce the individual to revolt against the world and the community of his fellow-men. This difference explains not only the problematic nature of characters such as Dostoevsky's Raskolnikov and Ivan Karamazov or Tolstoy's Pierre Bezukhov and Levin, not only these writers' gospel of love and faith, but the messianism of the whole of Russian literature.

The Russian novel is much more strictly tendentious than the novel of Western Europe. Social problems not only occupy much more space and a more central position, they maintain their predominance for a longer time and more undisputedly than in Western literature. The connection with the political and social questions of the day is closer here from the very outset than in the works of the French and English writers of the same period. In Russia despotism offers intellectual energies no other possibility of making themselves felt than through the medium of literature and the censorship forces social criticism into literary forms as the only possible outlet.[174] The novel, as the form of social criticism par excellence, here acquires an activisit, pedagogical and, indeed, prophetic character, such as it never possessed in the West, and the Russian writers still remain the teachers and prophets of their people, when the literati in Western Europe are already declining into absolute passivity and isolation. For the Russians, the nineteenth century is the age of enlightenment; they preserve the enthusiasm and optimism of the pre-revolutionary years a century longer than the peoples of the West. Russia did not experience the disillusionment of the treacherously defeated and adulterated European revolutions; there is no trace of the fatigue by which France and England are overcome after 1848. It is due to the youthful inexperience of the nation and its undefeated social idealism that, at a time when in France and England naturalism begins to develop into a passive impressionism, the naturalistic novel remains fresh and full of promise in Russia. Russian literature, which passes out of the hands of the tired and ill-fated gentry into those of a rising class, when the bourgeois cultured élite is already exhausted in the West and feels threatened by forces from below, not only overcomes the weariness of life which was beginning to make itself felt in the writings of the romantically inclined nobility, but also the mood of resignation and scepticism that dominates modern Western literature. In spite of its darker streaks, the Russian novel is the expression of an invincible optimism, evidence of a belief in the future of Russia and the human race; it is and remains inspired with a hopeful spirit of attack, an evangelical yearning for and certainty of redemption. This optimism is not by any means expressed in mere wish-fulfilment dreams and cheap 'happy endings', but in the certain faith that human sufferings and sacrifices have a meaning and are never in vain. The works of the great Russian novelists nearly always end in a conciliatory mood, though often very sadly; they are more serious than the novels of the French writers, but they are never so bitter, never so hopeless.

The miracle of the Russian novel consists in the fact that, in spite of its youth, it not only reaches the heights of the French and English novel, but takes over the lead from them and represents the most progressive and most vigorous literary form of the age. Compared with the works of Dostoevsky and Tolstoy, the whole of Western literature in the second half of the century seems weary and stagnant. *Anna Karenina* and *The Brothers Karamazov* mark the summit of European naturalism; they sum up and surpass the psychological achievements of the French and English novel without ever losing their feeling for the great superindividual relationships of life. Just as the social novel attains its perfection with Balzac, the 'Bildungsroman' with Flaubert, the picaresque novel with Dickens, so the psychological novel enters the phase of its full maturity with Dostoevsky and Tolstoy. These two novelists represent the close of the development which starts, on the one hand, with the sentimental novel of Rousseau, Richardson and Goethe, on the other, with the analytical novel of Marivaux, Benjamin Constant and Stendhal. Modern psychology begins with the description of the inner strife of the soul—of a dissension which cannot simply be reduced to a definite inner conflict. Antigone already wavers between duty and inclination, and Corneille's heroes can almost be said to know nothing but this struggle. Shakespeare makes the hero's indecision the main subject of the drama. The inhibitions are here not derived merely from a moral impulse, as in Sophocles and Corneille, but also from the nerves, that is, from an unconscious and uncontrolled region of the soul. But the antagonistic psychological inclinations still appear separated from one another and the characters' moral judgement on their own impulses is absolutely clear-cut and consistent. At most, they waver in their moral identification with one or the other part of their impulses. The disintegration of the personality, in which the emotional conflict goes so far that the individual is no longer clear about his own motives and becomes a problem to himself, does not take place until the beginning of the last century. The concomitants of modern capitalism, romanticism and the estrangement of the individual from society, first create the consciousness of spiritual dissension and hence the modern problematical character. The psychological contradictions in Shakespeare and the Elizabethans are mostly mere absurdities; they represent a stage of development *prior to* the synthesis of classicism. In other words: the dramatists have not yet learnt by experience how to draw characters who act uniformly and consistently, and they also attach no special importance to the uniformity of the total picture. The inconsistent characters of romantic literature, on the other hand, are the expression of a conscious and programmatically stressed reaction against the rationalism of classicistic psychology. Wild and fantastic figures are favoured, because chaotic feelings are considered more genuine and original than consistent and methodical reason. The most obvious, although still somewhat crude expression of the mind at variance with itself and no longer capable of being reduced to any rational unity is the idea of the 'double', which Dostoevsky takes over from the romantics as a standing requisite of character drawing and which he preserves to the end. It is, however, only the fight against romanticism and the constant wavering between the romantic and anti-romantic attitudes which brings about the absolute dissolution of the unity of the character, that is, the disintegration which consists not only in the incoherence of the constituents of the human soul, but also in their constant displacement and transformation, revaluation and reinterpretation. With Stendhal, who introduces this phase, we see the different components of the soul changing their nature before our very eyes. The provisional character of any description of a spiritual condition and the indefinable quality of spiritual attitudes now becomes the criterion of any feasible psychology and only an iridescent and kaleidoscopic picture of the human soul is now regarded as artistically interesting. The final stage in this development is reached with the absolute incalculability and irrationality of Dostoevsky's characters. The aspect of 'You are not what you seem to be' now becomes the psychological norm, and the strange and uncanny, the demonic and inscrutable, in man is regarded from now onwards as the presupposition of his psychological significance. Compared with Dostoevsky's characters, the figures of older literature always seem more or less idyllic and non-committal. Today, of course, we realize that even Dostoevsky's psychology is still full of conventional traits, and that it makes the most abundant use of the remains of romantic gruesomeness and Byronism. We see that Dostoevsky is not a beginning but an end and that, for all his originality and productivity, he is quite willing to take over the achievements of the West European psychological novel and develop them consistently.

Dostoevsky discovers the most important principle of modern psychology: the ambivalence of the feelings and the divided nature of all the spiritual attitudes which express themselves in exaggerated and over-demonstrative forms. Not only love and hate, but also pride and humility, conceit and self-humiliation, cruelty and masochism, the yearning for the sublime and the 'nostalgia for filth', are interconnected in his characters; not only figures like Raskolnikov and Svidrigailov, but also Myshkin and Rogozhin, Ivan Karamazov and Smerdyakov, belong together as variations of one and the same principle; every impulse, every feeling, every thought, produces its opposite, as soon as it emerges from the consciousness of these people. Dostoevsky's heroes are always confronted with alternatives, between which they ought to but cannot choose; hence their thinking, their self-analysis and self-criticism is a constant raving and raging against themselves. The parable of the swine possessed by evil refers not only to the characters of *The Possessed*, but more or less to the whole collection of people he describes in his novels. His novels take place on the eve of the Last Judgement; everything is in a state of the most fearful tension, of the most mortal fear, and the wildest chaos; everything is waiting to be purified, reassured and saved by a miracle—waiting for a solution based not on the power and acuteness of the mind and the dialectic of the reason, but on renunciation of this power and the sacrifice of reason. In the idea of intellectual suicide for which Dostoevsky pleads, is expressed the whole questionableness of his philosophy, in which he attempts to solve real problems and correctly posed questions in an absolutely unreal and irrational way.

Dostoevsky owes the depth and refinement of his psychology to the intensity with which he experiences the problematical nature of the modern intellectual, whereas the naïvety of his moral philosophy comes from his anti-rationalistic escapades, from his betrayal of the reason and his inability to resist the temptations of romanticism and abstract idealism. His mystical nationalism, his religious orthodoxy and his intuitive ethics form an intellectual unity, and obviously originate in the same experience, the same spiritual shock. In his youth, Dostoevsky belonged to the radicals and was a member of the socialistically-minded circle around Petrashevsky. He was condemned to death for the part he played here, and after all the preparations for his execution, he was pardoned and sent to Siberia. This experience and the years of imprisonment seem to have broken his rebelliousness. When he returns to St. Petersburg, after an absence of ten years, he is no longer a socialist and a radical, even though he is still far removed from his later political and religious mysticism. Only the terrible privations of the following period, his worsening illness and his vagabondage in Europe succeed in breaking his resistance completely. The author of *Crime and Punishment* and *The Idiot* already seeks for protection and peace in religion, but it is only the creator of *The Possessed* and *The Brothers Karamazov* who becomes an enthusiastic apologist of the ecclesiastical and secular authorities and a preacher of positive dogma. It is only in his later years that Dostoevsky becomes the moralist, the mystic and the reactionary that he is often summarily described to be.[175] But even with this qualification, it is not easy to classify him politically. His criticism of socialism is pure nonsense; the world he describes cries out for socialism, however, and for the deliverance of mankind from poverty and humiliation. In his case, too, one must speak of the 'triumph of realism', of the victory of the clear-sighted, realistically-minded artist over the bewildered, romantic politician. But with Dostoevsky the situation is much more complicated than with Balzac. In his art there is a deep sympathy and solidarity with the 'insulted and injured', which is completely lacking in Balzac, and in his work there is something in the nature of a nobility of poverty, even though there is much in his novels about the poor that is based only on literary convention and a stereotyped romantic pattern. Dostoevsky is at least one of the few genuine writers on poverty, for he writes not merely out of sympathy with the poor, like George Sand or Eugène Sue, or as a result of vague memories, like Dickens, but as one who has spent most of his life in need and has literarily starved from time to time. That is why, even when he is speaking of his religious and moral problems, the impression Dostoevsky makes is more rousing and revolutionizing than when George Sand and Dickens speak of the economic distress and social injustice of their time. But he is in no sense a spokesman of the revolutionary masses. In spite of his idealization of the 'people' and his Slavophil convictions, he has no intimate contact with the industrial proletariat and the peasantry.[176] It is only to the intellectual proletariat that he really feels drawn. He calls himself a 'literary proletarian' and a 'post-horse', who always works under the pressure of a contract, who has never in his life sold a work other than for payment in advance and often has no idea of the end of a chapter, when the beginning of it is already with the printers. He complains that work has stifled and consumed him; he has worked until his brain has become dull and broken. If only he could write a single novel as Turgenev and Tolstoy write their works! But proudly and challengingly he calls himself a 'man of letters', and considers himself the representative of a new generation and a new social class, which have never before had a chance to speak their mind in literature. And despite his opposition to the political aspirations of the intelligentsia, he is the first valid representative of this class in the history of the Russian novel. Gogol, Goncharov and Turgenev still express the outlook of the gentry, although they stand to some extent for very progressive ideas and, in contrast to their class-conditioned interests, are among the pioneers of the transformation of Russia into a bourgeois society. Dostoevsky rightly considers Tolstoy one of the representatives of this 'landowners' literature' and calls him the 'historian of the aristocracy', who keeps the form of the Aksakovian family chronicle in his great novels, above all in *War and Peace*.[177]

Most of Dostoevsky's heroes, especially Raskolnikov, Ivan Karamazov, Shatov, Kirilov, Stepan Verhovensky, are bourgeois intellectuals and Dostoevsky bases his analysis of society on their point of view, even though he never expressly identifies himself with them. But what decides the world-view of a writer is not so much whose side he supports, as through whose eyes he looks at the world. Dostoevsky envisages the social problems of his time, first of all the atomization of society and the deepening gulf between the classes, from the standpoint of the intelligentsia, and sees the solution in the reunion of the educated with the simple, faithful people, from whom they have become estranged. Tolstoy reviews the same problems from the standpoint of the nobility and bases his hopes for the recovery of society on an understanding between the landowners and the peasants. His thinking is still associated with patriarchal-feudal concepts, and even those characters who come nearest to the realization of his ideas, Levin and Pierre Bezukhov, are at best benefactors of the people, not really democrats. In Dostoevsky's world, on the other hand, a perfect intellectual democracy predominates. All his characters, both the rich and the poor, the aristocrats and the plebeians, wrestle with the same moral problems. The rich Prince Myshkin and the poor student Raskolnikov are both homeless vagabonds, déclassés and outlaws with no place in modern bourgeois society. All his heroes stand to some extent outside this society and form a classless world, in which only spiritual relationships prevail. They are present in all their activities with their whole nature, their whole soul, and in the midst of the routine of the modern world they represent a purely intellectual, spiritual, Utopian reality. 'We have no class interests, because strictly speaking we have no classes and because the Russian soul is wider than class differences, class interests and class law,' Dostoevsky writes in

An Author's Diary, and nothing is more characteristic of his way of thinking than the contradiction between this assertion and the consciousness of his class-determined divergence from his aristocratic colleagues. The same Dostoevsky who draws such a sharp dividing line between himself and the representatives of the 'landowners' literature' and bases his *raison d'être* as a writer on his plebeian intellectualism, denies the very existence of classes and believes in the primacy of a-social spiritual relationships.

Attention has repeatedly been drawn to the similarity between the social position of Dostoevsky and Dickens. It has been noticed that both were the sons of fathers with no very firm roots in society, and that they both knew the feeling of social insecurity and uprootedness from their youth upwards.[178] Dostoevsky was the son of a staff-doctor and of a merchant's daughter. His father acquired a small property and had his sons educated in a school otherwise attended only by the children of nobles. The mother died early and the father, who gave himself up to drink, was killed by his own peasants, whom he is said to have treated very badly. Dostoevsky now sank from a relatively respectable social level to that of the intellectual proletariat by which he felt alternately repelled and attracted. Nothing is more probable than that there was, in fact, a connection between the contradictory and often unclarified social outlook of both Dostoevsky and Dickens and the wavering social position of their fathers and their own early acquaintance with the feeling of having fallen in the social scale.

Dostoevsky's position in the history of the social novel is marked above all by the fact that the first naturalistic representation of the modern metropolis with its petty bourgeois and proletarian population, its small shop-keepers and officials, its students and prostitutes, idlers and down and outs, is his creation. Balzac's Paris was still a romantic wilderness, the scene of fantastic adventures and miraculous encounters, a theatrical setting painted in a chiaroscuro of contrasts, a fairyland in which dazzling riches and picturesque poverty live next door to each other. Dostoevsky, on the other hand, paints the picture of the big city in altogether sombre colours, as a place of utterly dark, colourless misery. He shows its drab official buildings, its gloomy gin-shops, its furnished rooms, these 'coffins' of rooms, as he calls them, in which the saddest victims of the life of a big city pass their days. All this has an unmistakable social significance and a political point; but Dostoevsky attempts to take away the class-determined coefficients from his characters. He demolishes the economic and social barriers between them and mixes them all up one with another, as if something in the nature of a common human destiny really did exist. His spiritualism and nationalism fulfil the same function: they create the legend of a moral being that leads a life ordered in accordance with higher laws and beyond the limitations of birth, class and education. With Goncharov, Turgenev and Tolstoy the class-determined features of the characters are not effaced; the fact that they belong to the nobility, the middle class or the common people is not overlooked or forgotten for a moment. Dostoevsky, on the other hand, often neglects these differences, and he sometimes seems to pass them over deliberately. The fact that the class character of his figures makes itself felt all the same, and that we feel, above all, his intellectuals as an exactly defined social group, is part of that triumph of realism which makes Dostoevsky a materialist in spite of himself.

This 'materialism' is, however, only one of the invisible and often unconscious presuppositions of his intellectuality—an intellectuality which is a real passion, a demoniac compulsion to reduce experience to its ultimate threads, to probe feelings to their last impulse, to think deeper and deeper, to experiment with all the consequences of thought and to descend into its deepest subconscious sources. Dostoevsky's heroes are impassioned, fearless, maniacal thinkers wrestling with their ideas and visions just as desperately as the heroes of the novels of chivalry wrestled with giants and monsters. They suffer, murder, and die for ideas; for them life is a philosophical task, and thought is the one and only constant occupation in their life, its sole content. They struggle with real monsters—with still unborn, indefinable ideas to which as yet no shape can be given, with problems which cannot be solved, cannot even be formulated. Dostoevsky is not only the first modern novelist to know how to give as concrete and evident form to an intellectual experience as to a sensual experience, but he also advances into regions of the mind into which no one before him had ever ventured. He discovers a new dimension, a new depth, a new intensity of thought. To be sure, the discovery owes its effect of novelty above all to the fact that romanticism has accustomed us to keep thoughts and feelings, ideas and passions in strictly water-tight compartments, and only regard feelings and passions as fit subjects for artistic treatment.[179] The real innovation in Dostoevsky's intellectual constitution is the fact that he is a romantic in the world of thought, and that the movement of thought has the same motive power and the same emotional, not to say pathological, impetus in him as the flood and stress of the feelings had in the romantics. The synthesis of intellectualism and romanticism is the epoch-making innovation in the art of Dostoevsky; it gives rise to the most progressive literary form of the second half of the last century, the form which best met the needs of this age with its indissoluble ties with romanticism and its impetuous striving after intellectualism.

Dostoevsky did not, however, move only on the heights, but also in the lowlands of romanticism. His work represented not merely the continuation of the romantic literature of confession, but also that of the romantic thriller.[180] In this respect, too, he was a genuine contemporary of Dickens—a writer who showed himself as indiscriminate in his choice of methods as the other purveyors of the serial novel. Perhaps he would actually have avoided certain lapses of taste and inaccuracies, if he had been able to work like Tolstoy and Turgenev. The melodramatic quality of his style was, nevertheless, inseparably bound up with his conception of the psychological novel and the drastic methods he employed were not merely a vehicle of thrilling exposition, but were intended to contribute to the creation of that overheated spiritual atmosphere without which the dramatic situations of his novels would be quite unthinkable. One can, if one likes, think of *The Brothers Karamazov* as a shilling-shocker, of *Crime and Punishment* as a detective novel, of *The Possessed* as a penny-dreadful, and *The Idiot* as a thriller; murder and crime, mysteries and surprises, melodrama and atrocities, morbid and macabre moods, play a leading part in them: but it would be a mistake to assume that all this is only to compensate the reader for the abstractness of the intellectual content, the author wants rather to induce the feeling that the spiritual processes on which the story hinges are just as elemental as the most primitive impulses. In Dostoevsky we find again the whole gallery of heroes from the romantic adventure novel: the handsome, strong, mysterious and lonely Byronic hero (Stavrogin), the wild, unbridled, dangerous but good-natured man of instinct (Rogozhin and Dimitri Karamazov), the angelic figures of light (Myshkin and Alyosha), the inwardly pure prostitute (Sonya and Nastasya Philippovna), the old debauchee (Fedor Karamazov), the escaped convict (Fedka), the dissolute drunkard (Lebyadkin), etc., etc. We find all the requisites of the thriller and the adventure novel: the seduced and forsaken girl, the secret marriage, the anonymous letters, the mysterious murder, the madness, the fainting fits, the sensational slap on the face and, above all and repeatedly, the explosive scenes of social scandals.[181] These scenes best show what Dostoevsky is capable of developing from the methods of the thriller. They not only serve, as one might think, to produce effective endings and brilliant 'coups de théâtre', but are present, as it were, from the very beginning as a threatening danger and produce the feeling that the great passions and elemental spiritual relationships always approach the limits of the conventional and the socially permissible. The Utopian isle of spiritual beings, on which Dostoevsky's heroes lead their moral life, turns out to be a narrow cage; wherever the immanence of their existence is broken through, a social scandal results. It is a characteristic feature of these scandal scenes that they take place in the presence of the most mixed society conceivable, with the participation of the socially most incompatible elements. Both in the great scandal scene in the house of Nastasya Philippovna, in *The Idiot*, and in that which takes place in the house of Varvara Petrovna, in *The Possessed*, all the participants in the drama are gathered together, as if the author were trying to prove that social differentiation is least capable of withstanding the universal dissolution. Each of these scenes seems like a fear-ridden dream, in which a crowd of human beings are squeezed together in an incredibly narrow room, and the nightmarish character which is peculiar to them shows what an uncanny power society, with its differences of class and rank, its taboos and vetos, had for Dostoevsky.

Most critics emphasize the dramatic structure of Dostoevsky's great novels; but they usually interpret this formal peculiarity merely as a means of achieving theatrical effects, and they contrast it with the broad-surging, epic flow of Tolstoy's novels. Dostoevsky does not, however, use a dramatic technique merely to create climaxes, in which the threads of the plot converge and the threatening conflict breaks out, he uses it rather to fill the whole plot with dramatic life and to express a world-view completely different from the epic outlook on life. According to Dostoevsky, the meaning of existence is not contained in its temporality, in the rise and fall of its aims, in memories and illusions, not in the years, days and hours which descend on one another and bury us, but in those high moments in which human souls are stripped bare and seem to be reduced to simple, unequivocal formulae, in which they feel they are their real unquestionable selves and in which they declare themselves one with themselves and one with their destiny. That there are such moments is the basis of Dostoevsky's tragic optimism, of that reconciliation with fate, which the Greeks called the catharsis in their tragedies. This is also the basis of his philosophy and its opposition to the pessimism and nihilism of Flaubert. Dostoevsky always described the feeling of greatest happiness and the most perfect harmony as an experience of timelessness; thus, above all, Myshkin's condition before his epileptic fits and Kirilov's 'five seconds', the ecstasy of which would, as he says, have been intolerable for any greater length of time. In order to describe the kind of existence that culminates in such moments, the Flaubertian conception of the novel, based entirely on the feeling of time, had to be changed so fundamentally that the result often seemed to have hardly anything in common with the usual idea of the novel. It is true that Dostoevsky's form represents the direct continuation of the social and psychological novel, but it also signifies the beginning of a new development. What is usually described as its dramatic structure depends on a formal principle quite different from that of the unity of the romantic novel which superseded the old picaresque form. It represents rather a return to the picaresque novel, inasmuch as its dramatic scenes are scattered and form several independent focal points. With this abolition of continuity in favour of a series of substantial, expressive, but mosaic-fashion combined episodes, it anticipates the formal principles of the modern expressionistic novel. The narrative recedes in favour of the explication, the psychological analysis and the philosophical discussion, and the novel develops into a collection of dialogue scenes and internal monologues to which the author adds an accompaniment of commentaries and digressions.

This method is often as remote from the style of naturalism as from the novel as an epic genre. Dostoevsky represents, as far as sharpness of psychological observation is concerned, the most highly developed form of the naturalistic novel, but if one understands by naturalism the representation of the normal, the average and the everyday, then one is bound to see in his fondness for situations with a quality of dreamlike exaggeration and fantastically overdone characters a reaction against naturalism. Dostoevsky himself defines his position in the history of literature with perfect exactness: 'I am called', he says, 'a psychologist, that is wrong, I am only a realist on a higher level, in other words, I describe all the depths of the human soul.' These depths are, for him, the irrational, the demonic, the dreamlike and ghostlike in man; they call for a naturalism that is not the truth of the surface; they point to phenomena, in which the elements of real life intermingle, displace and outbid each other in a fantastic way. 'I love realism in art beyond all measure,' he declares, 'the realism which approaches the fantastic. . . . What can be more fantastic and unexpected for me than reality? In fact, what can be more improbable than reality?' There could be no more exact definition of expressionism and surrealism. That which in Dickens is still a merely occasional and usually unconscious contact with the no man's land between reality and dream, experience and vision, is here developed into a permanent openness of the spirit to the 'mysteries of life'. The break with scientism, which was expressed in nineteenth-century naturalism, is here being made ready. A new spiritualism is in process of arising from the reaction against the scientific outlook, from the revolt against naturalism, from the distrust in the rationalistic mastery of the problems of life. Life itself is felt to be something essentially irrational, mysterious voices are supposed to be audible from all directions, and art becomes the echo of these voices.

In spite of the deepest conceivable antithesis, there is a basic unity between Dostoevsky and Tolstoy in their attitude to the problem of individualism and freedom. Both regard the emancipation of the individual from society, his loneliness and isolation, as the greatest possible evil. Both desire to ward off the chaos that threatens to invade the individual estranged from society by all the means at their disposal. Above all in Dostoevsky, everything hinges on the problem of freedom, and his great novels are fundamentally nothing but analyses and interpretations of this idea. The problem itself was by no means new; it had always occupied the romantics, and from 1830 onwards it had held a central place in political and philosophical thought. For romanticism, freedom meant the victory of the individual over convention; it regarded a personality as free and creative only if it had the intellectual force and courage to disregard the moral and aesthetic prejudices of its own age. Stendhal formulated the problem as that of the genius, especially that of Napoleon, for whom success, as he thought, was a question of the ruthless enforcement of his will, of his great personality and impetuous nature. The arbitrariness of the genius, and the victims which it demands, seemed to him the price the world has to pay for the sight of its spiritual heroes. Dostoevsky's Raskolnikov represents the next stage in the development. He stands for an abstract, virtuoso-like form, as it were a play form, of the individual genius. The personality requires its victims no longer in the interest of a higher idea, of an objective goal, or a materially valuable achievement, but merely in order to prove that it is capable of free and sovereign action. The deed itself becomes absolutely immaterial; the question that is to be settled is a purely formal one: is personal freedom a value in itself? Dostoevsky's answer is by no means so clear-cut as it might appear to be at first sight. Individualism certainly leads to anarchy and chaos—but where then do coercion and order lead to? The problem is given its final and deepest setting in the story of *The Grand Inquisitor*, and the solution to which Dostoevsky comes can be regarded as the sum-total of his whole philosophy of morals and religion. The abolition of freedom produces rigid institutions and replaces religion by the Church, the individual by the state, the restlessness of questioning and seeking by the reassurances of dogma. Christ signifies inward freedom but, therefore, an endless struggle; the Church implies an inner compulsion, but also peace and security. One can see how dialectically Dostoevsky thinks, and how difficult it is to give a clear definition of his moral and socio-political views. The reactionary and dogmatist of ill-repute ends his work with an open question.

It is true that the problem of freedom does not play anything like so important a part in Tolstoy's work as in that of Dostoevsky, but even with him it forms the key to an understanding of his psychologically most interesting and morally most revealing characters. Levin, above all, is wholly conceived as the exponent of this problem and the violence of his inner struggles shows how seriously Tolstoy wrestled with the idea of the estrangement and the spectre of the individual left to his own devices. Dostoevsky was right: *Anna Karenina* is not an innocuous book at all. It is full of doubts, scruples and apprehensions. Here too the basic idea, and the motif which connects the story of Anna Karenina with that of Levin, is the problem of the detachment of the individual from society and the danger of homelessness. The same fate to which Anna falls victim as a result of her adultery, threatens Levin as a result of his individualism, his unconventional outlook on life and his strange problems and doubts. Both are threatened by the danger of being expelled from the society of normal, respectable people. Only whereas Anna forgoes the consent of society from the very outset, Levin does everything in order not to lose the hold which he has on society. He bears the yoke of his marriage, manages his estate, like his neighbours, submits to the conventions and prejudices of his environment, in short, he is prepared to do anything, merely not to become an uprooted outlaw, an eccentric and a crank.[182]

But the anti-individualism of Dostoevsky and Tolstoy reveals the whole difference in their way of thought. Dostoevsky's objections are of a more irrational and mystic nature; he interprets the 'principium individuationis' as a defection from the world-spirit, from the prime original, from the divine idea, which make themselves known in a concrete historical form in the common people, the nation and the social community. Tolstoy, on the other hand, rejects individualism on purely rational and eudemonist grounds; personal detachment from society can bring man no happiness and no satisfaction; he can find comfort and contentment only in self-denial and in devotion to others.

In the relationship between Tolstoy and Dostoevsky the significant, paradigmatic, fundamentally typical spiritual relationship is repeated which existed between Voltaire and Rousseau and which has an analogy in that which existed between Goethe and Schiller.[183] In all these cases rationalism and irrationalism, sensuality and intellectuality, or as Schiller himself puts it, the naïve and the sentimental, confront each other. In all three cases the conflict of outlook can be traced back to the social gap between the protagonists; in each an aristocrat or a patrician confronts a plebeian and a rebel. Tolstoy's aristocratic nature is, above all, responsible for the fact that his whole art and thought are rooted in the idea of the physical, the organic and the natural. Dostoevsky's spiritualism, his speculative mind, his dynamic, dialectical mode of thinking, can be traced back just as definitely to his bourgeois descent and plebeian uprootedness. The aristocrat owes his position to his mere existence, his birth, his race, whereas the plebeian owes it to his talent, his personal ability and achievements. The relationship between the feudal lord and the scribe has not changed much in the course of the centuries—even though some of the lords have become 'scribes' themselves.

The contrast between Tolstoy's discretion and Dostoevsky's exhibitionism, between the restraint of the one and the 'dancing about naked in public' of the other—as someone says in *The Possessed*—is attributable to the same social gap as separated Voltaire from Rousseau. It is more difficult to ascribe to definite sociological causes such qualities of style and taste as moderation, discipline and order, on the one side, and shapelessness, chaos and anarchy, on the other. In certain circumstances extravagance is just as characteristic of the aristocratic as of the plebeian attitude, and the bourgeois philosophy of art often shows, as we know, just as rigoristic tendencies as that of the courtly class. As far as the composition of his works is concerned, Tolstoy is often just as extravagant and arbitrary as Dostoevsky; in this respect they are both anarchists. Tolstoy is only more restrained in his exposure of the 'depths' of the soul and more discriminating in the means he uses to obtain emotional effects. His art is much more elegant, much more settled and much more graceful than that of Dostoevsky; he has been rightly called a child of the eighteenth century, in contrast to this typical representative of the nervous nineteenth century. Compared with the romantic, mystical 'dionysianly' ecstatic Dostoevsky, he always seems more or less classical, or, to keep to Nietzsche's terminology, 'apollonian', plastic, statuesque. In contrast to Dostoevsky's problematical nature, his whole character has a positive quality in the sense understood by Goethe when he said he wanted to hear other people's opinions expressed in a 'positive' form, since he had enough 'problems' in himself already. This might well have been said by Tolstoy, if not in the same words, for he did, in fact, once say something very similar in connection with Dostoevsky. He compared Dostoevsky with a horse that makes a quite magnificent impression at first sight and seems to be worth a thousand roubles; but suddenly one notices that it has something wrong with its legs and limps, and one concludes with regret that it is not worth twopence. There was indeed 'something wrong' with Dostoevsky's legs and, compared with the robust and healthy Tolstoy, there always seems something pathological about him, just as there does about Rousseau when compared with Voltaire, the well-balanced man of reason. But the categories cannot be divided so sharply as in the case of Voltaire and Rousseau. Tolstoy himself manifests a whole series of Rousseauist characteristics and in some respects stands closer to Rousseauism than Dostoevsky. His striving for simplicity, naturalness and truthfulness is merely a variant of Rousseau's discomfort with culture, and his yearning for the idyllic life of the patriarchal village no more than the renewal of the old romantic antagonism to modern civilization. It is not for nothing that he quotes Lichtenberg's remark that humanity will be finished when there are no more savages.

But this Rousseauism is again merely an expression of Tolstoy's fear of loneliness, uprootedness and social homelessness. He condemns modern culture on account of the differentiation and segregation which it produces, and the art of Shakespeare, Beethoven and Pushkin, because it splits men up into different strata instead of uniting them. That which might be spoken of as collectivism and the fight against class distinctions in Tolstoy's theories, has hardly anything to do, however, with democracy and socialism; it is more the nostalgia of a lonely intellectual for a community from which he awaits above all his own redemption. —When Christ called upon the rich young man to distribute all his possessions among the poor, he wanted, according to Henry George's interpretation, to help the rich young man, not the poor. Tolstoy also thought that it was the 'rich young man' who needed helping. Self-perfection and spiritual salvation are his own goal. This spiritualism and self-centredness explain the unreal, Utopian character of his social gospel and the inner contradictions of his political doctrine. It is this private moral ideal that determines his quietism, his rejection of violent resistance to evil and his endeavour to reform souls, instead of social realities. 'Nothing does more harm to men', he writes in his appeal 'To the Working Class' after the Revolution of 1905, 'than the idea that the causes of their distress lie not in themselves but in external conditions.' Tolstoy's passive attitude to external reality is in accordance with the pacifism of the saturated ruling class and, with its brooding, self-accusing, self-torturing moralism, it expresses an approach completely alien to the thinking and feeling of the common people.

But Tolstoy can no more be forced into a narrow political category than Dostoevsky. He is an incorruptible observer of social reality, a sincere friend of truth and justice and an unsparing critic of capitalism, although he judges the inadequacies and sins of modern society purely and simply from the point of view of the peasantry and agriculture in general. He fails, on the other hand, to recognize the real causes of the grievances and he preaches a morality which implies an *a priori* renunciation of all political activity.[184] Tolstoy is not only no revolutionary, but he is a decided enemy of all revolutionary attitudes; what distinguishes him, however, from the advocates of 'order' and appeasement in the West, the Balzacs, Flauberts and Goncourts, is the fact that he shows even less understanding for the terrorism of the government than for that of the revolutionaries. The murder of Alexander II leaves him quite unmoved, but he protests against the execution of the assassins.[185] In spite of his prejudices and errors, Tolstoy represents an enormous revolutionary force. His fight against the lies of the police state and the Church, his enthusiasm for the community of the peasantry and the example of his own life are, whatever may have been the inner motives of his 'conversion' and his ultimate flight, among the ferments which undermined the old society and promoted not merely the Russian revolution but also the anti-capitalistic revolutionary movement in the whole of Europe. In the case of Tolstoy one can, in fact, speak not only of a 'triumph of realism', but also of a 'triumph of socialism', not only of the unprejudiced description of society by an aristocrat, but of the revolutionary influence of a reactionary.

Its uncompromising rationalism preserves Tolstoy's art and philosophical doctrine from the fate of sterility and ineffectiveness. His sharp and sober eye for physical and psychical facts, and his aversion to lying to himself and others, keep his religiosity free from all mysticism and dogmatism and allows his belief in Christian morality to develop into a political factor of great influence. Dostoevsky's enthusiasm for Russian orthodoxy is just as foreign to him as the ecclesiastical bias of the Slavophils in general. He reaches his faith by a rational, pragmatic and thoroughly unspontaneous way.[186] His so-called conversion is an entirely rational process, which takes place without any direct religious experience. It was, as he says in his *Confession*, 'a feeling of fear, of being orphaned and lonely' that made him a Christian. Not a mystical experience of God and the supernatural, but dissatisfaction with himself, the attempt to find a purpose and an aim in life, despair at his own nothingness and instability, and, above all, his boundless fear of death turn him into a believer. He becomes the apostle of love, because he himself is lacking in love, he glorifies human solidarity, to make up for his mistrust of and contempt for man, and he proclaims the immortality of the human soul, because he cannot bear the thought of death. But his flight from the world has more the character of aristocratic lordliness than of Christian humility; he renounces the world because it cannot be completely mastered and possessed.

The concept of grace is the only irrational element in Tolstoy's religious philosophy.—He admits into his 'folk tales' an old legend based on medieval sources: Long ago there lived a pious hermit on a lonely island. One day fishermen landed near his hut, amongst them an old man who was so simple-minded that he could barely express himself, indeed he could not even pray. The hermit was profoundly upset by such ignorance and with great trouble and pains taught him the Lord's prayer. The old man thanked him kindly and left the island with the other fishermen. After some time, when the boat had already vanished in the distance, the holy man suddenly saw a human figure on the horizon walking towards the island on the surface of the water. Soon he recognized the old man, his pupil, and went towards him, speechless and perplexed, to meet him as he set foot on the island. Stammering, the old man gave him to understand that he had forgotten the prayer. '*You* do not need to pray,' replied the hermit, and left the old man hurrying back over the water to his fishing boat.—The meaning of this story lies in the idea of a certainty of salvation which is tied to no moral criteria. In another story of his later years, *Father Sergius*, Tolstoy represents the theme from the opposite angle; the grace which is bestowed on one man without effort, and apparently without merit, is denied to another, in spite of all manner of torment and agony, in spite of the most superhuman sacrifices and the most heroic self-conquest. This conception of grace, which places election above merit and equates predestination with gift and chance, is obviously more deeply related to Tolstoy's aristocratic background than to his Christianity.

The optimism of the healthy, self-confident aristocrat, who turns *War and Peace* into an apotheosis of organic, vegetative, endlessly creative life, into a great idyll, a 'naïve heroic epic', on whose highest point, as Merezhkovsky remarks with such relish, the novelist plants the napkins of Nastasya's babies 'as the guiding banner of mankind'[187]—this pantheistic optimism is obscured in *Anna Karenina* and approaches the pessimistic mood of Western literature, but the disillusionment with the conventionalism and obtuseness of modern culture expressed here is utterly different from that of Flaubert or Maupassant. The triumph of real life over the romanticism of the emotions was already intermingled with some melancholy in *War and Peace*, and Tolstoy had already struck a Flaubertian note in his earlier work, thus for example in *Family Happiness*, by describing the degeneration of the great passions, especially the transformation of love into friendship. The discrepancy between the ideal and the reality, between poetry and prose, youth and old age, never seems so bleak, however, in Tolstoy as in the French writers. His disillusionment never leads to nihilism, never leads to an impeachment of life in general. The novel of Western Europe is always full of a querulous self-pity and self-dramatization of the hero in conflict with reality; here external conditions, society, the state, the social environment, always bear the blame for the antagonism. With Tolstoy, on the other hand, the subjective personality is just as much to blame as objective reality, if it comes to a clash.[188] For, if the life which disillusions is too soulless, the disillusioned hero is too soulful, too poetic, too Utopian; if the one is lacking in tolerance for dreamers, the other lacks a sense of reality.

The fact that the form of Tolstoy's novels is so different from the West European is bound up in the main with this concept of the self and the world and its deviation from the Flaubertian conception. The distance from the naturalistic norm is here, in fact, just as great as in Dostoevsky, only Tolstoy's remoteness from it lies in the opposite direction. If Dostoevsky's novels have a dramatic structure, then Tolstoy's have an epic—epopee-like—character. No attentive reader can ever have failed to feel the surging Homeric flow of these novels, or ever have failed to experience the panoramic, all-embracing picture of the world which they unfold. Tolstoy himself compared his novels to Homer, and the comparison has become a stock formula of Tolstoy criticism. The unromantic, undramatic and unemphatic quality of the form, the forgoing of all theatrical climaxes and intensity, have always been regarded as Homeric. The dramatic concentration of the novel, which first took place with the transformation from the picaresque form of the eighteenth century to the biographical form of pre-romanticism, was not yet adopted by Tolstoy in *War and Peace*. He considers the conflict between the individual and society not as an unavoidable tragedy, but as a calamity which he attributes, following the eighteenth-century view, to a lack of insight, understanding and moral seriousness. He still lives in the age of the Russian enlightenment, in an intellectual atmosphere of faith in the world and faith in the future. But while he is working at *Anna Karenina*, he loses this optimism, and above all his belief in art, which he declares to be absolutely useless, indeed harmful, unless it renounces the refinements and subtleties of modern naturalism and impressionism and turns a luxury article into the universal possession of mankind. In the estrangement of art from the broad masses and the restriction of its public to an ever smaller circle Tolstoy had recognized a real danger. There is no doubt but that the extension of this circle and contact with culturally less exclusive strata of society might well have had fruitful results for art. But how was such a change to be brought about methodically and according to plan, unless the artists who had grown up and were firmly rooted in the tradition of modern art were not prevented from producing works of art and unless it was not made as easy as possible for the dilettanti, who were foreign to this tradition, to engage in artistic activities—to the disadvantage of the others? Tolstoy's rejection of the highly developed and refined art of the present, and his fondness for the primitive, 'universally human' forms of artistic expression, is a symptom of the same Rousseauism with which he plays off the village against the town and identifies the social question with that of the peasantry. It is quite easy to understand why Tolstoy had not much use for Shakespeare, for example. How could a puritan, who hated all exuberance and virtuosity, have found any pleasure in the mannerism of a poet, even though he were the greatest poet of all time? But it is inconceivable that a man who created such artistically exacting works as *Anna Karenina* and *The Death of Ivan Ilych* accepted without reservations out of the whole of modern literature, apart from *Uncle Tom's Cabin*, only Schiller's *Robbers*, Hugo's *Misérables*, Dickens' *Christmas Carol*, Dostoevsky's *Memoirs from Underground* and George Eliot's *Adam Bede*.[189]

Tolstoy's relationship to art can only be understood as the symptom of a historic change, as the sign of a development which brings the aesthetic culture of the nineteenth century to an end and a generation to the fore that judges art once again as the mediator of ideas.[190]

What this generation revered in the author of *War and Peace* was by no means merely the great novelist, the creator of the greatest novel in the literature of the world, but above all the social reformer and the founder of a religion. Tolstoy enjoyed the fame of Voltaire, the popularity of Rousseau, the authority of Goethe and, more than that—he became a legendary figure, whose prestige was reminiscent of that of the old seers and prophets. Yasnaya Polyana became a place to which the members of all nations, social classes and cultural strata went on pilgrimage, and admired the old count in the peasant's smock as if he were a saint. Gorky will not have been the only one to have seen him and thought 'This man is like to God!', a confession with which the unbeliever ends his memories of Tolstoy.[191] Many will certainly have had the feeling, as did Thomas Mann, that Europe became 'without a master' after his death.[192] But these were only feelings and moods, words of gratitude and loyalty. Tolstoy was doubtless something very much like the living conscience of Europe, the great teacher and educator, who expressed, as did no other, the moral unrest and desire for spiritual renewal of his generation, but, with his naïve Rousseauism and quietism, he would never have been able to remain—if he ever really was—the 'master' of Europe. For, it may well be sufficient for an artist, as Chekhov thought, to put the right questions, but a man who was to rule over his century would also have to answer them aright.

4. IMPRESSIONISM

The frontiers between naturalism and impressionism are fluid; it is impossible to make a clear-cut historical or conceptual distinction between them. The smoothness of the stylistic change corresponds to the continuity of the simultaneous economic development and the stability of social conditions. 1871 is of merely passing significance in the history of France. The predominance of the upper middle class remains essentially unchanged and the conservative Republic takes the place of the 'liberal' Empire—that 'republic without republicans',[193] which is acquiesced in only because it seems to guarantee the smoothest possible solution of the political problems. But a friendly relationship is established with it only after the supporters of the Commune have been rooted out and comfort has been found in the theory of the necessity and the healing power of bleeding.[194] The intelligentsia confronts events in a state of absolute helplessness. Flaubert, Gautier, the Goncourts, and with them most of the intellectual leaders of the age, indulge in wild insults and imprecations against the disturbers of the peace. From the Republic they hope at the most for protection against clericalism, and they see in democracy merely the lesser of the two evils.[195] Financial and industrial capitalism develops consistently along the lines long since laid down; but, under the surface, important, though for the time being still unobtrusive changes are taking place. Economic life is entering the stage of high capitalism and developing from a 'free play of forces' into a rigidly organized and rationalized system, into a close-meshed net of spheres of interest, customs territories, fields of monopoly, cartels, trusts and syndicates. And just as it was feasible for this standardization and concentration of economic life to be called a sign of senility,[196] so the marks of insecurity and the omens of dissolution can be recognized throughout middle-class society. It is true that the Commune ends with a more complete defeat for the rebels than any previous revolution, but it is the first to be sustained by an international labour movement and to be followed by a victory for the bourgeoisie associated with a feeling of acute danger.[197] This mood of crisis leads to a renewal of the idealistic and mystical trends and produces, as a reaction against the prevailing pessimism, a strong tide of faith. It is only in the course of this development that impressionism loses its connection with naturalism and becomes transformed, especially in literature, into a new form of romanticism.

The enormous technical developments that take place must

not induce us to overlook the feeling of crisis that was in the air. The crisis itself must rather be seen as an incentive to new technical achievements and improvements of methods of production.[198] Certain signs of the atmosphere of crisis make themselves felt in all the manifestations of technical activity. It is above all the furious speed of the development and the way the pace is forced that seems pathological, particularly when compared with the rate of progress in earlier periods in the history of art and culture. For the rapid development of technology not only accelerates the change of fashion, but also the shifting emphases in the criteria of aesthetic taste; it often brings about a senseless and fruitless mania for innovation, a restless striving for the new for the mere sake of novelty. Industrialists are compelled to intensify the demand for improved products by artificial means and must not allow the feeling that the new is always better to cool down, if they really want to profit from the achievements of technology.[199] The continual and increasingly rapid replacement of old articles in everyday use by new ones leads, however, to a diminished affection for material and soon also for intellectual possessions, too, and readjusts the speed at which philosophical and artistic revaluations occur to that of changing fashion. Modern technology thus introduces an unprecedented dynamism in the whole attitude to life and it is above all this new feeling of speed and change that finds expression in impressionism.

The most striking phenomenon connected with the progress of technology is the development of cultural centres into large cities in the modern sense; these form the soil in which the new art is rooted. Impressionism is an urban art, and not only because it discovers the landscape quality of the city and brings painting back from the country into the town, but because it sees the world through the eyes of the townsman and reacts to external impressions with the overstrained nerves of modern technical man. It is an urban style, because it describes the changeability, the nervous rhythm, the sudden, sharp but always ephemeral impressions of city life. And precisely as such, it implies an enormous expansion of sensual perception, a new sharpening of sensibility, a new irritability, and, with the Gothic and romanticism, it signifies one of the most important turning points in the history of Western art. In the dialectical process represented by the history of painting, the alternation of the static and the dynamic, of design and colour, abstract order and organic life, impressionism forms the climax of the development in which recognition is given to the dynamic and organic elements of experience and which completely dissolves the static world-view of the Middle Ages. A continuous line can be traced from the Gothic to impressionism comparable to the line leading from late medieval economy to high capitalism, and modern man, who regards his whole existence as a struggle and a competition, who translates all being into motion and change, for whom experience of the world increasingly becomes experience of time, is the product of this bilateral, but fundamentally uniform development.

The dominion of the moment over permanence and continuity, the feeling that every phenomenon is a fleeting and never-to-be-repeated constellation, a wave gliding away on the river of time, the river into which 'one cannot step twice', is the simplest formula to which impressionism can be reduced. The whole method of impressionism, with all its artistic expedients and tricks, is bent, above all, on giving expression to this Heraclitean outlook and on stressing that reality is not a being but a becoming, not a condition but a process. Every impressionistic picture is the deposit of a moment in the perpetuum mobile of existence, the representation of a precarious, unstable balance in the play of contending forces. The impressionistic vision transforms nature into a process of growth and decay. Everything stable and coherent is dissolved into metamorphoses and assumes the character of the unfinished and fragmentary. The reproduction of the subjective act instead of the objective substratum of seeing, with which the history of modern perspective painting begins, here achieves its culmination. The representation of light, air and atmosphere, the dissolution of the evenly coloured surface into spots and dabs of colour, the decomposition of the local colour into *valeurs*, into values of perspective and aspect, the play of reflected light and illuminated shadows, the quivering, trembling dots and the hasty, loose and abrupt strokes of the brush, the whole improvised technique with its rapid and rough sketching, the fleeting, seemingly careless perception of the object and the brilliant casualness of the execution merely express, in the final analysis, that feeling of a stirring, dynamic, constantly changing reality, which began with the re-orientation of painting by the use of perspective.

A world, the phenomena of which are in a state of constant flux and transition, produces the impression of a continuum in which everything coalesces, and in which there are no other differences but the various approaches and points of view of the beholder. An art in accordance with such a world will stress not merely the momentary and transitory nature of phenomena, will not see in man simply the measure of all things, but will seek the criterion of truth in the 'hic et nunc' of the individual. It will consider chance the principle of all being, and the truth of the moment as invalidating all other truth. The primacy of the moment, of change and chance implies, in terms of aesthetics, the dominion of the passing mood over the permanent qualities of life, that is to say, the prevalence of a relation to things the property of which is to be non-committal as well as changeable. This reduction of the artistic representation to the mood of the moment is, at the same time, the expression of a fundamentally passive outlook on life, an acquiescence in the rôle of the spectator, of the receptive and contemplative subject, a standpoint of aloofness, waiting, non-involvement—in short, the aesthetic attitude purely and simply. Impressionism is the climax of self-centred aesthetic culture and signifies the ultimate consequence of the romantic renunciation of practical, active life.

Stylistically, impressionism is an extremely complex phenomenon. In some respects it represents merely the logical development of naturalism. For, if one interprets naturalism as meaning progress from the general to the particular, from the typical to the individual, from the abstract idea to the concrete, temporally and spatially conditioned experience, then the impressionistic reproduction of reality, with its emphasis on the instantaneous and the unique, is an important achievement of naturalism. The representations of impressionism are closer to sensual experience than those of naturalism in the narrower sense, and replace the object of theoretical knowledge by that of direct optical experience more completely than any earlier art. But by detaching the optical elements of experience from the conceptual and elaborating the autonomy of the visual, impressionism departs from all art as practised hitherto, and thereby from naturalism as well. Its method is peculiar in that, whilst pre-impressionist art bases its representations on a seemingly uniform but, in fact, heterogeneously composed world-view, made up of conceptual and sensual elements alike, impressionism aspires to the homogeneity of the purely visual. All earlier art is the result of a synthesis, impressionism that of an analysis. It constructs its particular subject from the bare data of the senses, it, therefore, goes back to the unconscious psychic mechanism and gives us to some extent the raw material of experience, which is further removed from our usual conception of reality than the logically organized impressions of the senses. Impressionism is less illusionistic than naturalism; instead of the illusion, it gives elements of the subject, instead of a picture of the whole, the bricks of which experience is composed. Before impressionism, art reproduced objects by *signs*, now it represents them through their components, through *parts* of the material of which they are made up.[200]

In comparison with the older art, naturalism marked an increase in the elements of the composition, in other words, an extension of the motifs and an enrichment of the technical means. The impressionistic method, on the other hand, involves a series of reductions, a system of restrictions and simplifications.[201] Nothing is more typical of an impressionist painting than that it must be looked at from a certain distance and that it describes things with the omissions inevitable in them when seen from a distance. The series of reductions which it carries out begins with the restriction of the elements of the representation to the purely visual and the elimination of everything of a non-optical nature or that cannot be translated into optical terms. The waiving of the so-called literary elements of the subject, the story or the anecdote, is the most striking expression of this 'recollection by painting of its own particular means'. The reduction of all motifs to landscape, still life and the portrait, or the treatment of every kind of subject as a 'landscape' and 'still life', is nothing more than a symptom of the predominance of the specifically 'painterly' principle in painting. 'It is the treatment of a subject

ATMOSPHERICAL EFFECTS

1. MONET: GARE SAINT-LAZARE IN PARIS. *1877. New York, Maurice Wertheim Collection.*

2. MANET: THE ROAD-MENDERS OF THE RUE DE BERNE. *1878. London, formerly Courtauld Collection.*

THE EFFECTS OF DAYLIGH

1. MONET: ROUEN CATH
FORENOON. *1894. Paris, L*

2. PISSARRO: BOULEVARD
ITALIENS. AFTERNOON. *18*

HINE AND SHADE

IR: DANCING IN THE MOULIN DE LA GALETTE (*Detail*). *1876. Paris, Louvre.*

IMPRESSIONISM OF MOVEMENT

1. DEGAS: BEFORE THE TRIBUNES. *About 1871. Paris, Louvre.*
2. TOULOUSE-LAUTREC: THE JOCKEY. *1899.*
3. TOULOUSE-LAUTREC: JANE AVRIL DANCING. *1892. Paris, Louvre.*

THE ACCIDENTAL CHARACTER OF THE IMPRESSIONISTIC REPRESENTATION OF REALITY

1. DEGAS: PLACE DE LA CONCORDE. *About 1873. Berlin, Gerstenberg Collection.*

2. MONET: ANGLERS NEAR POISSY. *1882.*

THE SYNTHESIS OF CÉZANNE AS TRANSITION FROM IMPRESSIONISM TO CUBISM

1. CÉZANNE: GUSTAVE GEFFROY. *1895. Paris, Lecomte-Pellerin Collection.*

2. CÉZANNE: LAC D'ANNECY. *1897. London, Courtauld Collection.*

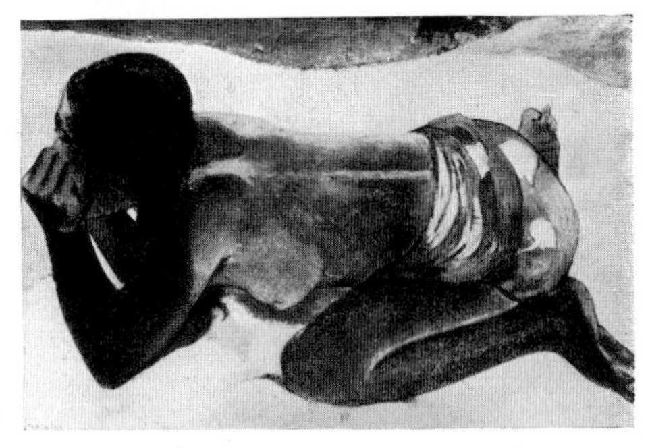

STYLIZATION OF GAUGUIN AND VAN GOGH AS TRANSITION FROM IMPRESSIONISM TO EXPRESSIONISM

:GAS: THE TUB. *About 1895. Paris, Louvre.*

UGUIN: OTAHI.

N GOGH: THE RAILWAY BRIDGE OF ARLES. *1888. Porto Ronco, E. M. Remarque ction.*

1. GEORGES BRAQUE: LIFE. *Paris, Musée N d'Art moderne.*

2. PICASSO: TÊTE AN 1925. *Paris, Musée N d'Art moderne.*

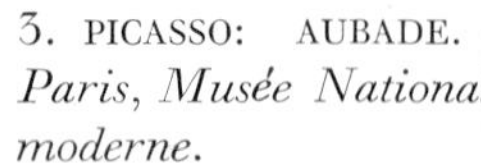

3. PICASSO: AUBADE. *Paris, Musée National moderne.*

for the sake of the tones, and not for the sake of the subject itself, that distinguishes the impressionists from other painters,' as one of the earliest historians and theorists of the movement points out.[202] This neutralization and reduction of the motif to its bare material essentials can be considered an expression of the anti-romantic outlook of the time and seen as the trivialization and stripping bare of all the heroic and stately qualities of the subject-matter of art, but it can also be regarded as a departure from reality, and the restriction of painting to subjects of 'its own' can be looked upon as a loss from the naturalistic point of view. The 'smile' that the Greeks discovered in the plastic arts and that, as has been observed, is being lost in modern art[203] is sacrificed to the purely pictorial aspect; but it means that all psychology and all humanism disappears from painting altogether.

The replacement of tactile by visual values, in other words, the transfer of physical volume and plastic form to the surface, is a further step, bound up with the new 'painterly' trend, in the series of reductions to which impressionism subjects the naturalistic picture of reality. This reduction is, however, in no sense the aim, but only a by-product of the method. The emphasis on colour and the desire to turn the whole picture into a harmony of colour and light effects is the aim, the absorbing of the space and the dissolving of the solid structure of the bodies nothing more than a concomitant. Impressionism not only reduces reality to a two-dimensional surface but, within this two-dimensionality, to a system of shapeless spots; in other words, it forgoes not only plasticity but also design, not only spatial but also linear form. That the picture makes up in energy and sensual charm for what it loses in clarity and evidence is obvious, and this gain was also the main concern of the impressionists themselves. But the public felt the loss more strongly than the gain and now that the impressionistic way of looking at things has become one of the most important components of our optical experience, we are unable even to imagine how helplessly the public confronted this medley of spots and blots. Impressionism formed merely the last step in a process of increasing obscurity that had been going on for centuries. Since the baroque, pictorial representations had confronted the beholder with an increasingly difficult problem; they had become more and more opaque and their relation to reality more and more complex. But impressionism represented a more daring leap than any single phase of the earlier development and the shock produced by the first impressionist exhibitions was comparable to nothing ever experienced before in the whole history of artistic innovation. People considered the rapid execution and the shapelessness of the pictures as an insolent provocation; they thought that they were being made fun of and the revenge they took was as cruel as they were able to contrive.

With these innovations, however, the succession of reductions employed by the impressionist method is by no means exhausted. The very colours which impressionism uses alter and distort those of our everyday experience. We think, for example, of a piece of 'white' paper as white in every lighting, despite the coloured reflexes which it shows in ordinary daylight. In other words: the 'remembered colour' which we associate with an object, and which is the result of long experience and habit, displaces the concrete impression gained from immediate perception;[204] impressionism now goes back behind the remembered, theoretically established colour to the real sensation, which is, incidentally, in no sense a spontaneous act, but represents a supremely artificial and extremely complicated psychological process.

Impressionistic perception, finally, brings about one further and very severe reduction in the usual picture of reality, inasmuch as it shows colours not as concrete qualities bound to a particular object, but as abstract, incorporeal, immaterial phenomena—as it were colours-in-themselves. If we hold a screen with a small opening in front of an object that is big enough to reveal the colour, but not big enough to enlighten us as to the form of the object and the relationship of the colour in question to the object, it is a well-known fact that we get an indefinite, hovering impression, which is very different from the character of the colours adherent to plastic form we habitually see. In this way the colour of fire loses its radiance, the colour of silk its lustre, the colour of water its transparency, etc.[205] Impressionism always represents objects in these incorporeal surface colours, which make a very direct and lively impression, owing to their freshness and intensity, but considerably reduce the illusionistic effect of the picture and most strikingly reveal the conventionality of the impressionistic method.

In the second half of the nineteenth century painting becomes the leading art. Impressionism here develops into an autonomous style at a time when in the literary world a conflict is still raging around naturalism. The first collective exhibition of the impressionists takes place in 1874, but the history of impressionism begins some twenty years earlier, and already comes to an end with the eighth group exhibition in the year 1886. About this time impressionism as a uniform group movement breaks up and a new, post-impressionist period begins which lasts until about 1906, the year of Cézanne's death.[206] After the predominance of literature in the seventeenth and eighteenth centuries and the leading part played by music in the age of romanticism, a change in favour of painting occurs about the middle of the nineteenth century. The art critic Asselineau places the dethronement of poetry by painting as early as 1840,[207] and, a generation later, the Goncourt brothers already exclaim with enthusiasm in their voices: 'What a happy profession that of the painter is compared with that of the writer!'[208] Painting dominates all the other arts not only as the most progressive art of the age, but its productions also surpass the literary and musical achievements of the same period qualitatively, especially in France, where it was perfectly correct to maintain that the great poets of this period were the impressionist painters.[209] It is true that nineteenth-century art remains romantic to some extent and the poets of the century profess a belief in music as the highest artistic ideal, but what they understand thereby is more a symbol of sovereign, unfettered creation, independent of objective reality, than the concrete example of music. Impressionist painting discovers, on the other hand, sensations which poetry and music also attempt to express and in which they adapt their means of expression to painterly forms. Atmospherical impressions, especially the experience of light, air and colour, are perceptions native to painting, and when the attempt is made to reproduce moods of this kind in the other arts, we are quite within our rights to speak of a 'painterly' style of poetry and music. But the style of these arts is also painterly, when they express themselves, forgoing distinct 'contours', with the aid of colour and shade effects, and attach more importance to the vivacity of the details than the uniformity of the total impression. When Paul Bourget points out that, in the style of his time, the impression made by the single page is always stronger than that of the whole book, that made by a sentence deeper than that of a page and that of the single words more striking than that of a sentence,[210] what he is describing is the method of impressionism—the style of an atomized, dynamically-charged world-view.

Impressionism is not, however, merely the style of a particular period dominating all the arts, it is also the last universally valid 'European' style—the latest trend based on a general consensus of taste. Since its dissolution it has been impossible to classify stylistically either the various arts or the various nations and cultures. But impressionism neither ends nor begins abruptly. Delacroix, who discovered the law of complementary colours and the coloration of shadows, and Constable, who established the complex composition of colour effects in nature, already anticipate much of the impressionistic method. The energizing of vision, which is the essence of impressionism, at any rate begins with them. The rudiments of plein-airism in the painters of Barbizon represent a further step in this development. But what contributes to the rise of impressionism as a collective movement is above all, on the one hand, the artistic experience of the city, the beginnings of which are to be found in Manet, and, on the other hand, the amalgamation of the young painters which is brought about by the opposition of the public. At first sight, it may seem surprising that the metropolis, with its herding together and intermingling of people, should produce this intimate art rooted in the feeling of individual singularity and solitude. But it is a familiar fact that nothing seems so isolating as the close proximity of too many people, and nowhere does one feel so lonely and forsaken as in a great crowd of strangers. The two basic feelings which life in such an environment produces, the feeling of being alone and unobserved, on the one hand, and the impression of roaring traffic, incessant movement and constant variety, on the other, breed the impressionistic outlook on life in which the most subtle moods are combined with the most rapid alternation of sensations. The negative attitude of the public as a motive for the rise of impressionism as a movement seems just as surprising at first sight. The impressionists never behaved aggressively towards the public; they had every desire to remain within the framework of tradition, and often made desperate efforts to be recognized in official quarters, above all in the Salon, which they considered the normal road to success. At any rate, the spirit of contradiction and the desire to attract attention by flabbergasting the public play a much smaller part with them than with most romantics and many naturalists. All the same, there may never have existed such a deep divergence between official circles and the younger generation of artists, and the feeling of being jeered at may never have been so strong as now. The impressionists certainly did not make it easy for people to understand their artistic ideas—but in what a bad way the art appreciation of the public must have been to allow such great, honest and peaceable artists as Monet, Renoir and Pissarro almost to starve.

Impressionism also had nothing of the plebeian about it, to make an unfavourable impression on the bourgeois public; it was rather an 'aristocrats' style', elegant and fastidious, nervous and sensitive, sensual and epicurean, keen on rare and exquisite subjects, bent on strictly personal experiences, experiences of solitude and seclusion and the sensations of over-refined senses and nerves. It is, however, the creation of artists who not only come very largely from the lower and middle sections of the bourgeoisie, but who are much less concerned with intellectual and aesthetic problems than the artists of earlier generations; they are less versatile and sophisticated, more exclusively craftsmen and 'technicians' than their predecessors. But there are also members of the well-to-do bourgeoisie and even of the aristocracy amongst them. Manet, Bazille, Berthe Morisot and Cézanne are the children of rich parents, Degas is of aristocratic and Toulouse-Lautrec of high aristocratic descent. The refined intellectual style and cultivated well-bred manners of Manet and Degas, the elegance and delicate artistry of Constantin Guys and Toulouse-Lautrec, show the genteel bourgeois society of the Second Empire, the world of the crinoline and the décolleté, the equipages and the riding horses in the Bois, from its most attractive side.

The history of literature reveals a much more complicated picture than that of painting. As a literary style, impressionism is, intrinsically, not a very sharply defined phenomenon; its beginnings are hardly recognizable within the total complex of naturalism and its later forms of development are completely merged with the phenomena of symbolism. Chronologically, too, a certain discrepancy is to be observed between impressionism in literature and painting; in painting, the most productive period of impressionism is already past, when its stylistic characteristics are first beginning to emerge in literature. The most fundamental difference, however, is that in literature impressionism loses the connection with naturalism, positivism and materialism comparatively early and becomes almost from the outset the champion of that idealistic reaction which finds expression in painting only after the dissolution of impressionism. The main reason for this is that the conservative élite plays a much more important rôle in literature than in painting, which, as a result of its stronger roots in craft traditions, puts up greater resistance to the spiritualistic aspirations of the age.

The crisis of naturalism, which is only a symptom of the crisis of positivism, does not become evident until about 1885, but the omens are already apparent around 1870. The enemies of the Republic are mostly also enemies of rationalism, materialism and naturalism; they attack scientific progress and expect that a religious revival will also bring about an intellectual rebirth. They talk about the 'bankruptcy of science', the 'end of naturalism', the 'soulless mechanization of culture', but they always mean the Revolution, the Republic and liberalism when they storm against the intellectual poverty of the age. The conservatives have lost their influence on the government, it is true, but they have kept their strong position in public life. They still continue to occupy the most important posts in the administration, diplomacy and the army and they dominate public education, especially in its higher branches.[211] The *lycées* and the University belong as much as ever to the domain of the clergy and high finance, and the cultural ideals which they spread abroad have a stronger currency in literature than ever. We come across academically educated writers in much greater numbers than hitherto and, under their influence, intellectual life acquires a predominantly reactionary character. Flaubert, Maupassant and Zola were not writers of learning, whereas Bourget and Barrès represent the spirit of the Academy and the University; they feel themselves to some extent responsible for the cultural inheritance of the nation and come forward as the competent intellectual leaders of youth.[212] This intellectualization of literature is perhaps the most striking and most universally valid characteristic of the period; it finds expression in both the progressive and the conservative writers.[213] In this respect there is not the slightest difference between Anatole France and his clerical and nationalistic colleagues. And although there is only one Anatole France alongside Bourget, Barrès, Brunetière, Bergson and Claudel, the esteem in which this Voltairian is held proves that the spirit of the enlightenment is by no means dead in France. On the other hand, incidents like the Dreyfus affair and the Panama scandal are needed to awaken it from its trance.

Around 1870 France goes through one of its most serious intellectual and moral crises, but its 'intellectual Sedan' is in no way connected with its military defeat, as Barrès maintains,[214] and its 'fatal weariness of life' is not derived from its materialism and relativism, as Bourget thinks. Bourget and Barrès are no less affected by this weariness of life than are Baudelaire and Flaubert. It is part of the romantic sickness of the whole century, and Zola's naturalism, which the generation of 1885 treats as a scapegoat, actually represents the only serious, though inadequate, attempt to overcome the nihilism which had seized men's minds. From the later 'eighties onwards the literary situation is dominated by the attacks on Zola and the disbandment of naturalism as the leading movement. That is the strongest impression that emerges from the answers to the inquiry organized by Jules Huret, a contributor to the *Écho de Paris*, which also appeared in book form in 1891 under the title *Enquête sur l'évolution littéraire* and which represent one of the most important sources for the intellectual and cultural history of the period. Huret asked the sixty-four most prominent French writers of the day what they thought of naturalism, whether, in their opinion, it was already dead, or whether it could still be saved, and if not what literary trend would take its place. The overwhelming majority of those questioned, with most of Zola's former disciples at the head, thought the case hopeless. Only the ever-faithful Paul Alexis hastened to wire, 'Naturalisme pas mort. Lettre suit', as if he were anxious to prevent the spread of a dangerous rumour. But his haste was of no avail. The rumour did spread and naturalism was denied even by those who owed it their whole artistic existence. And this meant most of the creative writers of the age. For what was the most influential literature up to the turn of the century, and what is it partly still today, if not naturalistic, form-demolishing literature bent on the expansion of the content of experience? What, above all, was the 'psychological novel' of Bourget, Barrès, Huysmans and even Proust, if not the result of naturalistic observation interested in the 'document humain'? And what is the whole modern novel, in the last analysis, but the exact, minute and increasingly precise description of concrete spiritual reality? It is quite true that certain anti-naturalistic characteristics are as inseparably connected with impressionism in literature as they are in painting, but these, too, grow out of the soil of naturalism. At first sight, therefore, the violence of the public reaction seems inexplicable. The arguments against naturalism were by no means new, the curious thing was simply that, at a time when naturalism already seemed to have won the day, it was attacked with such bitterness. What was it that people could not forgive in naturalism or pretended not to be able to forgive? Naturalism, it was asserted, was an indelicate, indecent and obscene art, the expression of an insipid, materialistic philosophy, the instrument of clumsy, heavy-handed democratic propaganda, a collection of boring, trivial and vulgar banalities, a representation of reality which, in its portrayal of society, described only the wild, ravenous, undisciplined animal in man and only the works of disintegration, the dissolution of human relationships, the undermining of the family, the nation and religion, in short, it was destructive, unnatural, hostile to life. The generation of 1850 merely defended the interests of the upper classes against the inroads of naturalism, that of 1885 defends humanity, creative life, God himself. In the interim there has been an increase of religion, perhaps, but not of sincerity.

People drivel about the mysteries of being and the depth of the human soul; they call the rational flat and want to explore and divine the unknown and the unknowable. They profess a belief in world-renouncing, 'ascetic ideals', but they omit to ask, with Nietzsche, why they really seem to be necessary. Symbolism is the most celebrated literary trend of the day; Verlaine and Mallarmé stand in the centre of public interest. The greatest names of the romantic movement, Chateaubriand, Lamartine, Vigny, Musset, Mérimée, Gautier, George Sand, are not mentioned at all in the answers which Huret receives.[215] Instead, Stendhal and Baudelaire are discovered, there is enthusiasm for Villiers de l'Isle-Adam and Rimbaud, the vogue of the Russian novel, of English Pre-Raphaelism and German philosophy is predominant. But the deepest and most fruitful influence emanates from Baudelaire; he is regarded as the most important predecessor of symbolist poetry and the creator of the modern lyric in general. It is he who leads the generation of Bourget and Barrés, Huysmans and Mallarmé back to the path of romantic aestheticism and teaches it how to reconcile the new mysticism with the old fanatical devotion to art.

Aestheticism reaches the pinnacle of its development in the age of impressionism. Its characteristic criteria, the passive, purely contemplative attitude to life, the transitoriness and non-committing quality of experience and hedonistic sensualism, are now the standards by which art in general is judged. The work of art is not only considered an end in itself, not only a self-sufficient game, whose charm is apt to be destroyed by any extraneous, extra-aesthetic purpose, not only the most beautiful gift which life has to offer, for the enjoyment of which it is one's duty devotedly to prepare oneself, it becomes, in its autonomy, its lack of consideration for everything outside its sphere, a pattern for life, for the life of the dilettante, who now begins to displace the intellectual heroes of the past in the estimation of poets and writers and represents the ideal of the *fin de siècle*. What distinguishes him above all is the fact that he strives to 'turn his life into a work of art', in other words, into something costly and useless, something flowing along freely and extravagantly, something offered up to the beauty, the pure form, the harmony of tones and lines. Aesthetic culture implies a way of life marked by uselessness and superfluousness, that is to say, the embodiment of romantic resignation and passivity. But it outdoes romanticism; it not only renounces life for the sake of art, it seeks for the justification of life in art itself. It regards the world of art as the only real compensation for the disappointments of life, as the genuine realization and consummation of an existence that is intrinsically incomplete and inarticulate. But this not only means that life seems more beautiful and more conciliatory when clothed in art, but that, as Proust, the last great impressionist and aesthetic hedonist, thought, it only grows into significant reality in memory, vision and the aesthetic experience. We live our experiences with the greatest intensity not when we encounter men and things in reality—the 'time' and the present of these experiences are always 'lost'—but when we 'recover time', when we are no longer the actors but the spectators of our life, when we create or enjoy works of art, in other words, when we remember. Here, in Proust, art takes possession of what Plato had denied it: ideas—the true remembrance of the essential forms of being.

The theoretical foundations of modern aestheticism as the philosophy of the absolutely passive, contemplative attitude to life can be traced back to Schopenhauer, who defines art as the deliverance from the will, as the sedative which brings the appetites and passions to silence. The philosophy of aestheticism judges and evaluates the whole of life from the point of view of this art free from will and passion. Its ideal is a public entirely made up of real or potential artists, of artistic natures for whom reality is merely the substratum of aesthetic experience. It regards the civilized world as a great artist's studio and the artist himself as the best connoisseur. D'Alembert had still said: 'Woe betide the art whose beauty only exists for artists.' The fact that he felt induced to utter such a warning proves, however, that the danger of aestheticism had already existed in the eighteenth century; in the seventeenth that kind of idea would not yet have occurred to anyone. For the nineteenth century D'Alembert's fear again ceased to have any meaning. The Goncourts describe his words as the greatest stupidity imaginable,[216] and are convinced of nothing more deeply than that the precondition of an adequate appreciation of art is a life dedicated to art, in other words, the practice of art.

The aesthetic philosophy of impressionism marks the beginning of a process of complete inbreeding in art. Artists produce their works for artists, and art, that is, the formal experience of the world *sub specie artis*, becomes the real subject of art. Raw, unformed nature untouched by culture loses its aesthetic attraction and the ideal of naturalness is thrust aside by an ideal of artificiality. The city, urban culture, urban amusements, the 'vie factice' and the 'paradis artificiels', seem not only incomparably more attractive, but also much more spiritual and soulful than the so-called charms of nature. Nature itself is ugly, ordinary, shapeless; art alone makes it enjoyable. Baudelaire hates the country, the Goncourts regard nature as an enemy and the later aesthetes, especially Whistler and Wilde, speak of it in a tone of contemptuous irony. This is the end of the pastoral, of the romantic enthusiasm for the natural and the belief in the identity of reason and nature. The reaction against Rousseau and the cult of the state of nature initiated by him now comes to its definite conclusion. Everything simple and clear, instinctive and unsophisticated, loses its value; the consciousness, the intellectualism and the unnaturalness of culture are now sought after. Intelligence and the functions of the critical faculty are again stressed in the process of artistic creation. The imagination of the artist continually produces good, middling and bad things—says Nietzsche —it is his discernment that first rejects, selects and organizes the material to be used.[217] This idea, like the whole philosophy of the 'vie factice', comes fundamentally from Baudelaire, who desires to 'transform his delight into knowledge' and to let the critic in the poet always have his say,[218] in whom the enthusiasm for everything artificial goes, in fact, so far that he even considers nature morally inferior. He maintains that evil takes place without effort, that is to say, naturally, whereas goodness is always the product of design and purpose, and is, therefore, artificial and unnatural.[219]

The enthusiasm for the artificiality of culture is in some respects again only a new form of romantic escapism. Artificial, fictitious life is chosen, because reality can never be so beautiful as illusion and because all contact with reality, all attempts to realize dreams and wishes must lead to their corruption. But people now take refuge from social reality not in nature, as the romantics had done, but in a higher, more sublimated and more artificial world. In Villiers de l'Isle-Adam's *Axel* (1890, posthumous), one of the classical portrayals of the new attitude to life, the intellectual and imaginary forms of being always stand above the natural and practical, and unrealized desires always seem more perfect and more satisfying than their translation into ordinary, trivial reality. Axel wants to commit suicide with Sara whom he loves. She is quite willing to die with him, but she would like, before they die, to know the happiness of one night of love. Axel fears, however, that, afterwards, he would no longer have the courage to die and that their love, like all realized dreams, would not stand the test of time. He prefers the perfect illusion to the imperfect reality. The whole thought of neo-romanticism more or less depends on this feeling; everywhere we come across Lohengrins who, as Nietzsche says, leave their Elsas in the lurch on the wedding night. 'Life?' asks Axel. 'Our servants see to that for us.' In Huysmans' *À rebours* (1884), the principal document of this anti-natural and anti-practical aestheticism, the replacement of practical life by the life of the spirit is carried through even more completely. Des Esseintes, the famous hero of the novel, the prototype of all the Dorian Grays, seals himself off from the world so hermetically that he does not even dare to go on a journey since he is afraid of being disappointed by reality. It is the same crippling, life-destroying subjectivism that finds expression in the aesthete's boredom with nature. 'The age of nature', says Des Esseintes, 'is past; it has finally exhausted the patience of all sensitive minds by the loathsome monotony of its landscapes and skies.' For such minds there is but one way: to make themselves absolutely independent and replace nature by the mind, reality by fiction. They have to make everything straight crooked and to bend all natural instincts and inclinations into their opposite. Des Esseintes lives in his house as in a monastery, he visits no one and receives no one, he neither writes nor receives letters, he sleeps by day and reads, indulges in fancies and speculates by night; he creates his own 'artificial paradises' and gives up everything in which ordinary mortals delight. He invents symphonies in colours, scents, drinks, artificial flowers and rare jewels; for the instruments of his spiritual acrobatics must be rare and costly. Natural, cheap, insipid and plebeian are synonyms in his vocabulary.

Perhaps the mysticism of this whole philosophy is, however, expressed nowhere so strongly as in Villiers de l'Isle-Adam's short story *Véra.*[220] Véra is the idolized, early departed wife of the hero, who refuses to acknowledge the fact of her death, because he could not endure the consciousness of it. He throws the key of the vault in which she lies buried back through the grating, goes home and begins a new, artificial life, that is, he continues his former life, as if nothing had happened. He goes in and out, talks and acts, as if she were still alive and beside him. His behaviour is such a consistent and unbroken chain of attitudes and actions that nothing but the physical presence of Véra is needed to make his conduct absolutely reasonable. But she is so completely present spiritually and the radiation of her personality so immediate, so overwhelming that her fictitious life has a much deeper, truer and more genuine reality than her actual death. She does not die until, all at once, these words escape the sleep-walker's lips: 'I remember . . . You are really dead after all!' No intelligent reader will overlook the analogy between this obstinate refusal to admit the relevance of reality and the Christian denial of the world, but none will also fail to recognize the difference between the stubbornness of an obsession and the imperturbability of a religious faith. It is impossible to imagine anything more unchristian, more foreign to the spirit of the Middle Ages than *ennui*, this new, impressionistic form of romantic *Weltschmerz*. This is the expression of a feeling of disgust at the monotony of life,[221] therefore, the precise opposite of the dissatisfaction which, as has been pointed out, earlier ages, in which faith in the divine order was still alive, had felt with the unpleasant aspects of things here on earth.[222] In former ages the fickleness of Fortuna, the inconstancy and incalculability of fate, had been viewed with alarm, there was a general yearning for peace and security, for the monotony and boredom of peace; for the modern aesthete, on the other hand, it is the ordered security of bourgeois life that he finds most intolerable of all. The impressionists' attempt to arrest the fleeting hour, their surrender to the passing mood, as the highest and least replaceable value, their aim of living in the moment, of being absorbed by it, is only the result of this unbourgeois view of life, of this revolt against the routine and discipline of bourgeois practice. Impressionism, too, is the art of an opposition, like all progressive tendencies since the romantics, and the rebelliousness which is latent in the impressionistic approach to life, although the impressionists are not always aware of it, is part of the reason why the bourgeois public rejected the new art.

In the 'eighties people are fond of describing the aesthetic hedonism of the time as 'decadence'. Des Esseintes, the refined epicurean, is at the same time the prototype of the pampered 'décadent'. The concept of decadence, however, contains traits which are not necessarily contained in that of aestheticism, thus above all the feeling of doom and crisis, that is, the consciousness of standing at the end of a vital process and in the presence of the dissolution of a civilization. The sympathy with the old, exhausted, over-refined cultures, with Hellenism, the later years of the Roman Empire, the rococo and the mature, 'impressionistic' style of the great masters, is part of the essence of the feeling of decadence. The awareness of being witnesses of a turning point in the history of civilization was nothing new, but whereas people in former times had deeply lamented the fate of belonging to an ageing culture, as Musset had done for instance, the idea of intellectual nobility is now connected with the concept of old age and fatigue, of over-cultivation and degeneration. Men are seized by a real frenzy of change and decay—by a feeling that is again not entirely new, but much stronger than ever before. The analogies with Rousseauism, the Byronic weariness of life and the romantic passion for death are obvious. It is the same abyss that attracts both the romantic and the decadent, the same delight in destruction, self-destruction, that intoxicates them. But for the decadent 'everything is an abyss', everything replete with the fear of life, with insecurity: 'Tout plein de vague horreur, menant on ne sait où,' as Baudelaire says.

'Who knows whether truth is not sad,' writes Renan—words of the deepest scepticism, to which none of the great Russians would have subscribed. For them it was possible for everything, except truth, to be sad. But how much more sinister are the words of Rimbaud: 'Ce qu'on ne sait pas, c'est peut-être terrible' (*Le Forgeron*). One has but an inkling of the kind of unfathomable and inexhaustible riddles he feels himself surrounded by, even though he immediately adds: 'Nous saurons.' The abyss which, for the Christian, was sin, for the knight, dishonesty, for the bourgeois, illegality, is, for the decadent, everything for which he lacks concepts, words and formulae. Hence his desperate struggle to achieve form and his unconquerable abhorrence for everything unformed, untamed and natural. Hence his fondness for the ages which had the most, if not always the deepest, formulae, which had at their disposal a word, albeit often only a feeble word, for everything.

Verlaine's 'Je suis l'empire à la fin de la décadence' becomes the signature of the age, and although, as the apologist of the period of Roman decline, he has his forerunners in Gérard de Nerval,[223] Baudelaire and Gautier,[224] nevertheless, he utters the catchword at the right moment and lends to what had hitherto been the expression of a mere mood the character of a cultural programme. There have been periods of culture which did not know or refused to know anything of a Golden Age, but, before the decadents of the nineteenth century, there had never been a generation which had decided against the Golden in favour of the Silver Age. This choice implied not only the awareness of being the mere descendants of great ancestors, not only the modesty of belated heirs, but also a kind of consciousness of guilt and a feeling of inferiority. The 'decadents' were hedonists with a bad conscience, sinners who threw themselves, like Barbey d'Aurevilly, Huysmans, Verlaine, Wilde and Beardsley, into the arms of the Catholic Church. This feeling of guilt was expressed more directly than anywhere else in their conception of love, which was completely dominated by the psychological puberty of the romantics. For Baudelaire, love is the essence of the forbidden, the fall of man, the irreparable loss of innocence; 'faire l'amour, c'est faire le mal', he says. But his romantic satanism transforms this sinfulness itself into a source of lust: love is not only the intrinsically evil, its highest pleasure consists precisely in the consciousness of doing evil.[225] The sympathy for the prostitute, which the decadents share with the romantics, and in which Baudelaire is again the intermediary, is the expression of the same inhibited, guilt-laden relationship to love. It is, of course, above all the expression of the revolt against bourgeois society and the morality based on the bourgeois family. The prostitute is the déracinée and the outlaw, the rebel who revolts not only against the institutional bourgeois form of love, but also against its 'natural' spiritual form. She destroys not only the moral and social organization of the feeling, she destroys the bases of the feeling itself. She is cold in the midst of the storms of passion, she is and remains the superior spectator of the lust that she awakens, she feels lonely and apathetic when others are enraptured and intoxicated—she is, in brief, the artist's female double. From this community of feeling and destiny arises the understanding which the artists of decadence show for her. They know how they prostitute themselves, how they surrender their most sacred feelings, and how cheaply they sell their secrets.

This declaration of solidarity with the prostitute completes the estrangement of the artists from bourgeois society. The bad schoolboy sits in the 'back row', as Thomas Mann said of one of his heroes, and feels the relief which one feels on leaving the scene of public strife, and stays in the 'back row', despised but unmolested. It would be curious if, in a thinker such as Thomas Mann, whose whole outlook on life hinges on a single central problem, namely the position of the artist in the bourgeois world, even this apparently innocuous remark were not connected in a way with his interpretation of the artist's way of life. The particular existence the artist leads, which must strike the bourgeois mind as lacking all ambition, is in fact very much like a 'back row' which relieves him of all responsibility and all need to account for his actions. In any case, Thomas Mann's emphatically 'bourgeois' outlook, as also, for example, the 'correct' social philosophy of Henry James, can only be understood as a reaction against the way of life of the type of artist who has taken his seat ostentatiously in the 'back row' and with whom people refuse to have anything to do. Thomas Mann and Henry James know, however, only too well that the artist is forced to lead an extra-human and inhuman existence, that the ways of normal life are not open to him and that spontaneous, unself-conscious, warm human feelings have no relevance to his purpose. The paradox of his lot is that it is his task to describe life from which he himself is excluded. This situation is followed by serious, often insoluble complications. Paul Overt, the younger of the two writers who confront each other in Henry James's *The Lesson of the Master*, revolts in vain against the cruel monastic discipline to which a life devoted to art is subjected and struggles to no avail against the forgoing of all personal and private happiness which Henry St. George, the master, demands of him. He is full of impatience and bitterness against the merciless tyranny of the power to which he has sold himself. 'You don't imagine, by any chance, that I'm defending art?' the master replies to him. 'Happy the societies in which it hasn't made its appearance.' And Thomas Mann's reproach to art is just as stern and implacable. For when he shows that all problematical, ambiguous and disreputable lives, all the feeble, the diseased and degenerate, all the adventurers, swindlers and criminals and, finally, even Hitler are spiritual relations of the artist,[226] he formulates the most dreadful charge ever brought against art.

The age of impressionism produces two extreme types of the modern artist estranged from society: the new bohemians and those who take refuge from Western civilization in distant, exotic lands. Both are the product of the same feeling, the same 'discomfort with culture', the only difference being that the first choose 'internal emigration', the others real flight. But both lead the same abstract life severed from immediate reality and practical activity; both express themselves in forms which must inevitably appear increasingly strange and unintelligible to the majority of the public. The voyage into remote lands, as an escape from modern civilization, is as old as the bohemian protest against the bourgeois way of life. Both have their source in romantic unreality and individualism, but they have become transformed meanwhile and the form in which they now enter the artist's experience is attributable once again above all to Baudelaire. The romantics were still searching for the 'blue flower', for the land of dreams and ideals, 'Mais les vrais voyageurs', says Baudelaire, 'sont ceux-là seuls qui partent Pour partir. . . .' That is the real escape, the voyage into the unknown, which is undertaken not because one is enticed, but because one is disgusted by something.

> O Mort, vieux capitaine, il est temps! levons l'ancre!
> Ce pays nous ennuie, o Mort! Appareillons!
> Si le ciel et la mer sont noirs comme l'encre,
> Nos coeurs que tu connais sont remplis de rayons!

Rimbaud intensifies the pain of departing—'La vie est absente, nous ne sommes pas au monde'—but he scarcely intensifies the beauty of Baudelaire's words of farewell, which are unparalleled in the whole of modern poetry. Nevertheless, he is Baudelaire's only real heir, the only one who realizes the master's imaginary voyages, and turns into a way of life what before him had been mere escapades into the world of bohemianism.

In France the bohème is not a uniform and clear-cut phenomenon. There is no need of special evidence to prove that the frivolous and lovable young people in Puccini's opera have nothing in common with Rimbaud and his possession by the spirit of evil, or with Verlaine and his wavering between criminality and mysticism. But Rimbaud's and Verlaine's genealogy has many ramifications, and to describe it, it is necessary to distinguish between three different phases and forms of artist life: the bohème of the romantic, of the naturalistic and of the impressionistic age.[227] The bohème was originally no more than a demonstration against the bourgeois way of life. It consisted of young artists and students, who were mostly the sons of well-to-do people, and in whom the opposition to the prevailing society was usually a product of mere youthful exuberance and contrariness. Théophile Gautier, Gérard de Nerval, Arsène Houssaye, Nestor Roqueplan and all the rest of them, parted from bourgeois society, not because they were forced, but because they wanted to live differently from their bourgeois fathers. They were genuine romantics, who wanted to be original and extravagant. They undertook their excursion into the world of the outlaws and the outcasts, just as one undertakes a journey into an exotic land; they knew nothing of the misery of the later bohème, and they were free to return to bourgeois society at any time. The bohème of the following generation, that of the militant naturalism with its headquarters in the beer-cellar, the generation to which Champfleury, Courbet, Nadar and Murger belonged, was, on the other hand, a real bohème, that is, an artistic proletariat, made up of people whose existence was absolutely insecure, people who stood outside the frontiers of bourgeois society, and whose struggle against the bourgeoisie was no high-spirited game but a bitter necessity. Their unbourgeois way of life was the form which best suited the questionable existence that they led and was in no sense any longer a mere masquerade. But just as Baudelaire, who belongs to this generation chronologically, marks, intellectually, a reversion to the romantic bohème, on the one hand, and an advance to the impressionistic, on the other, Murger also represents, albeit in a different sense, a transitional phenomenon. Now that the bohème ceases to be 'romantic', the bourgeoisie begins to romanticize and idealize it. In this process Murger plays the part of the *maître de plaisir*, and represents the Quartier Latin tamed and cleansed. For this service he himself is promoted, as he deserves, into the ranks of the authors acknowledged by the middle class. The philistine regards the bohème on the whole as an underworld. It attracts him and it repels him. He flirts with the freedom and irresponsibility which reign supreme in it, but shrinks from the disorder and anarchy which the realization of this freedom implies. Murger's idealization is intended to make the danger which threatens bourgeois society from this side seem more harmless than it is and to allow the unsuspecting bourgeois to continue luxuriating in his equivocal wish-fulfilment dreams. Murger's figures are usually gay, somewhat frivolous, but thoroughly good-natured young people, who will remember their bohemian life when they grow old, as the bourgeois reader remembers the riotous years when he was a student. In the eyes of the bourgeois this impression of the provisional took the final sting out of the bohème. And Murger was by no means alone in his views. Balzac also described the bohemian life of the young artists as a transitional stage. 'The bohème consists', he writes in *Un Prince de la Bohême*, 'of young people, who are still unknown, but who will be well known and famous one day.'

In the age of naturalism, however, not only Murger's conception but also the actual life of the bohemians is still an idyll, compared to the life of the poets and artists of the next generation who shut themselves off from bourgeois society—Rimbaud, Verlaine, Tristan Corbière and Lautréamont. The bohème had become a company of vagabonds and outlaws, a class in which demoralization, anarchy and misery dwell, a group of desperados, who not only break with bourgeois society, but with the whole of European civilization. Baudelaire, Verlaine and Toulouse-Lautrec are heavy drinkers, Rimbaud, Gauguin and Van Gogh tramps and homeless globe-trotters, Verlaine and Rimbaud die in hospital, Van Gogh and Toulouse-Lautrec live for some time in a lunatic asylum, and most of them spend their lives in cafés, music-halls, brothels, hospitals or on the street. They destroy everything in themselves that might be of use to society, they rage against everything that gives permanence and continuity to life and they rage against themselves, as if they were anxious to exterminate everything in their own nature which they have in common with others. 'I am killing myself', Baudelaire writes in a letter of 1845, 'because I am useless to others and a danger to myself.' But it is not merely the consciousness of his own unhappiness that fills him, but also the feeling that the happiness of others is something banal and vulgar. 'You are a happy man,' he writes in a later letter. 'I feel sorry for you, sir, for being happy so easily. A man must have sunk low to consider himself happy.'[228] We find the same contempt for the cheap feeling of happiness in Chekhov's short story *Gooseberries*. And that is no accident in the case of a writer who feels so much sympathy for bohemianism. 'Tell me why you lead such a monotonous life?' the hero of one of his short stories about artists asks his host. 'My life is tedious, dull, monotonous, because I am a painter, a queer fish, and have been worried all my life with envy, discontent, disbelief in my work: I am always poor, I am a vagabond, but you are a wealthy, normal man, a landowner, a gentleman—why do you live so tamely and take so little from life?'[229] The life of the older generation of bohemians was, at least, full of colour; they put up with their misery, in order to live colourfully and interestingly. But the new bohemians live under the pressure of a dull, fusty and stifling boredom; art no longer intoxicates, it only narcotizes.

Yet neither Baudelaire nor Chekhov nor the others had any idea what a hell life could develop into for a man like Rimbaud. Western culture had to reach the stage of its present crisis before such a life could become conceivable at all. A neurasthenic, a ne'er-do-well, an idler, a thoroughly malignant and dangerous man who, wandering from country to country, manages to scrape a living for himself as language teacher, street hawker, circus employee, docker, agricultural day-labourer, sailor, volunteer in the Dutch army, mechanic, explorer, colonial trader and heaven knows what else, catches an infection somewhere in Africa, has to have a leg amputated in a hospital in Marseilles, in order, at the age of thirty-seven, to die piecemeal in the most terrible agony; a genius who writes immortal poems at the age of seventeen, gives up writing poetry completely at the age of nineteen, and in whose letters there is never a mention of literature during the rest of his life; a criminal towards himself and others, who throws away his most precious possessions and completely forgets, completely denies that he has ever possessed them; one of the pioneers and, as many people maintain, the real founder of modern poetry, who, when the news of his fame reaches him in Africa, refuses to listen and dismisses it with a 'merde pour la poésie': can one imagine anything more appalling, anything more in conflict with the idea of a poet? Is it not, as Tristan Corbière says: 'His poems were by another; he had not read them'? Is it not the most terrible nihilism conceivable, the extremity of self-denial? And that is the real fruit of the seed sown by the respectable, decent-minded and fastidious bourgeois Flaubert and his sophisticated, cultivated and art-minded friends.

After 1890 the word 'decadence' loses its suggestive note and people begin to speak of 'symbolism' as the leading artistic trend.

Moréas introduces the term and defines it as the attempt to replace reality in poetry by the 'idea'.[230] The new terminology is in accordance with Mallarmé's victory over Verlaine and the shift of emphasis from sensualistic impressionism to spiritualism. It is often very difficult to distinguish symbolism from impressionism; the two concepts are partly antithetical, partly synonymous. There is a fairly sharp distinction between Verlaine's impressionism and Mallarmé's symbolism, but to find the proper stylistic category for a writer like Maeterlinck is by no means so simple. Symbolism, with its optical and acoustic effects, as well as the mixing and combining of the different sense data and the reciprocal action between the various art forms, above all what Mallarmé understood by the reconquest from music of the property of poetry, is 'impressionistic'. But, with its irrationalistic and spiritualistic approach, it also implies a sharp reaction against naturalistic and materialistic impressionism. For the latter, sense experience is something final and irreducible, whereas for symbolism, the whole of empirical reality is only the image of a world of ideas.

Symbolism represents, on the one hand, the final result of the development which began with romanticism, that is, with the discovery of metaphor as the germ-cell of poetry, and which led to the richness of impressionistic imagery, but it not only disowns impressionism on account of its materialistic world-view and the Parnasse on account of its formalism and rationalism, it also disowns romanticism on account of its emotionalism and the conventionality of its metaphorical language. In certain respects symbolism can be considered the reaction against the whole of earlier poetry;[231] it discovers something that had either never been known or never been emphasized before: 'poésie pure'[232]— the poetry that arises from the irrational, non-conceptual spirit of language, which is opposed to all logical interpretation. For symbolism, poetry is nothing but the expression of those relationships and correspondences, which language, left to itself, creates between the concrete and the abstract, the material and the ideal, and between the different spheres of the senses. Mallarmé thinks that poetry is the intimation of hovering and ever evaporating images; he asserts that to *name* an object is to destroy three-quarters of the pleasure which consists in the gradual divining of its true nature.[233] The symbol implies, however, not merely the deliberate avoidance of direct naming, but the indirect expression of a meaning, which it is impossible to describe directly, which is essentially indefinable and inexhaustible.

Mallarmé's generation by no means invented the symbol as a means of expression; symbolic art had also existed in previous ages. It merely discovered the difference between symbol and allegory, and made symbolism as a poetic style the conscious aim of its endeavours. It recognized, even though it was not always able to give expression to its insight, that allegory is nothing but the translation of an abstract idea into the form of a concrete image, whereby the idea continues to a certain extent to be independent of its metaphorical expression and could also be expressed in another form, whereas the symbol brings the idea and the image into an indivisible unity, so that the transformation of the image also implies the metamorphosis of the idea. In short, the content of a symbol cannot be translated into any other form, but a symbol can, on the other hand, be interpreted in various ways, and this variability of the interpretation, this apparent inexhaustibility of the meaning of the symbol, is its most essential characteristic. Compared with the symbol, the allegory always seems like the simple, plain and to some extent superfluous transcription of an idea which gains nothing by being translated from one sphere to another. The allegory is a kind of riddle, the solution to which is obvious; whereas the symbol can only be interpreted, it cannot be solved. The allegory is the expression of a static, the symbol that of a dynamic process of thought; the former sets a limit and a boundary to the association of ideas, the latter sets ideas in motion and keeps them in motion. High medieval art is expressed chiefly in symbols, late medieval art in allegories; the adventures of Don Quixote are symbolical, those of the heroes of the novels of chivalry which Cervantes takes as his model are allegorical. But in almost every age allegorical and symbolical art co-exist, and one often finds them intermingled in the works of one and the same artist. Lear's 'wheel of fire' is a symbol, Romeo's 'night's candles' an allegory; but the very next line in Romeo—'the jocund day

Stands tiptoe on the misty mountain tops'—has again a symbolic ring about it.

Symbolism is based on the assumption that poetry's task is to express something that cannot be moulded into a definite form and cannot be approached by a direct route. Since it is impossible to utter anything relevant about things through the clear media of the consciousness, whereas language discloses as it were automatically the secret relationships existing between them, the poet must, as Mallarmé intimates, 'give way to the initiative of the words'; he must allow himself to be borne along by the current of language, by the spontaneous succession of images and visions, which implies that language is not only more poetic but also more philosophical than reason. Rousseau's concept of a state of nature, which is allegedly better than civilization, and Burke's idea of an organic historical development, which supposedly produces more valuable things than reformism, are the real sources of this mystical poetic theory, and they are still discernible in the Tolstoyan and Nietzschean notion of the body that is wiser than the mind, and in the Bergsonian theory of the intuition that is deeper than the intellect. But this new mysticism of language, this 'alchimie du verbe', comes, like the whole hallucinatory interpretation of poetry, immediately from Rimbaud. He it was who made the statement that has had a decisive influence on the whole of modern literature, namely that the poet must become a *seer* and that it is his task to prepare himself for this by systematically weaning his senses from their normal functions, by denaturalizing and dehumanizing them. The practice which Rimbaud recommended was not only in accordance with the ideal of artificiality, that all the decadents had in mind as their ultimate ideal, but already contained the new element, namely that of deformity and grimace as a means of expression, that was to become so important for modern expressionistic art. It was based in essentials on the feeling that the normal, spontaneous spiritual attitudes are artistically sterile and that the poet must overcome the natural man within himself, in order to discover the hidden meaning of things.

Mallarmé was a Platonist, who regarded ordinary empirical reality as the corrupted form of an ideal, timeless, absolute being, but who wanted to realize the world of ideas, at least partly, in the life of this world. He lived in the vacuum of his intellectualism, completely cut off from ordinary practical life, and had almost no relationships at all with the world outside literature. He destroyed all spontaneity inside himself and became as it were the anonymous author of his works. No one ever followed Flaubert's example more faithfully. 'Tout au monde existe pour aboutir à un livre'—the master himself could not have put it more Flaubertishly. 'À un livre', Mallarmé says; but what results is, in fact, hardly a book. He spends his whole life writing, rewriting and correcting a dozen sonnets, two dozen shorter and about six larger poems, a dramatic scene and some theoretical fragments.[234] He knew that his art was a blind alley leading nowhere,[235] and that is why the theme of sterility takes up so much space in his poetry.[236] The life of the refined, cultured and clever Mallarmé ended in just as dreadful a fiasco as Rimbaud's vagabond existence. They both despaired of the meaning of art, culture and human society, and it is difficult to say which of the two acted more consistently.[237] Balzac proved himself a good prophet in his *Chef-d'œuvre inconnu*; in estranging himself from life, the artist has become the destroyer of his own work.

Flaubert had already thought of writing a book without a subject, which would be pure form, pure style, mere ornament, and it was he on whom the idea of 'poésie pure' first dawned. Perhaps Mallarmé would not have literally made his own the dictum that 'a beautiful line without meaning is more valuable than a less beautiful with meaning'; he did not actually believe in the renunciation of all intellectual content in poetry, but he demanded that the poet should renounce the rousing of emotions and passions and the use of extra-aesthetic, practical and rational motifs. The conception of 'pure poetry' can be considered, at least, the best summing-up of his views on the nature of art and the embodiment of the ideal he had in mind as a poet. Mallarmé began writing a poem without knowing exactly where the first line would lead; the poem arose as the crystallization of words and lines which combined almost of their own accord.[238] The doctrine of 'poésie pure' transposes the principle of this creative method into a theory of the receptive act, and lays down that for a poetic experience to take place it is not absolutely necessary to know the whole poem, however short; often one or two lines are sufficient, sometimes only a few verbal scraps, to produce in us the mood corresponding to the poem. In other words: to enjoy a poem, it is not necessary or it is, at any rate, not sufficient to grasp its rational meaning, indeed, it is, as folk poetry shows, not at all necessary that the poem itself should have an exact 'meaning'.[239] The similarity of the mode of reception described here to the contemplation of an impressionistic painting from a suitable distance is obvious, but the conception of 'pure poetry' contains features which are not necessarily contained in that of impressionism. It represents the purest and most uncompromising form of aestheticism, and expresses the basic idea that a poetic world wholly independent of ordinary, practical, rational reality, an autonomous, self-contained aesthetic microcosm revolving around its own axis, is thoroughly possible.

The aristocratic aloofness expressed in this estrangement and isolation of the poet from reality is still further intensified by the deliberate vagueness of expression and the intentional difficulty of the poetic thought. Mallarmé is the heir of the 'dark rhyming' of the troubadours and the erudition of the humanist poets. He looks for the indefinite, the enigmatical, the obscure not only because he knows that the expression seems to be the more richly allusive the vaguer it is, but also because a poem must, in his opinion, 'be something mysterious to which the reader has to search for the key'.[240] Catulle Mendès expressly refers to this aristocratism of the poetic practice of Mallarmé and his followers. To the question of Jules Huret as to whether he reproaches the symbolists for their obscurity, he replies: 'By no means. Pure art is becoming more and more the possession of an élite in this age of democracy, the possession of a bizarre, morbid and charming aristocracy. It is right that its level should be upheld and that it should be surrounded by a secret.'[241] From the discovery that rational understanding is not the characteristic mental approach to poetry Mallarmé derives the conclusion that the basic feature of all great poetry is the incomprehensible and the incommensurable. The artistic advantages of the elliptic mode of expression, of which he is thinking, are obvious; by omitting certain links in the chain of association a speed and intensity is achieved which is lost when the effects are developed slowly.[242] Mallarmé makes full use of these advantages and his poetry owes its attraction above all to the compression of the ideas and the leaps and bounds of the images. The reasons why he is difficult to understand are not, however, by any means always implicit in the artistic idea itself, but are often connected with quite arbitrary and playful linguistic manipulations.[243] And this ambition to be difficult for the sake of difficulty reveals the poet's very intention to isolate himself from the masses and restrict himself to as small a circle as possible. In spite of their apparent indifference to political affairs, the symbolists were essentially reactionary-minded; they were, as Barrès remarks, the Boulangists of literature.[244] The poetry of the present day, partly for the same reason as that of Mallarmé, seems esoteric and undemocratic and as if it were deliberately shutting itself off from the wider public, different as the political convictions of the individual poets are and much as we know that this difficulty is the result of a development that has been in preparation for a long time and which it is impossible for modern culture to circumvent.

Since the Restoration, England had never been so strongly under French influence as in the last quarter of the nineteenth century. After a long period of prosperity, the British Empire now passes through an economic crisis, which develops into a crisis of the Victorian spirit itself. The 'great depression' begins around the middle of the 'seventies and scarcely lasts longer than a decade, but during this time the English middle class loses its former self-confidence. It begins to feel the economic competition of foreign, mostly younger nations, such as the Germans and the Americans, and finds itself involved in a fierce contest for the possession of the colonies. The direct effect of the new situation is the retrogression of the economic liberalism which the English middle class had hitherto regarded, in spite of all criticism, in the light of an irrefutable dogma.[245] The decline in exports reduces production and depresses the standard of living of the working class. Unemployment increases, strikes multiply and the socialist movement, which had come to a standstill after the revolutionary years in the middle of the century, now not only acquires new strength, but becomes conscious for the first time in England of its real aims and power. This change has far-reaching consequences for the intellectual development of the country. The consciousness of confronting foreign countries capable of competing in the world market brings about the end of British isolationism[246] and prepares the ground for foreign intellectual influences. Amongst these that of French literature is of prime importance; the influence of the Russian novel, of Wagner, Ibsen and Nietzsche, supplements the stimuli coming from France. Much more important than the external influences, indeed, their real precondition, is the fact that, with the shaking of middle-class self-confidence and the belief in England's divine mission in the world, but above all with the new socialistic movement of the 'eighties, a renewed struggle for individual freedom sets in and gives the whole intellectual development, the progressive literature and the way of life of the younger generation the stamp of a fight for freedom. The intellectual disposition of the period shows hardly a feature which is independent of this fight against tradition and convention, puritanism and philistinism, barren utilitarianism and sentimental romanticism. Youth fights the older generation for the possession and enjoyment of life. Modernism becomes the aesthetic and moral slogan of youth 'knocking at the door' and demanding to be let in. Ibsen's ideal of self-realization, the will to give expression to one's own personality and to obtain recognition for it, becomes the aim and content of life. And unclarified as what is understood by this 'self-realization' usually remains, the moral security of the old bourgeois world collapses under the attack of the new generation. Until about 1875 youth confronts a generally speaking stable society, self-confident in its traditions and conventions and respected even by its opponents. One feels not only with a Jane Austen but even with a George Eliot that they face a social order which, if not exactly ideal and to be accepted unconditionally, is, at any rate, by no means negligible or simply replaceable, whereas now all the norms of social life suddenly cease to be recognized as valid; everything begins to waver, to become problematical and open to discussion.

The liberal tendency in the English literature and art of the 'eighties represents an unpolitical individualism, even though there is a close connection between the younger generation's quest for self-realization and its fight against the old superindividual forms and the new political and social situation.[247] This younger generation is absolutely hostile to the bourgeoisie, but it is, on the whole, by no means democratic or even socialistic. Its sensualism and hedonism, its aim of enjoying life and becoming enraptured with it, of turning every hour of this life into an unforgettable and irreplaceable experience, often assumes an antisocial and a-moral character. The anti-philistine movement is not directed against the capitalistic, but against the dull, art-despising bourgeoisie. In England the whole movement of modernism is dominated by this hatred for the philistine which, incidentally, becomes a new mechanical convention. Most of the changes which impressionism undergoes in this country are also conditioned by it. In France, impressionist art and literature was not expressly anti-bourgeois in character; the French had already finished with their fight against philistinism and the symbolists even felt a certain sympathy for the conservative middle class. The literature of decadence in England has, on the other hand, to undertake the work of undermining which had been carried out in France partly by the romantics, partly by the naturalists. The most striking feature of the English literature of the period, in contrast to the French, is the proneness to paradox, to a surprising, bizarre, deliberately shocking mode of expression, to an intellectual smartness, the coquettish complacency and utter lack of concern for truth of which seems in such bad taste today. It is obvious that this fondness for paradox is nothing but the spirit of contradiction and has its real origin in the desire to 'épater le bourgeois'.

All the peculiarities and mannerisms of language, thought, clothing and way of life of the rebels are to be regarded as a protest against the outlook of the dull, unimaginative, mendacious and hypocritical philistine. Their extravagant dandyism is as much a protest as the colourful language in which all the treasures of the impressionistic style are paraded. The English decadent movement has been rightly described as a fusion of Mayfair and Bohemia. In England we find neither a bohemianism as absolute as the French, nor such uncompromising, unapproachable ivory-tower existences as that of Mallarmé. The English middle class still has sufficient vigour to absorb them or to segregate them. Oscar Wilde is a successful bourgeois writer, so long as he seems endurable to the ruling class, but as soon as he begins to disgust them, he is mercilessly 'liquidated'. In England the dandy takes the place of the bohemian to some extent, just as he was already his counterpart in France. He is the bourgeois intellectual taken out of his proper class into a higher one, whilst the bohemian is the artist who has sunk down to the proletariat. The fastidious elegance and extravagance of the dandy fulfils the same function as the depravation and dissipation of the bohemians. They embody the same protest against the routine and triviality of bourgeois life, the only difference being that the English resign themselves to the sunflower in the buttonhole more easily than to the open neck. It is a well-known fact that the prototypes of Musset, Gautier, Baudelaire and Barbey d'Aurevilly were already Englishmen; Whistler, Wilde and Beardsley, on the other hand, take over the philosophy of dandyism from the French. For Baudelaire, the dandy is the living indictment of a standardizing democracy. He unites within himself all the gentlemanly virtues that are still possible today; he is a match for every situation and is never astonished at anything; he never becomes vulgar and always preserves the cool smile of the stoic. Dandyism is the last revelation of heroism in an age of decadence, a sunset, a last radiant beam of human pride.[248] The elegance of dress, the fastidiousness of manners, the mental austerity, are only the external discipline which the members of this higher order impose upon themselves in the trite world of today; what really matters is the inward superiority and independence, the practical aimlessness and disinterestedness of life and action.[249] Baudelaire places the dandy above the artist;[250] for the latter is still capable of enthusiasm, still strives, still works—is still banausic in the ancient meaning of the word. The cruelty of Balzac's vision is here surpassed: the artist not only destroys his work, he also destroys his claim to fame and honour. When Oscar Wilde ranks the work of art that he intends to make out of his life, the art with which he shapes his conversations, relationships and habits, above his literary works, he has Baudelaire's dandy in mind—the ideal of an absolutely useless, purposeless and unmotivated existence.

But how complacent and coquettish this forgoing of the artist's honour and fame is, is shown by the strange combination of dilettantism and aestheticism which typifies the English decadents. Art had really never been taken so seriously before as it was now; never had so much trouble been taken to write skilfully chiselled lines, a flawless prose, perfectly articulated and balanced sentences. Never had 'beauty', the decorative element, the elegant, the exquisite and the costly played a greater rôle in art; never had it been practised with so much preciosity and virtuosity. If painting was the model for poetry in France, then it was the goldsmith's art in England. It is not for nothing that Wilde speaks so enthusiastically of Huysmans' 'jewelled style'. Colours like the 'jade-green piles of vegetables' in Covent Garden are his personal contribution to the inheritance of the French. G. K. Chesterton remarks somewhere that the scheme of the Shavian paradox consists in the author saying 'light-green grapes' instead of 'white grapes'. Wilde, who, in spite of all the differences, has so much in common with Shaw, also bases his metaphors on the most obvious and trivial details, and it is precisely this combination of the trivial and the exquisite which is so characteristic of his style. It is as if he were trying to say that there is beauty in even the most commonplace reality, as he had learnt from Walter Pater. 'Not the fruit of experience, but experience itself, is the end . . . to maintain this ecstasy, is success in life,' as we read in the Conclusion of *The Renaissance*, and these sentences contain the whole programme of the aesthetic movement. Walter Pater completes the trend which begins with Ruskin and is continued in William Morris, but he is no longer interested in his predecessors' social aims; his only aim is hedonistic: the heightening of the intensity of the aesthetic experience. With him impressionism is no more than a form of epicureanism. Since 'everything is in flux' in the Heraclitean sense, and life roars past us with uncanny speed, there is only one truth for us—that of the moment—and only so much delight and pleasure as we can wrest from the moment. All we can do is not to let a moment pass without enjoying its own peculiar charm, its inner power and beauty.—One realizes best how far the aesthetic movement in England departed from French impressionism, if one thinks of such a phenomenon as Beardsley. It is impossible to imagine a more 'literary' art than his, or one in which psychology, the intellectual motif and the anecdote play a greater rôle. The most essential element of his style is the merely ornamental calligraphy that the French masters tried so painfully to avoid. And this calligraphy is the starting point of the whole development which leads to the fashionable illustrators and stage decorators so beloved by the semi-educated and well-placed bourgeoisie.

The intellectualism which, in spite of the strong intuitionistic current, forms the predominant trend in French literature, also represents the main characteristic of the new literature in England. Wilde not only accepts Matthew Arnold's view that it is the critic who determines the intellectual climate of a century,[251] and not only assents to Baudelaire's statement that every genuine artist must also be a critic, he even places the critic above the artist and tends to look at the world through the eyes of the critic. This explains the fact that his art, like that of his contemporaries, usually seems so dilettante. Everything they produce seems like the virtuoso playing of very gifted people who are not, however, professional artists. But that was, if one may believe them, precisely the impression they wanted to create. Meredith and Henry James move on the foundations of the same intellectualism, though on a much higher level. If there is a tradition in the English novel connecting George Eliot and Henry James,[252] then it lies without any doubt in this intellectualism. From a sociological point of view, a new phase in the history of English literature began with George Eliot—the rise of a new and more exacting reading public. But, although she represented an intellectual stratum high above the Dickens public, it was still possible for comparatively large sections of the public to enjoy George Eliot, whereas Meredith and Henry James are read only by a quite small stratum of the intelligentsia, the members of which no longer expect a novel to provide them with a thrilling plot and colourful characters, as did the public of Dickens and George Eliot, but above all with a faultless style and mature, discriminating judgements on life. What is usually sheer mannerism in Meredith is often a real intellectual obsession in Henry James, but both are the representatives of an art whose relations with reality are often rather abstract, and whose figures seem to move in a vacuum compared with the world of Stendhal, Balzac, Flaubert, Tolstoy and Dostoevsky.

Towards the end of the century impressionism becomes the predominant style throughout Europe. From now onwards a poetry of moods, of atmospherical impressions, of the declining seasons of the year and the fugitive hours of the day is to be found everywhere. People spend their time puzzling over lyrics which express fleeting, scarcely palpable sensations, indefinite, indefinable sensual stimuli, delicate colours and tired voices. The undecided, the vague, that which moves on the nethermost boundaries of sensual perception, becomes the main theme of poetry; it is, however, not objective reality with which the poets are concerned, but their emotions about their own sensitiveness and capacity for experience. This unsubstantial art of moods and atmosphere now dominates all forms of literature; they are all transformed into lyricism, into imagery and music, into timbres and nuances. The story is reduced to mere situations, the plot to lyrical scenes, the character drawing to the description of spiritual dispositions and trends. Everything becomes episodical, peripheral to a life without a centre.

In literature outside France the impressionistic features of the exposition are more strongly marked than the symbolistic. With only French literature in mind, one is easily tempted to identify impressionism with symbolism.[253] Thus even Victor Hugo called the young Mallarmé 'mon cher poète impressioniste'. But the differences are unmistakable on closer examination; impressionism is materialistic and sensualistic, however delicate its motifs, whereas symbolism is idealistic and spiritualistic, although its world of ideas is only a sublimated world of the senses. But the most fundamental difference is that whilst French symbolism, to which must also be added, above all, Belgian symbolism, together with its offshoots, that is to say, Bergson's vitalism, on the one hand, and the catholicism and royalism of the *Action française*, on the other, represents a tendency which is always about to turn into activism, the impressionism of the Viennese, the Germans, the Italians and the Russians, with Schnitzler, Hofmannsthal, Rilke, D'Annunzio and Chekhov as the leading personalities, expresses a philosophy of passivity, of complete surrender to the immediate environment and of unresisting absorption in the passing moment. But how deep the relations between impressionism and symbolism are, how easily the irrational factor gets the upper hand in both, and passivity turns into activism, is shown by the development of such poets as Stefan George and D'Annunzio. One would be quite prepared to connect the latter's lapses into bad taste, his chronic intoxication with life and his sumptuous verbal draperies with his fascist inclinations, if in Barrès and Stefan George the same political tendency were not connected with taste and literary manners of such greater quality.

The Viennese represent the purest form of the impressionism which forgoes all resistance to the stream of experience. Perhaps it is the ancient and tired culture of this city, the lack of all active national politics and the great part played in literary life by foreigners, especially Jews, which gives Viennese impressionism its peculiarly subtle and passive character. This is the art of the sons of rich bourgeois, the expression of the joyless hedonism of that 'second generation' which lives on the fruits of its fathers' work. They are nervous and melancholy, tired and aimless, sceptical and ironical about themselves, these poets of exquisite moods which evaporate in a trice and leave nothing behind but the feeling of evanescence, of having missed one's opportunities, and the consciousness of being unfit for life. The latent content of every kind of impressionism, the coincidence of the near and far, the strangeness of the nearest, most everyday things, the feeling of being for ever separated from the world, here becomes the basic experience.

> Wie kann das sein, dass diese nahen Tage
> fort sind, fuer immer fort und ganz vergangen?
>
> (How can it be that these recent days
> are gone, gone for ever and completely lost?)

asks Hofmannsthal, and this question contains almost all the others: the horror at the 'here and now, that is, at the same time, the beyond', the amazement at the fact that 'these things are different and the words we use different again', the consternation over the fact that 'all men go their own ways' and, finally, the last great question: 'When a man has passed on, he takes a secret with him: how it was possible for him, just him—to live in the spiritual sense of the word.' If one thinks of Balzac's 'Nous mourons tous inconnus', one sees how consistently the European outlook on life has developed since 1830. This outlook has one constant, always predominant and ever more profoundly rooted characteristic: the consciousness of estrangement and loneliness. It may sink down to the feeling of absolute god- and world-forsakenness or rise, in the moment of exuberance, which is often that of the greatest despair, to the idea of superhumanity; the superman feels just as lonely and unhappy in the rarified air of his mountain heights as the aesthete in his ivory tower.

The most curious phenomenon in the history of impressionism in Europe is its adoption by Russia and the emergence of a writer like Chekhov, who can be described as the purest representative of the whole movement. Nothing is more surprising than to meet such a personality in a country that not long before has lived in the intellectual atmosphere of the enlightenment and to which that aestheticism and decadentism which accompany the rise of impressionism in the West had been completely foreign. But in a technical century like the nineteenth, the spread of ideas proceeds rapidly and the adoption of the industrial forms of economy now creates conditions in Russia which lead to the rise of a social structure corresponding to that of the Western intelligentsia and of an outlook on life similar to that of *ennui*.[254] Gorky understood from the very beginning the decisive rôle that Chekhov was to play in Russian literature; he saw that with him a whole epoch had come to an end and that his style had an attraction for the new generation which they could no longer forgo. 'Do you know what you are doing?' he writes to him in 1900. 'You are slaying realism. . . . After any of your stories, however insignificant, everything appears crude, as if written not by a pen but by a cudgel.'[255]

As the apologist of inefficiency and failure, it is true that Chekhov has his predecessors in Dostoevsky and Turgenev, but they had not yet regarded lack of success and loneliness as the inevitable fate of the best. Chekhov's philosophy is the first to hinge on the experience of the unapproachable isolation of men, their inability to bridge the last gap that divides them, or, even if they do sometimes succeed in doing that, to persist in an intimate nearness to one another, which is so typical of the whole of impressionism. Chekhov's characters are filled with the feeling of absolute helplessness and hopelessness, of the incurable crippling of the will-power, on the one hand, and on the fruitlessness of all effort, on the other. This philosophy of passivity and indolence, this feeling that nothing in life reaches an end and a goal, has considerable formal consequences; it leads to stress being laid on the episodical nature and irrelevance of all external happenings, it brings about a renunciation of all formal organization, all concentration and integration, and prefers to express itself in an ex-centric form of composition in which the given framework is neglected and violated. Just as Degas moves important parts of the representation to the edge of the picture, and makes the frame overlap them, Chekhov ends his short stories and plays with an anacrusis, in order to arouse the impression of the inconclusiveness, abruptness and casual, arbitrary ending of the works. He follows a formal principle that is in every respect opposed to 'frontality', one in which everything is aimed at giving the representation the character of something overheard by chance, intimated by chance, something that has occurred by chance.

The feeling of the senselessness, insignificance and fragmentariness of external happenings leads in the drama to the reduction of the plot to an indispensable minimum and to the forgoing of the effects which were so characteristic of the 'pièce bien faite'. The effective stage drama owes its success fundamentally to the principles of classical form: to the uniformity, conclusiveness and well-proportioned arrangement of the plot. The poetic drama, that is, both the symbolical drama of Maeterlinck and the impressionistic drama of Chekhov, renounces these structural expedients in the interest of direct lyrical expression. Chekhov's dramatic form is perhaps the least theatrical in the whole history of the drama—a form in which 'coups de théâtre', the stage effects of surprise and tension, play the smallest rôle. There is no drama in which less happens, in which there is less dramatic movement, less dramatic conflict. The characters do not fight, do not defend themselves, are not defeated—they simply go under, founder slowly, are swallowed up by the routine of their eventless, hopeless lives. They endure their fate with patience, a fate that is consummated not in the form of catastrophes, but of disappointments.

Ever since the existence of this kind of play without action and without movements, doubts have been expressed as to its *raison d'être* and the question has been raised whether it is real drama and real theatre at all, that is to say, whether it will prove capable of surviving on the stage.

The 'pièce bien faite' was still a drama in the old sense which, although it had indeed assimilated certain elements of naturalism, still kept on the whole both to the technical conventions and heroic ideal of the classical and romantic drama. It is not until the 'eighties that naturalism conquers the stage, that is, at a time when naturalism in the novel is already on the decline. Henri Becque's *Les Corbeaux*, the first naturalistic drama, is written in the year 1882, and Antoine's 'Théâtre libre', the first naturalistic theatre, is founded in 1887. To begin with, the bourgeois public's attitude is absolutely negative, although Henri Becque and his direct successors merely turn to good account for the stage what Balzac and Flaubert had long since made common literary property. The naturalistic drama in the narrower sense comes into being outside France, in the Scandinavian countries, in Germany and Russia. The public gradually accepts its conventions and, as far as the plays of Ibsen, Brieux and Shaw are concerned, merely protests against the immoderately aggressive attacks on bourgeois morality. Finally, however, even the anti-bourgeois drama conquers the bourgeois public and even Gerhart Hauptmann's socialistic drama celebrates its earliest and greatest triumphs in the bourgeois West End of Berlin. The naturalistic theatre is merely the path leading to the intimate theatre, to the psychological differentiation of the dramatic conflict and to a more immediate contact between the stage and the public. It is true that the all too obvious expedients of stagecraft, the complicated intrigue and the artificial tension, the delays and surprises, the great scenes of conflict and the violent curtains, are held in honour for a longer period than the corresponding expedients in the novel, but they suddenly begin to seem ridiculous and have to be replaced or concealed by more subtle effects. Without the conquest of comparatively large sections of the public, the naturalistic drama would never have become a reality in the history of the theatre; for a volume of lyrical poetry can appear in a few hundred, a novel in one or two thousand copies, but a play must be seen by tens of thousands to pay. The new naturalistic drama had long since proved itself capable of surviving from this point of view, at a time when the critics and aesthetic theorists were still racking their brains about its admissibility. They found it impossible to emancipate themselves from the classicistic conception of the drama and even the most reasonable and those with the greatest taste for art among them considered the naturalistic theatre a 'contradiction in terms'.[256] They found it impossible, in particular, to disregard the fact that the economy of the classical drama was being neglected, that unconstrained, free-and-easy conversation was being carried on on the stage, problems discussed, experiences described, no end of subjects thrashed out, as if the time of performance were unlimited and the play had never to come to an end. They criticized the naturalistic drama for not having arisen 'from a consideration of destiny, character and action, but from a detailed reproduction of reality';[257] in fact, nothing had happened, however, except that reality itself, with its concrete limitations, was felt to be heavy with destiny, and that 'characters' were no longer interpreted as clear-cut stage puppets, but as many-sided, complicated, inconsistent and, in the old sense of the word, 'unprincipled' people, who, as Strindberg explained in the Preface to *Miss Julia* in 1888, were the product of particular situations, of heredity, of the milieu, of education, of natural disposition, of the influences of place, season and chance, and whose decisions were conditioned not by a single but by a whole series of motives.

The preponderance in the drama of inwardness, mood, atmosphere and lyricism over the plot is, incidentally, the result of the same progressive elimination of the story element as in impressionist painting. The whole art of the period shows a tendency to the psychological and the lyrical, and the escape from the story, the replacement of external by internal movement, of the plot by a philosophy and interpretation of life, can be described as the really basic characteristic of the new trend in art which is everywhere coming to the fore. But whilst anecdotal painting had found hardly any advocates amongst the art critics, the dramatic critics protested most emphatically against the neglect of the plot in the drama. They speak, especially in Germany, of a fateful separation of the drama from the theatre, of the decisive rôle played by suitability for the stage in theatrical experience, of the mass character of this experience and the fundamental absurdity of the intimate theatre. The motives inspiring the opposition to the naturalistic drama were of many kinds; the reactionary political tendency did not always play the chief part and often found expression only in a roundabout way; of more decisive importance was the toying with the idea of the 'monumental theatre', which was played off, again above all in Germany, against the intimate theatre, that is to say, against the really topical form of theatre, and the ambition to create a theatre for the masses which certainly existed, but did not constitute a theatre public. It was typical of the whole confusion of ideas that the classicism of the old aristocracy and bourgeoisie was alleged to be the style suitable for the future people's theatre as against the naturalism rooted in the democratic outlook on life.

The most serious reproach levelled against the new drama was on account of the determinism and relativism which are inseparable from the naturalistic outlook. It was pointed out that where internal and external freedom, absolute values and objective, universally acknowledged, unquestionable moral laws are non-existent, no real, that is, no tragic drama is possible either. The determinism of moral norms and the appreciation of antithetical moral points of view made a real dramatic conflict impossible from the very outset, so it was said. When one can understand and forgive everything, then the hero fighting at the risk of his life must ultimately seem like a stubborn fool, the conflict must lose its inevitability and the drama acquire a tragicomic and pathological character.[258] The whole train of thought teems with a confusion of ideas, with pseudo-problems and sophisms. First of all, the tragic drama is here identified with the drama as such or, at any rate, represented as its ideal form, a preconception which is in itself very relative, because historically and sociologically conditioned. In reality, not only the non-tragic, but also the drama without a clear-cut conflict is a legitimate form of theatre, which is, therefore, perfectly compatible with a relativisitic outlook on life. But even if one considers conflict an indispensable element of the drama, it is difficult to see why shattering conflicts should take place only when absolute values are at stake. Is it not just as shattering when men are fighting for their ideologically conditioned moral principles? And even if their struggle were necessarily tragi-comic, is not tragi-comedy one of the strongest dramatic effects in an age of rationalism and relativism? But the presupposition of the whole argument, that is to say, the assumption that lack of freedom and moral relativism make tragedy impossible, is open to question. It is by no means an established fact that only absolutely free, socially independent people, kings and generals, for instance, are the most suitable heroes in tragedy. Is not the fate of Hebbel's Meister Anton, Ibsen's Gregers Werle, Hauptmann's Fuhrmann Henschel, tragic? Even if one admits without qualification that tragic and sad are not one and the same thing. It would be 'undemocratic', to say the least, to maintain with Schiller that there can be nothing tragic about the theft of silver spoons. Whether a situation is tragic or not depends solely on the measure of power with which irreconcilable moral principles are found in a human soul. For a tragic impression to be made, it is not even necessary that a public that believes in absolute values should see these questioned, and even less so with a public that has lost the belief in such values.

The central figure in the history of the modern drama is Ibsen, not merely because he is the greatest theatrical talent of the century, but also because he gives the most intense dramatic expression to the moral problems of his age. His settlement of accounts with aestheticism, the crucial problem of his generation, marks the beginning and the end of his artistic development. He writes to Björnson as early as 1865: 'If I were to tell at this moment what has been the chief result of my stay abroad, I should say that it consisted in my having driven out of myself the aestheticism which had a great power over me—an isolated aestheticism with a claim to independent existence. Aestheticism of this kind seems to me now as great a curse to poetry as theology is to religion.'[259] To all appearances, Ibsen achieves his mastery of this problem under the influence of Kierkegaard, who may have played a very important rôle in his development, even though, as he himself admits, he did not understand much of the philosopher's teaching.[260] Kierkegaard, with his categorical 'Either-Or', will have given the decisive impulse to the development of Ibsen's moral austerity.[261] Ibsen's ethical passion, the consciousness of having to choose and decide for oneself, his conception of art as 'passing sentence on oneself', all that has its roots in Kierkegaardian ideas. It has often been observed that Brand's 'All or Nothing' corresponds to Kierkegaard's 'Either-Or', but Ibsen owes more than that to the uncompromisingness of his teacher—he owes him his whole unromantic and totally unaesthetic concept of the ethical attitude. The short-sightedness of the romantics consisted above all in the fact that they saw all the things of the mind in terms of aesthetics and that all values had a more or less genius-like character in their eyes. Kierkegaard was the first to emphasize, in opposition to romanticism, that religious and ethical experience has nothing to do with beauty and genius, and that a religious martyr is absolutely different from a poet or philosopher. Apart from him, there was no one in the post-romantic West who had grasped the limitations of the aesthetic and who would have been capable of influencing Ibsen in this direction. How far Ibsen was otherwise influenced by Kierkegaard in his criticism of romanticism is hard to say. The unreality of romanticism represented a general problem of the age and he certainly did not need a particular stimulus to set him grappling with it. The whole of French naturalism hinged on the conflict between the ideal and reality, between poetry and truth, poetry and prose, and all the important thinkers of the century recognized the lack of a sense of reality as the curse of modern culture. In this respect Ibsen merely continued the struggle of his predecessors and stood at the end of a long succession in which the opponents of romanticism were united. The fatal blow which he struck at the enemy consisted in his exposure of the tragi-comedy of romantic idealism. It is true that there had been nothing absolutely new about that since the appearance of *Don Quixote*, but Cervantes had still treated his hero with a good deal of sympathy and forbearance, whereas Ibsen completely destroys his Brand, Peer Gynt and Gregers Werle. The 'ideal demands' of his romantics are revealed as pure egoism, the harshness of which is scarcely mitigated by the artlessness of the egoists themselves. Don Quixote asserted his ideals above all against his own interests, whereas Ibsen's idealists are merely distinguished by their intolerance towards others.

Ibsen owed his European fame to the social message of his plays, which was reducible, in the final analysis, to a single idea, the duty of the individual towards himself, the task of self-realization, the enforcement of one's own nature against the narrow-minded, stupid and out-of-date conventions of bourgeois society. It was his gospel of individualism, his glorification of the sovereign personality and his apotheosis of the creative life, that is, once again a more or less romantic ideal, that made the deepest impression on the younger generation, and that was not only akin to Nietzsche's ideal of the superman and Bergson's vitalism, but also found an echo in Shaw's idea of the 'life-force'. Ibsen was fundamentally an anarchistic individualist, who regarded personal freedom as life's supreme value, and based his whole thought on the idea that the free individual, independent of all external ties, can do very much for himself, whereas society can do very little for him. His idea of self-realization had in itself a very far-reaching social significance, but the 'social problem' as such hardly worried him at all. 'I have really never had a strong feeling for solidarity,' he writes to Brandes in 1871.[262] His thinking revolved around private ethical problems; society itself was for him merely the expression of the principle of evil. He saw in it nothing but the rule of stupidity, of prejudice and force. Finally, he attained that aristocratically conservative master morality, to which he gave the clearest expression in *Rosmersholm*. In Europe he was regarded, as a result of his modernism, his anti-philistinism and his embittered struggle against all conventions, as a thoroughly progressive mind, but in his own country, where his political views were seen in a more adequate context, he was considered, in contrast to Björnson the radical, the great conservative writer. Outside Norway, however, his historical importance was assessed more accurately. There he was looked upon as one of the few representative personalities of the age—if not the only one who could be compared with Tolstoy. He too, like Tolstoy himself, owed his reputation and influence not so much to his literary work, as to his activity as a teacher and an agitator. He was honoured, above all, as the great moral preacher, the passionate accuser and the fearless champion of the truth, for whom the stage was merely the means to a higher end. But Ibsen had nothing positive to say to his contemporaries as a politician. His whole outlook on life was shot through with a profound contradiction: he fought against conventional morality, bourgeois prejudices and the prevailing society on behalf of an idea of freedom in the realizability of which he himself did not believe. He was a crusader without a faith, a revolutionary without a social ideal, a reformer who finally turned out to be a sad fatalist.

In the end he stopped precisely at the point where Balzac's Frenhofer or Rimbaud and Mallarmé had stopped. Rubek, the hero of his last play, the purest embodiment of his idea of the artist, disowns his work and feels what more or less every artist had felt since the romantic movement, that he had lost life itself by living only for art. 'A summer night on the Vidda! With thee! With thee! Ah, Irene, that could have been our life!' This exclamation contains a judgement on the whole of modern art. From the apotheosis of the 'summer nights' of life there has developed an unsatisfying substitute and an opiate, which blunts the senses and makes men incapable of enjoying life itself.

Shaw is Ibsen's only real disciple and successor—the only one to continue the fight against romanticism effectively and to deepen the great European discussion of the century. The unmasking of the romantic hero, the shattering of the belief in the great, theatrical and tragic gesture, is consummated by him. Everything purely decorative, grandiosely heroic, sublime and idealistic becomes suspect; all sentimentality and refusal to face reality is revealed as humbug and fraud. The psychology of self-deception is the source of his art and he is not merely one of the bravest and most uncompromising, but also one of the most buoyant and amusing unmaskers of the self-deceivers. He can in no way deny his descent from the enlightenment, the origin of his whole legend-destroying and fiction-revealing thought, but through his philosophy of history, which has its roots in historical materialism, he is at the same time the most progressive and the most modern writer of his generation. He shows that the angle from which people see the world and themselves, the lies that they proclaim as the truth or allow to prevail as such and for which they are in certain circumstances capable of doing anything, are ideologically conditioned, that is, by economic interests and social aspirations. The worst thing is not that they think irrationally—they often think only too rationally—but that they have no sense of reality, that they refuse to admit facts as facts. Hence it is realism and not rationalism that is the object of Shaw's striving, and the will, not the reason, that is the *faculté maîtresse* of his heroes.[263] That also partly explains why he became a dramatist and found the most adequate medium for his ideas in the most dynamic literary genre.

Shaw would not have been the perfect representative of his age, if he had not shared its intellectualism. In spite of the stirring dramatic life that pulses in them, in spite of their effectiveness on the stage, which often reminds us of the 'pièce bien faite', and their somewhat crude melodramatics, his plays have an essentially intellectualistic character; they are plays of ideas to an even higher degree than the plays of Ibsen. The hero's self-recollection and the intellectual tussles between the dramatis personae are not peculiar to the modern drama; the dramatic conflict demands rather, if it is to achieve an appropriate intensity and significance, the full consciousness in the persons involved in the struggle of what is happening to them. No really dramatic, above all no tragic, effect is possible without this intellectuality of the characters. Shakespeare's most artless and impulsive heroes becomes geniuses in the moment in which their fate is to be decided. The 'dramatic debates', as Shaw's plays have been called, seemed indigestible merely because they were preceded by the meagre intellectual diet of the successful plays of entertainment of the time, so that the critics and the public first had to get used to the new fare. Shaw kept more strictly to the intellectual quality of the dramatic dialogue than his predecessors, but, surely, no public was more fitted to find pleasure in such an offering than the theatre-goers at the turn of the century. And they enjoyed, in fact, without the slightest restraint even the most daring intellectual acrobatics presented to them, as soon as they were convinced that Shaw's attacks on bourgeois society were nothing like so dangerous as they seemed, and, above all, that he had no desire to take their money from them. In the end, it turned out that he felt fundamentally at one with the bourgeoisie, and that he was merely the mouthpiece of that self-criticism that had always been part of the intellectual make-up of this class.

The psychology which determines the direction of the outlook on life at the turn of the century is a 'psychology of exposure'. Both Nietzsche and Freud start out from the assumption that the manifest life of the mind, that is to say, what men know or pretend to know about the motives of their behaviour, is often merely a concealment and distortion of the real motives of their feelings and actions. Nietzsche attributes the fact of this falsification to the decadence that has been discernible since the advent of Christianity and to the attempt to represent the weakness and resentments of degenerate humanity as ethical values, as altruistic and ascetic ideals. Freud interprets the phenomenon of self-deception, which Nietzsche exposes with the aid of his historical criticism of civilization, through individual psychological analysis, and establishes that the unconscious stands behind human consciousness as the real motor of human attitudes and actions, and that all conscious thinking is only the more or less transparent cloak masking the instincts which form the content of the unconscious. Now, whatever Nietzsche and Freud knew and thought of Marx, when they were developing their theories, they followed the same technique of analysis in their revelations as had first been used in historical materialism. Marx also emphasizes that human consciousness is distorted and corrupt and that it sees the world from a false angle. The concept of 'rationalization' in psycho-analysis corresponds exactly to what Marx and Engels understand by the formation of ideology and 'false consciousness'. Engels[264] and Jones[265] define the two concepts in the same sense. Men not only act, they also motivate and justify their actions in accordance with their particular, sociologically or psychologically determined approach. Marx is the first to point out that, driven by their class interests, they not only commit isolated mistakes, falsifications and mystifications, but that their whole thinking and their whole world-view is crooked and false, and that they cannot see and judge except in accordance with the presuppositions contained in the facts of their economic and social circumstances. The doctrine on which he bases his whole philosophy of history is that in a society differentiated and riven by class distinctions, correct thinking is impossible from the very outset.[266] The recognition that it is chiefly a matter of self-deception, and that the separate individuals are by no means always aware of the motives conditioning their actions, was of basic importance for the further development of psychology.

But historical materialism with its technique of exposure was itself a product of that bourgeois-capitalistic outlook on life the background of which Marx wanted to expose. Before economics had achieved its primacy in the life of Western man, such a theory would have been unthinkable. The decisive experience of the post-romantic age was the dialectic of everything that comes to pass, the antithetical nature of being and consciousness, the ambivalence of feelings and intellectual relationships. The basic principle of the new technique of analysis was the suspicion that behind all the manifest world is hidden a latent world, behind all consciousness an unconscious and behind all apparent uniformity a conflict. In view of the commonness of this approach, it was by no means necessary for all the individual thinkers and scholars to be conscious of their dependence on the method of historical materialism; the idea of the unmasking technique of thought and the psychology of exposure was part of the property of the century and Nietzsche was not so much dependent on Marx, Freud not so much on Nietzsche, as all were dependent on the general atmosphere of crisis which marked the whole age. They discovered, each in his own way, that the self-determination of the mind was a fiction and that we are the slaves of a power working inside us and often against us. The doctrine of historical materialism was, like later that of psycho-analysis, though with a more optimistic upshot, the expression of a frame of mind in which the Western world had lost its exuberant belief in itself.

Even the most rationalistic and self-conscious thinkers by no means always take the ultimate philosophical presuppositions of their thinking as the starting point in the development of their theories. They often only become aware of them later and, in some cases, never at all. Freud, too, did not recollect the experience in which the problems of his psycho-analysis were rooted until he had reached a comparatively advanced stage in his development. This experience, which was the origin of every pertinent intellectual and artistic utterance at the turn of the century, was described by Freud himself as the 'sense of discomfort with civilization' (*das Unbehagen in der Kultur*). This expressed the same feeling of estrangement and loneliness as the romanticism and aestheticism of the age, the same anxiety, the same loss of confidence in the meaning of culture, the same concern at being surrounded by unknown, unfathomable and indefinable dangers. Freud traced back this uneasiness, this feeling of an unstable and precarious balance, to the injury that had been inflicted on the life of the instincts, especially the erotic impulses, thereby completely leaving out of account the part played by economic insecurity, lack of social success and political influence. Now, there is no doubt that neuroses are part of the price we have to pay for our civilization, but they are only a part and often only a secondary form of our tribute to society. As a consequence of his strictly scientific outlook, Freud is unable to appreciate the sociological factors in man's spiritual life, and although he discerns in the super-ego the judicial representative of society, he denies that social developments can bring about essential changes in our biological and instinctive constitution. In his view, cultural forms are not historical and sociological products, but the more or less mechanical expressions of the instincts. In bourgeois-capitalistic society analerotic instincts are expressed, wars are the work of the death-instinct, the discomfort of living in a civilized society is attributable to the suppression of the libido. Even the theory of sublimation, which is one of the greatest achievements of psycho-analysis, leads to a dangerous simplification and coarsening of the concept of culture, when the sexual instinct is made the sole or even the most important source of creative intellectual work. The Marxists are right to reproach psycho-analysis for moving in a vacuum with its a-historical and unsociological method and for retaining in its idea of a constant human nature a remnant of conservative idealism. Their objection, on the other hand, that psycho-analysis is the creation of the decadent bourgeoisie and must perish with that class, is all the more dogmatic. What living intellectual values do we possess—including historical materialism—that are not the creation of this 'decadent' society? If psycho-analysis is a decadent phenomenon, then the whole naturalistic novel and the whole of impressionist art are too—then everything that bears the marks of the discord of the nineteenth century is decadent.

Thomas Mann points out that Freud is deeply involved in the irrationalism of the beginning of the new century because of the nature of the material of his enquiry, the unconscious, passions, instincts and dreams.[267] But Freud is really connected not only with this neo-romantic movement, in which the subterranean regions of the life of the mind are the central point of interest, but at the same time with the beginning and origins of the whole aspect of romantic thought which goes back to the pre-civilized and the pre-rational. There is still an abundant share of Rousseauism in the pleasure with which he describes the freedom of the uncivilized man of instinct. And even though he does not assert, for instance, that the natural man who slew his father and enjoyed cohabiting with the women members of his family can be called 'good' in Rousseau's sense of the term, at any rate, he doubts whether man has become much better or even happier in the course of the process of civilization. The real danger of irrationalism consists, for psycho-analysis, not in its choice of material and in its sympathy for the primitive man unmolested by culture, but in the foundation of its theory on mere instinct and nature. All undialectic concepts of man based on the assumption that human nature is an historically unchangeable constant contain an element of irrationalism and conservatism. Whoever does not believe in man's capacity for development usually does not want man, and society with him, to change. Pessimism and conservatism here condition each other reciprocally. But Freud is no more a real pessimist than he is a conservative or even an irrationalist. In spite of all its questionable factors, his work bears the unmistakable evidence of a spontaneous affection for mankind and of a progressive mind. It is not necessary to prove this, but there is no lack of proof. Freud certainly has doubts in the power of the reason over the instincts, but he emphasizes that we have no other means of controlling them but our intelligence. And that is not a statement quite without hope. 'The voice of the intellect is a soft one,' he says, 'but it does not rest until it has gained a hearing. . . . This is one of the few points in which one may be optimistic about the future of mankind, but in itself it signifies not a little. And one can make it a starting point for yet other hopes. The primacy of the intellect certainly lies in the far, far, but still probably not infinite distance.'[268]

Freud resists the evils of his age, he fights against the dark irrational forces to which it has sold its soul, but he is and remains tied by innumerable threads to both its achievements and its limitations. The principle of his psychology of exposure itself, in which individual differences play so much greater a part than in Marx, is most intimately connected with the impressionistic outlook on life and the relativistic philosophy of the age. The concept of deception, which is rooted in the experience that our feelings and impressions, moods and ideas are always changing, that reality makes itself known to us in ever varying, never stable forms, that every impression we receive from it is knowledge and illusion at the same time, is an impressionistic idea, and the corresponding Freudian notion, that men spend their lives concealed from themselves and others, would have been hardly conceivable before the advent of impressionism. Impressionism is the style in which both the thinking and the art of the period are expressed. The whole philosophy of the last decades of the century is dependent on it. Relativism, subjectivism, psychologism, historicism, anti-systematism, the principle of the atomization of the world of mind and the doctrine of the perspective nature of truth are elements common to the theories of Nietzsche, Bergson, the pragmatists and all the philosophical trends independent of German academic idealism.

Nietzsche says: 'Truth has never yet hung on the arm of an absolute.' Science as an end in itself, truth without presuppositions, disinterested beauty, selfless morality, are fictions for him and his contemporaries. What we call truths are, he asserts, in reality nothing more than life-promoting, power-increasing lies and deceptions which are necessary for life to continue,[269] and, in essentials, pragmatism adopts this activistic and utilitarian concept of truth. Truth is what is effective, useful and profitable, what stands the test of time and 'pays', as William James says. It is impossible to imagine a theory of cognition more in harmony with impressionism. Every truth has a certain actuality; it is valid only in quite definite situations. An assertion can be true in itself, and yet absolutely meaningless in certain circumstances, because without relation to anything else. If to the question, 'How old are you?', someone replies, 'The earth turns round the sun', then these words, in spite of the possible truth of the statement, represent a perfectly irrelevant and meaningless assertion in the given situation. Reality is an unanalysable subject-object relationship, the individual components of which are quite unascertainable and unthinkable independently of one another. We change and the world of objects changes with us. Statements about natural and historical happenings, which may have been true a hundred years ago, are no longer true today, for reality, like ourselves, is involved in a process of constant movement, development and change, it is the sum-total of ever new, unexpected, chance phenomena, and can never be considered finished. The whole pragmatic school of thought springs from the artist's impressionistic experience of reality; for here, in the sphere of art, the relation to truth is, in fact, exactly what this philosophy assumes it to be for the whole of experience. The Shakespeare of Dr. Johnson, Coleridge, Hazlitt and Bradley no longer exists; the great dramatist's works are no longer the same as they were. The words may still be the same; works of literature do not consist, however, merely of words, but also of the meaning of words, and this meaning changes from one generation to another.

Impressionistic thinking finds its purest expression in the philosophy of Bergson, above all in his interpretation of time—the medium which is the vital element of impressionism. The uniqueness of the moment, which has never existed before and will never be repeated, was the basic experience of the nineteenth century, and the whole naturalistic novel, especially that of Flaubert, was the description and analysis of this experience. But the main difference between Flaubert's philosophy and Bergson's was that he still saw time as an element of disintegration by which the ideal substance of life is destroyed. The change in our conception of time and hence of the whole of our experience of reality took place step by step, first in impressionist painting, then in Bergson's philosophy, and finally, most explicitly and significantly of all, in the work of Proust. Time is no longer the principle of dissolution and destruction, no longer the element in which ideas and ideals lose their value, and life and mind their substance, it is rather the form in which we obtain possession and become aware of our spiritual life, our living nature, which is the antithesis of dead matter and rigid mechanics. What we are, we become not only in time but through time. We are not merely the sum-total of the individual moments of our life, but the result of the ever-changing aspect which they acquire through each new moment. Time that is past does not make us poorer; it is this very time that fills our lives with content. The justification of Bergson's philosophy is the Proustian novel; it is here that Bergson's conception of time first becomes really creative. Existence acquires actual life, movement, colour, an ideal transparency and a spiritual content from the perspective of a present that is the result of our past. There is no other happiness but that of remembrance and the revival, resuscitation and conquest of time that is past and lost; for, as Proust says, the real paradises are the lost paradises. Since romanticism, art had been made responsible for the loss of life, and Flaubert's 'dire' and 'avoir' had been regarded as a tragic alternative; Proust is the first to see in contemplation, in remembrance and in art not only one possible form but the only possible form in which we can possess life. The new conception of time does not, it is true, alter the aestheticism of the age, it merely gives it a more conciliatory appearance—and nothing but the appearance of conciliation; for Proust's philosophy is merely the self-consolation and self-deception of a sick man, of a man already buried alive.

CHAPTER VIII

THE FILM AGE

THE 'twentieth century' begins after the first world war, that is to say, in the 'twenties, just as the 'nineteenth century' did not begin until about 1830. But the war marks a turning point in the development only in so far as it provides an occasion for a choice between the existing possibilities. All three main trends in the art of the new century have their predecessors in the foregoing period: cubism in Cézanne and the neoclassicists, expressionism in Van Gogh and Strindberg, surrealism in Rimbaud and Lautréamont. The continuity of the artistic development corresponds to a certain steadiness in the economic and social history of the same period. Sombart limits the lifetime of high capitalism to a hundred and fifty years and makes it end with the outbreak of the war. He wants to interpret the system of cartels and trusts of the years 1895–1914 itself as a phenomenon of old age and as an omen of the impending crisis. But in the period before 1914 only the socialists speak of the collapse of capitalism, in bourgeois circles people are certainly aware of the socialist danger, but believe neither in the 'internal contradictions' of the capitalist economy, nor in the impossibility of overcoming its occasional crises. In these circles there is no thought of a crisis in the system itself. The generally speaking confident frame of mind even continues in the first years after the end of the war and the atmosphere in the bourgeoisie is, apart from the lower middle class, which has to struggle against fearful odds, by no means hopeless. The real economic crisis begins in 1929 with the crash in America which brings the war and post-war boom to an end and unmistakably reveals the consequences of the lack of international planning of production and distribution. Now people suddenly begin to talk everywhere about the crisis of capitalism, the failure of the free economy and liberal society, about an imminent catastrophe and the threat of revolution. The history of the 'thirties is the history of a period of social criticism, of realism and activism, of the radicalization of political attitudes and the increasingly widespread conviction that only a radical solution can be of any help, in other words, that the moderate parties have had their day. But there is nowhere a greater awareness of the crisis through which the bourgeois way of life is passing than in the bourgeoisie itself, and nowhere is there so much talk of the end of the bourgeois epoch. Fascism and bolshevism are at one in considering the bourgeois a living corpse and in turning with the same uncompromisingness against the principle of liberalism and parliamentarianism. On the whole, the intelligentsia takes its stand alongside the authoritarian forms of government, demands order, discipline, dictatorship, is inspired with enthusiasm for a new Church, a new scholasticism and a new Byzantinism. The attraction of fascism for the enervated literary stratum, confused by the vitalism of Nietzsche and Bergson, consists in its illusion of absolute, solid, unquestionable values and in the hope of being rid of the responsibility that is connected with all rationalism and individualism. From communism the intelligentsia promises itself a direct contact with the broad masses of the people and the redemption from its isolation in society.

In this precarious situation the spokesmen of the liberal bourgeoisie can think of nothing better than to stress the characteristics that fascism and bolshevism have in common, and to discredit one by the other. They point to the unscrupulous realism peculiar to both and they find in a ruthless technocracy the common denominator to which their forms of organization and government can be reduced.[1] They wilfully neglect the ideological differences between the various authoritarian forms of government and represent them as mere 'techniques', that is, as the province of the party expert, the political administrator, the engineer of the social machine, in a word, of the 'managers'. There is, no doubt, a certain analogy between the different forms of social regulation, and if one proceeds from the mere fact of technicism and the standardization connected with it, one can even discern a likeness between Russia and America.[2] No state machinery today can wholly dispense with the 'managers'. They exercise political power on behalf of the more or less broad masses, just as the technicians manage their factories and the artists paint and write for them. The question is always merely in whose interest power is being exerted. No ruler in the world today dares to admit that he has not the interests of the people exclusively at heart. From this point of view, we are, in fact, living in a mass society and a mass democracy. The broad masses have, at any rate, a share in political life in so far as the powers that be are forced to take pains to lead them astray.

Nothing is more typical of the prevailing philosophy of culture of the period than the attempt to make this 'revolt of the masses'[3] responsible for the alienation and degradation of modern culture and the attack which is made on it in the name of the mind and spirit. Most of the extremists profess a belief in the usually somewhat confused cultural criticism which underlies this philosophy. It is true that the two parties take it as meaning absolutely different things and wage their war against the 'soulless' scientific world-view with positivism in mind, on the one side, and capitalism, on the other. But the way the intelligentsia is divided into the two camps is very unequal right up to the 'thirties. The majority are consciously or unconsciously reactionary and prepare the way for fascism under the spell of the ideas of Bergson, Barrès, Charles Maurras, Ortega y Gasset, Chesterton, Spengler, Keyserling, Klages and the rest. The 'new Middle Ages', the 'new Christendom', the 'new Europe', are all the old romantic land of counter-revolution, and the 'revolution in science', the mobilization of the 'spirit' against the mechanism and determinism of the natural sciences, nothing but 'the beginning of the great world reaction against the democratic and social enlightenment'.[4]

In this period of 'mass democracy' there is an attempt to make pretensions and demands in the name of ever larger groups, so that, in the end, Hitler does the trick of ennobling the overwhelming majority of his people. The new 'democratic' process of aristocratization begins by playing off the West against the

East, against Asia and Russia. West and East are contrasted as representing order and chaos, authority and anarchy, stability and revolution, disciplined rationalism and unbridled mysticism respectively,[5] and post-war Europe under the spell of Russian literature is emphatically warned that with its cult of Dostoevsky and its Karamazovism it is treading the path to chaos.[6] At the time of Vogüé, Russia and Russian literature were by no means 'Asiatic', they were, on the contrary, the representatives of the genuine Christianity which was set up as a model for the pagan West. At that time there was, however, still a Czar in Russia. The new crusaders do not, incidentally, really believe that the West can be saved at all and they clothe the hopelessness of their political outlook in a general shroud of pessimism. They are determined to bury the whole of Western civilization along with their political hopes and, as the genuine heirs of decadence, they accept the 'decline of the West'.

The great reactionary movement of the century takes effect in the realm of art as a rejection of impressionism—a change which, in some respects, forms a deeper incision in the history of art than all the changes of style since the Renaissance, leaving the artistic tradition of naturalism fundamentally unaffected. It is true that there had always been a swinging to and fro between formalism and anti-formalism, but the function of art being true to life and faithful to nature had never been questioned in principle since the Middle Ages. In this respect impressionism was the climax and the end of a development which had lasted more than four hundred years. Post-impressionist art is the first to renounce all illusion of reality on principle and to express its outlook on life by the deliberate deformation of natural objects. Cubism, constructivism, futurism, expressionism, dadaism and surrealism turn away with equal determination from nature-bound and reality-affirming impressionism. But impressionism itself prepares the ground for this development in so far as it does not aspire to an integrating description of reality, to a confrontation of the subject with the objective world as a whole, but marks rather the beginning of that process which has been called the 'annexation' of reality by art.[7] Post-impressionist art can no longer be called in any sense a reproduction of nature; its relationship to nature is one of violation. We can speak at most of a kind of magic naturalism, of the production of objects which exist alongside reality, but do not wish to take its place. Confronted with the works of Braque, Chagall, Rouault, Picasso, Henri Rousseau, Salvador Dali, we always feel that, for all their differences, we are in a second world, a super-world which, however many features of ordinary reality it may still display, represents a form of existence surpassing and incompatible with this reality.

Modern art is, however, anti-impressionistic in yet another respect: it is a fundamentally 'ugly' art, forgoing the euphony, the fascinating forms, tones and colours of impressionism. It destroys pictorial values in painting, carefully and consistently executed images in poetry and melody and tonality in music. It implies an anxious escape from everything pleasant and agreeable, everything purely decorative and ingratiating. Debussy already plays off a coldness of tone and a pure harmonic structure against the sentimentality of German romanticism, and this anti-romanticism is intensified in Stravinsky, Schoenberg and Hindemith into an anti-*espressivo*, which forswears all connection with the music of the sensitive nineteenth century. The intention is to write, paint and compose from the intellect, not from the emotions; stress is laid sometimes on purity of structure, at others on the ecstasy of a metaphysical vision, but there is a desire to escape at all costs from the complacent sensual aestheticism of the impressionist epoch. Impressionism itself had no doubt already been well aware of the critical situation in which modern aesthetic culture finds itself, but post-impressionist art is the first to stress the grotesqueness and mendacity of this culture. Hence the fight against all voluptuous and hedonistic feelings, hence the gloom, depression and torment in the works of Picasso, Kafka and Joyce. The aversion to the sensualism of the older art, the desire to destroy its illusions, goes so far that artists now refuse to use even its means of expression and prefer, like Rimbaud, to create an artificial language of their own. Schoenberg invents his twelve-tone system, and it has been rightly said of Picasso that he paints each of his pictures as if he were trying to discover the art of painting all over again.

The systematic fight against the use of the conventional

means of expression and the consequent break up of the artistic tradition of the nineteenth century begins in 1916 with dadaism, a war-time phenomenon, a protest against the civilization that had led to the war and, therefore, a form of defeatism.[8] The purpose of the whole movement consists in its resistance to the allurements of ready-made forms and the convenient but worthless, because worn-out, linguistic clichés, which falsify the object to be described and destroy all spontaneity of expression. Dadaism, like surrealism, which is in complete agreement with it in this respect, is a struggle for directness of expression, that is to say, it is an essentially romantic movement. The fight is aimed at that falsification of experience by forms, of which, as we know, Goethe had already been conscious and which was the decisive impulse behind the romantic revolution. Since romanticism the whole development in literature had consisted in a controversy with the traditional and conventional forms of language, so that the literary history of the last century is to some extent the history of a renewal of language itself. But whereas the nineteenth century always seeks merely for a balance between the old and the new, between traditional forms and the spontaneity of the individual, dadaism demands the complete destruction of the current and exhausted means of expression. It demands entirely spontaneous expression, and thereby bases its theory of art on a contradiction. For how is one to make oneself understood—which at any rate surrealism intends to do—and at the same time deny and destroy all means of communication?—The French critic Jean Paulhan differentiates between two distinct categories of writers, according to their relationship to language.[9] He calls the language-destroyers, that is to say, the romantics, symbolists and surrealists, who want to eliminate the commonplace, conventional forms and ready-made clichés from language completely and who take refuge from the dangers of language in pure, virginal, original inspiration, the 'terrorists'. They fight against all consolidation and coagulation of the living, fluid, intimate life of the mind, against all externalization and institutionalization, in other words, against all 'culture'. Paulhan links them up with Bergson and establishes the influence of intuitionism and the theory of the 'élan vital' in their attempt to preserve the directness and originality of the spiritual experience. The other camp, that is, the writers who know perfectly well that commonplaces and clichés are the price of mutual understanding and that literature is communication, that is to say, language, tradition, 'worn-out' and, precisely on that account, unproblematical, immediately intelligible form, he calls the 'rhetoricians', the oratorical artists. He regards their attitude as the only possible one, since the consistent administration of the 'terror' in literature would mean absolute silence, that is, intellectual suicide, from which the surrealists can only save themselves by constant self-deception. For there is actually no more rigid and narrow-minded convention than the doctrine of surrealism and no more insipid and monotonous art than that of the sworn surrealists. The 'automatic method of writing' is much less elastic than the rationally and aesthetically controlled style, and the unconscious—or at least as much of it as is brought to light—much poorer and simpler than the conscious mind. The historical importance of dadaism and surrealism does not consist, however, in the works of their official representatives, but in the fact that they draw attention to the blind alley in which literature found itself at the end of the symbolist movement, to the sterility of a literary convention which no longer had any connection with real life.[10] Mallarmé and the symbolists thought that every idea that occurred to them was the expression of their innermost nature; it was a mystical belief in the 'magic of the word' which made them poets. The dadaists and the surrealists now doubt whether anything objective, external, formal, rationally organized is capable of expressing man at all, but they also doubt the value of such expression. It is really 'inadmissible'—they think—that a man should leave a trace behind him.[11] Dadaism, therefore, replaces the nihilism of aesthetic culture by a new nihilism, which not only questions the value of art but of the whole human situation. For, as it is stated in one of its manifestos, 'measured by the standard of eternity, all human action is futile'.[12]

But the Mallarmé tradition by no means comes to an end. The 'rhetoricians' André Gide, Paul Valéry, T. S. Eliot and the later Rilke continue the symbolist trend in spite of their affinity to surrealism. They are the representatives of a difficult and exquisite art, they believe in the 'magic of the word', their poetry is based on the spirit of language, of literature and tradition. Joyce's *Ulysses* and T. S. Eliot's *The Waste Land* appear simultaneously, in the year 1922, and strike the two keynotes of the new literature; the one work moves in an expressionistic and surrealistic, the other in a symbolistic and formalistic direction. The intellectualistic approach is common to both, but Eliot's art springs from the 'experience of culture', Joyce's from the 'experience of pure, prime existence', as defined by Friedrich Gundolf, who introduces these concepts in the preface to his book on Goethe, thereby expressing a typical thought-pattern of the period.[13] In one case historical culture, intellectual tradition and the legacy of ideas and forms is the source of inspiration, in the other the direct facts of life and the problems of human existence. With T. S. Eliot and Paul Valéry the primary foundation is always an idea, a thought, a problem, with Joyce and Kafka an irrational experience, a vision, a metaphysical or mythological image. Gundolf's conceptual distinction is the record of a dichotomy which is being carried through in the whole field of modern art. Cubism and constructivism, on the one side, and expressionism and surrealism, on the other, embody strictly formal and form-destroying tendencies respectively which now appear for the first time side by side in such sharp contradiction. The situation is all the more peculiar as the two opposing styles display the most remarkable hybrid forms and combinations, so that one often acquires more the impression of a split consciousness than that of two competing trends. Picasso, who shifts from one of the different stylistic tendencies to the other most abruptly, is at the same time the most representative artist of the present age. But to call him an eclectic and a 'master of pastiche',[14] to maintain that he only wants to show to what an extent he has command of the rules of art against which he is in revolt,[15] to compare him with Stravinsky and to recall how he, too, changes his models and 'makes use of' Bach, then Pergolesi, then again Tchaikovsky for the purposes of modern music,[16] is not to tell the whole story. Picasso's eclecticism signifies the deliberate destruction of the unity of the personality; his imitations are protests against the cult of originality; his deformation of reality, which is always clothing itself in new forms, in order the more forcibly to demonstrate their arbitrariness, is intended, above all, to confirm the thesis that 'nature and art are two entirely dissimilar phenomena'. Picasso turns himself into a conjurer, a juggler, a parodist, out of opposition to the romantic with his 'inner voice', his 'take it or leave it', his self-esteem and self-worship. And he disavows not only romanticism, but even the Renaissance, which, with its concept of genius and its idea of the unity of work and style, anticipates romanticism to some extent. He represents a complete break with individualism and subjectivism, the absolute denial of art as the expression of an unmistakable personality. His works are notes and commentaries on reality; they make no claim to be regarded as a picture of a world and a totality, as a synthesis and epitome of existence. Picasso compromises the artistic means of expression by his indiscriminate use of the different artistic styles just as thoroughly and wilfully as do the surrealists by their renunciation of traditional forms.

The new century is full of such deep antagonisms, the unity of its outlook on life is so profoundly menaced, that the combination of the furthest extremes, the unification of the greatest contradictions, becomes the main theme, often the only theme, of its art. Surrealism, which, as André Breton remarks, at first revolved entirely round the problem of language, that is, of poetic expression, and which, as we should say with Paulhan, sought to be understood without the means of understanding, developed into an art which made the paradox of all form and the absurdity of all human existence the basis of its outlook. Dadaism still pleaded, out of despair at the inadequacy of cultural forms, for the destruction of art and for a return to chaos, that is to say, for romantic Rousseauism in the most extreme meaning of the term. Surrealism, which supplements the method of dadaism with the 'automatic method of writing',[17] thereby already expresses its belief that a new knowledge, a new truth and a new art will arise from chaos, from the unconscious and the irrational, from dreams and the uncontrolled regions of the mind. The surrealists expect the salvation of art, which they forswear as such just as much as the dadaists and are only prepared to accept it at all as a vehicle of irrational knowledge, from a plunging into the unconscious, into the pre-rational and the chaotic, and they take over the psycho-analytical method of free association, that is, the automatic development of ideas and their reproduction without any rational, moral and aesthetic censorship,[18] because they imagine they have discovered therein a recipe for the restoration of the good old romantic type of inspiration. So, after all, they still take their refuge in the rationalization of the irrational and the methodical re-production of the spontaneous, the only difference being that their method is incomparably more pedantic, dogmatic and rigid than the mode of creation in which the irrational and the intuitive are controlled by aesthetic judgement, taste and criticism, and which makes reflection and not indiscrimination its guiding principle. How much more fruitful than the surrealists' recipe was the procedure of Proust, who likewise put himself into a kind of somnambulistic condition and abandoned himself to the stream of memories and associations with the passivity of a hypnotic medium,[19] but who remained at the same time a disciplined thinker and in the highest degree a consciously creative artist.[20] Freud himself seems to have seen through the trick perpetrated by surrealism. He is said to have remarked to Salvador Dali, who visited him in London shortly before his death: 'What interests me in your art is not the unconscious, but the conscious.' [21] Must he not have meant by that: 'I am not interested in your simulated paranoia, but in the method of your simulation.'

The basic experience of the surrealists consists in the discovery of a 'second reality', which, although it is inseparably fused with ordinary, empirical reality, is nevertheless so different from it that we are only able to make negative statements about it and to point to the gaps and cavities in our experience as evidence for its existence. Nowhere is this dualism expressed more acutely than in the works of Kafka and Joyce, who, although they have nothing to do with surrealism as a doctrine, are surrealists in the wider sense, like most of the progressive artists of the century. It is also this experience of the double-sidedness of existence, with its home in two different spheres, which makes the surrealists aware of the peculiarity of dreams and induces them to recognize in the mixed reality of dreams their own stylistic ideal. The dream becomes the paradigm of the whole world-picture, in which reality and unreality, logic and fantasy, the banality and sublimation of existence, form an indissoluble and inexplicable unity. The meticulous naturalism of the details and the arbitrary combination of their relationships which surrealism copies from the dream, not only express the feeling that we live on two different levels, in two different spheres, but also that these regions of being penetrate one another so thoroughly that the one can neither be subordinated to[22] nor set against the other as its antithesis.[23]

The dualism of being is certainly no new conception, and the idea of the 'coincidentia oppositorum' is quite familiar to us from the philosophy of Nicholas of Cusa and Giordano Bruno, but the double meaning and the duplicity of existence, the snare and the seduction for the human understanding which lies hidden in every single phenomenon of reality, had never been experienced so intensively as now. Only mannerism had seen the contrast between the concrete and the abstract, the sensual and the spiritual, dreaming and waking in a similarly glaring light. The emphasis which modern art lays not so much on the coincidence of the opposites themselves, as on the fancifulness of this coincidence, is also reminiscent of mannerism. The sharp contrast, in the work of Dali, between the photographically faithful reproduction of the details and the wild disorder of their grouping corresponds, on a very humble level, to the fondness for paradox in the Elizabethan drama and the lyric poetry of the 'metaphysical poets' of the seventeenth century. But the difference of level between the style of Kafka and Joyce, in which a sober and often trivial prose is combined with the most fragile transparency of ideas, and that of the manneristic poets of the sixteenth and seventeenth centuries is no longer so great. In both cases the real subject of the representation is the absurdity of life, which seems all the more surprising and shocking the more realistic the elements of the fantastic whole are. The sewing machine and the umbrella on the dissecting table, the donkey's corpse on the piano or the naked woman's body which opens like a chest of drawers, in brief, all the forms of juxtaposition and simultaneity into which the non-simultaneous and the incompatible are pressed, are only the expression of a desire to bring unity and coherence, certainly in a very paradoxical way, into the atomized world in which we live. Art is seized by a real mania for totality.[24] It seems possible to bring everything into relationship with everything else, everything seems to include within itself the law of the whole. The disparagement of man, the so-called 'dehumanization' of art, is connected above all with this feeling. In a world in which everything is significant or of equal significance, man loses his pre-eminence and psychology its authority.

The crisis of the psychological novel is perhaps the most striking phenomenon in the new literature. The works of Kafka and Joyce are no longer psychological novels in the sense that the great novels of the nineteenth century were. In Kafka, psychology is replaced by a kind of mythology, and in Joyce, although the psychological analyses are perfectly accurate, just as the details in a surrealistic picture are absolutely true to nature, there are not only no heroes, in the sense of a psychological centre, but also no particular psychological sphere in the totality of being. The de-psychologization of the novel already begins with Proust,[25] who, as the greatest master of the analysis of feelings and thoughts, marks the summit of the psychological novel, but also represents the incipient displacement of the soul in the balance of reality. For, since the whole of existence has become merely the content of the consciousness and things acquire their significance purely and simply through the spiritual medium by which they are experienced, there can no longer be any question here of psychology as understood by Stendhal, Balzac, Flaubert, George Eliot, Tolstoy or Dostoevsky. In the novel of the nineteenth century, the soul and character of man are seen as the opposite pole to the world of physical reality, and psychology as the conflict between the subject and object, the self and the non-self, the human spirit and the external world. This psychology ceases to be predominant in Proust. He is not concerned so much with the characterization of the individual personality, although he is an ardent portraitist and caricaturist, as with the analysis of the spiritual mechanism as an ontological phenomenon. His work is a

'Summa' not merely in the familiar sense of containing a total picture of modern society, but also because it describes the whole spiritual apparatus of modern man with all his inclinations, instincts, talents, automatisms, rationalisms and irrationalisms. Joyce's *Ulysses* is therefore the direct continuation of the Proustian novel; we are here confronted literally with an encyclopaedia of modern civilization, as reflected in the tissue of the motifs which make up the content of a day in the life of a great city. This day is the protagonist of the novel. The flight from the plot is followed by the flight from the hero. Instead of a flood of events, Joyce describes a flood of ideas and associations, instead of an individual hero a stream of consciousness and an unending, uninterrupted inner monologue. The emphasis lies everywhere on the uninterruptedness of the movement, the 'heterogeneous continuum', the kaleidoscopic picture of a disintegrated world. The Bergsonian concept of time undergoes a new interpretation, an intensification and a deflection. The accent is now on the simultaneity of the contents of consciousness, the immanence of the past in the present, the constant flowing together of the different periods of time, the amorphous fluidity of inner experience, the boundlessness of the stream of time by which the soul is borne along, the relativity of space and time, that is to say, the impossibility of differentiating and defining the media in which the mind moves. In this new conception of time almost all the strands of the texture which form the stuff of modern art converge: the abandonment of the plot, the elimination of the hero, the relinquishing of psychology, the 'automatic method of writing' and, above all, the montage technique and the intermingling of temporal and spatial forms of the film. The new concept of time, whose basic element is simultaneity and whose nature consists in the spatialization of the temporal element, is expressed in no other genre so impressively as in this youngest art, which dates from the same period as Bergson's philosophy of time. The agreement between the technical methods of the film and the characteristics of the new concept of time is so complete that one has the feeling that the time categories of modern art altogether must have arisen from the spirit of cinematic form, and one is inclined to consider the film itself as the stylistically most representative, though qualitatively perhaps not the most fertile genre of contemporary art.

The theatre is in many respects the artistic medium most similar to the film; particularly in view of its combination of spatial and temporal forms, it represents the only real analogy to the film. But what happens on the stage is partly spatial, partly temporal; as a rule spatial and temporal, but never a mixture of the spatial and the temporal, as are the happenings in a film. The most fundamental difference between the film and the other arts is that, in its world-picture, the boundaries of space and time are fluid—space has a quasi-temporal, time, to some extent, a spatial character. In the plastic arts, as also on the stage, space remains static, motionless, unchanging, without a goal and without a direction; we move about quite freely in it, because it is homogeneous in all its parts and because none of the parts presupposes the other temporally. The phases of the movement are not stages, not steps in a gradual development; their sequence is subject to no constraint. Time in literature—above all in the drama—on the other hand, has a definite direction, a trend of development, an objective goal, independent of the spectator's experience of time; it is no mere reservoir, but an ordered succession. Now, these dramaturgical categories of space and time have their character and functions completely altered in the film. Space loses its static quality, its serene passivity and now becomes dynamic; it comes into being as it were before our eyes. It is fluid, unlimited, unfinished, an element with its own history, its own scheme and process of development. Homogeneous physical space here assumes the characteristics of heterogeneously composed historical time. In this medium the individual stages are no longer of the same kind, the individual parts of space no longer of equal value; it contains specially qualified positions, some with a certain priority in the development and others signifying the culmination of the spatial experience. The use of the close-up, for example, not only has spatial criteria, it also represents a phase to be reached or to be surpassed in the temporal development of the film. In a good film the close-ups are not distributed arbitrarily and capriciously. They are not cut in independently of the inner development of the scene, not at any time and anywhere, but only where their potential energy can and should make itself felt. For a close-up is not a cut-out picture with a frame; it is always merely part of a picture, like, for instance, the repoussoir figures in baroque painting which introduce a dynamic quality into the picture similar to that created by the close-ups in the spatial structure of a film.

But as if space and time in the film were interrelated by being interchangeable, the temporal relationships acquire an almost spatial character, just as space acquires a topical interest and takes on temporal characteristics, in other words, a certain element of freedom is introduced into the succession of their moments. In the temporal medium of a film we move in a way that is otherwise peculiar to space, completely free to choose our direction, proceeding from one phase of time into another, just as one goes from one room to another, disconnecting the individual stages in the development of events and grouping them, generally speaking, according to the principles of spatial order. In brief, time here loses, on the one hand, its uninterrupted continuity, on the other, its irreversible direction. It can be brought to a standstill: in close-ups; reversed: in flash-backs; repeated: in recollections; and skipped across: in visions of the future. Concurrent, simultaneous events can be shown successively, and temporally distinct events simultaneously—by double-exposure and alternation; the earlier can appear later, the later before its time. This cinematic conception of time has a thoroughly subjective and apparently irregular character compared with the empirical and the dramatic conception of the same medium. The time of empirical reality is a uniformly progressive, uninterruptedly continuous, absolutely irreversible order, in which events follow one another as if 'on a conveyor belt'. It is true that dramatic time is by no means identical with empirical time—the embarrassment caused by a clock showing the correct time on the stage comes from this discrepancy—and the unity of time prescribed by classicistic dramaturgy can even be interpreted as the fundamental elimination of ordinary time, and yet the temporal relationships in the drama have more points of contact with the chronological order of ordinary experience than the order of time in a film. Thus in the drama, or at least in one and the same act of a drama, the temporal continuity of empirical reality is preserved intact. Here too, as in real life, events follow each other according to the law of a progression which permits neither interruptions and jumps, nor repetitions and inversions, and conforms to a standard of time which is absolutely constant, that is, undergoes no acceleration, retardation or stoppages of any kind within the several sections (acts or scenes). In the film, on the other hand, not only the speed of successive events, but also the chronometric standard itself is often different from shot to shot, according as to whether slow or fast motion, short or long cutting, many or few close-ups, are used.

The dramatist is prohibited by the logic of scenic arrangement from repeating moments and phases of time, an expedient that is often the source of the most intensive aesthetic effects in the film. It is true that a part of the story is often treated retrospectively in the drama, and the antecedents followed backwards in time, but they are usually represented indirectly—either in the form of a coherent narrative or of one limited to scattered hints. The technique of the drama does not permit the playwright to go back to past stages in the course of a progressively developing plot and to insert them *directly* into the sequence of events, into the dramatic present—that is, it is only recently that it has begun to permit it, perhaps under the immediate influence of the film, or under the influence of the new conception of time, familiar also from the modern novel. The technical possibility of interrupting any shot without further ado suggests the possibilities of a discontinuous treatment of time from the very outset and provides the film with the means of heightening the tension of a scene either by interpolating heterogeneous incidents or assigning the individual phases of the scene to different sections of the work. In this way the film often produces the effect of someone playing on a keyboard and striking the keys ad libitum, up and down, to right and left. In a film we often see the hero first at the beginning of his career as a young man, later, going back to the past, as a child; we then see him, in the further course of the plot, as a mature man and, having followed his career for a time, we, finally, may see him still living after his death, in the memory of one of his relations or friends. As a result of the discontinuity of time, the retrospective development of the plot is combined with the progressive in complete freedom, with no kind of chronological tie, and through the repeated twists and turns in the time-continuum, mobility, which is the very essence of the cinematic experience, is pushed to the uttermost limits. The real spatialization of time in the film does not take place, however, until the simultaneity of parallel plots is portrayed. It is the experience of the simultaneity of different, spatially separated happenings that puts the audience into that condition of suspense, which moves between space and time and claims the categories of both orders for itself. It is the simultaneous nearness and remoteness of things—their nearness to one another in time and their distance from one another in space—that constitutes that spatio-temporal element, that two-dimensionality of time, which is the real medium of the film and the basic category of its world-picture.

It was discovered in a comparatively early stage in the history of the film that the representation of two simultaneous sequences of events is part of the original stock of cinematic forms. First this simultaneity was simply recorded and brought to the notice of the audience by clocks showing the same time or by similar direct indications; the artistic technique of the intermittent treatment of a double plot and the alternating montage of the single phases of such a plot only developed step by step. But later on we come across examples of this technique at every turn. And whether we stand between two rival parties, two competitors or two doubles, the structure of the film is dominated in any case by the crossing and intersecting of the two different lines, by the bilateral character of the development and the simultaneity of the opposing actions. The famous finish of the early, already classical Griffith films, in which the upshot of an exciting plot is made to depend on whether a train or a car, the intriguer or the 'king's messenger on horseback', the murderer or the rescuer, reaches the goal first, using the then revolutionary technique of continuously changing pictures, flashing and vanishing like lightning, became the pattern of the dénouement since followed by most films in similar situations.

The time experience of the present age consists above all in an awareness of the moment in which we find ourselves: in an awareness of the present. Everything topical, contemporary, bound together in the present moment is of special significance and value to the man of today, and, filled with this idea, the mere fact of simultaneity acquires new meaning in his eyes. His intellectual world is imbued with the atmosphere of the immediate present, just as that of the Middle Ages was characterized by an other-worldly atmosphere and that of the enlightenment by a mood of forward-looking expectancy. He experiences the greatness of his cities, the miracles of his technics, the wealth of his ideas, the hidden depths of his psychology in the contiguity, the interconnections and dovetailing of things and processes. The fascination of 'simultaneity', the discovery that, on the one hand, the same man experiences so many different, unconnected and irreconcilable things in one and the same moment, and that, on the other, different men in different places often experience the same things, that the same things are happening at the same time in places completely isolated from each other, this universalism, of which modern technics have made contemporary man conscious, is perhaps the real source of the new conception of time and of the whole abruptness with which modern art describes life. This rhapsodic quality, which distinguishes the modern novel most sharply from the older novel, is at the same time the characteristic accountable for its most cinematic effects. The discontinuity of the plot and the scenic development, the sudden emersion of the thoughts and moods, the relativity and the inconsistency of the time-standards, are what remind us in the works of Proust and Joyce, Dos Passos and Virginia Woolf of the cuttings, dissolves and interpolations of the film, and it is simply film magic when Proust brings two incidents, which may lie thirty years apart, as closely together as if there were only two hours between them. The way in which, in Proust, past and present, dreams and speculation join hands across the intervals of space and time, the sensibility, always on the scent of new tracks, roams about in space and time, and the boundaries of space and time vanish in this endless and boundless stream of interrelations: all this corresponds exactly to that mixture of space and time in which the film moves. Proust never mentions dates and ages; we never know exactly how old the hero of his novel is, and even the chronological relationships of the events often remain rather vague. The experiences and happenings do not cohere by reason of their proximity in time and the attempt to demarcate and arrange them chronologically would be all the more nonsensical from his point of view as, in his opinion, every man has his typical experiences which recur periodically. The boy, the youth and the man always experience fundamentally the same things; the meaning of an incident often does not dawn on him until years after he has experienced and endured it; but he can hardly ever distinguish the deposit of the years that are past from the experience of the present hour in which he is living. Is one not in every moment of one's life the same child or the same invalid or the same lonely stranger with the same wakeful, sensitive, unappeased nerves? Is one not in every situation of life the person capable of experiencing this and that, who possesses, in the recurring features of his experience, the one protection against the passage of time? Do not all our experiences take place as it were at the same time? And is this simultaneity not really the negation of time? And this negation, is it not a struggle for the recovery of that inwardness of which physical space and time deprive us?

Joyce fights for the same inwardness, the same directness of experience, when he, like Proust, breaks up and merges well-articulated, chronologically organized time. In his work, too, it is the interchangeability of the contents of consciousness which triumphs over the chronological arrangement of the experiences, for him, too, time is a road without direction, on which man moves to and fro. But he pushes the spatialization of time even further than Proust, and shows the inner happenings not only in longitudinal but also in cross-sections. The images, ideas, brain-waves and memories stand side by side with sudden and absolute abruptness; hardly any consideration is paid to their origins, all the emphasis is on their contiguity, their simultaneity. The spatialization of time goes so far in Joyce, that one can begin the reading of *Ulysses* where one likes, with only a rough knowledge of the context—not necessarily only after a first reading, as has been said, and almost in any sequence one cares to choose. The medium in which the reader finds himself, is in fact wholly spatial, for the novel describes not only the picture of a great city, but also adopts its structure to some extent, the network of its streets and squares, in which people stroll about, walking in and out and stopping when and where they like. It is supremely characteristic of the cinematic quality of this technique that Joyce wrote his novel not in the final succession of the chapters, but—as is the custom in the production of films—made himself independent of the sequence of the plot and worked at several chapters at the same time.

We meet the Bergsonian conception of time, as used in the film and the modern novel—though not always so unmistakably as here—in all the genres and trends of contemporary art. The 'simultanéité des états d'âmes' is, above all, the basic experience connecting the various tendencies of modern painting, the futurism of the Italians with the expressionism of Chagall, and the cubism of Picasso with the surrealism of Giorgio de Chirico or Salvador Dali. Bergson discovered the counterpoint of spiritual processes and the musical structure of their interrelationships. Just as, when we listen properly to a piece of music, we have in our ears the mutual connection of each new note with all those that have already sounded, so we always possess in our deepest and most vital experiences everything that we have ever experienced and made our own in life. If we understand ourselves, we read our own souls as a musical score, we resolve the chaos of the entangled sounds and transform them into a polyphony of different parts.—All art is a game with and a fight against chaos; it is always advancing more and more dangerously towards chaos and rescuing more and more extensive provinces of the spirit from its clutch. If there is any progress in the history of art, then it consists in the constant growth of these provinces wrested from chaos. With its analysis of time, the film stands in the direct line of this development: it has made it possible to represent visually experiences that have previously been expressed only in musical forms. The artist capable of filling this new possibility, this still empty form, with real life has not yet arrived, however.

The crisis of the film, which seems to be developing into a chronic illness, is due above all to the fact that the film is not finding its writers or, to put it more accurately, the writers are not finding their way to the film. Accustomed to doing as they like within their own four walls, they are now required to take into account producers, directors, script-writers, cameramen, art-directors and technicians of all kinds, although they do not acknowledge the authority of this spirit of co-operation, or indeed the idea of artistic co-operation at all. Their feelings revolt against the idea of the production of works of art being surrendered to a collective, to a 'concern', and they feel that it is a disparagement of art that an extraneous dictate, or at best a majority, should have the last word in decisions of the motives of which they are often unable to account for themselves. From the point of view of the nineteenth century, the situation with which the writer is asked to come to terms is quite unusual and unnatural. The atomized and uncontrolled artistic endeavours of the present now meet for the first time with a principle opposed to their anarchy. For the mere fact of an artistic enterprise based on co-operation is evidence of an integrating tendency of which—if one disregards the theatre, where it is in any case more a matter of the reproduction than the production of works of art—there had really been no perfect example since the Middle Ages, and, in particular, since the masons' lodge. How far removed film production still is, however, from the generally accepted principle of an artistic co-operative group, is shown not only by the inability of most writers to establish a connection with the film, but also by such a phenomenon as Chaplin, who believes that he must do as much as possible in his films on his own: the acting of the main part, the direction, the script, the music. But even if it is only the beginning of a new method of organized art production, the, for the present, still empty framework of a new integration, nevertheless, here too, as in the whole economic, social and political life of the present age, what is being striven for is the comprehensive planning without which both our cultural and material world threaten to go to pieces. We are confronted here with the same tension as we find throughout our social life: democracy and dictatorship, specialization and integration, rationalism and irrationalism, colliding with each other. But if even in the field of economics and politics planning cannot always be solved by imposing rules of conduct, it is all the less possible in art, where all violation of spontaneity, all forcible levelling down of taste, all institutional regulation of personal initiative, are involved in great though certainly not such mortal dangers as is often imagined.

But how, in an age of the most extreme specialization and the most sophisticated individualism, are harmony and an integration of individual endeavours to be brought about? How, to speak on a practical level, is the situation to be brought to an end in which the most poverty-stricken literary inventions sometimes underlie the technically most successful films? It is not a question of competent directors against incompetent writers, but of two phenomena belonging to different periods of time—the lonely, isolated writer dependent on his own resources and the problems of the film which can only be solved collectively. The co-operative film-unit anticipates a social technique to which we are not yet equal, just as the newly invented camera anticipated an artistic technique of which no one at the time really knew the range and power. The reunion of the divided functions, first of all the personal union of the director and the author, which has been suggested as a way to surmount the crisis, would be more an evasion of the problem than its solution, for it would prevent but not abolish the specialization that has to be overcome, would not bring about but merely avoid the necessity of the planning which is needed. Incidentally, the monistic-individual principle in the discharge of the various functions, in place of a collectively organized division of labour, corresponds not merely externally and technically to an amateurish method of working, but it also involves a lack of inner tension which is reminiscent of the simplicity of the amateur film. Or may the whole effort to achieve a production of art based on planning only have been a temporary disturbance, a mere episode, which is now being swept away again by the torrent of individualism? May the film be perhaps not the beginning of a new artistic era, but merely the somewhat hesitant continuation of the old individualistic culture, still full of vitality, to which we owe the whole of post-medieval art?—Only if this were so, would it be possible to solve the film crisis by the personal union of certain functions, that is, by partly surrendering the principle of collective labour.

The film crisis is, however, also connected with a crisis in the public itself. The millions and millions who fill the many thousands of cinemas all over the world from Hollywood to Shanghai and from Stockholm to Cape Town daily and hourly, this unique world-embracing league of mankind, have a very confused social structure. The only link between these people is that they all stream into the cinemas, and stream out of them again as amorphously as they are pumped in; they remain a heterogeneous, inarticulate, shapeless mass with the only common feature of belonging to no uniform class or culture. This mass of cinema-goers can hardly be called a 'public' proper, for only a more or less constant group of patrons can be described as such, one which is able to some extent to guarantee the continuity of production in a certain field of art. Public-like agglomerations are based on mutual understanding; even if opinions are divided, they diverge on one and the same plane. But with the masses who sit together in the cinemas and who have undergone no previous common intellectual formation of any kind, it would be futile to look for such a platform of mutual understanding. If they dislike a film there is such a small chance of agreement amongst them as to the reasons for their rejection of the film that one must assume that even general approval is based on a misunderstanding.

The homogeneous and constant public units which, as mediators between the art producers and the social strata with no real interest in art, had always discharged a fundamentally conserving function were, as we know, dissolved with the advancing democratization of the enjoyment of art. The bourgeois subscription audiences of the state and municipal theatres of the last century still formed a more or less uniform, organically developed body, but with the end of the repertory theatre even the last remains of this public were scattered and since then an integrated audience has come into being only in particular circumstances, though in some cases the size of such audiences has been bigger than ever before. It was on the whole identical with the casual cinema-going public which has to be caught by new and original attractions every time and over and over again. The repertory theatre, the serial performance theatre and the cinema mark the successive stages in the democratization of art and the gradual loss of the festive character that was formerly more or less the property of every form of theatre. The cinema takes the final step on this road of profanation, for even to attend the modern metropolitan theatre showing some popular play or other still demands a certain internal and external preparation—in most cases seats have to be booked in advance, one has to keep to a fixed time and to prepare for an occupation that will fill the whole evening—whereas one attends the cinema *en passant*, in one's everyday clothes and at any time during the continuous performance. The everyday point of view of the film is in perfect accordance with the improvisation and unpretentiousness of cinema-going.

The film signifies the first attempt since the beginning of our modern individualistic civilization to produce art for a mass public. As is known, the changes in the structure of the theatre and reading public, connected at the beginning of the last century with the rise of the boulevard play and the feuilleton novel, formed the real beginning of the democratization of art which reaches its culmination in mass attendance of cinemas. The transition from the private theatre of the princes' courts to the bourgeois state and municipal theatre and then to the theatre trusts, or from the opera to the operetta and then to the revue, marked the separate phases of a development characterized by the effort to capture ever wider circles of consumers, in order to cover the costs of the growing investments. The outfit for an operetta could still be sustained by a medium-sized theatre, that of a revue or a large ballet had already to travel from one big city to the next; in order to amortise the invested capital, the cinema-goers of the whole world have to contribute to the financing of a big film. But it is this fact that determines the influence of the masses on the production of art. By their mere presence at theatrical performances in Athens or the Middle Ages they were never able to influence the ways of art directly, only since they have come on the scene as consumers and paid the full price for their enjoyment, have the terms on which they hand over their shillings become a decisive factor in the history of art.

There has always been an element of tension between the quality and the popularity of art, which is not by any means to say that the broad masses of the people have at any time taken a stand against qualitatively good art in favour of inferior art on principle. Naturally, the appreciation of a more complicated art presents them with greater difficulties than the more simple and less developed, but the lack of adequate understanding does not necessarily prevent them from accepting this art—albeit not exactly on account of its aesthetic quality. Success with them is completely divorced from qualitative criteria. They do not react to what is artistically good or bad, but to impressions by which they feel themselves reassured or alarmed in their own sphere of existence. They take an interest in the artistically valuable, provided it is presented so as to suit their mentality, that is, provided the subject-matter is attractive. The chances of success of a good film are from this point of view better from the very outset than those of a good painting or poem. For, apart from the film, progressive art is almost a closed book today for the uninitiated; it is intrinsically unpopular, because its means of communication have become transformed in the course of a long and self-contained development into a kind of secret code, whereas to learn the newly developing idiom of the film was child's play for even the most primitive cinema public. From this happy constellation one would be inclined to draw far-reaching optimistic conclusions for the future of the film, if one did not know that that kind of intellectual concord is nothing more than the state of a paradisian childhood, and is probably repeated as often as new arts arise. Perhaps all the cinematic means of expression will no longer be intelligible even to the next generation, and certainly the cleft will sooner or later arise that even in this field separates the layman from the connoisseur. Only a young art can be popular, for as soon as it grows older it is necessary, in order to understand it, to be acquainted with the earlier stages in its development. To understand an art means to realize the necessary connection between its formal and material elements; as long as an art is young, there is a natural, unproblematical relation between its content and its means of expression, that is to say, there is a direct path leading from its subject-matter to its forms. In the course of time these forms become independent of the thematic material, they become autonomous, poorer in meaning, and harder to interpret, until they become accessible only to a quite small stratum of the public. In the film this process has hardly begun, and a great many cinema-goers still belong to the generation which saw the birth of the film and witnessed the full significance of its forms. But the process of estrangement already makes itself felt in the present-day director's forgoing of most of the so-called 'cinematic' means of expression. The once so popular effects produced by different camera-angles and manoeuvrings, changing distances and speeds, by the tricks of montage and printing, the close-ups and the panoramas, the cut-ins and the flash-backs, the fade-ins, fade-outs and dissolves, seem affected and unnatural today, because the directors and cameramen are concentrating their attention, under the pressure of a second, already less film-minded generation, on the clear, smooth and exciting narration of a story and believe they can learn more from the masters of the 'pièce bien faite' than from the masters of the silent film.

It is inconceivable that, in the present stage of cultural development, an art could begin all over again, even though, like the film, it has completely new means at its disposal. Even the simplest plot has a history and bears within it certain epic and dramatic formulae of the older periods of literature. The film, whose public is on the average level of the petty bourgeois, borrows these formulae from the light fiction of the upper middle class and entertains the cinema-goers of today with the dramatic effects of yesterday. Film production owes its greatest successes to the realization that the mind of the petty bourgeois is the psychological meeting place of the masses. The psychological category of this human type has, however, a wider range than the sociological category of the actual middle class; it embraces fragments of both the upper and the lower classes, that is to say, the very considerable elements who, where they are not engaged in a direct struggle for their existence, join forces unreservedly with the middle classes, above all in the matter of entertainment. The mass public of the film is the product of this equalizing process, and if the film is to be profitable, it has to base itself on that class from which the intellectual levelling proceeds. The middle class, especially since the 'new middle class', with its army of 'employees', minor civil servants and private officials, commercial travellers and shop-assistants, has come into being, has hovered 'between the classes' and has always been used to bridge the gaps between them.[26] It has always felt menaced from above and below, but has preferred to give up its real interests rather than its hopes and alleged prospects. It has wanted to be reckoned as part of the bourgeois upper class, although in reality it shared the lot of the lower class. But without a clear-cut and clarified social position no coherent consciousness and consistent outlook on life is possible, and the film producer has been able to rely quite safely on the disorientation of these rootless elements of society. The petty bourgeois attitude to life is typified by a thoughtless, uncritical optimism. It believes in the ultimate unimportance of social differences and, accordingly, wants to see films in which people simply walk out of one social stratum into another. For this middle class the cinema gives the fulfilment to the social romanticism which life never realizes and the lending libraries never realize so deceptively as the film with its illusionism. 'Everyone is the architect of his own fortune', that is its supreme belief and climbing the basic motif of the wish-fantasies which entice it into the cinema. Will Hays, the one-time 'film czar', was well aware of that when he included in his directions for the American film industry the instruction, 'to show the life of the upper classes'.

The development of moving photography to the film as an art was dependent on two achievements: the invention of the close-up—attributed to the American director D. W. Griffith—and a new method of interpolation, discovered by the Russians, the so-called short cutting. The Russians did not, however, invent the frequent interruption of the continuity of a scene, the Americans had long had this means of producting excited atmospheres or dramatic accelerations at their disposal; but the new factor in the Russian method was the restriction of the flashes to close-ups—forgoing the insertion of informative long-shots—and the shortening, pushed to the limits of perceptibility, of the individual shots. The Russians thereby succeeded in finding an expressionistic film style for the description of certain agitated moods, nervous rhythms and tearing speeds, which made possible quite new effects, unattainable in any other art. The revolutionary quality of this montage technique consisted, however, less in the shortness of the cutting, in the speed and rhythm of the change of shots and in the extension of the boundaries of the cinematically feasible, than in the fact that it was no longer the phenomena of a homogeneous world of objects, but of quite heterogeneous elements of reality, that were brought face to face. Thus Eisenstein showed the following sequence in *The Battleship Potemkin*: men working desperately, engine-room of the cruiser; busy hands, revolving wheels; faces distorted with exertion, maximum pressure of the manometer; a chest soaked with perspiration, a glowing boiler; an arm, a wheel; a wheel, an arm; machine, man; machine, man; machine, man. Two utterly different realities, a spiritual and a material, were joined together here, and not only joined but identified, in fact, the one proceeding from the other. But such a conscious and deliberate trespassing presupposed a philosophy which denies the autonomy of the individual spheres of life, as surrealism does, and as historical materialism has done from the very beginning.

That it is not simply a question of analogies but of equations, and that the confrontation of the different spheres is not merely metaphorical, becomes even more obvious when the montage no longer shows two interconnected phenomena but only one and, instead of the one to be expected from the context, a substituted one. Thus, in the *End of St. Petersburg*, Pudovkin shows a trembling crystal chandelier for the shattered power of the bourgeoisie; a steep, endless staircase on which a small human figure is laboriously climbing up for the official hierarchy, its thousands of intermediary stages and its unattainable summit. In Eisenstein's *October*, the twilight of the Czars is represented by dark equestrian statues on leaning pedestals, quivering statues of the Buddha used as knick-knacks and shattered negro idols. In the *Strike*, executions are replaced by slaughter-house scenes. Throughout things take the place of ideas; things which expose the ideological character of ideas. A social-historical situation has hardly ever found a more direct expression in art than the crisis of capitalism and the Marxist philosophy of history in this montage technique. A tunic covered with decorations but without a head signifies the automatism of the war machine in these

Russian films; new, strong soldiers' boots, the blind brutality of military power. Thus, in *Potemkin*, we see again and again only these heavy, indestructible and merciless boots, instead of the steadily advancing Cossacks. Good boots are the precondition of military power, that is the meaning of this 'pars pro toto'-montage, just as the meaning of the earlier example from *Potemkin* was that the victorious masses are nothing but the personification of the triumphant machine. Man, with his ideas, faith, and hope is merely a function of the material world in which he lives; the doctrine of historical materialism becomes the formal principle of the art of the Russian film. One must not forget, however, how far the film's whole method of presentation, especially its technique of the close-up, which favours the description of the material requisites from the outset and is calculated to give them an important motivating rôle, comes to meet this materialism half-way. On the other hand, the question whether the whole of this technique, in which the properties are put in the foreground, is not itself already a product of materialism cannot simply be dismissed. For the fact that the film is the creation of the historical epoch which has witnessed the exposure of the ideological basis of human thought is no more pure coincidence than the fact that the Russians have been the first classical exponents of this art.

Film directors throughout the world, irrespective of national and ideological divergences, have adopted the stock forms of the Russian film and thereby confirmed that as soon as the content has been translated into form, form can be taken over and used as a purely technical expedient, without the ideological background from which it has emerged. The paradox of historicity and timelessness in art, to which Marx refers in his *Introduction to the Critique of Political Economy*, is rooted in this capacity of form to become autonomous: 'Is Achilles conceivable in an era of powder and lead?' he asks. 'Or for that matter the *Iliad* at all in these days of printing-press and press-jacks? Do not song and legend and muse necessarily lose their meaning in the age of the Press? But the difficulty is not that Greek art and epic are connected with certain forms of social development, but rather that they still give us aesthetic satisfaction today, that in a sense they act as a norm, as an unattainable paragon.'—The works of Eisenstein and Pudovkin are in some respects the heroic epics of the cinema; the fact that they are regarded as models, independent of the social conditions which made their realization possible, is no more surprising than the fact that Homer still gives us supreme artistic satisfaction.

The film is the only art in which Soviet Russia has important achievements to its credit. The affinity between the young communist state and the new form of expression is obvious. Both are revolutionary phenomena moving along new paths, without a historical past, without binding and crippling traditions, without presuppositions of a cultural or routine nature of any kind. The film is an elastic, extremely malleable, unexhausted form which offers no inner resistance to the expression of the new ideas. It is an unsophisticated, popular means of communication, making a direct appeal to the broad masses, an ideal instrument of propaganda the value of which was immediately recognized by Lenin. Its attraction as an irreproachable, that is to say, historically uncompromised, entertainment was so great from the point of view of communist cultural policy from the very outset, its picture-book-like style so easy to grasp, the possibility of using it to propagate ideas to the uneducated so simple, that it seemed to have been specially created for the purposes of a revolutionary art. The film is, moreover, an art evolved from the spiritual foundations of technics and, therefore, all the more in accordance with the problems in store for it. The machine is its origin, its medium and its most suitable subject. Films are 'fabricated' and they remain tied to an apparatus, to a machine in a narrower sense than the products of the other arts. The machine here stands both between the creative subject and his work and between the receptive subject and his enjoyment of art. The motory, the mechanical, the automatically moving, is the basic phenomenon of the film. Running and racing, travelling and flying, escape and pursuit, the overcoming of spatial obstacles is the cinematic theme par excellence. The film never feels so much in its element as when it has to describe movement, speed and pace. The wonders and mischievous tricks of instruments, automata and vehicles are among its oldest and most effective subjects. The old film comedies expressed sometimes naïve admiration, at others arrogant contempt for technics, but they were in most cases the self-teasing of man caught in the wheels of a mechanized world. The film is above all a 'photograph' and is already as such a technical art, with mechanical origins and aiming at mechanical repetition,[27] in other words, thanks to the cheapness of its reproduction, a popular and fundamentally 'democratic' art. It is perfectly comprehensible that it suited bolshevism with its romanticism of the machine, its fetishism of technics and its admiration for efficiency. Just as it is also comprehensible that the Russians and the Americans, as the two most technically-minded peoples, were partners and rivals in the development of this art. The film was, however, not only in accord with their technicism, but also with their interest in the documentary, the factual and the authentic. All the more important works of Russian film art are to some extent documentary films, historical documents of the building up of the new Russia, and the best we owe to the American film consists in the documentary reproduction of American life, of the everyday routine of the American economic and administrative machine, of the skyscraper cities and the Middle West farms, the American police and the gangster world. For a film is the more cinematic, the greater the share extra-human, material facts have in its description of reality, in other words, the closer the connection in this description between man and the world, the personality and the milieu, the end and the means.

This tendency to the factual and the authentic—to the 'document'—is evidence not only of the intensified hunger for reality characteristic of the present age, of its desire to be well informed about the world, with an activistic ulterior motive, but also of that refusal to accept the artistic aims of the last century which is expressed in the flight from the story and from the individual, psychologically differentiated hero. This tendency, which is tied up, in the documentary film, with an escape from the professional actor, again signifies not only the desire that is always recurring in the history of art, to show the plain reality, the unvarnished truth, unadulterated facts, that is, life 'as it really is', but very often a renunciation of art altogether. In our age the prestige of the aesthetic is being undermined in many ways. The documentary film, photography, newspaper reports, the reportage novel, are no longer art in the old sense at all. Moreover, the most intelligent and the most gifted representatives of these genres do not in any way insist that their products should be described as 'works of art'; they rather take the view that art has always been a by-product and arose in the service of an ideologically conditioned purpose.

In Soviet Russia it is regarded wholly as a means to an end. This utilitarianism is, of course, conditioned above all by the need to place all available means in the service of communist reconstruction and to exterminate the aestheticism of bourgeois culture which, with its 'l'art pour l'art', its contemplative and quietistic attitude to life, implies the greatest possible danger for the social revolution. It is the awareness of this danger that makes it impossible for the architects of communist cultural policy to do justice to the artistic developments of the last hundred years and it is the denial of this development which makes their views on art seem so old-fashioned. They would prefer to put back the historical standing of art to the level of the July monarchy, and it is not only in the novel that they have in mind the realism of the middle of the last century, in the other arts, particularly in painting, they encourage the same tendency. In a system of universal planning and in the midst of a struggle for mere existence, art cannot be left to work out its own salvation. But regimentation of art is not without risks even from the point of view of the immediate aim; in the process it must also lose much of its value as an instrument of propaganda.

It is certainly correct that art has produced many of its greatest creations under compulsion and dictation, and that it had to conform to the wishes of a ruthless despotism in the Ancient Orient and to the demands of a rigid authoritarian culture in the Middle Ages. But even compulsion and censorship have a different meaning and effect in the different periods of history. The main difference between the situation today and that of former ages is that we find ourselves at a point in time after the French Revolution and nineteenth-century liberalism and that every idea that we think, every impulse that we feel, is permeated by this liberalism. One might well argue that Christianity also had to destroy a very advanced and comparatively liberal civilization and that medieval art sprang from very modest beginnings; one must not forget, however, that early Christian art did in fact make an almost completely fresh start, whereas Soviet Russian art starts out from a style which was historically already highly developed, although it is much behind the times today. But even if one were willing to assume that the sacrifices demanded are the price of a new 'Gothic', there is no kind of guarantee that this 'Gothic' would not again become, as in the Middle Ages, the exclusive possession of a comparatively small cultured élite.

The problem is not to confine art to the present-day horizon of the broad masses, but to extend the horizon of the masses as much as possible. The way to a genuine appreciation of art is through education. Not the violent simplification of art, but the training of the capacity for aesthetic judgement is the means by which the constant monopolizing of art by a small minority can be prevented. Here too, as in the whole field of cultural policy, the great difficulty is that every arbitrary interruption of the development evades the real problem, that is, creates a situation in which the problem does not arise, and therefore merely postpones the task of finding a solution. There is today hardly any practicable way leading to a primitive and yet valuable art. Genuine, progressive, creative art can only mean a complicated art today. It will never be possible for everyone to enjoy and appreciate it in equal measure, but the share of the broader masses in it can be increased and deepened. The preconditions of a slackening of the cultural monopoly are above all economic and social. We can do no other than fight for the creation of these preconditions.

NOTES

VI. ROCOCO, CLASSICISM AND ROMANTICISM

1. Paul Hazard: *La Crise de la conscience européenne*, 1935, I, pp. i–v.
2. Cf. Bédier-Hazard: *Hist. de la litt. franç.*, II, 1924, pp. 31–2.
3. Germain Martin: *La Grande industrie en France sous le règne de Louis XV*, 1900, p. 15.
4. F. Funck-Brentano: *L'Ancien régime*, 1926, pp. 299–300.
5. Alexis de Tocqueville: *L'Ancien régime et la Révolution*, 1859, 4th edit., p. 171.
6. Henri Sée: *La France écon. et soc. au 18e siècle*, 1933, p. 83.
7. Albert Mathiez: *La Révolution franç.*, I, 1922, p. 8.
8. Karl Kautsky: *Die Klassengegensaetze im Zeitalter der franz. Rev.*, 1923, p. 14.
9. Franz Schnabel: 'Das XVIII. Jahrh. in Europa'. In *Propylaeen Weltgesch.*, VI, 1931, p. 277.
10. Joseph Aynard: *La Bourgeoisie française*, 1934, p. 462.
11. F. Strowski: *La Sagesse française*, 1925, p. 20.
12. J. Aynard, op. cit., p. 350.
13. Ibid., p. 422.
14. André Fontaine: *Les Doctrines d'art en France*, 1909, p. 170.
15. Pierre Marcel: *La Peinture franç. au début du 18e siècle*, 1906, pp. 25–6.
16. Louis Réau: *Hist. de la peint. franç. au 18e siècle*, I, 1925, p. x.
17. Louis Hourticq: *La Peinture franç. au 18e siècle*, 1939, p. 15.
18. Wilhelm v. Christ: 'Gesch. d. griech. Lit.' In I. v. Mueller's *Handbuch d. klass. Altertumswiss.*, VII 2/1, 1920, p. 183.
19. Francesco Macrì-Leone: *La bucolica latina nella lett. ital. del sec. XIV*, 1889, p. 15.—Walter W. Greg: *Pastoral Poetry and Pastoral Drama*, 1906, pp. 13–14.
20. T. R. Glover: *Virgil*, 1942, 7th edit., pp. 3–4.
21. M. Schanz-C. Hosius: 'Gesch. d. roem. Lit.' In I. v. Mueller's *Handbuch d. klass. Altertumswiss.*, II, 1935, p. 285.
22. W. W. Greg, op. cit., p. 66.
23. J. Huizinga: *The Waning of the Middle Ages*, 1924, p. 120.
24. M. Fauriel: *Hist. de la poésie provençale*, 1846, II, pp. 91–2.
25. Mussia Eisenstadt: *Watteau's Fêtes galantes*, 1930, p. 98.
26. G. Lanson: *Hist. de la litt. franç.*, 1909, 11th edit., pp. 373–4.

27. Cf. Albert Dresdner: 'Von Giorgione zum Rokoko'. *Preussische Jahrbuecher*, 1910, vol. 140.—Werner Weisbach: 'Et in Arcadia ego'. *Die Antike*, VI, 1930, p. 140.

28. Boileau: *L'Art poétique*, III, vv. 119 ff.

29. P. Marcel, op. cit., p. 299.

30. Nikolaus Pevsner: *Academies of Art*, 1940, p. 108.

31. G. Lanson, op. cit., p. 374.

32. Cf. Petit de Julleville: *Hist. de la litt. franç.*, IV, 1897, p. 419.

33. Ibid., IV, p. 459; V, 1898, p. 550.

34. Émile Faguet: *Dixhuitième siècle*, 1890, p. 123.

35. Arthur Eloesser: *Das buergerliche Drama*, 1898, p. 65.

36. Diderot: *Oeuvres*, 1821, VIII, p. 243.

37. Paul Mantoux: *La Révolution industrielle au 18e siècle*, 1906, p. 78.

38. *The English Revolution, 1640*. Three essays, edited by Christopher Hill, 1940, p. 9.

39. R. H. Gretton: *The English Middle Class*, 1917, p. 209.

40. W. Warde Fowler: *Social Life at Rome in the Age of Cicero*, 1922, pp. 26 ff.—J. L. and B. Hammond: *The Village Labourer* (1760–1832), 1920, pp. 306–7.

41. A. de Tocqueville, op. cit., p. 146.—J. Aynard, op. cit., p. 341.

42. G. Lefèbvre, G. Guyot, Ph. Sagnac: *La Révolution française*, 1930, p. 21.

43. A. de Tocqueville, op. cit., pp. 174–5.

44. Herbert Schoeffler: *Protestantismus und Literatur*, 1922, p. 181.

45. Alexandre Beljame: *Le Public et les hommes de lettres en Angleterre au 18e siècle*, 1881, p. 122.

46. H. Schoeffler, op. cit., pp. 187–8.

47. Ibid., p. 192.

48. Ibid., pp. 59, 151 ff. and passim.

49. A. S. Collins: *The Profession of Letters*, 1928, p. 38.

50. G. M. Trevelyan: *English Social History*, 1944, p. 338.

51. A. Beljame, op. cit., pp. 236, 350.

52. Leslie Stephen: *Engl. Lit. and Soc. in the 18th Cent.*, 1940, p. 42.

53. A. Beljame, op. cit., pp. 229–32.

54. Ibid., p. 368.

55. A. S. Collins: *Authorship in the Days of Johnson*, 1927, p. 161.

56. Levin L. Schuecking: *The Sociology of Literary Taste*, 1944, p. 14.

57. A. S. Collins: *Authorship*, etc., pp. 269–70.

58. Leslie Stephen, op. cit., p. 148.—George Sampson: *The Concise Cambridge Hist. of Lit.*, 1942, p. 508.

59. Quoted by F. Gaiffe: *Le Drame en France au 18e siècle*, 1910, p. 80.

60. L. L. Schuecking, op. cit., pp. 62 ff.

61. J. L. and B. Hammond: *The Rise of Modern Industry*, 1944, 6th edit., p. 39.

62. J. L. and B. HAMMOND: *The Town Labourer* (1760–1832), 1925, pp. 37 ff.

63. PAUL MANTOUX, op. cit., pp. 376 ff.—JOHN A. HOBSON: *The Evolution of Modern Capitalism*, 1930, p. 62.

64. WERNER SOMBART: *Der moderne Kapitalismus*, II/1, 1924, 6th edit. —Cf. OTTO HINTZE: 'Der mod. Kapitalismus als hist. Individuum'. *Hist. Zschr.*, 1929, vol. 139, p. 478.

65. Cf. LEWIS MUMFORD: *Technics and Civil.*, 1934, pp. 176–7.

66. ARNOLD TOYNBEE: *Lectures on the Industrial Revolution of the 18th Cent. in Engl.*, 1908, p. 64.

67. LEO BALET-E. GERHARD: *Die Verbuergerlichung der deutschen Kunst, Lit. u. Musik im 18. Jahrh.*, 1936, pp. 116–17.

68. DANIEL MORNET: *La Nouvelle Héloïse de J.-J. Rousseau*, 1943, pp. 43–4.

69. OSWALD SPENGLER: *Der Untergang des Abendlandes*, I, 1918, pp. 362–3.

70. GEOFFREY WEBB: 'Architecture and Garden'. In *Johnson's England*, edited by A. S. Turberville, 1933, p. 118.

71. W. L. PHELPS: *The Beginnings of the English Romantic Movement*, 1893, pp. 110–11.

72. Cf. JOSEPH TEXTE: *J.-J. Rousseau and the Cosmopolitan Spirit in Lit.*, 1899, p. 152.

73. H. SCHOEFFLER, op. cit., p. 180.

74. W. L. CROSS: *The Development of the English Novel*, 1899, p. 38.— H. SCHOEFFLER, op. cit., p. 168.

75. Cf. Q. D. LEAVIS: *Fiction and the Reading Public*, 1932, p. 138.

76. W. L. CROSS, op. cit., p. 33.

77. DIDEROT: 'De la poésie dramat.' In *Oeuvres compl.*, edited J. Assézat, 1875–7, VII, p. 371.

78. Cf. IRVING BABBITT: *Rousseau and Romanticism*, 1919, pp. 75 ff.

79. Cf. JEAN LUC: *Diderot*, 1938, pp. 34–5.

80. J. S. PETRI: *Anleitung zur praktischen Musik.*, 1782, p. 104.—Quoted in HANS JOACHIM MOSER: *Gesch. d. deutschen Musik*, II/1, 1922, p. 309.

81. On the uniformity of theme and mood in a movement: HUGO RIEMANN: *Handb. d. Musikgesch.*, II/3, pp. 132–3.

82. On the antithesis of the 'sequential type' and the 'song type': WILHELM FISCHER: 'Zur Entwicklung des Wiener klass. Stils'. In *Beihefte der Denkmaeler der Tonkunst in Oesterreich*, III, 1915, pp. 29 ff.—On the antithesis of fugal and sonata form, cf. AUGUST HALM: *Von zwei Welten der Musik*, 1920.

83. H. J. MOSER, op. cit., pp. 314–15.

84. L. BALET-E. GERHARD, op. cit., p. 403.

85. H. J. MOSER, op. cit., p. 312.

86. GEORGE LILLO: *The London Merchant or the History of George Barnwell*, 1731, IV/2.

87. L. Stephen, op. cit., p. 66.

88. Mercier: *Du Théâtre ou Nouvel essai sur l'art dramatique*, 1773.—Quoted by F. Gaiffe, loc. cit., p. 91.

89. Clara Stockmeyer: *Soziale Probleme im Drama des Sturmes und Dranges*, 1922, p. 68.

90. Beaumarchais: *Essai sur le genre dramatique sérieux*, 1767.

91. Rousseau: *La Nouvelle Héloïse*, II, Lettre 17.

92. Diderot: 'Entretiens sur le Fils naturel'. *Oeuvres*, 1875–7, VII, p. 150.

93. Georg Lukács: 'Zur Soziologie des Dramas'. *Archiv f. Sozialwiss. u. Sozialpolit.*, 1914, vol. 38, pp. 330 f.

94. A. Eloesser, op. cit., p. 13.—Paul Ernst: *Ein Credo*, 1912, I, p. 102.

95. Cf. G. Lukács, loc. cit., p. 343.

96. A. Eloesser, op. cit., p. 215.

97. Fritz Brueggemann: 'Der Kampf um die buergerliche Welt- und Lebensanschauung i.d. deutschen Lit. d. 18. Jahrh.' *Deutsche Viertelsjahrsschr. f. Literaturwiss. u. Geistesgesch.*, III/1, 1925.

98. Karl Biedermann: *Deutschland im 18. Jahrh.*, 1880, 2nd edit., I, pp. 276 ff.

99. Werner Sombart: *Der Bourgeois*, 1913, pp. 183–4.

100. Jacques Bainville: *Hist. de deux peuples*, 1933, p. 35.

101. Cf. G. Barraclough: *Factors in German Hist.*, 1946, p. 68.

102. Count Mantaeuffel in a letter to the philosopher Wolf. Quoted by K. Biedermann, loc. cit., II/1, p. 140.

103. Ibid., p. 23.

104. Ibid., p. 134.

105. W. H. Bruford: *Germany in the 18th Cent.*, 1935, pp. 310–11.

106. Wilhelm Dilthey: *Leben Schleiermachers*, I, 1870, pp. 183 ff.—The same, *Das Erlebnis und die Dichtung*, 1910, p. 29.

107. Ibid., p. 30.

108. Johann Goldfriedrich: *Gesch. des deutschen Buchhandels*, 1908–9, III, pp. 118 ff.

109. Cf. Georg Lukács: 'Fortschritt u. Reaktion i.d. deutschen Lit.' *Internationale Literatur*, 1945, XV, No. 8/9, p. 89.

110. Franz Mehring: *Die Lessing-Legende*, 1893, p. 371.

111. Cf. Karl Mannheim: 'Das konservative Denken'. *Archiv f. Sozialwiss. u. Sozialpolit.*, 1927, vol. 57, p. 91.

112. A. de Tocqueville, op. cit., pp. 247–8.—Cf. K. Mannheim, loc. cit.

113. Christian Friedr. Weiser: *Shaftesbury u. d. deutsche Geistesleben*, 1916, pp. ix, xii.

114. Cf. Rudolf Unger: *Hamann u. d. Aufklaerung*, 1925, 2nd edit., I, pp. 327–8.

115. Cf. B. Schweitzer: *Der bildende Kuenstler u. der Begriff des*

Kuenstlerischen in der Antike, 1925, p. 130.—ALFRED STANGE: 'Die Bedeutung des subjektivistischen Individualismus fuer die europaeische Kunst von 1750–1850.' *Deutsche Vierteljahrsschrift f. Literaturwiss. u. Geistesgesch.*, vol. IX, No. 1, p. 94.

116. L. BALET-E. GERHARD, op. cit., p. 228.

117. HAMANN'S *Leben u. Schriften von C. H. Gildemeister*, 1857–73, vol. V, p. 228.

118. K. MANNHEIM, loc. cit., p. 470.

119. FRIEDRICH MEUSEL: *Edmund Burke u. d. franz. Revol.*, 1913, pp. 127–8.

120. HANS WEIL: *Die Entstehung des deutschen Bildungsprinzips*, 1930, p. 75.

121. JULIUS PETERSEN: *Die Wesensbestimmung der deutschen Romantik*, 1926, p. 59.

122. H. A. KORFF: 'Die erste Generation der Goethezeit'. *Zeitschr. f. Deutschkunde*, 1928, vol. 42, p. 641.

123. VIKTOR HEHN: *Gedanken ueber Goethe*, 1887, p. 65.

124. Ibid., p. 74.

125. Ibid., p. 89.

126. HEINE: *Die romantische Schule*, I, 1833.

127. THOMAS MANN: *Goethe als Repraesentant des Buergertums*, 1932, p. 46.

128. Cf. ALFRED NOLLAU: *Das lit. Publikum des jungen Goethe*, 1935, p. 4.

129. GEORG KEFERSTEIN: *Buergertum und Buergerlichkeit bei Goethe*, 1933, pp. 90–1.

130. Ibid., pp. 174–5.

131. Cf. H. A. KORFF: *Geist der Goethezeit*, II, 1930, p. 353.—LUDWIG W. KAHN: *Social Ideals in German Lit.* (1770–1830), 1938, pp. 32–4.

132. Cf. FRITZ STRICH: *Goethe und die Weltliteratur*, 1946, p. 44.

133. As in WILHELM HAUSENSTEIN: *Der nackte Mensch*, 1913, p. 151, and F. ANTAL: 'Reflections on Classicism and Romanticism'. *The Burlington Magazine*, 1935, vol. 66, p. 161.

134. POPE: *Essay on Man*, I, v. 233 ff.

135. HEINRICH WOELFFLIN: *Kunstgeschtliche Grundbegriffe*, 1927, 7th edit., p. 252.—HANS ROSE: *Spaetbarock*, 1922, p. 13.

136. Cf. H. WOELFFLIN, op. cit., p. 35.

137. CARL JUSTI: *Winckelmann u. seine Zeitgenossen*, 1923, 3rd edit., III, p. 272.

138. MAURICE DREYFOUS: *Les Arts et les artistes pendant la période révolutionnaire*, 1906, p. 152.

139. ALBERT DRESDNER: *Die Entstehung der Kunstkritik*, 1915, pp. 229–30.

140. WALTER FRIEDLAENDER: *Hauptstroemungen der franz. Mal. von David bis Cézanne*, I, 1930, p. 8.

141. François Benoit: *L'Art franç. sous la Révol. et l'Empire*, 1897, p. 3.

142. Ibid., pp. 4–5.

143. Jules David: *Le Peintre David*, 1880, p. 117.

144. Edmond and Jules Goncourt: *Hist. de la société franç. pendant la Révol.*, 1880, p. 346.

145. Louis Madelin: *La Révolution*, 1911, pp. 490 ff.

146. George Plekhanov: *Art and Society*, 1937, p. 20.—Louis Hourticq: *La Peinture franç. au 18e siècle*, 1939, pp. 145 ff.—Albert Thibaudet: *Hist. de la litt. franç. de 1789 à nos jours.* (1936), p. 5.

147. Jules David, op. cit., p. 57.

148. Karl Marx: *Der 18. Brumaire des Louis Napoleon*, 1852.

149. Louis Hautecœur: 'Les Origines du Romantisme'. In *Le Romantisme et l'art*, 1928, p. 18.

150. Léon Rosenthal: *La Peinture romantique* (1903), pp. 25–6.

151. F. Benoit, op. cit., p. 171.

152. Louis Madelin: *La Contre-Révolution et la Révolution*, 1935, p. 329.

153. Ibid., pp. 162, 175.

154. Jules Renouvier: *Hist. de l'art pendant la Révol.*, 1863, p. 31.

155. Joseph Aynard: *La Bourgeoisie franç.*, 1934, p. 396.

156. Cf. Étienne Fajon: 'The Working Class in the Revolution of 1789'. In *Essays on the French Revolution*, edited by T. A. Jackson, 1945, p. 121.

157. Petit de Julleville, op. cit., VII, p. 110.

158. Henri Peyre: *Le Classicisme franç.*, 1942, p. 37.

159. A. Dresdner, op. cit., p. 128.

160. Ibid., pp. 128–9.

161. André Fontaine: *Les Doctrines d'art en France*, 1909, p. 186.—F. Benoit, op. cit., p. 133.

162. A. Dresdner, op. cit., p. 180.

163. Ibid., p. 150.

164. Joseph Billiet: 'The French Revol. and the Fine Arts'. In *Essays on the French Revolution*, edited by T. A. Jackson, 1945, p. 203.

165. F. Benoit, op. cit., p. 180.

166. M. Dreyfous, op. cit., p. 155.

167. F. Benoit, op. cit., p. 132.

168. Ibid., p. 134.

169. Quoted from F. L. Lucas: *The Decline and Fall of the Romantic Ideal*, 1937, p. 36.

170. Cf. on the concept of the 'epochal consciousness', Karl Jaspers: *Die geistige Situation der Zeit*, 1932, 3rd edit., pp. 7 ff.

171. G. Lanson, op. cit., p. 943.

172. Marcel Proust: *Pastiches et mélanges*, 1919, p. 267.

173. Joseph Aynard: 'Comment définir le romantisme?' *Revue de litt. comparée*, 1925, vol. V, p. 653.

174. F. BENOIT, op. cit., pp. 62–3.

175. Cf. ALBERT POETZSCH: *Studien zur fruehromant. Politik u. Geschichtsauffassung*, 1907, pp. 62–3.

176. ORTEGA Y GASSET: 'History as a System'. In *Philosophy and History*. Essays presented to Ernst Cassirer, edited by R. Klibansky and J. H. Paton, 1936, p. 313.

177. EMIL LASK: *Fichtes Idealismus u. die Geschichte*, 1902, pp. 56 ff., 83 ff.—Cf. ERICH ROTHACKER: *Einleitung i. d. Geisteswissenschaften*, 1920, pp. 116–18.

178. ARNOLD RUGE: *Die wahre Romantik. Ges. Schriften*, III, p. 134.—Quoted from CARL SCHMITT: *Politische Romantik*, 1925, 2nd edit., p. 35.

179. KONRAD LANGE: *Das Wesen der Kunst*, 1901.

180. COLERIDGE: *Biographia Literaria*, chap. XIV.

181. Cf. ALBERT SALOMON: 'Buergerlicher u. kapitalistischer Geist'. *Die Gesellschaft.*, 1927, IV, p. 552.

182. LOUIS MAIGRON: *Le Romantisme et les mœurs*, 1910, p. v.

183. Quoted from RICARDA HUCH: *Ausbreitung u. Verfall der Romantik*, 1908, 2nd edit., p. 349.

184. ERWIN KIRCHNER: *Die Philosophie der Romantik*, 1906, pp. 42–3.

185. DIDEROT: *Paradoxe sur le comédien.*

186. C. SCHMITT, op. cit., pp. 24 ff., 120 ff., pp. 148–9.

187. A. POETZSCH, op. cit., p. 17.

188. FRITZ STRICH: 'Die Romantik als europaeische Bewegung'. *Woelfflin-Festschrift*, 1924, p. 54.

189. GEORG BRANDES: *Hauptstroemungen der Lit. des 19. Jahrhunderts*, 1924, I, pp. 13 ff.

190. Cf. ERNST TROELTSCH: 'Die Restaurationsepoche am Anfang des 19. Jahrhunderts'. *Vortraege der Baltischen Lit. Ges.*, 1913, p. 49.

191. CHARLES-MARC DES GRANGES: *La Presse litt. sous la Restauration*, 1907, p. 44.

192. A. THIBAUDET, op. cit., p. 107.

193. PIERRE MOREAU: *Le Classicisme des romantiques*, 1932, p. 132.

194. HENRY A. BEERS: *A Hist. of Engl. Romanticism in the 19th Cent.*, 1902, p. 173.

195. A. THIBAUDET, op. cit., p. 121.

196. G. BRANDES, op. cit., III, p. 9.

197. Ibid., p. 225.

198. Ibid., II, p. 224.

199. GRIMROD DE LA REYNIÈRE in *Le Censeur dramatique*, I, 1797.

200. MAURICE ALBERT: *Les Théâtres des Boulevards* (1789–1848), 1902.

201. CH.-M. DES GRANGES: *La Comédie et les mœurs sous la Restauration et la Monarchie de Juillet*, 1904, pp. 35–41, 43–6, 53–4.

202. W. J. HARTOG: *Guilbert de Pixerécourt*, 1913, pp. 52–4.

203. PAUL GINISTY: *Le Mélodrame*, 1910, p. 14.

204. ALEXANDER LACEY: *Pixerécourt and the French Romantic Drama*, 1928, pp. 22–3.

205. ÉMILE FAGUET: *Propos de théâtre*, II, 1905, pp. 299 ff.

206. W. J. HARTOG, op. cit., p. 51.

207. Ibid.

208. PIXERÉCOURT: *Dernières réflexions sur le mélodrame*, 1843, quoted by HARTOG, op. cit., pp. 231–2.

209. FAGUET, loc. cit., p. 318.

210. ALFRED COBBAN: *Edmund Burke and the Revolt against the 18th Cent.*, 1929, pp. 208–9, 215.

211. C. DAY LEWIS: *The Poetic Image*, 1947, p. 54.

212. H. N. BRAILSFORD: *Shelley, Godwin and their Circle*, 1913, p. 226.

213. FRANCIS THOMPSON: *Shelley*, 1909, p. 41.

214. Cf. F. STRICH: *Die Romantik als europ. Bewegung*, p. 54.

215. H. Y. C. GRIERSON: *The Background of Engl. Lit.*, 1925, pp. 167–8.

216. JULIUS BAB: *Fortinbras oder der Kampf des 19. Jahrhunderts mit dem Geist der Romantik*, 1914, p. 38.

217. W. P. KER: *Collected Essays*, 1925, I, p. 164.

218. H. A. BEERS, op. cit., p. 2.

219. J. M. S. TOMPKINS: *The Popular Novel in England* (1770–1800), 1932, pp. 3–4.

220. LOUIS MAIGRON: *Le Roman historique à l'époque du romantisme*, 1898, p. 90.

221. GEORG LUKÁCS: 'Walter Scott and the Historical Novel'. *International Literature*, 1938, No. 12, p. 80.

222. *Ivanhoe*, chap. XLI.

223. LÉON ROSENTHAL, op. cit., pp. 205–6.

224. 'Le premier mérite d'un tableau est d'être une fête pour l'œil.'

225. DELACROIX: *Journal*, i.a. the entry of 26th April 1824.

226. Ibid., 14th February 1850.

227. L. ROSENTHAL, op. cit., pp. 202–3.

228. PAUL JAMOT: 'Delacroix'. In *Le Romantisme et l'art*, 1928, p. 116.

229. Ibid., p. 120.

230. Ibid., pp. 100–1.

231. ANDRÉ JOUBIN: *Journal de Delacroix*, 1932, I, pp. 284–5.

232. ALFRED EINSTEIN: *Music in the Romantic Era*, 1947, p. 39.

233. DELACROIX: *Journal*, passim, i.a. the entry of 30th January 1855.

VII. NATURALISM AND IMPRESSIONISM

1. HENRI GUILLEMIN: *Le Jocelyn de Lamartine* (1936), p. 59.

2. Cf. for the following JEAN-PAUL SARTRE: 'Qu'est-ce que la littérature?' *Les Temps Modernes*, 1947, II, pp. 971 ff.—Also in: *Situations*, II, 1948.

3. Ibid., p. 976.

4. Ibid., p. 981.

5. S. Charlety: 'La Monarchie de Juillet'. In E. Lavisse, *Hist. de France contemporaine*, V, 1921, pp. 178–9.

6. Werner Sombart: *Der moderne Kapitalismus*, III/1, pp. 35–8, 82, 657–61.

7. Werner Sombart: *Der Bourgeois*, 1913, p. 220.

8. Cf. Louis Blanc: *Histoire de dix ans*, III, 1843, pp. 90–2.—Werner Sombart: *Die deutsche Volkswirtschaft des 19. Jahrhunderts*, 7th edit., 1927, pp. 399 ff.

9. Emil Lederer: 'Zum sozialpsych. Habitus der Gegenwart'. *Archiv fuer Sozialwiss. u. Sozialpolit.*, 1918, vol. 46, pp. 122 ff.

10. Paul Louis: *Hist. du socialisme en France de la Révolution à nos jours*, 1936, 3rd edit., pp. 64, 97.—J. Lucas-Dubreton: *La Restauration et la Monarchie de Juillet*, 1937, pp. 160–1.

11. Paul Louis, op. cit., pp. 106–7.

12. Friedrich Engels: *Die Entwicklung des Sozialismus von der Utopie zur Wissenschaft*, 4th edit., 1891, p. 24.

13. Robert Michels: 'Psychologie der antikapitalistischen Massenbewegungen'. *Grundriss der Sozialoekon.*, IX/1, 1926, pp. 244–6, 270.

14. W. Sombart: *Die deutsche Volkswirtsch.*, p. 471.

15. Sainte-Beuve: 'De la littérature industrielle'. *Revue des Deux Mondes*, 1839. Also in: *Portraits contemporains*, 1847.

16. Jules Champfleury: *Souvenirs et portraits*, 1872, p. 77.

17. Eugène Gilbert: *Le Roman en France pendant le 19e siècle*, 1909, p. 209.

18. Nora Atkinson: *Eugène Sue et le roman-feuilleton*, 1929, p. 211.—Alfred Nettement: *Études critiques sur le feuilleton-roman*, 1845, I, p. 16.

19. Cf. Maurice Bardèche: *Stendhal romancier*, 1947.

20. André Breton: *Le Roman français au 19e siècle*, I, 1901, pp. 6–7, 73.—Maurice Bardèche: *Balzac romancier*, 1947, pp. 2–8, 12–13.

21. Ch.-M. Des Granges: *La Presse littéraire sous la Restoration*, 1907, p. 22.

22. H. J. Hunt: *Le Socialisme et le romantisme en France*, 1935, pp. 195, 340.

23. Ibid., pp. 203–4.—Albert Cassagne: *Le Théorie de l'art pour l'art en France*, 1906, pp. 61–71.

24. Cf. Edmond Estève: *Byron et le romantisme franç.*, 1907, p. 228.

25. Cf. Pierre Moreau: *Le Classicisme des romantiques*, 1932, pp. 242 ff.

26. Charles Rémusat's article of March 12 1825.—Quoted by A. Cassagne, op. cit., p. 37.

27. A. Cassagne, ibid.

28. José Ortega y Gasset: *La Deshumanización del Arte*, 1925, p. 19.

29. H. J. Hunt, op. cit., pp. 157–8.

30. Ibid., p. 174.

31. Georg Lukács: *Goethe und seine Zeit*, 1947, pp. 39–40.

32. M. BARDÈCHE: *Balzac romancier*, pp. 3, 7.
33. Quoted by JULES MARSAN: *Stendhal* (1932), p. 141.
34. M. BARDÈCHE: *Stendhal romancier*, p. 424.
35. ALBERT THIBAUDET: *Stendhal*, 1931.—HENRI MARTINEAU: *L'Œuvre de Stendhal*, 1945, p. 198.
36. Cf. JEAN MÉLIA: 'Stendhal et Taine'. *La Nouvelle Revue*, 1910, p. 392.
37. PIERRE MARTINEAU: *Stendhal*, 1934, p. 302.
38. H. MARTINEAU, op. cit., p. 470.
39. ÉMILE FAGUET: *Politiques et moralistes*, III, 1900, p. 8.
40. M. BARDÈCHE: *Stendhal romancier*, p. 47.
41. SAINTE-BEUVE: *Port-Royal*, 1888, 5th edit., VI, pp. 266–7.
42. ÉMILE ZOLA: *Les Romanciers naturalistes*, 1881, 2nd edit., p. 124.
43. Cf. PAUL BOURGET: *Essais de psychologie contemp.*, 1885, p. 282.
44. ANDRÉ DE BRETON: *Balzac*, 1905, pp. 70–3.
45. M. BARDÈCHE: *Balzac romancier*, p. 285.
46. BERNARD GUYON: *La Pensée politique et sociale de Balzac*, 1947, p. 432.
47. V. GRIB: *Balzac*. Critics Group Series, 5, 1937, p. 76.
48. MARIE BOR: *Balzac contre Balzac*, 1933, p. 38.
49. E. BUTTKE: *Balzac als Dichter des modernen Kapitalismus*, 1932, p. 28.
50. BALZAC: *Correspondance*, 1876, I, p. 433.
51. ERNEST SEILLIÈRE: *Balzac et la morale romantique*, 1922, p. 61.
52. ANDRÉ BELLESSORT: *Balzac et son œuvre*, 1924, p. 175.
53. KARL MARX and FREDERICK ENGELS: *Literature and Art*, 1947, pp. 42–3.—Also in *International Literature*, July, 1933, No. 3, p. 114.
54. MARCEL PROUST: *La Prisonnière*, I.
55. E. PRESTON: *Recherches sur la technique de Balzac*, 1926, pp. 5, 222.
56. THOMAS MANN: *Die Forderung des Tages*, 1930, pp. 273 ff.
57. HUGO VON HOFMANNSTHAL: *Unterhaltungen ueber literarische Gegenstaende* (1904), p. 40.
58. A. CERFBERR-J. CHRISTOPHE: *Répertoire de la Comédie humaine*, 1887.
59. TAINE: *Nouveaux essais de critique et d'histoire*, 1865, pp. 104–13.
60. Cf. TOCQUEVILLE'S speech in the National Assembly quoted by P. LOUIS, op. cit., II, p. 191.
61. Ibid., pp. 200–1.
62. Ibid., p. 197.
63. PIERRE MARTINO: *Le Roman réaliste sous le second Empire*, 1913, p. 85.
64. ALBERT THIBAUDET: *Hist. de la litt. franç. de 1789 à nos jours*, 1936, p. 361.
65. ÉMILE BOUVIER: *La Bataille réaliste*, 1913, p. 237.

66. JULES COULIN: *Die sozialistische Weltanschauung i. d. franz. Mal.* (1909), p. 61.

67. ÉMILE ZOLA: *La République et la litt.*, 1879.

68. OLIVER LARKIN: 'Courbet and his Contemporaries'. *Science and Society*, 1939, III/1, p. 44.

69. E. BOUVIER, op. cit., p. 248.

70. Cf. LÉON ROSENTHAL: *La Peinture romant.* (1903), pp. 267–8.—HENRI FOCILLON: *La Peinture aux XIXe et XXe siècles*, 1928, pp. 74–101.

71. H. J. HUNT, op. cit., pp. 342–4.

72. Vide i.a. the letter to Victor Hugo of 15th July 1853: FLAUBERT, *Correspondance*, edited by Conrad, 1910, III, p. 6.

73. Ibid., II, pp. 116–17, 366.

74. Ibid., III, pp. 120, 390.

75. E. and J. DE GONCOURT: *Journal.* The entry of 29th January 1863. Édit. Flammarion-Fasquelle, II, p. 67.

76. FLAUBERT: *Corresp.*, III, pp. 485, 490, 508.—*Éducation sentimentale*, II/3.—ERNEST SEILLIÈRE: *Le Romantisme des réalistes: Gustave Flaubert*, 1914, p. 257.—EUGEN HAAS: *Flaubert und die Politik*, 1931, p. 30.

77. Letter to Mlle Leroyer de Chantepie of 18th May 1857. *Corresp.*, III, p. 119.

78. E. GILBERT, op. cit., p. 157.

79. *Corresp.*, III, pp. 157, 448, etc.

80. *Le Moniteur*, 4th May 1857.—*Causeries de Lundi*, XIII.

81. ÉMILE ZOLA: *Les Romanciers naturalistes*, 1881, 2nd edit., pp. 126–9.

82. *Corresp.*, II, p. 182; III, p. 113.

83. Ibid., II, p. 112.

84. A. THIBAUDET: *Gustave Flaubert*, 1922, p. 12.

85. *Corresp.*, II, p. 155.

86. GEORG LUKÁCS: 'Theodor Storm oder die Buergerlichkeit und l'art pour l'art'. *Die Seele und die Formen*, 1911.—THOMAS MANN: *Betrachtungen eines Unpolitischen*, 1918, pp. 69–70.

87. GEORG KEFERSTEIN: *Buergertum und Buergerlichkeit bei Goethe*, 1933, pp. 126–223.

88. *Corresp.*, I, p. 238, Sept. 1851.

89. Ibid., IV, p. 244, Dec. 1875.

90. Ibid., III, p. 119.

91. ÉMILE FAGUET: *Flaubert*, 1913, p. 145.

92. *Corresp.*, II, p. 237.

93. Ibid., III, p. 190.

94. Ibid., III, p. 446.

95. Ibid., II, p. 70.

96. Ibid., II, p. 137.

97. Ibid., III, p. 440.

98. Ibid., II, pp. 133, 140–1, 336.

99. JULES DE GAULTIER: *Le Bovarysme*, 1902.

100. ÉDOUARD MAYNIAL: *Flaubert* (1943), pp. 111–12.

101. PAUL BOURGET: *Essais de psych. contempt.*, 1885, p. 144.

102. *Corresp.*, I, p. 289.

103. GEORG LUKÁCS: *Die Theorie des Romans*, 1920, p. 131.

104. ÉMILE ZOLA: *La Roman experimental*, 1880, 2nd edit., pp. 24, 28.

105. CHARLES-BRUN: *Le Roman social en France au 19e siècle*, 1910, p. 158.

106. ANDRÉ BELLESSORT: 'La Société française sous le second Empire'. *Revue hebdomaire*, 1932, No. 12, pp. 290, 292.

107. FRANCISQUE SARCEY: *Quarante ans de théâtre*, I, 1900, pp. 120, 122.

108. Ibid., pp. 209–12.

109. J.-J. WEISS: *Le Théâtre et les mœurs*, 1889, pp. 121–2.—Cf. RENAN: *Preface to the Drames philosophiques*, 1888.

110. A. THIBAUDET, op. cit., pp. 295 ff.

111. SARCEY, op. cit., V, p. 94.

112. Ibid., p. 286.

113. Cf. JULES LEMAÎTRE: *Impressions de théâtre*, I, 1888, p. 217.

114. SARCEY, op. cit., VI, 1901, p. 180.

115. S. KRACAUER: *Jacques Offenbach und das Paris seiner Zeit*, 1937, p. 349.

116. Ibid., p. 270.

117. Cf. FLEURY-SONOLET: *La Société du second Empire*, III, 1913, p. 387.

118. PAUL BEKKER: *Wandlungen der Oper.*, 1934, p. 86.

119. LIONEL DE LAURENCIE: *Le Goût musical en France*, 1905, p. 292.—WILLIAM L. CROSTEN: *French Grand Opera*, 1948, p. 106.

120. ALFRED EINSTEIN: *Music in the Romantic Era*, 1947, p. 231.

121. FRIEDRICH NIETZSCHE: *Der Fall Wagner*, 1888.—*Nietzsche contra Wagner*, 1888.

122. Cf. THOMAS MANN: *Betrachtungen eines Unpolitischen*, 1918, p. 75.—*Leiden und Groesse der Meister*, 1935, pp. 145 ff.

123. A. PAUL OPPÉ: 'Art'. In *Early Victorian England*, edited by G. M. Young, 1934, II, p. 154.

124. RUSKIN: *Stones of Venice*, III.—*Works*, 1904, XI, p. 201.

125. H. W. SINGER: *Der Praeraffaelismus in England*, 1912, p. 51.

126. Cf. A. CLUTTON-BROCK: *William Morris. His Work and Influence*, 1914, p. 9.

127. D. C. SOMERWELL: *English Thought in the 19th Century*, 1947, 5th edit., p. 153.

128. CHRISTIAN ECKERT: 'John Ruskin'. *Schmollers Jahrbuch.*, 1902, XXVI, p. 362.

129. E. BATHO-B. DOBRÉE: *The Victorians and After*, 1938, p. 112.

130. A. CLUTTON-BROCK, op. cit., p. 150.

131. Ibid., p. 228.

132. WILLIAM MORRIS: *Art under Plutocracy*, 1883.

133. LOUIS CAZAMIAN: *Le Roman social en Angleterre* (1830–1850), II, 1935, pp. 250–1.

134. Ibid., I, 1934, pp. 11–12, 163.

135. W. L. CROSS: *The Development of the English Novel*, 1899, p. 182.

136. L. CAZAMIAN, op. cit., I, p. 8.

137. A. H. THORNDIKE: *Literature in a Changing Age*, 1920, pp. 24–5.

138. Cf. Q. D. LEAVIS: *Fiction and the Reading Public*, 1939, p. 156.

139. G. K. CHESTERTON: *Charles Dickens*, 1917, 11th edit., pp. 79, 84.

140. AMY CRUSE: *The Victorians and their Books*, 1936, 2nd edit., p. 158.

141. OSBERT SITWELL: *Dickens*, 1932, p. 15.

142. Cf. L. CAZAMIAN, op. cit., I, pp. 209 ff.

143. T. S. JACKSON: *Charles Dickens*, 1937, pp. 22–3.

144. HUMPHREY HOUSE: *The Dickens World*, 1941, p. 219.

145. Cf. the speech Dickens made in Birmingham on 27th September 1869.

146. Cf. HUMPHREY HOUSE, op. cit., p. 209.

147. TAINE: *Hist. de la litt. angl.*, 1864, IV, p. 66.

148. O. SITWELL, op. cit., p. 16.

149. Q. D. LEAVIS, op. cit., pp. 33–4, 42–3, 158–9, 168–9.

150. M. L. CAZAMIAN: *Le Roman et les idées en Angleterre*, I, 1923, p. 138.—ELIZABETH S. HALDANE: *George Eliot and her Times*, 1927, p. 292.

151. P. BOURL'HONNE: *George Eliot*, 1933, pp. 128, 135.

152. ERNEST A. BAKER: *History of the English Novel*, VIII, 1937, pp. 240, 254.

153. E. BATHO-B. DOBRÉE, op. cit., pp. 78–9, 91–2.

154. *Middlemarch*, XV.

155. M. L. CAZAMIAN, op. cit., p. 108.

156. J. W. CROSS: *George Eliot's Life as related in her Letters and Journals*, 1885, p. 230.

157. F. R. LEAVIS: *The Great Tradition*, 1948, p. 61.

158. ALFRED WEBER: 'Die Not der geistigen Arbeiter'. *Schriften des Vereins fuer Sozialpolitik*, 1920.

159. GEORG LUKÁCS: 'Moses Hess und die Probleme der idealistischen Dialektik'. *Archiv f.d. Gesch. d. Sozialismus u. die Arbeiterbewegung*, 1926, XII, p. 123.

160. KARL MANNHEIM: *Ideology and Utopia*, 1936, pp. 136 ff.—*Man and Soc. in an Age of Reconstruction*, 1940, pp. 79 ff.

161. Cf. HANS SPEIER: 'Zur Soziologie der buergerl. Intelligenz in Deutschland'. *Die Gesellschaft*, 1929, II, p. 71.

162. D. S. MIRSKY: *Contemp. Russian Lit.*, 1926, pp. 42–3.

163. D. S. MIRSKY: *A Hist. of Russian Lit.*, 1927, pp. 321, 322.

164. M. N. POKROVSKY: *Brief Hist. of Russia*, I, 1933, p. 144.

165. D. S. MIRSKY: *Russia. A Social History*, 1931, p. 199.

166. JANKO LAVRIN: *Pushkin and Russian Lit.*, 1947, p. 198.

167. D. S. MIRSKY: *A Hist. of Russian Lit.*, pp. 203–4.

168. Ibid., p. 204.

169. Ibid., p. 282.

170. TH. G. MASARYK: *The Spirit of Russia*, 1919, I, p. 148.

171. Turgenev in a letter to Herzen of 8th November 1862.

172. E. H. CARR: *Dostoevsky*, 1931, p. 268.

173. NICOLAS BERDIAEFF: *L'Esprit de Dostoievski*, 1946, p. 18.

174. D. S. MIRSKY: *A Hist. of Russian Lit.*, p. 219.

175. E. H. CARR, op. cit., pp. 281 ff.

176. Ibid., pp. 267–8.

177. DOSTOEVSKY: *An Author's Diary*, February 1877.

178. EDMUND WILSON: *The Wound and the Bow*, 1941, p. 50.—REX WARNER: *The Cult of Power*, 1946, p. 41.

179. DMITRI MEREJKOWSKI: *Tolstoi as Man and Artist*, 1902, p. 251.

180. VLADIMIR POZNER: 'Dostoievski et le roman d'aventure'. *Europe*, XXVII, 1931.

181. Ibid., pp. 135–6.

182. Cf. LEO SCHESTOW: *Dostojewski und Nietzsche*, 1924, pp. 90–1.

183. THOMAS MANN: 'Goethe und Tolstoi'. In *Bemuehungen*, 1925, p. 33.

184. N. LENIN: 'L. N. Tolstoi' (1910). In N. LENIN-G. PLECHANOW: *L. N. Tolstoi im Spiegel des Marxismus*, 1928, pp. 42–4.

185. D. S. MIRSKY: *Contemp. Russian Lit.*, p. 8.

186. Ibid., p. 9.—JANKO LAVRIN: *Tolstoy*, 1944, p. 94.

187. D. S. MERESCHKOWSKI, op. cit., p. 213.

188. LUKÁCS GYÖRGY: *Nagy orosz realisták, Budapest*, 1946, p. 92.

189. TOLSTOY: *What is Art?*, XVI.

190. Cf. THOMAS MANN: *Die Forderung des Tages*, 1930, p. 283.

191. MAXIM GORKY: *Literature and Life*, 1946, p. 74.

192. THOMAS MANN: *Die Forderung des Tages*, p. 278.

193. ANDRÉ BELLESSORT: *Les Intellectuels et l'avènement de la troisième République*, 1931, p. 24.

194. PAUL LOUIS: *Hist. du socialisme en France*, pp. 236–7.

195. A. BELLESSORT, op. cit., p. 39.

196. WERNER SOMBART: *Der mod. Kapit.*, III/1, pp. xii/xiii.

197. PAUL LOUIS, op. cit., pp. 242, 216–7.

198. Cf. HENRY FORD: *My Life and My Work*, 1922, p. 155.

199. W. SOMBART: *Der mod. Kapit.*, III/2, pp. 603–7.—*Die deutsche Volkswirtschaft*, pp. 397–8.

200. Cf. PIERRE FRANCASTEL: *L'Impressionnisme*, 1937, pp. 25–6, 80.

201. GEORG MARZYNSKI: 'Die impressionistische Methode'. *Zeitschr. f. Aesth. u. allg. Kunstwissenschaft*, XIV, 1920.

202. GEORGES RIVIÈRE: 'L'Exposition des Impressionnistes'. In *L'Impressioniste. Journal d'Art*, 6th April 1877.—Reprinted in L. VENTURI: *Les Archives de l'Impressionnisme*, 1939, II, p. 309.

203. André Malraux: 'The Psychology of Art'. *Horizon*, 1948, No. 103, p. 55.
204. G. Marzynski, loc. cit., p. 90.
205. Ibid., p. 91.
206. John Rewald: *The History of Impressionism*, 1946, pp. 6–7.
207. Albert Cassagne: *La Théorie de l'art pour l'art en France*, 1906, p. 351.
208. E. and J. de Goncourt: *Journal*. 1st May 1869, III, p. 221.
209. Henri Focillon: *La Peinture aux 19e et 20e siècles*, 1928, p. 200.
210. Paul Bourget, op. cit., p. 25.
211. Charles Seignobos: 'L'Évolution de la troisième République'. In E. Lavisse: *Hist. de la France contempt.*, VIII, 1921, pp. 54–5.
212. Henry Bérenger: *L'Aristocratie intellectuelle*, 1895, p. 3.
213. A. Thibaudet: *Hist de la litt. franç.*, p. 430.
214. E. R. Curtius: *Maurice Barrès*, 1921, p. 98.
215. Jules Huret: *Enquête sur l'évolution litt.*, 1891, pp. xvi-xvii.
216. E. and J. de Goncourt: *Idées et sensations*, 1866.
217. Nietzsche: *Menschliches Allzumenschliches*, 155.
218. Baudelaire: *Richard Wagner et Tannhaeuser à Paris*, 1861.
219. Baudelaire: *Le Peintre de la vie moderne*, 1863. Reprinted in Baudelaire: *L'Art moderne*, edited by E. Raynaud, 1931, p. 79.
220. Villiers de l'Isle-Adam: *Contes cruels*, 1883, pp. 13 ff.
221. Émile Tardieu: *L'Ennui*, 1903, pp. 81 ff.
222. E. von Sydow: *Die Kultur der Dekadenz*, 1921, p. 34.
223. Peter Quennell: *Baudelaire and the Symbolists*, 1929, p. 82.
224. Max Nordau: *Entartung*, 1896, 3rd edit., II, p. 102.
225. Baudelaire: *Journaux intimes*, edited by Ad. van Bever, 1920, p. 8.
226. Thomas Mann: 'Kollege Hitler'. *Das Tagebuch*, edited by Leopold Schwarzschild, 1939.
227. Cf. René Dumesnil: *L'Époque réaliste et naturaliste*, 1945, pp. 31 ff.—Ernest Raynaud: *Baudelaire et la religion du dandysme*, 1918, pp. 13–14.
228. Baudelaire: *Œuvres posthumes*, edited by J. Crépet, I, pp. 223 ff.
229. Chekhov: *The House with the Mezzanine. A Painter's Story*, translated by S. S. Koteliansky, Everyman's Library.
230. *Le Figaro*, 18th September 1886.
231. A. Thibaudet: *Hist de la litt. franç.*, p. 485.
232. Ibid., p. 489.
233. J. Huret, op. cit., p. 60.
234. Cf. Ernest Raynaud: *La Mêlée symboliste*, 1920, II, p. 163.
235. John Charpentier: *Le Symbolisme*, 1927, p. 62.
236. Charles Mauron: Introduction to Roger Fry's translation of Mallarmé's poems, 1936, p. 14.
237. Georges Duhamel: *Les Poètes et la poésie*, 1914, pp. 145–6.

238. Cf. ROGER FRY: *An Early Introduction to Mallarmé's Poems*, 1936, pp. 296, 302, 304–6.

239. HENRI BREMOND: *La Poésie pure*, 1926, pp. 16–20.

240. E. and J. DE GONCOURT: *Journal*. 23rd February 1893, IX, p. 87.

241. J. HURET, op. cit., p. 297.

242. Cf. C. M. BOWRA: *The Heritage of Symbolism*, 1943, p. 10.

243. G. M. TURNELL: 'Mallarmé'. *Scrutiny*, 1937, V, p. 432.

244. J. HURET, op. cit., p. 23.

245. H. M. LYND: *England in the Eighteen-Eighties*, 1945, p. 17.

246. Ibid., p. 8.

247. BERNHARD FEHR: *Die engl. Lit. des 19. u. 20. Jahrhunderts*, 1931, p. 322.

248. BAUDELAIRE: *Le Peintre de la vie moderne*, loc. cit., pp. 73–4.

249. J.-P. SARTRE: *Baudelaire*, 1947, pp. 166–7.

250. BAUDELAIRE: *Le Peintre de la vie mod.*, p. 50.

251. M. L. CAZAMIAN: *Le Roman et les idées en Angleterre* (1880–1900), 1935, p. 167.

252. F. R. LEAVIS: *The Great Tradition*, 1948, passim.

253. H. HATZFELD: *Der franzoesische Symbolismus*, 1923, p. 140.

254. Cf. D. S. MIRSKY: *Modern Russian Lit.*, 1925, pp. 84–5.

255. JANKO LAVRIN: *An Introduction to the Russian Novel*, 1942, p. 134.

256. THOMAS MANN: 'Versuch ueber das Theater'. In *Rede und Antwort*, 1916, p. 55.

257. PAUL ERNST: *Ein Credo*, 1912, I, p. 227.

258. PAUL ERNST: *Der Weg zur Form*, 1928, 3rd edit., pp. 42 ff.

259. IBSEN: *Correspondence*, edited by Mary Morison, 1905, p. 86.

260. HALVDAN KOHT: *The Life of Ibsen*, 1931, p. 63.

261. M. C. BRADBROOK: *Ibsen*, 1946, pp. 34–5.

262. IBSEN: *Corresp.*, p. 218.

263. HOLBROOK JACKSON: *The Eighteen-Nineties*, 1939 (1913), p. 177.

264. Letter to Mehring of 14th July 1893. MARX-ENGELS: *Correspondence*, 1934, pp. 511–12.

265. ERNEST JONES: 'Rationalism in Everyday Life'. Read at the First Internat. Psycho-Analytic Congress, 1908. In *Papers on Psycho-Analysis*, 1913.

266. KARL MANNHEIM: *Ideology and Utopia*, 1936, pp. 61–2.

267. THOMAS MANN: 'Die Stellung Freuds in der modernen Geistesgeschichte'. In *Die Forderung des Tages*, 1930, pp. 201 ff.

268. S. FREUD: *The Future of an Illusion*, translated by W. D. Robson-Scott, 1928, p. 93.

269. NIETZSCHE: *Werke*, 1895 ff., XVI, p. 19.

VIII. THE FILM AGE

1. HERMANN KEYSERLING: *Die neuentstehende Welt*, 1926.—JAMES BURNHAM: *The Managerial Revolution*, 1941.

2. M. J. Bonn: *The American Experiment*, 1933, p. 285.

3. José Ortega y Gasset: *The Revolt of the Masses*, 1932.

4. Ernst Troeltsch: 'Die Revolution in der Wissenschaft'. *Gesammelte Schriften*, IV, 1925, p. 676.

5. Henri Massis: *La Défense de l'Occident*, 1927.

6. Hermann Hesse: *Blick ins Chaos*, 1923.

7. André Malraux: *Psychologie de l'art*, 1947.

8. André Breton: *What is Surrealism?*, 1936, pp. 45 ff.

9. Jean Paulhan: *Les Fleurs de Tarbes*, 1941.

10. Jacques Rivière: 'Reconnaissance à Dada'. *Nouvelle Revue Française*, 1920, XV, pp. 231 ff.—Marcel Raymond: *De Baudelaire au surréalisme*, 1933, p. 390.

11. André Breton: *Les Pas perdus*, 1924.

12. Tristan Tzara: *Sept manifestes dada*, 1920.

13. Friedrich Gundolf: *Goethe*, 1916.

14. Michael Ayrton: 'A Master of Pastiche'. *New Writing and Daylight*, 1946, pp. 108 ff.

15. René Huyghe-Germain Bazin: *Hist. de l'art contemp.*, 1935, p. 223.

16. Constant Lambert: *Music ho!*, 1934.

17. Edmund Wilson: *Axel's Castle*, 1931, p. 256.

18. André Breton: (*Premier*) *Manifeste du surréalisme*, 1924.

19. Louis Reynaud: *La Crise de notre littérature*, 1929, pp. 196–7.

20. Cf. Charles du Bos: *Approximations*, 1922.—Benjamin Crémieux: *XXe siècle*, 1924.—Jacques Rivière: *Marcel Proust*, 1924.

21. J. Th. Soby: *Salvador Dali*, 1946, p. 24.

22. André Breton: *What is Surrealism?* p. 67.

23. André Breton: *Second Manifeste du surréalisme*, 1930.—Maurice Nadeau: *Histoire du surréalisme*, 1945, 2nd edit., p. 176.

24. Julien Benda: *La France byzantine*, 1945, p. 48.

25. Cf. E. R. Curtius: *Franzoesischer Geist im neuen Europa*, 1925, pp. 75–6.

26. Cf. Emil Lederer-Jakob Marschak: 'Der neue Mittelstand'. *Grundriss der Sozialoekonomik*, IX/1, 1926, pp. 121 ff.

27. Walter Benjamin: 'L'Œuvre d'art à l'époque de sa reproduction mécanisée'. *Zeitschrift fuer Sozialforschung*, 1936, V/1, p. 45.

INDEX OF SUBJECTS

Absolute monarchy, 438
  and the social classes, 439
Absolutism, 364
  and classicism, 442
Academicism, 385 f., 447 f.
Académie de Rome, 445
Académie Royale de Peinture et de Sculpture, 444 f.
Academies of art, 304, 383 ff., 444–8, 450
Accademia del Disegno, 383, 386
Accademia di S. Luca, 384
Acropolis, 90
Adolphe, 570
Aegina pediments, 86
Aesthetic hedonism, 884
  movement in England, 905 f.
  nihilism, 787
Aestheticism, 111 f., 270, 332, 339 f., 435, 621, 668, 787, 883–8, 914 f.
Agon, 86
Aix-la-Chapelle, 160, 161, 204
'Alchimie du verbe', 898
Amadis, 523
Amateurs, 165, 301
Amiens Gospel-Book, 193
Aminta, 519
Amsterdam, 464, 472
Anabaptism, 367
Ancient-Oriental art, and cultus, 48
    impersonal character of, 49
    practical tasks of, 48 f.
    as a profession, 45
  city life, 44 f.
  money economy, 45
  political coercion and artistic quality, 46
Ancient-Oriental priests and kings as patrons, 47 f.
  sepulchral art, 48 f.
  temple and palace households, 47
  trade and handicraft, 45
  traditionalism, 45
Anglo-Saxon miniatures, 150, 162
Animism, 33, 35
  and art, 33
  and magic, 33
Anna Karenina, 737, 848, 861, 866, 868
Anti-impressionism, 930 f.
Anti-naturalism, 930 f.
  and conservatism, 880 ff.
Anti-philistinism, 902 f., 916 f.
  in England, 902 f.
Antigone, 108
Antwerp, 365, 396, 466, 467, 472
Apoxyomenos, 105
Arabic court poetry, 221
Arazzi (Raphael), 346
Arcadian ideal, 515, 520
Archaeological classicism, 631–4
Archaeology and anthropology, 37
Archaic 'Apollos', 86
Architecture as a profession, 335 f.
Areté, 84, 113
Argonautica, 213
Aristocratic moral concepts, 439 f.
Aristocracy and the bourgeoisie, amalgamation of, 506 f.
'Arsenal', 678, 681
À rebours, 886 f.
Armance, 749
Art, collectors, 300 f.
  criticism, 386 f.

Art as an educator, 340
  exhibitions, 649 f., 681
  and handicraft, 127, 821–4
  and industrialization, 819, 821 ff.
  instruction, 383 ff., 651
  and leisure, 41 f.
  and machine, 822 f.
  market, 127, 300, 653
  and prosperity, 40, 94
  public, 450, 469, 648 f.
    progressive and conservative, 449 f.
  as pure form, 91 f., 94
  as relaxation, 796 f.
  and religion, 89 f.
  and science, 321 f., 332 f.
'Art of Versailles', 449
Artificiality, cult of, 885 ff.
Artist, as a craftsman, 76, 124, 127
  colonies, 777 f.
  freedom and security of, 473
  -magician, 39 f., 72
  and the work of art, 109 f., 125, 129 f., 319, 326, 328 f.
Artists, and art dealers, 468 f.
  and the bourgeoisie, 786 f., 890 f.
  and posterity, 328 f.
  and prostitutes, 890
  way of life of, 786 f.
  workshop organization of, 470
Artistic activity as a side-line, 41
'Artistic intention' (*Kunstwollen*), 135, 475, 660
  and technique, 241
Artistic proletariat, 787
  quality and sociology, 103
Arts, order of precedence in, 322, 384
  unity of, 387
Asia Minor, 76, 81, 93
Astrée, 519, 736
Assyrian art, 66
  'Doorkeepers', 65
Athens, 89, 95, 96, 97, 100, 103, 111, 113, 127, 281, 284
Athletic contests, 126, 127
Aucassin et Nicolette, 267
Audiences, 98, 99
Augustan age, 119, 120
Autobiography, 117
'Automatic method of writing', 935 f.
Autonomy of art, 91–4, 330 ff.
  of cultural forms, 91–4, 136
  of mind, 667
Avignon, 289, 341
Axel, 886

Babylonian art, 65 f.
  commerce and finance, 65
'Bad taste', 533, 796 f.
Barbizon, School of, 777 f., 805, 878
Bards, 77 f.
Baroque, 626, 627, 631
  a-tectonic structure of, 427
  basic concepts of, 426–9
  of the Catholic Church, 423, 435 ff.
  Church art, 433, 436
  cinematic features of, 427
  and classicism, 627
  classicism of, 423 f., 441–4, 452
    dissolution of, 503 f., 512
    and the Middle Ages, 442, 444
  concept of, 423–33
  concept of the Universe, 431 f.
  cosmic world-view of, 431 f.
  of the courts, 423, 440–8
  democratization of Church art, 435
  devotional image, 434
  dynamic quality of, 426 f.
  and impressionism, 425
  and mannerism, 423, 433, 436, 437
  naturalism of, 424
  official and non-official trend of, 449
  papal art patronage, 436
  painterly quality of, 426
  piety, 435
  ramifications of, 423 f., 431
  and Renaissance, 428 f., 432
  revaluation of, 424 f.
  -rococo tradition, 502

Baroque, sociological presuppositions of, 426
space, 426 f.
striving for the infinite, 428, 432 f.
striving for unity, 428
Bayeux Tapestry, 195 f.
Bayreuth, 811
Benedictine rule, 152, 174
Beowulf, 75, 164, 165, 166
Bildungsroman, 737, 739, 848
Biography, 103, 112, 117 f.
Boetian peasantry, 81
Bohème, 681 f., 683, 702, 709, 774, 781, 891–5, 903 f.
ramifications of, 892–5
Bohemianism, 339 f., 621
Bologna, 279, 323, 518
Bonapartism, 685, 748
Boulevard theatres, 687–90
Bourgeois classicism, 731, 734
'idealism', 795
self-criticism, 785, 919
Bourgeoisie, and aristocracy in the Middle Ages, 256
and art, 620 f.
in the 19th century, 715, 722 f., 757, 759, 769, 770 f.
crisis of, 928
'Bovarysm', 790
Bozzetti, 328
Breton romances, 212
Brothers Karamazov, The, 848, 851, 856
Brumaire 18, 639
Brussels, 396, 467
Bucolic ideal, 514 f., 520
Building-site and workshop, 250 f.
Burgundian court, 262
Bushman art, 37
Byronic hero, 699–702
Byzantine architecture, 143 f.
aristocracy, 140
art, 142–5, 149 f., 162, 189
formalism of, 143, 150
tradition, 287
Byzantine court, 139, 141
art at, 142 f.
economy, 139
image worship, 147 f.
landowners, 140, 142, 145 f.
miniature painting, 144
monastic art, 144, 150
monasticism, 148 ff., 152
mosaics, 143 f.
portraiture, 145
theocracy, 141
urban life, 140
Byzantium, 138–41

Caesaropapism, 140
Capitalism, 284 ff., 296, 363 ff., 402, 813, 870
in the 19th century, 716, 720–3, 755 ff., 759, 770
crisis of, 927 f.
and individualism, 186
Cappella Paolina, 371, 376
Carolingian art, 161 ff., 189, 190, 195
civilization, nomadic character of, 163
court style, 161
impressionism, 161
miniature painting, 162 f.
monastic workshops, 163
Renaissance, 160–2, 172
and Christian antiquity, 160
Cassoni, 301, 314, 318
Castle of Otranto, 561
Catacomb paintings, 134
Cathedral schools, 158
Céladon, 523
Central perspective, 273 f., 277, 333 ff.
Change of style, 430
Chanson de la mal mariée, 222
Chanson de Roland, 170, 172, 173, 228
Chansons de geste, 170 f., 212, 215, 227

Charlemagne's court, 160
 literary academy, 160
 palace school, 160
 palace workshop, 160, 163
Chartres, 178, 235, 248, 267
Chartreuse de Parme, 728, 740, 741, 746, 748, 749
Chef-d'œuvre inconnu, 767, 837
Child art, 24
Chivalry, 396–9, 401, 405 f.
 defeat of, 254 f.
 novels of, 396, 399
 parody of, 399 f.
Christ, image of, 135, 143, 147, 195
Cid, 626
Cinematographic style, 122
Cinquecento, 324, 332, 342, 344–52, 354
 anti-emotionalism of, 347
 authoritarian principles of, 348
 classicism of, 344–8
 formalism of, 347 f., 352
Ciompi revolt, 282, 288, 292
Clans, in Greece, 78
Clarissa Harlowe, 737
Class struggle, 716, 717, 720, 758
 in England, 815, 832
Classicism, 344–52, 354 f., 443 f., 623–35
 and the aristocracy, 451 f., 623, 626 f.
 and the bourgeoisie, 451 f., 623, 626, 627
 formalism of, 630
 and idealism, 97
 and naturalism, 452
 and rationalism, 451 f., 625 f.
 and republican virtues, 635
 and the Revolution, 635
 and romanticism, 644
'Closed household economy', 184
Cluniac movement, 187, 193
Collective art production, 180, 247, 947
'Collective genius', 77
Cologne, 176, 248
Colonate, 124, 182
Comédie humaine, 755, 758, 761, 763, 764, 765, 767, 790
Commedia dell'arte, 417, 688
Commercialism, 285
Common people and art, 395 f.
Communal poetry, 165
Competition, lack of, in the Middle Ages, 185
Compostella, 170, 171
Concordat, 646, 724
 and art, 646
'Condition-of-England' problem, 824
Conférences of the Paris Academy, 385, 447 f.
Connoisseurs, 301, 310
 and laymen, 450
'Conscious self-deception', 400
'Conspicuous leisure', 130
Constant factors of evolution, 271
Consulate, 639, 646
Constantinople, 138–41
'Continuous' representation, 122, 238, 273, 490
Convention, 665, 724
Copernican world-view, 431 f.
Corbie, 176
Cortegiano, 306
Council of Trent, 368, 372, 375–9
Counter-Reformation, 341, 359, 368, 372, 375–9
 and art, 375 f.
 and baroque, 379
 and mannerism, 379
Country folk in art, 395
Courtly art, 501
Courtly-chivalric love, and clerical literature, 223
 cult of, 214–21
 fictitiousness of, 216 f.
 romances, 227 f., 231 f.
 sexual-psychological motives of, 218 f.
 moral concepts, 210

Courtly-chivalric poetry, 164 f., 214–24
culture, feminine character of, 212 f.
Crécy, 255
Cretan art, 66
anti-naturalistic conventions of, 69
courtly-chivalrous features of, 69
'modernity' of, 69
naturalism of, 68 f.
stylistic freedom of, 67 f.
standardization of, 70
city life, 67
social system, 67
Crime and Punishment, 851, 856
Cromwell (V. Hugo), 681
Cross-vaulting, 240 f.
Cubism, 934, 946

Dadaism, 932 f.
Dame aux camélias, 526, 799
Dandyism, 903 f.
'Dark rhyming', 225
Darwinism in art theory, 475
Decadent movement, 888 f.
and dandyism, 904
in England, 903 f.
Decamerone, 306
'Decline of the West', 930
'Deliberate self-deception', 665
Demi-monde, 799
Democracy and individualism, 95
Democratization of art, 959
Demodokos, 74, 75, 78
Des Esseintes, 886 f., 888
Des Grieux, 523, 524
'Detached intelligentsia', 108, 837
Diable boiteux, 524, 737
Dialectic of artistic development, 630
Dialectical thinking, 654
Dichtung und Wahrheit, 697
Dilettantism, 41, 336
Dionysus worship, 100, 118
Dipylon style, 81 f.
Directoire, 639 ff.
Dischi di parto, 301
Discobolos, 101
'Discomfort with culture', 891, 921
Disegno, 384
Documentary film, 957 f.
Domestic industry, 41
Dominicans, 289
Don Carlos, 592, 618
Don Juan, 702
Don Quixote, 254, 398–401, 406, 544, 736, 916
Dorian invasion, 76
nobility, 88
peasantry, 81
sculpture, 83
Doryphoros, 194
Dramatic unities, 443 f., 625
and naturalism, 625
Drawings, 328
in the Middle Ages, 329
in the Renaissance, 329
Dual morality, 374
'Duality of truth', 235
Dutch art market, 463, 465–70
patronage, 463
production, 466 f.
public, 463–7, 469
stratification of, 463 ff.
artists' workshop, 471
bourgeoisie, 459 f.
capitalism, 460
economic prosperity, 459 f.
fine art trade, 467–70
liberalism, 459
middle-class art, 462
middle-class culture, 461, 464
nobility, 460 f.
painters, economic situation of, 467, 469–70, 472
painting, 433
classical-humanistic tendencies in, 463 f.
genres of, 461 f.
middle-class character of, 461 ff.

Dutch painting, naturalism of, 462, 464
specialization in, 468 f.
Protestantism, 458 f.
and art, 461

Early Christian art, 132
anti-naturalism of, 133, 137 f.
frontality of, 133, 138
simplifications of, 135, 138
Eclecticism, 115, 771, 934
École de bon sens, 731, 734
Economic liberalism, 555, 813, 814
rationalism, 274, 284 ff., 397, 716
'Economy without outlets', 184
Enlightenment, 266, 534, 544, 556, 568 f., 593, 606, 610, 813
and Germany, 593, 604
rationalism of, 593, 604 f.
Edict of Toleration and art, 135
Éducation sentimentale, 734, 738, 781, 783, 789, 790, 791, 792
Egyptian aristocracy, 58, 62, 64
and art, 61
art, academic character of, 52
in the age of Akhenaton, 59 f.
'completing' technique of, 56
conventionalism of, 54, 60
education, 52
formalism of, 56, 58
frontality of, 56 f.
of the Middle Kingdom, 53 ff.
naturalism of, 55, 59, 60
of the New Kingdom, 60
of the Old Kingdom, 53
stereotyping of, 54
artistic production, rationalization of, 52
artists, social position of, 49 f.
bazaar system, 50
bureaucracy, 62
common people and art, 61, 63
death masks, 55 f.
'folk art', 60, 62
middle class and art, 61 f.
Egyptian provincial art, 64
scribe and artist, 50
stylistic dualism, 62 f.
temple and palace workshops, 50 f.
Eighteenth-century drama, 578 f.
characters of, 584 f.
and classical drama, 578, 580 ff., 583 f.
freedom and necessity in, 588
heroes of, 580 f.
milieu description in, 583
morality of, 587
optimism of, 589 f.
problem of guilt in, 585
psychological motivation in, 586 f.
Eighteenth century music, 573–7
audiences of, 575 f.
expressionism of, 576 f.
and the middle class, 576
Lied- and sonata form of, 574
El Amarna, 49, 56, 64
Elizabethan courtly literature, 408 f.
drama, 418 f., 420
England, 415
patronage of literature, 410
professional writers, 409 f.
theatre, 409–15
Émigré literature, 673, 677, 699
Emma Bovary, 570, 785, 790
Emotionalism, 112, 347, 450, 629
Emperors' Gospel-Books, 162
Empire (of Napoleon), 639 f., 645 f., 647, 674
and art, 640 f., 645, 648, 653
and romanticism, 646
style, 640
Encyclopédie, 570
England in the eighteenth century, 534, 537 f.
English aristocracy, 534–9
and bourgeoisie, 403
bourgeoisie, crisis of, 901 f.
capitalism, 535 f.
garden, 561
gentry, 401 f.

English lending libraries and literary production, 704
  liberalism, 534
    crisis of, 901 f.
  literary market in the eighteenth century, 548 ff.
  literary patronage, 542–6
  middle class, 401 ff., 538 f., 559 ff.
  monarchy and Parliament, 535 ff.
    and the social classes, 534–9
  nobility, 401 ff., 405, 408
  novel, 703 f.
  Parliament, 534, 536 f.
  periodicals in the eighteenth century, 542 f., 548
  reading public, 539–42, 548, 563, 703 f., 824–9, 834 f., 906
  Renaissance literature, 408 f.
  Revolution, 536
  romanticism, 673 f., 680, 695, 697 f.
    and conservatism, 695 f., 705
    and French romanticism, 695, 699, 705
    and the Industrial Revolution, 696
    and liberalism, 695 f.
    and Napoleon, 695 f.
    and the novel, 703 ff.
  society in the eighteenth century, 537 ff.
  upper classes, 534 f.
  writers in the eighteenth century, social and economic situation of, 545–9
Ennui, 887, 909
Equivocations, 39
Eroica, 577
Estrangement, idea of, in Russian literature, 860, 863 f.
Eugénie Grandet, 756, 765
Expressionism, 934, 946

Fable, 258 f.
Fabliau, 203, 231
Fabrice del Dongo, 743, 744, 746, 750
Fame, 73, 165
Fa-presto-technique, 336
February revolution, 725
Ferme générale, 509, 532
Fermiers généraux, 635
Ferrara, 279, 305, 307, 518
Fêtes galantes, 513 f., 520, 522
Feudal and urban nobility, 256
Feudalism, 124, 145, 156 f., 181 ff., 187
Feuilleton, 726 f.
Feuilleton novel, 726–9, 755
Film, 121, 122, 358, 809, 939–43, 946–58
  and artistic co-operation, 947 f.
  crisis of, 946
  and democratization of art, 949 f.
  documentary value of, 957 f.
  and drama, 940–2
  and dynamization of space, 940 f.
  and historical materialism, 954 f.
  and political propaganda, 956
  public, 949–53
  simultaneity in, 943
  in Soviet-Russia, 956 ff.
  and space, 940 f.
  and spatialization of time, 942 f.
  and technics, 956 f.
  time in, 939–44, 946
  and writers, 947 f.
Fine art trade, 302, 467–70
Flanders, and France, 457
  organization of art production in, 470
  Spanish rule in, 456 f.
Flemish aristocracy, 457 ff.
  art, 457
  Catholicism, 457 ff.
  and Dutch baroque, 458
  society, 457
Florence, 278, 279, 280–4, 288 ff., 291–7, 305, 308 f., 315, 318, 322, 340 f., 343, 360, 362 f., 383 f., 389 f., 518

Florence, Baptistry, 285, 299, 317, 336
  Campanile, 287, 299
  Cathedral, 287, 307
  S. Croce, 287, 300, 302
  S. Lorenzo, 300, 303
  S. Maria Novella, 287, 289, 318, 323
    Spanish Chapel, 289
Florentine art, 287, 289, 291–4
  mannerism, 387–90
Folk art, 42, 151
Folk epic, 164 f., 168 f., 173
Folk poetry, 154, 164, 168 f., 173, 258 f
Folk song, 222 f., 259
'Folk soul', 247
Folk theatre, 414
Folklore mysticism, 168 f.
Fontainebleau, 360
Forms, untruth of, 671
Formalism and conservatism, 97
Formalistic conception of art, 331, 341
Formalizing of spiritual activities, 92 f.
Fourierites, 717, 730, 734
Franciscan movement, 234, 276
Franco-Burgundian art, 272
Franco-Flemish Gothic, 276
Frankish aristocracy, 155 f.
Frédéric Moreau, 570, 790
'Free arts', 322
Free competition, 813
Freedom, problem of, in Russian literature, 861 ff.
French absolutism, 438 f.
    and art, 442
    academic art theory, 448 f.
    academies, 444–8, 450, 675
  Academy of Fine Arts, 521 f., 639, 649, 650 ff.
  aristocracy, 438
    and the bourgeoisie, 506 ff.
    in the eighteenth century, 506 ff.
    moral code of, 439 f.
French art market, in the seventeenth century, 470
  artists and writers, economic situation of, in the seventeenth century, 470
  baroque classicism, 441–4, 448, 451 f.
  bourgeoisie, 438, 506–12
    cultural ascent of, 508
    economic ascent of, 509
    and literature, 455, 510
    and the Revolution, 511
    Voltairianism of, 510
  classical art education, 444 ff.
  classical drama, 443 f.
  court art and literature, 440 ff., 446 f.
    dissolution of, 504 ff.
    society, 439 f.
  Revolution, 647, 674, 686, 688, 720, 724, 742, 755, 781 f.
    and Academy, 649, 650 ff.
    and art, 638, 642, 643, 646, 648, 650
    and art instruction, 651
    and artistic freedom, 644
    and artists, 652
    and the bourgeoisie, 647
    and the intelligentsia, 666
    and Napoleon, 640, 642
    and romanticism, 643, 653
    and theatre, 688 ff.
  romantic drama, 693 f.
    writers and painters, amalgamation of, 681
  romanticism, 673, 675–88
    anti-bourgeois mood of, 682 ff.
    aristocratism of, 682
    bohemianism of, 681 f., 683, 684
    and classicism, 675
    clericalism of, 678, 682
    conservatism of, 678
    coteries of, 678–81
    cult of youth of, 683
    disillusionment of, 677 f.

French romanticism, and English romanticism, 673 f., 680
and German romanticism, 680
'l'art pour l'art' of, 681, 684
liberalism of, 680 ff., 685 f.
and literary parties, 676 f.
pessimism of, 678
and political parties, 675
and the reading public, 676
royalism of, 678
school character of, 679
its struggle for the theatre, 684 f.
salons, 440, 452–5
and the court, 454
and literature, 454 f.
and modern psychology, 452 f.
society in the eighteenth century, 506–12
state patronage, 444 ff.
Frontality, 56 f., 63, 65, 83, 105, 123 f., 142, 143
Functionalism in art, 240, 476
'Fundamental aspects', 83, 102, 105

Generation of 1830, 715 f., 719, 768
disillusionment of, 719, 749
Generation of 1848, 773 f.
Génie du Christianisme, 646, 676
Genius, 108, 109 f., 128, 130, 265, 325, 326–30, 336, 549 f., 611 f.
Gentilhomme, 510
Geometrism, 30, 35, 41, 81 f., 475
German aestheticizing of world-view, 608
anti-rationalism, 607 f., 614 f.
classicism, 616–22
liberalism of, 619
middle-class character of, 619 f.
conservatism and liberalism, 613 ff.
idealism, 599, 605 f., 608 f.
intelligentsia, 598, 605, 607
anti-rationalism of, 607 f.
and enlightenment, 594
its estrangement from public life, 598 f.
German middle class, 594 f., 598–601, 604
middle-class culture, 599 f., 602, 619 f.
literature, 602 ff.
particularism, 595–600
princely courts, 597 f.
rationalism, 604, 613 ff.
Reformation, 596
rococo, 597, 602
romanticism, 634, 653–73
and Western romanticism, 653, 662 f.
Germany and the enlightenment, 593, 594, 606
Gesamtkunstwerk, 810
Ghent altar piece, 262
Gil Blas, 524, 737
Gongorism, 400, 454
Gothic, 266 ff.
Gothic accumulative composition, 272 f.
architecture, 192, 240, 242, 245 f.
functionalism of, 240
romantic interpretation of, 241
art, 197, 232, 243
cathedrals, 203 f., 244 ff.
cyclical composition, 239
description of nature, 234
dualism, 235–8
emotionalism, 243
idealism, 236 f.
individualism, 235
juxtaposition, 238
naturalism, 233 ff., 267, 290
pantheism, 234
rationalism and irrationalism, 239 ff.
and Romanesque composition, 238
sensitivity, 243
subjectivism, 234
virtuosity, 244, 252
Grand Cyrus, 736
Grand goût, 522
Grand Inquisitor, 860

'Grand Opera', 795, 809 ff.
Grand siècle, 441
Grande maniera, 353
Grande manière, 440
  dissolution of, 512 f.
Greek aestheticism, 111 f.
  archaic style, 82 f., 92
  aristocracy, 76, 80, 82, 83 ff., 88, 95, 96, 97, 102, 105, 114
    moral ideals of, 84, 104, 108
    poetry of, 84 f.
  aristocratic idea of beauty, 86
  art market, 116, 117
    patronage, 90, 108, 112, 127
    public, 116
    and religion, 89 f., 100
  artist as a craftsman, 76
    social status of, 72, 76, 127 ff.
  audiences, 77, 79, 85, 98, 99, 109, 110, 112
  bards, 75, 77 f.
  bourgeoisie, 84, 95, 96, 106, 110, 114, 116, 126
  capitalism, 105, 111 f., 113
  choirs, 85 f.
  clan state, 73, 78, 96, 102, 108
  class antagonisms, 80, 84, 89, 96
  classicism, 94 f., 101, 102
  collective poetry, 77, 87
  colonization, 82, 93 f.
  comedy, 96 f., 118
  commercial society, 85, 88, 117
  conservatism, 96, 97, 110 f.
  court poetry, 78 f.
  courtly art, 83
  cult of the noble families, 85, 100
  democracy, 77, 88, 94–7, 100, 105, 108, 126
  education, 103 f.
  elegists, 84
  emotionalism, 103, 112
  enlightenment, 103 ff., 106
  epic, 74, 76–9, 81
  feudalism, 73
  'folk epic', 78
Greek folk poetry, 74, 79, 80
  geometrism, 81 f., 83
  gnomic poets, 84
  heroic lay, 74 f., 76, 78 ff.
  idealism, 97, 110 f.
    and nobility, 97
  individualism, 87 f., 94 f., 98, 102, 105
  intelligentsia, 104, 108
  liberalism, 94, 105
  literary professionalism, 85, 107
  literary public, 107
  literati, 78, 79, 106, 107
    political outlook of, 96, 110
  lyric, 84 f., 87, 103
  mime, 99, 101, 110
  money economy, 84 f., 94
  naturalism, 83, 95, 97, 101, 103, 106, 110
    and aristocracy, 97
  peasant art, 81
  plutocracy, 84, 95, 96
  poet as an amateur, 75, 76, 85
    economic situation of, 107, 127 f.
    as a folk singer, 75
    as a professional singer, 75, 85
    and public life, 109
    as a seer and prophet, 71, 75
    social status of, 75, 76
    as a spiritual leader of the nobility, 84 f.
  poetic schools, guilds and groups, 76, 77 ff., 87
  polis, 98, 99, 114, 115
  portraiture, 86 f., 103, 112, 117, 120
  primitive community art, 72
  proletariat, 89, 113
  rationalism, 103 f.
  relativism, 104 ff.
  religion, 90, 100
  rhapsodes, 77 f., 85, 87, 104
  ritual poetry, 72
  statues of athletes, 86
  theatre, 98, 99, 118, 443

Greek tombstones, 103
tragedy, 73, 85, 97–101, 103, 106, 411, 415 f.
audience of, 98
and democracy, 97 f.
and happy ending, 106
and heroic world-view, 106
and individualism, 98
as an instrument of propaganda, 99 f.
and polis, 99 f.
and politics, 98, 100
and the problem of guilt, 107
and religion, 100 f.
and Sophistic movement, 106 f.
tragic chorus, 98, 99
tribal organization, 73, 78
Tyrants, 77, 83, 88–90, 92, 95, 100, 107
as patrons, 89 f.
art policy of, 89
courts of, 89
urban culture, 82 f.
urban society, 87
Guild Priors, 280, 282, 283
Guilds, 78, 248–50, 256, 279–82
and art production, 248 f.
Gulliver's Travels, 543 ff., 737
Guirlande de Julie, 454

Hard Times, 831 f.
Hellenism, 113–18
Hellenistic art production, 117
'baroque', 116, 117, 119, 124
bureaucracy, 115
classicism, 116
copying, 116 f.
cosmopolitan capitalism, 114
courts, 116 f.
eclecticism, 115 ff.
internationalism, 113 f.
materialism, 115
museums, 114, 115
naturalism, 116
Hellenistic organization of intellectual work, 114 f.
rationalism, 114
'rococo', 116, 119
social levelling, 113 f.
specialization, 115
world state, 114 f.
Herculaneum, 633
'Hereditary poetry', 173
Heretical movements and iconoclasm, 378
Hernani, 681, 684, 686, 693
Hero-worship, 118, 127, 817
Heroic age, 72 ff.
individualism of, 72, 74
saga, 169 f., 173
High capitalism, 870, 927
High Renaissance, 272, 274, 342, 344–52, 354 f., 624
Historical materialism, 661, 790, 919 f.
Historicism, 658–62
and conservatism, 662
and the social classes, 662
'History of art without names', 660 f.
Holy Alliance, 654, 674
Homeric age, 75
poems, 77 ff., 81, 93
social outlook of, 97 f.
Homeridai, 78
Honnête homme, 439, 510
Honour, aristocratic and middle-class conception of, 126 f.
Hôtel de Rambouillet, 454
Humanists, 310, 319, 322, 336–40
social origins of, 336 f.
and artists, 319 f., 330, 339 f.
political views of, 404
Humanist drama, 417 f.
Humour, 399 f.

Iconoclasm, 111, 146–50, 378
Idealists, in England, 813, 814 f., 825
Ideology, 920
Idiot, The, 851, 856, 857

Iliad, 80, 213
Illusionism, 102, 105, 121
Illusions perdues, 677, 738, 758, 760
Immanence of the history of art, 346, 429 f.
  of intellectual spheres, 667
Impressionism, 871–9
  and aestheticism, 883 ff.
  and the bourgeoisie, 879, 887, 903
  and city life, 871 f., 878
  development of, 878 f.
  international, 907–10
  and naturalism, 869, 870, 873 f., 880, 882
  in philosophy, 925
  and the public, 878 f.
  and symbolism, 880, 896, 907 f.
Impressionist conception of time, 925 f.
  drama, 910 f.
  method, 873–8
Impressionists, social origins of, 879
Individualism, 326 ff.
  problem of, in Russian literature, 861 ff.
  and the concept of the Renaissance, 269, 271
Industrial Revolution, 696, 812, 823, 824
Industrialism, 812 f.
  opposition to, 813 f., 817, 821 ff., 825
Industrialization of literature, 725 f., 729
Intellectual competition, 185
Intellectualism of modern literature, 881, 906, 918 f., 934
Intelligentsia, 104, 338 ff., 662 f., 837–41
  alienation of, 339 f.
  and authoritarianism, 929
  and the bohème, 840 f.
  and the bourgeoisie, 837 ff.
  in England, 813 f., 837
  and the French Revolution, 838
Intelligentsia and the Industrial Revolution, 839
  and the proletariat, 840
  and the propertied classes, 339
  in Russia, 841 ff.
Ionia, 76, 82, 87, 88, 91
Ionian natural philosophy, 93
  style, 83, 89
Irish miniatures, 150, 152, 154, 193
  monks, 152, 174
  poetry, 152 ff.
  poets, 154
Irrationalism in England, 813–17, 825
Ivan Karamazov, 846, 847, 850, 853

Jesuit order, 372
Jeune-France, 683
Jongleurs, 228, 230
Journalism, 725 ff.
Journal des Débats, 725, 726, 731
Julien Sorel, 570, 715, 741–5, 749, 750
July monarchy, 715, 718, 720–5, 730, 767, 770
  and capitalism, 720 f.
  political system of, 720 f.
  its politicization of literature, 720, 725
July revolution, 639, 685, 716, 769
Juste-milieu, 720, 722, 731

Ka, 55
Kabale und Liebe, 591
Kalokagathia, 84, 98, 101, 104, 110, 126, 135, 209, 349 ff., 361, 610
Knighthood, 206–10
  class-consciousness of, 207
  origins of, 206–9
Knightly culture, 211–26
  idealism, 255
  irrationalism, 255
  virtues, 209 f.
Kirilov, 846, 853, 858
Korai, 83, 90

Kunstwollen, 135, 475, 660

Laissez-faire, 552, 555 f.
  fight against, 825
Landscape, 707 f.
'L'art pour l'art', 91, 301, 638, 681, 684, 716, 725, 729, 730, 731–4, 765, 780, 783, 786, 800
  and the bourgeoisie, 786
Last Judgement, representation of, in the Middle Ages, 193, 194 f.
Last Judgement (Michelangelo), 370, 376 f.
Late Gothic, 261 f.
Late medieval courtly art, 263 f., 289 f.
  graphic arts, 264
  literature, 261
  miniature painting, 264
  naturalism, 261
  painting, 262–5
  revival of courtly-chivalric culture, 262
Late Roman art, 132
Leisure, 126
Levin (in *Anna Karenina*), 861
Liaisons dangereuses, 737
Liberalism, in England, 813 f.
  and the concept of the Renaissance, 268, 271
Light reading of the bourgeoisie, 795 f.
Linearism and colorism, 450
Literary coteries, 678–81
Literary proletariat, 852
Literary schools, 680
Lithography, 778
Louis-Seize, 630
Louvre, 437, 446, 651
Love in classical literature, 118, 213 f.
  in medieval literature, 214–25
  in modern literature, 523, 526 f.
'Love of the remote', 215
Lucien Leuwen, 740, 742
Lucien de Rubempré, 570, 715

Machiavellism, 373 f., 406
Madame Bovary, 734, 737, 779, 781, 783, 789, 790
Mme de Rênal, 743, 750
Magic, 26
  and animism, 33
  and art, 26 ff.
  and naturalism, 28 f.
  and religion, 26
Magical dances, 28, 40, 99
Maître Pathelin, 580
Mal de siècle, 699 f., 708
'Managerial revolution', 928 f.
Maniera, 353
Maniera grande, 344
Mannerism, 274, 328, 355 ff., 361, 387–95, 400 f., 624, 626
  and academicism, 383–6
  anti-classicism of, 354
  and art education, 383 ff.
  art theory of, 381 f.
  and baroque, 359, 379
  classicism of, 355
  concept of, 353–61
  its conception of space, 358, 370 f., 388 f.
  and Counter-Reformation, 379, 391
  as a court style, 360, 389
  eroticism of, 377
  and Gothic, 361
  intellectualism of, 355, 359
  internationalism of, 359, 360
  and knightly romanticism, 396–9, 405 f.
  and the Middle Ages, 357, 380
  and modern art, 356, 358
  naturalism of, 357
  pantheism of, 357
  and Reformation, 388
  and Renaissance, 357 f., 370 f., 387, 389
  and rococo, 390
  and Roman Catholic Church, 379 ff.
  spiritualism of, 355, 357, 361

Manneristic and mannered, 353
Mantua, 305, 307, 471
Manufacture des Gobelins, 446 f.
Manon Lescaut, 524, 737
Manual labour, 42, 50
  depreciation of, 124 ff., 129 f.
Marinism, 400, 454
Marivaudage, 527
Mary, images of, 143, 195
Masons' lodge, 244–50
  and film studio, 244
  and guild, 248 ff.
Mass democracy, 929
Mastersingers, 232, 260
Mastersingers, The, 810, 811
Mathilde de la Mole, 715, 743, 745
Mechanical reproduction of works of art, 264 f.
Mechanistic-materialistic art theory, 475
Medici tombs, 370
Medieval actors, amateurs, 260
    professionals, 260
  anti-feminist literature, 231
  apocalyptic mood, 187
  art, cyclic composition of, 196
    didactic character of, 136 f.
    spirituality of, 131 f.
    stylization of, 131
    symbolism of, 133
    transcendentalism of, 137
    trade, 204 f.
  artist, anonymity of, 179 f.
  artist-craftsmen, 177, 179
  artists' workshop, 250 ff.
  'authoritarian and coercive culture', 187
  authorship, 166
  bourgeoisie, 197, 202, 252 f., 256
    differentiation of, 256 f.
    as an upholder of culture, 258
  building trade, 245–8
  bureaucracy, 254
  capitalism, 199 f., 257
  chivalric conception of love, 214 ff.
Medieval church architecture, 179 f., 187 f.
  Church, and art, 146 f.
    authority of, 187 f.
    educational monopoly of, 158, 187, 204
    and feudalism, 187
  clergy and nobility, 181
  clerical poetry, 164, 166, 223 f.
  court poets, 165 ff., 171, 228 f.
  courts, 210 f.
    and women, 212
  courtly culture, 211 f.
  craftsmanship and art, 265
  craftsmen, 175, 198 f.
  drama, 239, 412, 418
  economic rationalism, 201
  education, 205
  epics, origins of, Bédier's theory, 169 ff.
    romantic theory, 168 f., 173
    song-theory, 170, 173
  eroticism, 219 ff.
  'folk epic', 164–70, 173
  heroic age, 164–8
  heroic lay, 164, 167–73
  heroic poetry, 164, 167–73, 188
  kings and nobility, 181 ff.
  landed property, 201 f.
  manor, 177, 184, 198, 201
  merchants, 198 ff.
  metaphysical world-view, 131 f., 135, 187
  middle-class art, 203, 232, 251 f., 258, 263 ff.
    literature, 231, 232
  money economy, 197, 199, 200 f.
  nobility, 181 ff., 206–10, 212, 253 f.
  organization of artistic production, 244–9
  poets, 231 f.
    social origins of, 203
    position of, 226
  rural culture, 157, 184

Medieval school poetry, 230
social antagonisms, 202 f., 252 ff.
changes, 205 f.
levelling, 253
stability, 185
theatre, 259 f.
theocracy, 140, 159, 187
town, 184, 198, 204
and country, 157
towns and poleis, 198
trade, 175, 198
tradesmen, 256
traditionalism, 185 f.
urban civilization, 198
decay of, 157
economy, 190, 199, 256 f.
wage-workers, 203
wandering scholar, 225 f., 229 ff.
wandering singer, 166
writing rooms, 162 f., 176
Méditations (Lamartine), 676
Melodrama, 689–95, 728
and romantic drama, 693 f.
and *tragédie classique*, 691 f.
Mendicant orders, 204
Menestrel, 228 f., 231
Menhirs, 30
Mercantilism, 364, 442 f.
Mercenary armies, 254
Merchant of London, 580
Merovingian art, 158 f.
benefice, 156
Merovingians, 155 ff.
Mesopotamian art, 64
Middle Ages, class struggles in, 278
cultural unity of, 327
universalism of, 271
Middle-class drama, 578 f., 581, 583, 586, 589, 591 f., 798
its alienation from the bourgeoisie, 592
apotheosis of the family in, 798 f.
as an instrument of propaganda, 800
Middle-class morality, 286
novel of family life, 562 ff.
spirit in medieval art, 251 f., 258, 263 ff.
'super-bourgeois' features of, 591 f.
virtues, 285 f.
Middle Latin poetry, 223, 230
Middlemarch, 836
Migration of the peoples, 138, 150
Migratory period, 150 f.
art of, 150 f.
economy of, 151
epic songs of, 164
peasant culture of, 151
Milan, 278, 279, 290, 291, 298, 303, 313
Milieu theory, 793
Mime, 99, 167, 171 f., 226, 231, 688, 691 f.
Ministeriales, 206 f., 550
Minstrel, 167, 171 f., 225 ff., 231
and knight, 226
Modernism in England, 902 f.
Modern Church art, 433 f.
individualism, 916 f.
landscape, origins of, 707 f.
painting, dehumanization of, 707
times and historical times, 714
Moissac, 193, 194
Monasteries, 174–80, 181
as art schools, 178
as cultural centres, 174 f.
organization of work in, 174, 175, 176 f.
rational economic organization of, 199
workshops of, 175 ff.
Monastic architecture, 178 f., 188
art, 176, 177, 179 f., 181
book-illumination, 176 f., 180
estates, 174, 198
handicraft, 174, 176 f.
reforms, 188
schools, 158
Monasticism, 174 f., 179

Money, 186
  and social dynamism, 200 f.
Monks and epics, 170 f.
Mourning Athena, 102
Mystères de Paris, 726, 729

Natural economy, 184
Naturalism, 266, 623 f., 706 f.
  and formalism, 623 f.
  historical priority of, 476
  and liberalism, 97, 781
  modern, 734, 735, 762 f., 772–81, 783, 858
    crisis of, 880–3
    and democracy, 775 f., 781
    and conservative criticism, 776, 780 f.
    political origins of, 774 f.
    and public, 778 f., 781
    scientific outlook of, 773, 793 f.
  and romanticism, 773, 779 f., 782–5, 794 f.
Naturalistic drama, 910 f.
    criticism of, 912 f.
    and determinism, 913 f.
    public of, 913
  landscape, 776 f.
Natureingang, 222
Naumburg, 235
Negro art, 37
Neo-classicism, 628 f.
Neo-Gothic, 561, 567
Neolithic art, 30, 33, 40
  economy, 31 f.
  geometrism, 30, 35, 36
  stylization, 33 f.
Neoplatonism, 128, 130, 214, 295, 303, 304, 331, 608, 609
Netherlandish bourgeoisie, 458 f.
  Catholicism and Protestantism, 458 f.
  culture, bifurcation of, 458
  monarchism and republicanism, 458
  Revolt, 458 f.
Neutralization of values, 92 f.
Nibelungenlied, 79, 173
Night Watch, 469, 472
Nineteenth century, 706 f.
  and the eighteenth century, 706
  foundations of, 715 f.
  and music, 713
  spirit of, 859 f.
Nominalism, 236 ff., 266
  and realism, 238
Nouvelle Héloïse, 571, 737
Novel, 716 f.
  adventure, 736
  and Bergsonian concept of time, 925 f., 939
  of chivalry, 736
  of disillusionment, 719
  history of, 719, 735–9, 848 ff.
  intellectualism in, 836 f., 855 f.
  love, 526 f., 736
  modern, 716 f., 719, 737 f.
    hero of, 737 f., 749 f., 752 f.
    psychology of estrangement in, 753
  naturalistic, 848, 859
  picaresque, 400, 524, 735, 737, 848, 858 f.
  psychological, 525, 752 f., 848, 858, 938
    crisis of, 938
    in England, 835 ff.
  psychology of self-estrangement in, 848 ff.
  publishing in England, 826 f.
    in monthly instalments, 827
  and the reading public in nineteenth-century England, 826–30, 834 f.
  social, 739 f., 754 f., 841, 847, 848, 853 ff., 858
    in England, 824 ff., 830–3, 835
  of terror, 693
  time in, 858
Nude, 83, 112

Oath of the Horatii, 634, 636 f., 642
Oath in the Tennis Court, 641, 642
Obermann, 570
Oceanic nations, 364
Odéon, 688, 689
Odyssey, 80, 213
Olympia, 83
  sculptures, 95, 101, 344
Olympic games, 83, 86
Onegin, 706
Opera buffa, 804
Operetta, 804–8
Oresteia, 108
'Original genius', 328
Originality, 326 ff.
'Oxford movement', 816

Padua, 290, 291
Palaeolithic art and livelihood, 25
  organization of artistic production, 40
Palais Royal, 505, 512
Pamela, 564
Panathenaeas, 77
Pantheism, 432
Pantomime, 690
Papal courts, 318, 341 ff.
Paradiso degli Alberti, 306
Parallelisms in the history of art, 429 f.
Paris, 248, 437, 442, 505, 513, 759, 771
Parnassiens, 769, 800
Parsifal, 811
Parthenon, 344, 346
  sculptures, 102
Parzival, 220
Passion of Christ, 194 f.
Passion plays, 239
Pastoral novel, 523
Pastoral in painting, 520 f.
  poetry, 515–21
    and courts, 516 ff.
Pastourelles, 518 f.
Patronage, 325 f., 338
Paulicians, 147
Pavia, Battle of, 362
  Certosa, 298
Paysage intime, 777
Peasant art, 36, 42, 151
Peasantry, conservatism of, 36
People's theatre, 98, 99
Periodicity in the history of art, 429 f.
Perugia, 279, 323
Philanthropism in England, 813, 815, 825
Phemios, 74, 75
Picaresque novel, 400, 524
Pictography, 37
Pièce bien faite, 694, 800–4, 910, 911
Pierre Bezukhov, 570, 847, 853
Pietà Rondanini, 371
Pisa, 278, 298
Platonic 'enthusiasm', 109, 697
  hostility to art, 111
  theory of Ideas, 110 f.
  Utopia, 111
Platonism, 660
Play forms, 92
Préiade, 625
Podestà, 279 f.
Poésie pure, 896 f., 899 f.
Poet, as the champion of an oppressed class, 80
  as an educator, 100
  as a seer and prophet, 71, 75, 100, 124
Poets and artists, social and economic position of, 107, 124 f., 127 f.
Poiein, 29
Political propaganda and art, 638, 642
  in English literature, 543–50
  realism, 367, 372–5, 397
Politicization of the spirit, 340
Pompeian style, IVth, 123
Pompeii, 633
Popular art, 99, 395
  theatre, 687–95
Pontifical state, 341
Popularity and quality in art, 827 ff.

Portraiture, 86 f., 103, 112
Possessed, The, 850, 851, 856, 857, 862
Post-impressionism, 930 f.
Post-revolutionary Europe and writers, 663
Poussinistes and Rubénistes, 449, 648
Pragmatism, 924
  and impressionism, 925
Prague, 360
Preciosity, 454 f.
'Pregnant moment', 101, 122, 238
Prehistoric art and sociology, 42 f.
  expressionism, 36
  naturalism, 23 ff.
Pre-magical age, 29
Pre-Raphaelism, 817, 818 f.
Pre-romantic 'discomfort with civilization', 568 ff.
  emotionalism, 550, 557, 568, 572
  escapism, 559
  individualism, 556 f.
  irrationalism, 568 f., 572 f.
  moralism, 558 f.
  novel, 562–6
    author and public of, 565 f.
    heroes and readers of, 565 f.
    of middle-class family life, 562 ff.
    moralism of, 564
  music, 573 f.
  pessimism, 559
  sense of nature, 560 f., 568 f.
  sentimentalism, 550, 557 f., 573
  subjectivism, 563, 570
Pre-romanticism, 550 f., 556–62, 566 ff., 568 ff., 573, 592 f., 706
  and romanticism, 550 f., 643
  and the bourgeoisie, 550
Prestige, 125 f.
Primitive art, 24
  individualism, 25
Prinz von Homburg, 585
Prince Myshkin, 850, 853, 858
Princesse de Clèves, 524, 736
Prize-songs, 165 f.
Professional differentiation, 39 f.
  poets, 165 f.
Proletariat of modern times, 716, 724, 758, 769 f.
Protestantism and the common people, 367
  and the middle class, 367, 368
  and the peasantry, 366 f.
  and the princes, 367, 368
Protestant clergy and secular literature, 540 f.
Proto-Renaissance, 267
Provençal love lyric, 212, 214–24
Psycho-analysis, 790, 919–23
  and historical materialism, 919–22
  and impressionism, 923
  and rationalism, 922 f.
  and Rousseauism, 922
  and sociology, 921 f.
Psychological novel, 525, 752 f., 848, 858, 938
Psychology of exposure, 452 f., 919 f., 923
Psychology and sociology, 221
Public, 98, 99, 107
Public concerts, origins of, 575 f.
  stylistic consequences of, 575 ff.
Publishing, 548, 826 f.
Puritanism, 407, 411
Pygmalion, 27, 768

Quality and popularity in art, 950 f.
'Quarrel between the Ancients and the Moderns', 504, 627, 676
Quattrocento, 272, 292–7, 301 f., 314, 316, 323, 332, 342, 345 f., 347, 348 f., 352

Rappresentazioni sacre, 308
Raskolnikov, 748, 846, 847, 850, 853, 860
Rastignac, 715, 755, 765
Rationalism, 593, 604 f., 613 ff., 622, f., 626 f., 814
  and the aristocracy, 451 f.
  and the bourgeoisie, 451 f.

'Rationalization', 919 f.
Ravenna, 204, 290
Reading public, 539–42, 548, 563, 703 f., 824–9, 834 f., 906
  origins of, 227 f.
Recitation, 78, 85, 166, 227
Reformation, 366–9
  and art, 378 f.
Régence, 503, 505, 506 f., 512, 513, 627 f.
Relativism, 104
  in modern philosophy, 923 f.
Renaissance, 354 f., 356 f., 358, 370, 372
  aristocracy, 279–82, 286, 343, 348–52
  art academies, 295, 304, 321
    appreciation, 307 ff.
    and craftsmanship, 301 f., 311, 314, 320, 325
    education, 312, 320 f.
    market, 300 f., 315 f., 318 f.
    public, 278, 307–10, 344
  artistic competitions, 298
    co-operation, 312
  artists, anecdotes about, 322
    apprenticeship of, 312, 320
    biographies of, 322
    and courts, 317
    economic situation of, 315–18
    and guilds, 311, 315, 317–20
    legend of, 326
    social status of, 311, 319, 323, 324 ff.
    veneration of, 324 ff.
    versatility of, 335
    virtuosity of, 336
    workshop of, 308, 312, 313, 314
  capitalism, 274, 275 f., 279, 284 ff.
  chivalric-romantic tendencies of, 278, 290, 296, 297, 305
  class struggles of, 279, 281
  and classical antiquity, 275 f.
  classicism of, 272, 274, 287, 344–52
  collectors, 300
Renaissance communes, artistic activity of, 297 f.
  concept of, 266–77
  concept of space, 490
  conservatism of, 345, 347, 352
  court society, 286, 292
  courtly culture, 305 ff.
    salons, 306 f.
    tendencies, 278, 290, 291, 292, 296, 341, 351 f.
  courts, 278, 290 f., 305 ff., 337, 341
  cultural élite, 309 f.
  democracy, 282, 283
  'discovery of the world and man', 267
  fine art trade, 302
  formalism, 331, 341
  Gothic-spiritualistic features of, 286, 293, 295 f.
  guilds, 279–82, 319 f.
    artistic activity of, 297 ff.
  individualism of, 326 f.
  and liberalism, 268 f.
  literary professionalism in, 336 ff.
  literary public of, 337 f.
  masters and assistants, 312
    and pupils, 312, 314, 320 f.
  and the Middle Ages, 266 ff., 271–7
  middle class, 278, 280 ff., 285 f., 292, 293, 294, 296, 305, 337 f.
  middle-class art, 287, 292 ff., 305 f.
  middle class, artistic activity of, 299
  national and racial criterion of, 271 f.
  naturalism of, 267 f., 277, 287, 288, 289, 291–4, 297
  novelle, 322
  origins of, 275 f.
  patronage of art, 302–5, 307, 338, 343
  popular art, 308
  princes, 306
    patronage of, 307
  principle of uniformity, 272 ff., 277

Renaissance, rationalism of, 274, 275 f., 278, 284 ff., 305
and religion, 268 f.
rentiers, 282, 286, 295, 337 f.
representation of space, 273, 288
secularization, 291
simultaneity of vision, 274
specialization, 335
universalism, 335
working-class, 281 f.
workshop community, 312, 313
workshop organization, 313
writers, social origins of, 336
René, 524, 570, 677, 678
Repoussoir figures, 426
Restoration, 653, 654, 673 ff., 682, 689, 718, 724, 742, 743, 746
'Reversed perspective', 133
'Revolt of the masses', 929
Révolution davidienne, 639
Revolution of 1848, 769, 773, 774
Revolutionary classicism, 634 f., 642
Revue des Deux Mondes, 727, 731, 732, 776, 795
Rhapsodes, 77 f.
Rheims, 162, 235, 248, 267
'Rhetoricians' (of Jean Paulhan), 933
Rider of Bamberg, 212
Ritual poetry, 165
Robinson Crusoe, 543 ff., 737
Rococo, 501 f., 528–32, 628, 631, 632, 634, 635, 636
and baroque, 501, 528 f.
and the bourgeoisie, 529 f., 532
classicism, 630 f., 635
eclecticism of, 631
eroticism of, 530
hedonism of, 530 f.
and impressionism, 531 f.
and l'art pour l'art, 531
and modern art, 529 f.
struggle against, 533 f.
Roman aestheticism, 130
ancestral portraits, 119
Roman aristocracy, 119 f.
and art, 120
art, 119–24
artists and poets, social and economic position of, 127–30
cultural tradition in the Middle Ages, 136, 154 ff., 158, 160
emperors as amateurs, 129
expressionism, 123, 132
'Imperial art', 119
impressionism, 120, 122, 123
naturalism, 120
painting, 120
patronage, 129
popular art, 120
portrait sculpture, 119 f., 132
predilection for pictures, 120
provincial art, 119
Roman-Catholic art, 434, 436 f.
reform movement, 368
Romanesque architecture, 188 f., 242
art, 181, 189, 243
dynamism of, 193
ecclesiastical and secular elements of, 189
expressionism of, 191 ff.
hieratic quality of, 190 f.
formalism of, 190 f.
stability of, 185
transcendentalism of, 194
manuscripts, 196
sculpture, 192
secular art, 196
Romanticism, 706, 709, 713, 716, 730, 731, 734, 738, 742, 747, 748, 749, 750, 811 f., 856
its ambivalent relationship to art, 668
antiformalism of, 671
and the aristocracy, 666 f.
and artistic freedom, 643 f.
and the bourgeoisie, 730, 785
and classicism, 644
concept of, 653 ff.

Romanticism, its emanatistic philosophy of history, 659 f.
and enlightenment, 666
escapism of, 655, 657, 663, 670
fight against, 716, 782 f., 785–90, 915 f., 917 f.
and the German intelligentsia, 662
and history, 657
and liberalism, 653
as a middle-class movement, 666 f.
and modern art, 656
molochism of, 708
its pathological features, 654 f., 670 f.
and realism, 653, 672 f.
and religion, 646
and the Restoration, 653 f., 672 f.
and the Revolution, 653 f., 672 f.
Romantic aestheticism, 668
historicisms, 657–62
homelessness, 664
individualim, 667 f.
irrationalism, 655 f.
music, 710–13
and the middle class, 711
'occasionalism', 672
painting, 706–9
sensibility, 655 f.
Rome, 318, 341–4, 362, 368, 383 f., 436 f.
Roncevaux, 170
Rossano Gospel-Book, 133
Rouge et Noir, 738, 740, 742 f., 745, 746, 747, 748, 752, 790
Rousseauism, 569 ff., 717, 748, 824, 844, 846, 863, 869, 935
Ruralization of culture, 184
Russian film montage, 953 f.
novel, 841, 847 f., 867

Sack of Rome, 359
Saint-Preux, 524, 570, 677, 699, 748
Saint-Simonites, 717, 730, 734
Salons (annual exhibitions), 513, 649, 650, 652, 681
Salons (literary), 506, 676, 678 f.
S. Vitale, Ravenna, 143, 145
Sancho Panza, 400 f., 406
Scavi, 633
Sceaux, 505
Scop, 165, 172, 231
Scriptoria, 162 f., 176
Second Empire, 767, 768–72, 781
and art, 796 f.
society of, 781, 805–9
theatre of, 797 f.
Second romanticism in England, 814 ff., 822
Serial novel, 726–9
Shakespeare's audience, 407, 411–15
baroque style, 422
concept of chivalry, 397, 401, 405 f.
dramatic form, 415–18
liberalism, 403, 405
mannerism, 422 f.
naturalism, 419 f.
political views, 403 ff.
psychology, 419 f.
social sympathies, 407
theatre, 411, 414
Siena, 288, 289
Sienese painting, 288
Signoria, 279
Simultaneity, experience of, and modern art, 939, 944 ff.
Skald, 166
Slavophils, 844 ff.
Social criticism in England, 816 f., 819–22
levelling, 403
lyrics, 165
novel in Russia, 841, 847, 853 ff.
Socialism, 716, 724, 769 f.
and art in England, 820 f.
and literature, 729 f., 734, 782
and naturalism, 734
Solignac, 178
Sophistic movement, 237, 368
Sophists, 85, 96, 103–7, 113, 115, 338, 658

Sophrosýne, 84, 110
Souillac, 193
Soviet-Russian art policy, 956 ff.
Space, and dynamic cultures, 388 f.
  representation of, 357 f., 370 f., 388 f., 490
Spain, 362, 397 ff., 518
Spatialization of time in modern art, 939
Specialization, 115, 126
Storm and Stress, 603 ff., 609, 610–13, 616, 618, 619, 621, 693
  and the concept of genius, 611 f.
  and enlightenment, 605, 610 f., 612 ff.
  irrationalism of, 604 f., 607, 610
  its 'philosophy of life', 613
Stoic ethics, 210
Stoics, 113
'Style Louis XIV', 441, 447
Subjectivism, 326 ff.
Subscription and publishing, 548
Surrealism, 358, 932–8, 946
  dualism of, 936 f.
  and mannerism, 937
  and psycho-analysis, 936
Symbol and allegory, 897
Symbolism, 393 f., 883, 895–8, 933 f.
  and aristocratism, 900 f.
  and estrangement, 899 f.
  and expressionism, 898
  and impressionism, 896
  and irrationalism, 896, 898
  and spiritualism, 896

'Tactile values', 289
Technicism, 871
  in art theory, 475
Technics, cultural problem of, 822 f.
'Terrorists' (of Jean Paulhan), 932 f.
Theatre and cinema, 949 f.
  and the French bourgeoisie, 625 f.
  public of the modern metropolis, 797 f.
Théâtre-Français, 687, 688, 689, 690
Thermidor 9, 639, 640, 652, 666
Time in the modern novel, 791, 925 f., 939, 944 ff.
Toledo, 392
Tom Jones, 737
Torquato Tasso, 587, 618
Tragédie classique, 417 f., 687
  and the middle class, 625
  and naturalism, 625
  origins of, 624 f.
  and rationalism, 625
Tragedy, idea of, and the Middle Ages, 416
  periods of, 589
  and political realism, 416
  and Protestantism, 417
Tragic and non-heroic outlook, 589
'Trahison des clercs', 340
Trajan's Column, 121, 134
'Travel landscape', 262
Trecento, 275, 287 ff., 291, 292
Tristram Shandy, 737
'Triumph of realism', 762, 781
Troubadour poetry, 216–26
  origins of, Arabic theory, 221
    classical theory, 222
    folk-song theory, 222 f.
    fiction theory, 216–19
Troubadours and clerics, 224
  and minstrels, 224–8
  social status of, 219, 224
'Twentieth century', 927
Twilight of the Gods, 811
'Two nations', 816
'Typical styles', 429 f.

Ultras and liberals, 675
Ulysses, 934, 939, 945
Universals dispute, 236 ff.
Uomo universale, 335
Urbino, 305, 518
Utilitarians, 813, 814
Utrecht Psalter, 162

Vagans, 225 f., 229 ff.

Vaudeville, 689, 692 f., 728, 804
Vautrin, 755, 758, 765
Venice, 278, 279, 284, 289, 323, 324, 369, 390 f.
  Scuola S. Rocco, 391
Véra, 887
Verona, 278, 290, 291
Versailles, 360, 431, 442, 446, 505, 513
Victorian compromise, 814, 815, 833
  England, 815
    and art, 817 f.
Vie factice, 885 ff.
Vie de Marianne, 526, 737
Viennese impressionism, 908 f.
Virtuosity, 336
Voltairianism, 510, 569, 685
  and Rousseauism, 570, 572
Votive offerings, 90

Waldenses, 378
Wandering court singer, 166 f.
  minstrel, 79
  scholar, 267
War and Peace, 853, 866, 867, 868, 869
Wars of religion, 435, 438
Wars of Roses, 401, 408
Weimar, 602, 616, 617 f., 633
Weltschmerz, 699 f., 887
Werther, 523, 524, 526, 570, 604, 617, 620, 677, 699, 719, 737
West and East, 930
Westernizers in Russia, 844 f.
Whigs, 546, 552
  and Tories, 536 f., 543–6
Wilhelm Meister, 618, 619, 621, 654, 720, 737, 738
'Wits', 541 f.
Women, artistic activity of, 41
  and artistic life, 306 f.
Work of art as a commodity, 265
Work, social estimation of, 126, 128
Workshop instruction and academies, 384
World Exhibition of 1851, 835
  of 1867, 808
World literature, 621 f., 703
Writers and public, 717 ff., 768

INDEX OF NAMES

Aachen, Hans von, 360
Abraham, Pol, 489
Achard, 178
Adam, L., 477
Addison, Joseph, 542 f., 545, 825
Aeschylus, 89, 96, 106, 108, 109, 118
Akhenaton, 59 f., 62, 66
Albert, Archduke, 457, 471
Albert, Maurice, 967
Alberti, Leon Battista, 283, 321 f., 333, 334, 345, 347, 494
Albertinelli, Mariotto, 313
Albizzi family, 283
Albrecht V, 360
Alcaeus, 87
Alexander the Great, 113, 118, 127
Alexander II, 865
Alexander Severus, 129
Alexis, Paul, 794, 882
Altdorfer, Albrecht, 600
Altoviti, 343
Amenhotep IV, 53, 59 f.
Anacreon, 89, 130
Angelico, Fra Giovanni, 293, 303, 314, 315, 342
Angers, David d', 681
Anne, Queen of England, 543, 546
Antal, Frederick, 492, 965
Apelles, 128
Apollonius, 213
Archilochus, 88, 130
Aretino, Pietro, 337, 494
Arion, 89
Ariosto, 399, 518
Aristhonothos, 87, 88
Aristophanes, 97, 800
Aristotle, 97, 112, 345
Armenini, Giov. Batt., 309, 493
Arnaut, Daniel, 226
Arnim, Achim von, 666
Arnold, Matthew, 697, 788, 906
Arpino, Cavaliere d', 437
Ashur-bani-pal, 66
Asselineau, Charles, 877
Asterius of Amasia, 147
Atkinson, Nora, 969
Attila, 164, 166, 167
Aubigné, Agrippa d', 626
Augier, Émile, 780, 796, 797, 798, 799, 800, 802, 804
Augustus, 303, 517
Aurelius, Marcus, 129, 160
Aurevilly, Barbey d', 889, 904
Austen, Jane, 541, 825, 828, 833, 835, 902
Aynard, Joseph, 498, 961, 962, 966
Ayrton, Michael, 977

Bab, Julius, 968
Babbitt, Irving, 963
Babeuf, 724
Bacchylides, 89
Bach, Joh. Seb., 573 f., 711, 712, 934
Bach, Phil. Emm., 576
Bacon, Francis, 39
Baglioni family, 279
Bainville, Jacques, 964
Baker, Ernest A., 973

Baldovinetti, Alessio, 302
Balet, Leo, 963, 965
Balzac, 405, 524, 565, 568, 570, 677, 681, 694, 703, 710, 715, 716, 717, 719, 723, 726, 727, 728, 729, 730, 731, 734, 735, 738, 739, 740, 741, 749, 753–68, 778, 779, 783, 784, 827, 829, 831, 833, 836, 837, 848, 852, 854, 864, 894, 899, 904, 907, 908, 911, 917, 938, 970
Bandello, Matteo, 494
Barberini family, 437
Bardèche, Maurice, 969, 970
Baron, Hans, 490
Barraclough, G., 964
Barrès, Maurice, 881, 882, 883, 901, 908, 929
Bartas, Baron du, 626
Bartolommeo, Fra, 311, 313, 344
Bartsch, Karl, 484
Batho, E., 972, 973
Baudelaire, 568, 684, 759, 765, 781, 806, 812, 881, 883, 885, 889, 890, 892, 893, 894, 895, 904, 906, 975, 976
Baudry, Paul, 772, 778
Baum, Julius, 486
Bax, E. Belfort, 495
Bayle, Pierre, 268, 503
Bazille, Frédéric, 879
Bazin, Germain, 977
Beardsley, Aubrey, 889, 904, 906
Beaumarchais, 456, 628, 964
Beaumont, Francis, 404, 411
Beazley, J. D., 480
Beccafumi, 355, 388
Becker, C. H., 483
Becque, Henri, 911
Bédier, Joseph, 169 ff., 484, 488, 489, 498, 961
Beenken, H., 485
Beers, Henry A., 967, 968
Beethoven, 531, 577, 710, 712, 751
Bek, 59
Bekker, Paul, 972
Belinsky, 844, 846
Beljame, Alexandre, 962
Bellange, Jacques, 626
Bellessort, André, 970, 972, 974
Bellini, Giovanni, 312
Bellori, 353, 495
Beloch, K., 480
Below, Georg von, 485, 488, 491
Benda, Julien, 494, 977
Benjamin, Walter, 476, 490, 977
Benoit, François, 966
Bentovogli family, 279
Béranger, 685 f.
Berchem, Nicolas, 463
Bercken, E. von, 496
Berdiaeff, Nicolas, 974
Bérenger, Henry, 975
Berenson, Bernard, 289, 333, 492, 494
Bergeret, P.-N., 509
Bergson, 881, 898, 907, 916, 925, 928, 929, 939, 946
Berlioz, 711, 712
Bernard of Clairvaux, 224
Bernart de Ventadour, 225
Bernini, Lorenzo, 423, 435, 437
Bernward, 178
Berri, Duc de, 264, 395
Berthelot, Philippe, 781
Bertin, aîné, 725, 780
Bertoldo di Giovanni, 304 f.
Bertran de Born, 225
Beth, K., 476
Bethe, E., 480
Bezold, Fr. von, 488, 495, 499
Bicci, Neri di, 309, 314
Biedermann, Karl, 964
Biese, Alfred, 488
Billiet, Joseph, 966
Birt, Th., 481
Bismarck, 808
Bisticci, Vespasiano, 303
Björnson, 914, 917
Blake, William, 655, 696

Blanc, Louis, 969
Bloch, Marc, 486
Blok, P. J., 499
Blunt, Anthony, 492, 495
Boccaccio, 266, 281, 286, 322, 336, 517
Bode, W. von, 492, 493, 499
Boehme, Jakob, 600
Bogart, Humphrey, 700
Boileau, 441, 442, 456, 470, 504, 523, 961
Boissonade, P., 484, 486
Bojardo, 305, 399
Bolingbroke, Vis., 545
Bonald, V. de, 667, 844
Bonn, M. J., 977
Bor, Marie, 970
Borchardt, Ludwig, 477
Borghese family, 437
Borghini, Raffaele, 376, 386, 495
Borghini, Vincenzo, 353, 376, 384
Borgia, Cesare, 324
Borgia, Lucrezia, 306
Borinski, Karl, 490, 494
Borromeo, Carlo, 372
Bossuet, 441, 504, 508, 736
Botticelli, 294, 297, 303, 311, 314, 315, 370
Boucher, 501, 521, 532, 533, 534, 631
Bouguereau, W., 778
Bouillon, Duke of, 437
Bouilly, Jean-Nicolas, 689
Boulanger, Louis, 681, 709, 778
Bourbon, House of, 686
Bourget, Paul, 747, 765, 878, 881, 882, 883, 970, 972, 975
Bourl'honne, P., 973
Bouvier, Émile, 970, 971
Bowra, C. M., 976
Bracciolini, Poggio, 269
Bradbrook, M. C., 976
Bradley, A. C., 497, 924
Brailsford, H. N., 968
Bramante, 335, 342
Brancacci family, 302
Brandes, Georg, 916, 967
Braque, Georges, 931
Bray, René, 498
Breasted, J. H., 477, 478
Brecht, Walter, 490
Bréhier, Louis, 483
Bremond, Henri, 976
Brentano, Lujo, 482
Breton, André, 935, 969, 970, 977
Breuil, Henri, 36, 476, 477
Bridges, Robert, 497
Brieger, Lothar, 493, 495
Brieux, Eugène, 911
Briggs, Martin S., 485
Brinkmann, Carl, 482
Brinkmann, Hennig, 486, 488, 497
Bronzino, 314, 355, 360, 387, 389 f.
Bruegel, Pieter, 355, 356, 357, 393–6
Brueggemann, Fritz, 964
Bruford, W. H., 964
Brunelleschi, 268, 284, 299, 302, 303, 311, 323, 335
Brunetière, Ferdinand, 785, 881
Bruni, Leonardo, 269
Bruno, Giordano, 382, 496, 937
Buecher, Karl, 184, 199, 476, 485, 486, 494
Buechner, L., 844
Buehler, Johannes, 485, 486
Buloz, François, 727, 730, 780
Bunyan, 563
Burckhardt, Jakob, 126, 267, 268, 269, 326, 356, 424, 429, 479, 481, 491, 493
Burdach, Konrad, 221, 276, 487, 488, 491
Burke, Edmund, 616, 815, 844, 898
Burkitt, M. C., 476, 477
Burn, A. R., 478, 479
Bury, J. B., 482
Butler, Joseph, 655
Buttke, E., 970
Byron, 667, 677, 695, 696, 699–703, 705, 709, 719, 730

Callot, Jacques, 357
Calvin, 268, 378
Campanella, Tommaso, 545
Campin, Robert, 277
Candid (Pieter de Witte), 360
Cangrande, 291
Canitz, Baron von, 601
Capponi family, 283
Caraffa, Cardinal Carlo, 369
Caravaggio, 424, 433 ff., 437, 449
Cardano, Girolamo, 335, 452
Carlyle, 814, 815, 816, 817, 819, 820, 824, 825, 831
Carr, E. H., 974
Carracci family, 433 f., 437
Carracci, Agostino, 433
Carracci, Annibale, 353
Carrara family, 291
Caruso, 823
Cassagne, Albert, 969, 975
Cassiodorus, 166
Cassirer, Ernst, 492
Castagno, Andrea del, 272, 293, 300, 311
Castiglione, Baldassare, 306, 324, 351 f., 494, 518
Cauer, Paul, 479
Cavalcanti, Guido, 322, 336
Caylus, Comte de, 521, 628, 632
Cazamian, Louis, 973
Cazamian, M. L., 973, 976
Cellini, Benvenuto, 452
Cennini, Cennino, 320
Cerfberr, A., 970
Cervantes, 268, 357, 394, 397, 398–401, 897, 916
Cézanne, 333, 877, 879, 927
Chadwick, H. M., 478, 479, 484
Chagall, Marc, 931, 946
Chambers, E. K., 487, 497
Chamisso, Adalbert von, 666
Champfleury, Jules, 774, 775, 893, 969
Chaplin, 947
Chardin, Jean-Siméon, 450, 501, 522, 531, 532, 533, 635
Charlemagne, 159–63, 164, 170, 189, 190, 204, 362
Charles I, 535, 580
Charles V, 324, 325, 362, 363 f., 373, 596
Charles VIII, 362
Charles X, 682
Charles-Brun, 972
Charlety, S., 969
Charpentier, John, 975
Chateaubriand, 646, 654, 666, 676, 677 f., 681, 682, 699, 700, 705, 709, 719, 747, 755, 883
Chaussée, P.-C. Nivelle de la, 690
Chekhov, 869, 894, 895, 908, 909 ff., 975
Chénier, 629, 630
Chernyshevsky, 843, 846
Chesterfield, Lord, 547
Chesterton, G. K., 828, 905, 929, 973
Chigi family, 437
Chigi, Agostino, 324, 343
Childe, V. Gordon, 31, 36, 476, 477
Chirico, Giorgio de, 946
Chledowski, Casimir de, 494
Chopin, 710, 712
Chrétien de Troyes, 227 f.
Christ, Wilhelm von, 961
Christophe, J., 970
Cimabue, 312, 322
Cino da Pistoja, 336
Cione, Nardo di, 289
Clark, Kenneth, 493, 494
Claudel, Paul, 881
Claude Lorrain, 430, 624
Cleisthenes, 100
Clement VII, 362, 368
Clement VIII, 377
Clement of Alexandria, 146
Clovio, Giulio, 496
Clovis, 166
Clutton-Brock, A., 972
Cobban, Alfred, 968

Cochin, Ch.-N., 470, 628, 632
Cock, Jeroome de, 468
Coelho, Claudio, 360
Coellen, Ludwig, 489
Cohen, Gustave, 484
Colbert, 442, 444–8
Coleridge, 404, 665, 696, 697, 705, 815, 924, 967
Collins, A. S., 962
Colonna, Vittoria, 369
Columbus, 268
Comte, Auguste, 724, 844
Congreve, William, 545, 547
Constable, John, 707, 777, 878
Constant, Benjamin, 648, 678, 699, 719, 848
Constantine the Great, 132, 134
Contarini, Gaspare, 369, 372
Conze, Alexander, 475 f.
Copernicus, 266, 431
Corbière, Tristan, 894, 895
Corneille, 441, 453, 454, 523, 582, 590, 626, 627, 687, 688, 808, 828, 848, 849
Cortona, Pietro da, 437
Cosimo I, de' Medici, 383
Cosimo, Piero di, 297, 314
Cossa, Francesco, 305 f.
Coulin, Jules, 971
Coulton, G. G., 484
Courajod, Louis, 276, 491
Courbet, 772, 774–7, 778, 893
Cousin, Jean, 626
Cousin, Victor, 725, 732
Couture, Thomas, 778
Coypel, Antoine, 632
Crébillon *fils*, 522
Croce, Benedetto, 424 f., 495, 498
Cross, W. L., 963, 973
Crosten, William L., 972
Crozat, 509, 521
Cruse, Amy, 973
Cunningham, W., 486, 495, 497
Curtius, E. R., 975, 977
Curtius, Ludwig, 477, 478, 479
Cuyp, Aelbert, 470
Cyrano de Bergerac, 545

Daddi, Bernardo, 289
Daiches, David, 497
D'Alembert, 507, 510, 564, 884
Dali, Salvador, 931, 936, 937, 946
Dalton, O. M., 482, 483
Danilevsky, 845
D'Annunzio, 908
Dante, 226, 235, 261, 266, 275, 276, 517, 709, 734
Danton, 654, 747
Daumier, Honoré, 776, 777, 778
D'Avenel, G., 499
David, Jacques Louis, 502, 531, 623, 630, 633, 634, 635–42, 644, 645, 646, 651, 652, 709
David, Jules, 966
Davidsohn, Robert, 491
Debussy, 931
Decamps, A. G., 709, 778
Defoe, Daniel, 541, 543 ff., 549, 825, 826
Degas, 25, 879, 910
Dehio, Georg, 160, 240, 483, 484, 485, 486, 490
Dejob, Charles, 496
Dekker, Thomas, 408, 418, 419
Delacroix, 531, 640, 681, 706–10, 713, 731, 811, 878, 968
Delaroche, 709
D'Ennery, 694
Descartes, 382, 441
Deschamps, Émile, 681
Des Granges, Charles-Marc, 967, 969
Desiderio da Settignano, 297, 300
Devéria, Eugène, 681
Dickens, 739, 814, 924, 825, 826, 827–35, 848, 852, 854, 856, 868, 906
Diderot, 504, 521, 525, 533 f., 567, 573, 582 ff., 586, 670, 690, 693, 740, 962, 963, 964, 967
Diehl, Charles, 482, 483

Diels, H., 479
Dietz, Friedrich, 487
Dill, Samuel, 483
Dilthey, Wilhelm, 332, 432, 494, 498, 672, 964
Dinamov, Sergei, 497
Dio Chrysostom, 128
Disraeli, Benjamin, 816, 824, 925
Dobrée, B., 972, 973
Dobrolyubov, 843
Dolce, Lodovico, 386
Dolmayr, Hermann, 494, 495
Donatello, 272, 293, 295, 303, 311, 313, 314, 315, 342
Dopsch, Alfons, 483, 484, 485
Dorat, C.-J., 549
Doren, Alfred, 491, 492
Dos Passos, 944
Dostoevsky, 373, 568, 570, 739, 749, 754, 842, 845, 846, 848, 849, 850–61, 862 f., 865, 867, 868, 907, 909, 930, 938, 974
Drake, Sir Francis, 402
Dresdner, Albert, 493, 494, 496, 498, 499, 961, 965, 966
Drey, Paul, 493, 499
Dreyfous, Maurice, 965, 966
Dreyfus, 881
Drost, Willi, 500
Droysen, J. G., 124
Dryden, John, 540
Du Bos, Abbé, 450
Du Bos, Charles, 977
Dubufe, Claude-Marie, 778
Ducis, Jean-François, 689
Ducray-Duminil, 755
Duhamel, Georges, 975
Dumas, Alexandre, 681, 682, 689, 693, 695, 726, 727, 728, 730, 731, 827
Dumas *fils*, 417, 526, 780, 796, 797, 798, 799, 800, 802, 803, 804
Dumesnil, René, 975
Durandus, 137
Duranty, Ph., 774
Dürer, 387 f., 600
Dutacq, 726
Dvořák, Max, 357, 481, 482, 483, 491, 495, 497
Dyck, Anthony van, 424

Eckert, Christian, 972
Ehrenberg, Richard, 495
Ehrenberg, Victor, 480
Ehrhard, Albert, 496, 498
Ehrismann, Gustav, 486
Eichendorff, 603, 666
Eicken, Heinrich von, 485, 487
Einhart, 164
Einstein, Alfred, 968, 972
Eisenstadt, Mussia, 961
Eisenstein, S. M., 954, 956
Eleanor of Aquitaine, 212
Eliot, George, 835 ff., 868, 902, 906, 938
Eliot, T. S., 933, 934
Elizabeth, Queen of England, 402, 407, 408
Elizabeth Charlotte, 505
Eloesser, Arthur, 962, 964
Empedocles, 96
Engels, Friedrich, 404, 495, 705, 724, 761, 920, 969, 970
Epicharmus, 89
Erasmus, 378, 463
Erman, Adolf, 57, 477
Ermaneric, 164
Ermengarde of Narbonne, 212
Ernst, Paul, 964, 976
Ernst, Viktor, 486
Essex, Earl of, 407
Este family, 279, 363
Estève, Edmond, 969
Euripides, 96, 97, 106–10, 117, 118, 213
Eusebius, 147
Evelyn, John, 466, 499
Eyck, Brothers van, 262
Eyck, Jan van, 266, 271

Fabriano, Gentile da, 266, 291, 315, 323, 342
Faguet, Émile, 694, 962, 968, 970, 971
Fajon, Étienne, 966
Falconet, 632
Faral, Edmond, 484, 488
Farnese family, 279, 437
Fauriel, M., 487, 961
Fehr, Bernhard, 976
Félibien, 448
Fénelon, 503
Ferri, Silvio, 481
Feuerbach, Ludwig, 836, 844
Feuerlicht, I., 487
Feuillet, Octave, 772, 780, 795 f.
Feydeau, Ernest, 789
Fichte, 603, 616, 654, 673
Ficino, Marsilio, 304
Fielding, Henry, 541, 547, 551, 568, 737, 825, 826, 828
Filarete, 323, 328
Fischer, Wilhelm, 963
Fisher, H. A. L., 495
Flach, Jacques, 487
Flaubert, 570, 684, 699, 716, 730, 734, 737, 739, 762, 765, 769, 772, 774, 779, 781–92, 793, 795, 800, 805, 806, 810, 812, 816, 831, 846, 848, 858, 864, 867, 870, 881, 895, 899, 907, 911, 925, 938, 971
Flavians, the, 119
Fléchier, 508
Fletcher, John, 404, 411
Fleury-Sonolet, 972
Fliche, A., 485
Flinck, Govert, 465
Floerke, Hanns, 499
Focillon, Henri, 489, 971, 975
Fontaine, André, 498, 961, 966
Fontenelle, 503, 507
Ford, Henry, 974
Ford, John, 419
Fouquet, Jean, 266
Fourier, Charles, 724, 844
Fowler, W. W., 962
Fragonard, 509, 522, 528, 531, 532, 631, 634, 654
Francastel, Pierre, 974
France, Anatole, 881
Francesca, Piero della, 272, 293, 294, 307, 333
Francia, Francesco, 311, 312, 323
Franciabigio, 313
Francis I, 360, 362, 438
Frankl, Paul, 489
Franz Joseph, 808
Frederick II, Emp., 280
Frederick II, 'the Great', 602
Freud, 373, 571, 919–23, 936, 976
Frey, Dagobert, 489, 490
Freymond, Émile, 488
Friedlaender, Ludwig, 481
Friedlaender, Max J., 500
Friedlaender, Walter, 495, 965
Fry, Roger, 976
Fugger family, 363
Funck-Brentano, F., 498, 961

Gabriel, Jacques Ange, 628
Gaddi, Taddeo, 289
Gaiffe, F., 962
Galileo, 332
Gall, Ernst, 240, 241, 489
Ganzenmueller, Wilhelm, 488
Garbo, Greta, 526
Gardner, E. A., 479
Garger, E. V., 482
Gaskell, Mrs., 824, 825, 835
Gaspary, Adolfo, 492
Gauguin, Paul, 894
Gaultier, Jules de, 971
Gauricus, Pomponius, 389, 496
Gautier, Théophile, 681, 682, 683, 684, 702, 710, 713, 730, 731, 787, 870, 883, 889, 892, 904
Gaye, 493
Gebhardt, Émile, 491
Gellert, 603

Genestal, R., 486
Geoffrin, Mme, 507
George, Henry, 864
George, Stefan, 908
Gérard, 645, 651, 652
Gerhard, E., 963, 965
Géricault, 531, 708
Gersaint, 521
Gessner, Salomon, 618
Ghiberti, 284, 299, 303, 311, 313, 315, 323, 336
Ghirlandajo, Domenico, 294, 297, 302, 306, 311, 312, 313, 314, 316, 318, 323, 335, 336
Gibbon, 658
Giberti, Giammateo, 369
Gide, André, 784, 933
Gierke, Otto von, 489
Gigoux, Jean, 681
Gilbert, Eugène, 969, 971
Gilio, Andrea, 376
Gilson, Étienne, 488
Ginisty, Paul, 967
Giotto, 266, 272, 276, 286 ff., 292, 312, 322, 335, 391, 623, 624
Girardin, Émile de, 726
Girodet, 644, 646
Glanville, R. K., 477
Glotz, G., 478
Glover, T. R., 961
Glück, Gustav, 496
Gobelin family, 446
Godwin, William, 695
Goerres, Joseph, 603, 654
Goethe, 424, 570, 573, 577, 587, 588, 591, 602, 604, 607, 609, 612, 616, 617–22, 633, 634, 654, 668, 670, 671, 673, 697, 699, 703, 709, 719, 737, 738, 739, 755, 786, 832, 848, 862, 869, 932
Gogh, Vincent van, 894, 927
Gogol, 852
Goldfriedrich, Johann, 964
Goldschmidt, Fritz, 496
Goldsmith, Oliver, 548, 560, 696, 826
Gombosi, Georg, 492
Goncharov, 852, 855
Goncourt, Edmond and Jules de, 774, 775, 781, 784, 795, 800, 809, 831, 864, 870, 877, 885, 966, 971, 975, 976
Gonzaga family, 363
Gonzaga, Ludovico, 306, 307
Gonzaga, Vincenzo, 471
Gorky, Maxim, 869, 909, 974
Gothein, Eberhard, 498
Gottsched, 601, 603
Goyen, Jan van, 423, 467, 469, 470
Gozzoli, Benozzo, 293, 294, 303, 314, 315, 342
Gracchus, Tiberius, 121
Graeven, H., 484
Granville, George, 545
Grautoff, O., 496
Greco, 355, 356, 357, 381, 392 ff.
Green, J. R., 497
Greg, W. W., 961
Gregory of Tours, 156
Gretton, R. H., 962
Greuze, 501, 502, 530, 533, 582, 631, 635
Grib, V., 970
Grierson, H. J. C., 497, 968
Griffith, D. W., 943, 953
Grigoriev, 845
Grimm, Brothers, 603
Grimm, Jakob, 168
Grimm, Melchior, 507
Groenbeck, V., 479
Gros, Baron, 644, 645
Grosse, Ernst, 476
Grossmann, Henryk, 498
Grupp, Georg, 482, 484
Gruyer, Gustave, 496
Guardi, 528, 532, 630
Guardini, 517, 518, 519
Guérin, 644
Guillemin, Henri, 968
Guinicelli, Guido, 322
Guizot, 721, 725

Gundolf, Friedrich, 934, 977
Guyon, Bernard, 970
Guys, Constantin, 759, 879

Haas, Eugen, 971
Habsburg, House of, 457
Hadrian, 129, 160
Haldane, Elizabeth S., 973
Halm, August, 963
Hals, Frans, 424, 467, 470
Hamann, Joh. Georg, 603, 612, 616, 844, 965
Hamann, Richard, 492
Hamilton, William, 632
Hammond, J. L. and B., 962
Hammurabi, 64, 65
Handel, 712
Harbage, Alfred, 497
Hardy, Alexandre, 626
Harkness, Margaret, 761
Harrison, J., 480
Hartog, W. J., 967, 968
Haskins, Ch. H., 484
Hassenfratz, J. H., 638
Hatzfeld, H., 976
Hauck, Albert, 486
Hauptmann, Gerhardt, 579, 911
Hausenstein, Wilhelm, 38, 477, 478, 965
Haussmann, Baron, 771, 795
Hautecoeur, Louis, 966
Haydn, 576, 577
Haym, R., 672
Hazard, Paul, 488, 489, 498, 961
Hazlitt, William, 924
Hearnshaw, F. J. C., 489
Hebbel, 106, 571, 586, 589, 702, 914
Heemskerck, Marten van, 357
Hegel, 758
Heichelheim, Fr. M., 477
Heideloff, Carl, 489
Hehn, Viktor, 965
Heine, 668, 685, 701, 705, 721, 807, 965
Heinse, 270, 490
Heinz, Josef, 360
Hell, J., 487
Helst, Bartholomaeus van der, 467
Helvétius, 622, 740, 747
Henri IV, 519, 624
Henrici, E., 487
Henriette, d'Angleterre, 736
Henry III, 324
Heraclitus, 96, 658
Herder, 603, 609, 615 f., 634, 658, 844
Herodotus, 51, 96
Herondas, 118
Herostratus, 74
Hertz, Wilhelm, 484
Herzen, Alexander, 845
Hesiod, 80
Hesse, Hermann, 977
Heusler, Andreas, 169, 484
Heywood, Thomas, 418, 419
Hiero, 89
Hildebrand, Adolf, 333, 494
Hilduard, 178
Hilka, Alfons, 488
Hill, Christopher, 962
Hindemith, Paul, 931
Hinks, Roger, 484
Hintze, Otto, 963
Hitler, 816, 891, 929
Hobbema, 467, 470
Hobson, John A., 963
Hoelderlin, 603, 699
Hoenigswald, Richard, 492
Hoerner, Margarete, 495
Hoernes, H., 36, 40, 68, 476, 477, 478
Hoffmann, E. T. A., 603
Hofmannsthal, Hugo von, 765, 908 f., 970
Hogarth, D. G., 478
Hogarth, William, 502, 564
Holbach, Baron d', 740
Hollanda, Francisco de, 330, 369
Homer, 71, 74, 77–81, 97, 173, 828, 867, 956
Hooch, Pieter de, 463, 467, 470

Hoogstraten, Samuel van, 463
Hosius, C., 961
Houdon, Jean Antoine, 652
Hourticq, Louis, 961, 966
House, Humphrey, 973
Houssaye, Arsène, 892
Huch, Ricarda, 967
Hugh of St. Victor, 224
Hugo, Victor, 678, 681, 682, 684, 685–8, 693, 695, 710, 730, 731, 760, 779, 799, 810, 811, 868, 907
Huizinga, J., 490, 494, 499, 961
Hull, Eleanor, 483
Hume, David, 549, 658
Hunt, H. J., 969, 971
Hunt, Leigh, 695
Huret, Jules, 881, 883, 900, 975, 976
Huth, Hans, 489
Hutten, Ulrich von, 366
Huxley, Thomas, 836, 841
Huyghe, René, 977
Huysmans, J. K., 882, 883, 886, 889, 905

Ibsen, 106, 417, 591, 592, 695, 764, 902, 911, 914–17, 918, 976
Inama-Sternegg, K. Th., 485
Ingres, 731, 778
Isabella, Archduchess, 457
Isabella d'Este, 306
Isabey, L. G. E., 651
Isembert, 178

Jackson, Holbrook, 976
Jackson, T. A., 497
Jackson, T. S., 973
Jacobi, Friedr. Heinr., 616
Jaeger, W., 479, 480
James I, 407
James II, 535
James, Henry, 890 f., 906, 907
James, William, 920
Jamot, Paul, 968
Jaspers, Karl, 966
Jeanroy, Alfred, 222, 487
Jerrold, M. J., 493
Jode, Geeraard de, 468
Johannot, 681
John of the Cross, 372
Johnson, Samuel, 546, 547, 549, 924
Jones, Ernest, 920, 976
Jones, G. P., 489
Jonson, Ben, 408, 421
Joubin, André, 968
Jouffroy, Th., 725
Joyce, James, 358, 931, 934, 936, 937, 938, 939, 945 f.
Joyce, P. W., 483
Julienne, 521
Julius II, 342, 343
Justi, Carl, 965
Justinian, 139, 140, 143

Kaegi, Werner, 490
Kaerst, Julius, 115, 480
Kafka, Franz, 358, 931, 934, 936, 937, 938
Kahn, Ludwig W., 965
Kant, 603, 605, 608, 609, 616, 667, 732, 790
Karlinger, H., 490
Karlstadt, 378
Karo, G., 478
Kaschnitz-Weinberg, Guido, 481, 485
Kaser, Kurt, 499
Kaufmann, Angelika, 636
Kautsky, Karl, 489, 961
Kautzsch, Rudolf, 481
Keats, 668, 696, 699, 702
Keferstein, Georg, 965, 971
Kehrer, H., 496
Kelly, J. F., 497
Kepler, 332
Ker, W. P., 484, 497, 968
Keyserling, Hermann Graf, 929, 976
Kierkegaard, 915
Kingsley, Charles, 824, 825, 835
Kirchner, Erwin, 967
Klages, Ludwig, 929

Kleist, Heinrich von, 571, 585, 666, 699
Klemperer, Viktor, 499
Klettenberg, Fraeulein von, 620
Klopstock, 602
Kluckhohn, Paul, 486, 487
Knebel, Karl Ludwig, 617
Knoop, G., 489
Koberstein, K. A., 484
Koch, Herbert, 481
Kock, Paul de, 789
Koegel, Rudolf, 484
Koemstedt, Rudolf, 482
Koerte, Alfred, 487
Koht, Halvdan, 976
Kondakoff, N., 482
Korff, H. A., 965
Koser, R., 498
Kotzebue, 618
Kracauer, S., 972
Kraus, Karl, 805
Kuehn, Herbert, 476, 477
Kulischer, Josef, 485

Labiche, Émile, 804
La Bruyère, 440
La Calprenède, 523
Lacey, Alexander, 968
Lachmann, Karl, 170, 172
Laclos, Choderlos de, 522, 525, 705
Lacroix, Paul, 693
Lactantius, 481
Lafayette, Mme de, 453, 524, 736
Lafayette, Marquis de, 747
Laffitte, Jacques, 721
Lafontaine, 441, 456
Lamartine, 667, 675, 678, 681, 682, 685, 701, 709, 716, 730, 883
Lambert, Constant, 977
Lamennais, F.-R. de, 667
Lamprecht, Karl, 475
Lancret, Nicolas, 521
Lange, Julius, 57, 83, 475
Lange, Konrad, 967
Lanson, Gustave, 961, 962, 966
Laplace, 509
Laqueur, Richard, 482
Largillière, 501, 513
Larkin, Oliver, 971
La Rochefoucauld, 441, 453, 455, 525
Lask, Emil, 967
Latini, Brunetto, 336
La Tour, Maurice Quentin de, 528
Laurence, R. V., 496
Laurencie, Lionel de, 972
Lautréamont, 894, 927
Lavater, 603, 611
Lavisse, Ernest, 495, 498
Lavrin, Janko, 973, 976
Leavis, F. R., 973, 976
Leavis, Q. D., 963, 973
Le Brun, 442, 445–50, 470, 504, 513, 532, 627, 639, 676
Leconte de Lisle, 684
Lederer, Emil, 969, 977
Lemaître, Jules, 972
Lemonnier, Henry, 498
Le Nain, Louis, 424, 441, 452, 626
Lenin, 956, 974
Lenz, Max, 489
Lenz, Reinhold, 603
Leo III, 147 ff.
Leo X, 342
Leonardo da Vinci, 303, 308, 312, 313, 316, 318, 320, 321, 324, 325, 341, 344, 346, 350, 429, 637
Leopardi, 667, 701
Lermontov, 667, 699
Lerner-Lehmkuhl, H., 493
Lesage, 525
Lessing, 49, 122, 322, 490, 502, 526, 582, 587, 590, 593, 602 f., 604, 616, 634
Le Sueur, 441
Lévy-Bruhl, 27, 476
Lewis, C. Day, 968
Lewis, Wyndham, 497
Lillo, George, 579, 581, 963

Lippi, Filippino, 302, 303, 314, 316, 318
Lippi, Filippo, 303, 311, 315, 323
Liszt, 710, 711, 712, 713
Locke, John, 545, 609, 622
Loesch, H. von, 489
Loewy, Emmanuel, 83, 475 f.
Logau, Friedrich von, 602
Lomazzo, Giov. Paolo, 375, 382, 387, 496
Lorenzetti, Ambrogio, 288, 289, 334
Lorenzo, Monaco, 293
Lot, Ferdinand, 483
Louis XIII, 440, 625
Louis XIV, 441, 445 ff., 450, 456, 470, 503 ff., 506, 508, 512, 513, 523, 530, 625, 629, 639, 675
Louis XV, 470, 504, 505, 507, 508, 530
Louis XVI, 504, 505, 507, 509
Louis Napoleon, 685
Louis-Philippe, 720–3
Louis the Pious, 164
Louis, Paul, 969, 974
Loyola, Ignatius, 373, 397, 435
Luc, Jean, 963
Lucas, F. L., 966
Lucas-Dubreton, J., 969
Luchaire, Julien, 491
Lucian, 130
Lucretius, 747
Ludovisi family, 437
Luecken, G. von, 485
Lukács, Georg, 964, 968, 969, 971, 972, 973, 974
Luquet, G. H., 476
Luther, 268, 366 f., 373, 378, 596
Lynd, H. M., 976
Lyly, John, 825
Lysippus, 105, 117

Machiavelli, 372 ff., 452, 495, 741
Macpherson, James, 551
Macrì-Leone, Francesco, 961
Madelin, Louis, 966
Maes, Nicolas, 464
Maeterlinck, Maurice, 896, 910
Mahaffy, J. P., 481
Maigron, Louis, 967, 968
Maine, Duchesse du, 505
Maintenon, Mme de, 504, 512
Mairet, 626
Maistre, Joseph de, 654, 666, 747, 844
Majano, Benedetto da, 303, 318, 335
Makart, Hans, 811
Malatesta, Sigismondo, 307
Mâle, Émile, 496, 498
Malebranche, 503
Mallarmé, Stéphane, 883, 896–901, 904, 907, 917, 933
Malraux, André, 975, 977
Malvasia, 353
Manet, 134, 878, 879
Mann, Thomas, 570, 606, 713, 764, 786, 869, 890 f., 922, 965, 970, 971, 972, 974, 975, 976
Mannheim, Karl, 480, 964, 965, 973, 976
Mantegna, 305 f., 307, 342
Mantoux, Paul, 962, 963
Manzoni, Alessandro, 667
Maquet, Auguste, 727
Marcabru, 225, 226
Marcel, Pierre, 961, 962
Marie de Champagne, 212
Marigny, 632
Marino, 518
Marivaux, 522, 525 ff., 531, 666, 705, 743, 848
Marlowe, 406, 408, 418
Marot, Clément, 517
Marsan, Jules, 970
Marschak, Jakob, 977
Martelli, Roberto, 303, 314
Martin, Alfred von, 486, 487, 494
Martin, E. J., 482, 483
Martin, Germain, 961
Martin, W., 499
Martineau, Henri, 970
Martini, Simone, 288, 322

Martino, Pierre, 970
Marx, 184, 373, 404, 571, 643, 739, 758, 919, 920, 923, 955, 966, 970
Marzynski, Georg, 974, 975
Masaccio, 272, 292, 293, 294, 295, 302, 315, 321, 342
Masaryk, Th. G., 974
Massis, Henri, 977
Mathiez, Albert, 961
Maupassant, 762, 781, 784, 792, 831, 867, 881
Mauron, Charles, 975
Maurras, Charles, 929
Maximian, 145
Maximilian I, 363, 397
Mayer, A. L., 496
Maynial, Edouard, 972
Mazarin, 441, 451
Meder, Joseph, 493, 494
Medici family, 279, 283, 297, 302, 360, 363
Medici, Alessandro, 363
Medici, Cosimo, 283 f., 295, 297, 300, 302, 303
Medici, Lorenzo, 269, 295 f., 300, 303 ff., 307, 340, 518
Medici, Piero, 300
Mehring, Franz, 499, 964
Meissner, Bruno, 478
Meissonier, 778
Mélia, Jean, 970
Melozzo da Forlì, 342
Mély, F. de, 485
Menander, 118
Mendès, Catulle, 900
Ménageot, 636
Menghin, O., 476, 477, 478
Mengs, Anton Raffael, 502, 632, 636, 650
Mercier, 579, 581, 690, 693, 964
Meredith, George, 906, 907
Merezhkovsky, D., 866, 867, 974
Mérimée, 684, 689, 701, 710, 730, 883
Mesnil, Jacques, 494
Metsu, 463
Metternich, 654
Meulen, van, 445
Meusel, Friedrich, 965
Meyer, Eduard, 478
Meyer, Kuno, 483
Meyerbeer, 713, 807, 809 ff.
Michelangelo, 313, 315, 316, 317, 318, 324 f., 335, 336, 342, 343, 344, 345, 350, 354, 356, 359, 369–72, 380, 384, 390, 391, 392, 422
Michelet, Jules, 268, 490, 725
Michelozzo, 303, 313, 323
Michels, Robert, 969
Michels, Wilhelm, 498
Middleton, Thomas, 419
Milizia, Francesco, 498
Mill, J. S., 836, 841
Millet, 776, 777
Miltiades, 96
Milton, 517, 540
Mirabeau, 747
Mirsky, D. S., 973, 974, 976
Misch, Georg, 477, 478, 480
Moeser, Justus, 844
Moleschott, Jakob, 844
Molière, 266, 441, 442, 445, 454, 456, 470, 504, 523, 527, 580, 581, 688, 691, 804
Mommsen, Th., 481
Monet, Claude, 879
Monnier, Philippe, 494
Montaigne, 268, 452
Montégut, Émile, 780
Montemayor, 517, 519
Montesquieu, 658
Mor, Anthony, 357
More, Thomas, 545
Moréas, Jean, 896
Moreau, Pierre, 967, 969
Morisot, Berthe, 879
Mornet, Daniel, 963
Moro, Ludovico, 316, 324

Morris, William, 820 f., 823 f., 905, 972
Moser, Hans Joachim, 963
Mozart, 531, 576, 577, 710, 712, 751, 784, 808, 810
Mulertt, W., 488
Mueller, Adam, 654, 844
Mueller, Eduard, 494
Muentz, Eugène, 496
Muller, Jan Hermensz de, 468
Mumford, Lewis, 484, 963
Murger, Henri, 774, 893, 894
Murray, Gilbert, 480
Musset, 667, 681, 684, 701, 702, 710, 730, 883, 888, 889, 904
Mussolini, 816
Myron, 95, 101

Nadar, 893
Nadeau, Maurice, 977
Nanteuil, Célestin, 681
Napoleon, 639 f., 642, 645, 646, 648, 673, 674 f., 677, 685, 689, 695, 696, 742, 745, 746, 747, 748 f., 860
Napoleon III, 770, 773, 808, 811
Naumann, Hans, 486
Neri, Filippo, 372
Nero, 129
Nerval, Gérard de, 681, 730, 889, 892
Netscher, Caspar, 463
Nettement, Alfred, 760, 969
Neumann, Carl, 276, 491, 500
Neumann, Friedrich, 487
Neumann, Karl, 482
Neurath, O., 478, 479, 480, 481
Neuss, Wilhelm, 482
Nicholas I, 845
Nicholas of Cusa, 937
Nicolai, Chr. Fr., 602
Nicoll, Allardyce, 497
Nietzsche, 270, 373, 490, 655, 811, 812, 863, 883, 885, 886, 898, 902, 916, 919, 920, 924, 928, 972, 975, 976
Nisard, D., 725, 732
Nodier, Charles, 678, 681, 693
Nollau, Alfred, 965
Nordau, Max, 975
Novalis, 603, 659, 664, 665, 666, 667, 670, 671

Obermaier, Hugo, 476, 477
Offenbach, 797, 805–8
Oldenbourg, Rudolf, 500
Olschki, Leonardo, 493
Oppé, A. Paul, 972
Oppenheimer, Franz, 495
Orcagna, Andrea, 289, 335
Ortega y Gasset, José, 659, 929, 967, 969, 977
Ossian, 551, 645
Ostade, Isaak van, 469, 470
Ostrogorsky, Georg, 482
Otto III, 193
Otto, Walter, 478
Otway, Thomas, 765
Ovid, 214, 222

Paganini, 712
Païva, La, 811
Palestrina, 378
Palla, Giov. Batt. della, 302
Palladio, 561
Palmer, John, 497
Panofsky, Erwin, 334, 490, 494, 496
Pamfili family, 437
Paris, Gaston, 170, 222, 483, 487, 488
Parmenides, 96
Parmigianino, 355, 356, 357, 380, 381, 389 f.
Pascal, 432, 441, 453
Pater, Jean Baptiste, 521
Pater, Walter, 267, 803, 905
Paul III, 372
Paul IV, 377
Paulhan, Jean, 932 f., 935, 977
Pausanias, 86, 90

Pazzi family, 302
Peele, George, 408
Penni, Francesco, 343
Pergolesi, 934
Periander, 89
Pericles, 96
Perugino, 272, 303, 311, 318, 323, 324, 341, 346, 370
Peruzzi family, 281, 287
Peruzzi, Baldassare, 336, 343
Pesellino, 293, 297, 306
Peter the Great, 844, 845
Petersen, Julius, 965
Petit de Julleville, 962, 966
Petrarch, 266, 275, 332, 336, 517
Petrashevsky, 851
Petrie, Flinders, 61, 478
Petri, J. S., 963
Pevsner, Nikolaus, 495, 496, 499, 962
Peyre, Henri, 966
Pfandl, Ludwig, 495, 496
Pharrhasius, 128
Phelps, W. L., 963
Phidias, 129
Philemon, 130
Philip of Orléans, 504 ff.
Philip II, 360, 364, 398, 458 ff.
Philippi, Adolf, 490
Phrynichus, 100
Piazzetta, Giambattista, 528
Picard, Roger, 499
Picasso, 931, 934 f., 946
Pierre, J.-B.-M., 642
Pigault-Lebrun, 755
Piles, Roger de, 450
Pillet, A., 487
Pindar, 84, 85, 86, 89, 104, 110
Pinder, Wilhelm, 489, 492, 495, 496, 497
Piombo, Sebastiano del, 317, 343
Piranesi, 633
Pirenne, Henri, 482, 483, 485, 486, 492, 499
Pisanello, 266, 271, 291, 335, 630
Pisarev, 846
Pisistratus, 89, 100, 479
Pissarro, Camille, 879
Pius V, 377
Pixerécourt, Guilbert de, 691–4, 968
Planche, Gustave, 732, 776, 780
Plato, 96, 109, 110–12, 126, 148, 214, 320, 339, 416, 697, 820, 884
Platzhoff, Walter, 498
Plekhanov, George, 966, 974
Pliny, 86
Plotinus, 128, 331, 608
Plutarch, 129, 130, 481
Poetzsch, Albert, 967
Poelenburgh, Cornelis van, 463
Poggi, Giov. Batt., 315
Pohlenz, M., 480
Pokrovsky, M. N., 973
Pole, Reginald, 369, 372
Pollajuolo, Brothers, 311
Pollajuolo, Antonio del, 294, 300, 303, 311, 312, 313, 314, 335
Polycletus, 102, 105, 129
Polycrates, 89, 479
Polygnotus, 97, 129
Pompadour, Mme de, 632
Ponsard, François, 731, 734
Pontmartin, Arnauld de, 780
Pontormo, 314, 355, 357, 380, 381, 387 ff.
Pope, Alexander, 541, 544, 546, 547, 628, 629, 666, 702, 965
Poussin, 424, 430, 441, 448, 451 f., 520, 626
Pozner, Vladimir, 974
Praxiteles, 105, 117
Predis, Evangelista da, 313
Preger, Arnulf, 489
Preston, E., 970
Prévost, Abbé, 522, 525–8, 666, 705, 779
Prior, Matthew, 545, 546
Priscus, 166, 167
Prochno, J., 486
Proudhon, Pierre Joseph, 775

Proust, 568, 570, 715, 736, 754, 760, 882, 884, 925 f., 936, 938, 939, 944 f., 966, 970
Prudhon, P., 645, 651
Puccini, 892
Pudovkin, V. I., 954, 956
Pulci, Luigi, 269, 305, 399
Pushkin, 667, 699, 702, 703, 705, 706, 842, 864

Quaratesi family, 299
Quaratesi, Castello, 302
Quennell, Peter, 975
Quercia, Jacopo della, 299

Rabelais, 268
Rachel, Mlle, 731
Racine, 441, 445, 456, 470, 504, 525, 526, 582, 623, 627, 688, 753, 828
Radcliffe, Mrs., 691
Rajna, Pio, 170, 172, 484
Raleigh, Sir Walter, 402
Rambaud, Alfred, 486
Rameau, 531
Raphael, 49, 272, 312, 318, 324, 335, 336, 340 f., 342, 343, 344, 346, 350, 352, 354, 359, 362, 429, 448, 471
Raynaud, E., 975
Read, Herbert, 477
Réau, Louis, 484, 961
Reich, Hermann, 479, 484
Reinach, Salomon, 476
Rembrandt, 422, 423, 424, 429, 448, 464, 465, 467, 469, 472 f.
Rémusat, Charles, 780, 969
Renan, 781, 889, 972
Renard, Georges, 490, 491
Renier, G. J., 499
Renoir, 879
Renouvier, Jules, 966
Restif de la Bretonne, 522
Retz, Cardinal de, 442, 453, 456
Reumont, Alfred von, 492
Rewald, John, 975
Reynaud, Louis, 486, 977
Reynière, Grimrod de la, 967
Reynolds, Sir Joshua, 628
Riario family, 279
Ribera, 424
Richardson, 502, 541, 551, 559, 562–6, 568, 622, 703, 825, 826, 833, 848
Richelieu, Card., 441, 451, 625
Richelieu, Marshal, 504
Richter, J. P., 494
Riegl, Alois, 135, 240, 356, 425, 429, 464, 472, 475, 499, 500, 660, 661
Riemann, Hugo, 963
Rigaud, Hyacinthe, 470
Rilke, Rainer Maria, 750, 908, 933
Rimbaud, 883, 889, 892, 894, 895, 898, 899, 917, 927, 931
Rimsky-Korsakov, 711
Rivière, Georges, 974
Rivière, Jacques, 977
Robbia, Luca della, 303, 313, 314, 336
Robespierre, 654
Rodenwaldt, G., 478, 481
Rodin, 425
Roeder, 477, 478
Roemer, Adolf, 480
Rohde, Erwin, 487
Romano, Giulio, 343
Ronsard, Pierre de, 517
Roqueplan, Nestor, 892
Rose, Hans, 498, 965
Rosenberg, Adolf, 499
Rosenthal, Léon, 966, 968, 971
Rospigliosi family, 437
Rosselli, Cosimo, 314
Rossini, 808, 810
Rosso, Fiorentino, 357, 381, 388
Rostovtzeff, M., 480
Rothacker, Erich, 967
Rothschild family, 721
Rouault, Georges, 134, 931

Rousseau, Henri, 931
Rousseau, J.-J., 502, 504, 509, 510, 511, 514, 525, 526, 551, 558, 560, 568–73, 609, 617, 618, 622, 631, 634, 645, 677, 690, 699, 700, 703, 719, 748, 753, 755, 779, 782, 785, 848, 862, 863, 869, 885, 898, 922, 931, 964
Rubens, 422, 423, 424, 429, 435, 437, 448, 457, 470 ff., 513, 708, 709
Rucellai family, 302
Rucellai, Giov., 299 f.
Rudel, Jaufre, 225
Rudolf II, 360
Rudge, Arnold, 967
Ruisdael, Jacob van, 467, 470
Runciman, Steven, 482
Ruskin, 816, 817, 819 f., 821 ff., 824, 831, 905, 972

Sabatier, Paul, 491
Sabouret, Victor, 489
Sacchetti, Franco, 322, 336
Sachs, Hans, 600
Sadoleto, Jacopo, 369, 372
St. Bernard of Clairvaux, 178
St. Elegius, 178
St. Nilus, 137
St. Patrick, 152
St. Paul, 138
St. Teresa, 372
Saint-Simon, Duc de, 453
Saint-Simon, Henri de, 724, 844
Sainte-Beuve, 527, 681, 725, 730, 751, 781, 783, 969, 970
Saitschick, Robert, 492, 493, 494
Salomon, Albert, 967
Salutati, Coluccio, 269
Salvini, Roberto, 492
Sampson, George, 962
Sand, George, 710, 730, 789, 852, 883
Sandeau, Jules, 780
Sangallo, Antonio da, 335
Sangallo, Giuliano da, 303
Sannazzaro, Jacopo, 517, 518
Sappho, 87, 88
Sarcey, Francisque, 797 f., 801, 805, 972
Sardou, Victorien, 803, 804
Sarto, Andrea del, 311, 313, 314, 345
Sartre, Jean-Paul, 968, 976
Sassetti family, 302
Savage, Richard, 546
Savonarola, 369, 378
Scaliger, J. C., 274, 490
Schaefer, Dietrich, 494
Schaefer, Heinrich, 477, 478
Schanz, M., 961
Scheffer, Ary, 709
Scheler, Max, 488
Schelling, 603, 668
Scheltema, Adama van, 476
Scheludko, D., 487
Scherer, Wilhelm, 484, 489
Schestow, Leo, 974
Schewill, Ferdinand, 491
Schiller, 516, 571, 591, 603, 609, 616, 617, 618, 664, 862, 868, 914
Schlegel, A. W., 488, 603
Schlegel, Friedrich, 616, 654, 659, 669, 698, 738
Schleiermacher, 603
Schlosser, Julius, 492, 493, 494, 496
Schmid, W., 479
Schmidt-Degener, E., 499, 500
Schmitt, Carl, 967
Schnabel, Franz, 961
Schneider, Hermann, 484
Schneider, Hortense, 808
Schnitzer, Josef, 496
Schnitzler, Arthur, 908
Schober, Arnold, 480
Schoeffler, Herbert, 540, 962, 963
Schoenemann family, 620
Schoenberg, Arnold, 931
Schopenhauer, 713, 884
Schrade, H., 490
Schroeter, F. R., 488
Schroeter, W., 487
Schubert, 709, 712

Schuchardt, Carl, 476, 483
Schuecking, L. L., 497, 498, 962
Schuhl, P.-M., 480
Schulte, Aloys, 484, 485
Schumann, Otto, 488
Schumann, Robert, 710, 712
Schurtz, Heinrich, 477
Schwarzlose, Karl, 482, 483
Schweitzer, Bernhard, 127, 128, 479, 481, 964
Scott, Walter, 695, 696, 703–6, 716, 755, 826
Scribe, 417, 689, 692, 730, 731, 798, 803, 804
Scudéry, Mlle de, 523
Sedaine, 690, 693
Sée, Henri, 495, 961
Seignobos, Charles, 486, 975
Seillière, Ernest, 970, 971
Semper, Gottfried, 33, 239, 240, 475, 489
Senancour, 664, 678, 699
Seneca, 129
Sercambi, 336
Sévigné, Mme de, 453, 456
Sforza, Francesco, 279, 298
Shaftesbury, Earl of, 609 f.
Shakespeare, 63, 118, 266, 268, 357, 394, 401–23, 586, 589, 590, 660, 697, 709, 788, 802, 803, 828, 848, 849, 868, 918, 925
Shaw, G. B., 404, 418, 592, 803, 905, 911, 916, 917 ff.
Sheavyn, Phoebe, 497
Shelley, 517, 667, 695, 696, 698 f.
Sidney, Sir Philip, 408, 517, 825
Sieveking, H., 482, 484
Signorelli, 272, 324
Simmel, Georg, 370, 486, 495
Simonides, 84, 85, 107, 322
Singer, H. W., 972
Sisson, C. J., 497
Sitwell, Osbert, 973
Sixtus IV, 342
Sixtus V, 436
Smetana, 711
Smirnov, A. A., 497
Smith, Adam, 556, 814
Smollett, 549, 704, 826
Snijder, G. A. S., 478
Soby, J. Th., 977
Soderini, Pietro, 340
Sodoma, 343
Solon, 84
Sombart, Werner, 484, 485, 489, 491, 927, 963, 964, 969, 974
Somerwell, D. C., 972
Sophocles, 73, 96, 97, 106, 108, 109, 110, 118, 828, 848
Soufflot, Jacques Germain, 628, 632
Southampton, Earl of, 407
Southey, Robert, 696
Spee, Friedrich von, 601
Speier, Hans, 973
Spencer, Herbert, 836
Spengler, Oswald, 389, 485, 496, 560, 616, 963
Spenser, Edmund, 517
Spiegelberg, W., 60, 477
Spinello, Aretino, 289
Spranger, Barth., 355, 360
Springer, Anton, 485
Squarcione, Francesco, 312, 314
Staehlin, O., 479
Staël, Mme de, 568, 607, 648, 678, 729
Stammler, Wolfgang, 488
Stange, Alfred, 965
Steele, Sir Richard, 542 f., 545, 546, 825
Steen, Jan, 464, 467, 469
Stein, Frau von, 617
Stendhal, 524, 684, 686, 710, 715, 716, 717, 719, 728, 730, 731, 734, 735, 738, 739, 740–53, 754, 828, 848, 849, 860, 907, 938
Stephen, Leslie, 962, 964
Sterne, Laurence, 551, 566, 666, 737
Stockmeyer, Clara, 964
Stoll, E. E., 497

Strabo, 137
Strauss, D. F., 836
Strauss, Johann, 808
Stravinsky, 931, 934
Strich, Fritz, 965, 967, 968
Strieder, Jakob, 491
Strindberg, 912, 927
Strowski, F., 961
Strozzi family, 299, 302
Stuart dynasty, 535
Stuart, Mary, 407
Sue, Eugène, 726, 727, 729, 730, 827, 852
Suessmilch, Holm, 488
Surrey, Earl of, 408
Sustris, 360
Swarzenski, Georg, 484
Swift, Jonathan, 543 ff., 666
Sydow, E. von, 975

Taine, 684, 767, 781, 792, 832, 970, 973
Talleyrand, M. de, 530
Tardieu, Émile, 975
Tasso, 357, 381, 517, 518, 519
Taylor, O. H., 487
Tchaikovsky, 934
Teniers, David the Younger, 468, 521
Terborch, Gerard, 463
Texte, Joseph, 963
Thackeray, 835
Themistocles, 96
Theocritus, 514, 516, 517, 519, 521
Theodora, 143
Theodoric, 164, 166
Theognis, 84
Theophilus, 177
Thibaudet, A., 488, 966, 970, 971, 972, 975
Thiene, Count Gaetano da, 369
Thierry, Augustin, 725
Thiers, Adolphe, 721, 725
Thode, Henry, 276, 491
Thompson, Francis, 968
Thompson, J. W., 484, 486
Thomson, George, 478, 479, 480
Thomson, James, 546, 551
Thorndike, A. H., 973
Thucydides, 96
Thurnwald, Richard, 478, 489
Thutmosis, 56
Tibullus, 222
Tillyard, E. M. W., 497
Tintoretto, 355, 356, 357, 390–3
Titian, 318, 324, 325, 345, 390, 391
Tischbein, Wilhelm, 636
Tocqueville, Alexis de, 504, 506, 535, 606, 721, 961, 962, 964, 970
Tolnai, Charles de, 497
Tolstoy, 148, 404, 570, 737, 739, 842, 846, 848, 852, 853, 855, 856, 858, 860, 861–9, 898, 907, 917, 938, 974
Tompkins, J. M. S., 968
Tornabuoni family, 302
Tornabuoni, Giov., 318
Toulouse-Lautrec, 25, 759, 879, 894
Touquet, 685
Toynbee, Arnold, 963
Trajan, 119, 121
Trevelyan, G. M., 962
Trinkaus, Ch. E., 494
Trivas, N. S., 499
Troeltsch, Ernst, 484, 485, 486, 490, 967, 977
Trollope, Anthony, 835
Tudor, House of, 401 f., 534
Tuotilo, 178
Turgenev, 852, 855, 856, 909
Turnell, G. M., 976
Tylor, E. B., 476
Tyrtaeus, 84
Tzara, Tristan, 977

Uccello, Paolo, 293, 300, 311, 315, 321, 329
Udine, Giovanni da, 343
Unamuno, Miguel de, 497
Unger, Eckhard, 478

Unger, Rudolf, 964
Urban VIII, 437
Urfé, Honoré d', 517, 519, 523
Uzzano family, 283

Valentinian I, 129
Valéry, Paul, 784, 933, 934
Valla, Lorenzo, 269
Valois, House of, 360
Vanbrugh, Sir John, 545
Vanloo, J. B., 534, 628
Vasari, 286, 315, 319, 324, 329, 336, 353, 360, 376, 377, 383, 385, 387
Veblen, Th., 125, 477, 481
Velde, Aert van der, 467
Veneziano, Domenico, 291, 293, 300
Venturi, L., 974
Verlaine, 759, 883, 889, 892, 894, 896
Vermeer van Delft, 464, 467
Vernet, Horace, 645
Véron, Dr., 727
Veronese, 376
Verrocchio, Andrea del, 294, 297, 300, 303, 311, 312, 313, 314
Veuillot, Louis, 760
Viau, Théophile de, 626
Vico, G. B., 658
Vien, 631, 632, 635, 636
Vierkandt, Alfred, 476
Vigée-Lebrun, Mme E. L., 652
Vigny, Alfred de, 667, 678, 681, 701, 730, 883
Villani, Giov., 281, 286, 322, 336
Villari, Pasquale, 495
Villemain, François, 725, 730
Villiers de l'Isle-Adam, 883, 886, 887, 975
Viollet-le-Duc, 240, 241, 250, 485, 489
Virgil, 214, 516 f.
Visconti family, 279, 298
Vitet, Louis, 689
Vitruvius, 345
Vitzthum, Georg Graf, 483
Voege, Wilhelm, 485, 488, 489
Vogt, Karl, 844
Vogüé, Melchior de, 930
Voigt, Georg, 493
Volbach, W. F., 483
Volpe, Gioacchino, 486
Voltaire, 268, 303, 421, 441, 509, 510, 525, 549, 551, 564, 570, 572, 573, 609, 628, 631, 648, 666, 678, 685 f., 737, 747, 782, 785, 801, 828, 844, 863, 869
Volterra, Daniele da, 377
Vondel, Joost van der, 465
Vos, Cornelis van, 468
Vossler, Karl, 488, 498
Vouet, Simon, 441
Vries, Adriaen de, 360

Wackenroder, 668
Wackernagel, Martin, 492, 493
Wagner, Richard, 568, 655, 712, 713, 764, 808, 810 ff., 902
Walpole, Horace, 547, 561, 564
Walpole, Sir Robert, 540, 543, 546
Walser, Ernst, 269, 490, 494
Walther von der Vogelweide, 225
Walzel, Oskar, 498
Watteau, 450, 513 f., 520 ff., 527 f., 531, 532, 708
Webb, Geoffrey, 963
Weber, Alfred, 480, 973
Weber, C. M. von, 712, 713
Weber, Max, 477, 480, 481, 486, 491
Webster, T. B. L., 479, 480
Wechssler, Eduard, 216 ff., 487, 488
Weil, Hans, 965
Weisbach, Werner, 491, 492, 495, 496, 498, 962
Weiser, Christ. Friedr., 964
Weiss, Charles, 760
Weiss, J.-J., 972
Werff, Adriaen van der, 463
West, Benjamin, 632

Whibley, L., 480
Whistler, 885, 904
Wickhoff, Franz, 122, 123, 480, 490
Wieland, 616, 617
Wilamowitz-Moellendorff, U. von, 112, 479, 480
Wilde, Oscar, 885, 889, 904, 905, 906
William III, 543
William IX, Count of Poitiers, 216 f., 225
Wilson, Edmund, 974, 977
Wilson, J. Dover, 497
Winckelmann, 424, 502, 603, 632, 633, 634, 658
Winterhalter, F. X., 778
Woelfflin, Heinrich, 354, 356, 422, 425–30, 495, 498, 630, 661, 965
Wolf, Fr. A., 170
Wolff, Max J., 497
Wolfram von Eschenbach, 220, 225, 261
Woolf, Virginia, 944
Wordsworth, 655, 696 f., 702, 705
Wulff, Oskar, 482, 483
Wundt, Wilhelm, 475
Wyatt, Sir Thomas, 408

Young, Edward, 549, 551, 611

Zadoks-Jitta, A., 481
Zeuxis, 128
Zilsel, Edgar, 479, 480, 481, 494
Zola, 752, 761, 764, 775, 781, 783, 790, 792–5, 799, 800, 811, 881, 882
Zuccari, Federigo, 382, 384, 387, 437, 496
Zuccari, Taddeo, 376
Zwingli, 378